SOCIOLOGICAL THEORIES OF TODAY

PITIRIM A. SOROKIN

Harper & Row, Publishers

NEW YORK AND LONDON

Library of Congress Catalog Card Number: 66-14173

CONTENTS

PART THREE: THEORIES OF CULTURAL SYSTEMS

PART FIVE: TAXONOMY AND CHANGE IN SOCIOCULTURAL SYSTEMS

BIBLIOGRAPHICAL KEY

AA: *American Anthropologist*

AJS: *American Journal of Sociology*

ASR: *American Sociological Review*

CST: P. A. Sorokin, *Contemporary Sociological Theories* (Harper & Row, 1928; 2nd ed., 1964)

SCP: P. A. Sorokin, *Society, Culture, and Personality* (Harper & Row, 1947; rev. ed., Cooper Square Publishers, 1962)

DYNAMICS: P. A. Sorokin, *Social and Cultural Dynamics,* 4 vols. (American Book Company, 1937–1941; rev. ed., The Bedminster Press, 1962)

PREFACE

This book, a companion volume to my *Contemporary Sociological Theories*,[covers the main currents of sociological thought for about the last forty years] It deals with the theories of general sociology that appeared after the publication of *Contemporary Sociological Theories* in 1928. [Taken together, the two volumes give a critical account of the state of general sociology from the end of the nineteenth century up to 1965]. Like the earlier volume, this work endeavors to [examine critically the principal types of recent theories, and the works of individual sociologists enter this examination only insofar as they represent these types] In other words, the book is not a gallery of individual sociologists; it is, rather,[a guide to orient the reader in the bewildering jungle of general sociologies] The objectives of this volume and its characteristics remain essentially similar to those outlined in the Introduction to *Contemporary Sociological Theories*. The differences between the two works and the limitations of the present book are delineated in Chapter 1. For this reason, there is no need to reiterate these matters here.

Since my age precludes the possibility of my writing another volume on the state of general sociology, I conclude this foreword with sincere thanks to my fellow sociologists all over the world for the considerable attention they have given my sociological works. I hope this volume, like its predecessor, may be of some help in the creative growth of general sociology.

PITIRIM A. SOROKIN

Winchester, Mass.
January, 1966

ACKNOWLEDGMENTS

I am deeply indebted to Mr. and Mrs. Eli Lilly for their friendly encouragement and unfailing financial help in the preparation of this volume, as well as in most of my scientific and cultural activities. I wish to express my sincere thanks to the Lilly Endowment for its financial support of the Harvard Research Center in Creative Altruism (now affiliated with the American Academy of Arts and Sciences). I am profoundly grateful to the American Sociological Association, the International Institute and Congress of Sociology, and the International Society for the Comparative Study of Civilizations for bestowing the honor of presidency upon me, and to the American and the Belgian Royal Academy of Arts and Sciences, to the National University of Mexico, and to other scientific institutions for conferring fellowships or doctorships *honoris causa* upon me.

My thanks are due also to Philip J. Allen, F. S. Cowell, A. Cuvillier, W. C. P. Fan, M. Fraga Iribarne, J. Gjermoe, J. J. Maquet, L. Mendieta y Nuñez, E. A. Tiryakian, and C. C. Zimmerman for writing, organizing, and publishing special volumes devoted to an analysis of my theories, and to the vast galaxy of other distinguished scholars who have written thoughtful essays about my works. The scholars, editors, translators, and publishers responsible for some fifty published translations of my volumes are sincerely thanked for their labors in making my writings accessible to the thinkers and readers of many countries. The kindness of authors and publishers in giving permission to quote from their works in this volume is also gratefully acknowledged.

Finally, my heartfelt thanks to my family: my wife, Dr. Helen P. Sorokin, and my two sons, Dr. Peter P. Sorokin and Dr. Sergei P. Sorokin. Their loving care and serene affections have been the greatest joy of my life and a most powerful incentive in my scientific labors.

P. A. S.

PART ONE

INTRODUCTION

CHAPTER 1

The General Sociologies

of the Period 1925–1965

THEIR DIFFERENCES FROM THE GENERAL SOCIOLOGIES
OF THE PRECEDING PERIOD

Compared with the period from the end of the nineteenth century to 1925, described in my *Contemporary Sociological Theories*,[1] the field of general sociology for the period 1925–1965 displays several—external and internal—differences. The external differences are: (1) an increase in and proliferation of sociological research and publications; (2) the adoption and introduction of sociological courses into a large number of universities, colleges, and even high schools; (3) the growth of academic and cultural prestige of sociology as a science; (4) an increased employment of sociologists as experts in government, business, education, law, medicine, ministry, armed forces, foreign affairs, labor unions, industrial corporations, and so forth; and (5) the penetration of sociological interpretations and viewpoints into biology, psychology, psychiatry, history, political science, economics, law, ethics, and philosophy. In brief, for the recent period, sociology has experienced a successful external growth, expansion, and solidification of its scientific prestige and practical social importance.

It is more difficult to point out the internal changes that general sociology has undergone in the recent period. Among the significant changes seem to have been the following: (1) In comparison with the previous period, recent sociological re-

[1] (New York, 1928). Hereafter referred to as *CST*.

search has concentrated more on the techniqueways of socio-logical investigation and somewhat less on the discovery and formulation of broad substantive theories concerning basic sociocultural problems, and (2) the bulk of recent sociological research has dealt mainly with comparatively narrow "micro-sociological" problems and only a minor part of it has investigated the fundamental problems of sociocultural reality. In its extreme form this preoccupation with narrow concrete phenomena has led many sociologists to eschew broad investigations of basic sociocultural forms and processes, "grand systems of sociology," and philosophical presuppositions and analysis. Recent sociological thought has also displayed (3) a strong proclivity for studying basic macrosociological phenomena with all the philosophical clarifications involved in such investigations and for abstract theorizing in building analytical conceptual schemes of general and special character. This proclivity has become so widespread that one sociologist remarked that it has reached the stage of: "Look, Ma, I'm theorizing." Both of these mutually contradictory trends have existed side by side in recent sociological research and have often been displayed by the same sociologists. (4) The clear-cut differences between various sociological schools of the preceding period have tended to become less sharp. Several of the schools have dropped their one-sided claims, have reconciled their previously irreconcilable differences, and have increased their substantive agreement in regard to a number of important points of general sociology. (5) Several of these schools have converged on what I call the "integral" type of sociological theory, which incorporates and reconciles in its broader and more adequate conceptions the valid claims of each school without accepting their erroneous contentions. (6) As a result of this *rapprochment* and convergence, today's realignment of various currents of sociological thought is tangibly different from that of the schools of the preceding period. This problem will be discussed in the next section of this chapter. (7) Finally, recent sociological research is marked by the following characteristics:

The bulk of it represents mainly a continuation, variation, and verification of most of the approaches to the study of the human universe given in my *Contemporary Sociological Theories*, beginning with the mechanistic and ending with the sociologistic schools. Most of the recent research has contributed predominantly to a refinement of the old methods and techniques of sociological investigation. A lesser part of this research has presented new variations on the old systems of general and special sociologies and has remodeled formulas of uniformities in the relationship of diverse sociocultural variables. Finally, a few works of the period have attempted to build new systems of sociology, to discover new methods of understanding sociocultural phenomena, and to formulate new uniformities in their relationships. With the possible exception of these few works, almost all the research represents refinements of the old sociological techniques and reformulations of the old theories and uniformities. Hardly any of it is revolutionary. It supplies us with vaster statistical samples and collections of "facts"; it suggests some improvements on the techniques of interviewing or questioning, of statistical sampling, data-processing, and content analysis, or of sociometric, psychometric, psychodramatic, scalogramatic, group-dynamic, operational, projective, cybernetic, semantic, experimental, and analytical research. It furnishes us with a number of allegedly more precise formulas of uniformities, indexes, and tests; and, once in a while, it offers an improved variation on an old sociological theory. When these refinements, improvements, and reformulations are viewed in the light of the preceding currents of sociological thought, however, they are found to be, at best, improvements of details only and, sometimes, even no improvement at all. In spite of an enormous amount of sociological research done in the period, it has been, with the exceptions mentioned, pedestrian, epigonic, and Alexandrian rather than truly creative. No new sociological Platos and Aristotles emerged during the period; not even many leaders of the caliber of the eminent sociologists of the end of the nineteenth and of the beginning of the twentieth century, like G. Tarde, E. Durkheim, M. Weber, V. Pareto, M. Scheler, O. Spengler, L. Ward, W. Sumner, W. Dilthey, L. von Wiese, and the like, emerged.

Sociological research of the period has increasingly assumed the forms of collective research. Thanks to the participation of a large army of researchers in the collective research projects, the steam shovels of the numerous investigating crews have dug up an enormous mass of facts. In this mass, some grains of cognitive gold have naturally been found; but the excavations have turned up only a few gold nuggets, much less struck a rich vein of new sociological knowledge. The few nuggets that have been discovered are the work of individual prospectors.

Such in general seem to be some of the internal characteristics of recent sociological research. In subsequent chapters, these characteristics will be developed and corroborated. For the present, the above outline is sufficient to introduce us to a more substantial examination, evaluation, and criticism of today's main currents of sociological thought.

The task of this volume consists not so much in an analysis of a limited number of individual sociological theories[2] as in a critical survey of the main currents of sociological thought in the field of general sociology. The theories of the individual sociologists are examined only insofar as they serve as significant examples of each current of general sociology. In this respect, I follow the procedure used in my *Contemporary Sociological Theories*.[3]

Three further limitations should be mentioned: First, my critical survey deals only with general sociological theories or systems. It does not include special sociologies (political, economic, rural, urban, etc.) or works dealing with narrow, specific topics—unless such works have a direct bearing upon or con-

---

[2] Recent good examples of such works are given in C. and Z. Loomis, *Modern Social Theories* (Princeton, N.J., 1961); H. E. Barnes, *An Introduction to the History of Sociology* (Chicago, 1948); and C. S. Mihanovich, *Social Theorists* (Milwaukee, Wis., 1953). A somewhat intermediate procedure is used in such works as R. Agramonte, *Estudios de Sociologia Contemporanea* (Mexico City, 1963); Paulo Dourado de Gusmao, *Theorias Sociologicas* (Rio de Janeiro, 1962); A. Poviña, *La Sociologia Contemporanea* (Buenos Aires, 1955); and G. Gurvitch and W. E. Moore, *Twentieth-Century Sociology* (New York, 1945).

[3] It is also used in Don Martindale's *The Nature and Types of Sociological Theory* (Boston, 1960); in N. S. Timasheff's *Sociological Theory* (New York, 1955), in A. Cuvillier's *Manuel de Sociologie* (Paris, 1962), and in other works mentioned later on.

tain in them a significant system of general sociology.[4] The whole field of today's general and special sociologies is so vast that to adequately cover it would require the lifetime work of a scholar and a team of capable investigators.

Second, even the field of general sociological theories is studied here only in its main currents. Many small rivulets of modern sociological thought are excluded from examination. The reason for this limitation is the same as for the first: The total field of recent general theories in sociology is so enormous, so complicated, and so confused that there is no possibility of covering it in all its ramifications in one volume.

Third, American sociological theories are examined in greater detail than those of other countries, not because of a scientific superiority of American sociology in comparison with sociologies of other countries but mainly because of the personal deficiency of the author: Due to his advanced age and ignorance of several foreign languages, he simply could not follow the sociological works of other countries as closely and easily as he could the works of American sociologists. This is especially true of sociological investigations of Latin American, Japanese, Chinese, Arabic, and other Asiatic and African sociologists. In a lesser degree this is also true in regard to European sociologists. Only the most important of their theories are covered in this volume.

MAIN CURRENTS OF SOCIOLOGICAL THOUGHT OF THE RECENT PERIOD

The new realignment of various currents of sociological thought does not mean that any of the schools of the preceding period have disappeared. It does mean, however, that, during the recent period, not all of them have developed and blossomed

[4] See, on the differences between general and special sociological theories, P. Sorokin, *Society, Culture, and Personality* (New York, 1962), ch. 1; R. K. Merton, L. Broom, L. S. Cottrell, Jr. (eds.), *Sociology Today* (New York, 1959), Parts I and II, and J. S. Rouček (ed.), *Contemporary Sociology* (New York, 1958). *Society, Culture, and Personality* will hereafter be referred to as *SCP*.

equally well. Some have been cultivated industriously whereas others have been greatly neglected. Almost all of the schools have undergone notable changes in their principles, generalizations, and claims. As a result, the total map of the main currents of sociological thought of the period 1925–1965 looks somewhat different from that of the preceding period. This problem has confronted practically all scholarly writers on recent sociological theories and has been solved, rightly or wrongly, by each in his own way. Here are some examples of these classifications:

Don Martindale classifies the main types of recent sociological theories as positivistic organicism, conflict theory, the formal school, social behaviorism, and sociological functionalism.[5] C. and Z. Loomis specify seven sociologists: typological analyst, generalizing and specializing analyst, interaction theorist, structural analyst, historical and systematic analyst, analyst of social institutions and systems, and the theorist of general social action and social systems.[6] A. Cuvillier outlines the following sociologies: biological, psychological, Durkheimean, metaphysical, systematic, phenomenological, relational, historical, behavioral, sociopsychological, instinctivist, and personalistic.[7] N. S. Timasheff distinguishes neopositivistic, ecological, functional, analytical, philosophical, and historical currents.[8] Paulo Dourado de Gusmao examines the encyclopedic, evolutionary-organic, economic, psychosociological, realistic-sociologistic, relational, mechanistic, *verstehende*, cultural, fluctuational, cyclical, phenomenological, sociometric, epistemological, and socioactional types of sociological theory. C. C. Zimmerman divides the main currents into static-structural, neopositivistic empirical, and neodynamic. O. D. Duncan and L. F. Schnore distinguish cultural, behavioral, and ecological approaches.[9]

---

[5] Martindale, *The Nature and Types of Sociological Theory*. In his recent Introduction to G. K. Zollschan and W. Hirsch (eds.), *Explorations in Social Change* (Boston, 1964), he divides these currents into holistic and atomistic types, a division similar to that carried on in this volume.

[6] Loomis and Loomis, *Modern Social Theories*.

[7] Cuvillier, *Manuel de Sociologie*, ch. II.

[8] Timasheff, *Sociological Theory*.

[9] Dourado de Gusmao, *Theorias Sociologicas*; O. D. Duncan and L. F. Schnore, "Cultural, Behavioral, and Ecological Approaches,"

Perhaps the most complex and detailed classification of modern sociological theories is given by H. R. Wagner. He divides all *types* of sociological theories into: (1) *positive*, subdivided into neopositivism, human ecology, structure-functionalism, social behaviorism, and bio-psychological theory of culture; (2) *interpretative*, subdivided into theory of cultural understanding, interpretative sociology of action and interaction, interpretative social psychology, and social phenomenology; and (3) *nonscientific or evaluative*, subdivided into social-philosophical theory, ideological-social theory, and humanitarian-reform theory. Each of the subclasses is subdivided in turn into several sub-subdivisions. The whole classificatory scheme is one of the most detailed and complicated ever devised.[10]

This multifariousness of classifications denotes a rather chaotic situation, but this is quite natural and not reprehensible at all. After all, classifications of multidimensional and somewhat overlapping phenomena depend upon, first, which of their numerous aspects are studied by which scholar. The difference of the aspects studied warrants a diversity of classifications of these phenomena by different investigators. Also, the total field of today's sociological theories is so vast that it can hardly be well mastered by any one scholar. Most of them know well only some of the numerous theories and construct their classifications of these theories without any regard to those that they do not know. Furthermore, different sociologists often differently evaluate the significance of various theories, which leads to notable differences in their classifications. These and other reasons account for the many different classifications outlined. Since none of the outlined and existing classifications meets fully the objective of my study of these theories and since my evaluation of the scientific importance of the various currents of sociological thought

---

American Journal of Sociology, LXV (1959), 132–146; and C. C. Zimmerman, "Contemporary Trends in Sociology," in J. Rouček (ed.), *Readings in Contemporary American Sociology* (Paterson, N.J., 1962), pp. 3–29.

[10] H. R. Wagner, "Types of Sociological Theory: Toward a System of Classification," *American Sociological Review*, October, 1963, pp. 735–742. The *American Journal of Sociology* and the *American Sociological Review* will henceforth be referred to by their initials, *AJS* and *ASR*, respectively.

seemingly differs from those of other scholars in this field, I am forced to take the liberty of making my own grouping of these currents. After all, as H. R. Wagner correctly remarks, the cognitive service of any classification is decided by its heuristic fruitfulness. "By their fruits ye shall know them."

The most significant currents of today's sociological thought are divided, first, into the following main classes:

1. Singularistic-Atomistic theories, divided into two main classes:
   Physicalistic-Mechanistic
   Quantitative-Atomistic
2. Systemic Theories, subdivided into four Macrosociologies of *Cultural* Systems and Supersystems or Civilizations:
   Totalitarian
   Nontotalitarian
   Dichotomic
   Typological
3. Systematic Theories of *Social* Systems, subdivided into six main classes:
   Social-Action and Analytical theories
   Functional-Structural and Nomenclature theories
   Dialectic theories
   Pseudo-Behavioral (Mixed) theories
   Mixed Taxonomies of Social Systems (Groups)
   Mixed Theories of Social Change
4. Integral system of structural and dynamic sociology

Each of the subclasses of these main currents is in turn divided into several sub-subclasses.

This classification allows for most of the significant theories of the recent period. It also allows for all the schools discussed in *Contemporary Sociological Theories.* Thus, almost all the theories of such schools as the mechanistic, the demographic, and the bio-psychological fall into the singularistic-atomistic class, whereas most of the organic and organismic, the sociologistic, and some of the psycho-sociologistic schools enter the systemic class. The rest of the schools, like the geographic, and other theories examined in that volume belong to the singularistic or the mixed-eclectic class. Finally, since many of the recent theories seem to converge to a new integralistic type, these theories, together with the already-developed integral systems of sociology, compose the integralistic class.

It is true that some of the theories put into the same class differ from one another in a few characteristics. However, these differences are well compensated for by a series of significant similarities. In recent theories, many of the distinctive features of previous schools, for instance, of the psychological, the sociologistic, and the psychosocial, notably softened and melted in the recent, more adequate conceptions of the psychosociologistic or integralistic theories. Instead of the previous specific characteristics of each "school," new—substantial and methodological—traits have become the important *differentia specifica* of recent theories. The outlined classification on p. 10 permits the grouping and subgrouping of these theories according to these new *differentia specifica*.

Some of the reasons for my classification and also for my critical survey of the theories of the four main classes are given in Chapter 2, which outlines the essentials of my theory of sociocultural phenomena, their componential structure, and their differentiation into cultural and social systems and congeries. The outline serves as a basis for the subsequent critical survey and analysis and makes understandable a number of my critical remarks.

The Bases of Critical Survey

and Analysis

The task of this chapter is to define the meanings of the basic terms used in this work and to orient ourselves in what looks like a jungle of diverse and often discordant theories. It also serves as a concise introduction to the subsequent critical survey of recent sociological theories. The chapter outlines the points of my integral system of sociology that are directly concerned with the problems of social and cultural systems and congeries in their structural and dynamic aspects.[1]

COMPONENTIAL STRUCTURE OF SOCIOCULTURAL PHENOMENA

In contradistinction to the inorganic phenomena that have only one physicochemical component, and to organic phenomena that have two components—physical and vital (life)—the sociocultural or superorganic phenomena have the "immaterial" (symbolic) component of meaning (or meaningful values or norms), which is superimposed upon the physical and vital components. This realm of meanings-values-norms is a form of being

---

[1] For a detailed development of my general theory of sociocultural phenomena and social, cultural, and personality systems, see *SCP* and my *Social and Cultural Dynamics* (Totowa, N.J., 1962), especially Vol. I, chs. 1–4, and Vol. IV, *passim*. For my personality system, see my *The Ways and Power of Love* (Boston, 1954), chs. 5, 6, and 7. In these works, I give a detailed blueprint of my general theory of sociocultural phenomena. I have tested the empirical building of sociology corresponding to this blueprint more systematically than has almost any other sociological or historico-philosophical theorist. An overwhelming part of recent sociological theories are still in the blueprint stage. *Social and Cultural Dynamics* will henceforth be referred to as *Dynamics*.

or reality different from the inorganic and organic forms of being. The component of "meaning" is decisive in determining whether a phenomenon is sociocultural (superorganic). Without it there are no sociocultural phenomena; its presence radically changes the very nature of the inorganic or organic phenomena upon which it is superimposed. Without its meanings, a book— say Plato's *Republic*—simply becomes a physical object possessed of a certain geometrical form, with certain physical and chemical properties that are noticeable even to mice and that mice may even nibble now and then. On the other hand, the meaning of Plato's *Republic* can be objectified and materialized not only in the paper book, but through quite different physical media, such as phonograph records, air-waves, and other physical vehicles. Without its meaning the "Venus de Milo" is just a piece of marble of a certain geometrical form and with certain physical properties. Without the component of meaning, there is no difference between rape, adultery, fornication, and lawful sexual relations in marriage, because the purely physical act of copulation may be identical in all these actions that vary so profoundly in their meaning, value, and sociocultural significance. A thousand-dollar bill handed by A to B with an identical motion of his hand can socioculturally mean now "a payment of debt," now "a charity contribution," now "bribery," now "investment," now "inducement to murder," and so on. And, vice versa, the same meaningful cultural phenomenon can be objectified or externalized through different "material" vehicles or actions of living human agents: Hatred of A for B may express itself in thousands of material and organic phenomena, such as annoyance, beating, poisoning, shooting, drowning, frightening, destroying B's property, inflicting pain upon his dear ones, and so on. Biologically, the organism of a king or dictator may be weaker than that of any of his subjects or victims; socioculturally, the power of an absolute monarch or dictator is incomparably greater than that of his biologically strongest subject. Physically and biologically there are no human organisms that are kings, patriarchs, popes, generals, scientists, laborers, peasants, merchants, prisoners, criminals, heroes, saints, and so on. All these and thousands of other "meanings" are superimposed upon biological organisms by the sociocultural world or by persons and groups functioning not only as physical objects and biological organisms but mainly as mindful human personalities, as bearers, creators, and agents of "immaterial" (symbolic) meanings, values, and norms. Thus any phenomenon that is an incarnation or objectification of mind and meanings superimposed upon its physical and/or biological properties is by definition a sociocultural phenomenon.

On this planet, such phenomena are found only in the world of mindful human beings, functioning as meaningful personalities, who meaningfully interact with one another and create, operate, accumulate, and objectify their meanings (or meaningful values and norms) in and through an endless number of material vehicles—all physical and biological objects and energies—used for a materialization of the immaterial meanings, values, and norms of the human mind. Beginning with the simplest tool made, or the simplest path cut in the wilderness, or the simplest hut built, and ending with all the gadgets, machinery, domesticated animals, palaces, cathedrals, universities, museums, all the cities and villages, all the pictures, statues, books, all the energies harnessed by man—heat, electricity, radio, atomic fission—all this makes up the material culture of humanity. It is made up of the totality of the biophysical objects and energies that are used as media for the objectification of meanings, values, and norms.

The totality of the immaterial meanings-values-norms, not objectified as yet through the material vehicles but known to some members of humanity, the totality of already-objectified meanings-values-norms with all their vehicles, and, finally, the totality of interacting mindful individuals and groups—past and present—these inseparable totalities make up the total manmade sociocultural world, superimposed on the physical and biological realms of the total universe.

As has been mentioned before, any meaning-value-norm that is superimposed on a physical or biological phenomenon radically changes its sociocultural nature. A religious value superimposed on a little stick (*churinga*) transforms it into a sacred totem. When a piece of cloth on a stick becomes a national flag, it becomes an object for which life is sacrificed. When a sickly organism is declared to be a monarch or a pope, it becomes a powerful, sovereign, sacrosanct "Majesty" or "Holiness." When these same monarchs, their organisms remaining unchanged, are stripped of their sociocultural meaning-value— are "deposed" or "overthrown"—their power, prestige, functions, social position, and personality change fundamentally. From "Majesty" and "Holiness" they are transformed into despised and hated outcasts.

Similarly, when an assortment of physical and biological objects, causally unrelated to one another, becomes a vehicle or "conserver" for the same system of meanings-values-norms, a causal or empirically tangible interdependence appears between the physical and biological members of this assortment. And, vice versa, causally connected physical and biological phenomena sometimes become causally unrelated when a meaningful component is superimposed on them. For instance, many persons, ash trays, books, glass flowers, instruments, trucks, buildings, and thousands of other physical objects are not causally connected with one another through their purely physical and biological properties. But when they become the vehicles and agents of a unified system of meanings-values-norms called Harvard University then a sort of causal interdependence connects them. An important change in one part of Harvard University—the destruction of its main library, for instance, or an important change in its faculty and administration—tangibly influences most of these objects and members. In the case of the destruction of the main library, the enormous expense of restoring it may lead to a notable decrease in the budget for all departments, which in turn may effect a decrease in salaries, in the number and quality of ash trays, instruments, paper, books, and diverse objects bought for the departments. When these objects and persons become the agents and vehicles of the same system of meanings and values, then they become "causally" connected with one another. Otherwise, their "causal" interdependence, on the basis of purely physical or biological properties, is nonexistent. Such, in brief, is the specific componential structure of sociocultural or superorganic phenomena, clearly distinguishing them from inorganic and organic phenomena. To sum up: All empirically rooted sociocultural phenomena are made up of three components: (1) meanings-values-norms; (2) biophysical vehicles (media) objectifying them; and (3) mindful or conscious human beings (and groups) that create, operate, and use them in the process of their meaningful interactional activities.

IDEOLOGICAL, BEHAVIORAL, AND MATERIAL CULTURES OF INDIVIDUALS AND GROUPS

An individual or group can possess a given cultural phenomenon in its ideological form only. For instance, an individual or group may well know the ideology—that is, the totality of meanings, values, and norms—of Communism or Buddhism without either practicing it or objectifying it through a set of material objects and vehicles, such as a Buddhist temple with its ritual objects, or a Communist club with its pictures of Marx, Lenin, and Stalin. Christians who ideologically profess the Sermon on the Mount but do not at all realize it in their behavior or in their material culture are only ideological Christians. The same is true of any cultural phenomenon that functions only on an ideological level without influencing the behavior and material culture of individuals and groups.

When individuals and groups in their overt actions begin to practice the ideologies of Communism, Christianity, or Buddhism, then the cultures of Communism, Christianity, or Buddhism become behavioral as well as ideological. When the ideologies are also realized through a number of material vehicles that "incarnate" and "objectify" them, Buddhism, Communism, or any other cultural (meaningful) phenomenon assumes a "material" form.

Thus, any cultural phenomenon can appear either in a purely ideological form, or in ideological and behavioral, ideological and material, and ideological, behavioral, and material forms. The purely ideological form is the least strongly rooted in the empirical universe. When it becomes rooted in the behavior and in the material objects of an individual or group, it becomes more deeply and more strongly grounded than when it remains a mere ideology. As a behavioral and material realization it becomes a factor in molding not only ideas and meanings, but also the overt behavior and the interrelationships of human beings and their physical and biological objects and processes.

To sum up: (1) The totality of meanings-values-norms possessed by individuals or groups makes up their ideological culture; (2) the totality of their meaningful actions, through which the pure meanings-values-norms are manifested and realized, makes up their behavioral culture; and (3) the totality of all the other vehicles, the material, biophysical things and energies through which their ideological culture is externalized, solidified, and socialized, makes up their material culture. Thus, the total empirical culture of a person or group is made up of these three cultural levels—the ideological, the behavioral, and the material.

MAIN FORMS OF THE INTERCONNECTION OF SOCIOCULTURAL PHENOMENA

A copy of *Look*, a broken whiskey bottle, a shoe, and an orange can lie side by side on the pavement, having been brought into close proximity by casual, incidental forces. *Spatial proximity* is the only connection between them. Aside from that, they are not bound together by either a causal or a logical tie. A dumping field near a city exhibits a vast number of various cultural objects lying in close proximity. Since this spatial juxtaposition is the only connection between them, one can change— add, take away, break into pieces—some of these objects without changing the rest of the dumped cultural objects. Any collection of cultural phenomena interrelated only by spatial adjacency (or time adjacency, like many newsreel events) makes the most conspicuous case of cultural congeries.

A somewhat more tangible connection exists between the phenomena X, Y, Z, each of which is neither causally nor meaningfully related to the others, but each and all of which are causally related to a common factor A, and through A they happen to be connected by an indirect causal bond. In my pockets I find a watch, keys, handkerchief, dollar bill, pen, pencil, and comb. None of these cultural objects demands one another either logically or causally. There is no direct causal relationship between the handkerchief, the keys, the dollar bill, and the comb, because ordinarily we find that a handkerchief is not in the company of any of these objects, and none of these objects is ordinarily accompanied by the others. Likewise, we can tear the handkerchief into pieces without in any way affecting the watch, keys, or the dollar bill. This means that there is no direct causal tie between them, because a causal relationship between A and B means that when A is given B is given (or vice versa in two-sided causal relations), and when one of these is changing the other is changing also.

However, if all these objects are found in my pockets, they are there, in close proximity, because each of them satisfies one of my needs (causal and meaningful ties with *me*). Being directly related to me as their common factor, they become related to one another not only by spatial (and time) proximity, but by an indirect causal relationship. This ties them together somewhat more closely than a mere spatial (and time) adjacency. The tie is, however, so indirect that they lose it as soon as their common factor disappears. Hence they are still congeries rather than real unities or systems, in which any important change of an important part tangibly influences the other parts and the whole. The sociocultural world is full of numerous collections of two or more cultural objects, phenomena, and processes of this type, lying between congeries and real unities. They may be called *semicongeries*.

Next we shall consider the totality of cultural objects, phenomena, and processes that are bound together into a real unity or system by a direct causal tie. They make causal cultural unities or systems. The explosion of war or famine or any other great emergency invariably leads to an expansion of governmental regimentation in all societies of a certain kind; and the termination of war, famine, or other emergency regularly leads to a quantitative and qualitative decrease in governmental regimentation. This is an example of two sociocultural phenomena bound into a causal unity by a direct causal tie. Within the limited budget of any nation an increased appropriation for military purposes calls forth a decrease in expenditures for nonmilitary needs. The excessive atomization of ethical and legal values tends to increase criminality. A rigid caste regime is causally connected with a low vertical social mobility in a given population. The northern climate causes fur and heavy cloth coats to be used in the winter months. These are examples of cultural phenomena connected by direct causal ties. The causal unities are real unities or systems.

In contradistinction to congeries or a conglomeration of meanings, like "two + Stalin + azalea + water + Jupiter + shoe + Baroque + fish + table," where the meanings are united only by spatial (or time) proximity, any proposition like "*A* is *B*" or "two and two make four" or "*A* is not *B*" is a meaningful little system where the logical subject and predicate are logically united to make one meaningful proposition. The totality of such meanings united into one logically consistent and comprehensible proposition makes up a meaningful system. Thus, mathematics is a vast, meaningful, eminently consistent system, for no important proposition can be changed without introducing inconsistency and making it necessary to change other mathematical equations and formulas to re-establish its consistency. The same, to a somewhat lesser degree, is true of physical, biological, and social sciences; the bulk of their propositions is a logically consistent whole (with a few congeries present). It is also true of all great philosophical systems of meanings. The bulk of propositions in Plato's *Republic* or Kant's *Critique of Pure Reason* or St. Thomas's *Summa Contra Gentiles* is mutually consistent (with some congeries here and there). This is no less true of the Christian credo or the credo of other great religions, of the great ethical systems, even of most of the law codes. Most of their main propositions are mutually consistent and make a *meaningful unity* or *system*. None of their main propositions can be radically changed without affecting the other main propositions and making it necessary to change them also in order to re-establish their consistency.

In aesthetic-cultural meanings, the aesthetic consistency of the content and style of the fine-arts phenomena occupies the place of logicomathematical consistency. Aesthetic congeries represent a hodgepodge of various disharmonious bits of content and form. A musical composition in which some bars are taken from Bach, some from Stravinsky, some from Brahms, some from Gershwin, some from Wagner, and some from jazz serves as an example of a musical hash. A literary composition written partly in Homeric style and partly in the styles of Dante, Rabelais, Gorki, Shelley, and Gertrude Stein is another example of an aesthetic congery. All great creations in music and literature, painting and sculpture, architecture and drama display a seamless unity of style and content (with a few "bridges" here and there).

This outlines the profound difference between *meaningful congeries* and *meaningful unities or systems*. The parts that make up a meaningful system are united by the tie of meaningful (logical or aesthetic) consistency or complementarity. Such unities are different from purely causal unities, for, in meaningful unities, the interdependence is logical or aesthetic, whereas in the causal it is neither logically nor aesthetically consistent or inconsistent; it is simply a relatively constant and tangible empirical interdependence of A and B in their coexistence or sequence or concomitant variation.

Finally, when a system of meanings is objectified by material vehicles and becomes not only an ideological but also a behavioral and material system, it becomes fully grounded in the empirical sociocultural world. As such it simultaneously becomes a causal-meaningful system or unity. Causal as well as meaningful ties bind together its parts into one ideological-behavioral-material system, because when diverse persons, material objects, or energies become agents and vehicles of the same system of meanings-values-norms, the component of meanings throws a causal net over all such persons and vehicles and introduces a causal dependence where it would otherwise not have existed. For this reason the overwhelming majority of grounded sociocultural systems are causal-meaningful unities, different from purely causal and purely meaningful unities. The causal-meaningful unities are thus the most integrated kind of sociocultural grounded systems, and the causal-meaningful interconnections among cultural phenomena are the closest possible ties.

All grounded cultural systems, whether they be mathematics or science generally, philosophy, religion, law, ethics, music, or the fine arts, generally become meaningful-causal sociocultural systems as soon as they become behavioral and material. Without their system of meanings or "ideology" they simply would not exist: There cannot be any mathematics without the system of mathematical meanings or propositions. When mathematics begins to be practiced, taught, objectified in books, computers, and other media used for study and practical purposes, it becomes a meaningful-causal system whose ideological, behavioral, and material aspects become tangibly interdependent with its human agents and material vehicles. The same is true of practically all other cultural systems grounded in empirical reality.

Thus we find that the interconnections among innumerable and immensely diverse grounded sociocultural phenomena are of five different kinds at least: (1) a mere spatial or time adjacency; (2) indirect causal relations; (3) direct causal connections; (4) meaningful unity; and (5) meaningful-causal ties. Correspondingly, all the combinations of two or more sociocultural phenomena give us: (1) pure sociocultural congeries; (2) semicongeries united by an indirect (or external) causal bond; (3) causal unities or systems; (4) meaningful systems; and (5) meaningful-causal systems or unities. All grounded sociocultural systems are meaningful-causal unities.

MAIN CULTURAL SYSTEMS AND SUPERSYSTEMS

In the total culture of any population, or of the whole of mankind, there exists a multitude of cultural congeries and of causal-meaningful systems. These range from the smallest (like "*A* is *B*") to ever-vaster ones. "Two times two make four" is a little system; the multiplication table is a larger system; arithmetic is a still larger system; all mathematics (arithmetic, algebra, geometry, calculus, etc.) is a vaster system; the entire field of science is a yet vaster system. Similarly, we find a wide range of systems, beginning with the smallest and ending with the vastest, in other fields of cultural phenomena.

The basic vast cultural systems are: language, science, philosophy, religion, the fine arts, ethics, law, and the vast derivative systems of applied technology, economics, and politics. The bulk of the meanings-values-norms of science or of great philosophical, religious, ethical, or artistic systems are united into one consistent ideological whole. When grounded empirically, this ideological system is, to a tangible degree, realized in all the material vehicles, or the material culture, and in the behavior of the creators, bearers, agents, or members of each of these systems. Scientific ideology (of any and all sciences) is objectified in millions of books, manuscripts, instruments, laboratories, libraries, universities, schools, and in practically all objects, gadgets, and machinery, from an axe or shovel up to the most complex atomic-radio-electrical-steam machinery invented, constructed, and made possible by science. Behaviorally, science is actualized in all educational and research activities of scientists, students, teachers, inventors, scholars, and millions of laborers and farmers, businessmen and technicians who apply scientific discoveries, behave scientifically, and use the utensils and gadgets invented by science according to the scientific technique prescribed by the meaningful norms of scientific methods. Taken as a whole, the total scientific system—in its ideological, material, and behavioral forms—occupies an enormous portion of the total cultural phenomena of mankind.

Religious ideology likewise is objectified in material objects, beginning with temple and cathedral buildings and ending with millions of religious objects. It is also objectified in overt actions by its members—its hierarchy and its ordinary followers—from a simple prayer to innumerable ritual actions, moral commandments, and charity. Taken in all its three forms—ideological, material, and behavioral—the religious system occupies a very large place in the human population's total culture. With a respective modification, the same can be said of the systems of language, fine arts, law and ethics, politics and economics. In their totality, these systems cover the greater part of the total culture of almost any population, the rest consisting partly of a multitude of other derivative systems, but mainly of a multitude of cultural congeries. They make up the central and the highest portion of any population's culture. Being essentially consistent, they are also a gigantic manifestation of human rational (and partly even superrational) creativity. Their very existence demonstrates the fallacy of all theories that view human beings and human culture as mainly irrational and nonrational. Congeries testify in favor of this nonrationality or irrationality, but, insofar as congeries are a minor part of humanity's total culture, these theories enormously exaggerate human irrationality and nonrationality.

Besides these vast cultural systems there are still vaster cultural unities that can be called cultural supersystems. As in other cultural systems, the ideology of each supersystem is based upon certain major premises or certain ultimate principles whose development, differentiation, and articulation makes up the total ideology of a supersystem. Depending upon the generality and nature of their major premises, there are different and varyingly vast supersystems. The vastest of these are the supersystems whose major premises or ultimate principles concern the nature of the ultimate true reality or the ultimate true value. Three main consistent answers have been given by humanity to the question, "What is the nature of the true, ultimate reality-value?" One is: "The true, ultimate reality-value is sensory. Beyond it there is no other reality or any other nonsensory value." This premise and the gigantic supersystem built upon it is called the *sensate* supersystem.

Another answer to this question is: "The true, ultimate reality-value is a supersensory and superrational God (Brahma, Tao, 'Divine Nothing,' and other equivalents of God). Sensory and any other reality or value is either a mirage or represents inferior and shadowy pseudoreality and pseudovalue." This premise and its corresponding cultural supersystem is called *ideational*.

The third answer to the question is: "The true, ultimate reality value is the Manifold Infinity, which contains all differentiations and which is infinite qualitatively and quantitatively. The finite human mind cannot grasp it or define it or describe it adequately in its infinite plenitude. This Manifold Infinity is ineffable and unutterable. Only by a very remote approximation can we discern three main aspects in it: the rational or logical, the sensory, and the superrational-supersensory. All three of these aspects harmoniously united in it are real; real also are its superrational-supersensory, rational, and sensory values. It has many names: God, Tao, Nirvana, the Divine Nothing of mystics, the Supra-Essence of Dionysius, Heidegger's Being, Jaspers' Transcendence, and Northrop's "undifferentiated aesthetic continuum." This typically three-dimensional conception of the ultimate and the supersystem built upon it is described as *idealistic* or *integral*.

Each of these three supersystems embraces in itself the corresponding type of the vast systems already described. Thus, the *sensate* supersystem is made up of sensate science, sensate philosophy, sensate religion of a sort, sensate fine arts, sensate ethics, law, economics and politics, along with predominantly sensate types of persons and groups, ways of life, and social institutions. Likewise, the *ideational* and *idealistic* or *integral* supersystems consist respectively of ideational and idealistic types of all these systems. In each of these supersystems the ideological, behavioral, and material elements articulate, in its main parts—in its science and philosophy, fine arts and religion, ethics and law, way of life, behavior, and social institutions— its major or ultimate premise concerning the nature of the true, ultimate reality-value.

Thus, for instance, in the medieval European culture, from the sixth to the end of the twelfth century, we find that the ideational supersystem was dominant and embraced the main portions of the total medieval culture. Its major premise was the Christian credo, with the superrational and supersensory Trinity representing the ultimate true reality and value. This credo was articulated by the dominant medieval "science," theology, philosophy, fine arts, law, ethics, economics, and politics. Medieval science was subordinate to theology, which was the queen of the sciences. The supreme truth was the revealed truth of religion. Medieval philosophy was hardly distinguishable from theology and religion. Medieval architecture and sculpture were but the same "Bible in stone," articulating the same credo. So also were its painting and music, literature and drama. From 85 to 97 percent of the total great fine arts of the Middle Ages was religious and Christian. Medieval law and ethics were but an articulation of the divine and natural law, formulated in the absolute, God-given Ten Commandments and the Sermon on the Mount, with canon law supplementing secular law. The medieval form of government was theocracy, with the spiritual power supreme over the secular. Even medieval economics was notably Christian-religious, tangibly "noneconomical" and "nonutilitarian." In brief, the major ideational premise was articulated by all the main compartments of medieval culture. On the basis of this premise there emerged, grew, and functioned a vast ideational supersystem, which was the dominant and most characteristic one of medieval culture. The sensate and idealistic systems and congeries were also present, but these were minor.

The total European culture after the sixteenth century and on up to the twentieth century presents an entirely different picture, for the sensate rather than the ideational supersystem dominates European culture. During these four centuries, the major parts of all the compartments of European culture have articulated the premise that the true, ultimate reality-value is sensate. All the compartments of this culture have become secularized. Religion and theology have declined in influence and prestige. Religiously indifferent, sometimes even irreligious, sensory science has become the supreme, objective truth. The real truth is now the truth of the senses, empirically perceived and tested. Sensate philosophy (materialism, empiricism, scepticism, pragmatism, etc.) and sensate literature, music, painting, sculpture, architecture, and drama have largely replaced the religious medieval philosophy and fine arts. Sensate, utilitarian, hedonistic, relative, manmade law and ethics have replaced the ideational, unconditional, God-revealed law and ethics of the Middle Ages. Material value, wealth, physical comfort, pleasure, power, fame, and popularity have become the main values for which modern sensate men have been fighting and struggling.

God and religion have gone by the board. Together with the values of the Kingdom of God they have been given lip service but have ceased to be really important. The predominant type of persons, their way of life, and their institutions also have become dominantly sensate. In brief, the major part of modern Western culture has been dominated by the sensate supersystem.

If, finally, we take Greek culture of the fifth century B.C., or European culture of the thirteenth century, we find that it was dominated by the idealistic or integral cultural supersystem. This culture, in all its main compartments, articulated the major idealistic or integral premise—that the true, ultimate reality-value is the Infinite Manifold, partly sensory, partly rational, and partly superrational and supersensory. These outlined supersystems are the vastest cultural systems that are known so far.[2]

SOCIAL SYSTEMS AND SOCIAL CONGERIES

The preceding paragraphs outlined the structure of the sociocultural world from the standpoint of its component of meanings (values and norms). The whole sociocultural universe of mankind appears, from this standpoint, as a cosmos of infinitely numerous and diverse meanings (values, norms), combined into innumerable congeries and systems of meanings, beginning with the smallest and ending with the vastest sensate, ideational, and idealistic (integral) supersystems. These supersystems have appeared only in a few great total cultures that achieved the highest form of integration. The majority of the total cultures of various peoples and periods achieve only narrower and looser forms of integration.

If now we view the sociocultural universe from the standpoint of the component of its human creators, agents, users, and operators, we observe that the human components of sociocultural phenomena appear also in the forms of social systems (or organized groups), social congeries (unorganized, disor-

---

[2] See a detailed analysis of these supersystems in my *Dynamics*, all four volumes.

ganized, and largely nominal plurels of individuals), and intermediary semiorganized groups of individuals of various degrees of organization. Which combinations of the mindful individuals are the social systems, the social congeries, and the intermediary groups is decided by the same criteria that determine the cultural systems, congeries, and the intermediary combinations of meanings. If an interacting group of individuals has as its *raison d'être* a consistent set of meanings-values-norms that satisfies their need(s) and for whose use, enjoyment, maintenance, and growth the individuals are freely or coercively bound together into one collectivity with a definite and consistent set of lawnorms prescribing their conduct and interrelationships, such a social group is a social system or organized group. These lawnorms are a part of a consistent set of meanings-values that are the *raison d'être* for a given organized group. If its central meanings-values are religious or scientific, political, artistic, or "encyclopedic," the group will be a religious, scientific, political, artistic, or "encyclopedic" social system. The nature of the meanings-values of the group determines the specific nature of the group itself. If the mindful individuals in a group do not interact with one another and are not interdependent in their mental and overt activities, such a group of, say, fifty Robinson Crusoes, each isolated on his island from the rest of the Crusoes, is only a nominal plurel of individuals, but not a real social group. If the mindful individuals do interact with each other, but do not have a consistent set of meanings-values-norms because of which and for the sake of which they interact, or a derivative set of consistent law-norms prescribing the forms of conduct and interrelationships of the individuals, such a group of "anarchically" interacting individuals represents a social congeries or unorganized social group. In between the perfectly organized and unorganized social groups there are many intermediary semiorganized groups of various degrees of organization.

To sum up, whether a real social group (in contrast to a nominal plurel of individuals) is a social system or a social congeries is decided, as in cultural systems and congeries, by the fact of the consistency or inconsistency of the central meanings-values-norms because of which and/or for the sake of which the individuals interact. This means, among other things, that each of the organized or unorganized real social groups is built around and contains a set of cultural meanings-values-norms as its "heart and soul," as its main unifying bond and the very reason for its existence. Thus, in any real group—be it a social system or a social congeries or an intermediary type—its "social" form of being is always inseparable from its "cultural" meanings-values-norms. Besides the dimension of personality of its members, any real human (superorganic) group is always a two-dimensional sociocultural reality. By definition and by its componential structure, any social human group is invariably a cultural phenomenon, and any living cultural phenomenon is always a social phenomenon. The different categories of "the cultural" and "the social" are thus inseparable in the empirical sociocultural universe of man.[3]

In view of the basic importance of the social systems, social congeries, and social semiorganized groups, it is advisable to investigate them further. The central meanings-values and law-norms[4] of organized groups determine in detail what the rights and duties of each member are; what, in regard to whom, when, how much, and under what conditions each member is entitled and obliged to do or not to do, to tolerate or not to tolerate; what the exact *functions or roles* are that a member has to play; and what the *status* of each member is in the system of inter-action as determined by the totality of his rights-duties, func-tions, and roles. The law-norms generate the official law and

---

[3] In purely biological aggregates of other species, like the societies of bees, wasps, or birds, there are real social groups without the super-organic or cultural components of meanings-values-norms. All such societies, having at best only the most rudimentary forms of thought, consciousness, or meaning, and being controlled mainly by reflexes and instincts, belong to the organic or biological realm of reality and not to the superorganic class of the total reality. The manmade superorganic universe is given only in the world of the mindful interacting human in-dividuals. All the above and subsequent statements concern only this manmade cosmos studied by homosociology. The ecology or biology of animal and plant aggregations does not concern us here, since such a discipline is outside of homosociology.

[4] See, for a precise definition of law-norms, L. Petrazycki's *Law and Morality* (Cambridge, Mass., 1955), and my *SCP*, ch. 4.

government of the group. By defining rights and duties, the law-norms clearly indicate what relationships or forms of interaction are required from the parties as obligatory; what are prohibited; and what are recommended, though not required, and under what conditions, when, and in regard to whom. Through their definition of the rights-duties, functions, and status of every member and through that of the obligatory, prohibited, and recommended relationships, the law-norms make a group of interacting individuals into a clearly differentiated and stratified body in which each member performs a specific task in the total functions of the group and in which each occupies a certain rank in its hierarchy of authorities. The group usually has an economic complex of vehicles, including material resources, possessed, used, and operated to carry on its functions and, often, to give to it its means of subsistence. The group ordinarily gets a name, sign, or symbol of its identity.

Additional characteristics of all organized groups or social and cultural systems are the group's or cultural system's reality, which is different from that of a mere sum of its parts or components; its individuality; and the triple interdependence of all of its important parts. Triple interdependence implies triple conductivity within the group or cultural system: when an important change occurs in one of its parts, it is transmitted to other parts by the interaction of the group's members and the component of the vehicles. Besides this general triple interdependence an organized group has differential interdependence and conductivity among its parts. Spatial compatibility of groups is also characteristic of organized groups. Two or more physical objects cannot occupy the same physical space at the same time, but two or more social systems can be spatially compatible: The same set of vehicles, for instance the NBC radio network, is used by hundreds of different groups broadcasting different programs; the same set of individuals listening can be members of several different organized groups, religious, political, occupational, ethnic, and so on. An organized group is able to maintain its continuity, individuality, and identity, despite a regular change of its members and vehicles. A change in togetherness of all important parts of the group and the group as a whole is also characteristic. Self-directing, immanent change in the group and in its life-career, with the role of external factors reduced to accelerating or retardating, facilitating or hindering the unfolding of the group's immanent potentialities, in extreme cases causes the destruction of the group, but as long as the group exists, change never neutralizes completely the group's self-directing control of its destiny and life-career. Any organized group or cultural-grounded system has a varying degree of autonomy from all forces of its environment. Any organized group or cultural system is a selective agency, taking into itself only certain elements of its environment and rejecting or leaving out of itself other elements. Any organized group or cultural system varies in its forms, but within certain limits. If it changes beyond these limits, it loses its identity and ceases to exist.

These are the exact characteristics of organized groups and social systems as distinguished from unorganized social congeries. The unorganized or disorganized group is amorphous: The rights, duties, possessions, functions, roles, social status, and position of its members are undetermined and undefined either in broad outline or meticulous detail, as are its categories of lawful, recommended, and prohibited forms of conduct and relationships; its official law and government; its social differentiation, stratification, and economic order; and its whole set of meanings-values-norms. It does not have any of the other characteristics of organized groups.

No doubt the passage from the absolutely unorganized to the perfectly organized groups or social systems of interaction is in reality gradual. We have a gradation from unorganized social groups through somewhat organized up to perfectly organized and integrated social bodies, where practically all the actions of the members and all their relationships are crystallized clearly and consistently and where each member has a definite norm for each of his roles in interaction for each configuration of circumstances. The main forms of unorganized and semi-organized groups are:

1. Externally united, as-if-organized group of individuals
2. Public
3. Crowd, mob, group of strangers

4. Seminominal plurel
5. Purely nominal plurel[5]

CLASSIFYING ORGANIZED GROUPS OR SOCIAL SYSTEMS

In the sociocultural universe there exist millions of different organized groups or social systems, beginning with organized dyads and triads and ending with vast social systems such as empires and world religious groups that have many millions of members and an enormous body of material vehicles that enables them to function. This immense multitude of social systems can be classified in many different ways, depending upon the purposes of classification. The classification below endeavors to indicate the important social groups—repeated in time and space —that have been exerting a powerful causal-meaningful influence upon enormous multitudes of individuals, upon other social groups, upon the course of historical life of mankind, and upon the sociocultural world in general. These groups are divided into the "unibonded" and the "multibonded" according to the unidimensional or multidimensional character of their set of meanings-values-norms:

I. *Important Unibonded Groups (built upon and centered around the main values) of*:
   A. *Biosocial Nature*: (1) Race; (2) Sex; (3) Age-values
   B. *Sociocultural Nature*: (4) Kinship; (5) Territorial proximity (Neighborhood groups); (6) Language, Ethnic, and Nationality groups; (7) the State; (8) Occupational groups; (9) Economic groups; (10) Religious; (11) Political groups; (12) Scientific, Philosophical, Aesthetic, Educational, Recreational, Ethical, and other "ideological" groups; (13) Nominal group of the elite: great leaders, men of genius, and historical persons.
II. *Important Multibonded Groups* (centered around a combination of two or more unibonded meanings-values-norms): (1) Family; (2) Clan; (3) Tribe; (4) Nation; (5) Caste; (6) Social Order or Estate (like the medieval nobility, clergy, bourgeoisie, free labor-peasant class, and unfree

[5] For the meaning of each of the forms of unorganized and semi-organized groups see *SCP*, chs. 4, 8.

serfs); (7) Social Class. These important unibonded and multibonded groups mark the main lines of social differentiation and stratification of the total human population.

By their *structural properties* all social systems exhibit the varieties of: large or small in size; well or poorly organized; centralized or decentralized; with monarchical, aristocratic, oligarchic, democratic, tyrannical, and other forms of government; stratified in various ways; antagonistic, solidary and mixed innerly and externally in relationship to other groups; long and short-lived; spontaneously grown and intentionally established; rich and poor in their components of meanings-values, in their material vehicles and means of living and functioning; completely open and comparatively closed; with intense and weak social and cultural mobility,[6] concrete and discrete-localized on a contiguous territory and scattered over various points of this planet.

This dry enumeration gives an idea of the diversity and multitude of the powerful social systems and also of the main lines of social differentiation and stratification of the whole of mankind into the main organized groups or social systems.

THE INTERRELATIONSHIP OF SOCIAL AND CULTURAL SYSTEMS

Though every organized social group has a set of meanings-values-norms and every living cultural system has a group of interacting individuals as its creators, operators, or agents, the map of cultural systems in mankind or in a given population does not coincide with the map of its social systems. As the bits of colored class in a kaleidoscope are never identical at different turns of the kaleidoscope, so the boundaries of these two systems are neither identical nor coterminal. There are several reasons for their noncoterminability and noncoincidentality. Many cultural systems, especially such vast systems as mathematics, biology, medicine, and science, enter the total culture of practically all social systems: The family, the business concern, the religious group, the state, the political party, the labor union, all use

[6] See the reasons for, and details of, this classification and analysis of these groups in *SCP*, chs. 9–20.

arithmetic or medicine or the rudiments of physical or biological science. The same is true of the language system. There are many diverse social groups that speak English. It is likewise true of religious cultural systems. Many social systems have as their religious system either Buddhism or Roman Catholicism or Protestantism or Confucianism. In all these cases the cultural systems are like a vast body of water surrounding a diverse multitude of islands (social groups or systems).

Social and cultural systems also differ from one another in that the total culture of any organized group, even of a single person, consists not of one central cultural system but of a multitude of peripheral vast and small cultural systems that are partly in harmony, partly out of harmony, with one another, as well as a multitude of congeries of various kinds. Even the total culture of practically any individual is not completely integrated into one cultural system but represents a multitude of coexisting cultural systems and congeries. These systems and congeries are partly consistent with, partly neutral toward, and partly contradictory to one another. Suppose Mr. X to be a Baptist, Republican, physician, baseball fan, lover of Gershwin music, a man who prefers blondes to brunettes, whiskey to wine, and so on. The total culture of X thus appears to be partly integrated and partly unintegrated. Neither logically nor causally does his Baptist affiliation require him to be Republican, or a physician, or a whiskey-lover; the Baptist church is neutral to the Republican Party, to X's occupational culture, and to his liking for baseball; it may even contradict X's preference for jazz, blondes, and whiskey. Causally, all these cultural systems or traits are unrelated. There are many Baptists who are Democrats or who do not belong to any political party. There are many Republicans who are not baseball fans or who do not have a preference for blondes or whiskey. And there are many lovers of whiskey who are neither Baptists, Republicans, nor physicians. Thus the total culture of an organized group or even of an individual is neither identical nor coterminal with any one cultural system. The total culture of even the individual (as the smallest culture-area) is not wholly integrated into one meaningful-causal system. It represents the coexistence of many cultural systems—

partly harmonious, partly indifferent, partly contradictory to one another—plus the coexistence of many congeries that have somehow entered the individual's total culture and settled there. With these concise propositions, which are developed in subsequent chapters, we can turn to our critical survey of recent sociological theories.

PART TWO

THE NOMINALISTIC-SINGULARISTIC-ATOMISTIC TREND IN CONTEMPORARY GENERAL SOCIOLOGY

CHAPTER 3

Singularistic-Atomistic Theories:
Physicalistic and Mechanistic Varieties

GENERAL CHARACTERISTICS

The proponents of singularistic-atomistic theories often do not see the forest for the trees. More exactly, their attention is given mainly to the trees, that is, to individuals, and much less, if at all, to the forest, or the total society, and to its ecological formations. The forest appears to singularistic-atomistic researchers as the mere sum of its trees with no reality or properties of its own.

They claim also that, ontologically, any social group is the mere sum of its interacting members and apart from them does not have any reality of its own. In this respect, their conception of society or a social group represents "a sociological variety of nominalism and atomism. . . . It is a kind of nominalistic-atomistic conception of society as an aggregate of singularistic or separate individuals and their social actions, behind and beyond which there is no ontological entity called society."[1]

This conception of society is expressed not only in a series of philosophical and sociological theories but also, and particularly sharply, in the legal theories of the juridical personality. In this field it has both theoretical and practical significance, as I point out in my *Dynamics:*

> By juridical personality in law is meant any body consisting of one or more individuals treated by the law as a unit, and

[1] *Dynamics*, Vol. II, pp. 263–264. See there a more detailed analysis of philosophical and sociological nominalism, its representatives, and its fluctuation in Greco-Roman and Western history from 600 B.C. up to A.D. 1920.

usually endowed with the right to perpetual succession and to act as a single person. Since the Roman Law, two main forms of the juridical personality have been distinguished: (1) Corporations (*universitas personarum* or the medieval *collegia personalia*) where the union of the members as persons is stressed—such as most of various corporations, incorporated societies, firms, etc. (2) Institutions (*universitas bonorum* or the medieval *collegia realia*) as a complex of property with a specific purpose, endowed by the law to act as a single person, such as various universities, asylums, etc. (3) Mixed juridical personalities, intermediary between the two (*collegia mixta*).

The problem of the nature and reality of the juridical personality has caused unspeakable difficulties and hardships to the jurists. What is juridical personality? Is it a true reality of the trans-subjective social world, different from that of its individual members, or is it a mere fiction, which does not have any trans-subjective reality beyond that of its members, but which, for practical purposes, may artificially be treated as if it had a reality similar to that of a single person?

For centuries, many theories have attempted to answer this question. Omitting secondary differences, these theories can be classed into three main groups: (1) The *realistic* asserts that the juridical personality is a transsubjective and superindividual reality that truly exists in the social world and that is neither derivative from the reality of its members nor coincidental with it. (2) The *nominalistic* contends there is no reality of the juridical personality different from that of its members, either in the transsubjective social world or even in our thought. The only real elements in the *nominalistic* group are its individual members with their social actions and various sensory objects attached to it artificially. It is a fiction created artificially for specific practical needs and conditionally treated "as if" (*als ob*) it were a unity or reality, though in fact it is not. (3) The *mixed* or *intermediary* falls between the realistic and the nominalistic.[2]

---

[2] See a detailed analysis of these conceptions in the *Dynamics*, Vol. II, ch. 8. From Roman times up to the present, in these theories of the juridical personality can be found all the varieties of recent sociological theories concerning the nature, reality, and properties of society, social groups, and social systems. Many of the Roman, medieval, and

Nominalistic theories of juridical personality excellently express the modern singularistic-atomistic views on society or social group. Singularistic-atomistic sociologists view human culture or the culture of any area as a mere conglomeration of singularistic persons, traits, objects, and events that are in the given area at a certain period. They do not draw any explicit division between sociocultural systems and congeries. If they make a "survey" of a culture area, be it the culture of County A or Tribe B or Nation C or State D, they merely enumerate certain persons and describe the composition of its population and certain of its actions, events, industries, agriculture, and other of its singularistic phenomena. They make no serious attempt to separate the cultural systems from the congeries. If some classifications are used, they are used as purely formal groupings of the elements of the cultural conglomeration studied under fictitious catalogue headings. As I point out in my *Dynamics*, "As a result we have the piling up of various bits of information into a number of chapters or volumes, without any comprehension of the structure of the culture area, without even an understanding of why, out of a potentially infinite number of singular cultural objects, events, and actions, only these, and not millions of others, are selected."[3]

If sociocultural atomists want to find out some quantitative uniformities among these singularistic phenomena they again take for their "variables" two or more of these phenomena without any regard as to whether their variables are congeries or parts of a system or a whole system. If they discover any uniformities, they are regarded as probabilistic, statistical chance uniformities:

---

later theories of juridical personality can successfully rival in ingenuity, logicity, and adequacy the best recent sociological theories of society and of social systems.

[3] This and the following two quoted passages are from the *Dynamics*, Vol. IV, pp. 102–103. See, in the *Dynamics*, a detailed analysis and criticism of singularistic-atomistic conceptions of the total culture of a given area, of a population, and of the whole of mankind, Vol. IV, pp. 98–106, 192–193, 433–435; Vol. I, ch. 1; Vol. II, chs. 5–8 and pp. 439–446.

If our atomists write a history or theory of a change in the total culture of a given area or population they similarly just catalogue some persons, describe size and composition of the population, depict some events, and objects as they happen to follow one another in time-proximity and in space-adjacency. They give us just a "chronicle" or a variety of history well represented by television news or by daily and weekly papers.

On the "screen" they flash a picture of yesterday's murderer, a celebrity, a notorious call girl, President Johnson, Leonid Brezhnev, today's big fire, Vietnamese Buddhists, a basketball play, a snowstorm, the Berlin Wall—all phenomena that have no interconnection except their time-proximity or space-contiguity. Chronicles and many histories are similar:

> They give us a description of Cleopatra or Cicero, followed by that of a certain battle of Caesar or Sulla, then say something of Lucretius, of the Roman Senate, the cult of Mithra or Isis, then give a few statistics on the wages of the period, bits of information about the political parties and the structure of the Roman Empire, about gladiators or an uprising of slaves, and so on, [presenting] one "picture" after another united only by time or space-proximity. . . . In vain one may ask why these, but not millions of other persons, objects, phenomena, events, are specifically picked out. What, if any, is the connection between them? In vain one might ask all these whys.

This atomistic standpoint is well voiced by the following statements of two eminent historians who deny the existence of almost any uniformities in historical events: "I can see only one emergency following upon another . . . only one great fact in respect to which, since it is unique, there can be no generalization, only one safe rule for the historian: that he should recognize in the development of human destinies the play of the contingent and the unforeseen."[4] And, "To my mind, history is not so much a record of Progress, or Evolution, but a series of happenings of various tendencies. . . . In short, let us never talk of the world stream, or of inevitability, but reflect that the human (historical) record is illogical, often cataclysmic."[5]

In the sociocultural world surrounding us the atomistic

---

[4] H. Fisher, *History of Europe* (London, 1935), Vol. I, p. vii.
[5] Sir Charles Oman, *On the Writing of History* (New York, 1939).

sociologists see mainly or exclusively objects, persons, actions, and values as singular facts of sociocultural reality. They analyze, compute, and measure them summatively just as so many single units, atoms, or variables. They do not distinguish clearly between a heap of atomistic conglomerations and a unified system or a whole. In this respect, they remind us of the proverbial group of tourists who visited a famous cathedral and spent their appointed time not in observing the cathedral as an architectural, religious, and cultural whole, but in trying to ascertain whether it had 700 columns, as their guidebook said it had.

Such an approach leads atomistic-singularistic investigators to concentrate their research on concrete, perceptional, largely "microsociological" phenomena, because only concrete things can be perceived as single or separate variables and because many vast unified wholes are discreet and do not have perceptional concreteness.

We cannot sensorily perceive the whole immense system of Christianity in all its dogmas, beliefs, philosophy, ethics, and other meanings-values-norms, in all its membership, hierarchical organization, and in all its "materialized vehicles"— buildings, ritual objects, religious ceremonies, and multifarious activities of its members. Nor can we sensorily perceive the system of science in all its ideological theories and behavioral and material manifestations. No better can we perceive in its ideological, behavioral, and material plenitude the idealistic system of philosophy, or the romantic school in literature, or the United States of America, or even the American Sociological Association.

The singularistic-atomistic approach is also responsible for the "analytical" method of research: When the atomistic sociologists are confronted with vast, discreet, and complex sociocultural structures and processes, they, imitating the method of the physical sciences, try to resolve them into "elementary units" or "components" or to chip off such totalities a few fragments in order that they can subsequently manipulate these "fragments" or "units" as empirical quantitative variables—to measure them in various ways, to compute their corelations and covariations, and to observe and describe them with "objective scientific preciseness."

At the bottom of all consistent singularistic-atomistic socio-logical theories (though very few of them are really consistent) lies a fundamental postulate: that *all sociocultural phenomena have only singularistic forms of being,* each phenomenon existing in a state of independence from the others, neither bound to other phenomena by causal or meaningful-causal ties nor making any kind of unified whole with the others. Now and then these singularistic phenomena can display in their relationships purely probabilistic, chance uniformities. Sociological atomists and singularists regard it as their supreme task to discover this sort of uniformity. In this point they also imitate one of the methods of the physical sciences.

To sum up, singularistic-atomistic sociological theories are marked by logico-ontological nominalism versus logico-onto-logical realism and partly by conceptualism; by ontological, sociocultural, and partly ethical singularism versus sociocultural and partly ethical universalism; and by temporalism versus eternalism.[6] They are also marked by their preferential treat-ment of microsociological, concrete, sensorily perceptible phe-nomena; their imitation of the methods and terminology of poorly understood physical sciences; their concentration on the quantitative aspects of the sociocultural phenomena studied; and, finally, their negative attitude toward "philosophizing," "specu-lative theorizing," and "grand systems of sociology." Nominal-ism-conceptualism-realism, singularism-universalism, and tem-poralism-eternalism all have a variety of extreme and moderate forms, and the singularistic-atomistic sociological theories also have diverse variations. For the purposes of our examination, these variations can be grouped into two classes: "physicalistic-mechanistic" and "quantitative," each of which has several sub-classes, given in this and following chapters.

[6] I do not want to give here a systematic analysis of these terms. Such an analysis can be found in the *Dynamics,* Vol. II, chs. 5, 6, and 7. The full meaning of singularistic-atomistic sociological theories can be grasped only after a careful study of these chapters. See there also the quantitative indicators of fluctuation of these currents of philosophical and sociological thought in the Greco-Roman and the Western world since the sixth century B.C. on up to A.D. 1920. On pp. 676 to 696 a fairly complete list of the thinkers of each of these currents is given.

THE RECENT UPSURGE OF SINGULARISTIC-ATOMISTIC THEORIES

As mentioned above, the recent field of general sociology has been marked by an upsurge of the singularistic-atomistic as well as of the systemic currents of sociological thought. The upsurge of the singularistic-atomistic theories is described by a Soviet sociologist:

> The works of the Fourth International Congress of the International Association at Stresa, Italy, in September, 1959, demonstrated an important feature; namely, the deep crisis of the bourgeois sociology. Beginning with the middle of the nineteenth century the dominant method of the bourgeois sociological research has become the method of positivism, reduced to the research of very narrow and insignificant facts mainly by the way of questionnaires and interviews of small and incidental samples of population. This has led to the dwarfing of the character of the bourgeois sociological investigations and to the reluctance of formulating significant sociological theories and generalizations. Instead of a systematic and generalizing view on society there appeared numerous empirical studies of incidental and mutually unrelated social phenomena. Bourgeois sociology disintegrated into fragmentary studies of a multitude of perfectly insignificant problems. . . . In recent years among the bourgeois sociologists there [have arisen] voices calling for paying more attention to theoretical generalizations and for returning to the theoretical works of the nineteenth and the twentieth centuries. Many of the bourgeois sociologists now begin to understand increasingly the sterility of positivism and empiricism. Life itself sets forth the big problems of social life from which it is impossible to hide by burying ourselves into the realm of empirical investigations of the second- and the third-class social phenomena.[7]

[7] V. S. Semenov, "Thchetvertyi Vsemirnyi Soziologichesky Kongress," *Vestnik Istorii Mirovoi Kultury*, No. 1 (1960), pp. 148–149. See also G. V. Osipov and V. V. Kolbanovsky, "Marksistkaya Soziologia," in *Nauchnuye Doklady Vuschey Shkoly*, No. 5 (1962); G. M. Andrejeva, *Sovremennaja bourgouaznaja empiricheskaja soziologia* (Moscow, 1965); F. Konstantinov, G. Osipov, and V. Semenov (eds.), *Marxistskaja i bourgouaznaja soziologia segondnia* (Moscow, 1964); and G. Osipov, *Sovremenaja bourgouaznaja soziologia* (Moscow, 1964).

The essential point of this diagnosis is confirmed by practically all the American sociologists who participated in the Symposium on the Changes in Sociology in 1956: E. Burgess, F. S. Chapin, J. L. Gillin, F. H. Hankins, W. E. Ogburn, S. A. Queen, J. F. Steiner, C. C. Taylor, K. Young, L. von Wiese, and myself.[8] All testify that during the last three decades "Sociological-system-building fell into disrepute, helped by many scornful remarks about 'arm-chair' philosophers";[9] that "early in the century there began a movement to abandon the attempts to make a grand system of sociology";[10] and that "today the grand-system-makers have almost vanished."[11]

> Perhaps the most conspicuous change, especially in American sociology, during the period considered consists in a sharp shift of sociological research of the younger generation of sociologists from a cultivation of general systems of sociology and a study of its basic problems to an "operational," "quantitative," "experimental," "precise" research of special problems of psychosocial sciences, including its methods and techniques. The bulk of the younger sociologists seem to have lost interest in "arm-chair" sociology, as they call the systems of sociology of the preceding generations, and they are trying to build "a natural-science sociology" as a replica of a physical science.[12]

A large number of other sociologists (R. Bierstedt, C. W. Mills, J. B. Ford, W. Record, L. F. Schnore, R. N. Bellah, J. Coleman, O. D. Duncan, and others) unanimously stress this change in recent, especially American, sociology.

If on this point there seems to be a complete agreement between the Soviet and the Western sociologists, the same is not true on the value of the shift from building grand systems of sociology to the research of special, narrow problems. Some participants in the Symposium, like Chapin, Ogburn, Burgess, Queen, and many of the younger generation of American sociologists, welcome the shift and view it as a real progress of sociology from the "speculative and philosophical" to the "scien-

---

[8] See "The Symposium," *Sociology and Social Research,* July–August, 1956.
[9] *Ibid.,* p. 392.
[10] *Ibid.,* p. 399.
[11] *Ibid.,* p. 402.
[12] *Ibid.,* p. 405.

tific" stage. Others, like the Soviet sociologists and an increasing number of Western sociologists (F. H. Hankins, J. F. Steiner, L. von Wiese, F. Znaniecki, R. Bierstedt, C. W. Mills, F. R. Cowell, J. B. Ford, C. C. Zimmerman, G. Gurvitch, myself, and others) view the shift with serious apprehensions and criticisms.

What does this shift mean? Is it really a notable progress of sociology toward its scientific maturity, or is it rather a sign of the fragmentation and decline of sociology in the sense of knowing more and more about less and less? Shall we view the sociological theorizing and "system-building" as perfectly needless and irrevocably obsolescent, or shall we deeply regret the scarcity of such systems and of their creators among the younger generation of sociologists and renew our efforts in creating ever better and grander systems of science?

Before answering these questions, let us carefully glance at some typical singularistic-atomistic theories.[13]

RECENT PHYSICALISTIC AND MECHANISTIC THEORIES

During the period considered, various currents of physicalistic or mechanistic interpretations of sociocultural and psychological phenomena continued to be laboriously cultivated, especially in the United States. In this country, particularly, the period is marked by the intensified invasion and diffusion of imitative natural-science sociology and psychology, social physics, social mechanics, mechanical psychology, and cybernetic sociology; by physicalistic pseudomathematical, pseudoexperimental, and operational research of psychosocial phenomena; and by the proliferation of a legion of mechanical tests applied to all sorts of psychosocial and cultural problems. In brief, the period has been a sort of a Golden Age for physicalistic sociology and psychology. This trend has expressed itself, first of all, in an increased imitation of the terms of physical science. "Valence" is used instead of "attractiveness," "locomotion" instead of "change" or "transformation," "social atom" instead of

[13] See the answer in Chapter 4, pp. 127–129.

"individual," "dimension" instead of "aspect," "field" instead of "class or category of phenomena," "cohesion" instead of "solidarity," and so on. Second, the trend has manifested itself in an intensified importation into sociology of the formulas, methods, models, and tests of macrophysics, geometry, chemistry, and biology; and, third, in the setting forth of a large number of physicalistic and mechanistic theories of psychosocial phenomena. So far, there is no clear sign that this trend is abating. Let us now outline the main currents of "modern" physicalistic sociology.

RECENT "SOCIAL PHYSICS"

We shall begin our survey of recent social physics with P. W. Bridgman's manifesto of physicalistic sociology.[14] Although Bridgman is an eminent physicist, he unfortunately knows little of sociology or psychology. As a result, his manifesto is marked by the same characteristics that usually stamp the credo of a person who invades a science little known to him—that is, by incompetence, mistakes, and by the "discovery" of laws that were discovered long ago.

The book opens with a repetitious proclamation of the all-too-familiar credo of physicalistic sociology:

> It is to be a fundamental thesis of this essay that the same principles which physics have discovered to control any valid reconstruction of its concepts also control any valid reconstruction of social concepts. . . . The parallelism in situation between physics and society is so close as to constitute more than a mere analogy, for it reveals a logical identity. . . . The physical approach [to social problems] thoroughly justifies itself.

He goes on to say that the operational method of studying social phenomena is the only reliable method, and so on. The

---

[14] P. W. Bridgman, *The Intelligent Individual and Society* (New York, 1938), pp. 7, 8, 12, and *passim*. See also his "The Task Before Us," *Proceedings of the American Academy of Arts and Sciences, 83*(1954), 97–112.

bulk of the book deals with the concepts and methods of physics with an insistent advice to sociologists to follow the physicalistic approach. The last part of the book is devoted to a discussion of social concepts and problems, such as duty, rights, morality, politics, and economics.

Bridgman's credo of physicalistic sociology does not have even the fascination of novelty, for our eminent physicist seems to be unaware of the fact that it is but a repetition of hundreds of other such credos promulgated by the partisans of "social physics" and "social mechanics" of the preceding centuries.[15] In his discussion of social problems—duty, rights, morality, "intelligent individual," "society," and so on—Bridgman seems to be unaware of the enormous amount of study that has already gone into these social and ethical problems. In comparison with the great ethical, political, and sociological theories in the field, Bridgman's views appear about as crude as Leucippus-Democritus' atomic theory does in comparison with the atomic theories of modern physics. No wonder that Bridgman's reconstruction of sociology along the patterns of physics does not go beyond purely wishful analogies; no wonder it stops short before it even clears the ground for the magnificent palace of "social physics."

A group of social physicists led by John Q. Stewart, an astrophysicist at Princeton, have gone somewhat further in this area than Bridgman. But, like other physicalistic sociologists, Stewart also assumes that sociology must pass through the stages of evolution analogical to those of physics, following, of course, the methods and concepts of physics. Stewart and his group use the familiar analogical arguments at all points of their presentation. Fortunately, the group does not stop at these misleading analogies, but tries to discover various uniformities of psychosocial phenomena and to describe them in terms of physical science. Let us glance at Stewart's social physics, its methods, uniformities, and other results of the group's labor:

> Our immediate quest is for uniformities in social behavior which can be expressed in mathematical forms more or less corresponding to the known patterns of physical science. Social

[15] See *CST*, ch. 1.

physics so defined analyzes demographic, economic, political, and sociological situations in terms of purely physical factors: time, distance, mass of material, and numbers of people, with recourse also to social factors which can be shown to operate in a similar way to two other physical agents, namely, temperature and electrical charge. . . . Social physics describes mass human relationships in physical terms, treating large aggregations of individuals as though they were composed of "social molecules"—without attempting to analyze the behavior of each molecule.[16]

His social physics thus views the social universe as six-dimensional or as made up of six "social quantities" or "fundamental categories": "distance, time, mass, temperature, electric charge, and number of molecules." We are told that "this list [of six dimensions] makes social physics in its dimensional structure isomorphic with physical science"—that is, "there is a complete and trustworthy analogy between two or more situations" that entitles us "to transfer equations from physics to politics."[17]

Having thus outlined the framework of social physics, Stewart proceeds to round up various social uniformities and to interpret them in terms of his six-dimensional categories. As the most important example of the uniformities, Stewart takes Zipf's "rank-size rule" (referred to below, p. 57), but extrapolates it much further than Zipf did. We shall see also that Zipf's rule is at best purely local and temporal and in no way as general as Zipf and, especially, Stewart claim. However, when Stewart is confronted with interpreting the rationale of this "rank-size rule," he completely fails to give any adequate explanation of it. "The rank-size rule is not at present derivable from general principles." Here we have the "widespread mathematical regularity for which no explanation is known."[18]

The failure leaves Stewart only one way out of the difficulty, namely, issuing a big check from social physics for an unknown bank of the future that "some day, somehow, by some bank" will be redeemed, "after much more study." This hope

[16] J. Q. Stewart, "A Basis for Social Physics," *Impact of Science on Society*, 3(1952), 110, 118.

[17] *Ibid.*, pp. 122–123.

[18] *Ibid.*, pp. 116–118.

for future banks where all doubtful checks of the present will be fully paid is also very familiar. However, it has nothing to do with a real scientific theory: Science does not ask us to believe in its future promises, but, so far as it claims its recognition at present, it pays its checks any time, anywhere, from its present capital of evidence.

Let us now glance closer at the social meaning of the six categories. First, we note that Stewart's "time" dimension is the uniform, evenly flowing, infinitely divisible time of macrophysics ("clock time"). Here he seems to forget that macrophysical time is not quite applicable to microphysical phenomena. And he seems to be unaware also that this time is only one of the "sociocultural times," which are in no way identical with the variety of "qualitative social times," which are neither uniform nor infinitely divisible. Stewart's time, a mere variety of empirical "tempus" tied up with ever-changing sensory phenomena, entirely misses two fundamental forms of time called by the medieval Scholastics *aeternitas* and *aevum*. *Aeternitas* deals with eternal or unchanging forms of being; *aevum* is the category for semieternal forms of being, like the truth of scientific propositions, which in their potentiality are viewed even by scientists themselves as tending to be eternal and invariant. (Otherwise the true propositions would not differ from ever-changing fallacies.)[19] The moral of these remarks is that in limiting his "time" to "clock time," Stewart cannot "locate" in the time process or measure in time units a large part of the sensory-empirical, and especially the eternal or semieternal values of the sociocultural universe.

His other five "dimensions-categories-social quantities" are

---

[19] These remarks are probably unclear to most modern sociologists and psychologists who hardly ever studied the meaning, forms, and functions of time and space, and especially of their sociocultural forms. Clarifying analyses of sociocultural time and space can be found in my *Sociocultural Causality, Space, Time* (New York, 1964), chs. 3 and 4; and in my *Dynamics*, Vol. IV, chs. 9, 10, and 11. See also G. Gurvitch, *Determinismes sociaux et liberté humaine* (Paris, 1955), where another pluralistic theory of time is developed; W. E. Moore, *Man, Time, and Society* (New York, 1963); and R. M. MacIver, *The Challenge of the Passing Years: My Encounter with Time* (New York, 1962).

still worse for cognitive purposes than his "time dimension." What, for instance, can he mean by "social mass," or "social electric charge," or "social temperature," or "social distance?" If these terms mean exactly what "mass," "electric charge," "temperature," and "distance" mean in the physical sciences, then the addition of the word social is superfluous. Physical sciences take good care of "mass," "electric charge," "temperature," and "distance" whenever and wherever they are found, including the human universe. If, however, these terms mean something different, then one has to show what each of them means and give a reason for calling them by the terms of physics —as well as a reason for calling the whole discipline "social physics."

In Stewart's use, these terms have meanings quite different from their meanings in physics. Thus, his "electric charge" does not mean electric charge at all, but rather "desire"; his "mass" means the "bodies of the people and of their domesticated animals, their stocks of harvested food, their clothing and personal equipment, artificial housing, buildings, and ships, plants of all sorts, the weight of material that had to be moved in constructing trails, roadways, railways, mines, harbor improvements, airports, dams. It includes water being circulated by pumps, and the mass of the tilled soil." Quite a "mass" indeed! Given such new meanings of "electric charge" and "mass," we are not surprised at the meaning of "social temperature," which signifies the "level of activity" of people and the intensity of their interaction; or by the meaning of "distance," which has very little relation to the "distance" of physics. Stewart gives several terms of the psychosocial sciences no less surprising (though not new) physicalistic meaning; for instance, the "politico-economical concept of liberty" is viewed as a form of "social enthropy."[20]

Stewart's "social physics" has no relation to physics at all.

---

[20] Stewart, *op. cit.*, pp. 118–129. In a letter to me, Professor Stewart states that "as the point of view of social physics develops further, you would be willing to consider that the dimensions of reason, feeling, and authority offer sufficient description of many sociocultural phenomena. This would leave time, distance, and mass as purely physical." (May 26, 1953.)

His physicalistic terms are likewise total strangers to similar terms of physics. The categories of "desire," "population and material culture" ("social mass"), "intensity of interaction and level of human activity," and so on, are just ordinary notions of traditional psychosocial sciences and do not make these sciences "physicalistic" at all. Stewart's term "social physics" is a misnomer in both its "physics" and its "social" components.

If we take Stewart's categories "desire," "level of activity," "the population and its material culture," "time," and "distance" in their real meanings, we can easily see that his framework of categories is neither adequate logically nor fruitful empirically. It is certainly more clumsy and defective than several other conceptual frameworks of general sociology. In addition, it combines several incommensurable notions, like "desire" and "social mass," or (in Stewart's letter) "time" and "reason," "distance and authority," and so on. In this respect, his framework is a bastard of pseudophysics and pseudosociology.

Unsatisfactory, also, are Stewart's dimensional categories. For instance, one can hardly use his category of "social mass" as an instrument for analyzing and measuring psychological and sociocultural phenomena. By itself this "social mass" is made up of so many, so different, and so difficult-to-measure and partly immeasurable quantities, that it is doomed to be a largely undefined, unmeasurable, and indeterminate variable or category.

One of the components of the "social mass" is the "bodies of the people." Now, suppose we find that one group of 100 individuals has the total weight (the "social mass") of 10,000 pounds (because it has many babies and children), whereas another group of 100 individuals has the total "social mass" of 16,000 pounds (partly because it has only a few babies and the adults are fatter and heavier). What sociological significance may such a difference have in the total weight of these two groups? And why is it important to know this "social mass," especially if we pay no attention to the age-sex-health composition of the groups, their somatotypes, their morbidity, their intelligence? If we pass from this component of the "social mass" to such components of it as the "mass of tilled soil" (not the acreage), we are confronted at once with the task of how to measure this mass of tilled soil. And why is such a mass more important than the fertility of the soil or the average amount harvested per acre? And is not the whole "social mass" an incomplete, cumbersome, and very inadequate form of material wealth or capital more easily and accurately measured by economics? Why does Stewart's "social mass" give an importance to merely "weight" and "bulkiness" of plants, buildings, tilled soil, amount of food, clothing, buildings, "roadways," "railways," and so on, without any consideration of their quality? A ruin of a medieval castle weighs more and is bulkier than a dozen modern houses; an old siege machine weighs more than a small atomic bomb; a haystack weighs more than a bottle of vitamins; an assortment of jazz instruments weighs more than one Stradivarius violin; thousands of factory-made pictures weigh more than one sketch by Raphael or el Greco. Does this mean that the group that possesses these heavy "masses" is more advanced, more creative, more civilized than the group that has lighter "masses"—an atomic bomb, vitamins, Raphael's picture, a Stradivarius—as Stewart seems to think? Shall we call a person who has a large library of detective stories, comics, grade-school texts, and popular magazines more cultured than a person whose library is limited to Plato's *Dialogues*, Kant's *Critique of Pure Reason*, Homer's *Iliad*, Shakespeare's *Hamlet*, and Dante's *Divine Comedy*?

Stewart's "social mass" cannot serve either as an index of material wealth and prosperity or as a measure of standard of living, cultural and social creativity, or level of culture and civilization. Nor can it measure hardly any other important sociocultural state of a person or group. It is perfectly useless and does not justify an astronomical load of work to obtain even its roughest measure. Stewart, an astronomer, has a meager knowledge of psychosocial sciences, and apparently assumes that these scientists hardly ever studied the problems of his social physics. His paper is interspersed with semisatirical remarks, such as "spaces which separate people are airily ignored [by social sciences]"; "demographers had never introduced a term to measure the influence of people at distance"; "the concept of the demographic field was unknown [to social scientists]"; "[social scientists] did not study intensively the phenomena of interaction," and so on. I can positively assure the author that not only have all psychological and sociocultural phenomena discussed by him been studied by the psychosocial sciences, but these sciences have investigated these problems with an incomparably greater care, adequacy, objectivity, and quantitative precision than Stewart's amateurish smattering does. Economics has handled and measured natural resources, wealth, and capital much more accurately than the "social mass" of Stewart does. Sociology has studied demographic phenomena, the phenomena of interaction, the influence of people at distance, social migrations and mobility, levels and forms of cultural and social activity, and so on, so much better than Stewart's "social mass" could that any comparison is superfluous.[21]

If Stewart had seriously studied economics, demography, sociology, psychology, philosophy, and previous attempts to create "social physics," he hardly would have come out with the amateurish "social mass," "social temperature," "desire," and other dimensional categories of his antiquated "social physics." If anything, it is even more primitive than some of the previous "social physics and mechanics" outlined in Chapter 1 of *Contemporary Sociological Theories*.

What is said of Stewart's "social physics" can be said, with still greater reason, of other modern "social physics," "social mechanics," "topological psychologies," "physicalistic politics," and so on. In spite of my criticism of Stewart's endeavor, his social physics is better than most of the other physicalistic speculations of our time.

IMITATIVE PHYSICALISTIC TRANSCRIPTIONS

Here are some transcriptive examples of these speculations. T. Parsons, R. F. Bales, and E. A. Shils in 1953 solemnly announced, in the impressive terms of the physicomathematical sciences, that they had "found four fundamental generalizations

[21] See on these matters, *CST*, chs. 1, 3, 7, and *passim*; *Dynamics*, Vol. IV, ch. 5; and *SCP*, *passim*.

for defining the equilibrium of a social system in terms of 'four-dimensional space.' "

> 1. The Principle of Inertia: A given process of action will continue unchanged in rate and direction unless impeded or deflected by opposite motivational forces.
> 2. The Principle of Action and Reaction: If, in a system of action, there is a change in the direction of a process, it will be balanced by a complementary change which is equal in motivational force and opposite in direction.

In similar terms, they formulated "The Principle of Effort" and "The Principle of System-Integration."[22]

These and similar "fundamental generalizations" merely repeat the transcriptions of practically all the earlier representatives of "social physics" (G. Berkeley, Saint-Simon, H. C. Carey, L. Winiarsky, A. P. y Barcelo, and others, outlined in Chapter 1 of *Contemporary Sociological Theories*). For this reason, Parsons-Bales' contention that they "have found" them is somewhat amusing. They did not find anything new. Furthermore, if their transcription of Newton's, d'Alambert's, Lagrange's, Le Chatelier's, and Bernoulli's "laws" aims at a mere popularization of these "laws," then, instead of their "home-made" versions of them, Parsons and Bales should have given the exact formulations of these great physicists and mathematicians. Also, if Parsons-Bales' propositions claim to be the basic principles of human social actions, then they become either meaningless or fallacious, because without the units of time, space, direction, change, and force neither the change of action nor its direction or motivational force nor "equal" and "opposing" forces can be determined, defined, and measured. Since the authors give none of these units, their propositions are meaningless, imitative verbiage.

If we try to apply these generalizations to empirical social actions, we see that they are obvious fallacies. According to

---

[22] T. Parsons, R. F. Bales, and E. A. Shils, *Working Papers in the Theory of Action* (Glencoe, Ill., 1953), p. 102. See a more detailed criticism of these "generalizations" in P. Sorokin, *Fads and Foibles in Modern Sociology* (Chicago, 1955), and of the concept of equilibrium in the *Dynamics*, Vol. IV, pp. 670–693.

Parsons-Bales' "principle of inertia," if one starts to eat or to micturate, one will be eating or micturating forever at the same rate and in the same direction, if there are no impeding and deflecting motivational forces. According to the "principle of action and reaction," no real change can take place in any system of action, because any tendency to change its direction "will tend to be balanced by a complementary change which is equal in motivational force and opposite in direction." Consequently, all actions will be forever frozen in the form in which they appeared for the first time. If one's primordial prototype action was, say, reading or chopping wood, one will be forever "frozen" in this action, unless some external force intervenes. The absurdities of these amateurish laws are due to a misinterpretation of the laws of physics by our homemade physicists, to a clumsy application of the laws of physics to phenomena to which they are inapplicable, to the authors' vague definition of the principle of equilibrium,[23] and, especially, to their forgetting two basic principles: the principle of immanent change of a system according to which any system or action, as a going concern, cannot avoid change from "within" even in the constant and unchangeable environment; and the principle of limit, according to which for any change in a certain direction there is always a limit.[24]

The criticisms of Parsons-Bales' transcription and misapplication of the laws and principles of physics can be applied to all other misuses of physical and mathematical sciences.

As a rule knowing poorly these sciences, our sociological physicists are so carried away by their enthusiasm for the natural sciences that they import their terms without any regard as to whether they are applicable to psychosocial phenomena. These sociologists are so obsessed by their desire to create a "natural-science sociology" that fairly often they give gibberish definitions

---

[23] They outline vaguely one of the five different meanings of the term "equilibrium," none of which is applicable to psychosocial systems and actions. See an analysis and criticism of all five concepts of equilibrium in the *Dynamics*, Vol. IV, pp. 677–694. See also O. Lange, *Catość i rozwój w świete cybernetyki* [*The Whole and Development in the Light of Cybernetics*], (Warsaw, 1962).

[24] See, on these principles, the *Dynamics*, Vol. IV, chs. 12–16, and *SCP*, ch. 46.

and propositions made up of terms of physics carelessly thrown together. Terms that have, in the natural sciences, clear and precise meanings are, when imported into sociology, given a meaning quite different from their original sense. In their new meanings they simply replace one of the traditional sociological terms without adding to it any cognitive value. Instead of making the traditional terms more precise, the imported terms must be explained by the traditional ones in order to have any meaning whatsoever. In this way, a large number of perfectly parasitic terms have been imported into sociology where they merely litter its field without rendering any fruitful service. Sociological language has become obtuse; it is full of sham scientific slang devoid of clear meaning, precision, and elementary elegance. Thus, "valence" is used instead of "attractiveness"; "syntality" instead of the "total performance of the group"; "synergy" instead of the "total energy of the group"; "locomotion" instead of "change"; "cathexis" instead of "pleasure-seeking and pain-avoiding or contacting"; "enthropy" instead of "habit"; and so on. The amusing side of all this is that the importers do not try to clarify the meaning of "attractiveness" by that of "valence," but define "valence" through "attractiveness," and so forth.[25]

When these physicalistic terms, emptied of their real meanings in the process of importation, are combined in a sentence, supposedly to give a precise definition of psychosocial phenomena, they make no sense whatsoever. Here are a few examples of this meaningless verbiage:

> "[An organism is] a system of energy operating within a field of forces."[26]
> "[An individual is] both a mechanical system . . . and a semantic self."
> "[Mind is] an organism's selection of particular kind of material operations to perform upon particular kinds of matter-energy

[25] See many examples of these terms in D. Cartwright and A. Zander (eds.), *Group Dynamics* (Evanston, Ill., 1953). (This and all further references are to the first edition. A greatly revised edition was published in 1960.) For a further criticism of this "fashion" see my *Fads and Foibles*, chs. 1 and 2.

[26] G. A. Lundberg, *Foundations of Sociology* (New York, 1939), p. 115.

in order to minimize the organism's own probable work."
"[An organism] is a movable mathematical point in space-time,
in reference to which matter-energy moves in such a way that
a physical situation exists in which work is expended in order
to preserve a physical system from a final gravitational and
electro-magnetic equilibrium with the rest of universe."[27]

Sometimes our innovators ponderously define mere platitudes, even tautological platitudes at that:

> From the definitions of promotively and contriently independ-
> ent goals, it appears that (a) any person, X, who has promo-
> tively interdependent goals with persons A, B, C, etc., will
> come to have promotively interdependent locomotions in the
> direction of his goal with persons A, B, C, etc.[28]

These examples show well the physicalistic obsession of
many a modern "natural-science sociologist," as well as the
cognitive fruitlessness of their imitative efforts. About all this
"jabberwocky" one can say with Alice: "It seems pretty, but
it's rather hard to understand! Somehow, it seems to fill my
head with ideas—only I don't exactly know what they are."
With Humpty-Dumpty we also can say: "There are plenty of
hard words there." Let us glance at other varieties of this
obsession.

RECENT "PSEUDOMATHEMATICAL IMITATIONS"

K. Lewin's and J. F. Brown's "topological" psychology
serves as another example of the meaningless transcription
of geometric and physicalistic terms, propositions, and signs.
They turn psychology into "psychological field" as a "space
construct" where space "is understood in its post-Riemannian
sense." To this "psychological field" they order all "psychological activities," and then transfer to it the terms of physics

---

[27] G. K. Zipf, *Human Behavior and the Principle of Least Effort*
(Cambridge, Mass., 1949), pp. 212, 253, 327–328.

[28] Morton Deutsch, "The Effects of Cooperation and Competition
upon Group Process," in *Group Dynamics* (1953 edition), Cartwright
and Zander, pp. 320–321.

and of geometrical space: "direction, vector, sense, magnitude, distance, force, continuity or discontinuity, liberty or restriction." They add to this assortment their own homemade terms: "purpose," "goal," "striving," "ambition," and so on—terms entirely alien to any geometric space or science of physics.[29]

These transcriptive operations are instructive only in their errors; they remain sterile in their cognitive fruitfulness. Their definition of psychology as "psychological field" or science of "psychological activities" is tautological. They distort the precise meanings of concepts of physics and geometry, giving to them psychological meanings entirely alien to the physical sciences. They distort the meanings of psychosocial terms like goal, purpose, and ambition by interpreting them in a spatial sense. For instance, they translate the term direction into goal and goal or purpose into direction. The term direction in physics or geometry means always "direction in space"; it has nothing to do with goal or purpose and is never used in this sense. Physics and geometry have no "spaceless goals," "aims to be achieved," or "ambitions to be realized." On the other hand, the psychosocial meaning of the terms goal and purpose is rarely spatial; as a rule they have no spatial connotation. The goal of X to become a millionaire or of Y to get his Ph.D. has no latitude, altitude, longitude, or any strictly spatial locus or direction. When these goals are called "spatial directions," the expression becomes meaningless. By declaring that the "points in the psychological field . . . may for the present only be nonmetrically defined," the authors make these terms void of any significance, for the nonmetric magnitude, force, direction, distance, and vector become the notions of a most indeterminate nature, hardly ever used in the physical sciences in this qualitative vague

---

[29] See K. Lewin, *Principles of Topological Psychology* (New York, 1936), and *Field Theory in Social Sciences: Selected Theoretical Papers* (New York, 1951); J. F. Brown, "On the Use of Mathematics in Psychological Theory," *Psychometrika*, I (1936), and *Psychology and Social Order* (New York, 1936); M. Lins, *Espaco-Tempo e relacões sociaes* (Rio de Janeiro, 1940); Pinto Ferreira, *Teoria do espaco social* (Rio de Janeiro, 1939); and Pontes de Miranda, *Introducção a sociologia geral* (Rio de Janeiro, 1927). For a more detailed criticism of these transcriptions, see my *Sociocultural Causality*, ch. 3.

form. By mixing together physical and psychosocial terms our authors produce meaningless bastards disserviceable to physical as well as to psychosocial disciplines. If Lewin, Brown, de Miranda, and others made some contribution to our knowledge of psychosocial phenomena, they made it in those of their non-imitative studies in which these transcriptive operations were absent.

"SHORTHAND" SOCIOLOGIES

Side by side with the imitative pseudophysical and pseudo-geometric sociological theories, the physicalistic trend of the period has also manifested itself in a veritable proliferation of pseudomathematical studies of psychosocial phenomena. Perhaps the most conspicuous examples of these sham mathematical sociologies are given by the theories that substitute shorthand symbols and empty formulas for the true mathematical ones. Here are a few samples of these sham mathematical imitations.

In his quantitative study of interaction as a specific social energy, A. Lysen tells us that social ties can be either positive or negative, and that the interacting agents can be either qualitatively equal (inorganic ties) or unequal (organic ties). Expressing both criteria "mathematically," Lysen denotes the quantities of social energy by the symbols a, b, and c and its qualities by those of x, y, and z. Having obtained his symbols, he proceeds to use them in the following manner: $ax = bx + x$ means a horde or the sum of persons devoid of social consciousness and held together only by instinct; $ax = bx - cx$ means the negative social ties or social conflicts; $ax = by \times cz$ means the positive organic ties or collective consciousness of the interacting individuals; $ax = by :: cz$ denotes the negative-organic ties or the sum of interacting persons aware of subordination, dependency, etc.[30]

---

[30] A. Lysen, "Anorganisches und Organisches in den sozialen Erscheinungen," *Kölner Vierteljahrshefte für Soziologie*, XI(1932), 139–153.

No lengthy comments are necessary. It is clear that the sham mathematical nature of the shorthand symbols hinders rather than helps his verbal definitions of social energy, positive and negative ties, and types of groups. His *ax, by, cz,* etc., do not mean anything clearly defined; neither do they mean any measurable quantity or definite quality; his $=$, $+$, $-$, $\times$, and $::$ signs are perfectly arbitrary and do not mean at all what they mean in mathematics. Why, for instance, is a group with collective consciousness denoted by the multiplication symbol, whereas a horde is denoted by the addition sign? Or why is the group with domination-subordination expressed by the equation $ax = by :: cz$, whereas the group with social conflicts is defined by the equation $ax = bx - cz$? Why division in one case and subtraction in the other? These formulas, symbols, and equations are nothing but a logical mess, mathematical nonsense, and empirical rubbish.

Another example of sham mathematics is given by many shorthand formulas of K. Lewin, J. F. Brown, T. Parsons, and others. For instance, Lewin expresses the notion that the "variety of behavior increases during childhood with normal development" by the following formula: $\mathrm{var}(B^{Ch})$ $\mathrm{var}(B^{Ad})$, "where *var* means variety, B^{Ch} the behavior of the child, and B^{Ad} the behavior of the adult." Or, "we call the totality of these factors the life-space ($L\ Sp$) of an individual and write $B = F(P, E) = F(S\ Sp)$." (B means behavior; P means person; E means environment.)[31]

Lewin's works are full of these homemade shorthand symbols. His cumbersome hieroglyphics have no relationship whatsoever to mathematics, and serve no useful purpose whatsoever.

---

[31] Lewin, *Field Theory in Social Sciences*, pp. 100, 239–240. Another example of the "shorthand" sociologies is given by the "most generalized formula for a system of action" of Talcott Parsons, *The Structure of Social Action* (New York), 1937, pp. 78–81. The formula is as follows:

$$A = S(M \text{ manifested in } T, t, r\ +$$
$$C \text{ manifested in } T, t, r\ +$$
$$i \text{ manifested in } T, t, r)$$
$$+ E + N \text{ (defined in terms of } T, t, r, i)$$
$$+ r$$
$$Z = (A_1 + A_2 + \ldots A_n) + R_{el} + R_1 + R_c$$

Also see there several other "shorthand" formulas having no relationship to any mathematical or physicochemical formulas whatsoever.

S. C. Dodd supplies another set of sham mathematical symbols. Like other formulas of this sort, they do not serve even the pedagogical function of enabling the reader to understand Dodd's verbal statements. Dodd's basic "*S*-theory" is an example of his formulas:

> Any quantitatively recorded societal situation(s) can be expressed as a combination of: 4 indexes [*I*], namely, of time [*T*], space [*L*], a human population [*P*], and indicators [*I*] of their characteristics, each modified by 4 scripts, namely, the exponent [I^s], and descripts denoting a series of classes [I_s], of class-intervals [$_sI$], and of cases [^sI]; all combined by 8 operators (;), namely, for adding [+], subtracting [−], multiplying [×], dividing [/], aggregating [:], cross-classifying [::], correlating [.], and identifying [′].

The *S*-theory is a system of hypotheses that asserts that combinations of the basic concepts (in brackets) will describe and classify every tabulation, graph, map, formula, prose paragraph, or other set of quantitative data in any of the social sciences.[32]

Here is the master formula of the *S*-theory: $S = \frac{s}{s}(T; L; P; Ipp, I_r)\frac{s}{s}$. Here *S* stands for recorded social situations; *T* denotes time; *L* distance; *P* number of people; *Ipp* indexes of population's characteristics; and I_r residual characteristics.

We should not be surprised at the sharp reaction of an eminent mathematician to this metrophrenic abracadabra:

> There is no more pathetic misapprehension of the nature and function of mathematics than the trite cliché that mathematics is a shorthand. . . . Mere symbolization of any discipline is not even a respectable parody of mathematics. . . . For all its symbols, a theory may take the name of mathematics in vain. . . . The S-theory has yet to take its first step toward generative mathematical symbolism. . . . No reckless abuse of the mathematical vocabulary can [of itself] transform a theory not yet mathematical into anything more substantially mathematical than a feeble mathematical pun. . . . [Dodd's] "Research Suggestions" contain several queries relating to possibilities for mathematical developments, for example, "Can dimensional analysis of societal situations be used, as dimen-

---

[32] S. C. Dodd, *Dimensions of Society: A Quantitative Systematics for the Social Sciences* (New York, 1942), frontispiece. See also Dodd, *Systematic Social Science: A Dimensional Sociology* (Beirut, 1947).

sional analysis is used in physics?" with a citation of P. W. Bridgeman's (*sic*) *Dimensional Analysis*. Offhand, a mathematician would say, probably not, at least until someone can give a meaningful answer to such exactly analogous questions as, "How many yards of buttermilk does it take to make a pair of britches for a bull?" Such queries as some of these in "Research Suggestions" may seem profound to the mathematically uninitiated; to at least one mathematician by trade they seem profoundly pretentious. . . . There is no mathematics in the book. As for the "geometric technique consisting of translating S-theory into terms of vectors with their points, lines, and angles," it seems to fritter out in a new "verbalistic nebulousness," evaporating finally in an unimplemented aspiration for a mathematical theory of human relationships.[33]

Any competent mathematician would give a quite similar appraisal of Dodd's metrophrenic shorthand with all the logical, mathematical, and empirical blunders inherent in such an abuse of mathematics and physics.[34] This appraisal may be applied also to Lysen's, Lewin's, Parsons' and other "shorthand" abuses of the mathematical, physical, and biological sciences.

CYBERNETIC SOCIOLOGIES

One of the most recent varieties of physicalistic sociology is represented by the imitations of cybernetic models in a study of psychosocial phenomena. An eminent mathematician, N. Wiener, who revived the term cybernetics means by it a science of "control and communication in the animal and machine," including man and his social environment. In his opinion the "operation of living individuals and the operation of some of the newer communication machines are precisely parallel."[35]

[33] E. T. Bell, "Review of Dodd's "Dimensions of Society," *ASR*, VII(1942), 707–709.

[34] See further criticism in my *Fads and Foibles*, ch. 7.

[35] N. Wiener, *The Human Use of Human Beings: Cybernetics and Society* (Boston, 1950), pp. 9, 15, 16. See also N. Wiener, *Cybernetics or Control and Communication in the Animal and Machine* (Cambridge, Mass., 1948); and F. D. Barrett and H. A. Shepard, "A Bibliography of Cybernetics," *Proceedings of the American Academy of Arts and Sciences*, *80*(1953), pp. 204–222. See also P. D. Bardis, "Cybernetics: Definition, History, Etymology," *Social Science*, October, 1965, pp. 226–228.

Another leader in cybernetics, D. M. MacKay, asserts, with some reservations, that the computing electronics machines can imitate human behavior on the same principles as those on which the brain works.[36] The cyberneticists claim that cybernetics not only clarifies the processes of message transmission, operation, and control, but that cybernetics furnishes a "new frame of reference for solution of such long-standing philosophical problems as free will, consciousness, teleology, [and the] scientific method."

For physicalistic sociologists and psychologists, cybernetics is a godsend for their mechanistic exploration of sociocultural and psychological phenomena. In contrast to the significance of the contributions of cybernetics to the problems of communication and control in machines and in the physical mechanisms of animals, sociological cybernetics has yielded, so far, very meager, and, now and then, even wrong results. The first reason for that meagerness is that sociological cybernetics is based on an old fallacy, the similitude of machine and human brain. Chapter 1 of *Contemporary Sociological Theories* shows that the theories of similarity, even identity, of man with machine are very old. They were voiced long ago by Hindu, Buddhist, Chinese, Greek, and Roman thinkers. In Europe, these "yarns" were developed by Descartes, Hobbes, Pascal, Leibnitz, Malebranche, Spinoza, Condillac, and others. Today's notions, based on the unsound logic of a misleading analogy ("Man has two eyes and cat has two eyes; therefore, man and cat are identical animals"), are but a variation on this old theme.

When the theory of similarity of man and machine is seriously examined by the foremost authorities in the field, like Sir Charles Sherrington, it is found to be fallacious: "Between the calculating machine and the human brain there is no basic similarity. The brain is a mystery—it has been—and still is. The facts we know concerning the brain . . . all fail to give a key to the mystery of how it creates our thoughts and feelings; that

[36] D. M. MacKay, "On Comparing the Brain with Machines," *American Scientist*, 42(1954), pp. 261–268. See also J. O. Wisdom, R. L. Spilsbury, and D. M. MacKay's paper in the "Symposium on Mentality in Machines," *Proceedings of the Aristotelian Society* (1952), Supplement.

is, . . . our mind."[37] The same conclusion is reached by MacKay: "I believe most seriously that man is 'more than' the physical organism. . . . This implies not necessarily that there must be gaps in the physical account of his activity, but that man has other *aspects* that are neither revealed by nor are contained in the physical man."[38]

The psychosocial aspects of man, his meaningful behavior and the meaningful aspects of social and cultural phenomena,[39] cannot be caught in the cybernetic net: They slip through its meshes.

This explains why cybernetic fishermen (K. Deutsch, L. K. Frank, R. D. Luce, A. Rapoport, A. Bavelas, C. M. Churchman, partly S. C. Dodd, and others)[40] have not caught any big psychosocial fish in their cybernetic nets. Although they have caught a few real fish when fishing with noncybernetic equipment, their cybernetic expeditions have yielded but empty shells, like the painfully elaborated "discovery" of the physical law of falling bodies, a law long ago discovered by Galileo and precisely formulated by physics. For obtaining their platitudes, tautologies, and homemade physical laws, no costly and painstaking experiments were needed. The mere exercise of an elementary logic and mathematics, plus the comfortable reading of some physics, history, sociology, and psychology, would have given all the sound results of these cybernetic explorations, and a great deal more. At the same time, it would have prevented

---

[37] Sherrington, "Mystery of Mysteries: The Human Brain," *New York Times Magazine*, December 4, 1949, pp. 19–20. See also W. Penfield, "The Physiological Basis of the Mind," in S. Farber and R. Wilson (eds.), *Control of the Mind* (New York, 1961).

[38] MacKay, "On Comparing the Brain with Machines," pp. 259–260.

[39] See, on the component of meaning as the main component of all psychosocial phenomena different from their physical components, *SCP*, ch. 3.

[40] See S. C. Dodd, "Can the Social Scientist Serve Two Masters?," *Research Studies of the State College of Washington, 21*(1953), pp. 195–213; A. Bavelas, "Communication Patterns in Task-Oriented Groups," *Journal of Acoustical Society of America, 22*(1950), pp. 725–730; A. Bavelas and F. D. Barrett, "An Experimental Approach to Organizational Communication," *Personnel*, April, 1951; and H. J. Leavitt, "Some Effects of Certain Communication Patterns on Group Performance, *Journal of Abnormal and Social Psychology, 46*(1951), pp. 38–50.

our cybernetic fishermen from catching nothing but shells in their nets.[41]

TESTOMANIC SOCIOLOGIES

In psychology and psychiatry, the physicalistic trend of the period has manifested itself in the development of a "robot psychology," in mechanical techniques and tests of personality characteristics, and in other currents of research dispensing largely with mind, mentality, consciousness, will, thought, and similar metaphysical entities of old-fashioned psychology. In the words of A. H. Maslow, the psychology of the period has been mainly "technique-centered" psychology, "playing down the meaningfulness, vitality, and significance of the problem and of creativeness in general."[42] Accordingly, the physicalistic psychosocial sciences of the period have "invented" hundreds of mechanical techniques believed to be capable of testing scientifically any and all characteristics of an individual or a group. A veritable plethora of these tests has invaded these sciences and vast numbers of "testers" have succeeded in selling their products to their fellow scholars, educators, governmental agencies, business and labor managers, and to the public at large. At the present time, in the West, almost every individual is tested from the cradle to the grave. We are living in an age of testocracy. By their tests of our intelligence, emotional stability,

---

[41] For a more detailed analysis and criticism of the cybernetic psychosocial theories, see *Fads and Foibles*, ch. 9. This criticism does not exclude a fruitful use of some of the principles of cybernetics in analyzing such problems as development, equilibrium, homeostasis, equifinality, and so on, when they are used competently, as O. Lange did in his *Catość i rozwój w świete cybernetyki* [*The Whole and Development in the Light of Cybernetics*], (Warsaw, 1962), and as several Soviet scientists do in their studies published in *Voprosy Filosofii*.

[42] A. H. Maslow, *Motivation and Personality* (New York, 1954), p. 13, and *Toward a Psychology of Being* (Princeton, N.J., 1962). See, on the recent dominant currents in psychology, G. W. Allport, *The Nature of Personality* (Cambridge, Mass., 1950), pp. 48–75, and *Becoming* (New Haven, Conn., 1955), *passim*. See also Björn Sjövall, *Höjdpsykologi* (Stockholm, 1959); and my *The Ways and Power of Love*.

aptitude, character, and unconscious drives, the testocrats largely decide our vocation, occupation, social position, promotion or demotion, normality or abnormality—in brief, a large part of our life. At the present time, the testocrats have at their disposal a vast battery of supposedly scientific tests.

This ever-growing battery contains dozens of intelligence tests; tests of aggressiveness, submission, caution, conformity, conscientiousness, originality, deception, and suggestibility; tests of instincts, "prepotent reflexes," and emotions; tests of moods, temperament, will power, and extroversion-introversion; tests of attitudes, interests, and preferences; tests of aptitudes, abilities, and leadership; tests of ethical judgments and values; tests of mental and moral normality or abnormality; tests of potential, general, and specific criminality, compatibility or incompatibility of prospective bridegroom and bride, loyalty and subversivity, successful or unsuccessful parole, and lying; tests of the "basic type of personality"; projective tests; sociometric and psychodramatic tests; and so on.[43]

This "test-centered" psychology and psychiatry are largely responsible for the affliction of sociology with testomania. The use of tests has become a sort of preliminary "must" in many modern sociological studies. A large portion of this research consists mainly of a statistical summary of various tests given to the persons or groups studied, beginning with their intelligence tests and ending with the Rorschach, or the sociometric, or the psychodramatic tests.

If these tests were scientific, and if they tested the respective traits of the individuals or groups as accurately as, say, the thermometer tests body temperature or the barometer tests barometric pressure, such tests and researches could only be welcomed. Unfortunately, the real situation is quite different. Almost all of the numerous tests are very far from adequate, reliable, or scientific. One can say of them what one of the pioneers of intelligence tests, E. L. Thorndike, says about mental tests:

---

[43] For a detailed discussion, analysis, and criticism of these tests, see *Fads and Foibles*, chs. 4, 5, and 6. See there also the literature on these problems.

"Just what they measure is not known; how far it is proper to add, subtract, multiply, divide, and compute ratios with the measures obtained is not known; just what the measures obtained signify concerning the intelligence is not known.[44] When the tests are tested in their testing adequacy, the results often show that either they do not test at all what they are supposed to be testing, or they test a given characteristic in an unreliable, sometimes in a misleading way, or they yield "quotients," "indexes," and "scores" as enigmatic as some of the utterances of the Pythia of Delphi or of a tea-leaves reading. Even the most carefully administered intelligence tests—such as those used by L. M. Terman and his associates in their classical selection of 1,070 potential geniuses (with I.Q.'s ranging from 135 to 200) out of some 250,000 California children—did not seem to select potential geniuses much better than a chance selection did. When Terman and his associates studied what happened to their 1,070 "potential geniuses" twenty-five years after their selection, the net results of this verifying study were fairly similar to the blind selection, picked without the battery of tests administered by the Terman group of investigators.[45]

When a competent team of psychologists, psychiatrists, and social scientists thoroughly tested the aptitudes and intelligence of some 5,391 recruits for the Office of Strategic Services and then, one year after the appointment of the testees to the overseas positions for which, according to the tests, they were most fit, tried to find out how successfully the testees performed their functions, the results were disappointing: "None of our statistical computations demonstrates that our system of assessment was of great value." The coefficients of correlation between the assessments of job rating (through the battery of tests) and

[44] E. L. Thorndike, *The Measurement of Intelligence* (New York, 1927), p. 1.

[45] See L. M. Terman and M. H. Oden, *Genetic Studies of Genius* (5 vols.; Stanford); Terman *et al.*, *Mental and Physical Traits of a Thousand Gifted Children*, Vol. I, 1925; C. M. Cox, *The Early Mental Traits of Three Hundred Geniuses*, Vol. II (1926); B. S. Burks, D. W. Jensen, and L. M. Terman, *The Promise of Youth: Follow-up Studies of a Thousand Gifted Children*, Vol. III (1930). See, for an analysis and substantiation of the above conclusions, my *Fads and Foibles*, ch. 5.

the actual performance of the testees ran between .08 and .37, mostly between .1 and .2.[46]

Still less reliable or less testing are other mechanical tests of personality: ascendance-submission, caution, compliance, perseverance, dominant interests, emotionality, will power, originality, aggressiveness, etc.[47]

The same can be said of the projective tests of the hidden, unconscious regions of personality: drives, complexes, repressions, basic types of personality, and so on. The thematic apperception test, the word-association test, the Rorschach test, the dream-interpretation test, the Rosenzweig P-F test, the story-completion test, tests through the interpretation of plays, drawings, and art, and the doll and puppet test are examples of the projective techniques that, according to their adepts, open to us the dark caverns of the unconscious inaccessible to the nonprojective tests. Critically examined the projective tests are full of holes. They are based on unproved theories and doubtful assumptions. The tests' nature is largely indeterminate. Interpretations of their results are quite arbitrary. Their validity is little demonstrated. When they are tested in their testing power, they are shown to be incapable of registering even the strongest biological and "unconscious" drives. For instance, a whole battery of these projective tests hardly registered the strong and persistent striving for food of thirty-six conscientious objectors kept on a semistarvation diet for six months during which they lost about a quarter of their initial body weight.[48]

The reasons for the fallibility of all the mechanical tests are at hand. The first of these reasons was mentioned long ago by

---

[46] See *Assessment of Men: Selection of Personnel for the Office of Strategic Services by the OSS Assessment Staff* (New York, 1948), pp. 5–8, 392, 423, 425. For details, see *Fads and Foibles*, ch. 5. See also A. W. Heim, *The Appraisal of Intelligence* (London, 1954), and J. W. Getzels and P. W. Jackson, *Creativity and Intelligence* (New York, 1962).

[47] See, for details, *Fads and Foibles*, ch. 6.

[48] See J. Brozek, H. Guetzkow, M. D. Baldwin, and R. Cranston, "A Quantitative Study of Perception and Association in Experimental Semi-Starvation," *Journal of Personality*, *19*(1951), 245–264; and G. W. Allport, "The Trend in Motivational Theory," *American Journal of Orthopsychiatry*, *23*(1953). For a comprehensive criticism of the projective techniques, see *Fads and Foibles*, ch. 6.

Montaigne: "Man is a marvelous, vain, fickle, and unstable subject, and on whom it is very hard to form certain and uniform judgment."[49] The highly complex, creative, and plastic nature of man is the main obstacle to the validity of the psychosocial tests generally, and of mechanical tests particularly. Man's nature is responsible for many a wrong appraisal of men of genius by capable observers, examiners, and teachers who knew them well. The creative ability of such men of genius as St. Ignatius Loyola, St. Thomas Aquinas, Vico, Newton, Hegel, Pushkin, Tolstoy, Beethoven, Bach, Verdi, and others was estimated by some of their contemporary "experts" as rather low. And, vice versa, many "smart Alecs" who did not create anything significant were often evaluated as geniuses.

The second main reason for the fallibility of the modern tests of personality and groups is the perfectly artificial and superficial character of the bulk of these tests. An overwhelming majority of them represent either written or vocal operations and responses of the testees to written questionnaires or to vocal interview and quiz questions. Only rarely do the tests test actual performance of, say, piano playing by the would-be musician, designing and constructing a new gadget by a prospective inventor, composing a poem by a would-be writer, and so on. The bulk of these tests, given mostly *ad hoc*, are of a short duration and are autocratically designed by the testers, who assume that the testees are capable of answering the questions instantaneously, ignoring the differences of the individuals, their mental state (moods, indisposition, blocking, etc.) at the moment of testing, and favoring fast and disfavoring slow test operations. Often the questions asked are vague; they frequently ask for preferences, aspirations, and hypothetical responses to imaginary situations and not for factual knowledge. A large part of the questions do not require a display of logical thought, originality, or real skill, but, rather, memorized information. For these reasons, the answers to this sort of question hardly reveal the difference between the competent and incompetent, skillful and unskilled, original and "rubber-stamped," talented and un-

---

[49] *The Essays of Michel de Montaigne* (London, 1913), Vol. I, p. 5.

talented persons. Probing questions in the psychosocial, ethical, political, economic, philosophical, and artistic fields often yield unreliable results because of the numerous divergent theories, approaches, generalizations, and values to which both testers and testees are exposed. The testers are all too human, and thus are inclined to regard as correct the answers and values that agree with their "denominational creed." This subjectivity contributes its share of errors to the test results.

The inadequacy of the tests is notably magnified by the subsequent interpretation and quantification of their results. In contrast to the precise and direct indication of body temperature by the thermometer and of barometric pressure by the barometer, indications that do not need any indirect interpretations, the results of the psychosocial tests, taken per se, are neither direct nor clear nor diagnostically meaningful. They acquire meaning only when they are "interpreted" by the tester. And the "interpretations" are usually quite different from the empirical nature of the results as such. Empirically, the results of a word-association test are but a number of various words uttered by the testee in response to the words of the tester. Perceptionally, the results of the Rorschach test are but a mass of various images evoked in the testee by an inkblot on a card. Neither the words nor the images have, per se, any diagnostic or other meaning. They acquire such a meaning only through the interpretation of the tester. Whether he wants to or not, *he must superimpose his interpretation upon the responses of the testee.* And these superimposed interpretations are quite different from the empirical or perceptional nature of the test results. A patient tells correctly his last-night's dream to his psychoanalyst. He tells that in his dream he was climbing a mountain, that when he was near its peak he suddenly lost his footing and began to fall, that this falling evoked in him a mortal fear, and that in this state of trepidation he awoke. Such is the empirical content of the dream. By itself it does not have any diagnostic or other meaning. To acquire this meaning, it has to be interpreted by the psychoanalyst. Is the dream part of the syndrome of some unconscious processes? If it is, does it manifest the Oedipus complex, or fear of castration, or a repressed wish, or something else? Whatever the interpretation, its diagnostic character is quite different from the content and character of the dream itself.

These interpretations open the royal road for all sorts of arbitrary, fanciful, and subjective misinterpretations of the tests and their results. The very assumption that a dream is part of a syndrome of this or that subconscious process is already an arbitrary assumption. That a *given* dream is part of a syndrome of a *certain* complex or a *particular* repressed wish is again an arbitrary conjecture, devoid of a minimum of scientific proof.

When carefully studied, most of the interpretations are found to be based not on a proved causal connection between the tests' results and the specific interpretation, but mainly on a dogmatic belief in the results as omens of certain—unconscious or conscious—entities and forces: repressed wishes, instinctive drives, various complexes, "native intelligence," "prepotent reflexes," or dominant interests of a certain variety, and so on. This is confirmed by fairly frequent discrepancies in the interpretations of the same results by different interpreters. To sum up, the interpretations import a large portion of nonscientific elements into the test results, and thereby notably contribute to their invalidity.

Still greater distortion of test results is introduced by their quantification. Our testers, obsessed by quantomania, indefatigably measure their test data and present them in an "exact" and "objective" form of numerical scores, indexes, and statistical tables, marvelously decorated with impressive-looking mathematical formulas and other simulacra of a precise quantitative research. A legion of psychosocial researchers sincerely believe that these impressive-looking scores, indexes, rows of figures, coefficients of correlations, probable errors, standard deviations, coefficients of reliability, and so on, deliver objectively studied and exactly measured "diamonds of a valid knowledge." As a matter of fact, the bulk of these "diamonds" are the testers' arbitrary, subjective, often fantastic, assumptions dressed up in quantitative costumes and wearing mathematical make-up.

The bulk of the tests' data is qualitative and, so far, is untranslatable into quantitative units. These data do not have objectively assigned quantitative points. They neither show how many score-points each test response has nor which response has a greater and which a lesser number of score-points. For this simple reason the points of each response cannot be counted, added, subtracted, divided, multiplied, or subjected to other mathematical operations.

This means that these quantitative units or scoring points with all the subsequent quantitative manipulations are largely the arbitrary creations of the quantifiers. They arbitrarily decide how many score-points to give to each of the numerous responses of the testees—that is, which responses are to get 10, 5, or 99 points. Their scoring would be no less arbitrary if they decided to give an equal number of points to all responses. If, instead of scoring points, the testers decided to rank the responses into a certain number of ranks, or numerical classes, such a decision is also arbitrary. The same is true of their placing each response into one of these ranks. If, instead of one tester, the ascription of points, weights, units, or ranks is done by 5 "expert" testers (and this subterfuge is frequently used), the quantification of 5 or 500 pseudoexperts still remains arbitrary, since none of them has any objective basis for his numerological distribution of points or weights or ranks.

For the present, the totality of the considerations given about the doubtful validity of the artificial psychosocial tests and about the conditions additionally damaging their adequacy are sufficient to justify a strongly sceptical attitude toward the scientific nature of these tests. All in all, they are hardly more scientific than a tea-leaves or coffee-grounds reading.[50]

Since the bulk of modern psychological and sociological research consists in constructing and using all sorts of artificial tests, with subsequent largely arbitrary quantification and interpretation of the tests' results, such research can hardly contribute much to our understanding of sociocultural and psychological phenomena. In spite of an enormous amount of labor and funds invested in this "testomanic" research, it has yielded a dispro-

---

[50] See, for a detailed criticism of the modern tests, *Fads and Foibles*, chs. 5, 6, and 7.

portionally meager knowledge of psychosocial phenomena. It has not disclosed to us any new significant uniformity, any valid causal or probabilistic relationship, or only deeper understanding of these phenomena. It has largely been busy with constructing many test-mirages and then in quantitatively investigating the relationship between various illusionistic variables of these mirages. Testomanic sociology, living and operating as it has in the world of these artificial mirages, has largely missed the genuine psychosocial reality, inevitably committed many blunders, and is now lost in the jungle of its own numerous tests and their indexes, scores, coefficients, and arbitrary interpretations. To be sure, the vast capital of labor and funds expended by the testomanic psychosocial science has yielded some modest dividends of real knowledge, though mainly of insignificant facts. But the bulk of the capital has been rather fruitlessly wasted in its hunt for mechanical tests of nonmechanical human beings, their properties, their societies, and their creative cultural achievements.

OPERATIONAL AND SO-CALLED EXPERIMENTAL SOCIOLOGIES

● Operationalism

The next manifestation of the physicalistic trend in the modern psychosocial sciences consists in the rapid spread of operational and/or experimental studies and methods. Though the experimental method was widely used in pre- and post-Newtonian physics, P. W. Bridgman gave to it a new name, "operationalism," and attempted to make it the only scientific method for physical and other sciences.[51]

The essential meaning of operationalism in physics is that physical concepts should be defined in terms of actual physical

[51] See P. W. Bridgman, *The Logic of Modern Physics* (New York, 1927); *The Nature of Physical Theory* (New York, 1936); and "Some General Principles of Operational Analysis," *Psychological Review,* *52*(1945).

operations. On this view there is no meaning to a concept unless it represents an operation which can be performed in a laboratory. Thus the term "pressure of gas" signifies nothing until an operation is described which constitutes the measurement of pressure [with the description of the apparatus like glass and rubber tubing, mercury, and the operations to get a pointer reading called the pressure of gas.][52]

So heralded by Bridgman and others, operationalism drew a legion of sociologists and psychologists into its fold. Operational method and definitions have become a sort of sociological and psychological "must" for a scientific researcher in these fields. Operational terms have become magic catchwords to which are ascribed infallibility, precision, objectivity, and other virtues.[53]

When the operational (experimental) method is carefully studied, however, one finds that its role, even in the physical sciences, has been much more modest than the operationalists claim, whereas in sociology and psychology operational approaches appear to have been mainly sham operational and largely unscientific with little in common with the real operational method of the natural sciences. In the natural sciences, the operational or experimental method has been highly fruitful within certain limits when it worked in cooperation with the logicomathematical (theoretical) and intuitional methods. It cannot be said, however, that all or even almost all scientific discoveries have been due exclusively to it. Most of these have been born of intuition, developed by logicomathematical thought, and, at the last stage, tested and verified through an experimental procedure. Without intuitional flash and logicomathematical reasoning, the operational (experimental) approach alone could hardly have discovered any of the basic generalizations and formulas of uniformity in these sciences. Bridgman's attempt to make the operational method the only scientific method has been rejected by most of the natural scientists, and,

[52] R. B. Lindsay, "A Critique of Operationalism in Physics," *Philosophy of Science,* 4(1937), p. 456.
[53] See E. G. Boring, "The Use of Operational Definitions in Science," *Psychological Review,* 52(1952). On rapidly growing operationalism in psychology, see G. Allport, *The Nature of Personality,* pp. 57–58.

in his latest work, Bridgman himself seems to have abandoned his excessive claims.[54]

Many experimental (operational) discoveries, such as the Compton effect, the value of the charge on the electron, and so on, are contradictory and questionable. The contradictions have been removed only through the use of nonoperational (theoretical) logical deductions and mathematical inferences. An experiment performed for the sake of experiment, and not for testing a nonoperational hypothesis conceived before the experiment, is irrelevant and meaningless. Further, any operational experiment deals always with a narrow range of experience or reality. As such, it gives only fragmentary results significant from the standpoint of the operation performed, but irrelevant for, and contradictory to, the results obtained through *different operations*. There would be as many different results and concepts for as many different operations as are performed in a study of a given problem. None of these operations can give a general formula, concept, or uniformity valid for different operational manipulations. For instance, the concept of gas pressure measured by the ordinary U-tube is different from that measured by the ionization gauge; "intelligence" and I.Q. will be different when operations of testing them are different. At its best, the operational method can give different, though often contradictory, fragments of knowledge. This explains why practically all basic discoveries, generalizations, formulas, and concepts of the

---

[54] See Lindsay, "A Critique of Operationalism in Physics," and Allport, *The Nature of Personality*. See also H. Margenau, *The Nature of Physical Reality* (New York, 1950), and his "Physical vs. Historical Reality," *Philosophy of Science, 19*(1952), 203. About intuitional and logicomathematical methods, see my *The Ways and Power of Love*, ch. 6; M. Bunge, *Intuition and Science* (New York, 1962); R. Ulich, *Man and Reality* (New Haven, 1948); F. S. C. Northrop, *The Meeting of East and West* (New York, 1946); E. W. Sinnott, *Two Ways to Truth* (New York, 1953); P. W. Bridgman, "The Task Before Us," *Proceedings of the American Academy of Arts and Sciences, 83*, No. 3; and "The Present State of Operationalism," in P. G. Frank (ed.), *The Validation of Scientific Theories* (New York, 1961), as well as G. Bergmann's "Sense and Nonsense in Operationalism"; P. H. Prabhu, "The State of Psychology as a Science Today," *Fiftieth Indian Science Congress* (Calcutta, 1963); and V. A. Asmus, *Problema intuizii v filosofii i matematike* (Moscow, 1963).

natural sciences have been achieved only through the combined use of the intuitive, logicomathematical, and experimental methods. In these discoveries, the experimental method has ordinarily been not the first, but the last step in testing a theory that was conceived intuitionally and developed by logicomathematical thought.

If such are the limitations of the experimental-operational method in the natural sciences, still greater are they in the psychosocial sciences. In sociological research, the real operational method has hardly been used at all. Instead, under the name of operationalism its enthusiasts used procedures that have hardly anything in common with the real operational method. For instance, C. Kirkpatrick operationally defines "marital adjustment" as "that quality in marriage which causes one close friend to classify the couple as maladjusted. Marital adjustment was crudely defined in a similar way."[55] Other operational investigators of happiness in marriage, like E. W. Burgess, L. S. Cottrell, H. J. Lock, and L. M. Terman,[56] ask a lot of questions of the married couple, arbitrarily weigh, score, and tabulate their unchecked answers, and present the results in the form of many statistical tables as an example of an operational study of marriage-happiness. Similarly, instead of giving an analysis of the intra- and intergroup differentiation and stratification of 75 occupational groups as they really exist and function in the Danish population, K. Svalastoga simply gives the tabulated *opinions* of 2,422 males and 606 females who were asked to rank these 75 occupations, according to their "acceptability," into 5 and 9 hierarchical strata "from the highest to the lowest."[57] A majority of other psychosocial operationalists collect untested opinions—through questionnaires and interviews—then process this "hearsay stuff" (not admitted as evidence in any

[55] Kirkpatrick, "A Methodological Analysis of Feminism," *AJS*, XLIV(1939), 332.

[56] See E. W. Burgess and L. S. Cottrell, Jr., *Predicting Success or Failure in Marriage* (New York, 1939); E. W. Burgess and H. J. Lock, *The Family* (New York, 1945), pp. 458 ff.; and L. M. Terman, *Psychological Factors in Marital Happiness* (New York, 1938).

[57] K. Svalastoga, *Prestige, Class, and Mobility* (Toronto, 1959).

court, much less in science), and present to us a legion of figures, indexes, and coefficients as an operational scientific study.

Anyone who knows the A B C's of the true experimental or operational method, knows that these procedures have no relationship to the real thing. A physicist does not measure barometric pressure by asking the opinion of two or more persons. Instead, without asking anybody's opinion, he uses a barometer to obtain a fairly precise reading of the barometric pressure. Likewise, a physician desirous of finding out the temperature of his patient does not arrive at the answer by consulting his friends or even the patient himself. Instead, he uses a thermometer, which will provide the answer to his question.

Similarly, physicists, chemists, and biologists do not solve their problems by asking various persons what, in their opinion, is the structure of the atom, or the composition of a given chemical compound, or the nature and functions of chromosomes. Instead, they set forth an intuitional postulate, then make the deductions and inferences from it through their logicomathematical analysis, then test the inferences experimentally, without collecting any hearsay stuff from anybody. Replacing the scientific method by gathering untested opinions—through questionnaires or interviews—is an utter distortion of the operational-experimental method generally.

Another variation on the operational method, used by psychosocial scholars, represents an already-familiar transcription of concepts, definitions, and formulas of the physical sciences. The conceptual framework of the physical sciences was constructed for a study of physical phenomena and has a definite meaning, preciseness, and measurability. Applied to quite different psychosocial phenomena, this framework becomes meaningless and useless. S. C. Dodd's "system of operationally defined concepts for sociology" serves as an example of these meaningless "operational transcriptions."[58] He introduces the concepts of "time, space, population," and "all characteristics of people or of their environment" as the basic concepts of his operational

---

[58] S. C. Dodd, "A System of Operationally Defined Concepts for Sociology," *ASR*, 4(1939).

system of sociology. With the help of these concepts and of their symbols, T, S, P, and so on, he reveals to us that "all static or timeless data may be represented by a zero exponent on the time component: $T^0 = 1$. . . . . Acceleration is defined by dividing the speed by the over-all time period. The formula for it is $1/T^2$ or T^{-1}. . . . A societal force may be defined as an acceleration of change in a population and may be measured . . . as the product of acceleration and the population accelerated." Its formula is $F = T^{-2} \, IP$. And so on. In regard to all these transcriptions one can say, first, that none of these concepts is derived by Dodd from any operational procedure of his own, nor are they defined by him in any way; he simply takes them from physics. Second, since Dodd does not give any real unit for the measurement of societal force, or societal change, or acceleration, his definitions are empty and disoperative. Meaningless also are his statements like "A societal force . . . may be measured . . . as the product of the acceleration and the population accelerated," and his "shorthand" symbols like $F = T^{-2} \, IP$. Third, there is hardly any old-fashioned empirical study of psychosocial phenomena that does not use the concepts of time, space, population, environment, and other of Dodd's concepts. Why these all too familiar concepts are introduced as "operational" and allegedly new remains, therefore, a mystery. To sum up, Dodd's whole transcriptive operation has no relationship to the real experimental or operational method. It is but an imitative parody of it.

The same can be said of many other "operational" studies, including those that identify the terms operational and operationism with quantitative and measurement.[59] If we accept this identification, then the operational method with all its different meanings becomes a sort of money whose real value is unknown.

This conclusion is empirically confirmed by H. Hart's study "Toward an Operational Definition of the Term 'Operation.'"[60] Hart shows that in some 140 papers on operationalism the basic term operation is given very different meanings; it remains undefined and devoid of any precision. Its leaders seem to have

[59] See my criticism of these in *Fads and Foibles*, ch. 3.
[60] *ASR, 18*(1953), pp. 612–617.

"understood each other" only a "minor fraction of the time" and have hardly "achieved, and consistently maintained clearcut, operational concepts at crucial points."[61]

In psychosocial sciences the operational method has not been used in the sense of a genuine experimental method. The wide variety of its uses represents a distortion of this method and its remote relationship to any scientific method generally. No wonder, therefore, that it has been notably fruitless in its cognitive results.

● Sham Experimental Method

Since the real operational method is the experimental method—highly fruitful within its proper limits—and since almost all "operational" studies in psychosocial sciences have been pseudo-operational, the question arises as to what extent the experimental method is actually used in sociological research. If we are to believe the claims of the texts and research papers, the experimental method is flourishing in modern sociology. If, however, one keeps in mind the very essentials of the experimental method, one realizes that almost all the allegedly experimental studies in sociology are in fact sham experimental. Hardly any of these "experimental" studies meet the canon of inductive inference according to the rules of either agreement, or difference, or concomitant variation, or residue, and so on.[62]

---

[61] The same is true of A. Rapoport's attempt to define operationalism, operational definitions, and operational philosophy. Instead of giving clear concepts of these, he gives a wide variety of different, sometimes even contradictory, notions of operationalism. See his *Operational Philosophy* (New York, 1953).

[62] See, on this canon, J. S. Mill, *A System of Logic* (London, 1843), Book 3, and *passim*; J. Venn, *The Principles of Empirical and Inductive Logic* (London, 1889); F. Znaniecki, *The Method of Sociology* (New York, 1934); P. H. Furfey, *The Scope and Method of Sociology* (New York, 1953); R. Carnap, "Inductive Logic and Science," *Proceedings of the American Academy of Arts and Sciences*, 80(1953), pp. 189–197; F. S. Chapin, *Experimental Designs in Sociological Research* (New York, 1937); E. Greenwood, *Experimental Sociology* (New York, 1945); and G. and L. B. Murphy, *Experimental Social Psychology* (New York, 1931, and later editions).

If, according to F. S. Chapin, "the fundamental rule of the experimental method is to vary only one condition at a time and to maintain all other conditions rigidly constant," then none of the experiments analyzed in Chapin's and Greenwood's works referred to are real experiments. Likewise, except for purely physiological experiments, most of the experimental studies of strictly psychological phenomena are spurious, so far as their experimental character is concerned.

The most common "experimental" procedure in psychosocial research consists in matching the experimental and the control groups or persons or situations, or in observing the same group or person before and after exposing it to the conditions or agencies experimented with. The experimenters seemingly believe that by these matchings they make all the other conditions constant and vary only the condition experimented with. Though there are different degrees of matching, I hardly ever have met in this type of study any single study where the matching approaches the real experimental conditions. In practically all matching studies there are always dozens, even hundreds, of variables that are neither constant nor controlled, indeed, not even considered. Even the traits in which the experimented and controlled groups or persons are matched, say, age, sex, religion, political affiliation, or education, these matched traits are, as a matter of fact, not identical but very different variables.

Females or males of the same age and race display every imaginable variation in beauty, intelligence, somatic type, character, taste, etc. The Roman Catholicism of a new Chinese convert, of Jacques Maritain, of Dorothy Day, and of Cardinal Spellman are quite different from each other. The Republican party of Senator Barry Goldwater is very different from the Republican party of N.Y.C. Mayor John Lindsay. And so on. For these obvious reasons, the "matching" in such studies is not really a matching of identical traits, but a comparison of different traits *assumed* to be identical. As a result, such matching studies are comparing two phenomena different from one another not only in the unmatched, but also in the matched conditions. For these reasons, if a researcher finds some difference between the group being tested and the so-called control group, he does not have any solid basis for ascribing this difference to his experimental variable.[63] If he does so, he is a careless detective who arbitrarily picks up Mr. Jones out of hundreds of possible suspects, without even having any circumstantial evidence for picking him up. Such a procedure obviously has no relationship to the real experimental method.

The same can be said of practically all other procedures covered by the term experimental in sociology and psychology. So far, they represent mainly poor imitations of the real experimental method.[64]

The sham experimental nature of these studies is largely responsible for the comparative poverty of the results they yield, as well as for the contradictoriness of the results.[65]

We should by all means cultivate a real experimental method wherever it can be applied; the more it is used in psychosocial sciences the better. But we should avoid using sham experimental imitations of it. These cannot contribute to a real knowl-

[63] Recent "experimental" studies by S. Schachter, L. Festinger, L. Killian, and L. Coch, and by C. I. Hovland, A. A. Lumadaine, and F. D. Sheffield serve as examples of this sort of pseudoexperimental research. See Cartwright and Zander (eds.), *Group Dynamics* (Evanston, Ill., 1953; rev. ed., 1960), and C. I. Hovland and others, *Experiments on Mass Communication* (Princeton, 1950). Other examples are given in M. W. Riley, *Sociological Research* (New York, 1963), pp. 570–612, and in G. C. Homans, *Social Behavior* (New York, 1961). Practically all these allegedly experimental studies bear a very remote resemblance to genuine experimental investigations.

[64] See a development of this criticism in my *Fads and Foibles*, ch. 9; N. and A. Chapanis, "Cognitive Dissonance," *Psychological Bulletin, 61*(1964), 1–22; S. E. Asch, "Review of L. Festinger's *A Theory of Cognitive Dissonance*," *Contemporary Psychology* (1958), 194–195; and H. L. Zetterberg, *On Theory and Verification in Sociology* (Totowa, N.J., 1965).

[65] Compare, for instance, the results obtained by me in studies of the relationship between friendship and social distance, described in *The Ways and Power of Love*, pp. 21 ff.; by J. B. Maller, in his *Cooperation and Competition* (New York, 1929); by B. A. Wright, in her "Selfishness, Guilt-Feeling, and Social Distance," and "Fairness and Generosity" (unpublished theses, University of Iowa, 1940 and 1942); and by M. Deutsch, "The Effect of Cooperation and Competition upon Group Process," in Cartwright and Zander, *Group Dynamics* (1953 edition). Despite my sympathy for the real experimental method and despite the valiant efforts to use it in sociology, an overwhelming mass of so-called experimental studies in sociology are not genuinely experimental.

edge of psychosocial phenomena. If anything, they corrode the experimental studies and psychosocial science itself.

ATOMISTIC AND SMALL-GROUP SOCIOLOGIES

● The Hunt for Social Atoms

Recent "atomistic" and "small group" sociologies are also, to a large extent, a belated manifestation of the prevalent physicalistic trend in the psychosocial sciences. Since pre-twentieth-century physics dealt with atoms as the simplest units of physical phenomena, our physicalistic sociologists had to find the psychosocial counterpart of atoms. The main methodological rule of the biophysical sciences of the nineteenth century was to proceed from a study of the simplest atoms or organisms to the increasingly complex physical and biological phenomena; thus, the partisans of the "natural-science sociology or psychology" had to imitate this rule by assuming that "small groups" are the simplest social bodies and, as such, should be the starting point for a study of large and complex social organizations. Hence the contemporary preoccupation with "social atoms" and "small groups."

Of several recent theories of social atoms, J. L. Moreno's theory is possibly the best:

> The social atom is the nucleus of all individuals toward whom a person is emotionally related, or who are related to him at the same time [emotional relatedness means attraction or repulsion]. It is the smallest nucleus of an emotionally toned inter-personal pattern in the social universe. . . . The social atoms are the centers of attraction or rejection. It is the social atom which is the smallest social unit, not the individual. . . . The social atom is simply an individual and the people he is emotionally related to at the time.[66]

The web of emotional relationships between a newborn baby and his parents and siblings is, according to Moreno, the

---

[66] Moreno, *Psychodrama* (New York, 1946), Vol. I, pp. 184 and 229; and *Who Shall Survive* (Washington, 1934), pp. 77 ff., 96.

earliest social atom of an individual. "The volume of the social atom is in continuous expansion as we grow up. . . . These social atoms change from time to time in their membership."[67]

The shortcomings of this conception of social atoms are many. First, it considers only the emotional tone of social relations and completely ignores their intellectual and nonemotional aspects. Every individual is involved in a multitude of social relations that are emotionally neutral and yet have a very important effect on him. This means that a large part of the universe of social relationships is not covered by Moreno's social atoms. Second, out of a wide variety of emotions, Moreno considers only attraction and repulsion; he thus ignores many emotions that cannot strictly be categorized as either: compassion, forgiveness, sorrow, apathy, envy, generosity, joy, ecstasy, peace of mind, and so on. His "social atom" covers only a small number of the emotional relationships possible among individuals and groups. His social atom is not a social atom at all for a large portion of the universe of social relationships. In this point it differs sharply from the physical atom, which is considered to be a universal unit in *all* physical structures. Third, Moreno's atom differs from the physicochemical atoms in that some ninety physicochemical atoms—like hydrogen, oxygen, iron, gold, uranium—differ from each other not by one trait only (like mass or weight) but by several, particularly by the number and arrangement of the electrons around the central nucleus. Moreno's social atoms are distinguished from one another by one trait only: by either emotional attraction or rejection. The atom of physics and Moreno's social atom have very little in common: For this reason there is no basis for Moreno to borrow the term atom from physics and to give to it a meaning devoid of even a superficial similitude.

Fourth, contrary to Moreno's statement, his atom in no way is the simplest and smallest unit of all social relationships. The network of emotional attraction or rejection that centers around monarchs, dictators, presidents, popes, patriarchs, military lead-

[67] Moreno, "The Social Atom and Death," *Sociometry*, *10*(1947), 80–84.

ers, political leaders, captains of finance and industry, and so on, involves thousands, often millions, of individuals whom such leaders attract and reject, and by whom they are admired or hated. The total network of emotional relatedness of such social atoms is not the simplest and smallest unit, but is one of the vastest and most complex webs of social relationships in the whole range of human emotional interactions. Only euphemistically can such networks be called the "smallest" or the "simplest." Fifth, the physical atom of any of the ninety elements, for instance, oxygen, remains identical to itself in its essential traits. Moreno's atom incessantly changes, expands, and contracts in the number of its social relationships and in the kind of individuals with whom emotional rapport is established. There are many more defects in Moreno's social atom, but the following conclusions can be drawn on the basis of those cited:[68] In regard to the social world, Moreno's social atom does not play the same role that the physical atom plays in regard to the physical universe; neither does the former resemble the latter in its structure. For this reason, the term "social atom" is a misnomer for the network of emotional attractions and repulsions. It is neither the "smallest" nor the "simplest" unit of emotional or social relatedness. It does not cover all social relations—not even all emotionally colored social interactions. It is neither an ultimate nor a universal unit out of which all webs of social relationships are built, and to which they can be analytically reduced. It is so diverse in its structure and function, in its volume and properties—now embracing millions of persons, now involving only a few—and, at the same time, it so incessantly changes that it is not the same unit in all these diverse forms. The term covers rather a series of different phenomena. For these reasons, it cannot perform the functions of a simplest unit of social phenomena. The concept of the network of emotional rapports of an individual, though valuable, cannot serve the tasks of the social atom. In this point it is useless. Such, in

---

[68] See, on these defects, my *Fads and Foibles*, ch. 10; and G. D. Gurvitch, "Microsociology and Sociometry," *Sociometry, 12*(1949), 1–31.

brief, are the shortcomings of Moreno's social atom. Still more defective are the "social atoms" discovered by other sociologists.

The *coup de grâce* to Moreno's social atom, as well as to all searches for the social atom as the simplest unit of social relationship, was dealt by modern physics when it ceased to view the atom as the simplest unit of physical phenomena, replacing it with an ever-increasing number of progressively smaller and smaller "elementary particles." In about 1930, the electron and the proton replaced the atom as the simplest unit. During subsequent years, a number of other elementary particles were discovered: the "nonmaterial" photon, then the neutron, the positron, two kinds of meson, the neutrino, the antiproton, the antielectron, the antineutron, and the antineutrino. In this welter of elementary particles, the very terms elementary particle and ultimate particle have radically changed their meaning. In the words of an eminent physicist, "elementary" now seems to mean "the equivalent of cryptic, arcane, perplexing, enigmatic, inscrutable." Since many of these "enigmatic" particles do not have most of the characteristics of "matter," the term "material" has also become inapplicable to them and has had to be largely abandoned.[69]

Although the physical sciences have already abandoned the atom as the simplest unit of physical reality, our "sociological physicists" are still playing with atomic marbles—still looking for the social atom as the most elementary unit of social phenomena, relationships, and structures. It is high time to give up playing with marbles and to terminate the search for the sociological Humpty-Dumpty. In my works I have pointed out many times that there is *no* elementary "social atom" or any simplest unit of social phenomena.[70] Instead, we should look for the *generic model* of social phenomena that gives us the

[69] See E. Fermi, *Elementary Particles* (New Haven, 1951); E. Schrödinger's article in *Endeavour*, No. 35, 9(1950); H. Margenau, "The Meaning of 'Elementary Particle,'" *American Scientist*, 39(1951), 422–431; and V. S. Barashenkov, "Aktualnyje voprosy fisiki elementarnykh chastiz," *Voprosy Filosofii*, 9(1965), 84–94.

[70] See *SCP*, pp. 39–49, and *passim*.

traits and relationships common to all social phenomena. Our efforts should be concentrated on a study of this generic model and not on nonexisting social atoms.

● The Hunt for Elementary Small Groups

Following the precept of the biologists of the nineteenth century that a study of the structure and evolution of organisms should begin with their simplest and smallest forms, a number of sociologists and psychologists "discovered" in recent years the "small group" as the elementary social unit. Accordingly, they started an intense investigation of "small groups" as the most promising approach for discovering generalizations valid for larger groups and for the whole universe of social phenomena. The initial impetus to the study of the small groups was given by Moreno's theory of the social atoms and his "sociometry" and by K. Lewin's pseudomathematical schemes of "group dynamics." Under their influence a number of younger researchers—like the members of the "Group Dynamics," R. Bales, A. Bavelas, G. C. Homans, E. F. Borgata, and others[71]— have enthusiastically engaged in studies of small groups and made such studies fashionable. The partisans of this movement have increasingly extolled the revolutionary character of their discoveries and the exceptionally scientific nature of their studies. They claim to have studied the small group scientifically —experimentally, objectively, and quantitatively—for the first time in history. They also claim that before their scientific research the psychosocial sciences produced mainly a spectulative armchair philosophy.

When these claims are carefully examined, they are found to be largely baseless. When the research methods of these scientists are seriously considered, they turn out to consist

[71] Representative samples of small-group studies are P. Hare, E. F. Borgata, R. F. Bales (eds.), *Small Groups* (New York, 1955); R. F. Bales, *Interaction Process Analysis* (Cambridge, Mass., 1950); G. C. Homans, *The Human Group* (New York, 1950); and Cartwright and Zander, *Group Dynamics.*

mainly of sham experimental and sham quantitative procedures; when their discoveries are analyzed, they appear to be either rediscoveries of old laws, or insignificant trifles, or errors.

To begin with, the researchers of the small groups still do not have a satisfactory definition of a small group. Their definitions stress two *differentiae specificae* of small groups: (1) face-to-face interaction "in which each member receives some impression of each other member distinct enough so that he can give some reaction to each of the others as an individual person, even though it be only to recall that the other was present"; (2) a small membership of the group fluctuating from one to some twenty-five or so members. According to this definition, a face-to-face meeting of some twenty persons previously unknown to each other, where each member does not receive a "clear impression" of many members of the meeting —be it an incidental cocktail party, a spontaneous political gathering, or a religious revival—is not a small group. On the other hand, a series of meetings of some 600 members of a parliament where each member knows all the other members, or a Republican convention where more than a thousand delegates who probably all know one another, interact face to face has at least one of the two characteristics of a small group. In addition, we are told that even one person, when he talks with himself, is a "small group." Thus, according to the basic characteristics of the definition of a small group, many a large group is a small group, whereas many a small group is not a small group at all. As an additional surprise we learn that a small group can be so small that it consists of one person only. Using the terms small and large in senses almost opposite to what these terms usually mean does not contribute to the clarity of the definition. In fact, it hopelessly confuses the issue, and makes the concept of a small group exceedingly vague and even self-contradictory.

Furthermore, the definition of the small group does not describe any *homogeneous* class of social groups; instead, it delivers to us a veritable motley of the most *dissimilar* groups, because either one of the two characteristics may be found among most heterogeneous groups or gatherings of persons.

Thus face-to-face interaction takes place in the meeting of two lovers, of executioner and the condemned, in a family reunion, in the meetings of the directors of a business corporation, in the interactions of a milling and shouting crowd, in a discussion group, in a platoon on a battle field, in the session of a parliament, at a political convention, and so on. Mere face-to-face interaction does not make these and hundreds of other groups similar nor does it make them members of the same species of group. A "small" membership is found among the most dissimilar groups: in the family, in the board of directors of a corporation, in a group of revolutionary plotters, in a gang of criminals, in "exclusive" clubs of various kinds, and in hundreds of other groups as different from one another as they can be.

To unify the most heterogeneous groups into one class, "small groups," is contrary to the basic scientific rule of the classification of phenomena. It is as antiscientific as the unification into one "nosey" species of such different organisms as insect, fish, dog, bird, and man, or, into one "taily" species, snakes, ants, horses, and birds. We know well that such a species is not a species at all. For the same reason, the class of small groups is not a class at all. The very attempt to make a specific class of "small groups" is devoid of any logical, semantic, and empirical grounds. It is about as unscientific as would be the attempt of a botanist to make a special species of small plants out of all plants from 1 to 25 inches tall, or the endeavor of a zoologist to make a new species of small organisms out of all organisms weighing from 1 to 20 pounds. In biology, such taxonomic classes do not exist; if suggested, they would have no chance at all of being accepted. In sociology, unfortunately, they are still made and have a notable vogue at the present moment.

The initial "sin" of the partisans of small groups is that they have no real class of social groups for their study, and they do not know exactly what the small groups are that they are trying to investigate. This "sin" has been responsible for the many defects and errors of their industrious research—for example, their false assumption that a small group is the simplest unit of social groups or structures. By face-to-face interaction and by the size of its membership, the family is a small group; and yet, in its structure and functions it is one of the most complex and most encyclopedic groups among all social organizations.[72] By the size of their membership, many national and international associations, like the Democratic or Republican parties, the American Federation of Labor, or the National Association of Manufacturers, are vast groups with millions of members. Structurally and functionally, they are much simpler groups than the family. Structurally, the members of these vast associations are bound together by only one or a few bonds or interests—economic or occupational or recreational or religious or scientific—whereas the members of the family are bound together by many bonds or interests. Functionally, the activities of these vast organizations are also much less encyclopedic, more narrow and specialized, than the "encyclopedic" activities of the family. Generally, many a real community (*Gemeinschaften*) is ordinarily small in size in comparison with many an association (*Gesellschaften*), and yet, structurally and functionally, such communities are much more complex than many a vast association. The small size of a group does not necessarily make it a simple group, and vice versa. The partisans of small groups grossly err in equating small groups with simple groups. If we want to follow the precept "from the simplest to the more complex," a study of social groups does not necessarily have to begin with the smallest groups and then pass to the larger groups. This precept itself, however, is not a universal methodological principle: In many cases it is more advisable to follow the Aristotelian opposite precept, namely, the properties of an oak can be studied more fruitfully on a full-grown oak than on an acorn.

The study of small groups and the kind of groups selected for study by the small-group researchers has been haphazard and blundering. The bulk of the investigated groups represents an incidental, semiorganized, or nonorganized collection of students or soldiers or workers or dwellers of an establishment (room, apartment, classroom, factory room, etc.) previously unknown to one another and hastily gathered together, often by

[72] See, on the complexity of the family, *SCP*, pp. 246 ff.

command of their superiors or by promise of payment, for the sake of "discussion," "problem solving," "interviewing and questioning," and similar artificial purposes. These incidental gatherings can be described most accurately as "chatterbox groups." Now and then a quite heterogeneous, organized group, like the family in Tikopeia or a metropolitan club or a small religious sect or a political clique, is studied by the small-group researchers, who fail to stress the profound differences between organized, unorganized, and nominal groups: All are given the same treatment. No wonder that a study of this hash of groups has yielded meager results.[73]

The above criticism does not mean that the *specific forms* of small groups cannot or should not be studied. On the contrary, such small groups as dyads and triads, the family, a small aristocracy, a small business group, a small sect or political party, and so on, have been fruitfully studied. However, each of these collectivities has been investigated not just as a small group generally, but as a specific group whose structural, dynamic, and functional properties cannot be extended over all or many groups with small membership. The basic properties of the family and the relationships of husband-wife-child cannot be extrapolated much beyond the family triad and cannot be applied to all the dyads, triads, and small business-religious-criminal-educational-military-political collectivities. Nor can they be applied to the nonorganized and the nominal groups, and vice versa. If the properties of one of these specific groups are extrapolated to other groups, as is regularly done by our discoverers of small groups, the results are bound to be either meaningless, fallacious, or cognitively insignificant.

We reject the claim of the recent investigators of small groups that, before their research, small groups were hardly studied at all, and that they are the discoverers of small groups. These pretentious claims are baseless. Since Confucius, at least

---

[73] The organized groups so basically differ from the unorganized and both from the nominal plurels that no competent scholar can ignore this difference and indiscriminately unite them into a fictitious class of small groups. See, on the organized, unorganized, and nominal groups, *SCP*, ch. 4, and *passim*.

a series of specific small groups, beginning with the family, have been carefully studied by many thinkers. These thinkers investigated them as specific groups and wisely abstained from extrapolating their results beyond the group studied.

In this respect, their procedure was much more scientific than that of the recent researchers of the fictitious class of small groups generally. The family and the household, the dyads of teacher-pupil, master-slave, seller-buyer, employer-employee; the triads of a judge-accuser-accused, husband-wife-lover; small *Bruderschaften*, small guild, caste, village, and many other small collectivities have been well analyzed already by the authors of the Code of Hammurabi, by Confucius, Mo-ti, Mencius, the authors of the Indian Puranas, Tantras, Arthasastras, and Nitisastras; they have been studied in the Laws of Manu, in the Institutes of Vishnu, and by such authors as Kautilya, Plato, Aristotle, and especially by the great Roman jurists whose work is incorporated into the Corpus Juris Civilis. This corpus alone gives such adequate, detailed, and well-analyzed definitions of the main specific small (and large) groups, corporations, and institutions, that it still lives not only in the law codes but in the social life of the West. In comparison with these definitions, formulas, and analyses, those of the recent small-group researchers are but baby talk. The quicker these researchers drop their childish claims of being the discoverers of small groups, and the quicker they acquaint themselves with the Corpus Juris Civilis and with other ancient studies of the main types of organized small groups, the better for themselves and for sociology.

When we carefully examine the alleged experimental, operational, quantitative, and objective *methods* of the recent investigators of small groups, we find an already-familiar imitative veneer of these methods applied mainly to the familiar "hearsay stuff" of the participants of the hastily recruited "discussion" or "problem-solving" or, more exactly, "chatterbox" groups. At first glance, the setting and procedures of these researchers impress us as truly instrumental and objective. Their "small group" meets in a special laboratory equipped with a one-way mirror and with sound and interaction recorders. These gadgets allegedly permit the investigator to observe, to record, and to place each "unit of speech" of each member into one of his categories. R. F. Bales' classification can serve as a typical example of these categories. He classifies all possible speech-reactions and overt-actions of the members into the following classes: "(1) shows solidarity; (2) shows tension release; (3) agrees; (4) gives suggestion; (5) gives opinion; (6) gives orientation; (7) asks for orientation; (8) asks for opinion; (9) asks for suggestion; (10) disagrees; (11) shows tension; (12) shows antagonism."

At the end of the session, the investigator-observer has the record of all the speech-and-action units of each member, to whom each utterance or action is addressed, in what order, and to what category it belongs. These data are then statistically processed to supply us with hitherto unknown, scientific knowledge of the interaction process and the structure and dynamics of small groups of all sorts. The results obtained are usually generalized and applied to many other—small and large—groups. Bales' small groups fluctuated in size from two to ten and from three to six participants. Their members consisted of Harvard undergraduates, obtained through the Harvard employment bureau. The students did not know each other prior to the first meeting. Each group had four meetings for discussion of a "human relations case."[74]

In spite of all this scientific veneer, the whole procedure is in fact highly subjective, arbitrary, and based on exceedingly vague assumptions and doubtful notions. First, the central concepts of the study—the "speech-unit" and the "action-unit"— remain practically undefined. Shall we regard as a "speech-unit" every single word? or every proposition consisting of the subject-copula-predicate? or a series of propositions dealing with the same subject? or showing the same emotional tone? or addressed to the same member? or what? A very indeterminate and foggy outline of these units does not help at all in defining them. As a result, which words (or actions) make up a "speech-

[74] See R. F. Bales, "A Set of Categories for the Analysis of Small-Group Interaction," *ASR*, *15*(1950), pp. 257–263; R. F. Bales, "The Equilibrium Problem in Small Groups," in T. Parsons, R. F. Bales, and E. A. Shils, *Working Papers in the Theory of Action* (Glencoe, Ill., 1953); and R. F. Bales, *Interaction Process Analysis*.

unit" or an "action-unit" is quite arbitrarily decided by the observer. Since these central concepts are undefined, the whole huge analytical and statistical superstructure built upon them remains but a mirage.

No less arbitrary is the operation of pigeonholing each "speech-unit" and "action-unit" of every member in the incessant and rapidly moving stream of often simultaneous utterances and motions of the participants. In contrast to the electronic mathematical calculators, the "interaction-recorder" does not automatically classify the speech- and action-units into one of the twelve classes. The pigeonholing is done—again in a great rush—by the observer himself. He, of course, has no time to analyze carefully whether the words uttered belong to the category of "gives suggestion," of "gives opinion," or of "gives orientation"; whether they fall into the category of "disagrees," or of "shows tension," or of "shows antagonism." Even if he did have plenty of time, he would still find difficult, often impossible, an accurate pigeonholing, because the categories "gives opinion," "gives orientation," and "gives suggestion" are so similar that only by some supernatural intuition can one distinguish between them and unerringly categorize each one of them. The same can be said of the categories "disagrees," "shows tension," and "shows antagonism." Considering that the observer throughout the whole session of his "chatterbox" group has to record each "speech-unit" (undefined), each "action-unit" (also undefined), by whom it is uttered or done, to whom it is addressed, and to which of his poorly defined categories it belongs, considering that several members of the group may be simultaneously talking and acting, and considering the haste with which he must make all these recordings, analyses, and classifications, we conclude that no observer can perform these impossible tasks accurately and objectively. It is inevitable that he do them only impulsively, arbitrarily, and blunderingly. If thus two basic aspects of the whole study—the definition of the units of speech and action and the method of pigeonholing them—are predominantly subjective and arbitrary, most of the other data of the research, most of its statistical superstructure, and the bulk of the conclusions are also subjective, arbitrary, pseudoexperimental, and pseudoquantitative. No gadgets and one-way mirrors, no long series of figures and indexes, can hide the essentially unscientific nature of the whole research operation.

A number of other important defects further vitiate these research operations. The classification of the twelve categories is haphazard. It does not have any *fundamentum divisionis*. Several of its categories, like "gives suggestion," "gives opinion," and so on, are so similar and overlapping that a most careful investigator, with plenty of time, cannot decide to which of these categories this or that "speech-unit" belongs. On the other hand, the classification unites into one category words and actions notably dissimilar from one another. For instance, the category "gives orientation" embraces "information, repetition, clarification, and confirmation." "Repetition" is obviously not synonymous with "information," and "clarification" means something different from "confirmation." Such a logically and factually clumsy classification is a very poor tool for a study of the vocal and behavioral units, and it makes unavoidable a great deal of arbitrariness and subjectivity in the research operation.

Furthermore, the categories of the classification aim to describe only the speech-reactions of the participants; they are unfit to describe their nonvocal actions. Omitting almost entirely the overt behavior of the participants and the real motives of their actions, the studies of our investigators merely glide on the vocal surface without touching the overt behavior of the members of their incidental "chatterbox" group. In this sense, this research is superficial and almost completely dodges the real problems of social interaction and group phenomena.

The pretentious "discoveries" of these investigators are, in fact, either ponderously formulated platitudes, or tautologies screened by statistical tables, or revelations discovered long ago, or distorted transcriptions of the propositions of the physical sciences, or plain errors. Here are typical samples of these "discoveries." If need be, they can be multiplied ad libitum.

"Interaction is a process consisting of action followed by reaction."[75] What a marvelous tautology! "[For leadership] there

---

[75] R. F. Bales, "The Equilibrium Problem in Small Groups," in Parsons, Bales, and Shils, *op. cit.*, p. 121.

must be a group with a common task . . . and at least one member must have responsibilities which differ from those of the other members" (R. M. Stogdill).[76] How true! This is a discovery almost as new as the discovery that "after the spring comes the summer, and after the summer, the fall." However, as often happens with platitudes, the author of the statement forgets that sometimes the group and its common task are created by a leader.

"Some members [of a group] may be regarded as rating higher than others in leadership [because they have responsibility for making decisions] (Stogdill)."[77] Extraordinary new discovery, not a bit older than 5,000 years.

"A significant aspect of our society is that persons desire membership in groups" (L. Festinger).[78] What a revelation this is, especially after Aristotle's "Man is naturally a political animal" and "There is in all persons a natural impetus to associate with each other."[79]

No less striking is Festinger's "discovery" of "why people seek membership in groups." The answer is because "Groups frequently [help] the attainment of important individual goals." The activities of the group are frequently attractive to the member. And they are attractive "because people have needs that can be satisfied only in groups." The author forgets to mention several important limitations of these verities, such as the fact that millions of persons become members of a group automatically, regardless of their wishes. For example, state citizenship or caste membership is automatically imposed upon all born in such and such a state or to parents of such and such a caste; sometimes many individuals, such as prisoners of war or criminals, are coerced to belong to a group of inmates of a concentration camp or of a jail, contrary to their wishes. Such automatic and undesirable memberships play a no less important role in the life of hundreds of millions of people than voluntary or sought-for memberships.

---

[76] Cartwright and Zander, *Group Dynamics* (1953 edition), p. 42.
[77] *Ibid.*, p. 49.
[78] *Ibid.*, p. 92.
[79] Aristotle, *Politics*, p. 1253a.

The same conclusion applies to Festinger's "discoveries" about the relationship between friendship (or enmity) and territorial and "functional" propinquity and about the conditions of successful community action, and to practically all of his conclusions allegedly derived from his "experimental" studies of the Regent Hill and the Westgate groups—his studies of "cognitive dissonance."[80] Each of his conclusions was incomparably better formulated, developed, and demonstrated by many social investigators of the preceding generations.

Let us now take some discoveries concerning the "cohesiveness" of groups. The term cohesiveness, according to John Thibaut, means "the total field of forces, which acts on members to remain in the group."[81] The term, as well as its definition, is a distorted version of a proposition of mechanics borrowed from the physical sciences. It is an extremely vague and inadequate statement. Without a preliminary differentiation of the kind of groups whose "cohesiveness" is studied, no real understanding of the forms and the "forces" of cohesiveness is possible. The point is that there are "voluntary" and "coercive" groups or, more exactly, "familistic," "contractual," and "compulsory" groups. The basic difference in these groups manifests itself in a fundamental difference of the forces of cohesiveness active in each. The factors that unite the members of a family into one unity and that enable it to maintain its identity, "cohesiveness," and continuity are quite different from the factors that coerce the inmates of a prison to remain in the group. The forces that keep together the employees and the employer of a business firm are again different from those that keep together the family, a prison group, or the members of the American Sociological Association.

This differentiation of the types of groups that stay together and the types of bonds that keep them together is not made clear in Thibaut's study, or in others like it. As a result, all the industrious efforts of these sociologists to study scientifically the problems of the cohesiveness of small groups have not yielded any

---

[80] See N. and A. Chapanis, *Psychological Bulletin*, No. 1 (1964).
[81] Cartwright and Zander, *op. cit.*, p. 102.

significant new discovery. In comparison with the existing body of knowledge in this field, their theories, their "discovered" uniformities, and their total grasp of the problem in all its main ramifications still remain at a primitive stage—a stage long ago passed over by today's psychosocial sciences.[82]

The next discovery is: "The attraction to the group is a function of the resultant forces acting on the member." What "resultant forces"? and how do they act on the members? In mechanics, all these terms are strictly defined and measurable. Here they remain just vague words devoid of any definite meaning and measurement.

Let us continue to discover the "discoveries" of our "pioneers." Here are further examples of their tautologies: "The term [group] cohesiveness refers to phenomena which come into existence if, and only if, the group exists." [How wonderful!] "The members of a group who are . . . friends . . . are likely to be more interested in one another as persons, perhaps more supportive of each other, more cordial in interpersonal relations." [What a revelation again! Note especially the extreme "scientific" caution in this remarkable "perhaps."][83] Until this revelation, we had naïvely thought that, without any "perhaps," "friendship" implied mutual interest, cordiality, and support of friends. After reading these revelations, I am inclined to echo Saintsbury: "O clichés! O tickets! O fudge!"

"An increase in the frequency of interaction between persons may increase the strength of their favorable sentiment toward one another."[84] If so, then the more frequently Vietnamese and American soldiers fight (interact), the more favorable a sentiment they develop toward one another. Consequently, the fighting and hating interaction is as good a remedy for the development of mutual admiration, sympathy, and altruism as is mutual help. Fortunately for Homans, at the end of the paragraph stating and developing this "scientific" generalization, he seems to have grasped its one-sided fallacy. He adds, in just four words, two other possible consequences of the frequent inter-

---

[82] See the discussion in *SCP*, chs. 5, 6, 7, 8, 21, and 22.
[83] Cartwright and Zander, *op. cit.*, pp. 76, 79.
[84] G. C. Homans, *The Human Group*, p. 444.

action—namely, the development of "respect or, worse, antagonism."

"Splinter-group formation will disrupt the larger organization when the goals of the smaller group are incompatible with those of the larger." Again, what a beautiful tautology! Splinter groups tend to splinter or disrupt! But, as happens with many tautologies, the tautological statement in this form is inadequate, because, instead of disrupting the larger group, the splinter group more frequently is suppressed by the larger group. Empirically one-sided also is the statement that "the tendency to break apart would be more likely, the larger the group."[85] If this generalization were true, no large groups, like great empires, world religious organizations, or large labor unions, could emerge and exist for very long. As a matter of fact, however, during the historical existence of man there have always been large groups, and they have, as a rule, existed longer than small groups.[86]

R. F. Bales and associates start their paper with the following claim: "The frequencies of communication between members in small face-to-face groups show certain striking regularities which have not previously been described. . . . The detection of these regularities represents a significant gain in our knowledge about the distribution of communication in small groups, and provides a basic framework of order within which many more detailed analyses of the interaction process may be made."[87] Quite a modest claim! But just what are these "striking and significant regularities"? "The findings reported indicate that if participants in a small group are ranked by the total number of acts they initiate, they will also tend to be ranked: (1) by the number of acts they receive; (2) by the number of acts they address to specific other individuals; and (3) by the number of acts they address to the group as a whole."[88]

In plain words, these ponderous "uniformities" mean that

[85] Cartwright and Zander, *op. cit.*, p. 86.

[86] See, on the life-span, mortality, and resurrection of various groups, *SCP*, ch. 34.

[87] R. F. Bales, F. L. Strodtbeck, T. M. Mills, and M. E. Roseborough, "Channels of Communication in Small Groups," *ASR, 16*(1951), 461, 465.

[88] *Ibid.*, p. 468.

in a discussion group the most talkative members of a group talk more frequently than other members and are talked back to more frequently by the less talkative members. From this beautiful tautology we can derive an additional "striking and significant uniformity" overlooked by Bales: Persons who are silent talk less frequently than other members and are talked back to less frequently by the more talkative persons.

Like many other tautologies, Bales' tautology in no way can be considered a general empirical rule for all—small and large—groups. In the courtroom group consisting of the judge, the accused, the prosecuting and the defense attorneys, and the jury—most of the talks are addressed, contrary to Bales' uniformity, to the jury and the judge. The jury, as a rule, remains silent, instead of talking most; even the judge ordinarily talks less than the attorneys. A lecturer, a preacher, and a commander of a platoon issuing orders are the only talking members of their respective groups. And yet, they ordinarily are not talked back to at all by the other members of their groups. In a large number of various groups, all the talking members address their talk to the chairman, yet the chairman often talks the least in the group. And so on and so forth.

In an overwhelming majority of the small and large groups, Bales' "uniformities" are exceptions rather than the rule, from the standpoint of the real processes of who is talking, who is being talked to, and how frequently. And, what is still more important, no painstaking research of Bales' type is necessary for discovering the order, frequency, and kind of talks by various members of almost all organized groups: All this can easily be found in the constitution of such groups. The laws and bylaws of each organized group supply incomparably more accurate information on all these points than the vague and largely fictitious uniformities that the investigators of the small groups obtained with an enormous waste of time, energy, and funds.

If one were to go, page by page, through the published studies of the recent researchers of the small groups, one would find on almost every page "discoveries," concepts, definitions, and theories represented by the examples given above. Yet in carefully reading these works, I have not found any single new discovery of even tertiary importance. I *have* found a super-abundance of pseudodiscoveries. Our investigators, walking in a park of well-cultivated facts, seemingly imagine themselves as the great pioneer-explorers of a hitherto unknown land, or as the first climbers of scientific hills and peaks that were, in actuality, conquered long ago.

With this summary our exploration of the explorers of the small groups can be concluded.

CHAPTER 4

Singularistic-Atomistic Quantitative Sociologies

RECENT UPSURGE OF QUANTITATIVE STUDIES

The last few decades have been marked not only by the pseudomathematical and "shorthand" sociologies outlined in Chapter 3, but also by a notable upsurgence of more or less genuine quantitative studies of psychosocial and cultural phenomena. In part, this upsurgence is a manifestation of the physicalistic trend discussed in Chapter 3; however, a large portion of these quantitative studies represent a sincere effort to obtain real knowledge of the quantitative aspects of social, cultural, and psychological realities. Many of them have yielded fruitful results and have tangibly contributed to our knowledge of psychosocial and cultural realities, especially economic, demographic, and criminological phenomena. This sort of quantitative research should be encouraged.

Those quantitative studies that use quantitative methods incompetently, or apply them to phenomena that do not lend themselves, as yet, to quantification, or regard them as a sort of infallible magic that knows all and measures all should, on the other hand, be discouraged. Unfortunately, this sort of quantitative study occupies a large place in modern quantitative sociology.

Several varieties of recent quantitative investigations of psychosocial phenomena can be roughly reduced to two main categories: to strictly mathematical research, and to statistical research.

MATHEMATICAL MODELS

As mentioned, any genuine mathematical study of psychosocial problems is welcome. None of the criticism of sham mathematical investigations applies to true mathematical explorations, for true mathematicians well realize the enormous difficulties and limited possibilities of the use of mathematical tools in the analysis of social and psychological facts. The leading mathematical sociologists openly acknowledge that "no one can deny this fact" [of the unamenability of many social phenomena to mathematical treatment], that the mathematics used for such an analysis is often "too elementary," that many equations inferred "are of little practical value," that many assumptions made are "only the artifacts used for mathematical expediency," "too simple and hardly corresponding to reality," and so on.[1]

These and similar difficulties are responsible for the hitherto modest contributions of mathematical studies to our knowledge of the what, how, and why of psychosocial facts. These contributions have been more tangible in the field of those mass phenomena that have a measurable unit—and, therefore, lend themselves more easily to mathematical analysis—than in the field of singular and qualitative social facts. This explains why mathematical studies of demographic facts, that is, populations, their density, sex-age composition, size, vital processes, mor-

---

[1] N. Rashevsky, *Mathematical Theory of Human Relations* (Bloomington, Ind., 1947), pp. iii–xi, *passim*. N. Rashevsky, *Mathematical Biology of Social Behavior* (Chicago, 1950), pp. iii–ix, ch. 27. See also A. Tarsky, *Introduction to Logic* (Oxford, 1946), ch. 6; J. von Neumann and O. Morgenstern, *Theory of Games and Economic Behavior* (Princeton, 1947); I. Fisher, "The Application of Mathematics to the Social Sciences," *Bulletin of American Mathematical Society*, *36*(1930); R. Fisher, "The Expansion of Statistics," *American Scientist*, *42*(1954); R. R. Bush and F. Mosteller, *Stochastic Models for Learning* (New York, 1955); P. F. Lazarsfeld, *Mathematical Thinking in the Social Sciences* (Glencoe, 1954); F. A. Isambert, "La statistique bien temperée," *Cahiers Internationaux de Sociologie*, *18*(1955); M. W. Riley, *Sociological Research* (New York, 1963), units 6, 7, 8, 9, 10, and J. M. Beshers, "Mathematical Models in Social Change," in Zollschan and Hirsch, *Explorations in Social Change* (Boston, 1964), pp. 281–296.

bidity, migration, and mobility; of large-scale economic phenomena and processes; and of the incidence of, say, inventions or crimes, have been fairly fruitful both in establishing probabilistic, statistical "semiuniformities" and in constructing mathematical models as the postulational systems of closely related equations well fitted to the observed phenomena and, with some limitations, capable of predicting their future empirical course.

In contrast to the purely statistical procedures, the method of mathematical models starts with one or a few axioms or postulates, infers from these a series of equations, which in their totality make a self-contained mathematical system, and, finally turns to the empirical data in order to find out the degree of agreement between the inferred equations and the relevant observable facts. The routine statistical investigation does not postulate any axiom or derive a series of equations from it; it simply counts its items, classifies and summarizes them, and computes percentages, and, occasionally, the indexes or coefficients of association between its variables.

The mathematical method, although potentially very promising, may be difficult to apply to a study of psychosocial phenomena. An irreproachable mathematical system, derived from assumed postulates, may be likened to an elegant blueprint of a marvelous building for whose construction the necessary material is unavailable. This happens when the empirical data necessary for verifying its equations are either totally lacking or purely qualitative and thus unmeasurable. In mathematical economics, psychology, and sociology there are a number of such mathematical systems or models. For an understanding of empirical sociocultural facts, such models contribute little, if anything.

Of course, there are some mathematical models that have a small amount of measurable empirical material and whose equations sometimes indicate several unsuspected relationships between empirical variables, and sometimes even predict a future course of their empirical processes. The best "models" of Rashevsky, Neumann and Morgenstern, Bush and Mosteller,[2] S.

---

[2] Refer to their works quoted in the preceding footnote.

Karlin, H. Landau, L. F. Richardson, A. Rapoport, S. C. Dodd, O. Lange, and others are examples of this type of mathematical study.[3]

In spite of a considerable potential value, the actual contributions of these models to an understanding of the psychosocial world is still very limited—mainly because their equations remain valid in regard to empirical facts only within the limits of their postulates and of the several empirical assumptions that they have to make throughout the whole process of their mathematical analysis. If these postulates and assumptions correspond to the empirical reality they try to analyze, their equations and inferences give us a sound knowledge of the empirical facts involved. If they do not correspond to the respective empirical facts, then the inferred conclusions and formulas become inapplicable to psychosocial reality. To illustrate this, we can take Neumann and Morgenstern's admirable model of economic behavior. Their inferences or equations, however, fit the actual economic behavior only under the following assumptions: Utility is a linear quantity; there is a transitivity of preference among the utilities; means are scarce and transferable; individuals are rational; individuals have an equal access to information; individuals conform to certain accepted standards of conduct; individuals plan carefully a rational strategy of their economic actions, and so on. If, however, the empirical individuals are nonrational or ill-rational; if they do not have an equal access to information—and most of them quite often do not; if they do not always conform to the accepted standards of conduct—and they certainly break these standards quite frequently—then most of the inferences of this model become little applicable to this sort of human universe and to the economic behavior of its

---

[3] See S. Karlin, *A Mathematical Treatment of Learning Models*, Research Memorandum No. 921 (RAND Corporation, 1952); L. F. Richardson, "Generalized Foreign Policies," *British Journal of Psychology*, 23(1939); Landau's and Landahl's studies of imitation in *Bulletin of Mathematical Biophysics*, 12(1950); A. Rapoport and L. Rebhun, "On the Mathematical Theory of Rumor Spread," *Bulletin of Mathematical Biophysics*, 14(1952); and S. Dodd, "Can the Social Scientist Serve Two Masters?," *Research Studies of State College of Washington*, 21(1953); O. Lange, *Catość i rozwój w świete cybernetyki* (Warsaw, 1962), *passim*.

members. (Cf. on this C. Gini, *Patologia economica*, [Torino, 1952]).

The same can be said of other mathematical models. For this reason the actual applicability and predictive ability of mathematical models in regard to empirical psychosocial phenomena have been, so far, very modest.

When the empirical assumptions of a mathematical model grossly differ from the actual empirical situation, the conclusions and predictions of such a model become fallacious. Empirically, the model turns into a misleading preciseness or a rigorous fallacy parading in the guise of exact knowledge. Auguste Comte warned of this danger:

> The possibility of applying mathematical analysis to the study of phenomena is exactly in proportion to the rank which they hold in the scale of the whole. [It is decreasing as we pass from physical, to biological, and then to psycho-social facts.] We must be aware of confounding the degree of precision with the certainty of science itself. . . . The certainty of science and our precision in the knowledge of it are two very different things [confounded often]. . . . A very absurd proposition may be very precise [for instance, two plus two equals seven or a horse has six legs] . . . and a very certain proposition may be wanting in precision in our statement of it as, for instance, when we assert that every man will die.[4]

Unfortunately, more frequently than not the mathematical modelists make either fallacious or very doubtful empirical assumptions in their studies. As a result, their mathematical theories are fallacies rather than positive contributions to the psychosocial sciences.[5] Many mathematical sociologists and psychologists display a surprisingly uncritical attitude in making their empirical assumptions. As long as such a carelessness continues, their mathematical studies are bound to suffer from the above-mentioned defects and to be of very limited value in understanding the actual psychosocial and cultural universe.

---

[4] A. Comte, *System of Positive Polity* (London, 1875), Vol. I, p. 30.

[5] N. Rashevsky's "Outline of a Mathematical Approach to History" is an example of such a fallacy. See its outline and criticism in *Fads and Foibles*, ch. 8. See there also other examples of such erroneous mathematical theories.

The last few decades have also witnessed an enormous increase in statistical studies of psychosocial and cultural phenomena. This increase has occurred in both elementary and advanced studies. The main task of the unambitious statistical investigation consists of accurately counting and then classifying and summarizing the items investigated. An accurate census of a population exemplifies this sort of statistical inquiry. By simple arithmetical operations it delivers to us the desired quantitative information.

In spite of its elementary character, this unambitious statistical approach has given to us valuable quantitative information about a multitude of psychosocial and cultural phenomena. It has, possibly, delivered even a greater amount of correct knowledge than the more ambitious forms of statistical research. As long as the counting operations are done accurately and are applied to phenomena that have objective units for counting, such studies are bound to grow and to enrich our knowledge of psychosocial realities.

On the other hand, the quantitative knowledge supplied by elementary statistics is mainly informational, temporary, and local. This sort of statistical investigation does not pretend to give us general or "middle-range" uniformities, causal laws, or formulas valid for all times and for different societies. Quantitative data concerning the size of the United States population in 1960, its age-sex composition, its birth-death-marriage-divorce-morbidity rates, its occupational composition, and so on, are valid only for the American population at the moment of the census-taking. These data and rates cannot be extrapolated and applied to non-American populations, or to the American population of 1830 or of 1990. The temporary, local, and purely informational nature of the data supplied by "unambitious" statistics is their greatest limitation. Although we need to know the figures, rates, and percentages of a given class of social and cultural phenomena and although we need a repository for this material, such data do not give us a particularly valuable understanding of ourselves, our fellow men, or the sociocultural universe in which we live and act. The only thing we actually need to know in regard to this vast ocean of data is where we can find statistics on a particular item when we need them.

Advanced statistical studies set forth much more ambitious tasks, such as discovering the causal or probabilistic relationship between the variables studied, the existence or nonexistence of uniformities in the field explored, and past, present, and future trends and fluctuations in the field; analyzing and measuring the factors involved; predicting the future course of the empirical processes analyzed, and so on. These are the tasks of a generalizing or nomothetic science and they go far beyond the task of compiling statistics.

In spite of the enormous amounts of energy, labor, and funds invested in advanced statistical research, however, its contributions have been, so far, fairly modest. Impressive-looking indexes, coefficients, and formulas frequently have turned out to be uncertain, contradictory, and misleading.

The statistical exploration of causal, functional, or probabilistic relationships between psychosocial variables has been undertaken in the last few decades by a legion of sociologists and psychologists. When several coefficients of correlation between the same variables were obtained by several different studies, however, the coefficients displayed a striking discordance. Also, they often failed to register a stable or close relationship between two or more variables that was ascertained by different methods, and they often registered a highly significant association between variables that was denied by a more convincing body of evidence. The misbehavior of the coefficients has left no doubt as to the fallibility of correlational statistics in unraveling causal or probabilistic relationships among diverse variables in the psychosocial universe. Correlational statistics has shown itself wanting also in its predictive ability. Various studies investigating the relationship between intelligence and criminality in a total of some 163,000 cases have yielded discordant coefficients of correlation fluctuating all the way from minus .52 to plus .76. Similar discrepancies of coefficients are found between delinquency and illiteracy, delinquency and amount of schooling, criminality and school progress, and intelligence and morality.[6] But, after all these studies, we know as little of the real relationship between intelligence and morality (or criminality) as we did before.

Similar discordancies appear in correlational studies of the relationship between psychosocial variables when the probabilistic or causal association between the same variables happens to be investigated by several studies of different or even of the same investigators. For instance, some studies of comparative intelligence find boys' intelligence higher, whereas other studies yield higher I.Q.'s for girls. Some of the correlational investigations disclose the primacy of innate or hereditary factors, whereas others extol the preponderant role of environmental factors.[7] Discrepancies in the statistical indexes also exist in regard to the comparative intelligence of various ethnic, racial, occupational, national, and other groups.

Statistical results concerning the role of similarity and dissimilarity or agreement and disagreement in so-called assortative mating[8] are also discordant. Sometimes, two studies by different or even by the same authors give very divergent coefficients for the same variables.[9] No less discordant are the coefficients of cor-

---

[6] See, for details, C. F. Chassell, *The Relationship Between Morality and Intelligence* (New York, 1935), pp. 25–133, 377–470; J. W. Getzels and P. W. Jackson, *Creativity and Intelligence* (London and New York, 1962).

[7] See, for the actual figures, *CST*, ch. 13. See also Sorokin, Zimmerman, Galpin, *A Systematic Source Book in Rural Sociology* (Minneapolis, 1932; New York, 1966), Vol. III, ch. 20.

[8] Compare, for instance, the results of the studies of assortative mating in the following works: K. Pearson, *Grammar of Science* (London, 1902), pp. 431 ff.; H. E. Jones, "Homogamy in Intellectual Abilities," *AJS 35*(1929), 369–382; E. Burgess and P. Wallin, "Homogamy in Social Characteristics," *AJS*, *49*(1943), 102–124; and H. M. Richardson, "Studies of Mental Resemblance," *Psychological Bulletin*, *36*(1939), 104–120.

[9] Compare L. M. Terman, *Psychological Factors in Marital Happiness* (New York, 1938), with E. Burgess and L. Cottrell, *Predicting Success or Failure in Marriage* (New York, 1939), and the latter with Burgess and Wallin, "Homogamy in Social Characteristics." Cf. also P. Benson, "The Common-Interests Myth in Marriage," *Social Problems*, July, 1955, pp. 27–34; and G. Karlsson, *Adaptability and Communication in Marriage* (Uppsala, 1951).

relation between nonbattle casualties and willingness for combat; these coefficients range from minus .82 to minus .07. Coefficients between nonbattle casualties and confidence in combat skill range from plus .18 to minus .74.[10]

Where several correlational investigations of the relationship between the same or highly similar variables exist, a notable discordancy of the results can be reasonably expected. The correlational-statistical studies rarely deliver to us valid or accurate results; in most cases, these results are uncertain, doubtful, and contradictory; in some cases, they are fallacious. The same can be said of the other ambitious tasks of the advanced statistical explorations: statistical factor analysis, general theory of trends and cycles, discovery of constant or universal uniformities, and so on.

Still more contradictory and uncertain are percentages and other statistical indexes when they are extrapolated beyond the samples studied, and especially when they concern rapidly changing phenomena and fleeting situations. At best, these percentages give but a glimpse of ever-changing configurations. S. Stouffer's *American Soldier* is full of such discordant percentages. For instance, the percentage of privates ready for further combat according to the degree of vindictiveness are, in Division A, 26, 25, and 21; in Division B, however, the corresponding percentages are 67, 67, 59.[11] In one of two questionnaires about the incentives that make soldiers keep on fighting, "prayer" is not mentioned at all; in the other questionnaire, however, from 57 to 83 percent of the respondents state that prayer "helped a lot."[12] Which of these contrasting percentages is accurate? Which is more typical of the majority of privates in the American army? Why is there such an enormous difference in the percentages? If we do not know the reasons for these discrepancies, then what is the cognitive value of these and of many other—still more discordant—percentages? This doubtful value becomes still more

---

[10] See, for details, *Fads and Foibles*, ch. 8.

[11] S. Stouffer, *The American Soldier* (Princeton, 1949), Vol. II, p. 165.

[12] *Ibid.*, pp. 108, 174–175. See other examples in S. Stouffer's *Communism, Conformity, and Civil Liberties* (New York, 1955).

problematic when we consider that these discordant snapshots of opinions continuously change and, through change, become still more discordant and evanescent in their "typicality" and "accuracy." As most public and private opinions, wishes, evaluations, and vocal answers of polled groups undergo a change—now slow and gradual, now sudden and sharp—percentages and indexes become truly evanescent, and incidental snapshots of polled situations or of states of mind are antiquated by the time they are published.[13]

If these statistical snapshots are taken repeatedly with the same sample in about the same conditions, they can trace the main lines of fluctuation of reactions of the respondents, in which case the cognitive value of these polls naturally increases. But even such repeated snapshots can supply us with the information only for the groups polled and for the period studied. They cannot be extrapolated with a reasonable certainty either to predict future events, or in regard to groups and persons different from the polled groups. If such a blind extrapolation is made, the results are likely to be inaccurate and fallacious.[14] The notorious mispredictions of the Gallup and other polls of the Presidential election in 1948, as well as a host of other wrong predictions of the pollsters, give a striking confirmation of this danger.[15]

[13] See the concrete examples of such a change in J. S. Brunner, *Mandate from the People* (New York, 1944).

[14] If we grant some validity to Lazarsfeld, Berelson, and associates' factorial analysis of voting in Elmira and Erie Counties—though the analysis is very questionable in a number of points—in no way can the conclusions reached about the factors of voting in these samples of American voters be extended over many American voting groups, or over the foreign-born voters, or over different periods of voting even in these Elmira and Erie samples. Compare B. R. Berelson, Paul Lazarsfeld, and William N. McFee, *Voting* (Chicago, 1954); and P. Lazarsfeld and associates, *The People's Choice* (New York, 1948).

[15] Most of the supposedly careful precautions taken by the psycho-sociological statisticians against possible errors in the formation of variables, in multivariate analysis, in the study of trends and predictions, in adequate sampling, and so on, concern mainly the insignificant mistakes—"the gnats of inaccuracies." They rarely touch the basic errors—"the elephants of gross blunders." P. F. Lazarsfeld and M. Rosenberg's *The Language of Social Research* (Glencoe, Ill., 1954) gives an example of

Another shortcoming of ambitions statistics is a quantitatively disguised subjectivity. This subjectivity is injected into a statistical study of opinions, wishes, evaluations, likes and dislikes, and other states of mind of the respondents at its earliest planning stage through the character of the questions, their wordings, and their classifications into a number of classes and degrees of "intensity." For the kind of questionnaire already predetermines the kind of the answers, and a different wording and classification of the same questions gives, as a rule, different results. S. Stouffer's *American Soldier* inadvertently furnishes a number of examples of this sort of subjectivity. In the forementioned questionnaires about the incentives or motives that helped the soldiers "to keep fighting," "prayer" was not mentioned at all in one questionnaire and, therefore, none of the respondents mentioned it as an incentive in his answers. In the other questionnaire, prayer was put first among five classes of "relevant motivational forces"; as a result, from 57 to 83 percent of the respondents answered that prayer "helped a lot." In other words, it came out as about *the* most important motivational force. In the same two questionnaires, dealing with the same problem of the incentives or motives that help men keep fighting while the going is rough, but classifying these motives differently, "self-preservation" was mentioned by 6 percent of the respondents in one polling, and by zero percent in the other; "hatred and vengeance" was mentioned only by 2 percent in one and by 21 to 46 percent in the other.

Without giving specific cases here,[16] it can be said generally that by the kind of questions, by the questionnaire's classification of items, and by its grading of the "intensities" of the opinions or the states of mind investigated, the statistical researchers

---

such works. It warns against some of the statistical "gnats of inaccuracies." It mentions only in passing, however, those statistical "elephants of error" on which a superstructure of statistical analysis is built in many statistical studies. The preceding and the subsequent criticism of this chapter outlines some of these "elephants," that is, the doubtful major assumptions and proceedings frequently found in ambitious statistical research. Cf. P. Sorokin, "Reply to My Critics," in P. J. Allen, *Pitirim A. Sorokin in Review* (Durham, N.C., 1963), pp. 440–449.

[16] See, for other cases and details, *Fads and Foibles*, ch. 8.

already predetermine to a great extent the answers and thus the results of their study.

Subjectivity and errors also enter statistical studies during the unavoidable weighing, evaluating, scaling, ranking, scoring, and correcting of the raw data obtained. These operations are unavoidable in all statistical studies that deal with qualitative phenomena devoid of natural, objective, quantitative units. They are also unavoidable in all statistical studies that must score and rank various intensities of respective opinions, wishes, attitudes, and states of mind and in researches that have to make a unified, combined index out of several different items of the hearsay stuff collected. For instance, what weight or how many scoring points are to be assigned to each of the criteria of marriage-happiness in Terman's and Burgess-Cottrell's studies: to "table manners," to "frequency of kissing," to "bridge or golf playing," to "similarity in religion," or in "economic status," and to several other subfactors and symptoms of marital adjustment? This weighing and scoring, as a rule, is decided arbitrarily by the investigators or by some experts to whom they pass the buck. Since the experts do not have any objective basis for their weighing or ranking either, their opinions are also perfectly arbitrary. In this way, an enormous amount of subjectivity is introduced into all these statistical studies that try to quantify and scale phenomena that are either purely qualitative or that do not have distinct ranks, degrees, and scoring points. The bulk of recent quantitative sociological and psychological research is debilitated by the passion for measuring the intensities and qualities of opinions, beliefs, emotions, intelligence, ideologies, attitudes, and so on.

L. Guttman's "scalogram" method and P. F. Lazarsfeld's theory of the continuous "latent classes" represent two of the bravest ideologies of how to scientifically scale phenomena that do not have any objective scales, and how to measure nonmetric qualities and intensities.[17] The outcome of these and similar attempts could be foreseen: If the quantified phenomena

---

[17] See L. Guttman's and P. F. Lazarsfeld's studies in S. A. Stouffer, L. Guttman, P. F. Lazarsfeld, and others, *Studies in Social Psychology of World War II*, Vol. **IV**: *Measurement and Prediction* (Princeton,

have objective units, they can be scaled and measured and the results can be expressed in numbers. If the scaled qualities do not have objective units, the resultant measurements are bound to be largely fictitious. These conclusions are inadvertently confirmed by the authors themselves. Guttman, Suchman, and Lazarsfeld confess that "The bulk of social phenomena is too complex for one to expect many aspects to be scalable. . . . [In our research] it was a much more frequent experience not to find a series of items scalable."[18]

When, however, the few allegedly scalable areas of opinions (called by them "attitudes") are carefully examined, one finds that their scalability is mainly fictitious, due to the fact that in their questionnaires they had arbitrarily prearranged the scalability of the answers. Their questions ask for answers ranked in terms of "very much," "some," and "little." Having so predetermined the answers, the authors simply count the number of answers in each rank. In plain words, they substitute their own arbitrary ranking for objectively existing or nonexisting ranks in the phenomena studied. The questionnaire itself already contains the number and the character of the ranks or classes of intensities. This arbitrariness leads them to the further error of confusing two different phenomena: the *frequency of occurrence* of a symptom, say, of fear on a battle field, and fear-*intensity*. From the fact that only 9 percent of the soldiers questioned "urinate in pants" from fear, whereas a much larger percentage are vomiting in fear, it does not follow that one of these phenomena represents a more intense fear than the other. From the fact that the common cold is more frequent than cancer, it does not follow that the common cold is the more severe form of sickness. From the fact that, in the prearranged ranks of the intensity of a belief, 32 percent check the line "very much," 45 percent check the line "much," and the remaining 23 percent check the line "some," it does not follow that these percentages give the objectively existing number of scales of the intensity of

1950). See also Lazarsfeld and Rosenberg's *The Language of Social Research*, and Lazarsfeld's *Mathematical Thinking in the Social Sciences*.

[18] Guttman and Lazarsfeld in Stouffer, Guttman, Lazarsfeld, *et al.*, *op. cit.*, Vol. IV, pp. 157–158.

the belief and its exact measures. Instead, they give only the percentages of the number of respondents who checked each of the three—prearranged—classes of the intensity.

Insofar as L. Guttman derives the possibility of scaling the severity of the fear-symptoms from the premises that they all come from the same universe and are interdependent, these premises do not at all validate the quantification and scaling of unscalable qualities. First of all, not only fear-symptoms but all the important parts and changes in the individual, in an organism, and in a sociocultural system are interdependent; it does not follow at all, however, that "therefore" all these parts and changes are scalable and can be measured either in their importance, or intensity, or time-order, or frequency of occurrence. In brief, the concepts of "interdependence" and "scalability" or "measurability" are entirely different from one another, and in no way allow for deducing scalability from interdependence or vice versa. For this obvious reason, Guttman's identification of these concepts is an error.

No better is Lazarsfeld's hypothesis that "There exists a set of latent classes, such that the manifest relationship between any two or more items on a test can be accounted for by the existence of these basic classes and by these alone. . . . Any attitude has two aspects—one associated with the latent classes, and one which is specific to the item." For Lazarsfeld, "Attitude is inference from the latent classes tested by fitting to the manifest data. . . . The latent continuum is a hypothetical construct."[19] Here is an example of how, under the name of exact science, a bad metaphysics gets into modern psychosocial sciences. There are neither mathematical nor logical nor empirical grounds for his postulation that all manifestly nonscalar items represent in reality a scalar continuum and that, when all the latent classes of this continuum are considered, these apparently nonscalar or discontinuous items become continuous and scalar. Mathematics knows not only continuous but also discontinuous equations, like $B = \frac{1}{A}$ or $B = \sqrt{A^2 - 1}$. His theory of the latent continuum contradicts quantum-mechanics where discontinuity and

[19] *Ibid.*, pp. 5–7.

"quantum-jumps" are basic principles. It also contradicts the discontinuous "mutations" in biology and a legion of discontinuous facts and events in the psychosocial and cultural universe. Logically, it is tautologically circular: If some empirical data confirm the theory of the latent continuum, it is proved empirically; if the empirical data contradict it, then the contradiction can be accounted for by the nonapparency of some of the latent classes; if discovered in their completeness, they would fill the gaps in the manifest nonscalar items, and would thus confirm the hypothesis. In this respect, the hypothesis is uncomfortably like the belief in a latent continuum of animistic ghosts or hidden forces that are responsible for anything and everything in the manifest empirical world. According to this belief, if their nonmanifest existence and their latent ways of operation are uncovered, these animistic ghosts would well account for birth and death, happiness and unhappiness, even for the manifestly discontinuous and nonscalar phenomena. Stouffer is correct in saying that "there is still relatively little which is not controversial" in Lazarsfeld's and Guttman's hypotheses.[20] The inadequacy of Lazarsfeld's hypothesis is partly confirmed by its author. Failing to quantify many nonscalar phenomena, he was forced to introduce "the quasi-scales," which by their very name mean the arbitrary and fictitious scales.

So far no scientific theory and no scientific procedure has been formulated that would allow an *objective* quantification, scaling, ranking, and measuring of manifestly nonscalar, qualitative sociocultural and psychological phenomena. When such scaling and measurement are done—and they are done nowadays by thousands of psychosociological statisticians—it unavoidably introduces into the quantitative studies an enormous dose of nonscientific subjectivity and errors.

Another, quite common way of introducing serious errors into this sort of statistical studies is to treat basically different phenomena as identical and essentially similar phenomena as different. In the Burgess-Cottrell study of marriage-happiness, the frequency of kisses of the married couple is quantitatively measured as one of the variables in marriage adjustment. In their computation, the authors counted all kisses mentioned by the couples as identical units. From daily experience we know, however, that not all kisses are identical: There are passionate kisses, habitual kisses, Judas' kisses, and many other kisses profoundly different from one another. For this reason, all the kisses mentioned by the married couple cannot be taken as identical units, phenomena, or values. If they are, the results of the study are bound to be inaccurate and misleading. So long as this type of error is not avoided, these studies cannot be scientific and correct.

Finally, almost all the ambitious statistical studies suffer from a lack of distinction between sociocultural systems and congeries and from the ensuing error of treating all their variables (including the systems) as isolated congeries. By cultural congeries are meant two or more cultural phenomena that are united only by their spacial or time-proximity and by no other logically meaningful, causal, or tangible probabilistic ties. By social congeries are meant all the unorganized, semiorganized, and purely nominal groups. By social systems are understood all the organized groups in the exact sense of this term. Cultural systems are made up of two or more cultural phenomena that are united into one interdependent whole by logically or aesthetically consistent, meaningful, and causal ties. All the important parts of a social or cultural system display the triple tangible interdependence of each important part with the other parts and with the whole system, of the whole system with each and all of its important parts. In their triple interdependence, sociocultural systems are similar to biological systems or to the mechanical system of an assembled automobile, in contrast to an unassembled automobile whose congeries of parts are scattered on the floor of the garage. The difference between congeries and systems is a very basic difference. No scientific sociocultural or biophysical research can ignore it without committing a gross error.[21] It is a difference that requires very different methods of study.[22]

---

[21] See a detailed analysis of social and cultural systems and congeries in all four volumes of the *Dynamics* and in *SCP*, chs. 4, 8, 17, 18, 19, *passim*. Although it was criticized when the *Dynamics* was published,

In a study of singular, unique, or rarely occurring psycho-social and cultural phenomena, the statistical method is generally inapplicable: There is hardly anything to be counted and statistically manipulated. In the field of the sociological and cultural mass congeries, frequently repeated in time and space, the sound statistical method, free from its outlined defects, is the fruitful method of investigation of their quantitative aspects, including the probabilistic uniformities in the relationship and change of such mass congeries. Since these sociocultural congeries are not bound together by any meaningful causal ties, a statistician can take any congeries as his independent or dependent variables and endeavor to find the relationship between them. Here his choice of chance variables is free and unlimited.

Finally, in regard to social and cultural systems, the statistical method can also be used as a subsidiary one, but the statistician's choice of variables here is very rigorously limited, and the treatment of the variables must follow a different path

---

my theory of the profound differences between social and cultural systems and social and cultural congeries and my analysis of the structural and dynamic properties of the systems and congeries is at present largely accepted and reiterated—in somewhat abortive and distorted form—by many a sociologist, anthropologist, and psychologist. A more detailed analysis of systems and congeries is given in Chapters 5, 6, 7, 8, 9, 10, 11, and 12 of this work.

[22] Three different approaches to the study of psychosocial and cultural phenomena correspond to three different approaches of modern physics in the investigation of physical phenomena:

(a) The methods of quantum physics applied to small aggregations of atoms and to subatomic physical phenomena. This realm of the physical world is thought of as the "microcosm of lawlessness," of discontinuity, uncertainty, and, to a large extent, of the indeterminism and unpredictability of all the future continuous states of the particles and atoms. The unique and rarely repeated sociocultural phenomena correspond somewhat to this subatomic world. They do not lend themselves to a causal, experimental, and statistical analysis or to a formulation of uniformities and prediction of their future in this field of sociocultural "accidents." They can only be described and understood in the way of empathy, coliving and coexperiencing the respective states of mind, actions, and events.

(b) The statistical, probabilistic methods applied to the enormous aggregations of atoms or of macrophysical phenomena. Viewed as chance congeries, these phenomena lend themselves to a statistical treatment and display probabilistic uniformities in their structure, relationship, and change. This is the field of statistical inquiry and experimental method.

from that used in the investigation of the congeries variables. A statistician cannot take as his independent, dependent, and interdependent variables phenomena that are *parts of different systems*—for example, the buzzing of a bee, the switching of a horse's tail, and the flying of a bird, in a biological system; or the idea of the Trinity in Christianity, the technique of massproducing automobiles, and the judicial procedure in a court trial, in a cultural system. The absurdity of choosing such variables is rather obvious. Less evident, but not less absurd is the choice of such variables for a study of their relationships as the "economic factor" and "religious credo," "material and immaterial culture," and "industrial techniques and aesthetic, or legal ideologies." There are an enormous number of statistical (and other) investigations that study the relationships between these and similar variables. Numerous theories of a cultural lag and lead between material and nonmaterial cultures (F. Bacon, K. Marx, L. Weber, A. Coste, M. Tugan-Baranovsky, W. Ogburn, F. S. Chapin, M. and A. Weber, T. Veblen, R. MacIver, and others), the Marxian theories of conditioning all ideological superstructures by the economic factors of means and the instruments of production, the theories of determining many

---

The sociocultural mass phenomena, incessantly repeated in time and space—such as: births, marriages, divorces, crimes, economic fluctuations, and many others—correspond to the field of macrophysics studying the enormous mass aggregations of atoms. This realm of sociocultural mass phenomena is the proper field of statistical investigation. As a gigantic aggregation of chance congeries, it lends itself to statistical study and displays. Here a statistician can take as his independent and dependent variables any of the congeries and can try to find out what their relationship is to each other. In this field of macrosociology some probabilistic predictions are possible.

(*c*) The field of physical, biological, and sociocultural systems governed by the immanent "laws of direction" (A. Eddington), or by "self-regulation producing orderly events" (E. Schrödinger), or by "conscious, active, voluntaristic decision" (H. Margenau), or by "free will" (Max Planck), or by "creative potential" (E. W. Sinnott). A very small aggregation of atoms, like genes, is a biological example of such a system: In spite of the insignificant number of atoms in genes, these contain in themselves "the plenotype" of the future organism with all its essential characteristics. Genes are capable of preserving and transmitting this plenotype from generation to generation. The field of personal, social, and cultural systems corresponds to this field of physical and biological sciences. A knowledge of the nature of these systems and of their im-

ideological phenomena by the factor of technological inventions, and Max Weber's theory of the preponderant role of religion in conditioning economic and technological phenomena are just a few examples of theories that have used variables that are parts of different sociocultural systems. (For a detailed criticism, see subsequent chapters.)

Every sociocultural system has the following components:

a. A system of meanings or an ideological, "nonmaterial" culture—the meaning of a scientific theory, of a religious dogma, of moral and legal precepts, and of a painting or a piece of sculpture.

b. Sensory or material manifestations of its system of meanings—manuscripts, books, instruments, tools, buildings, and all sorts of gadgets and material objects through which and in which the ideological system of meanings is objectified, externalized, socialized, or congealed.

c. Its technique of functioning in the empirical world, carried on by the actions of its members and agencies: scientific research and teaching; performing religious rites; judicial procedure and legislation by legislative bodies; musical composition, playing musical instruments, and conducting the orchestra; painting, sculpture, and architecture; managing a business or industrial enterprise; warfare; and producing agricultural, industrial, religious, scientific, artistic, and judicial objects and instruments.

In brief, each sociocultural system has its ideological (non-

---

manent "law of direction," or "self-regulation," or "conscious decision" or "meaningful-causal" character permits us to grasp some uniformities and predict some future states of the systems. In the field of the systems, statistical method can be only a subsidiary method, and the statistician is very definitely limited in his freedom to take any part of a system or different parts of different systems as his variables. See, on these three realms of biophysical phenomena and on the scientific methods of their study: E. Schrödinger, *What Is Life?* (Cambridge, Mass., 1947), H. Margenau, "The Meaning of 'Elementary Particle'," *American Scientist, 39*(1951), 422–431, Margenau, "Physical vs. Historical Reality," *Philosophy of Science, 19*(1952), 203; E. C. Kemble, "Reality, Measurement, and the State of the System in Quantum Mechanics," *Philosophy of Science, 18*(1951), 273–299; and E. W. Sinnott, *The Biology of Spirit* (New York, 1955). See a detailed treatment of this problem and the additional literature in *Fads and Foibles*, ch. 8.

material) system of ideas, beliefs, theories, values, and dogmas, and its material and technological components.

For this reason, an investigator cannot take as his variables a material component of, say, the economic system and an ideological component of, say, the religious system, or a technological component of the judicial system and the ideological system of the science of biology. If a study of the relationship between the buzzing of a bee, the tail-switching of a horse, and the flying of a bird is a foolish enterprise, no less foolish is the study of the relationship between the "lead and lag" of different parts of different sociocultural systems. An investigator can investigate the relationship between different components of the same system or between the different systems taken as a whole, but he cannot expect any fruitful results from an investigation of the static and dynamic relationships between different components of different systems. If he does so, as he frequently does, the results are bound to be abortive and fallacious. No wonder, also, that they are, as a rule, mutually contradictory. Thus, when Marx and the Marxians take the *ideological* components of religion, or law, or of the fine arts and the *material-technological* components of economic phenomena, they arrive at the conclusion that the material-technological, economic phenomena lead and condition the ideological-religious, ethical, and aesthetic phenomena. When Max Weber takes similar variables he arrives at the opposite conclusion, that it is the religious-ethical variable that leads and conditions the economic-technological phenomena. As a result, we have two opposite equations: the Marxian: R is $f(E - T)$ and the Weberian: $E - T$ is $f(R - Et.)$. From a scientific standpoint both equations and theories are untenable. For the same reason, all the variations of the Marxian theory claiming the leading and conditioning role of the material culture and the lagging and conditioned role of the nonmaterial culture are wrong.[23] In a statistical study of systems a statistician cannot take different components of dif-

[23] See a detailed discussion and criticism of all the varieties of these theories in the *Dynamics*, Vol. IV, ch. 4, and in Chapter 10 of the present work.

ferent systems as his variables; his freedom of choice is strictly limited.

Likewise, he cannot cut a living system into slices or cubes or meat balls and then study the relationship between these dead variables—the parts of the system. W. L. Warner and P. S. Lundt's *The Social Life of a Community* furnishes us with a conspicuous example of this kind of butchering. These authors cut up an aggregation of many living sociocultural systems (Yankee City) and then statistically study the relationships between the slices, cubes, and meat balls. First, they mechanically divide Yankee City into six slices (the upper-upper, the lower-upper, the upper-middle, the lower-middle, the upper-lower, and the lower-lower strata); then, in a subsequent volume, they cut these slices into various cubes and meat balls. In this way they obtained, finally, eighty-nine artificial positions. A statistical study of the interrelationships of these eighty-nine variables makes the central topic of their second volume.[24] No wonder that the results of such a statistical study are as meaningless as would be the results of a biological study of a living organism turned into meat balls by slicing it horizontally, vertically, and diagonally. A sound statistical explorer cannot "murder" a living sociocultural system in this way, and cannot hope to obtain through such operations an accurate and valid knowledge of the system and of its internal and external relationship.

Nor can a statistician make a unified system out of various cultural and social congeries, or take such a nominal system as a variable of his study. Throwing diverse sociocultural systems and congeries together does not transform a "dump" of sociocultural phenomena into a unified sociocultural system. Eminent examples of such dumps of cultural phenomena, mistaken for vast sociocultural systems, are N. Danilevsky's, O. Spengler's, and A. Toynbee's unification of enormous numbers of socio-

---

[24] See their *The Social Life of a Community* (New Haven, 1941), and *The Status System of a Modern Community* (New Haven, 1942). These works are of some value, but their value consists of the descriptions of some of the traits of the various organized groups in Yankee City, not in their statistical explorations of the relationships they "discovered."

cultural phenomena into vast pseudosystems of "civilization" or "high type of culture," or "cultural-historical types." In Chapters 7 and 8, we shall see that none of their vast "civilizations" or "cultural types" is a sociocultural system; each of them is, in fact, a vast system mixed together with many other systems and congeries not bound together into one living and interdependent unity by meaningful causal ties.[25] On a less conspicuous scale, this mistake of taking a conglomeration of various sociocultural odds and ends for a clear-cut unified variable is frequently committed by statistical investigators, introducing thereby an additional error into the results of their studies.

A further example of the errors ensuing from disregarding the profound difference between psychosocial systems and congeries, or from a statistical treatment of systems as congeries and congeries as systems is that of *taking a part of a system as an independent variable (or as the determining factor) and the whole of the system as a dependent variable (or as an effect of the part).* If a biologist declares a mustache or the color of an eye or a single gland or an arm or any other part of an organism as the primary factor of the whole organism—of all its anatomical and physiological characteristics—his fallacy is obvious. If, further, he contends that all the anatomical, physiological, and psychological changes that an organism undergoes while passing from the state of childhood into that of maturity are due to the primary factor of an increased height or of an appearance of a mustache or of a change in a gland, his fallacy is again quite obvious. He has taken a part of an organism as the factor determining the whole organism, and made the part greater and more powerful than the whole biological system. Fortunately for biology there are no competent biologists of this sort and no credit is given to such "mustache" theories.

Unfortunately for sociology, however, "mustache" theories of the structure and dynamics of social and cultural systems still proliferate. Owing to an ignorance of the basic difference

---

[25] See the detailed criticism of these "philosophies of history" in P. Sorokin, *Modern Historical and Social Philosophies* (New York, 1963) and in Chapters 7 and 8 of the present work.

between sociocultural systems and congeries, a legion of statistical and nonstatistical sociologists, historians, anthropologists, psychologists, economists, and political scientists take for their preponderant or main factor either the economic, or the political, or the religious, or the scientific, or the racial, or the legal, or the demographic, or the sexual, or the artistic variable, and, through their pet factor, try to account for the structure and dynamics of the whole sociocultural system or supersystem of which this pet factor is only one part. Conspicuous examples of this error are given again by Karl Marx's and Max Weber's theories. When Marx and other partisans of an economic interpretation of history make the economic factor of the means and instruments of production the main factor of the structure and change of all other sociocultural systems and of the whole supersystem of Western culture, they take a part of a given sociocultural system and try to account for the whole system. They commit the blunder of the *pars pro toto*. When Max Weber takes the religious system and its *Wirtschaftethik* as the preponderant factor of the economic system, he commits the reverse form of the same error. When both of these theories are carefully tested, we find that the economic system of capitalism did not produce and determine the emergence and growth of Protestantism, as Marx contended, and that Protestantism with its *Wirtschaftsethik* was not the preponderant factor in the emergence and development of capitalism, as Weber contended. Instead, both systems, capitalism and Protestantism, together with the Sensate system of truth and science, Sensate philosophy (materialism, empiricism, singularism, relativism, etc.), Sensate systems of painting, sculpture, architecture, literature, and drama, Sensate utilitarian, hedonistic, and relativistic ethics and law, Sensate politics and economics, and the Sensate way of life and mentality, have been developing interdependently as parts of a still larger Sensate supersystem that emerged after the twelfth century and have become the dominant supersystem in Western culture of the last four centuries.

At the present time, this supersystem and all its Sensate systems are disintegrating, including capitalism and the Sensate part of Protestant religiosity. All these Sensate systems and their supersystem have been interdependent in their emergence, growth, and decline, and the growth and decline of the Sensate supersystem itself has been interdependent with those of all its Sensate systems.[26] The static and dynamic triple interdependence of these systems, united into their supersystem, is very similar to the triple interdependence in an organism as a biological system. When a human organism passes from the stage of childhood into that of maturity, a host of anatomical, physiological, and psychological changes occur in all its main organs (subsystems). These changes are not due to a mustache factor or to an increased weight factor or to a change in any single part of the organism; they proceed simultaneously and interdependently. The same criticism can be applied to other sociological theories of a pet factor—to demographic or racial or political or scientific or philosophical or moral or sexual theories —that view the rest of the sociocultural systems as mere dependent variables of this pet factor. These theories, which are unaware of the properties of the systems, and particularly of the triple interdependence of each important part of the system with its other important parts and with the whole of the system, and of the interdependence of the whole system with all its parts, replace this triple interdependence with unilinear dependence of all the parts of the system and of the system as a whole upon one of the parts, the pet factor. No wonder that the psychosocial sciences are crowded with a multitude of diverse and mutually contradictory theories of pet factors, with strikingly inadequate "philosophies of history," and with all sorts of "mustache" conceptions of sociocultural statics and dynamics.

Disregarding the possibility of the variables being a part of a system, and treating practically all sociocultural variables as congeries, many a statistician daily commits, on a smaller scale, this error of the *pars pro toto*—of picking up a part of a system as its variable, and of treating the parts as congeries-variables. Such a procedure cannot help arriving at contradictory and fallacious results, indexes, and coefficients.

---

[26] See the *Dynamics,* all four volumes, particularly Vol. II, p. 500, and Vol. IV, *passim.*

Such are some of the errors, shortcomings, and limitations of the ambitious statistical study of sociocultural phenomena. They explain why, in spite of the potential fruitfulness, these studies have yielded, so far, a very modest harvest of significant discoveries and valid generalizations. As long as these errors and difficulties prevail in statistical research, it is likely to remain fairly sterile and in part misleading. If the psychosocial sciences want to move along the royal road of significant discoveries, they must get off the back road of sham mathematical and sham quantitative research.[27]

CRITICISM OF THE BASIC POSTULATE OF THE SINGULARISTIC-ATOMISTIC THEORIES

Further logical and empirical objections to the basic postulates and assumptions of singularistic-atomistic theories are, first, that the postulate that sociocultural reality is made up of purely separate, "free," singularistic phenomena existing independently from each other, not unified—causally or meaningfully—into *Ganzheiten*, or systems, is empirically fallacious. Some physical, biological, and sociocultural phenomena possibly exist in this singularistic "free" form of reality. But the elementary particles, atoms and molecules in the physical world

[27] Cf. for similar conclusions G. Gurvitch, *Determinismes Sociaux et Liberté Humaine* (Paris, 1955), pp. 27–29, 109–110; A. Cuvillier, *Où va la sociologie française?* (Paris, 1953); B. B. Wolman, *Contemporary Theories and Systems in Psychology* (New York, 1960), pp. 504 ff.; P. H. Prabhu, "The State of Psychology as a Science Today," *Fiftieth Indian Science Congress* (Calcutta, 1963); C. Burt, "The Concept of Consciousness," *British Journal of Psychology*, August, 1962; H. J. Eysenck, *Sense and Nonsense in Psychology* (New York, 1957); H. Cantril and others, "Psychology and Scientific Research," in F. H. Kilpatrick, *Explorations in Transactional Psychology* (New York, 1961), pp. 15 ff.; S. S. Stevens, *Handbook of Experimental Psychology* (New York, 1951), pp. 3 ff.; "Problems and Methods of Psychophysics," *Psychological Bulletin*, July, 1958, pp. 177–196; E. Schrödinger, *Über Indeterminismus in der Physik* (Leipzig, 1932); W. Heisenberg, *Wandlungen in der Grundlagen der Naturwissenschaft* (Leipzig, 1935); and most of the literature mentioned in Chapter 5 of the present work.

exist in fantastically multifarious forms of unified systems; the same is true of cells, tissues, organs, and organisms in the biological world. And the same is true of sociocultural phenomena. This proposition is axiomatic and is unconditionally accepted as valid by the physical and biological sciences. It is no less valid and axiomatic for the psychosocial sciences. The next chapters will give adequate evidence of the correctness of this proposition.

All atomistic-singularistic theories that deny the "systemic" part of the inorganic, the organic, and the superorganic reality and that in their studies attempt to treat, to view, and to cognize the systemic part of these realms of reality summatively (as a mere sum or conglomeration of singularistic phenomena) are utterly wrong. Their approach is correct only in regard to the phenomena that have a singularistic, separate, "free" existence.

The criticized postulate is also faulty *logically*. Logically, it means that all singularistic phenomena are in a state of complete independence or separateness from one another, that all their mutual relationships are purely chance relationships, and that no causal or uniformly close, stable, and repeated relationships exist in the whole universe of physical, biological, and superorganic phenomena.

If this were true, however, then all scientists, including the atomists-singularists, should "abandon any search for causal or meaningful relationships and respective uniformities and quietly content themselves with the physical, biological, and sociocultural chaos of absolute casualness, contingency, and fancifulness of the world of congeries."[28] The search for uniformities[29] has been possibly the highest objective of scientific research, but this search is now to be canceled and all scientific research is to be reduced to a mere description of some of the infinitely numerous singularistic phenomena. I am afraid that the postulate and its consequences would hardly be accepted

[28] The *Dynamics*, Vol. IV, p. 134.

[29] See a detailed logical and empirical criticism of atomistic-singularistic theories, including the singularistic contentions of some of the "antisystemic" historians, in the *Dynamics*, Vol. I, ch. 1, and pp. 167 ff.; and Vol. IV, pp. 98–99, 102–106, 129–133, 433–435.

by scientists, including the atomists-singularists themselves. If it were accepted it would deal the deathblow to the most important and creative part of science, and to the prestige and value of science itself.

CONCLUDING REMARKS

The preceding survey of comparatively important samples of singularistic-atomistic theories permits us now to answer the questions asked in Chapter 3 about (1) the claim of this current of sociological thought to being strictly scientific in its methods, and (2) the justification for its revolt against "philosophizing," "speculative theorizing," and "grand systems of sociology." My critical remarks about the false pretenses of each of the representative theories examined have already given an answer to these questions. Three objective criteria essentially reinforce the validity of my criticisms. They are, first, whether the singularistic-atomistic revolters against other types of sociological theories, and especially against the "grand systems" of sociology and their makers, actually practice what they preach. If, despite their contempt of these systems, they themselves use them, or attempt to build their own, then we can assume that this is convincing evidence of the unavoidable need for such systems. The second criterion is whether the singularistic-atomistic "fact-finders" and investigators of the narrow, specific problems of sociology produce actual scientific results. If the harvest of their large-scale research is truly rich and significant, if it has given to us a new, deep, and more adequate insight into the mysteries of man, human behavior, and social and cultural processes, if it has discovered a set of universal, or, at least, R. Merton's "middle-range" uniformities applicable to many persons, groups, and cultures, and, finally, if it has notably increased sociology's ability to predict future events and processes, then this would be a sufficient vindication of the revolters and their research methods. If, on the contrary, the results of their massive efforts have been modest in all these respects, then this would be sufficient proof against their pretentious claims and methods. The third criterion is whether their research has produced general-logical, epistemological, and phenomenological considerations that show the correct way of evaluating the current of thought discussed. Let us now apply each of these criteria to their work.

Do the critics of the "grand systems" of sociology use the principles and generalizations of these systems in their own works either for explaining or corroborating or generalizing or analyzing their findings and conclusions? The answer is, Yes, a great many of them do. One finds, as a rule, that they use the theories, principles, and generalizing conclusions of M. Weber, E. Durkheim, F. Tönnies, S. Freud, K. Marx, A. Comte, H. Spencer, G. Tarde, G. Simmel, V. Pareto, W. G. Sumner, C. Gini, C. H. Cooley, W. I. Thomas, G. Sorel, O. Spengler, B. Malinowski, C. Ellwood, L. von Wiese, R. Park, E. A. Ross, and of many other "system-builders." Furthermore, these theories and conclusions are used by the revolters as scientifically ascertained and authoritative. Not infrequently some of the physicalistic-quantitative fact-finding, operational, experimental, and empirically precise researches represent but mere illustrations of, or variations on, the themes of the grand-system-makers.

Do many of the revolters try to "theorize" and build their own generalizing systems of sociology? In Chapter 1, this proclivity was mentioned as one of the notable features of today's sociology. Subsequent chapters will give sufficient proof of this theorizing and generalizing bent of modern sociologists. Rather than rejecting the systematic theories, social philosophies, and "unscientific speculations" of the grand-system-makers, many of the revolters are quite busy formulating a multitude of special theories for interpreting and explaining the concrete results of their studies, general analytical conceptual schemes supposedly applicable to all societies and cultures, and methodological rules for any and all sociological research.

Regardless of the validity of this theorizing, the fact of its proliferation among physicalistic and other revolters is undeniable. This fact notably undermines the position of the revolters, for it demonstrates the unavoidable need and paramount value of generalizing and interpretative theories for the scientific progress of sociology.

This conclusion is strongly confirmed, according to our second and third criteria, by the results of the massive research done by the rebels. Their theories are full of big holes from logical, epistemological, and empirical standpoints. The net cognitive result of their massive research has been fairly modest and has given to us hardly any universal or "middle-range" uniformities, or any deeper understanding of the mysteries of human nature and social and cultural life. Nor has it delivered a new sociological Principia, which, like Newton's, could serve as a true foundation of sociology for the next two centuries. Something, of course, has been achieved, but this achievement is much smaller than the revolters boastfully claim. At any rate, it does not entitle them to declare the "grand systems" of sociology obsolescent and their own brand of sociology impeccably scientific. It contains only a few grains of real cognitive gold in the enormous mass of excavated pseudophysical, pseudomathematical, and pseudoexperimental stuff.[30]

[30] This conclusion contradicts that of Berelson and Steiner, who lists 1,045 "findings" (empirical scientific discoveries) of the recent "behavioral sciences." When one carefully examines these "findings," it is obvious that about 90 percent of them are either truisms and "discoveries" made long ago by philosophers, biologists, and other scientists, rather than by recent "behavioral scholars," or they represent disguised philosophical, methodological, and speculative propositions that can hardly be called empirical scientific discoveries. Their inventory of recent scientific discoveries in "behavioral sciences" is greatly inflated. On the other hand, it overlooks a considerable number of important, middle-range empirical findings by recent sociologists. See B. Berelson and G. A. Steiner, *Human Behavior: An Inventory of Scientific Findings* (New York, 1964).

PART THREE

THEORIES OF CULTURAL SYSTEMS

CHAPTER 5

Recent Upsurge of Systemic

Theories in the Physical, Biological,

and Psychological Sciences

GENERAL CHARACTERISTICS OF SYSTEMIC THEORIES

The difference between the singularistic-atomistic theories, which often do not see the forest for the trees, and the systemic theories is that the latter see the forest as a unified ecosystem and study its trees as interdependent parts or components of the forest as a whole. In their opinion, the forest has a reality, properties, and functions quite different from those of the sum of its singularistic trees. Likewise, the systemic theorists insist that an assembled automobile represents a reality, properties, and functions quite different from those of the totality of its unassembled parts scattered on the floor of a factory. They make the same distinction between unified systems and mere singularistic congeries in regard to physical, biological, psychological, and sociocultural phenomena. In the sociocultural world, these theories stress a profound difference between unified sociocultural wholes (*Ganzheiten*) and a mere assemblage of individuals or of a singularistic conglomeration of sociocultural facts and events. According to the systemic theorists the organized social groups (social systems) or cultural systems have a reality of *sui generis,* and in their structures, properties, and behavior display most significant differences from those of a mere sum of their unassembled and unintegrated components.

The essential differences between singularistic congeries and unified systems or wholes was noticed long ago. For many centuries, philosophers, social thinkers, and eminent jurists have carefully distinguished the *differentia specifica* of the unified systems from the merely summative conglomeration of their singularistic elements.[1] An analysis of the specific traits of a unified system involves a careful analysis of such concepts and realities as whole and parts, unity and multiplicity, one and many, integration, coherency, consistency, and so on. Without a clarification of these concepts and corresponding realities no adequate conception of the wholes, or unified systems, has been possible.[2]

Systemic theories have also been brilliantly developed by eminent jurists in their interpretations of the nature and reality of the juridical personality. All realistic conceptions of it are systemic in their nature. As mentioned in Chapter 3, the realistic theories of juridical personality view it as a transsubjective and superindividual reality that truly exists in the social world and that is neither derivative from the reality of its members nor coincidental with it. It is neither fiction nor mere artificial device but rather the reality that exists side by side and above that of its members.

There are several variations on this realistic conception: The *transcendental* variety sees the reality of juridical personality in some supersensory or transcendental essence or entity that permeates it. The "charismatic conception" of the early

---

[1] Almost all the proponents of ontological and sociological realism, universalism, and eternalism are partisans of the systemic approach to the study of physical, biological, and psychological realities in the world at large and in the sociocultural human universe. See a fairly detailed list of such thinkers from the Greco-Roman and the Western societies from the sixth century B.C. to A.D. 1920 in the *Dynamics*, Vol. II, pp. 684–696.

[2] This sort of analysis has been continued up to this time. See, for instance, H. Rickert, *Das Eine, die Einheit und die Eins* (Berlin, 1911); G. Galli, *L'uno e molti* (Torino, 1939); C. P. Wikner, *Über Einheit und Vielheit* (Uppsala, 1863); F. Altheim, "Einheit und Einzelheit," *Der Monat* (April, 1956); P. Martinetti, *Introducione alla Metafisica* (Milan, 1929); I. V. Blauberg, *Problema tzelostnosti v Marxistskoi filosofii* (Moscow, 1964); and especially A. M. Moschetti, *L'unità come categoria* (2 vols.; Milan, 1952), with its meaningful motto: "L'uno se non è niente é." Without a preliminary definition of these concepts—which, as we shall see, is rarely given in most sociological works on "social and cultural systems"—respective systemic theories are bound to be vague and deficient.

Christian church, in which all and everything Christian is united in God, is an example of this transcendental realism. The *empirico-organismic* variety views the juridical personality as a real superindividual organism, with its own body and its own system, partly corporeal, partly psychological. The *psychological-realism* variety sees the reality of it in some superindividual psychological entity, like public opinion, group mind, common will, group interests, group values, and so on. The *functional* variety finds the reality of the juridical personality in its functional unity, which sensorily appears as a reality of *sui generis,* different from its members. "The idea of community, for instance, [is] associated with land and persons who are in certain relationships between themselves, [and] corresponds to the reality. It is not a result of a phantasy, as some think, but of common sense."

If one carefully studies all the varieties of juridical interpretations of the juridical personality, one finds in these conceptions all the varieties of the recent systemic sociological theories of society, social group, and social and cultural systems.[3]

In the multitude of definitions of the *Ganzheiten* or unified systems and their *differentia specifica,* St. Thomas Aquinas' definition remains the best.[4] According to this definition, the unified wholes or systems have a mutual triple dependence of each important part of the system upon all its important parts and upon the whole system, and of the whole system upon all its important parts. Mere summative conglomerations of singularistic phenomena do not have this triple interdependence. As we shall see, all the recent definitions of the unified systems confirm and reiterate the Thomistic definition—fully or in part —and hardly any new conception of the *Ganzheiten* excels it.

In their philosophical presuppositions, the systemic theories adhere to ontological, sociological, and ethical realism versus

---

[3] See a detailed analysis of the realistic interpretations of the juridical personality, corporations, and institutions, together with their eminent theorizers, in the *Dynamics*, Vol. II, ch. 8.

[4] St. Thomas Aquinas, *Decem libros ethicorum*, Bk. I, sect. i; *Summa theologica*, IIa, IIae, q. 58 and q. 47, 11.

nominalism, universalism versus singularism, and eternalism versus temporalism.[5] Of the systemic sociological theories of the preceding period (examined in *Contemporary Sociological Theories*), the theories of the organic and the sociologistic schools are most typical for the systemic sociological approach.[6]

Additional characteristics of recent systemic sociological theories have been their concentration on macrosocial and macrocultural systems rather than on microsocial and microcultural ones; their qualitative as well as quantitative investigation of these macrosociological systems; their use of deductive, inductive, dialectic, and intuitional methods of research; a careful analysis of the philosophical presuppositions they accept as the basis of their theories; their more favorable attitude toward "philosophizing," theoretical analysis of the inner, subjective, and meaningful aspect of sociocultural phenomena and to the grand systems of sociology; and a comparative freedom from imitation of the methods and terminology of the natural sciences so conspicuous in the singularistic-atomistic theories.

RECENT UPSURGE OF SYSTEMIC THEORIES IN ALL BASIC SCIENCES

Because the singularistic-atomistic theories deliver, at best, a valid knowledge of only one or of a few of many aspects of sociocultural phenomena, and because these investigations, as we have seen, contain not the whole truth and nothing but the truth but only a part of the truth frequently mixed with error, their recent upsurge has been counteracted and complemented by an upsurge of systemic theories not only in recent sociology but also in physics, chemistry, biology, psychology, and the social sciences.[7]

---

[5] See the meaning of these terms in the *Dynamics*, Vol. II, chs. 5, 6, 7, and 8.

[6] Cf. *CST*, ch. 8.

[7] Besides the cognitive reasons, the existential-cultural factor has played an important part in both upsurges. This sociocultural factor has consisted: (*a*) in the decline of the hitherto dominant sensate cultural

This upsurge is well outlined in the following excerpts from V. G. Afanassiyeff's paper:

In this age when mankind is entering the period of scientific-technological revolution, a study of the problem of wholeness, structure, organization acquires great important. The successes of today's science and practice convincingly testify to the fact that the world surrounding us consists of not separate things isolated from one another but of a multitude of mutually bound and interacting objects—certain kinds of the unified formations or wholenesses. Investigation of the unified systems has a great significance for a study of the forms of movement of matter, classification of sciences, clarification of possibilities of application of mathematical and physico-chemical methods to a study of various regions of reality, for theory and practice of (scientific) models, for establishment and utilization of cybernetic systems and also for solution of a series of scientific and technical problems. The problem of wholeness (*Ganzheit*) has many philosophical aspects. [One of these is classification of the holistic systems and of the basic types of *Ganzheiten*.]

On what basis, on what principles should such a classification be made? In order to answer this question it is necessary to define what is meant by the unified system and wholeness. In Soviet and foreign literature the concept of the whole is identified with that of a system. No doubt each wholeness (*Ganzheit*) is a system; but is each system a whole? In my opinion, no. . . . In science . . . system is usually understood [as] a complex of interacting components. According to this definition several or even two molecules of gas colliding with each other in mechanical interaction will be a system. Nevertheless this is not a *holistic* (unified) but a merely *summative* system insofar as this mechanical interaction does not generate any new (holistic) properties. In difference from this in the

---

supersystem that has stimulated an upsurge of extreme singularistic-atomistic theories and (*b*) in the emergence of a new integral-cultural order that favors the upsurge of the systemic theories. Substantial evidence given in the *Dynamics* shows that nominalism-singularism-temporalism are congenial to, and are tangibly associated with, the sensate cultural supersystem, whereas systemic realistic-universalistic-eternalistic philosophies and theories are predominant in ideational and integral cultures. See the reasons and corroborations of this uniformity in the *Dynamics*, Vol. II, chs. 5–8. The contemporary decline of the sensate supersystem and the emergence of the integral cultural order are analyzed in detail in the *Dynamics* and concisely outlined in P. Sorokin, *The Basic Trends of Our Time* (New Haven, 1964).

interaction of 10^{22} molecules their system becomes a thermo-dynamic whole: it clearly displays new integrative properties (temperature, pressure) which are lacking in the isolated molecules. The same can be observed in any other holistic system—in the nucleus of atom, in atom, molecule, living cell, organism and so on. For this reason we could define the wholeness (*Ganzheit*) or unified system as a totality of objects whose interaction generates new integrative qualities absent in their isolated parts. This characteristic clearly indicates the difference of the unified (holistic) system from the merely summative system (a pile of stones and the like) whose properties are identical with a mere sum of the properties of its parts. By introducing new or eliminating old components of the summative system neither the system nor its components undergo any tangible qualitative change; the system merely either decreases or increases in its volume. Each component of the summative system remains autonomous; the cohesive force among the components has a purely external, unstable character. Quite a different picture represents a unified (holistic) system. Cohesion among its components is so close and organic that a change in one of the components necessarily determines a change in other components and quite frequently in the whole system. For this reason in various processes of inter-action with its environment the holistic system functions as a unity. This unity is due to the fact that the cohesion among its components is greater and more stable than their cohesion with the formations of their environment. . . .

After this definition Dr. Afanassiyeff enumerates the specific characteristics of all holistic systems. They are:

A. The unified system actively influences its components and often modifies them according to its own nature. As a result, its parts undergo serious changes: they lose some of their properties they had before their entrance into the system and they acquire some new qualities. For example, a neutron after its entrance into a nucleus of an atom becomes more stable, while in its "free" state it exists only a short time and dissociates into proton, electron and neutrino. The properties of atoms, ions, radicals tangibly change when they enter a molecule. . . . Especially close is the cohesion of the components (organs, cells, tissues) with one another and with the whole system in a living organism. There, as V. I. Lenin wrote, the parts "only in their unity with one another are that what they are. A hand separated from its body becomes only a terminological hand." Isolated from the unified system a part loses its living properties and changes into the products of chemical dissociation.

B. Each unified system (*Ganzheit*) has its own specific—quantitative and qualitative—organization of its components or parts. . . . Thus, an atom as a unity is made up of its nucleus and electronic wall; an organism, of organs, tissues, and cells, and so on.

C. Specific kinds of internal mutual cohesion of the components or of their organization make the *structure* of the unified system. Structure of an atom consists of electromagnetic interaction of its nucleus with electrons, etc.

D. Each unified system (*Ganzheit*) exists not in isolation, by itself, but in a certain relationship with its environment. Different kinds of systems have different forms of interaction with their milieu and the higher the level of the development of the system the more complex and diverse its interaction with the milieu. Some of the systems are comparatively *closed*, some others (many physical and chemical systems) are more *open* (they exchange only energy with their environment) while third type of systems (living organisms) are *open* and exchange with their environment energy as well as matter.

E. Each unified system changes in the course of time and has its own history. Being genetically connected with the preceding unified systems it, in its turn, becomes a material or foundation for formation of new unified systems.

F. Finally, each unified system has its own specific functions, qualities and properties determined by the nature of its components and their mutual cohesion, by its interaction with the environment and by its historico-genetic conditions. The totality of these characteristics determines the integrative properties of each system (property of association and disassociation of chemical systems, of assimilation and dissimilation, self-reproduction, etc., of living organisms).[8]

This gives us an idea of the systemic investigations of the unified physical systems beginning with the macrophysical metagalaxies and other galactic systems and ending with the microphysical structures of molecules, atoms, elementary parti-

[8] V. G. Afanassiyeff, "O prinzypakh klassificatzii tzelostnykh system" ["Principles of Classification of the Unified Systems"], trans. P. Sorokin, *Voprosy Filosofii*, No. 5 (1963), pp. 31–33. See especially O. Lange, *Całość i rozwój w świetle cybernetyki* [*The Whole and Development in the Light of Cybernetics*], (Warsaw, 1962).

cles.[9] During the last few decades, great progress in systemic research of physical and chemical systems has been accomplished. Numerous types of these systems have been studied, several classifications of these physical *Ganzheiten* have been formulated, and a series of uniformities in this field have been discovered.[10]

● Upsurge of Systemic Theories in the Biological Sciences

Still more conspicuous has been the upsurge of systemic theories in biology. Its essentials are well described by L. von Bertalanffy, one of the leaders in the field of general theory of systems and especially of biological systems:

> In our time a fundamental change of scientific conceptions has occurred. The revolutions in modern physics are widely known. . . . Less obvious, but perhaps no less significant in their consequences, are the changes that have taken place in biological thought. . . . If we retain the term *"organismic conception"* we shall consider it merely as a convenient denomination for an attitude which has already become very general and largely

---

[9] See on these astrophysical systems in S. B. Pikelner, *Fisika mejzvesdnoy sredy* [*Physics of the Interstarry Environment*], (Moscow, 1959); L. O. Valt, "So-otnosheniye struktury i elementov" ["Relationship between Structure and Elements"], *Voprosy Filosofii*, No. 5 (1963), pp. 44–53.

[10] Of the vast literature in this field, only a few works can be mentioned here: *General Systems: Yearbook of the Society for the Advancement of General System Theory* (Ann Arbor, 1956–1963), Vols. I–VIII; B. M. Kedrov, *Filosofskiye problemy sovremennago estestvoznaniya* (*Philosophical Problems of Contemporary Natural Science*) (Moscow, 1959); J. C. Smuts, *Holism and Evolution* (London, 1927); V. N. Sadovsky, *Problemi metodologii i logiki nauk* (*Problems of Methodology and Logic of Sciences*) (Tomsk, 1962); a series of research papers by V. I. Kremiansky, I. V. Blauberg, V. I. Sividersky, N. T. Abramova, V. N. Kondratiev, and others published in *Voprosy Filosofii* for 1959–1964; a series of monographs of eminent physicists like I. E. Tamm, *Osnovy teorii elektritchestva* (*Foundations of the Theory of Electricity*) (Moscow, 1957); V. Hukkel, *Himitcheskaia Sviaz* (*Chemical Cohesion*) (Moscow, 1960). A vast bibliography of the Western works about physical and biological systems is given in L. von Bertalanffy's *Problems of Life* (New York, 1960), pp. 205–211.

anonymous. . . . Biological research and thought have *hitherto* been determined by three leading ideas, which may be called the *analytical and summative*, the *machine-theoretical*, and the *reaction theoretical conceptions*. . . .

It appeared to be the goal of biological research to resolve the complex entities and processes that confront us in living nature into elementary units—to *analyze* them—in order to explain them by means of the juxtaposition of *summation* of these elementary units and processes. Thus chemistry resolves material bodies into elementary components—molecules and atoms; physics considers a storm that tears down a tree as the sum of movements of air particles, the heat of a body as the sum of the energy of motion of molecules, and so on. A corresponding procedure was applied in all biological fields. Thus biochemistry investigates the individual chemical constituents of living bodies and the chemical processes going on within them. . . . The classical cell theory considered cells as the elementary units of life comparable to atoms as the elementary units of chemical compounds. So a multicellular organism appeared morphologically as an aggregate of such building units. . . . The same point of view was applied to the embryonic development of organisms. . . . The classical theory of reflexes, centers, and localization . . . considered (the nervous system) as a sum of apparatuses established for individual functions. . . . Accordingly, the behavior of animals was resolved into a sum or chain of reflexes. . . . These examples . . . show that the *principle of analysis and summation* has been directive in all fields. Analysis of the individual parts and processes in living things is *necessary* and is the prerequisite for all deeper understanding. Taken alone, however, analysis is *not sufficient*. First, [because] every organism represents a *system*, by which term we mean a complex of elements in mutual interaction, it is impossible to resolve the phenomena of life completely into elementary units [because] the behavior of an isolated part is, in general, different from its behavior within the context of the whole. . . . If cells are explanted from the organism and are allowed to grow as a tissue culture in an appropriate nutrient, their behavior will be different from that within the organism. . . . Thus the characteristics of life are characteristics of a system arising from, and associated with, the organization of materials and processes. They are altered with alterations in the whole, and disappear when it is destroyed. . . .

Secondly, the actual whole shows properties that are absent from its isolated parts. The problem of life is that of *organization*. As long as we single out individual phenomena we do not discover any fundamental difference between the living and the non-living. . . . [The specific organization of all parts and processes in organisms] basically distinguishes events in a living organism from reactions taking place in non-living systems or in a corpse. . . . Thus the problem of wholeness and organization sets a limit to the analytical and summative description and explanation. [According to the hitherto prevalent machine theory] the order in vital phenomena was to be interpreted in terms of *structures*, mechanisms in the widest sense of the word. Examples of this conception are Weismann's theory of embryonic development or the classic reflex and centre theory. . . . Structural conditions are to a large extent present in the living organism. . . . Nevertheless, we *cannot consider structures as the primary basis of the vital order* for a fixed structure (and its mechanism) can respond to certain definite exigencies only, not just to any one whatever (as it is shown by all organisms). . . . There is a fundamental difference between the structure of a machine and that of an organism. The former consists always of the same components, the latter is maintained in a state of continuous flux, a perpetual breaking down and replacement of its building materials. *Organic structures are themselves the expression of an ordered process, and are only maintained in and by this process.* Thirdly, ontogenetically and philogenetically we find a transition from less mechanized and more regulable states to more mechanized and less regulable ones. . . .

We come therefore to the following conclusion. Primarily organic processes are determined by the mutual interaction of the conditions present in the *total system,* by a *dynamic* order as we may call it. This is at the basis of organic regulability. . . . The primary nature of a dynamic as opposed to a structural or machine-like order is seen in fields as diverse as those of cell structures, embryonic development, secretion, phagocytosis, the theory of reflexes and centres, of instinctive behavior, *gestalt* perception, etc. Organisms *are not* machines, but they can to a certain extent *become* machines, congeal into machines. Never completely, however, for a thoroughly mechanized organism would be incapable of regulation following disturbances, or of reacting to the incessantly changing conditions of the outside world.

The comparison of the organism with a machine also leads to what we call the *reaction theory*. The organism was considered as a sort of an automaton . . . as an essentially passive system set into action only through outside influences, the so-called stimuli. This "stimulus-response scheme" has been of fundamental importance, especially in the theory of animal behavior. In fact, however, the organism is, even under constant external conditions and in the absence of external stimuli, not a passive but basically *active* system. This is obvious in the fundamental phenomenon of life, metabolism. . . . Modern research has shown that we have to consider [the] autonomous activity of [the] organism as the primary phenomenon rather than [its] reflexes and reactivity.

We can therefore summarize the leading principles of an organismic conception in the following way: The *conception of the system as a whole* as opposed to the *analytical and summative* points of view; the *dynamic* conception as opposed to the *static and machine-theoretical* conceptions; the consideration of the organism as a *primary activity* as opposed to the conception of its *primary reactivity*.[11]

This theory of organismic systems is different from the hitherto prevailing—mechanistic and vitalistic—theories. "Organization and wholeness considered as principles of order, immanent to organic systems, and accessible to scientific investigation, involve a basically new attitude."

Important characteristics of living organisms are their incessant change and the open character of their system. A crystal is built of unchanging components that persist perhaps for millions of years, but "a living organism only appears to be persistent and invariable; in truth it is the manifestation of a perpetual flow. As a result of metabolism its components are not the same from one moment to the next."[12]

From the standpoint of *physics* the living organism is not a closed system with respect to its surrounding but an *open system* which continually gives up matter to the outer world and takes in matter from it, but which maintains itself in this continuous exchange in a *steady state*. . . . So far physical chemistry has been concerned almost exclusively with processes in closed systems. Such processes lead to chemical equilibria. Chemical equilibria are also basic for certain processes within the organism. . . . *The organism as a whole is, however, never in true equilibrium*, and the relatively slow processes of metabolism lead only to a *steady state*, maintained at a constant distance from true equilibrium by a continuous inflow and outflow, building up and breaking down of the component

[11] L. von Bertalanffy, *Problems of Life*, pp. 9–20.
[12] *Ibid.*

material. . . . The theory of open systems has opened up an entirely new field of physics. . . .[13]

I. Prigogine has noted that "The two principles of classical thermodynamics hold only for the *closed* systems, which exchange energy, but not matter, with the outside world. Thermodynamics is an admirable but *fragmentary* theory, and this fragmentary character originates from the fact that it is applicable only to *states of equilibrium in closed systems.* Therefore, it is necessary to establish a broader theory, comprising states of non-equilibrium as well as those of equilibrium."[14]

Furthermore, biological systems as well as the totality of known systems in the cosmos can be classified in various ways and hierarchical orders. The systemic standpoint leads to a modification of the principles of scientific explanation of the phenomena studied:

> On the one hand, every system in the hierarchical order, from the ultimate physical units to the atoms, molecules, cells, and organisms, exhibit new properties and modes of action that cannot be understood by a mere summation of the properties and modes of actions of the subordinate systems. The properties of living cells are very different from the properties of the component proteins, and so on.
>
> On the other hand, it is just the business of physics to explain higher levels in terms of the lower ones. Hence the question arises as to what the supposed "nonsummativity" of higher levels with respect to the lower ones really means, and in how far the former are explicable in terms of the latter. The answer is simple. The properties and modes of action of higher levels are not explicable by the summation of the properties and modes of actions of their components *taken in isolation.* If, however, we know the ensemble of components and *the relations existing between them,* then the higher levels are derivable from the components. In order to know a given system we must know not only its "parts" but also the "relations" between them.[15]

[13] *Ibid.,* pp. 123–125.

[14] Prigogine, *Etude thermodynamique des phénomènes irreversibles* (Liege, 1947). See also O. Lange, *The Whole and Development in the Light of Cybernetics.*

[15] Bertalanffy, *op. cit.,* pp. 147–150. See there a vast bibliography on biological systems.

These excerpts outline the essential principles of biological systemic theories. Detailed research on many a basic problem of biology from this standpoint has given a number of significant variations of these general principles and has opened several new vistas and interpretations of living systems. The vast literature in this field clearly confirms the vigorous resurgence of the systemic viewpoint in today's biology.

● Upsurge of Systemic Theories in Individual Psychology

An upsurge of the systemic theories similar to that in the physical and biological sciences has been occurring also in the science of individual psychology. Though in all these disciplines singularistic-atomistic research still probably predominates, systemic theories have emerged and have been growing in recent years. Professor Gordon W. Allport in his thoughtful lectures divides various currents of today's psychological thought into two main streams: the Lockean and the Leibnitzian traditions. These two streams are not fully identical with our streams of singularistic and systemic thought, but they are quite congenial to them. For this reason Allport's examination of the Lockean and Leibnitzian currents can serve as our guide and can save us a great deal of time and energy in outlining the upsurge of systemic theories in individual psychology.

John Locke viewed the mind of the individual as a *tabula rasa* at birth and the intellect itself as a passive recipient of sensations. Sensations furnished to it its content and shaped its structure:

> To Leibnitz the intellect was perpetually active in its own right, addicted to rational problem solving, and bent on manipulating sensory data according to its own inherent nature. For Locke the organism was reactive when stimulated; for Leibnitz it was self-propelled. . . . The Lockean point of view has been and still is dominant in Anglo-American psychology. Its representatives are found in associationism of all types, including environmentalism, behaviorism, stimulus-response psychology, and all other stimulus-oriented psychologies, in positivism and operationism, in mathematical models—in short, in most of

what today is cherished in our laboratories as truly "scientific" psychology.[16]

The presuppositions and general characteristics of this Lockean current largely coincide with those of the singularistic-atomistic theories in sociology. According to Allport, "They hold that what is external and visible is more fundamental than what is not." Mind and organism, he says, are viewed as passive and determined mainly by external stimuli, and "the 'cause' remains external to organism." For these theories "what is small and molecular (Locke's 'simple ideas') is more fundamental than what is large and molar (Locke's 'complex ideas'). Human personality is regarded as a concatenation of reflexes or of habits. For Hull as for Watson it is a habit-hierarchy. . . . The upper reaches of the hierarchy receive little attention. . . . Since man is an animal, why not take animals that are simpler—the rat, for instance—as a prototype of the more complicated animal?" These theories concentrate on a study of animals and unhesitatingly transfer upon and apply to man the results of their research of rats, pigeons, dogs, and so on. They assume also "that what is earlier is more fundamental that what is late in development." Hence their preoccupation with childhood learning-fixations-conditioning. "All of these Lockean presuppositions are congenial to modern positivism. . . . The idea (of these theories) is to bring psychology into line with physics and mathematics."[17]

In accordance with these presuppositions, this stream of psychological research avoids "the investigations of consciousness as a datum, as well as of personality as a complex structure," for in these domains the operational method, experimentation with external traits or fragments of behavior, is difficult to apply and to make repeatable and public.[18]

As a result, the main research of this current deals with external and simple fragments of reflexes, overt actions, various

---

[16] G. W. Allport, *Becoming* (New Haven, 1955), pp. 7–8.

[17] This and preceding quotations are from Allport, *Becoming*, pp. 9–11.

[18] *Ibid.*, pp. 11–12.

"complexes," "attitudes," and drives isolated from the total personality and from one another. It takes little interest in "the existential richness of human life" and in the deep, inner world of man. Its techniques and tests are predominantly mechanical and designed to test some presumed singularistic properties of the individuals, like depression, aggressiveness, submission, I.Q., decision, speed, honesty, disposition, motivation, aptitude, preference, and other isolated characteristics that are often poorly defined.[19]

In contrast to the Lockean, "The Leibnitzian tradition maintains *that the person is not a collection of acts; the person is the source of acts.* And activity itself is not conceived as agitation resulting from pushes by internal or external stimulation. It is purposive."[20] Aristotle's entelechy, St. Thomas Aquinas's doctrine of intention, and Spinoza's *conatus*-striving toward self-preservation and self-affirmation anticipated the Leibnitzian conception of intellect.

Later on, Kant, with his a priori categories of the human mind, and almost all the representatives of the neo-Thomist, the intuitivist, and the rationalist currents of philosophical and psychological thought, as well as a great number of scientists[21] maintained and asserted the active, creative, unified, and self-regulative nature of the highest forms of the human psyche and of its subsystems. Temporarily, during the twentieth century, this Leibnitzian or systemic current has been reduced to a minor stream compared with that of the Lockean or singularistic currents, especially in the United States. Nevertheless, in recent times, the systemic approach to the study of the human personality, mind, psyche, and of the total inner experience of man, including man's overt behavior, has been growing in Europe and America. This upsurge has manifested itself in many forms and currents of psychological thought.

[19] For a criticism of these tests, see my *Fads and Foibles*, chs. 4, 5, 6.

[20] Allport, *Becoming*, pp. 12–13.

[21] See their names and works in my *Dynamics*, Vol. IV, pp. 746–764, Vol. II, pp. 635–642; and in *The Ways and Power of Love*, chs. 5, 6, 7.

It was apparent, at least partly, even in the theories of early "associationists" like Herbart, Brentano, and Wundt (in their conceptions of creative apperceptive synthesis) and in the Würzburg doctrines of attitude and tendency. Then a systemic theory of psychological *Ganzheiten* or systems, developed by Ch. v. Ehrenfels and F. Krueger at the turn of this century,[22] resulted in the powerful Gestalt movement in psychology of today represented by Krueger, Wellek, Metzger, Wertheimer, Koffka, Köhler, Katz, and others. Beginning with Ehrenfels' discovery of the "qualities of configuration" in our perception, subsequent Gestalt psychologists have demonstrated the presence of several holistic structures and processes that in the development of normal individuals, tangibly integrate the central part of the individual's personality into a sort of a whole distinct from its surroundings. These structures and processes are articulate, supersummative, governed centrally, self-regulative, equipped with assimilatory and regenerative powers, holistically determined, and "stylistically" shaped into a "form or die—cast alive and developing."[23]

The second systemic current in recent psychology is represented by the existential-phenomenological philosophy in its ontological and phenomenological analysis of the "authentic self" and the unauthentic forms of being in the human individual. In accordance with their acceptance of a transcendent reality quite different from the reality of the empirical world (and called God by Kierkegaard, Transcendence by Jaspers, and Being by Heidegger), they and other phenomenologists and existentialists (Berdyaev, Unamuno, Sartre, Buber, Marcel, Husserl) have discovered in the individual, side by side with the temporal, superficial, unauthentic forms of his being, the unified, authentic self. Kierkegaard's "self," eternal in time, is the intersection of the individual's infinite soul with his finite body—an intersection realized at the moment of a "passionate

[22] See O. Anderle, "Die Ganzheitstheorie, ein historisch-systematischer Überblick," *Zeitschrift für Ganzheitsforschung, Neue Folge,* IV (1960), 2–18. See also F. Weinhandl (ed.) *Geschtalthaftes Sehen, Festgabe zum 100. Geburstag Ch. v. Ehrenfels* (Darmstadt, 1960).

[23] Cf., for a holistic or Gestalt analysis of personality, A. Wellek, *Person, Personlichkeit und Charakter* (Mesenheim, 1951).

choice," Heidegger's "authentic" (*eigentlich*) man, Jaspers' "selfhood" (*Selbstsein*) as the ultimate ground of our being, Berdyaev's "ego" as the "constant unity underlying all change," and Marcel's *"l'universel"* (creative, sublime love) are other forms of the "self" in the individual. The individual's empirical forms of being are more than a merely incidental succession of fragmentary reflexes, drives, sensations, images, emotions, volitions, and desires; they represent several integrated *Ganzheiten* or unified hierarchical levels: Jaspers' integral man is an empirical, finite being or organism, a participant in the universal reason and consciousness (*Bewusstsein überhoupt*), and a participant in the spirit (*Geist*); Berdyaev's breakdown of the total man into ego, personality, and individuality, and so on. This brief discussion clearly shows the systemic character of the philosophical and psychological theories of existentialism and phenomenologism.[24]

Systemic strains also permeate Freudian, Adlerian, Jungian, and other varieties of psychoanalytical theories. Freudianism views human personality as dominated (and therefore notably unified) by libidinal and destructive forces. It divides the personality into three distinct systems or levels, *id, ego,* and *superego,* and distinguishes in each of these regions several subsystems or "complexes," the Oedipus, the Narcissus, and so on. Jungians distinguish several systems: the whole psyche as a unified form of being, the instincts, the racial archetypes, and the special subsystems of the unconscious, the conscious ego, and the integrated self (outlined vaguely).[25] In Adler's psychology, the systemic strains manifest themselves in his conception of personality as dominated by a struggle for power and then in his "lasting style of life" of the individual as a system.

[24] See, for a systematic analysis of these theories from the standpoint of the category of unity, A. M. Moschetti, *L'unità come categoria,* Vol. II, ch. 3, and *passim*; see there a bibliography of existentialism. See also E. Tiryakian, *Sociologism and Existentialism* (New York, 1962); E. Rothacker, *Die Schichten der Personlichkeit* (Munich, 1951), and R. Jolivet, *Les doctrines existentialistes de Kierkegaard à Sartre* (Abbaye St. Wandrille, 1948).

[25] Of the many works of C. G. Jung, see especially his "The Spirit of Psychology" in W. Burnett (ed.), *This Is My Philosophy* (New York, 1957), pp. 114–167.

Still more conspicuous is the systemic approach in the psychological theories of neo-analysts like E. Fromm, K. Abraham, F. Alexander, S. Ferenczi, A. Kardiner, K. Horney, and others. Some of them, like Horney, even explicitly call their theory the theory of the "whole man."[26]

In various forms the psychoanalytical currents use the systemic approach and demonstrate in the field of human psyche the presence and functioning of several integrated regions and unified systems or complexes. They view the total human personality not as a dumping field of congeries of psychological odds and ends but as integrated by dominant forces into tangible unities or types.

Largely systemic also are the neo-Thomistic theories of personality and all the theories that represent a variation of the structure of personality. These theories consist of three coexisting and interdependent systems of forces: the unconscious controlled by the reflexological mechanism of our body, the consciously rational, and the superconscious-superrational (called pneuma, soul, spirit, genius, the divine in man, nous, atman, tao, self, purusha, prajna, jnana, and so on). In the old as in the new theories of this triadic division of personality, each of the three regions is viewed as a tangibly unified system and all three systems are viewed as tangibly interdependent with one another. In some individuals they are in harmonious relation with each other, and integrate the total personality. Variations on this type of psychological theory have been increasing in recent years. In contrast to Freud's "depth psychology," Sjövall calls this triadic conception of personality "height psychology," following Kafka's happy dictum that "the deepest in man is his highest."[27]

The systemic approach also dominates most of the recent theories that integrate into one dominant system, if not the total,

[26] See A. Adler, "The Fundamental Views of Individual Psychology," *International Journal of Individual Psychology*, I (1935); and A. Kardiner and R. Linton, "The Concept of Basic Personality Structure" in R. Linton (ed.), *The Science of Man in the World Crisis* (New York, 1945).

[27] See, on this type of recent theories, M. B. Arnold and J. A. Gasson, *The Human Personality: An Approach to an Integral Theory of Personality* (New York, 1954); P. Sorokin, *The Ways and Power of*

then at least an essential part of the personality (the part with many structural and dynamic subsystems in it). Many of these systemic theories do not admit any transcendent or even empirical "self," but all of them—in diverse ways and from different standpoints—acknowledge, in the words of G. W. Allport, that "the most comprehensive units (or systems) in personality are broad intentional future pointed dispositions (*Leitmotiven*, 'lasting styles of life'). These characteristics are unique for each person and tend to attract, guide, and inhibit the more elementary units to accord these with the major intentions themselves. This proposition is valid in spite of [all] the . . . unordered, impulsive, and conflictful behavior in every life. . . . These cardinal characteristics are not infinite in number, but for any given life in adult years are relatively few and ascertainable."[28] This approach is represented now by diverse currents of psychological thought, such as the theories of G. W. Allport, A. H. Maslow (his "psychology of being"), K. Goldstein, V. E. Frankl, J. L. Moreno (his tele, spontaneity-creativity, and his conception of the total man), C. Roger, A. Angyal, H. Cantril, P. Lecky, R. May, C. Murphy, H. Eysenck, C. Blondel, I. Progoff, A. Vexliard, W. J. Revere, H. Erikson, R. Assagioli and the "Psychosynthesis School," D. McClelland, P. Bertocci, P. H. Prabhu, and many others.[29] Though differing in many respects from each other these theories have a common characteristics: They are all systemic.

The systemic trend in recent psychological theories has shown itself also in those *theories dealing with various types of personality*. Each type represents the integration of certain characteristics into one living form dominant in the individuals of this type. This theory is represented by many typologies, which, in a modified form, continue the typological theories of the past: the typologies of psychotic, psychoneurotic, and nor-

---

Love, chs. 5, 6, 7; Björn Sjövall, *Höjdpsykologi* (Stockholm, 1959); J. Maritain, *Elements de philosophie*; *Reflexions sur l'intelligence et sur sa vie propre* (Paris, 1930), and his *The Degree of Knowledge* (New York, 1938); and R. Assagioli, *Psychosynthesis* (New York, 1965).

[28] Allport, *Becoming*, p. 92.

[29] See the bibliography in A. H. Maslow, *Toward a Psychology of Being* (Princeton, 1962).

mal personality types of Kraepelin, Janet, Jung, Kretschmer, Sholl, Spearman, Külpe, Jaensch, and Wertheimer; and recent typological theories of temperament and character connected with constitutional or environmental factors.[30]

In recent years, a number of sociopsychological typologies of personality or types of mentality have been offered by sociologists, anthropologists, social psychologists, and philosophers. Pareto's types of the *speculatori* and the *rentieri* are earlier examples of this sort of theory; William James' types of the "sick soul" and the "healthy-minded" are examples in the field of religious experience. Recent examples are David Riesman's "inner-directed" and "other-directed" types; Sorokin's ideational, idealistic, and sensate types; and, in the field of altruistic mentality and behavior, the "fortunate," "catastrophic," and "intermediary" types; K. Mannheim's "conservative" and "progressive or revolutionary" types; T. W. Adorno's "authoritarian personality"; and J. Ortega y Gasset's, Berdyaev's, Jaspers', Marcel's, and Heidegger's "mass-man."[31]

● Upsurge of Systemic Theories in the Historical Sciences

Perhaps still greater is the upsurge of systemic theories in the historical disciplines. An ever-increasing number of social and historical thinkers in the last few decades have criticized traditional, chronological history as the discipline giving, at best,

---

[30] See various typological theories in J. McV. Hunt, *Personality and the Behavior Disorders*, Vol. I (New York, 1944). See also G. W. Allport, *Personality: A Psychological Interpretation* (New York, 1937), especially its latest edition. See also C. S. Hall and G. Lindzey, *Theories of Personality* (New York, 1957). See also several papers in S. Koch, *Psychology: A Study of a Science* (5 vols.; New York, 1959–1962).

[31] See D. Riesman, N. Glazer, R. Denny, *The Lonely Crowd* (New Haven, 1953); P. Sorokin, the *Dynamics, passim,* and *The Ways and Power of Love,* ch. 9; K. Mannheim, *Ideology and Utopia* (New York, 1936); T. W. Adorno *et al., The Authoritarian Personality* (New York, 1950); J. Ortega y Gasset, *The Revolt of the Masses* (New York, 1932); M. Heidegger, *Being and Existence* (Chicago, 1960); N. Berdyaev, *Solitude and Society* (London, 1947); and K. Jaspers, *Man in the Modern Age* (London, 1951); A. Vexliard, "Sorokin's Psychological Theories" in P. J. Allen's *P. A. Sorokin in Review.*

only a "subjective" knowledge of a few singularistic events, as "only cutting separate trails through the jungle of events" and hardly ever explaining all the important what's, how's, and why's of history. Many of these scholars have suggested that the proper duty of history is to analyze the important social systems or unified sociocultural structures or ensembles, their structuralization and destructuralization, their relationship to one another, and their relationship to the external physical and biological world. Some of the extreme structuralists have gone so far along this line as to forecast the end of traditional, ideographic, singularistic history. A sharp argument between the singularistic, ideographic historians and the systemic social investigators is going on at present in most Western countries, particularly in France.[32]

● **Other Signs of an Upsurge of Systemic Theories**

The upsurge of systemic theories has manifested itself also in the establishment of a special Society for the Advancement of General Systems Theory, which, in its *Yearbook*, publishes studies of various general systems; the establishment of *Zeitschrift für Ganzheitsforschung,* a special journal devoted to research papers dealing with various unified systems; and an increase in studies in this field. The problem of unified systems has been made the central topic of national and international scientific congresses, like the First International and the Second International Congress of the Society for the Comparative Study of Civilizations. The first Congress is devoted to the study of

[32] See a report on this struggle and on the arguments of each side in H. Lefebvre, "Réflexions sur le structuralisme et l'histoire," and in F. Dumont, "Ideologie et savoir historique," *Cahiers internationaux de sociologie,* XXXV(1963), 3–24, 43–60; C. Lévy-Strauss, "Introduction à l'oeuvre de Mauss," *Sociologie et Anthropologie* (Paris, 1960); G. Granger, "Evénement et structure dans les sciences de l'homme," *Cahiers de l'I.S.E.A.,* series M, No. 6; H. I. Marrou, *De la connaissance historique* (Paris, 1955); and L. Goldman, *L'homme et l'histoire* (Paris, 1952). See also P. Sorokin, "Theses on the Role of Historical Method in the Social Sciences," *Transactions of the Fifth World Congress of Sociology* (Washington, 1962), Vol. I, pp. 235–254.

civilizations as macrosocial systems;[33] the second deals with *Ganzheiten* in physical, biological, and psychosocial sciences, and in philosophy and religion.[34]

This chapter has outlined the recent upsurge of systemic theories in all sciences and humanities. Subsequent chapters will give evidence of this upsurge in sociology.

[33] Its proceedings are published under the title *The Problems of Civilizations* (The Hague, 1964). It is edited by O. F. Anderle, with my preface. The volume contains the papers and discussions of the main problems of civilizations by distinguished historians, sociologists, archeologists, psychologists, economists, jurists, political scientists, and philosophers of various countries.

[34] The volume of its proceedings will be published in the near future.

CHAPTER 6

"Totalitarian" Theories of

Culture Integration

MAIN CHARACTERISTICS OF TOTALITARIAN THEORIES

At the beginning of Chapter 5, I briefly indicated that the systemic conception of sociocultural phenomena has been, from the remote past on up to the present time, one of the main currents of thought in philosophy, law, the humanities, and the psychosocial sciences. In the natural sciences, the systemic approach has in some periods almost disappeared, but in the history of Greco-Roman and Western philosophical, juristic, and psychosocial thought, from 600 B.C. to A.D. 1920, the systemic-realistic current was dominant for all but three centuries. Although the period 1700-1920 was marked by a decrease of the systemic-realistic current, this current was still about as strong as the nominalistic-singularistic current. (Comparative indicators for the systemic-realistic and nominalistic currents for 1700–1800 are 38–38; for the period 1800–1900, 41–38; and for 1900–1920, 36–42. For systemic universalism and singularism for the same periods the indicators are, respectively, 40–52, 52–45, and 45–55).[1] In sociology, despite an upsurge of singularistic-atomistic theories during the eighteenth, nineteenth, and twentieth centuries, the systemic current has still been almost as strong as the singularistic-atomistic current.

Since the introduction of the term sociology and the official

---

[1] See the indicators of the comparative "weight" of these currents from 600 B.C. to A.D. 1920 by 20- and 100-year periods in the *Dynamics*, Vol. II, pp. 252–260 and 273–304. For the names of the eminent earlier representatives of the systemic sociological theories see also my *CST*, pp. 197–200 and 435–438.

establishment of this discipline by Auguste Comte, the systemic current of sociological thought has been represented by Comte and the "systemic positivists"[2] (like E. Durkheim and E. de Roberty), by the organic school (in its four basic forms, philosophical organicism, psychosocial organicism, bio-organismic, and functionalism), by the sociologistic school in all its varieties, and by the universalistic theories of O. Spann and his school.[3]

Recent sociological and anthropological theories of cultural and social systems have many forms. These range all the way from theories of complete integration of many total cultures through several intermediary forms up to the seminominal theories of cultural systems and pass imperceptibly into singularistic-atomistic conceptions. The same can be said of the theories of social systems, which also range from clearly defined social systems (or organized groups) through intermediary forms up to theories hardly distinguishing social systems from social congeries (unorganized and semiorganized social groups).

In this and the following chapters we shall examine the main types of theories of cultural systems. Then we shall ex-

---

[2] Soon after Comte introduced the term "positivism," it acquired a "singularistic-atomistic" meaning entirely different from the "systemic" meaning given to it by Comte. From the standpoint of this "singularistic-atomistic positivism," Comte himself—especially in a later period of his writings, e.g., his *Positive Polity* and others—is certainly not a "positivist," nor can these singularistic-atomistic theories of positivism be regarded as Comtean theories.

[3] See, on these "schools" and other systemic theories, my *CST*, chs. 4–10. The bio-organismic theories of H. Spencer, A. Schäffle, P. Lilienfeld, and R. Worms correctly outlined the *differentia specifica* of social and cultural systems, despite the organismic analogies they used as a mere "scaffolding to help in building up a coherent body of sociological induction" (H. Spencer). Spencer introduced even the term *social system*, which he used interchangeably with *social organism* in his *Principles of Sociology*. (See especially Vol. I of this work (London, 1885), pp. 435–588.) On these points see *CST*, pp. 207–218. Don Martindale is correct in his statement that the "fundamental explanatory model (of contemporary) functionalism is that of the organic system." His subsequent statements that, in its difference from the contemporary functionalism, organicism was "dominated by the conception of large-scale, total organic structure" are, however, questionable. (Don Martindale, *The Nature and Types of Sociological Theory* (Boston, 1960), p. 449.) Spencer and

amine theories of social systems. Among the theories of cultural systems (and congeries) we can distinguish the following main types:

1. "Totalitarian" theories of the complete integration of the total culture of individuals; of small groups or preliterate and civilized culture areas (we can call these theories microsociological totalitarian); and of vast cultural continents, civilizations, high cultures, national cultures, cultures of the East and West, and so on (which can be called macrosociological totalitarian).

2. Intermediary theories of culture integration, which claim that only a part of any total culture—of individuals, small and large social groups, small and vast culture areas, including civilizations, high cultures, and so on—is integrated into a multitude of small and big cultural—causal and meaningful—systems. In great civilizations and high cultures the integrated part can be unified into a few vast supersystems, but none of the total cultures of even a single individual, of even the smallest culture area, and still less of any social group, cultural continent, civilization, or high culture is completely integrated into one—causal and meaningful—system. In any total culture there is always a coexistence of several different cultural systems subordinated to, coordinated with, neutral, and contradictory to each other, and a coexistence of many cultural congeries within the systems and outside of them. In highly integrated total cultures, there may be one or two dominant or main supersystems, several other systems or minor supersystems, and a multitude of congeries.

---

other organicists dealt not only with many subsystems like "the sustaining, the distributing, and the regulating," but also with several subsubsystems like "the domestic, the ecclesiastic, the ceremonial, the professional, the industrial," and other institutions. If anything, H. Spencer and other organicists analyzed and classified these subsystems and subsubsystems more thoroughly and clearly than most of today's "functionalists structuralists." This is especially true of the Neo-organicism of C. Gini, Marotta, Castellano, and others. See on this school M. Marotta, *Organicismo e Neo-Organicismo* (Milan, 1959), *CST*, pp. 422 ff.

3. Theories of the ideal or highest or "normative" or genuine vs. spurious cultural systems, which bestow the name of culture or civilization not upon all causal or meaningful cultural systems but only upon those that they consider to be the systems of genuine or highest unified cultural values.

4. Seminominal theories of cultural systems represent the formal classification of cultural phenomena into several artifical divisions. Some of these theories imperceptibly merge into either purely nominal or singularistic-atomistic systems.

MICROSOCIOLOGICAL TOTALITARIAN THEORIES OF CULTURE INTEGRATION

The central point of the totalitarian microsociological and macrosociological theories of cultural systems is their claim that the total culture of individuals, small and large groups, small culture areas, and vast cultural continents is unified into one system in which all the important parts are tangibly interdependent and, as a rule, harmoniously function in maintaining the life, identity, and continuity of the given total culture of the individuals and the social group that has and maintains it.

● The Total Culture of the Individual

We shall begin our examination of this thesis with the total culture of an individual as the smallest possible culture area. Before proceeding with this examination, we shall agree what we mean by the terms culture, cultural system, unified culture, integrated culture, unified structure, interdependence, function, and other derivative terms. This agreement is necessary because all these terms have been given quite different meanings by different scholars. Furthermore, we shall soon see that the main shortcoming of most of the theories of cultural and social systems has been the vagueness of their definitions of these terms. This vagueness and the variations in the meanings of these terms have been largely responsible for the mutual discordancy of systemic sociological theories and for the proliferation of a multitude of sterile "paradigms" and overcomplicated schemes in that field.[4]

I shall be using the terms culture, cultural system, integrated or unified culture, social system (organized social group), and cultural and social congeries exactly as they were defined in Chapter 2 of this work. Their detailed analysis is given in my *Dynamics, Society, Culture and Personality*, and *The Ways and Power of Love*. The reader should keep in mind the three-componental structure of sociocultural phenomena: meanings-values-norms; physical and biological objects and energies as the "vehicles" through which meanings-values-norms are objectified, materialized, or conserved; and human agents, who create, use, and realize these meanings-values-norms as either their ideological and/or material and/or behavioral culture in the process of interacting and' in establishing and carrying on mutual relationships.

I shall distinguish further five basic combinations of two or more cultural phenomena: (1) cultural congeries united only by spatial-time-mechanical proximity; (2) cultural semicongeries united by indirect causal ties (through the common factor or agent with which each of these cultural variables is causally or meaningfully related); (3) causal systems tied together by the tangible, regularly repeated, triple interdependence of each variable-part with other variables-parts, of each part with the whole system, and of the system with each of its important parts; (4) meaningful systems whose meanings make one consistent or complementary logical or aesthetic-intelligible whole (proposition, theory, aesthetic masterpiece marked by stylistic consistency of form and content); and (5) causal-meaningful systems whose parts display meaningful consistency as well as triple causal interdependence.

In other words, the term cultural system (ideological,

---

[4] See the samples of the widely different meanings that are given to the terms *integration* and *unification* in my *SCP*, pp. 337–341. These terms cover the phenomena of interaction, adjustment, adaptation, organization, concentration, coordination, centralization, control, interdependence, order, and many others.

material, and behavioral) designates only the causal, meaningful, or causal-meaningful complexes of cultural phenomena. The complexes united by spatial-time-mechanical proximity represent cultural congeries; those united by indirect causal relationships are called cultural semicongeries.

The term social system is applied only to those interacting groups of individuals that exhibit all six traits of the organized groups enumerated in Chapter 2. All interaction groups that do not have these characteristics will be called social congeries (unorganized and disorganized groups), or social semicongeries (intermediary, partly organized systems of interaction).

Finally, the reader should keep in mind the difference between social and cultural systems: Though both have three-componential structure and in part overlap, nevertheless social and cultural systems are not identical. Their boundaries, their modes of functioning, and their life careers do not coincide and display several *differentiae specificae*. The same is true of social and cultural congeries and semicongeries.

Now let us examine the total culture of the individual to determine whether it is completely integrated into one causal-meaningful consistent system, or if not, whether it represents a conglomeration of singularistic-ideological, behavioral, or material-cultural congeries, or the coexistence of many systems and congeries.

In Chapter 5, we noted that the atomistic-singularistic (Lockean) theories view the total ideological, behavioral, and material culture of the individual as a mere conglomeration of cultural congeries, whereas most of the systemic (Leibnitzian) theories affirm the coexistence of small and vast systems and congeries in the individual's total culture. Some systemic scholars insist on the complete integration of the total culture of the individual into one consistent cultural system:

Personality, insofar as it is not sick, meaning psychotic, is described by modern holistic psychology positively as a well-integrated whole in the strictest sense of the word, distinct from its surroundings, unified into a system, articulate, interdependent, supersummative, governed centrally, self-regulative, fitted with assimilatory and regenerative powers, holistically determined in its developmental process, "stylistically determined," a form, die-cast but alive and developing.[5]

Similar views are expressed by many other theories that, according to G. W. Allport, "do little more than assert personality to be an 'Indivisible Whole,' 'a total integrated pattern of behavior,' an *Unteilbarkeit*, an *in sich geschlossene Ganzheit*."[6] Many Oriental and Occidental, ancient, medieval, and modern philosophical and theological theories of personality, like the theories of Kierkegaard, Heidegger, Jaspers, and Marcel, see the supreme integration of personality in a transempirical "soul," "atman," "authentic being," "transcendence," "pneuma," "conatus," and similar metaphysical entities. And, in a milder form, they are also articulated by scientists: by physiologists who stress the self-preserving, self-repairing, self-regulating processes of the body, and by psychologists who see the unity of personality in its "striving," "conation," "congruence," or in the core of its "topological structure."[7]

These totalitarian theories are largely defective. Their first shortcoming is their vagueness. Their assertions of the complete unity of personality or the complete integration of the total culture of the individual rarely, if ever, specify exactly what they mean by unity and integration—whether they mean the causal or meaningful or causal-meaningful unity of the individual and of his ideological and/or behavioral and/or material culture; whether they mean the complete emotional, volitional, and cognitive harmony and the absence of conflicts in the inner life and overt behavior of the individual; or whether they view the individual as merely a biological organism and/or as a mindful, rational thinker and sociocultural being. Their propositions are

---

[5] O. Anderle, "Sorokin and Cultural Morphology," P. J. Allen (ed.), *P. A. Sorokin in Review*, p. 116.

[6] G. W. Allport, *Personality: A Psychological Interpretation* (New York, 1937), p. 343.

[7] See a survey of such theories in G. W. Allport's *Personality*. Samples of these sorts of theories are given in A. Wellek's *Person, Persönlichkeit und Charakter* (Mesenheim, 1951); E. Rothacker's *Die Schichten der Persönlichkeit* (München, 1951); E. Spranger, *Types of Men* (New York, 1928); W. Stern, *Allegemeine Psychologie* (1935); and K. Lewin, *Principles of Topological Psychology* (New York, 1936).

so general and so indefinite that to a large extent they become meaningless.

Their second defect is the theory of personality's structure and behavior.

Their third—and most important—defect is their blindness to many disharmonies, conflicts, inconsistencies, and contradictions given in the individual as a biological organism, as a mindful person, and as a sociocultural being.

This blindness is largely responsible for the totalitarian claims of these theories. Meanwhile, there is hardly any doubt that on all these levels there are many disharmonies, conflicts, and contradictions in the biological life, mentality, and behavior of normal individuals.

As a biological organism, the human individual is a causal unity in which each important part tangibly depends upon other important parts and upon the whole organism, and the whole organism depends upon its important parts. The causal system of the organism persists throughout its whole life—in periods of well-being and of illness, of healthy growth and of deterioration.

This triple causal interdependence in the organism does not mean, however, that all its parts or organs always function in mutual harmony, never conflict with one another, and never urge the organism to mutually contradictory actions. The existence of a multitude of various diseases and the early death of many individuals are uncontroversial proofs of the malfunctioning of various organs of the organism: If they were all functioning harmoniously, there would be few, if any, illnesses and deaths at an early age. If homeostasis were functioning unfailingly there would not be abnormal temperatures or other disequilibriums in the organism. The hypertrophical development of some tissue or organ at the cost of some other tissue or organ is clear evidence of conflict. Finally, the diverse biological drives of the organism frequently press it to mutually contradictory actions: hunger is now and then suppressed by a fear of, say, contaminated food; hunger now and then conflicts with sex impulse; sex impulse may conflict with other biological drives. The causal unity of the organism in no way guarantees either the mutual harmonious functioning of all its organs, or the absence of conflict.

Still more numerous are the conflicts and disharmonies between biological drives and the meaningful values and norms of the individual as a sociocultural conscious being: between the sex impulse and norms prohibiting unlawful sex relationships; between the temptation to overeat and rational consideration of its harm for the person with a defective heart or high blood pressure; between the spontaneous impulse to take revenge and moral commandments forbidding it; between the satisfaction of important biological needs and the ascetic vows taken by a monk or a nun. A multitude of such conflicts take place in the life of not only the abnormal but also in almost all normal persons.

No less numerous are the disharmonies and contradictions between the ideological, behavioral, and material cultures of the individual. Although there are many Christians who profess the ideological moral precepts of the Sermon on the Mount there are very few (if any) who realize these precepts in their behavioral and material cultures. The same can be said of the partisans of Judaism, Taoism, Confucianism, Hinduism, and Mohammedanism: Their overt conduct rarely, if ever, fully follows their moral commandments. Highfalutin ideological precepts and values are, as a rule, very rarely practiced in the behavioral and material cultures of almost all normal persons. Their overt deeds regularly contradict their noble preachings, and these noble preachings are often used to beautify the ugly deeds of the noble preachers. With a slight modification, the same can be said of the great chasm that separates the ideological and the material culture of the individual. Conflict and contradiction among the individual's ideological, behavioral, and material cultures is common to all normal and abnormal individuals.

Another set of meaningful conflicts, inconsistencies, and contradictions, experienced by almost all individuals, is the conflict between various egos or roles of the same individual. The individual often belongs to mutually antagonistic groups. Voluntary or involuntary membership in any group imposes upon its members a set of specified ideological, behavioral, and material rights and duties: Our family confers upon us the rights and duties of a father-mother-son-daughter; our occupational group requires from us a time-consuming set of activities; our state imposes upon us the many-sided duties of citizenship; our religious group and political party prescribe to us our religious and political ideologies and activities. Each group seeks to impress upon its members its own image; each attempts to mold us after its own pattern; each prescribes to us a detailed course of conduct; each demands from us a portion of our time and energy, a pound of our flesh, and a part of our soul or conscious mind. In this way each of the important groups installs into the individual its own ego, clearly specifying the role this ego has to play as long as the individual remains a member of the group.

These remarks explain the proposition that each of us has as many conscious sociocultural egos as there are organized groups of which we are members. The totality of these egos occupies almost the whole field of our conscious mentality, and the totality of these roles and activities fills a major part of our time, activities, and life. If the groups to which a given individual belongs are in a solidary relationship with one another, if they all urge the individual to think, feel, and act in the same or concordant way, push him toward the same or concordant goals, and prescribe to him the same or concordant duties and rights, then the different egos of the individual that reflect these groups will also be in harmony with one another, unified into a single, large harmonious ego. On the sociocultural level he will be blessed with peace of mind and consistency in his conduct. If the groups to which an individual belongs are in conflict, if they urge him to contradictory ideas, values, convictions, duties, and actions, then the individual's respective egos will be mutually antagonistic. The individual will be a house divided against himself and split by inner conflicts. His conduct will be irresolute, inconsistent, and contradictory; so also will be his thoughts, emotions, volitions, and utterances.

In a modern, greatly differentiated, and stratified society, an overwhelming majority of the individuals belong to many diverse groups. Their membership in some groups is voluntary, whereas in others—like citizenship in the state, compulsory draft into the army, or membership in a poverty-stricken group —it is often involuntary. As a result, among the several groups to which the individual belongs there almost always are two or more that are mutually antagonistic. Membership in such groups generates in the so-situated individual the conflicts and contradictions of those egos that are installed by these antagonistic groups. As long as the individual remains a member of such groups, his ideological, behavioral, and material conflicts, contradictions, inconsistencies, anxieties, hesitations, and emotional and mental disturbances will continue to deprive his personality of unity and to deprive him of real integration into his total culture.

Finally, if we examine the content of the individual's total culture, as we briefly did in Chapter 2, we shall certainly see that very few, if any, individuals have succeeded in unifying into one consistent ideological system all their ideas and beliefs, all their meaningful values, all the norms of conduct, and all their preferences and tastes. As a rule, the total ideological culture of practically all individuals represents a coexistence of a few vast and of many small ideological systems and a multitude of ideological semicongeries and congeries coexisting outside and inside of these systems. Some of the ideological systems are in consistent or mutually complementary relationships with one another, some are in neutral and some in mutually contradictory relationships to one another. Only in a small fraction of individuals are most of their ideological systems unified into one *Ganzheit*.

If we examine the content of the individual's ideological culture, as we did in Chapter 2, we find it to consist of many scientific, philosophical, religious, ethical, political, aesthetic, economic, and technical ideas, beliefs, values, norms, preferences, and tastes.

Our further examination of this ideological conglomeration discloses that some of these ideas-values-norms and tastes are unified into many logically and aesthetically consistent or complementary systems, whereas many others represent ideological fragments of odds and ends related to each other and to the systems only by spatial or time proximity. We observe that several of these systems are unified into vast consistent systems (by logical or aesthetic coordination, subordination, and complementariness), whereas several other systems are meaningfully neutral or even contradictory to one another and to the vaster systems.

In the total ideological culture of a few individuals we find now and then among its vast systems one dominant ideological supersystem that unifies not the total ideological culture of such persons but most of its vast and significant systems. Outside of this dominant supersystem in the total ideological culture of such individuals there are always several systems and congeries foreign or even inimical to it.

The presence of the dominant ideological supersystem in the total ideological culture of a person ordinarily signifies a notably higher degree of the integration of the ideological culture than when several systems and congeries coexist side by side without being unified into a vast dominant supersystem.

This higher degree of integration still falls short of the absolute or complete integration of the total ideological culture of an individual into one consistent supersystem. Regardless of the desirability or nondesirability of such a complete integration, it hardly ever exists in the total ideological culture of any individual, and remains extremely hypothetical.

In concrete analogical terms the outlined theory of the integration of the total culture of an individual compares the individual with a partly defective phonograph that now and then gets out of order. The phonograph represents the biological causal system, which now and then functions defectively. The ideological, behavioral, and material culture of the individual is represented by the records played by the phonograph—by the biological system of the human organism. According to the totalitarian theories this phonograph only plays those records that are installments of one logically and aesthetically unified story.

My criticism of these totalitarian theories is that the human phonograph (the individual) ordinarily plays records telling various kinds of stories or records of various kinds of music. Some human phonographs play many varied types of records. Some play their favorite records more frequently than those they do not particularly like. Finally, some phonographs play regularly records of a certain type: Baroque music, say, or Renaissance music or plays of a particular classical writer. But even these individuals, motivated either by their curiosity, or a desire to be modern, or just for the sake of variety, will occasionally play a very different kind of record. There are few individuals who prefer throughout their life to listen to only one kind of record or to see only one sort of movie, just as there are few individuals whose total culture consists of one completely unified cultural supersystem. The totalitarian integrators can hardly even find a single individual of that sort.

If we examine the behavioral and material culture of the individual, we observe that many mutually neutral or contradictory systems of actions and complexes of material cultures exist side by side with mutually harmonious systems of actions and material cultures, sometimes even unified into a behavioral or material supersystem.

Theories of the complete integration of the total culture of the individual are no less fallacious than the atomistic theories, which depict the total culture of the individual as a mere dump for a multitude of ideological, behavioral, and material congeries in mutually neutral or contradictory relationships to one another. Both individuals—totalitarian and atomistic—are a myth rather than a reality. On the empirical level, individuals range from those comparatively scatterbrained persons whose total culture represents a coexistence of many mutually consistent, neutral, and contradictory systems and congeries devoid of any unification into a supersystem to those persons whose total culture is integrated into a dominant supersystem. But the total culture even of scatterbrained persons is a unification of many meaningful and meaningful-causal systems; on the other hand, the dominant supersystem of highly integrated individuals hardly ever unifies their total culture into one consistent whole. It unifies only a large part of the significant systems of the total ideological, behavioral, and material culture. "The unity of personality is always a matter of degree. To be sure unity is never perfect, but only 'high level' concepts of consistency are capable of depicting adequately such unity as exists."[8]

If we examine this problem from the standpoint of the

[8] G. W. Allport, *Personality*, pp. 363 and 560.

integral theory of personality structure, we arrive at the same conclusion. Since an outline and analysis of this theory would unduly prolong the discussion of these problems I shall merely refer to works where such an analysis can be found.[9]

● The Total Culture of Small Groups or Small Areas

Another microsociological variety of the totalitarian theories is represented by several anthropological and sociological theories of the culture integration of small groups. Here are some typical formulas of such theories:

> A culture is a functioning dynamic unit and the various traits which compose it are interdependent. A culture trait does not function in isolation nor independently of other traits of the culture, but each is influenced by a change in any phase of the culture. . . . Since the traits which comprise a culture are interrelated, an innovation affects the entire culture.[10]

> To a greater or less extent, every cultural element is inextricably interconnected with other cultural elements and with the general cultural milieu itself. A culture is more than the simple mathematical addition of its individual parts.[11]

> No one would deny so obvious a statement that all aspects of a culture are interrelated.[12]

---

[9] See *The Ways and Power of Love,* chs. 5, 6, 7; my *SCP,* chs. 17, 18, 19, 35; and the *Dynamics,* Vol. IV, ch. 16. The main conclusion following from the integral theory of personality structure is that the complete integration of the total ideological, behavioral and material culture of the individual is possible only when: (*a*) the "supraconscious" in man completely controls the "rational-conscious egos" and the "bioconscious" and "unconscious" energies of man; (*b*) when the "socioconscious egos" are in harmonious relationship with one another and the "supraconscious" forces effectively and rationally control the bioconscious and unconscious forces of the human organism. These conditions are rarely, if ever, fully met by the human individuals; therefore, the completely integrated person is a very rare phenomenon in the human universe. (*Note:* the term "supraconscious" does not mean a supernatural or metaempirical force, but rather the highest form of creative energy ("genius") known in the empirical reality.)

[10] W. D. Wallis, *Culture and Progress* (New York, 1930), pp. 11, 12.
[11] S. Winston, *Culture and Human Behavior* (New York, 1933), p. 32.
[12] M. J. Herskovits, *Acculturation* (New York, 1930), p. 21.

With slight variations, this thesis of the complete integration of the total culture of many preliterate groups, small civilized groups, and culture areas has been stated by many functional and nonfunctional anthropologists, including B. Malinowski, R. Benedict, A. R. Radcliffe-Brown, C. Lévy-Strauss, M. Mead, E. Sapir, C. Wissler, R. B. Dixon, M. J. Herskovits, F. Graebner, W. Schmidt, and several functional sociologists and historians.[13]

They all seem to claim that any total culture is a unity, a functional whole, and that it has its own pattern and requires to be studied in its whole configuration if its separate traits are to be properly understood and interpreted.

Explicitly or implicitly the main thesis of the totalitarian integrators is also supported by all sociological theories of the main sociocultural factor, which supposedly tangibly determines all the other parts or compartments of a given total culture. "Such a dependence upon one and the same 'axis' (the main factor or variable or basic principle) of all the cultural phenomena makes all of them interdependent and bound together into one system."[14] Some sociological theories, like the Marxian, consider the economic factor as a unifying axis; other theories stress the geographic, the biological, the technological, the religious, the racial, the ethical, or the scientific factor as the integrating axis.[15] Any theory that contends that its main factor definitely conditions all the other parts of a given total culture

---

[13] See B. Malinowski, "Culture," in the *Encyclopedia of the Social Sciences*, Vol. 4; and A. R. Radcliffe-Brown, "On the Concept of Function in Social Science," *American Anthropologist* (1935). Also C. Wissler, *Man and Culture* (New York, 1923); R. B. Dixon, *The Building of Cultures* (New York, 1928); and R. Benedict, *Patterns of Culture* (Boston, 1934). See additional literature in R. Merton, *Social Theory and Social Structure*, ch. 1; D. Martindale, *The Nature and Types of Sociological Theory*, pp. 442–463; my *Dynamics*, Vol. I, ch. 1, and Vol. IV, ch. 3; P. L. van den Berghe, "Dialectic and Functionalism," *ASR*, October, 1963, p. 695. See also the papers of R. F. Spencer and I. C. Jarvie in D. Martindale (ed.), *Functionalism in the Social Sciences* (Philadelphia, 1965); and Claude Lévy-Strauss, *Structural Anthropology*, tr. by C. Jacobson and B. Schoepf (New York, 1963).

[14] The *Dynamics*, Vol. IV, p. 129. See there a development of this point.

[15] See the theories of this type in *CST*, *passim*.

is a variety of the totalitarian theory of the complete integration
of a given total culture.

To the group of totalitarian integrators belong also all those
historians and "culturologists" whose position is well voiced by
H. Becker in the following statement:

> Can historical data be torn out of their full context? Dare we
> assume when we begin an investigation that we can tear a
> closely-woven tapestry apart, sew the fragments on a "timeless"
> background, and get anything but a crazy quilt for our labor?
> . . . In order for separate characteristics . . . to have meaning,
> they must be considered with reference to the whole problem
> and to each other—they must be considered as a configuration
> united by logic of internal relationship. . . . Otherwise we shall
> have nothing left but a scattered collection of *disjecta membra*
> that helps us to explain nothing.[16]

It is on these grounds that many historians deny a sociology
that allegedly "tears historical data out of their full context."[17]

Some of the discussed "totalitarian integrators," like B.
Malinowski, steadily maintain their thesis of the complete integration of any total culture; others, like R. Benedict and C.
Kluckhohn, make reservations somewhat contradicting their
main thesis. On one page of Benedict's work we read: "A culture, like an individual, is a more or less consistent pattern of
thought and action. . . . This integration of cultures is not in the
least mythical. . . . Cultures at every level of complexity, even

[16] H. Becker, "Culture Case Study," *Social Forces* (1934), 399.

[17] See, for instance, H. Fisher, *History of Europe* (London, 1935),
Vol. I, p. vii; Charles Oman, *On the Writing of History* (New York,
1939); G. von Below, *Soziologie as Lehrfach* (Munich, 1920). On the
other hand, the denials by such historians of uniformities in historical
processes and their strictly ideographic standpoint of viewing all historical events as the unique phenomena unrepeated in time and space puts
them in the atomistic-singularistic group. The reason for this is that the
totalitarian and the atomistic theories are similar in their claim that all
historical and sociocultural phenomena are identically related to one another—either all are unified into one system (the totalitarian thesis) or
all exist as isolated singularistic-atomistic phenomena. Both currents of
thought fail to see the differences between sociocultural or historical
congeries related to one another only by spatial or time proximity and
causal and causal-meaningful systems: One drowns the difference by
submerging all systems in singularistic congeries; the other drowns the
congeries in one unified system.

the simplest, have achieved it." On the next page we read: "Some cultures . . . fail of such integration. . . . This lack of integration seems to be as characteristic of certain cultures as extreme integration is of others."[18]

These theories are suffering from diseases similar to those that affect the theories of the complete integration of the total culture of individuals. Most of these theories stop their analysis of culture-integration where it should begin. We may agree with Malinowski or Radcliffe-Brown that the total culture of the Trobrianders or the Andaman Islanders looks compact in the limited territorial culture-area inhabited by these tribes. But if we ask these scholars what kind of unifying ties bind together *all* traits, elements, and parts of each of these total cultures, we do not receive any answer to our question. Most of the totalitarian integrators fail to specify whether these ties are those of a mere spatial proximity, or of indirect causal bonds, or of tangible causal interdependence, or of meaningful and causal-meaningful binding relationships. We do not know whether the total culture of the Trobrianders or the Andamanese represents a mere spatial congeries or a semicongeries or causal or meaningful or causal-meaningful systems. If they are merely spatial congeries, then such a conglomeration cannot be called a unity or unified system. If they are semicongeries whose parts are unified by indirect causal ties, the investigators must show this—something they all fail to do. If each of these total cultures is one causal unity, they should prove this by demonstrating that in all groups where the Trobrian economic kula-kula transaction exists, the Trobrian type of kinship-marriage-magic-chieftainship and other cultural traits exist (because a causal relationship of A and B means that where A is given B is given, and where A is changing B is changing, or, if the causal relationship of A and B is twosided, then it signifies the coexistence and covariation of A and B; otherwise their relationship is not causal).

No attempt at such a proof can be found in the works of the totalitarian integrators. If they claim that the total culture of the Trobrianders or the Andamanese or the Samoans or the

[18] R. Benedict, *Patterns of Culture*, pp. 46–48.

Melanesians represents a causal-meaningful unity bound to-gether by meaningful consistency and tangible causal interde-pendence of all components and traits, then they should demonstrate the existence of such a unity and ties. Their hazy statements on the complete unity or integration of any total cul-ture are fairly meaningless and entirely indetermined.

The same can be said of C. Wissler's theory of the unified culture of the United States. According to Wissler, the dominant complexes of this unified culture are mechanical invention, mass education, universal suffrage, nationalism, militarism, the Bible, the sacred seventh day, and commercialism.[19] Let us agree that this is so. If, however, we ask by what sort of ties these dominant complexes are unified into one system and the nature of this system (is it a congeries? a semicongeries? a causal unity? a causal-meaningful unity?), we receive no answer.

Other integralists, like Radcliffe-Brown, endeavor to but-tress their claim by the argument that all elements of a given total culture are unified by being functions of the same organism, of the same unified system. "The function of a particular social usage is *the contribution it makes to the social life* as the func-tioning of the *total social system.* Such a view implies that a social system has a certain kind of unity which we may speak of as a *functional unity.* We may define it as a condition in which *all parts of the social system* work together with a sufficient degree of harmony or internal consistency; i.e., without pro-ducing persistent conflicts which can neither be resolved nor regulated."[20]

Arguments of this sort, offered by most of the functionalists, suffer from several diseases. First, they assume what has to be proved, namely, that all cultural phenomena are causally or meaningfully interdependent, and then proceed to claim that the whole culture is one unified system. In other words, the argument is but the old *petitio principii.* The absurdity of the claim is evident from the following reasoning: If the statement

[19] C. Wissler, *Man and Culture,* pp. 11 ff., 25 ff.
[20] Radcliffe-Brown, "On the Concept of Function in Social Science," p. 397.

is taken at its face value, it would mean that whatever two or more cultural phenomena (adjacent in space and time) we take, they are surely causally connected, because all cultural phenomena are causally interdependent. This implies that social science has reached such a height that there is no longer any need to study whether A and B are causally connected. We are told they are. There is no need to look for noncausal or accidental relationships between cultural phenomena found in any area or in any social group: Such relationships simply do not exist, because all cultural phenomena are interdependent. There is no need of any experimental, statistical, or other determination of the existence or nonexistence of causal relationships or uniformities between any adjacent cultural phenomena. We are assured that they are all tied together into one interdependent system. Therefore, the victory of A in a bridge contest, a sermon of Pope Paul, the birth of quintuplets in village M, a bullish trend in the stock market, an epidemic of influenza, and all the millions of phenomena and processes that seem to be little connected with one another *are* connected; we are assured of this by our "totalitarian interdependence" theories. If these theories were true, all the research institutions in the field of cultural phenomena, all the studies concerning relationships between cultural phenomena—statistical, experimental, clinical, etc.—all must be closed tomorrow. Since all cultural phenomena are interdependent, these researches and studies are a mere waste of time: They try to discover what has already been discovered once and for all by the universal formula of a universal interdependence of all cultural phenomena upon one another.[21]

Besides these grave logical errors, Radcliffe-Brown's and similar totalitarian and functionalist theories represent a sort of logico-empirical hash of spatial congeries, indirect causal, strictly causal, meaningful, and causal-meaningful relationships. This

---

[21] The *Dynamics*, Vol. IV, pp. 132–133. See there a development of this and other criticisms of the "totalitarian theories" discussed. This argument is equally applicable to the atomistic-singularistic theories claiming a universal accidental or chance relationship among all singularistic phenomena existing in a state of separation or isolation from one another.

hash is peppered by organic analogies and teleological ingredients. It contributes little, if anything, to our knowledge of the kinds of relationships between congeries and unities of cultural phenomena.[22]

In subsequent chapters it will be shown that this criticism is equally applicable to almost all the theories of cultural and social systems that use the terms equilibrium, adjustment, adaptation, interdependence, unity, and integration without either clearly defining them or differentiating congeries and semicongeries from causal and causal-meaningful systems. Most of the functional, totalitarian, and atomistic theories are badly infected with these diseases.

If we carefully analyze the total culture of any preliterate tribe, we find in it without any difficulty a multitude of congeries, semicongeries, and causal and meaningful-causal systems. If all these are found in the total culture of an individual, they are still more certainly present in the total culture of a tribe or of any—small or vast—organized group.

In some tribes, like the Dobu or the Zuni or the Hopi, the integration of the total culture may reach a comparatively high level, as, for instance, the Dionysian, Apollonian, ideational, or sensate supersystem unifying a large part of the important sys-

---

[22] "If by "functional" Radcliffe-Brown means the causal connections of the parts of a given cultural conglomeration, then it is hard to talk of such connections in the terms of harmony or disharmony, of inner consistency or inconsistency, because causal relationships are neither harmonious nor disharmonious, neither consistent nor inconsistent. They are simply either causal or not. The terms harmonious and the like are suitable as indications of the existence of logicomeaningful relationships between the parts. But Radcliffe-Brown nowhere mentions such relationship and talks of functionalism in the sense of causal functionalism. On the other hand, taking his definition of functionalism, one cannot separate a mere spatial congeries from causal unity. Any part of any spatial congeries "contributes something to the whole" of which it is a part. This, however, does not mean that it is causally connected with the rest of the congeries (dump of which it is a part). In brief, in his words "function" and "functionalism" he includes many different things, from the biological meaning of the terms in the connotation function-organ, to the fusion of spatial, external, causal, meaningful, and meaningful-causal forms of relationship. He does not have any means for separating the really causal-functional from the accidental." *Dynamics*, Vol. I, pp. 42–43.

tems of their total culture.[23] But even in such total cultures their unification into one dominant supersystem is never complete: Side by side with the parts unified into one dominant supersystem there are always other parts partly neutral and partly contradictory to the dominant supersystem.

The same can be said of such an "advanced" total culture as that of the United States. We may conditionally agree with C. Wissler in his enumeration of the dominant complexes of the total culture of the United States. But from the coexistence of these complexes in the total American culture it does not follow at all that these and other complexes of the American culture are united into one causal or one causal-meaningful supersystem.[24] For such a claim one has to prove that we cannot find nationalism without the other complexes; the veneration of the Bible without mechanical inventions; commercialism without mass education; militarism without universal suffrage, and so on. If someone contends that the total culture of the United States is unified into one meaningful-causal supersystem, then such a scholar has to prove that logically or aesthetically militarism is inextricably connected with mass education, that both logically require the veneration of the Bible, that this veneration requires commercialism, and so on.

It is perfectly obvious that neither Wissler nor anyone else can prove this. Empirically, militarism is found in cultures that have neither veneration of the Bible nor mass education nor any other of the dominant complexes of Wissler. Logically and aesthetically there is hardly any connection between these phenomena.

Finally, if we turn our attention to those totalitarian theories that try to buttress their thesis by making all traits, complexes, and elements of a total culture mere dependent variables of their

---

[23] See R. Benedict, *Patterns of Culture*, ch. IV; and L. Thompson, "Logico-Aesthetic Integration in Hopi Culture," *American Anthropologist* (1945), 540–553.

[24] C. Wissler's characterization of American culture as "unique," "typical," and as "a unity" is quite ambiguous. See his *Man and Culture*, pp. 11, 25 ff. More discerning, though still somewhat ambiguous, is R. M. Williams' theory of the unity of American society and culture outlined in his *American Society* (New York, 1961), ch. XIII.

main factor (or variable or principle), we shall see that none of these theories has succeeded as yet in proving either the all-powerful influence of the main factor (a part of the total culture) upon all other parts of the given total culture, or supported its claims by presenting the very minimum of evidence necessary for such a validation.[25] If this claim is largely invalid (in its fallacious statement that a part of a complex determines the whole complex), invalid also becomes the derivative thesis that through its main factor all cultures are unified into one causal or causal-meaningful unity.

All totalitarian theories of the complete integration of the total cultures of small areas or groups are largely fallacious. This conclusion is in substantial agreement with a similar conclusion of Merton that "The assumption of the complete functional unity of human society (or total culture) is repeatedly contrary to fact," and with the conclusions of D. Martindale, R. Lowie, A. Kroeber, C. Kluckhohn, and of many other investigators of these problems.[26]

[25] See the criticism of all such claims and theories in *CST, passim.*
[26] See R. Merton, *Social Theory and Social Structure* (Glencoe, Ill., 1957), p. 27; D. Martindale (ed.), *Functionalism in the Social Sciences* (Philadelphia, 1965), pp. 454–461; R. Lowie, *The History of Ethnological Theory*, pp. 234–235; A. L. Kroeber and C. Kluckhohn, *Culture* (Cambridge, Mass., 1952), p. 159.

CHAPTER 7

Recent "Totalitarian" Macrosociologies
of Civilizations and High Cultures

THE TOTALITARIAN MACROSOCIOLOGIES OF CULTURE

The last few decades have produced along with the upsurge of atomistic-singularistic and microsociological systemic theories, a rich harvest of impressive macrosociologies of great cultural and social systems. These theories, despite their shortcomings, are perhaps the greatest achievements of recent sociology and related sciences.

N. Danilevsky calls these vast cultural systems "culture-historical types," O. Spengler calls them "high cultures" (*die Hochkulturen*), A. J. Toynbee refers to them as "civilizations" or "intelligible fields of historical study," A. L. Kroeber calls them "high-value culture patterns," F. S. C. Northrop calls them "cultural systems" or "world cultures," N. Berdyaev calls them "great cultures," and I call them "vast cultural systems and supersystems." Whatever the name, practically all eminent investigators agree that they are real, causal-meaningful wholes, different from all cultural congeries and small cultural systems as well as from the state, the nation, political, religious, racial, ethnic, and other social groups.

The investigators seem to agree also that these civilizations, or cultural supersystems, like deep cultural undercurrents, largely determine most of the surface ripplings of the sociocultural ocean: the life, organization, and functions of smaller groups and cultural systems, the mentality and behavior of individuals, and a multitude of concrete historical events, trends, and processes. For this reason, a study of these vast sociocultural entities has not only theoretical but also great practical importance.

Without more or less adequate knowledge of these sociocultural continents, we cannot adequately know the what, how, and why of the structures and changes in the human universe, nor can we guide and control historical processes in a desirable direction.

Recent macrosociological studies of civilization and vast cultural supersystems display a variety of approaches and theories. I shall begin this examination with the totalitarian theories of civilizations and great cultures. Like other totalitarian theories they claim that each civilization or high culture is a vast cultural system unifying into one integrated whole the total culture of comparatively large, often supernational, contiguous culture-continents and of their populations. The most important examples of the macrosociological totalitarian theories are those of Oswald Spengler, Arnold Toynbee, and Nikolai Danilevsky. We shall begin our examination of these theories with Danilevsky's sociology of the great culture-historical types.

N. DANILEVSKY'S MACROSOCIOLOGICAL THEORY OF CIVILIZATIONS[1]

Nicolai J. Danilevský (1822–1885) first published *Russia and Europe* in the Russian Journal *Zaria* in 1869.[2] The conceptual framework of his theory is so similar to those of Spengler and Toynbee that it needs to be briefly outlined as the closest predecessor of Spengler's and Toynbee's theories.

Danilevsky sets forth his theory of the structure and dynamics of "historico-cultural types" not so much for its own sake as for the sake of explaining the much narrower problem

[1] A much more substantial analysis of Danilevsky-Spengler-Toynbee's theories is given in P. Sorokin, *Modern Historical and Social Philosophies* (New York, 1964), chs. 3, 4, 5. The book is also available in Spanish, German, and British editions under its previous title, *Social Philosophies of an Age of Crisis* (Boston, 1950).

[2] An abbreviated French translation of it under the title *La doctrine Panslavist d'après N. J. Danilevsky* was published in 1890 and its German translation, *Russland und Europa,* translated by K. Nötzell, was published in Berlin in 1920. A full bibliography of Danilevsky's publications is given in N. Danilevsky, *Sbornik polititsheskykh i economitcheskykh statey* (St. Petersburg, 1890), pp. 673–676.

of why Europe (and the West) remains perennially inimical to Russia:

> Europe does not consider Russia as its own part. . . . Europe sees in Russia and in Slavhood not only foreign, but an inimical force. . . . Russia and Slavhood have been hated not by some single European party or faction, but by all European parties. . . . No matter what interests divide Europe, all its parties unite together in their animosity towards Russia.[3]

And this animosity has persisted despite all the great sacrifices and services Russia made for Europe. Though Russia never invaded Europe, Europe has invaded Russia many times, forcing her to defend herself and expel her invaders.[4] Danilevsky finds no rational basis for the European animosity toward Russia:

> There is nothing conscious in this hatred for which Europe can account rationally. The real cause lies deeper. . . . It lies in those unfathomed depths of tribal sympathies and antipathies which are a sort of historical instinct of peoples and lead them towards a goal unknown to them. This unconscious tendency is responsible for Europe's hatred toward Russia.

This raises the question of why and how this antagonism between the Russian and the Teutonic-Romanic peoples appeared, has persisted, and is going to persist. Danilevsky's answer is that Europe and Russia belong to historico-cultural types alien to each other.

Europe is not merely a geographical entity but a unified historico-cultural whole. It is "an area of the Germano-Romanic civilization or . . . Europe is the Germano-Romanic civilization itself. These two terms are synonymous." This Germano-Romanic civilization is not universal but only one of several great civilizations that have flourished in human history. The widespread idea that European civilization is identical with universal civilization is based upon the fallacy that it is the only great civilization that is progressive and creative, in contrast to all

[3] All quotations are taken from the first edition of Danilevsky's *Rossia i Evropa* in *Zaria* (1869), nos. 1–9.

[4] See a corroboration of this in Toynbee's *Civilization on Trial* (New York, 1948), pp. 166–169.

other cultures, which are viewed as static and uncreative. The division, generally accepted by European historians, of historical events into the ancient, the medieval, and the modern periods is an example of these wrong assumptions. Western historians take the downfall of the Roman Empire as the event separating the ancient from the medieval periods and the discovery of America as the landmark between medieval and modern history. Logically as well as factually, this periodization is entirely fallacious. If its downfall in 476 A.D. was an important event for the Roman Empire, it was of no concern to China, India, and the greater part of mankind, which continued their course undisturbed by events in Roman history. As Danilevsky points out:

> Generally speaking, there is no single event which could reasonably divide the destiny of all of mankind into periods applicable to all humanity, for there never has been and hardly ever will be any event that will syncronously mean the same and be of the same importance to all of humanity. . . . [The] "ancient history" [of European historians] is but a replica of the artificial Linnaean classification of plants . . . whereby Greeks, Egyptians, and Chinese are lumped together simply because they all lived before the downfall of the Roman Empire. While Egypt, India, China, Babylon, Assyria, Iran, Greece, and Rome, each of which passed through several stages of development, are placed in one and the same group of ancient history, the stages of development of the Germano-Romanic peoples are divided into the Medieval and Modern periods.

As a result of this senseless periodization, Cato, Constantine the Great, Solomon, Ramses, Pericles, and the Gracchi are united into one group and one period (the ancient). Rudolf Hapsburg, the Emperor Maximilian, Philip the Fair, Louis XI, and even the Sultans Bayaset and Suleiman are separated from each other and put into different periods (the medieval and modern). "Such a classification," says Danilevsky, "is identical to that which puts a crow and an oyster into the same species because both of them do not have four legs."

This periodization and the assumption that European civilization is universal and the measure of all other civilizations is due to the European historians' false perspective: The close time proximity of European events and the superpatriotism of European historians make the differences between the European medieval and modern periods appear so great that the historians regard the numerous preceding centuries as mere background. But, as Danilevsky points out, "Strictly speaking, Rome, Greece, India, Egypt and all historical peoples each had its own Ancient, Medieval, and Modern periods; like any organism each of these had its own phases of development, though the number of these phases is not necessarily three."

Danilevsky concludes that just as modern biology replaced the artificial (Linnaean) classification of plants and animals with natural classification into a number of different types (genera and species) of organisms, each perfect in its own way, so also there are not one but many civilizations, each perfect in its own way and all together manifesting the infinitely rich creative genius of humanity. Only within the history of each of these types of civilizations can one talk of its ancient, middle, and modern phases of development. "Each civilization emerges, develops its own morphological form, its own values, thus enriching the total treasury of human cultural achievement, and then passes away without being continued in its specific and essential form by any other civilization."

Danilevsky divides, first, all peoples—past and present—into three main classes: the positive agents of history, the peoples who created great civilizations or historico-cultural types; the negative agents of history, the peoples and tribes, who, like the Huns, the Mongols, and the Turks, did not create great civilizations but as historical tornadoes or "whips of God" rendered the *coup de grâce* to senile, dying civilizations, helped them to die, scattered their remains, returned to their previous nothingness, and disappeared from the front stage of history; and the peoples and tribes whose creative *élan* is, for some reason, arrested at an early stage and who therefore are destined to be neither constructive nor destructive, neither positive nor negative agencies of history. They represent only ethnographic material used by creative peoples for the fertilization and enrichment of *their* civilizations. Most of the "unhistorical" tribes and peoples belong to this last class. Sometimes dead or decayed civilizations disintegrate to the level of "ethnographic material," until a new formative (creative) principle unites their elements with other elements into a new historical organism or civilization. The peoples that created the Roman Empire disintegrated after the fall of this empire into ethnographic material; eventually, however, after experiencing the influence of the Germanic formative principle, they re-emerged in a new form known as the Romanic peoples.

Only comparatively few peoples or tribes have been able to create great civilizations or to become "historico-cultural types." Danilevsky's list of such civilizations includes the Egyptian, the Assyro-Babylonian-Phoenician-Chaldean or Ancient Semitic, the Chinese, the Hindu-Indian, the Iranian, the Hebrew, the Greek, the Roman, the Neo-Semitic or Arabian, and the Germano-Romanic or European. Two civilizations, one Mexican, one Peruvian, met violent death at an early stage. Only peoples from these historico-cultures have been positive agents in the history of mankind. All of them developed in their own way the creative potential inherent in their spiritual nature as well as in the specific conditions of their environment, and thus enriched the common treasure of humanity.

Danilevsky then formulates the basic uniformities or laws governing the emergence, growth, and decay of civilizations, of the destructive type of peoples, and of the ethnographic-material peoples. In a schematic formulation these laws (again greatly and brilliantly developed) are as follows:

Law 1. Every tribe or family of peoples identified by a common language or by a group of languages whose resemblance is perceived directly, without deep philological explorations, constitutes an original historico-cultural type if it is mentally or spiritually capable of historical development and has already outgrown its childhood.

Law 2. It is necessary that a people enjoy political independence if its potential civilization is to be actually born and developed.

Danilevsky points out that the peoples of the ten creative civilizations had their own language or a language belonging to the same family of languages (say, the Semitic or the Aryan family of languages). "No civilization," he says, "has been conceived and developed without political independence, though after it has reached maturity a civilization (as exemplified by Greece) can live for a limited time after it has lost its independence. . . . The development of peoples who live in a state of political dependence is obstructed because such peoples are turned into a mere instrumentality serving the purposes of other peoples." Conquest and subjugation, together with unfavorable geographic and social conditions, account for the inability of an overwhelming majority of tribes to create their own civilization.

> Law 3. The basic principles of a civilization of one historico-cultural type are not transmissible to the peoples of another historico-cultural type. Each type creates its own civilization under the greater or lesser influence of alien-preceding or synchronous-civilizations.

Each of the ten civilizations diffused in its entirety only among the peoples of the common origin and of the common language—be it Egyptian or Semitic or Chinese. The Hebrew culture-type could not be transmitted to any of the non-Hebrew neighboring peoples. The numerous efforts to spread Greek civilization among the non-Aryan or Oriental peoples—even by means of Alexander the Great's conquest—all failed. In Egypt, where the Greek civilization blossomed for some time, it was carried on not by the Egyptians but by persons and groups of Greek origin. Learned Alexandria was but a Greek colony. Despite all efforts the Greek civilization could not be transmitted to Egypt and the Orient.

Today we can observe a similar failure by the English to transmit European civilization to India. Despite all efforts of the English to "europeanize" India, India still remains a Hindu or Indian and not a European type of civilization in its religious, aesthetic, and social life, political organization, and ethical folkways and mores. The same is true of other civilizations. Law 3, however, does not apply to the elements or features of a civilization. They can be transmitted from one civilization to another. The simplest way of diffusing civilization is by *colonization*. "In this way the Phoenicians handed their civilization to Carthage, the Greeks to Southern Italy and Sicily, and the

English to North America and Australia. The second way of diffusion is by *grafting.*" By grafting a scion into an alien plant we turn the plant into a mere means for the scion, which remains an alien, parasitical body in the grafted plant, exploits it, gets from it its nourishment, and does not benefit it in any way. Hellenic Alexandria, for instance, was such a cultural scion on the Egyptian tree, Roman culture on the Celtic trunk, and European culture on the body social of its African and Asiatic colonial peoples. The third way of influencing one civilization by another is by *fertilization* or *mutual cross-fertilization,* by borrowing the values of a civilization or by incorporating as a kind of fertilizer the ethnographic material of nonhistorical peoples or the debris of disintegrated civilizations. In science and technology such borrowing or fertilization is comparatively easy; with religious, philosophical, aesthetic, social, and ethical values it is more difficult. Any original civilization is a highly selective organism: It takes only those values or features of other civilizations that fit it and rejects those that do not harmonize with it.

Law 4. A civilization of a given culture-historical type reaches its fullness, variety and richness only when its "ethnographic material" is diverse and if the civilization enjoys political independence.

Law 5. The course of development of historico-cultural types is similar to the life-course of those perennials whose period of growth lasts indefinitely, but whose period of blossoming and fruitbearing is relatively short and exhausts them once and for all.

The earliest period of an emerging great culture can last for a long time. This period ends when the culture emerges from a merely ethnographic form of existence into a patterned form. During its second stage its cultural and political independence are established; its third, blossoming, phase represents a full development of all its creative potentials and the realization of its ideas of justice, freedom, wisdom, social, and individual well-being. This period ends when the civilization's fund of creative forces is exhausted. When this happens, some nations, like China, become petrified and uncreative or disintegrate into insoluble contradictions, inner conflicts, and disillusion. Of these three phases, the first (the "ancient") and the second (the "medieval") can last for an indefinite time; the last, the "modern" blossoming phase, is ordinarily fairly short, lasting on an average from 400 to 600 years. The subsequent phase of decline and distintegration sets in somewhat earlier than is observable. Thus, European civilization began to decline after the seventeenth century, but only in the nineteenth century when it was at the zenith of its blossoming did the first signs of its decline become noticeable. (This pattern is due to the same order of things that is observed in the temperature of a day. The highest culmination point of the sun is at noon, but the temperature on earth continues to rise some two or three hours after the sun has already begun to go down.)

Danilevsky has observed that most civilizations create only in one or a few fields and none is encyclopedic in its creative achievements. Thus, Greek civilization realized *beauty* to an extent unexcelled by any other civilization; it was creative in philosophy as well, but uncreative in many other fields. The main contribution of the Semitic civilizations has been religion; of the European, science and technology; of the Roman, law and political organization; of the Chinese, the practical, the useful; of the Indian, imagination, fantasy, and mysticism. When a civilization has fulfilled its creative mission, it is bound to die as a creative whole.

The real progress of mankind's life-course, according to Danilevsky, is not in a perennial linear movement in one and the same direction but of multilinear and multidirectional movements that cover the whole field of humanity's historical activities. The same is true of all great civilizations, each of which creates one or a few values and all of which together cover the field of creativity in all its main directions. No one civilization can boast that it is better than the preceding ones in all aspects of progress. Nobody can say that Cuvier was more intelligent than Aristotle; that Laplace was more intelligent than Archimedes; that Kant thought better than Plato; that Napoleon was a greater military genius than Caesar or Hannibal; or that Canova understood beauty better than Phidias or Praxiteles.

Danilevsky's work has contributed a great deal to what we

call the sociology of knowledge (*Wissensoziologie*) and to the comparative psychology of nations. He also formulated a few uniformities of lead and lag: that the blossoming of fine arts precedes that of science in the same civilization, and that political independence and unification precede cultural blossoming.

Finally, Danilevsky, in answering his initial question of why Europe hates Russia, delineates in detail the nature, interrelationship, and future of the European and Slavic historico-cultural types. Europe hates Russia and Slavhood because they represent different civilizations and because Europe has already entered its period of decline, whereas Slavic civilization is just about to enter its blossoming and most creative period. The European or Germano-Romanic civilization is a double civilization creative mainly in the political-economic and scientific-technological fields. The emerging Russian-Slavic civilization tends to be a triple or even quadruple type of civilization that creates in four fields of culture: religious, scientific-technological, political-economic and aesthetic, but mainly in the socioeconomic field through the building of a new and just socioeconomic order. European civilization is some 500 years older than the Russian-Slavic. The decline of European civilization manifests itself in many forms and syndromes: in the growing cynicism of Europe, in her de-Christianization, in her weakening creativity, and especially in her unsatiable lust for power and world domination. Such domination by any single civilization would mortally endanger humanity, would preclude the emergence and growth of a new type of civilization, and would put an end to the creative mission of mankind:

> Only united Slavhood can fight the united Europe. The united Slavhood does not threaten world domination but, on the contrary, it is the only possible guarantee for preserving world equilibrium and the only protection against the world domination of Europe. . . . As soon as Europe settles its own affairs, it will again invade Russia under the first handy pretext as was the case in the Crimean War.

However, federated Slavhood and its own emerging civilization will be able to withstand any onslaught by semisenile Europe, will take up the torch of world creative leadership from the exhausted European civilization, and will carry it on in the future until Slavic civilization itself begins to decline or to merge with the world civilization.

Such are the essentials of Danilevsky's macrosociological theory of civilizations. Begun as a political pamphlet of the highest grade, it became a brilliant and significant treatise on the philosophy of history or cultural sociology, and ended up by being an unusually shrewd and essentially correct piece of political prognostication and prophecy. *Russia and Europe* forecast, almost a century ago, the subsequent invasions of Russia by Europe and the continued struggle between the Europeanized West and Russian-Slavic world. If one removes the Marxist terminology and other secondary details from the policies and ideologies of Soviet leaders, one finds that Danilevsky's and the Soviet leaders' ideas regarding Russo-European relationships are essentially similar. In this matter, a most conservative Slavophil and a Communist Politbureau member can shake hands. Perhaps this fact has a much greater symptomatic significance than that of mere historical coincidence.

OSWALD SPENGLER

Spengler's *Der Untergang des Abendlandes* (*The Decline of the West*), published in 1918, has proved to be one of the most influential, controversial, and durable masterpieces of the first half of the twentieth century in the fields of cultural sociology, the philosophy of history, and German philosophy. Though in its total character *The Decline of the West* is quite different from Danilevsky's work, nevertheless its basic conceptual framework resembles Danilevsky's in all important points.

Like Danilevsky, Spengler (1880–1936) ridicules as "incredibly jejune and meaningless" the European division of history into ancient, medieval, and modern periods.[5] He replaces

---

[5] O. Spengler, *The Decline of the West* (New York, 1947), Vol. I, pp. 94 ff. All subsequent quotations are taken from this English translation of Spengler's work. A fuller analysis of Spengler's theory is given

this division by the "Copernican viewpoint," which considers every "High Culture" as important in the scheme of history as the Western or Classical cultures.

Like Danilevsky he considers human history not as a linear progress of one culture but as the "drama of a number of mighty Cultures, each springing with primitive strength from the soil of a mother-region to which it remains firmly bound throughout its whole life-cycle." Like flowers, the cultures grow with a superb aimlessness.

"Cultures are õrganisms," he says, "and world history is their collective biography." They emerge, grow, and having fulfilled their destiny, die:

> A culture is born in the moment when a great soul awakens out of the proto-spirituality of ever childish humanity, detaches itself, and becomes a form from the formless, a bounded and mortal thing from the boundless and enduring. . . . It blooms. . . . It dies when this soul has actualized the full sum of its possibilities in the shape of peoples, languages, dogmas, arts, states, sciences, and reverts into the proto-soul. . . . The aims once attained—the idea, the entire content of inner possibilities, fulfilled and made externally actual—the Culture suddenly hardens, it mortifies, its blood congeals, its (creative) force breaks down, and it becomes Civilization. . . .

Each culture . . . has its childhood, youth, manhood and old age. When the fire in the Culture's soul dies down, it enters its last phase—that of Civilization: "Every Culture has its own Civilization." Civilizations are the last, the most artificial states of Cultures:

> They are a conclusion. . . . Death following life, rigidity following expansion, intellectual age and . . . the petrifying world-city following mother-earth and the spiritual childhood of Doric and Gothic. They are an end of Cultures. They may, like a worn-out giant of the primeval forest, thrust their de-

---

in P. Sorokin, *Modern Historical and Social Philosophies*, ch. IV. For a comparison of Spengler's theory of civilizations with Sorokin's theory of cultural supersystems, see Gert Müller, "P. Sorokin und Oswald Spengler," in *Zeitschrift für philosophische Forschung*, *19*(1965), No. 1 and 2, pp. 110–134, 328–348.

caying branches toward the sky for hundreds or thousands of years as we see in China, in India, in the Islamic world.

In this petrified form they may even distort and hinder a full development of a newly emerging young Culture (so-called pseudomorphosis).

This stage of civilization is marked by cosmopolitanism and the megalopolis versus home, blood group, and fatherland; scientific irreligion or abstract dead metaphysics instead of the religion of the heart; mass instead of folk; money value instead of fruitful earth and real values; *panem et circenses* in lieu of religious and spontaneous folk festivals; and sex instead of motherhood. Urbanization, imperialism, the cult of bigness, syncretism, the lust for power, class-struggle, and the outward-directed man instead of the inward-directed are additional characteristics of the Civilization stage. In this agonizing or petrified state, Civilizations may last for long periods. Sometimes, they may even somewhat revive and have an "Indian summer." But, "finally, weary, reluctant, cold, Culture [in its Civilization phase] loses its desire to be, and wishes itself out of the overlong daylight and back in the darkness of proto-mysticism, in the grave." It reverts, in Danilevsky's terms, to "mere ethnographic material"—historyless and formless.

Before its death, however, the Civilization experiences the "spell of second religiosity," the fever of a new religious movement, a wave of mysticism or gnosticism such as the spread of the cults of Mithra, Isis, the Sun, or of Christianity (in ancient Rome). This "spell of second religiosity" marks the end of the life-course of the Culture and possibly the emergence of a new culture.

Spengler analyzes in detail each phase of culture in this life cycle. Instead of Danilevsky's ten great cultures, Spengler mentions only eight: the Egyptian, the Babylonian, the Indian, the Chinese, the Classical or Apollinian (Greco-Roman), the Arabian or Magian, the Mexican, and the Western or Faustian (which emerged around 1000 A.D.). He mentions the Russian as the next possibility. Of these nine cultures the Mexican died by violent death, the Magian (Arabian) and the Russian underwent "pseudomorphosis" at an early age—a partial suppression and distortion under the all-powerful influence of the older, "petri-fied" alien Civilizations. Spengler deals in detail with three of these cultures: the Classical or Apollinian, the Arabian or Magian (a designation including Arabic, Islamic, Iranian, Jew-ish, Syrian, Byzantine, Manichean, and early Christian), and the Western or Faustian. All these great cultures have passed through the described life-cycle of the High Cultures and are now either dead or in decline. Each of these Cultures passes from one phase to another in about the same length of time. The whole process has 50-, 100-, 300-, and 600-year periodicities.

Each of the great cultures is based on its own premise or "prime symbol." "The choice of prime symbol in the moment of the Culture soul's awakening into self-consciousness . . . decides all." This major premise or prime symbol determines the essential characteristics of the given culture: the character of its science and philosophy, of its mentality, of its art and beliefs, of its way of thinking, living, and acting. A given great culture articulates its prime symbol in all its main compartments.

Since the major premises of the High Cultures are different from each other, there is not one concept of numbers or mathe-matics, physics or chemistry, not one concept of the soul or mind, not one pattern of philosophy or religion or of the fine arts, but many such concepts and patterns—exactly as many as there are different cultures with their different prime symbols. The idea that there is or can be only one mathematics, one psychology, one sociology, one physics, or one biology is a myth, denied by historical as well as natural science evidence. Spengler develops this thesis and gives a body of evidence to corroborate it. This part of his work represents an important contribution to sociology of knowledge and of mental life.

The prime symbol of the Classical or Apollinian (Greco-Roman) Culture is the "sensuously present individual body as the ideal type of the extended." "Pure and limitless space" is the prime symbol of the Western or Faustian Culture. "The nude statue is Apollinian, the art of the fugue is Faustian." Apollinian are mechanical statics, the sensuous cult of the Olympian gods, the city-state, the doom of Oedipus, and the phallic symbol. Faustian are Galilean dynamics, Catholic and

Protestant dogmatics, the Baroque's great dynasties, the destiny of Lear and of the Madonna-like Beatrice. Mount Olympus, abode of the Classical gods, is a tangible geological formation. Valhalla, in Norse mythology, the hall where Odin receives the souls of slain heroes, is devoid of any sensory traits; it floats in a limitless space and is Faustian. So is the solitude of the Faustian souls—Siegfried, Parsifal, Tristan, Hamlet, and Faust himself: They are the loneliest heroes in any Culture. Along these lines Spengler draws a long series of examples showing the organic manifestations of the Faustian or Apollinian prime symbols in all main aspects of each of these cultures. He gives examples of how the prime symbol—the "stone" of Egyptian Culture and "the cavernous, eternal, vaulted space" of the Magian Culture are articulated in the science, philosophy, religion, psychology, fine arts, ethics, law, and politics of each of these cultures. "The prime symbol" of the Russian Culture is "plain without limit," of the Chinese Culture is tao—an indefinable, indeterminate, wandering, multilinear *way*. Spengler's whole work is a systematic demonstration of the cultural determination of all mental productions from numbers and mathematics to the notion of soul, mind, personality, the style of arts, ethics, politics, and economics. To repeat, this part of Spengler's work is one of the important examples of the *Wissensoziologie*.

If we ask how and why the High Culture originates, and why it runs its outlined life-cycle, Spengler's answer to these questions follows from his dualistic division of reality or "existence" or the world into two main aspects: the World-as-Nature and the World-as-History. The World-as-Nature is the image in which the man of higher culture interprets the impressions of his senses. The World-as-History is the image that he intuitively, instinctively, and then rationally creates in order to comprehend the world in relation to his own life. The World-as-Nature is an already fulfilled reality, the thing become, extended in space, static and dead, with invariable uniformities repeated again and again. It is studied along the principles of timeless causality by the physical sciences, which look for quantitative mechanical uniformities in the interrelationships of its "variables," and sum them up in formless, colorless formulas or generalized laws. The World-as-History is a living potentiality (life, soul) in a state of incessant becoming that fulfills its unique life-course or destiny in the time-process, never reversing its course and flowing from the past through the present to the future. Instead of causality it has destiny as an organic necessity of potentiality passing into actuality. It has rhythm in its becoming, full-blooded individuality, form, physiognomy, and unique events or facts. It is studied by historical "physiognomic," and is based upon the immediate, intuitive apprehension of the living potentiality (life, soul) by co-living or living into (*erfühlen*) the object, as opposed to dissecting it, by contemplating its destiny, and by the logic of time. Historical cognition or comprehension is therefore basically different from natural-science cognition. History is art rather than science: It is neither true nor false (as science) but, as art, is either deep or shallow.

These two aspects of the world manifest themselves in two different types of consciousness—historical and natural scientific—and lead to two different morphologies in the historical and the natural-science disciplines.

To the question, What are the factors governing the emergence of a High Culture and of its destined life-cycle?, Spengler replies that these matters are a mystery "that is not to be explained by any why and wherefore" because the causality principle is inapplicable to the World-as-History.

Here the inward necessity of direction or destiny, grasped by intuition, reigns supreme and is an explanation in itself. "We observe that swift and deep changes assert themselves in the history of great Cultures, without assignable causes, influences or purposes of any kind. . . ." The sudden emergence in the ocean of "primitive culture" of the High Culture of Egypt and Babylon or Sumer is an unforeseen incident and a mystery from a causal standpoint. It is not due to specific geographic, racial, or other causal factors, because it is not a given tribe or race that selects the Culture; rather, it is the suddenly emerging Culture that makes the choice of which tribe or people becomes its instrumentality, its living agents. This choice is made by cosmic forces, which determine which of many prehistorical cultures becomes a High Culture.

The life-cycle of great cultures and the place and time of their appearance are also concealed in the cosmic universe, and are beyond our causal understanding. But the destiny-cycle of these cultures is somewhat known to us by the way of instinctive, intuitional "historical logic of destiny."

The preceding is a concise outline of Spengler's macrosociology of the High Cultures. He outlines, also more cursorily, the social forms or social systems corresponding to the childhood, youth, maturity, and old age of the great Cultures.

In the pre-Cultural stage, early man is a carnivorous, raging animal, nomadic, keen, fighting hostile nature. With the development of agriculture, man becomes a peasant, settled and rooted in the earth; he discovers a soul in nature and nature becomes for him *Mother* Earth. The peasant is historyless, an eternal man, independent of every culture. His piety is older than any organized religion; his ethics and metaphysics lie outside of all religious and spiritual history—in fact they have no history at all. In this pre-Cultural stage there are no classes, no mass, no state, no politics. There are only blood-related nomadic and agricultural tribes with their chiefs and their protomystical "souls." They serve as "ethnographic material" for others.

The early period of the rising culture consists of two social phases: feudalism and the aristocratic state. The emergence of Culture is marked by two epoch-making phenomena: the emergence of the city and of the primary classes of the nobility and the priesthood. The pre-Cultural tribes and folk begin to organize into a feudal nation and state. Intellect emerges in the form of religious-chivalric ideas, idealism, and values. Subsequently, feudalism with its economics, politics, and values dissolves and is replaced by the aristocratic state. The role of the city and intellect increases. The early phase of Culture begins to pass into its late phase, in which the idea of the state and national government is realized in its full form. A third class—the bourgeoisie— emerges and grows. The city begins to dominate the countryside politically, economically, technically, and intellectually. Urban values replace agricultural ones. Money emerges victorious over landed property and values. The bourgeoisie grows in its influence and prestige. Politically, this phase has three subphases:

the structuralization of states and their forms; the absolutization of the state and the establishment of absolute monarchies, and the coordination of the nobility, clergy, and bourgoisie into a unified nation; the breakdown of the absolute state and absolutism, and the revolution and victory of "the people" over the privileged, of intelligentsia over tradition, of money over property, of urbanization over agriculturalism.

In the last, Civilization phase of Culture, the body of the people, now predominantly urban, dissolves into a formless mass. The state, the nation, and the social estates tend to disintegrate. The city grows into an artificial, cosmopolitan, pathological megalopolis. With it appears the fourth estate—the "masses." In the process of revolutions and anarchy, "Caesarism" emerges, a tyrannical dictatorship of various upstarts and politicians. Just as in the late period of culture money becomes victorious over aristocratic policies and values, so now the politics of rude force triumphs over money and the money policies of the bourgeoisie.

The megalopolitan cities are "wholly intellect." They are not "home." Their disproportional growth, their contrasts of poverty and riches, their artificial life and *taedium vitae* hastens their death. Today, the lord of the world, Western man, is becoming the slave of the machine. All organic things are dying in the grip of this megalopolitan machine organization. The machine in the end defeats its own purpose. In the stone-steel cage of his cities, Western man begins to be sick of machines and civilization and starts returning to simple forms of life, to Nature. Second religiosity is already under way. The exploited colonial peoples are rising against the megalopolitan white man. The machine civilization is beginning to destroy itself and one day "will lie in fragments, forgotten, our railways and steamships as dead as the Roman roads and Chinese wall, our giant cities and skyscrapers in ruins like old Memphis and Babylon. The history of the megalopolitan machine technics is fast drawing to its inevitable close. It will be eaten up from *within*, like the grand form of any and every Culture. When, and in what manner, we know not."

In a similar way, money and democracy undermine themselves and are "eaten up from within," giving way to the victorious policy of undisguised force and Caesarism. The passage of Democracy into Caesarism—the government of formless dictatorial arbitrariness—is marked by the following steps. At its outset, democracy is controlled by the responsible, noble, and pure intellect. It introduces a bill of rights and equality under the law. Soon, however, it turns out that one can enjoy his constitutional rights only if one has money. The leadership thus passes from the idealist intellect to the shrewd money-maker, the bourgeois. Money begins to control the vote and the voters through its political machinery. Democracy through its newspapers and mass magazines eventually expels the book from the people's mental life. Through the press, mass education, and mass propaganda, it teaches the people to think less and less for themselves and to accept what is offered by mass media. The book world that compelled the individual to think, select, and criticize now becomes the possession of only a few. The people read the one paper, "their paper," which spellbinds the intellect from morning to night, brainwashes its readers, drives serious books into oblivion, promotes the books it wants, and kills the books it disapproves of. What is truth under democracy? That which the press (and other mass media of communication) wills. The press evokes, transforms, interchanges, and manipulates truth as it pleases. After three weeks of press propaganda, the "truth" is acknowledged by everybody. Of course, there is freedom of speech in a democracy, but the press is free to notice or not to notice what the citizen says. It can condemn any "truth" to death simply by passing it by in silence, by not communicating it to the world. In lieu of the inquisitorial stake and faggot there is the great silence, which paves the way for the Caesars. The party leaders indoctrinate their followers with articles, telegrams, and pictures until the masses clamor for weapons and, seemingly force their leaders to the dictatorship at which, of course, they have carefully aimed. In the world of truth it is proof that decides all, but in the world of this sort of politics it is success that counts. The mass media are the means by which the power elite controls the masses, their minds and their actions. Parliaments, congresses, and elections are a mere preconcerted game, a farce, staged in the name of people's freedom and self-determination. "This is the end of Democracy," says Spengler; "Through money, democracy becomes its own destroyer, after money has destroyed intellect." Noble intellectual and moral leaders of the beginning of democracy are now replaced by unscrupulous and nonintellectual politicians. Government of the people, by the people, and for the people is replaced by "government of politicians, by politicians, and for politicians." Fights, disturbances, and insecurity become chronic. Tired and disgusted with the bickering, the people begin to hope for salvation from some other source and are ready to exchange their illusory "inalienable rights" for the security and order promised by a would-be Caesar. Caesarism grows on the soil of degenerated democracy and sooner or later conquers it. It establishes a money economy and a simulacrum of political order. Caesarism is the final phase of civilization. Eventually, barbarization sets in, and the culture's social form steadily disintegrates. It ends with "second Religiosity" and with the forms that it—and its church— imposes upon the remnants of the culture's life-cycle. Its social and creative history is ended.

Such in brief is the cycle of *social* forms or systems corresponding to the main phases of the culture's life-history. The many pages that Spengler devotes to a detailed analysis of these transformations are fresh, penetrating, and classic— worthy of Plato's and Aristotle's analyses of how the main political regimes pass into one another, from the government of philosophers into that of tyrants and mobs.

Spengler's views concerning the diffusion and transferability of one culture to another are similar to Danilevsky's. Each culture is unique and can be fully understood only by men of this culture. When one culture borrows the elements of another they serve merely as material for the self-expression of the borrowing culture. The Western interpretation of Plato is mainly a misinterpretation. Present-day Roman law is quite different from the Roman law of the Romans. The Christianity (Spengler ascribes its creation to the Arabian or Magian, and not to the Classical or the Western cultures) of the Western world after the eleventh century, with its dogmas, ritual, hierarchy, and spirit, would be rejected by St. Paul and St. Augustine, for it is basically different from the Magian Christianity of the first centuries of our era. In brief, each culture is closed to all who are alien to it and is fully comprehensible only to itself and to its own members.

Despite its defects, *The Decline of the West* is likely to survive as one of the most important works of the first half of the twentieth century.

ARNOLD J. TOYNBEE

Arnold J. Toynbee's theory of civilization can be regarded as the culmination of the theories of civilizations exemplified by the works of Danilevsky and Spengler. Conceived independently from their works and based on incomparably more solid historical evidence, Toynbee's monumental *Study of History*[6] is a real masterpiece of historical and macrosociological knowledge. The following discussion of his theory gives only an idea of his magnificent and full-blooded interpretation of social, cultural, and historical processes. The outline follows Toynbee's theory as it was developed in the first six volumes of his work. He made important changes in this early version in the last six volumes of his work, especially in the twelfth volume, *Reconsiderations*, and these will be briefly mentioned after a discussion of the first version of his comparative study of great cultures or civilizations.

Toynbee (1889–   ) begins with the thesis that the proper field of historical study is neither a description of singularistic happenings contiguous in space or time nor a history of the states and bodies politic or of mankind as a "unity": "The 'intelligible fields of historical study' . . . are societies which

---

[6] Arnold J. Toynbee, *A Study of History* (12 vols.; London, New York, Toronto, 1939–1961). Subsequent quotations are taken from these volumes. An abridged version of these volumes is given in D. O. Somervell's *A Study of History* (2 vols.; New York, London, 1957). See further, Arnold J. Toynbee, *An Historian's Approach to Religion* (London, New York, Toronto, 1956).

have a greater extension, in both Space and Time, than national states or city-states, or any other political communities. . . . Societies, not states, are 'the social atoms' with which students of history have to deal."

He perceives "civilization," with its religious, territorial, and political traits, as the proper object of historical study, for a "civilization" is a "species of society." Of such civilizations, he takes twenty-three full-blown, "related and unrelated" species: the Western, two Orthodox Christian (in Russia and the Near East), the Iranic, the Arabic, the Hindu, two Far Eastern, the Hellenic, the Syriac, the Indic, the Sinic, the Minoan, the Sumeric, the Hittite, the Babylonic, the Andean, the Mexic, the Yucatec, the Mayan, the Egyptiac, and four "arrested civilizations"—the Eskimo, Nomadic, Ottoman, and Spartan—and five "abortive" ones.

Toynbee attacks, first, the problem of the genesis of civilizations: Why do some societies, like many primitive groups, become static at an early stage of their existence and fail to emerge as civilizations, whereas other societies do reach this level? His answer is that the genesis of civilization is due neither to the race factor nor to geographic environment as such but to a specific combination of two conditions: the presence of a creative minority in a given society, and an environment that is neither too unfavorable nor too favorable. The groups that had these conditions emerged as civilizations; the groups that did not have them remained on the subcivilization level. The mechanism of the birth of civilization in these conditions is formulated as an interplay of challenge and response, with the environment incessantly challenging the society, and the society, through its creative minority, successfully responding to the challenge and solving the need. A new challenge follows, and a new response successfully ensues; and so the process continues. In these conditions no possibility of rest exists, the society is on the move all the time, and such a move brings it, sooner or later, to the stage of civilization.

The next problem of the study is why and how the Far Western Christian, Far Eastern Christian, Scandinavian, and Syriac civilizations proved abortive and why and how the

Eskimo, Nomadic, Spartan, and Ottoman civilizations were arrested in their growth at an early stage. The answer evidently depends upon the meaning of growth and its symptoms. In Toynbee's opinion, the growth of civilization is not, and is not due to, a geographic expansion of the society. If anything, the geographic expansion of a society is positively associated with retardation and disintegration but not with growth. Likewise, the growth of civilization does not consist in, and is not due to, technological progress and to the society's increasing mastery over the physical environment: "There is no correlation between progress in technique and progress in civilization." The growth of civilization consists in "a progressive and cumulative inward self-determination or self-articulation" of the civilization; in a progressive and cumulative "etherialization" of the society's values and a "simplification of the civilization's apparatus and technique." Viewed from the standpoint of intrasocial and interindividual relationships, growth is an incessant creative "withdrawal and return" of the charismatic minority of the society in the process of the ever new successful responses to ever new challenges of the environment. A growing civilization is a unity. Its society consists of the creative minority freely imitated and followed by the majority—the Internal Proletariat of the society and the External Proletariat of its barbarian neighbors. In such a society there is no fratricidal struggle, no hard and fast division. It is a solidary body. A growing civilization unfolds its dominant potentialities, which are different in different civilizations: aesthetic in the Hellenic civilization; religious in the Indic and Hindu; scientifically mechanistic in the Western; and so on.

The third main problem of the study is how and why civilizations break down, disintegrate, and dissolve. They evidently do so, for, of some thirty species of civilizations, "only four have miscarried as against twenty-six that have been born alive," and "no less than sixteen out of these twenty-six are by now dead and buried" (the Egyptiac, the Andean, the Sinic, the Minoan, the Sumeric, the Mayan, the Indic, the Hittite, the Syriac, the Hellenic, the Babylonic, the Mexic, the Arabic, the Yucatec, the Spartan, and the Ottoman). Of the remaining ten civilizations living, "the Polynesian and the Nomadic civilizations are now in their last agonies and seven out of eight others are all, in different degrees, under threat of either annihilation or assimilation by our own civilization of the West."

The main difference between the process of growth and the process of disintegration is that in the growth phase the civilization successfully responds to a series of ever new challenges, whereas in the disintegration stage it fails to give such a response. The author's verdict is that civilizations perish through suicide, not by murder. In his words, "the nature of the breakdowns of civilizations can be summed up in three points: a failure of creative power in the minority, an answering withdrawal of mimesis on the part of the majority, and a consequent loss of social unity in the society as a whole."

Expanding on this, he says:

> When in the history of any Society a Creative Minority degenerates into a mere Dominant Minority which attempts to retain by force a position which it has ceased to merit, this fatal change in the character of the ruling element provokes, on the other hand, the secession of a Proletariat (the majority) which no longer spontaneously admires or freely imitates the ruling element, and which revolts against being reduced to the status of an unwilling "underdog." This Proletariat, when it asserts itself, is divided from the outset into two distinct parts. There is an "Internal Proletariat" (the majority of the members) and . . . an "External Proletariat" of barbarians beyond the pale who now violently resist incorporation. And thus the breakdown of a civilization gives rise to a class-war within the body social of a society which was neither divided against itself by hard-and-fast divisions nor sundered from its neighbors by unbridgeable gulfs so long as it was in growth.

This decline phase consists of three subphases: the breakdown of the civilization; its disintegration; and its dissolution. The breakdown and dissolution are often separated by centuries, even thousands of years, from one another. For instance, the breakdown of the Egyptiac civilization occurred in the sixteenth century B.C., and its dissolution only in the fifth century A.D. For the 2,000 years between breakdown and dissolution it lived a "petrified life in death." The Far Eastern civilization is in a similar "petrified" state at the present time; it has lingered on in

China since its breakdown in the ninth century A.D. About 1,000 and 800 years, respectively, elapsed between the breakdown and dissolution of the Sumeric and Hellenic civilizations. Like a petrified tree trunk, such a society can linger in that stage of life-in-death for centuries, even for thousands of years. Nevertheless, the destiny of most, if not all, civilizations, seems to be to come to final dissolution sooner or later. As for Western society, though it seems to have had all the symptoms of breakdown and disintegration, the author is noncommital. He still leaves a hope for a miracle.

Toynbee analyzes in detail the uniformities, symptoms, and phases of the decline of civilizations in Volumes IV, V, and VI. Only a few of these uniformities can be touched on here. In the growth period, the "Creative Minority" gives a series of sucessful responses to ever new challenges, whereas in the disintegration period it fails to do so. Instead, intoxicated by victory, it begins to "rest on its oars," to "idolize" the relative values as absolute; it loses its charismatic attraction and is not imitated and followed by the majority. Therefore, it must increasingly use force to control the internal and the external proletariat. In this process it creates a universal state, like the Roman Empire, which was created by the Hellenic dominant minority, as a means of keeping itself and the civilization alive. It engages in war, becomes a slave of intractable institutions, and works its own and its civilization's ruin.

The internal proletariat now secedes from the minority, becomes dissatisfied and disgruntled and often creates a universal church—for instance, Christianity or Buddhism. The universal state of the dominant minority is doomed, but the universal church of the inner proletariat (for instance, Christianity) serves as a bridge and foundation for a new civilization "apparented" by and "affiliated" with the old one.

In his *Civilization on Trial,* however, Toynbee somewhat changes his position and maintains that the successive rises and falls of civilizations foster the growth of religion: They become "steppingstones to higher things on the religious plane."

The external proletariat now organizes itself and begins to attack the declining civilization, instead of striving to be incorporated by it. In this way schism enters both the body and soul of civilization. It results in an increase of strife and in fratricidal wars that lead to ruin. The schism in the soul manifests itself in the profound change of the mentality and behavior of the members of the disintegrating society. It leads to an emergence of four types of personality and "Saviors": Archaist, Futurist (Saviors by Sword), detached and indifferent Stoic, and— finally—Transfigured Religious Saviors, posited in the ᶜ super- sensory world of God. Drift and sin begins to grow; promiscuity and syncretism become dominant. Vulgarization and proletari- zation" invade the arts and sciences, philosophy and language, religion and ethics, manners and institutions.

But all in vain. With the exception of the "Transfigured Saviors," nothing halts the disintegration. The only fruitful way is the way of Transfiguration, the way of transferring the goal and values to the supersensory Kingdom of God. It may not stop the disintegration of the given civilization, but it may serve as a seed for the emergence and development of a new affiliated civilization, which is a step forward in the eternal process of elevating Man to Superman and "the City of Man to the City of God"—their ultimate terminal points. The volumes close with an almost apocalyptic note: "The aim of Transfigura- tion is to give light to them that sit in darkness. . . . It is pursued by seeking the Kingdom of God in order to bring its life . . . into action. . . . The goal of Transfiguration is thus the Kingdom of God."

The whole human history or the total civilization process thus turns into a creative theodicy. Through separate civiliza- tions and their uniform, but concretely different, rhythms, the reality unfolds its richness and leads from "under-Man" and "under-Civilization," to Man and Civilization, and finally to Superman and Transfigured Ethereal Super-Civilization of the Kingdom of God.

In *Civilization on Trial,* Toynbee contends that the move- ment of civilizations may be cyclic and recurrent, whereas the movement of religion may be on a single continuous upward level. "It may be served and promoted in its Heavenwardly progress by the cycles of birth and death of civilizations."

Christianity appears to be the final goal of human history and the highest measure of man's greatest good on earth.

In the twelfth volume of his work, Toynbee summed up a number of the important changes he had made in the outlined, earlier formulation of his theory of civilizations.[7] His first list of civilizations was as follows:

I. *Full-blown Civilizations*
  A. First Generation, Unaffiliated to others: Egyptiac, Andean
  B. First Generation, Unaffiliated to others: Sumeric, Minoan, Indus, Shang, Mayan
  C. Second Generation, Affiliated to others: Babylonic (to Sumeric); Hittite (to Sumeric); Hellenic (to Minoan); Syriac (to Minoan); Indic (to Indus); Sinic (to Shang); Yucatec (to Mayan); Mexic (to Mayan)
  D. Third Generation, Affiliated to others: Orthodox Christian, main body (to Hellenic); Orthodox Christian, Russian offshoot (to Hellenic); Western (to Hellenic); Arabic Muslim (to Syriac); Iranic Muslim (to Syriac); Hindu (to Indic); Far Eastern, main body (to Sinic); Far Eastern, Japanese offshoot (to Sinic)
II. *Arrested Civilizations*: Eskimo, Nomadic, Osmanli, Spartan
III. *Abortive Civilizations*: First Syriac, Far Eastern Christian, Far Western Christian, Scandinavian, Medieval Western City-State Cosmos

His revised list of civilizations is as follows:

I. *Full-blown Civilizations*
  A. Independent, unrelated to others: Middle American, Andean
     Unaffiliated to others: Sumero-Akkadian, Egyptiac, Aegean, Indus, Sinic
     Affiliated to others (first batch): Syriac (to Sumero-Akkadian, Egyptiac, Aegean, and Hittite); Hellenic (to Aegean); Indic (to Indus)
     Affiliated to others (second batch): Orthodox Christian, Western, Islamic (all affiliated to both Syriac and Hellenic)
II. *Abortive Civilizations*
     First Syriac (eclipsed by Egyptiac); Nestorian Christian

---

[7] For the reasons and details of this resurvey and reclassification of civilization see Volume XII of *A Study of History*, pp. 546–561.

(eclipsed by Islamic); Monophysite Christian (eclipsed by Islamic); Far Western Christian and Scandinavian (eclipsed by Western); Medieval City-States Cosmos (eclipsed by Modern Western)

A diagram accompanying the outline clearly sums up the periods of emergence, "pre-universal-state phase," and "universal-state phase" of each of these civilizations between 3000 B.C. and A.D. 2000. Toynbee's commentaries on the reasons for his revision of the first list of civilizations are most informative and give an up-to-date account of the extant historical and archeological knowledge of this problem.

Toynbee, in Volume XII, replaces his theory of the univariant life-cycle of civilizations by a theory of multivariant ones. In the first six volumes of his work his view of this problem was similar to those of Danilevsky and Spengler: All civilizations undergo a univariant cycle in their life-course; they emerge, grow, and then decay. Toynbee's subsequent study of this problem led him to the conclusion that "I have been at fault in having been content to operate with the Hellenic model (of civilization) only. Though this particular key has opened many doors, it has not proved omnicompetent. For example, it has not opened the door to an understanding of the structure of Egyptian history." As a result of this more careful investigation he replaced his earlier univariant theory by at least three different models of the life-course of civilizations as exemplified by the Hellenic, the Chinese, and the Jewish civilizations.[8]

EMERGENCE OF THE SCIENCE OF CULTURAL MORPHOLOGY OR CULTUROLOGY

Partly independently from Spengler but also partly under the influence of his theory of the *Hochkulturen*, a series of investigations has led, particularly in Austria and Germany, to the emergence and development of the science of cultural morphology, or culturology, a science specifically devoted to

[8] *Reconsiderations*, p. 186.

the study of vast sociocultural systems.[9] The essential points of this science are outlined by a leading Austrian cultural morphologist, Othmar Anderle:

> The lethal threat to which the Western World has been exposed since the end of World War II, has awakened an awareness among the peoples of the Occident that they form a community with a destiny. . . . The expression of this unity has been discovered in the concept of civilization (*Hochkultur*) which, since Spengler's *Decline of the West,* has been on everybody's tongue and has become replete with content. . . .
>
> The concept of civilization has become, for us, a dominant historico-sociological category similar to the earlier concept of nation, which was a predominant historico-sociological category before. "Thinking in terms of civilizations has supplanted thinking in terms of nations. . . ." This has become apparent also in science, where the emphasis has been shifted from peoples and nations to more comprehensive structures and processes in civilizations. . . . Since Spengler, we have called the science which deals with what is formal in the structural aspects of cultural phenomena "cultural morphology." This term was, however, not introduced by Spengler, but by Leo Frobenius. Today Spengler is looked upon as the classical cultural morphologist. As far as the subject itself is concerned, there have been cultural morphologists long before Spengler (like Giambattista Vico).[10]

[9] Several scholars of various countries have advocated the establishment of a special science of culturology devoted to a study of cultural phenomena, differentiated from the science of sociology, which deals with social phenomena. Later on, something more will be said about culturology as a special science. On the science of culturology, see Leslie White's *The Science of Culture* (New York, 1949); A. L. Kroeber, *The Nature of Culture* (Chicago, 1952), essays 13, 14, and *passim*; A. Hilckman, "Geschichtsphilosophie, Kulturwissenschaft, Soziologie," in *Saeculum,* XII, 405–420; and Wen-shan Huang, *Collected Essays on Culturology* (Canton, 1939), and the *Theoretical Trends of Culturology* (Taipei, 1959). As distinguished from the Austrian-German cultural morphology, most of these culturologies do not fully subscribe to the main theses of totalitarian theories of culture integration. For this reason, they are not outlined in this chapter.

[10] Othmar F. Anderle, "Sorokin and Cultural Morphology," in P. J. Allen (ed.), *P. A. Sorokin in Review,* pp. 94–95. As a matter of fact, a number of problems of cultural morphology were discussed by many thinkers before Vico, especially in connection with the problems of social, cultural, and personal unity, cycles, rhythms, and periodicities in the life-courses of such unities or systems. See a history of such theories in

Structured cultural wholes are, according to Anderle, (*Ganzheiten*) "very precise nonhomogeneous units of any substratum whatever which are more or less clearly distinguishable from their surroundings, are more or less abundantly articulated and logically, as well as ontologically antecedent to the members or parts which are discernible in the whole. . . . The existence of such structures is a relatively recent discovery."[11]

Influenced by Spengler, Toynbee, Koneczny, and partly by myself a group of scholars during the last few decades or so have become absorbed in the systematic elaboration of cultural morphology as a science of cultural and social *Ganzheiten,* particularly of civilization. They have concentrated, so far, on clarifying the concept of sociocultural *Ganzheiten* and, to a lesser degree, on the comparative study of civilizations. For these purposes they established a special journal, *Zeitschrift für Ganzheitforschung*, and, in cooperation with many scholars interested in the study of the cultural and social systems, though not necessarily along the Spenglerian line, they established in 1960 the International Society for the Comparative Study of Civilizations, with me as its president and O. F. Anderle as its secretary general.[12] Dr. Anderle has published in his numerous papers the leading principles of cultural morphology in its narrow (Spenglerian) sense.

P. Sorokin, the *Dynamics*, Vol. IV, chs. 8, 9, 10; A. M. Moschetti, *L'Unitá come categoria* (2 vols.; Milan, 1952–1959); G. E. Cairns, *Philosophies of History* (New York, 1962); O. F. Anderle, "Die Ganzheitstheorie, ein historisch-systematische Ueberblick," *Zeitschrift für Ganzheitsforschung*, Neue Folge, IV (1960), 2–18; G. Müller, "Oswald Spenglers Bedeutung," and "Pitirim Sorokin und Oswald Spengler," in *Zeitschrift für Philosophische Forschung*, Vols. XVII and XIX (1963, 1965); G. Müller, "Universalgeschichte im Zeitalter globaler Einheit," *Geschichte in Wissenschaft und Unterricht*, 12(1961); and "Toynbee's Reconsiderations," *Saeculum*, XV, No. 4 (1964).

[11] Anderle in Allen, *P. A. Sorokin in Review*, pp. 99–101.

[12] In October, 1961, the Society had its First International Congress at Salzburg, at which the basic problems of civilizations (*Die Problematik der Hochkulturen*) was the main topic. The deliberations of the Congress are now published in a volume: O. F. Anderle (ed.), *The Problems of Civilization* (The Hague, 1964).

In 1964, the Society had its Second International Congress devoted to the problems of holism (*Ganzheiten*). The volume of its proceedings is going to be published in the near future.

Sociocultural structures and processes, according to cultural morphology, "would have to be understood by no means additively, nor 'by starting with the parts' but, although complex, immediately as such, in their totality, with their holistic characteristics."[13]

Substantively, cultural morphology concentrates on the study of civilizations in the Danilevsky-Spengler-Toynbee sense. These civilizations are real holistic structures: They satisfy the criteria of *Ganzheit* established by Ehrenfels, Köhler, and Sanders-Volkelt; they have systematic unity, nonhomogeneity, internal articulation, interdependence of parts, supersummation, logical and ontological priority of the whole over its parts, ability to be transposed, and they are distinct from their environment.

Other points of cultural morphology in Anderle's formulation are particularly apparent in his countercriticism of my criticism of Danilevsky-Spengler-Toynbee's theory of civilizations, and in my reply to his countercriticism.[14]

FRAGMENTARY-TOTALITARIAN THEORY OF FELIKS KONECZNY

Somewhat totalitarian also is the theory of civilizations of the Polish historian Feliks Koneczny (1862–1949).[15] Since some scholars, especially A. Toynbee, O. Anderle, and A. Hilckman, evaluate it highly, a concise outline of it seems to be advisable.[16]

[13] Besides his forementioned works, see O. F. Anderle's "The Revolution in the World-View of History," *Diogenes*, No. 9 (1955); "Das Integrationsproblem in der Geschichtswissenschaft," *Schweitzer Beitrage zur allgemeinen Geschichte, XV* (1957); "Die Toynbee-Kritik," *Saeculum*, IX (1958); *Das Universalhistorische System of A. J. Toynbee* (Frankfurt, 1955).

[14] See full text of our dialogue in P. J. Allen (ed.), *P. A. Sorokin in Review*, pp. 95–121, 414–426.

[15] See his *O. Wielości cywilizacyj* (Cracow, 1935). English translation: *On the Plurality of Civilizations* (London, 1962).

[16] In his Preface to the volume, Toynbee calls it an "important contribution," "one of studies of the structure of human affairs on the largest scale." A. Hilckman in his "Introduction" to the book, states that "a comparison of Koneczny's doctrine with all the previous philosophy

The first few chapters of his work sketch the prehistorical "nuclei of all civilizations," namely, the invention of fire, the domestication of animals, the oldest associations (based mainly on sex differentiation), the role of tradition, and prehistorical economy. Despite very limited sources on out-of-date literature, Koneczny does not hesitate to make a number of dogmatic assertions, such as that the earliest form of marriage was monogamic, that polyandry or polygamy appeared at a later stage of man's history, and that communal possession and totemism never existed in any preliterate group. In these categoric statements, hardly supported by any evidence, the dogmatic bent of Koneczny's thought shows itself clearly. Contrary to Dr. Hilckman's assertion, this bent is responsible for many of Koneczny's questionable conclusions and for making several of his theories speculative and dogmatic rather than scientific and empirically exact.

Koneczny's conception of civilization is somewhat unclear and ambiguous. *"Civilization is the system on which communal life is organized.* This definition is wide enough to include art and science, ethics and law, economics, education, and communications, for all these belong to communal life. The isolated man does not create civilization but the sociable man among men."[17]

This is the fullest definition of civilization found in Koneczny's work. Taken at face value, it is identical with what I call the undifferentiated total culture of any group. It is a totalitarian conception of civilization that does not differentiate between congeries, semicongeries, or the causal or causalmeaningful systems that appear in practically every total culture.

---

of history makes it quite clear that it is only with him that the science of civilizations becomes a special science—one is almost tempted to say an exact science—of the same level and rank as the other special philosophical disciplines. . . . It is only with Koneczny that this science appears for the first time as a branch of learning, with a sphere of tasks delimited with precision and with its own *a posteriori*, empirical, exact method which can be verified in every detail." *On the Plurality of Civilizations*, pp. vii, 1–10.

[17] *On the Plurality of Civilizations*, p. 168.

The definition ends the analysis of the structures of the total culture where it should begin.

Koneczny possibly understood this weakness, for at other places in his work he supplements his definition by additional characteristics of civilization. All parts of a civilization, he says, have a "consistency and commensurability" of its "material institutions and a moral intellectual system such that all departments of life, feeling, thought and action are harmoniously and logically coordinated." Civilizations are "the largest extant fraction of humanity" that "have existed and exist [as] natural associations on the largest scale and more powerful than all powers and armies." "They [civilizations] resist every attempt at the artificial creation of large-scale associations which take no account of differences in civilizations. Often civilizations—as the highest forces of mankind—overturn and undo all that has been artificially created without reckoning with them." As such a system, civilization is not identical with the state, or the nation, or any other group.[18]

If by the "consistency and commensurability" of civilization Koneczny means the causal-meaningful consistency of its ideological-behavioral-material components and if by "natural associations on the largest scale" he means what I call the "cultural supersystem," then his conception of civilization is similar to my conception of the cultural supersystem. Unfortunately, Koneczny hardly uses this more adequate conception of civilization in his analysis of the concrete historical civilizations.[19]

Of Koneczny's theory of civilization the following main points are to be mentioned:

1. The identity and diversity of civilizations is based upon the following components: the character of the "triple law," the

---

[18] *Ibid.*, pp. 160–169.

[19] In other places in his work, Koneczny identifies civilization with almost any system of communal life of small and vast social groups. "Civilization of some kind exists everywhere communal life exists" (p. 169). "Every epoch has its civilizations" (p. 287). By not distinguishing "civilizational" (cultural) systems from the social system (organized group), he mars somewhat the clarity of his discussion.

"family law," the "property law," and the "inheritance law"; the character of the "quincunx of existential values or categories of being": health, economic well-being, the true, the good, and the beautiful, realized in a given civilization; and the conception and control of time, of private and public law, of ethics, and of national consciousness articulated by a given civilization and prevalent in the human group that has it.[20] If these components (or subsystems) are different in different groups their difference results in different kinds of civilizations. For instance, the associations with the socially sanctioned monogamous family law are bound to have civilizations different from those with polygamous or polyandrous family law; the same goes for the other components of civilization.

2. Due to the different character and combinations of the components of civilization, there have been and there are many diverse civilizations. "The number of systems for the organization of communal life is clearly unlimited; that is, the number of civilizations is unlimited. How many civilizations there have been and how many there are cannot be expressed in numbers in the present state of knowledge."

Since not all of the five existential values discussed above have been fully realized in many civilizations, there have been and are "incomplete, defective, fragmentary civilizations, one-sided, many-sided, universal, uniform and more or less mixed, original, and derivative in whole or part, unsuccessful, and primitive civilizations."[21] At any historical period several civilizations die and new ones are born. Among civilizations, particularly important are the sacral, semisacral, and nonsacral types.

3. The plurality and variety of civilizations is not primarily due to economic and technological factors (technological "homo faber" is not their architect and builder); nor are they determined by racial factors, by language systems, or, except

---

[20] How "the triple law," "the quincunx of values," and the conception of time, of private-public law, ethics, and national consciousness are interrelated with one another, and what their relationship is to fine arts, religion, language, science, and social institutions—is not clarified or analyzed.

[21] Koneczny, *On the Plurality of Civilizations,* pp. 168–169, 287.

the sacral civilizations, by religious factors. Homo faber (the economic-technological factor) did not establish civilization, nor did it make civilizations different. It has only contributed to the attainment of their higher level. "No civilization is the property of any race, and no race is confined to a certain civilization, still less to one level of it." "Language is neither the creator nor the creation of communal mentality." "Religion creates civilization only when it draws under its sacral legislation the five categories of being, when it is the determining factor not only for morals but also in categories of health, the struggle for existence, art and learning."[22] Still less can the variety of civilizations be explained by geographic or biological conditions. The identity and multiplicity of civilizations are due to spiritual factors, which are more powerful than material ones. This tentative answer hardly clears up the problems of the emergence, development, and individuality of all nonsacral civilizations.

4. Different civilizations have not a uniform but diverse life-courses and different life-durations. Only a few of them pass through the organic life-cycle of youth, maturity, and death. Some fully and harmonious developed civilizations, like the Roman-Latin-Western, can live an indefinitely long life.

5. Each civilization is a closed system and cannot be successfully crossed with a different civilization. All attempts to create "synthetic" or "hybridized" civilizations have failed.

---

[22] *Ibid.*, pp. 179–216, 243, 249, chs. IV, V, VII. This sort of procedure, applied to a unified system, is very doubtful. It takes as an independent variable a part of a civilization (economic-technological, religious, linguistic) and turns the civilization (minus these parts) into a "dependent variable." No wonder that the results of such an operation are puzzling. Factually, such an operation consists in carving out of the unified system-civilization (or an organism) several of its vital parts (language system, religious and economic systems or, in an organism, its heart, lungs, and other organs), which cannot normally function separated from their supersystem (civilization or organism) and in confronting these carved-out parts with the mutilated remnants of the supersystem, which cannot normally function without these parts. In Chapters 4, 5, and 6 of this work and in my *Fads and Foibles* (pp. 161–172), I repeatedly indicated the nonscientific nature of this sort of investigation. It is applicable to the congeries but not to the unified systems. Besides its odd character, it tries to explain the *whole system by one of its parts*— an operation logically, empirically, and obviously fallacious.

"Synthesis is possible only between cultures (subsystems) of the same civilization, not between civilizations. . . . Between civilizations, only a mechanical mixture is possible. This happens rarely, but always leads to the lowering of the civilization, sometimes to its downfall, to a state directly a-civilizational." "There are no syntheses but only poisonous mixtures. All Europe is now ill of the mixing of civilizations; here lies the cause of all crises." "It is not possible to be civilized in two ways."[23]

6. Every civilization, while it remains vital, aims at expansion so that wherever two vital civilizations meet they *must* fight each other. Every vital civilization is aggressive. The struggle lasts until one of the fighting civilizations is destroyed. "If civilizations sit side by side in peaceful indifference, evidently both are without vital force. A case of that kind often ends in some compromise mechanical mixture, stagnation ensues on both hands, and in time a real swamp of a-civilization develops."[24]

7. Of the contemporary civilizations Koneczny takes as "an experimental field" of his study "seven main civilizations in existence today—Jewish, Brahmin, Chinese, Turanian, Arabic, Byzantine and Latin."[25]

8. Of these and of all other civilizations that have existed in human history only one, the Latin (Roman and—its continuation—Latin European), is the best civilization. It is the only civilization which, under the beneficient influence of the Catholic Church, "has family emancipation and monogamy, historical and national consciousness, rests the State on society, demands ethics in public life, and recognizes the supremacy of spiritual forces."[26] All other civilizations failed to realize fully these five main values, and thus failed to achieve the control of time and other prerequisites of a perfect civilization. The few pages devoted to a characterization of each of these seven civilizations glorify the Roman and Latin European civilization and the

23 Koneczny, *On the Plurality of Civilizations,* pp. 319–320, 322.
24 *Ibid.,* pp. 318–319.
25 *Ibid.,* pp. 289 ff.
26 *Ibid.,* pp. 315 ff.

Catholic Church and scorn, with ludicrous vituperation, all other civilizations. One wonders whether this idealization of the Latin civilization is due to an astounding ignorance on Koneczny's part or to his emotional involvement in these problems. Whatever the reason, this aspect of his work is glaringly incorrect and represents not a scientific portraiture of these civilizations but purely political propaganda of the superiority of the Latin Catholic civilization, a superiority that never existed in historical reality. Koneczny easily explains defects in the Latin Catholic civilization by attributing them to the poisonous influence of the Byzantine, Turanian, Greek, or Arabic civilizations.[27] The incompetent and grossly inaccurate character of this part of Koneczny's work is not present in other parts of his theory of civilizations. He makes several generalizations, which though not new are nevertheless roughly correct. These points are discussed in the following chapter.

---

[27] Perhaps this glorification of the Roman-Latin civilization and the degradation of all other civilizations is the reason for the particularly high estimation of Koneczny's theory of civilization by all those who share his questionable propaganda.

CHAPTER **8**

Criticism of the Macrosociological

Totalitarian Theories

WHAT SORT OF UNITY IS CIVILIZATION?

Danilevsky, Spengler, Toynbee, Koneczny and other cultural morphologists all repeatedly contend that their "civilizations" or "high cultures" are real holistic *Ganzheiten* or unified systems. Toynbee asserts that:

> Civilizations are wholes whose parts all cohere with one another and all affect one another reciprocally. . . . It is one of the characteristics of civilizations in the process of growth that all aspects and activities of their social life are coordinated into a single social whole, in which the economic, political, and cultural elements are kept in a nice adjustment with one another by an inner harmony of the growing body social.[1]

This assertion raises the momentous question: *What kind of unities are these civilizations?* In my terms (outlined in Chapter 2), are they just spacial congeries? Or are they indirect causal semicongeries? Or causal unities? Or meaningful unities? Or meaningful-causal systems? If "civilization" is none of these unities then what sort of unity is it? Unfortunately, our eminent scholars do not give a clear answer to this question. They do not distinguish the congeries, semicongeries, causal, meaningful, and causal-meaningful unities from one another; they simply assert that civilizations are "wholes" or unified systems in which all elements are interdependent and adjusted to one another. Such an answer is highly indefinite and leads, among other

---

[1] A. Toynbee, *A Study of History*, Vol. III, pp. 380, 152; Vol. I, pp. 34 ff., 43 ff., 149–153 ff.

things, to a mixture of these five different relationships with one another, of mere spatial conglomeration with causal and meaningful-causal unities. It ends the analysis of the unities of civilizations where it should begin.

After carefully analyzing the concept of civilization brilliantly sketched by Danilevsky and magnificently developed by Spengler, Toynbee, and other cultural morphologists, I have made the following diagnosis of it in terms of my categories:

1. Most of these "civilizations" seem to represent not so much "cultural systems" as important *social groups* (*social systems*) with a central set of cultural meanings-values-norms or interests because of which, for the sake of which, and around which these groups are organized and function. (Any organized social group has such a central ideological-behavioral-material cultural set or system.)[2]

2. The social groups called "civilizations" or "high cultures" in the works of our scholars do not belong to the same kind of social systems, but rather to different kinds of social groups. Some of their civilizations, like the Tartar, Greek, or Arabic civilizations, are just *language* or *ethnic groups*—groups united by a common language or ethnic background. Such groups usually live in territorial propinquity, often have common ancestors (real or mythological), and are hardly ever united into *one* sovereign state. Their other "civilizations" are either pure *state* groups or *state groups combined with a respective language group* (a two-bonded group bound together by common language and state citizenship) like the Iranic, Russian, Mexic, and Roman "civilizations." Certain other "civilizations," like the Islamic, the Orthodox Christian, and the Nestorian, are mainly religious groups, while still others, like the Far Eastern or Mesopotamian, represent several complex "multibonded" groups. Finally, some of their civilizations, like Toynbee's Hellenic, Danilevsky's Assyro-Babylonian-Phoenician-Chaldean, or Spengler's Magian, are a veritable sociocul-

---

[2] See an exact analysis of the structure and properties of organized, semiorganized, unorganized, and disorganized groups in P. Sorokin, *SCP*, chs. 4, 8, 9; a brief sketch of these is given in Chapter 2 of the present work.

tural potpourri made up of several wholes, halves, and quarters of diverse language-state-religious-economic-territorial groups and unorganized populations. These scholars do not have a systematic taxonomy or classification of social groups[3]; thus they put into one "basket of civilization" most heterogeneous social groups and their total cultures.[4] The essentially different nature of these groups clearly displays the misleading "pseudounity" of their "civilizations."

3. The main organized group with its central cultural system makes up the core of those "civilizations" that have such a group as its *raison d'être*. Besides this main group, each civilization contains one or more alien groups with their own group culture different from the central culture of the main group. These alien groups live in the given civilization, but they are not an organic part of it, nor is their group culture necessarily consistent with the central culture of the main group.

4. In addition each civilization is connected—mainly through indirect causal relationships—with several outside groups and their group cultures, which enter the total culture of given civilizations as congeries.

5. The *total* culture of practically every individual and of each small or vast social group consists not of one cultural system uniting into one consistent whole millions of meanings-values-norms-interests but, rather, of a multitude of ideas-values-interests-aspirations-precepts that are partly neutral, partly even contradictory to one another. Thus, it is fairly certain that the *total culture of each civilization contains, side by side with the central cultural system of its main group, a multitude of different, partly neutral, partly contradictory, cultural systems and congeries.*

6. All this means that "carving" the "civilizations" out of an enormous mass of other cultural complexes and classifying them is done, without any uniform *fundamentum divisionis,* on the basis of different and somewhat indefinite criteria.

[3] See my systematic taxonomy of main social groups in *SCP*, chs. 10–16.
[4] This is acknowledged by Toynbee in his *Reconsiderations*, pp. 548 ff.

7. If these conclusions are correct, then the most serious errors of these theories consist in: mixing up and identifying cultural systems with social systems (groups); calling essentially different social groups and their total cultures—now ethnic, now religious, now state, now territorial, now various "multi-bonded" groups, and now even an agglomeration of various societies with their total cultures—civilizations or high culture; ascribing to the *total culture* of each of these groups a meaningful consistency and causal interdependence of all its parts with one another, with the whole system and of the whole system with each and all its important parts. In this point the theories commit the errors of all totalitarian and of many "functional" theories that maintain there is an integrated unity of the total culture of each organized group.[5]

This assumption is hardly tenable. In the preceding chapters it has been shown (and will be additionally demonstrated further) that social group (system) and cultural system are different kinds of systems, neither coextensive nor identical with each other. It is illogical and unscientific to term as "civilizations" quite different social groups with diverse total cultures. The error consists in a wrong identification of phenomena that are different.

8. Finally, if the *total* culture (ideological, behavioral, and material) of a single individual is hardly ever completely integrated and, as a rule, represents a dominant cultural system (though many eclectics and scatterbrained persons do not even have a dominant system) that coexists with many minor systems and with a multitude of congeries, partly neutral, partly contradictory to the dominant system and to one another, then obviously the total culture of such vast agglomerations of social groups as the "Hellenic," or the "Indic" or the "Syriac," or the "Sinic," or the "Western" has never been totally integrated into one consistent causal-meaningful system. As a matter of fact, the total culture of each of such territorially bounded civilization has represented a sort of a vast dumping place in which, besides the central system of meanings-values-norms-interests,

[5] See *SCP*, pp. 337–341.

have coexisted a multitude of other cultural systems unrelated to this central set and to each other and a still larger multitude of cultural congeries partly neutral, partly contradictory to each other and to the central system and to many cultural systems.

9. These basic errors seriously vitiate these otherwise most significant theories. Despite the efforts of Danilevsky, Spengler, Toynbee, and Koneczny, their concepts of "civilization" and "high culture" remain poorly delineated. This is strikingly corroborated by their disagreements with each other. What Danilevsky considers one civilization, for instance, his Assyro-Babylonian-Phoenician-Chaldean or Ancient Semitic Civilization, Toynbee treats as several, different civilizations (the Babylonic, the Hittite, the Sumeric, and the Syriac). Spengler, on the other hand, treats it as two: the Magian and the Babylonian. Spengler's Magian civilization is viewed by Danilevsky as two different civilizations, the Iranian and the Arabic, and by Toynbee as four, the Iranic, the Syriac, the Arabic, and the Orthodox-Byzantine. Toynbee's one Hellenic civilization is considered by Danilevsky as two civilizations, the Greek and the Roman. Koneczny's Brahmin and Turanian civilizations differ again from those of Danilevsky, Spengler, and Toynbee. Thus, where one of our scholars sees one cultural organism, the others see two or more, and vice versa. These spectacular discrepancies additionally testify against these "civilizations" being real *Ganzheiten*, or integrated unities. For, if they were real unified systems, each single civilization would have been clearly discernible, similarly identified and demarcated, and all civilizations would have been similarly classified by our eminent scholars.

Toynbee frankly acknowledged this defect in the latest volume of his *A Study of History*. In answering the criticisms of his earlier list of civilizations, and especially P. Bagby's statement (similar to mine)[6] that "Toynbee's list (of civilizations) . . . is a peculiar jumble of incompatible and incomparable entities," he frankly acknowledges that his "criterion for identifying civilizations is not uniform. In some cases it is

---

[6] See P. Bagby, *Culture and History* (London, 1958), p. 177; P. Sorokin, *Modern Historical and Social Philosophies*, ch. XII.

material culture, in others religion, in others race." He further admits that there were several arbitrary and "subjective elements in my original identification and demarcation of civilizations."[7] These reasons influenced Toynbee to revise seriously his concept of civilization and to replace his earlier list of civilizations by the different one (see pp. 203–204).[8]

FALLACY OF THE ORGANISMIC UNIVARIANT LIFE-COURSE OF CIVILIZATIONS

The second mistake of Danilevsky, Spengler, and Toynbee (in his earlier volumes) is their contention that the life-course of all civilizations runs one univariant "organic" cycle: They all are born, then grow, and eventually disintegrate and die. This unduly generalized model of the life-course of civilizations can, at best, be applied to some of the organized social groups as the central agency of each of their "civilizations." Social organized groups have different life-spans ranging from a few hours to centuries and even millennia.[9] Most of these groups are mortal and sooner or later die and disappear as individualities in the sociocultural universe of groups and human popula-

---

[7] Toynbee, *Reconsiderations*, pp. 548 ff.

[8] R. W. Wescott, in his paper "Counting and Classifying Urban Civilizations," sums up various classifications of civilizations by seven different cultural taxonomists (Gobineau, Danilevsky, Spengler, Toynbee, Wescott, Bagby, and Sedgwick) as follows:

I. Civilizations recognized by all seven taxonomists: Egyptian, Mesopotamian, Indic, Chinese, Hellenic, Western.

II. Civilizations recognized only by some of these taxonomists: Mexican, Peruvian, Russian, Levantine, Syrian, Persian, Roman, Byzantine, Cretan.

III. Civilizations recognized by only one taxonomist: Sumerian, Hittite, Judaic, Arabian, Islamic, Hindu, Far Eastern, Japanese, Tartar, Aegean, Mayan, Yucatec.

In his paper "Historiology and Anthropology," Wescott gives a list of about 300 civilizations—arranged in a five-level hierarchy of world civilizations up to local, urban civilizations.

This discrepancy reinforces the above criticisms of the theories discussed. (These papers were kindly given to me by Dr. Westcott before their publication.)

[9] See, on the life-spans of different social systems or groups, *SCP*, ch. 34.

tion. Some of the cultural systems, including the central one of "civilizations," can also disintegrate and die as unified systemic individualities.[10] But in no way can the univariant model of birth, maturity, and death be applied to any of the "civilizations." Since the *total culture* of each of these "civilizations" has never been integrated into one consistent system, it evidently cannot disintegrate. If the total culture of each "civilization," all the meanings-values-norms-interests-aspirations, in their ideological-behavioral-material forms, has never been a living causal or meaningful or meaningful-causal unity, it obviously cannot be born, grow, reach maturity, and die. None of these terms is applicable to, and none of these processes takes place in, a "cultural dumping place." The vast pile of heterogeneous cultural congeries and systems on such a vast territorial ground and in such a large population can be mechanically rearranged, increased, or decreased, and some of its systems and congeries may disintegrate, but the total cultural dump cannot disintegrate because it has never been integrated. Likewise it cannot die in its totality because it has never been born as a real *Ganzheit*.[11] It is unfortunate that our eminent scholars accepted an "organismic" model as the univariant model of the life-course of their civilizations. The slightest analysis of what they mean by birth, growth, maturity, breakdown, disintegration, and death at once shows the meaninglessness as well as the fallacy of these terms when they are applied to their civilizations in the sense of the total conglomeration of cultural systems and congeries contained in each "civilization." None of their theories clearly defines and indicates when each "civilization" in the sense of its total culture is born and what are the signs of its birth; likewise, none of them clearly

---

[10] Their longevity also ranges from a few moments to millennia. *Ibid.*, ch. 47. Some of these systems are sometimes reviving and having "resurrection."

[11] Some of the sociologists, like Don Martindale, put my theory into the school of the "idealistic organicists" and ascribe to me a theory of the organismic life-cycle of cultural systems. This is quite wrong. In my *Contemporary Sociological Theories* and in my *Dynamics, SCP,* and *Social Philosophies of an Age of Crisis,* I severely criticized all organismic sociological theories and clearly rejected them. Don Martindale, *The Nature and Types of Sociological Theories* (Boston, 1960), pp. 115–118.

points out when each civilization dies and what the criteria are of its death. Since the total culture of each of their "civilizations" has never been united into one causal or causal-meaningful *Ganzheit*, it is but natural that even most distinguished scholars cannot indicate when this sort of "cultural dumping place" is born or dies. Thus, for instance, if we ask them when Western civilization (or any other) was born, we do not receive any clear answer. Was it born with the emergence of the early barbaric states? or of the Merovingian? or Carolingian? or the Holy Roman Empire of the German Nation? or at the moment of the emergence and legalization of Christianity? or at the time of the Carolingian Renaissance or the later Italian Renaissance? or at the time of the Counter-Reformation? or after the discoveries of Galileo, Copernicus, and Newton? or after the discovery of America? or after the so-called fall of the Roman Empire? or with establishment of Gothic architecture? or when?

We can indicate when some of the organized social groups, like some of the states or big economic corporations or the Christian religious institutions or this or that university emerged in the sociocultural universe, and when other social or cultural systems, like Plato's Republic or Bach's Mass in B-Minor or Newton's Principia, were established ("born"), but since "civilizations" are not real unities, neither Danilevsky nor Spengler, nor Toynbee can indicate when Western civilization was born. The same is still more true in regard to their other "civilizations."

Likewise, it is exceedingly difficult to point out clearly when each "civilization" grew and reached the zenith of its development. In regard to the organized groups or cultural systems this can be done in many cases, if the criteria of growth are clearly delineated; but nobody can say authoritatively when a "cultural dumping place" reaches the peak of its "creative growth."

Similarly, it is impossible to indicate when a "civilization" dies. If our scholars mean by the death of civilization the disappearance from the living historical scene *all* the groups and *all* the cultural systems of a "dead civilization," then the statement is grossly incorrect. Despite the alleged "death" of the Greco-Roman or Hellenic "civilization," the Greek and the Latin languages are still alive; still more alive are all the great philosophical systems of the "pre-Socratics," of Democritus, Plato, Aristotle, Plotinus and others; the Doric, the Ionic, and the Corinthian orders of architecture; the aesthetic systems of Homer, Hesiod, Sophocles, Aristophanes; the Roman Corpus Juris Civilis; Spartan totalitarian or Athenian democratic sociopolitical systems; the Roman imperial organization in its monarchical and republican forms; and the scientific discoveries of the Greeks and the Romans. These and a multitude of other Greco-Roman cultural and social systems are still imitated, studied, practiced, recreated, and incorporated in our civilization, culture, institutions, in our mentality, conduct, and relationships. They live, function, and influence us—ideologically, behaviorally, and materially—much more than last year's best seller or yesterday's fads and fashions. With a proper modification, the same can be said of many of the social and cultural systems of practically all of Toynbee's "sixteen dead civilizations."

In many cases we can fairly precisely state when social and cultural systems became extinct as *Ganzheiten*. In regard to the unintegrated "civilizations" it is impossible, as a rule, to indicate even roughly the moment of their "death." For instance, when did the Greek or the Roman or the Hellenic or the Sinic or the Indic "civilizations" die? At the moment of the Peloponnesian War? or after the loss of the political independence of all Greek states? or after the division of the Roman Empire into the Western and Eastern empires? or after the so-called fall of the Western Roman Empire? If any of these events can be taken for the death of the Greek or the Roman civilizations, the events signify, at best, the death of the Greek states or the Roman Empire[12] as organized social systems; in no way do

---

[12] Toynbee often correctly indicates the beginnings, breakdowns, and disintegration of some of his "civilizations," because he really deals with the state, and various political groups, but not much with civilizations or cultures. "Culture itself as something substantive is hardly examined by Toynbee except incidentally. His study emanates from mainly political history," Kroeber correctly notes. See A. Kroeber, *Style and Civilization* (Ithaca, N.Y., 1957), p. 120.

they signify the extinction of an enormous number of other scientific, philosophical, aesthetic, ethical, and juridical social groups and cultural systems or even supersystems created by the Greek and Roman populations.[13]

Factually, when we study the life-course of either an organized social group or a cultural system—each of which represents a causal-meaningful unity—we can much more exactly indicate when it was "born," or when it appeared in the empirical sociocultural world, when it—quantitatively or qualitatively—grows or declines (in its membership, in its vehicles, and its system of meanings-values-norms-aspirations), through what phases it passes in its lifetime, the length of its life, and, finally, when it "dies," or looses its unity and individuality and disappears as a *Ganzheit* from the living empirical sociocultural universe.

A factual study of the life-course of the organized social systems (groups) and of cultural systems[14] shows, first, that their life-course is exceedingly multivariant and can in no way be reduced to one organismic univariant cycle; second, that their "birth" or emergence as a concrete empirical *Ganzheit* in the empirical sociocultural world is diverse for social groups (whereas cultural systems emerge in three uniform phases of, conception, objectification, and socialization); third, that their life-span ranges from a few seconds to millennia and virtual immortality (so long as the creative human race survives); and fourth, that in their life-course some of the organized social groups and some of the cultural systems run only one cycle of emergence, existence for some time, and final disintegration; in contrast, some other social and cultural systems have several waves of growth and decline, blossoming and withering; some even temporarily disintegrate, only to be reborn at a later time. Great cultural systems like science, great systems of philosophy, religion, fine arts, ethics, law, economics and politics, and especially what I call ideational, sensate, and integral cultural

[13] See a development of these criticisms in my *Modern Historical and Social Philosophies*, pp. 218 ff.

[14] See a systematic analysis of these problems in *SCP*, chs. 21–47; and in *Modern Historical and Social Philosophies*, pp. 209–233.

supersystems, are virtually immortal and can have any number of fluctuations in their temporary transformations, decline, and renaissance. The social systems (groups) seem to be more limited than cultural systems in these fluctuations as well as in their life-span. Fifth, organized social groups and cultural systems range in activity and creativity all the way from a business firm manufacturing sun glasses or a cultural system describing the characteristics of a defectively printed stamp to progressively wider, many-sided, and important forms of activity and creativity up to the almost "encyclopedic" form carried on by such social groups as the family or the totalitarian state or the *Gemeinschaft* type of community or by vast cultural systems like science, philosophy, ethics, law, religion, fine arts, economic and political systems, and especially by the vast Sensate, Ideational, and Integral supersystems.

FALLACY OF THE SPECIFIC CREATIVITY OF CIVILIZATIONS

In the light of these propositions several other mistakes of the criticized theories become quite discernible. For instance, their claim that each "civilization" throughout its whole life is creative only in one or at the best in two or three fields of creativity: the Hellenic civilization only in the aesthetic field, the Indic only in the field of religion, the Western only in the field of science and technology. Factually, each of these "civilizations"—or, more exactly, respective conglomerations of social groups that created and maintained each "civilization"—has been creative in various fields of culture at various periods of their existence, and all "civilizations" have been creative not in one but in several cultural fields: All have been autochtonous in various degrees. For instance, Western "civilization" in its medieval period was highly creative in religion, scholastic philosophy, universal and absolute ethics, sacral law, and ideational fine arts; it was little creative in science, technology, politics, and economics. The same civilization (that is, the social groups of the Western populations from the fifteenth to the twentieth centuries) has been little creative in religion, universal ethics, and ideational fine arts, and magnificently creative in science, technology, sensate fine arts, utilitarian and hedonistic ethics, economics and politics. The same can be said of other "civilizations."

A few abridged summaries of the creative periods in specified fields of culture in Egypt, India, Greece, the Islamic (Arabic) world, and France[15] are shown below.

Summaries of the Creative Periods

Egypt

Religion	c. 3500–3000 B.C., c. 2500–2300 B.C., c. 1580–1490 B.C., c. 1370–1352 B.C.
The state and economics	2895–2540 B.C., 2000–1785 B.C., 1580–1200 B.C., 663–525 B.C.
Science	c. 4241 B.C., 1900–1500 B.C.
Literature	2000–1225 B.C., 1300–900 B.C.
Sculpture	2840–2575 B.C., 1580–1350 B.C.
Architecture	1590–1250 B.C.
Music	1411–1284 B.C.
Painting	1580–1250 B.C., 750–525 B.C.

India

Religion	c. 1000 B.C., c. 600–400 B.C., c. 272–232 B.C. c. A.D. 1–100, c. A.D. 788–860
The native state and economics	c. 321–186 B.C., A.D. 78–96, A.D. 320–500, A.D. 606–647, A.D. 1350–1600
Philosophy	600–400 B.C., A.D. 100–500, A.D. 600–1000
Science	700–500 B.C., A.D. 400–1150 (climax c. A.D. 500–625)
Literature	c. 400 B.C.–A.D. 100, A.D. 350–750

Greece

Religion	850–500 B.C., 350–300 B.C.
The state and economics	750–430 B.C., 500–300 B.C.
Philosophy	585–270 B.C.
Science	585 B.C.–A.D. 100
Music	750–600 B.C., 450–350 B.C.
Literature	800–700 B.C., 550–350 B.C.
Architecture	550–430 B.C.
Sculpture	559–350 B.C.
Painting	450–300 B.C.

[15] See *SCP*, pp. 548–551. See there the periods of blossoming in various fields of cultural creativity in the history of China, Japan, Rome, Germany, Great Britain, Italy, and Russia.

Arabic (Islamic) World

Religion	A.D. 622–1258
The state	A.D. 632–833
Philosophy	A.D. 800–1200
Science	A.D. 750–1250
Literature (sculpture, painting, and drama are poorly developed)	A.D. 530–1200

France

Religion	Decline after the thirteenth century
The state	1050–1325, 1600–1715, 1800–1815, 1850–1870, 1890–1940
Economics	1100–1325, 1475–1560, 1840–1914
Philosophy	1075–1160, 1300–1350, 1600–1700, 1750–1850
Science	1580–1660, 1750–1870
Architecture	1050–1350
Sculpture	1140–1325, 1450–1550, 1850–1910
Music	1100–1350, 1650–1750, 1850–1910
Painting	1620–1670, 1760–1890
Literature	1070–1300, 1520–1580, 1630–1700, 1780–1900

However approximate, these data, together with all other considerations given above, show that the fields of creativity of all "civilizations," and especially those which have had a long life-span, have notably shifted, at different periods of their existence; these civilizations have had not one but several creative periods even in the same field of culture. The thesis of invariable specificity of creativeness of each civilization throughout its whole life-span is contradicted by a solid body of empirical evidence.

The validity of most of these criticisms has been frankly acknowledged by Toynbee. As mentioned before, in the twelfth volume of his *A Study of History* he abandoned his earlier theory of the univariant life-course of all civilizations and admitted at least three different models of their life-history. If instead of his "civilizations" Toynbee had studied the life-courses of the vast and small social and cultural systems he would undoubtedly have found more numerous different models of the life-courses of these systems, as well as basic differences between those of social and cultural systems and congeries.

Other—weak and sound—points of criticized theories can be further elucidated by summing up here Dr. Othmar Anderle's and Toynbee's countercriticisms of my criticisms and my reply to their remarks.[16] This dialogue outlines also several points in today's cultural morphology not mentioned before.

O. ANDERLE'S COUNTERCRITICISMS

His first defense of the unified, "holistic" structure of "civilizations" consists in his reference to the supposedly modern theory of *Ganzheiten* (wholes) as it is developed by von Ehrenfels, Köhler, Sanders-Volkelt, Wellek, Netzger, Wertheimer, Koffka, Katz, Lewin in psychology, Drisch, Bertalanffy, Troll, Portmann, and others in biology, and Spann, Friedman and Burkamp in philosophy and sociology. I do not have any quarrel with the method of the holistic morphologists of grasping and understanding each of the *Ganzheiten* first as a whole, in its totality, with its holistic characteristics, and then analyzing its elements and parts. But I find it difficult, practically impossible, to apply their diagnostic criteria of the concrete and compact *Ganzheiten* (biological organisms, human individuals) to the discontiguous, discreet, noncompact cultural complexes and social groups. Some of these characteristics, such as the "systematic unity," "logical and ontological articulation," "supersummativity," and "independence" of the *Ganzheiten*, are really not diagnostic criteria of the *Ganzheiten* that can help to distinguish the *Ganzheiten* from the *non-Ganzheiten* but mere synonyms for that word. Other diagnostic traits such as the distinguishability of *Ganzheiten* from their environment, their transposability, and the noninterchangeability of their parts are either inapplicable to discontiguous, discreet, often sensorily imperceptible cultural systems and congeries, social groups, and con-

---

[16] The papers of O. Anderle and A. J. Toynbee and my reply to them are published in Allen, *P. A. Sorokin in Review.*

glomerates of populations, or are wrong criteria of the *Ganzheiten*. How, for instance, can mathematics or idealistic systems of philosophy or Romantic music or Communist and Capitalist ideologies be "distinguishable from environment"? How can they be "transposed" and in what kind of space? If in some way these operations can be done, they can also be done even more easily with a heap of numbers or an eclectic philosophy or cacophonous musical sounds or an incoherent pile of various ideas and notions. How, on the basis of these criteria, can we find in the ocean of humanity such nonterritorial discontiguous groups as the International Sociological Society, or the Roman Catholic Church, or the Communist International, whose members are scattered all over the world and are not attached or bound to any contiguous territory? These simple questions show that these criteria of the *Ganzheiten* do not help us much to distinguish a multitude of real cultural and social systems from a jumble of cultural and social congeries. This means that Dr. Anderle's defense of the *total* unity of "civilization" through a reference to the Ehrenfels-Köhler-Volkelt "morphological criteria" of *Ganzheiten* does not prove his point.

Neither do his other arguments substantially disarm and neutralize my criticisms. Despite his valiant defense of the unifying role of Spengler's "prime symbols" of civilizations, Anderle does not give any proof that the prime symbol of "stone" unifies into one consistent whole the total culture—that is, millions of ideological, behavioral, and material culture systems and congeries—of the Egyptian civilization; or that the *Ursymbol* of the "sensuous individual body" does this in regard to the Greek ("Apollinian") civilization; or that "pure limitless space and voluntarism" does it in regard to the Western (Faustian) civilization. All of these prime symbols are chosen arbitrarily and the few impressionistic associations that Spengler tries to build around them are neither logical nor meaningful nor causal. Instead of stone, one can, perhaps with greater reason, take the sun, boat, Apis, or any of dozens of other symbols that played an important role in the Egyptian religion, morality, mythology, and fine arts. Likewise, why cannot Platonic "ideal forms" serve as the prime symbol of Greek civilization? Or the "sensuous individual body" for the sensate period of Western civilization with its emphasis on libido, sex, materialism, sensuality, and hedonism? These and many other prime symbols can be chosen with as much intuitive, logical, or empirical foundation as any of the Spenglerian prime symbols. At best, they serve as a premise for a meaningful integration of some of the cultural systems and congeries of Spengler's or Toynbee's "civilizations." But this integrated system remains only one among many systems and congeries in the total Egyptian, Apollinian, Magian, Faustian, and other "civilizations." I am reasonably certain that no logician or historian can demonstrate the meaningful or causal relatedness of millions of cultural phenomena of the total culture of each of the civilizations to Spengler's prime symbols and still less a real unification of these phenomena into one meaningful consistent whole or into one causal system.[17]

One of Anderle's main arguments consists in ascribing to me not only a rigorous distinction between cultural and social systems (which is correct) but in overly exaggerating this distinction: "Sorokin . . . does not even wish to admit their overlapping," he says, and then proceeds to demolish my criticisms of the unity of civilizations. Meanwhile my real views in this point can be seen from the following passage:

> An integrated cultural system in each and all three (ideological, behavioral, and material) levels, and an organized social group, are not identical unities. *Only in part do they coincide and overlap, namely, insofar as any organized group has a set of meanings, values, and norms as the* raison d'être *of its existence; and this set must be and usually is integrated in the bulk of its meanings, values and especially in its law-norms, and in the respective actions and vehicles of the group en-*

---

[17] In this particular point, I grant a much more limited unifying role to these prime symbols, and I value more highly other Spenglerian points than Kroeber does. See A. Kroeber, *Style and Civilization*, pp. 38 ff. G. Müller, in his "Toynbee's Reconsiderations," *Saeculum*, XV, No. 4 (1964), 311–326, gives a long series of philosophical, empirical, and other contradictions of Toynbee's "philosophy of history" that are summed up in his *Reconsiderations: A Study of History*. R. Coulborn points out several factual shortcomings of Toynbee's *Reconsiderations* in "Toynbee's *Reconsiderations*: A Commentary," *Journal of World History*, No. 1 (1964).

forced by it. Except for this set . . . an organized group and cultural system are different unities, having different boundaries, even within the same population.[18]

We have seen that each organized group has, besides its main cultural system, which is its *raison d'être*, a multitude of other cultural systems and congeries, partly neutral, partly contradictory to each other and to the group's "core system." On the other hand, almost all great cultural systems, like mathematics, languages, religion, philosophy, technology, law codes, art, and even such cultural objects as whiskey, lipsticks, television, or radio, spread over, are taken in, and become an integral part of the total cultures of numerous and heterogeneous social groups. From this, several other differences in the life-span and life-carriers of cultural and social systems follow.[19]

FALLACY OF THE CLOSED SYSTEM OF CIVILIZATION

Contrary to the claim of Danilevsky, Spengler, Anderle, and Koneczny that each civilization is a closed system whose culture cannot be transmitted to other cultures, a multitude of cultural systems and congeries can and do migrate and get rooted from the culture of the group or person that created them into the cultures of many other groups and persons. Again, contrary to their claim that with the disintegration or death of the creator-group or person their cultural system dies also, great cultural systems as a rule do not die with their creators but with or without some modification continue to live a vigorous life in many total cultures (or civilizations) of numerous heterogeneous social groups.

In contrast to the theory of the closed character of "civilization," M. Mauss defines the phenomena of civilization as "essentially international and extranational," as common to many more or less similar societies, as migrating from one so-

---

[18] *SCP*, p. 335. See there the development of, and evidence for, these statements, pp. 335–341, *passim*.

[19] See on the difference of life-spans and life-careers of social groups and cultural systems, *SCP*, chs. 34 and 47.

ciety to others. He notes its difference from those cultural traits that exist only within the culture of one group and cannot diffuse beyond it.[20]

Several generalized propositions of mine even more precisely and correctly define under what conditions any cultural system can be transmitted from group to group, person to person, and "civilization to civilization," and how much such a system is to be changed in the process of this transmission and in rooting itself as an integral part in the culture of its immigration.

> When a cultural object or value—be it a simple element or a cultural complex or system—moves from one cultural center to another, a) it may remain essentially unchanged if the culture of its immigration is similar to the culture from which it departed; b) it changes if the cultures of immigration and departure are different; and the greater the contrasts between these, the greater the transformation of the migrating cultural value or system in the process of its migration and incorporation into the culture which it enters; c) if the cultures of departure and of arrival are profoundly different, certain cultural systems of the first cannot penetrate and be rooted in the second culture at all. Even cultural congeries absolutely uncongenial to the culture of immigration find enormous difficulty in rooting themselves in a new culture.

> If we hold the difference between two cultures constant, then the magnitude or profundity of the transformation of the migratory cultural system depends upon its nature, and particularly upon the degree of its complexity, delicacy, and intricacy. Other conditions being equal, the more complex, refined, intricate the cultural system is and the greater ability, qualification, and training it requires for its adequate understanding and use, the more profoundly it transforms in the process of its passage from culture (or person) A to culture (or person) B, and in that of its infiltration and incorporation into B.

These propositions are applicable to and valid for the migration of cultural phenomena from person to person, from group to group, and from civilization to civilization, in horizontal

---

[20] M. Mauss, "Les Civilisations," in L. Febvre and M. Mauss, *Civilisations: Le mot et l'idée* (Paris, 1930), pp. 83–86.

as well as vertical migration of cultural congeries, complexes, and systems. These propositions seem to define the problems discussed more precisely and adequately than Danilevsky, Spengler, Anderle, Koneczny, and Mauss do.[21]

Anderle's final argument for the unity of civilization is his reference to holistic psychology, which "describes personality as a well-integrated whole, distinct from its surrounding, unified into a system, articulate, interdependent, supersummative, self-regulative . . . stylistically determined, a form, die-cast but alive and developing. . . . Individuals are integrated holistically in their psychic-spiritual makeup, insofar as they are normal."

The doubtful nature of this proposition was discussed in Chapter 6. Here we can simply say that the total psychic and spiritual make-up of the individuals rarely, if ever, give the happy, completely integrated "holistic unity" so beautifully described by Dr. Anderle. If indeed his picture of a "holistic man" were true then we would have to conclude that all normal human beings are perfectly rational and happy persons, invariably at peace with themselves and the world, free from any nonrationality and irrationality, inner conflicts, emotional upheavals, and so on. Unfortunately, the stubborn ugly facts do not allow us to accept this wonderful picture of man.

With these remarks I end my defense against the penetrating criticisms of Dr. Anderle. Our disagreement on a number of points does not prevent our agreement on a number of others.

TOYNBEE'S REPLY TO MY CRITICISM

In his masterful essay, "Sorokin's Philosophy of History,"[22] Toynbee gives a thoughtful countercriticism of my criticism of his theory. Only one of his arguments needs to be mentioned

---

[21] See detailization, analysis, and evidence for these and other uniformities in the field of mobility, diffusion, and transformation of cultural phenomena in my *Dynamics*, Vol. IV, pp. 252–253, and ch. 5, reproduced in my *Social and Cultural Mobility* (New York, 1959), pp. 549–640.

[22] In Allen, *P. A. Sorokin in Review*, pp. 67–95.

here. This is Toynbee's assertion that the unity, individuality, and specific creativity of each of his civilizations comes out clearly in their fine arts. Each civilization creates its own form of fine arts and keeps this form or style throughout its whole life-cycle.

I do not deny the distinctive unity and individuality of the great fine arts. They represent a real, meaningful-causal cultural system. But from the unity and individuality of Greek integral fine arts of the fifth century B.C. it does not follow that in the same period in Greece there did not coexist, as minor currents, the "Archaic"—ideational—and "Modern"—sensate—art. Nor does it follow that the *total* Greek culture or the *total* Hellenic civilization (in all its compartments) of this period was unified into one consistent, meaningful-causal *Ganzheit*. It is true that a large part of the highest level of this total culture or civilization was unified into one integral supersystem. But even this cultural supersystem did not unify the *total* Greek culture or civilization: Side by side with it coexisted the survivals of the preceding ideational supersystem, the beginnings of the emerging sensate supersystem, and a legion of heterogeneous and eclectic systems and congeries. In other words, from the unity and individuality of a great aesthetic system we are not entitled to conclude that the total culture in which this aesthetic system appeared is also unified into one meaningful-causal *Ganzheit*.[23]

---

[23] This also answers Kroeber's somewhat ambivalent theory of the "style of civilization" or culture. On the one hand, he states that "it is only sense to expect that Spengler's assertion that everything in a culture must be equally tinctured with one quality characteristic of the culture is untrue because it is an oversimple absolute." On the other, he says "it is only sense to realize that a flat denial of any and all stylistic congruence within a culture would be as extreme [an] absolute as Spengler's total affirmation. The truth evidently lies between." It lies, according to Kroeber, in a unity of style, "perhaps something like what I call a super-style, or style of styles: a total style of life." When we try to grasp what Kroeber means by "a total style of life" of a civilization, we get the terms: "coherence," "conformity," "similarity of forms," and "consistency," none of which indicates whether these terms mean a mere spatial proximity or indirect causal or direct causal or meaningful-causal (logical and aesthetic) relationships among the millions of sociocultural phenomena of a civilization or culture.

In other words Kroeber does not specify what sort of unity of

I deny also that most of the distinctive characteristics of the fine arts of a given total culture or civilization remain unchanged in the course of time. I humbly claim that the fine arts of different cultures clearly exhibit similarities in style and content if and when these cultures are in the same—ideational, or sensate, or idealistic—dominant phase, or, according to W. Deonna, in the same "archaic," "classical," and "decadent" phase. In Volume I of my *Dynamics*, I endeavored to prove these points through the quantitative and qualitative analysis of enormous numbers of pictures, sculptures (more than 100,000), buildings, musical compositions, and some examples of the literature of the Greco-Roman and the Western world throughout the whole historical existence of these cultures.[24] So far nobody as yet has even attempted to prove that either my samples were nonrepresentative or my analysis and statistics (more correctly, simple arithmetic) were wrong. Deonna (and other historians of the fine arts), analyzing the paleolithic, neolithic, Greco-Roman, and Christian sculpture and painting, convincingly shows that the traits and style, and even topics, of all four types of art are strikingly homogeneous.

> The similarity is so great that the statues of early medieval Europe (before the twelfth century A.D.) can easily be mistaken for those of archaic Greece (before the sixth century B.C.), and vice versa. Likewise, comparing the Aurora of

---

civilization or total culture he means. If by his "total style of life" of a civilization, that is, of the total culture of a given group, Kroeber means its main cultural system(s), and if he agrees that this central system(s) unifies a large part of the total culture (civilization) but not all of its systems and congeries, and if he admits that in any civilization, besides its main meaningful-causal systems in their ideological, behavioral, and material forms, there always are purely spatial and indirect-causal congeries, several causal and causal-meaningful systems neutral or contradictory to the main system(s)—then there is no disagreement between his and my position. It is the position that lies between two extreme absolutes. In the light of this statement, his ascription to me of "the radical denial of any unified part of the total culture or civilization" is obviously incorrect. It contradicts the spirit as well as the letter of my theory. (See A. Kroeber, *Style and Civilization*, pp. 70 ff., 88 ff., 150.) In the next chapter, in my examination of Kroeber's theory of civilization or culture, this point will be clarified further.

[24] See the *Dynamics*, Vol. I, chs. 5–13.

Michaelangelo with the Niobe of Rome; the Nymphs of the Fountain by Jean Goujon (sixteenth century A.D.) with the Dancing Woman figure of Pergamum (third-second century B.C.), geometric statues of the archaic paleolithic with the archaic of the neolithic, the archaic Greek and Medieval one cannot fail to see a striking similarity between them, even though they be separated from one another by centuries, even by thousands of years.[25]

Some of the statutes of Acropolis are remarkably similar to the works of Mino da Fiesole, Francia and Desiderio da Settignano, some of the sculptures of the Scopa School in Greece (fourth century B.C.) to the sculptures of Francia, some of the Greek and Pompeian vase paintings to the paintings of Mantegna, R. Van Weyden, Titian, and so on.

I do not claim that the similarities of the fine arts of various cultures in the same phase of their development are necessarily greater than the similarities of the fine arts of the same culture at different stages of its development; we hardly have an objective measuring stick to clear up this problem. But I contend that an essential similarity of the fine arts of different cultures in the same predominantly ideational or sensate or idealistic phase cannot be denied.

I also claim that the styles (and the inner meanings) of architecture, sculpture, painting, music, and literature of the same "civilization" change at different periods of its existence. To see this it is enough to compare Western Romanesque and Gothic architecture with Victorian and modern architecture, the bulk of Western medieval sculpture, painting, music, and literature with Victorian and Modern. If we did not know that all these styles were created in the Western culture, we would hardly have guessed that they all appeared in the same "civilization" during different periods of its existence. For this reason my propositions are in no way "paradoxical."

[25] Sorokin, *Modern Historical and Social Philosophies*, pp. 29–30. For a detailed documentation of Deonna's thesis, see his *L'archéologie, sa valeur, ses méthodes* (3 vols.; Paris, 1912).

OTHER SHORTCOMINGS OF THE DISCUSSED THEORIES OF CIVILIZATIONS[26]

The examined theories do not give satisfactory answers to a number of other problems. Why, for instance, has only an exceedingly small number of tribes or groups been able to build a great civilization or high culture? Why has an overwhelming majority of human preliterate groups remained on a "precivilizational" level or on the level of mere "ethnographic material"? What, generally, are the factors of cultural creativity?

We agree with our authors that the total number of civilizations or cultures that have created great cultural systems and supersystems in human history is very small, fluctuating somewhere between nine and forty. The majority of tribes and "peoples" or linguistic groups of human history have remained on preliteral, precivilizational cultural levels. They have not created great cultural systems.

Spengler practically ignores these questions. He views the whole matter of the emergence and growth of a "high culture" as resulting from an interference of mysterious cosmic forces in the life of this planet and especially in human affairs. Such an answer does not help us to understand the why and how, the when, where, and who of the emergence of great civilizations.

Danilevsky and Toynbee try to answer these problems in terms of empirical factors of cultural or civilizational creativity. Danilevsky stresses two factors particularly: the political independence of linguistically related groups, and the diversity and richness of the ethnographic or cultural material accessible to them. Toynbee explains the emergence of a great civilization by triple factors: a geographic milieu that is neither too hard nor too comfortable; the presence of a creative minority; and an incessant interplay of challenge and response, withdrawal and return. If the environment is too hard, the development of a great civilization is either arrested or its birth becomes abortive. If the

---

[26] A more substantial discussion of these shortcomings is given in my *Modern Historical and Social Philosophies*, pp. 229–243. Here I am giving only my conclusions about these shortcomings.

milieu is too soft, there is no strong challenge incessantly stimulating the group's maximum creative effort to meet it successfully. Their classification of factors is defective in several respects. It is incomplete. Some of their factors are very doubtful; others are very vague; still others are possibly wrong. Thus, Danilevsky's factor of political independence does not seem to be absolutely essential for a group to be creative in many fields of culture. Sometimes political power and independence can facilitate cultural creativity; at other times they can hinder it; and, again, they may have no effect. More accurate is the factor of *cultural freedom*, which allows the creators to create without being suffocated in their creative activities by all sorts of censorship and regimentation arising especially from their political or religious governing powers-that-be.

Toynbee's factor of a geographical environment that is neither too hard nor too comfortable is vague. Who knows exactly what environment is hard or soft for any given group at any given time? In addition, it is hardly possible to establish that all great civilizations emerged in such an environment. On the other hand, one can state with a reasonable degree of certainty that the environment of hundreds of preliterate groups has been of a "moderate" kind, neither too severe nor too soft. Yet these groups have not reached the level of Toynbee's civilization.

Also unsatisfactory is Toynbee's factor of a creative minority. He rejects the factor of racial and biological heredity. If we exclude these factors, then whence and how could Toynbee's creative minority appear, and how could it become creative? Unless he follows Spengler's theory of the "cosmic creative grace" that chooses in a mysterious way its "elect" and makes them a "creative minority," the what, how, whence, and why of the emergence and disappearance of Toynbee's minority remains a complete mystery.

Finally, his factors of challenge and response, withdrawal and return, are not very enlightening. As long as any group lives, it is incessantly challenged or stimulated by millions of external and internal stimuli and incessantly responds to these challenges. There is no living group or person, including the most uncreative, that is not subject to this factor. Since it is universal, continuous, and common to all living groups and individuals, it evidently cannot be a factor that operates only for creative groups and persons. The same can be said about the factor of withdrawal and return.

On the other hand, Toynbee and Danilevsky do not mention some of the factors that are indispensable for a person's or a group's eminent creativity. Among several as yet little-known factors of creativity, the following seem to be indispensable:

1. *Suprasensory and suprarational genius,* resulting either from "fortunate heredity," of which little is known at the moment, or coming from some other, unknown source.

2. The *social need* for a new system, whether scientific, technological, military, religious, ethical, artistic, or other. Without such a need being felt, a given group or person does not set out to do the requisite creative work.

3. *Cross-fertilization of cultural streams,* the factor stressed by Danilevsky.

4. *Cultural freedom* (discussed above).

5. *Luck,* a residual factor of an incidental favorable situation or constellation of circumstances that suggests an idea, like the swaying lamp noted by Galileo in the cathedral at Pisa, or the apple falling with a thud in the garden of Isaac Newton.

Each of these factors taken separately is insufficient to account for creativity; taken together, they account a little bit more for the creativity of persons and groups, though the whole problem of creativity and its factors still remains a mystery.

Unsatisfactory also are the examined theories in their analyses of growth and disintegration of civilizations. Since, according to their scheme, civilizations must undergo breakdown, disintegration, and death, these writers must either bury them or consider them "abortive," "arrested," and so forth.

These authors are not deterred by the fact that some of the civilizations which, according to their scheme, ought to have been dead long ago, have survived for centuries and longer, and are still very much alive. These writers—especially Toynbee—dispose of the difficulty by the simple device of postulating a "petrified" civilization. Thus China, Egypt, and the Hellenic cultures have been or were "petrified" for thousands of years.

All of Roman history was, in Toynbee's scheme, but an incessant disintegration from the very beginning to the end. In such a scheme, civilizations hardly have time to live and grow. If they are not born abortive—as some are—they are arrested. If they are not arrested, they break down almost immediately after they are born and then begin to disintegrate or become a "petrified trunk."

The foregoing explains why in Toynbee's work especially, and to a lesser degree in Danilevsky's and Spengler's, little analysis is found of the phase of the growth of civilizations. Only indefinite statements are to be found to the effect that in that phase there is a "creative minority" successfully meeting the challenge, that there is no class war, no intersociety war, and that everything goes well there, moves, and becomes more and more "etherialized." That is about all that is said of this phase. Such an idyllic characterization of the process of growth of Toynbee's twenty-one civilizations is evidently fantastic. If we have to believe it, we seemingly have to accept that in Greece before 431–403 B.C. (Toynbee's date for the Hellenic breakdown) there were no wars, no revolutions, no class struggle, no slavery, no traditionalism, no uncreative minority, and that all these "plagues" appeared only after the Peloponnesian War. On the other hand, we shall expect that, after this war, creativeness ceased in Greece and Rome, and that there was no Plato, no Aristotle, no Epicurus, no Zeno, no Plotinus, no Polybius, no Church Fathers, no Aristophanes, no Lucretius, no scientific discovery. As a matter of fact, the situation in all these respects was very different before and after the breakdown. The "indicators" of war (magnitude measured by war casualties) per million of the population for Greece were 29 for the fifth, 48 for the fourth, and 18 and 3, respectively, for the third and second centuries B.C. "Indicators" of internal disturbances (revolutions) were 149, 468, 320, 259, and 36, respectively, for the centuries from the sixth to the second B.C., inclusive. This shows that the real movement of wars and revolutions in Greece was very different from what Toynbee tells us. The same is true of Rome.[27]

Scientific, philosophical, and religious creativeness likewise

[27] See the detailed data in the *Dynamics*, Vol. III.

reached its peak in and after the fifth century B.C. rather than before that time.[28] In regard to Western civilization, as mentioned, Toynbee's diagnosis is somewhat ambiguous. In many places he says that its breakdown is already in process; in other places he is noncommital. Whatever his diagnosis, he regards Western civilization before the fifteenth century as in the phase of growth. If this is so, then, according to his scheme, no revolutions, serious wars or hard-and-fast class divisions existed in Europe before that century. Factually, however, in the history of Europe the thirteenth and fourteenth centuries were the most revolutionary up to the twentieth century; likewise, serfdom and class divisions were hard and fast, and there were many wars—small and great.

Finally, medieval Western civilization of the period of growth does not exhibit many of the traits of Toynbee's growing civilizations; it displays instead a mass of traits characteristic of Toynbee's disintegrating civilizations. The same is true of his other civilizations. This means that Toynbee's uniformities of growth and decline of the civilizations are not borne out by the facts. With some modification, this criticism can also be applied to Danilevsky's and Spengler's outlines of this phase.

These defects do not disvalue the outstanding significance and scientific importance of the theories discussed. The works of Spengler and Toynbee are and will probably remain in their field great masterpieces.

[28] *Ibid.*, Vol. II, ch. 3.

CHAPTER 9

Recent Macrosociologies of Cultural

Systems and Supersystems

THE NONTOTALITARIAN MACROSOCIOLOGIES OF CULTURAL SYSTEMS AND SUPERSYSTEMS

The recent crop of macrosociologies of culture is not exhausted by the totalitarian theories examined in the preceding chapters, for there are also certain nontotalitarian theories. The nontotalitarian theories do not share the basic assumption of the totalitarian theories that the total culture of any individual, group, or area, and especially of vast "cultural continents" called civilizations, is a completely unified causal or meaningful or meaningful-causal system. Such an assumption, these theorists point out, is neither warranted logically, nor supported by relevant empirical evidence: It is largely due to vague and loose criteria of unity or integration expressed in such unclear terms as "interdependence," "coherence," "adjustment," "prime symbol," "style," "function," and the like. As soon as we apply more rigorous criteria of unity, we realize that total cultures or civilizations are only partially unified into many cultural systems and congeries that coexist with the dominant system, if it is present in a given total culture or civilization.

This conclusion, reached by many scholars of culture, has induced them to approach the study of the problems of civilizational or cultural *Ganzheiten* from a different standpoint. Instead of assuming the total integration of the whole civilization or of any total culture, these scholars have proceeded in a less postulational and more inductive way in their investigation of cultural wholes. First, these "culturologists" defined rigorously the nature and criteria of civilizational or cultural unity. Second, armed with their rigorous criteria of cultural *Ganzheiten*, they proceeded to survey and to study various cultural systems, small and vast, given in the total cultural universe of man. Third, they discovered the existence of an enormous number of various causal and causal-meaningful cultural systems in the total culture of mankind as well as in that of any population, any social group, any culture-area, any individual. They discovered that hundreds and thousands of *small* cultural systems of the type "A is B," or "C is not D," "two and two make four," "snow is cold," "thou shall or shall not," a pictorial design, a folksong, and a simple utensil are living in ideological or behavioral and material forms in the *total* culture of individuals and groups, and they began to develop *a sociology of cultural systems.* Fourth, further study of cultural *Ganzheiten* disclosed that most of these small cultural systems have been combining together and producing vaster meaningful and causal-meaningful cultural systems, which, in turn, have formed still vaster cultural *Ganzheiten* up to the vastest possible cultural supersystems. "Two and two make four" is a mere "subsystem" in a vaster system of the table of multiplication, this table in turn is a subsystem in a vaster system of arithmetics, which is a subsystem in a still vaster system of mathematics; mathematics, in turn, is a subsystem in a still larger system of science. A similar unification of small systems into progressively vaster systems is given in other fields of culture: religious, philosophical, artistic, ethical, legal, economic, and political meanings-values-norms in their ideological, behavioral, and material forms.[1]

Fifth, many culturologists have concentrated on a study of vast cultural systems like language, science, philosophy, religion, law, ethics, fine arts, politics and economics (again in their ideological, behavioral, and material forms). Out of this sort of studies have grown *special, cultural sociologies:* the sociology of language,[2] of science, of religion, of philosophical *Weltan-*

---

[1] See a development of these statements in P. Sorokin, *SCP*, chs. 17, 18, 19, 35; and in the *Dynamics*, Vol. IV, chs. 1–4.

[2] See the literature on it in H. G. Rasch, "Sprachsoziologie" in K. C. Specht, H. G. Rasch, and H. Hofbauer, *Studium Sociale* (Cologne, 1963). See also F. de Saussure, *Cours de linguistique générale* (Paris, 1962).

schauungen, of law, of fine arts, of ethics, of political, economic, and other *cultural* systems.

Sixth, some cultural sociologists have gone still further and discovered the existence and functioning—not in all but in some of the total cultures—of still vaster supersystems that unify in themselves a large portion of many cultural unities. The theories of "material" and "non-material," of "sacral" and "secular," of "reality-culture" and "value-culture," of "ideational, integral, and sensate" cultural *Ganzheiten* are examples of the vastest supersystems rightly or wrongly discovered by some of the culturologists.

Seventh, in most of their studies of vast cultural systems and supersystems the culturologists deal with real cultural *Ganzheiten* whose important parts articulate consistent and complementary sets of meanings-values-norms in ideological-behavioral-material forms and are bound together by the triple causal dependence of each important part upon the other important parts, of all important parts upon the whole system or supersystem, and of the whole system or supersystem upon its important parts.

Eighth, as a result of these findings, the total cultures of individuals, groups, or culture-areas appear to be causally and meaningfully unified exactly in those portions of total culture which have cultural systems and supersystems. This means that any such total culture is, at least, partly unified. The greater the portion of it that is integrated into ideological-behavioral-material systems, the more fully the ideological form of each system is realized in its behavioral and material forms; the vaster these systems, the more consistent or complementary they mutually are; and the greater the proportion of them that are unified into one supersystem, the greater and closer is the integration of a given total culture.

Ninth, many of these systems and supersystems are not territorially bound to any definite contiguous territory. Ideologically, behaviorally, and materially they exist and live everywhere where there are individuals and groups that realize them ideologically or behaviorally or materially. Such individuals, groups, and "material objectifications" are often scattered over the whole planet, as is the case with such cultural systems as the Platonic system of philosophy, mathematics, Beethoven's music, the automobile-aeroplane-television complex, Gothic architecture, and Marxian or utilitarian ethics.

Tenth, the totality of these mutually harmonious systems unified into one supersystem gives to each total culture (that reaches this level of integration) its *dominant* physiognomy, style, or individuality.

Eleventh, not all the total cultures of individuals, of groups, or of culture-areas reach this high degree of unification. Many of these have only a multitude of small systems and a few vast systems meaningfully neutral or contradictory to each other and causally independent from one another. Such total cultures, having no dominant physiognomy, individuality, or style, can be called eclectic or "scatterbrained." They are like "cultural dumps" in which various cultural phenomena, not bound by either meaningful or causal ties, are piled together. They exhibit a multitude of small systems, but in their totality these cover only a small portion of such eclectic cultures. Hardly any of the "scatterbrained" cultures ever reaches a real greatness or plays a creatively important role in the cultural history of mankind. In Danilevsky's terms, such total cultures are largely "ethnographic material" in the total cultural universe of man.

Twelfth, even the highly integrated total cultures are never integrated in 100 percent of all their cultural phenomena, for there always coexist several vast systems and a multitude of small systems and congeries meaningfully neutral or contradictory to the supersystem and causally independent from it. As minor currents they run in the river-bed of the same total culture in which flows the main current of the dominant supersystem fed by the currents of all its tributary systems.

These theses show clearly the substantial difference between the totalitarian macrosociologies of civilizations and those of cultural systems, supersystems, and congeries. We shall now review some recent macrosociological theories of cultural systems and supersystems. Their main forms are well exemplified by the theories of Northrop, Kroeber, Znaniecki, Ortega, Becker, and by the "dichotomic" and other analyses of cultural *Ganzheiten.*

F. S. C. NORTHROP (1893–)[3]

Among Northrop's works, *The Meeting of East and West: An Inquiry Concerning World Understanding*[4] is most important for our purposes, for it shows that the total culture of any nation is neither a completely unified *Ganzheit* nor a mere dumping place for innumerable cultural congeries. Besides congeries, a vast total culture consists of one or several large cultural systems, occasionally crowned by a supersystem. The supersystem and the vast cultural systems are based on certain philosophical presuppositions. In unfolded form these presuppositions are articulated and objectified in the main compartments of each total culture—in arts and philosophy, religion and law, economics and politics, manners and mores, in the prevalent type of personality, and in basic social institutions.

> Cultures with differing political, economic, aesthetic and religious ideals or values are grounded in differing philosophical conceptions of the nature of man and of the universe. . . . Actually in any culture there are as many different theoretical beliefs as there are different individuals or different opinions of the same individual at different times. Usually, however, certain beliefs capture a majority opinion. (*The Meeting of East and West*, pp. 14, 249, 437.)

These general conceptions give to cultures their individuality and specific "physiognomy."

In the last analysis, the "philosophical presuppositions" (or "major premises" or "prime symbols") of each cultural system are based upon the state of science or the basic scientific theories existing in a given culture.

> Mathematical and natural science, as its facts are made theoretically systematic and articulate, gives rise to [a corresponding] philosophy, and this philosophy . . . gives technical meaning and—since it is scientifically determined—publicly valid empirical justification to the claim of [a corresponding] religion

---

[3] See a more detailed analysis of Northrop's theory in my *Modern Historical and Social Philosophies*, chs. 8, 13.

[4] (New York, 1946).

and morality; and these in turn and the science and philosophy from which they stem, when applied, generate the [corresponding] arts of poetry, painting, music, sculpture, architecture, and governmental and ecclesiastical polity in their normative character, as well as engineering and technocracy. . . . In short, philosophy . . . is natural science made articulate with respect to its basic assumptions on the theoretical side. (*Ibid.*, pp. 288 ff.)

The real significance of Northrop's propositions is twofold. By arriving at these conclusions independently he additionally confirms their validity and demonstrates this validity admirably, especially in the cases of the Mexican and the United States cultures.

Having taken the *total* culture of Mexico, Northrop convincingly shows that it is made up largely of five coexisting systems of culture, each grounded in its own philosophical principles (and a corresponding state of natural science). At Mexico City, he points out, one meets, within one square mile, shops and parks reminiscent of Paris, Manhattan skyscrapers, the Spanish Hotel Majestic, the colonial Catholic cathedral and National Palace, and the distinctly Mexican Zocalo, whose lawns cover the Aztec ruins: "There they were. All within one square mile. Five distinct and unique cultures: ancient Aztec, Spanish Colonial, positivistic French nineteenth century, Anglo-American economic, and contemporary Mexican. Harmonious, yet competitively diverse." (*Ibid.*, p. 15.)

Subsequently, Northrop analyzes in detail the purely Indian, precolonial culture of Mexico in all its main variations and manifestations, with its underlying science and philosophy, its theoretic and aesthetic principles, beginning with the Place of the Gods (Teotihuacán) and Pyramid of the Sun and ending with the fresco, with its naturalistic colors, recently unearthed behind the Pyramid of the Sun. In a similar manner, he analyzes the Spanish colonial culture that replaced the almost completely destroyed high Aztec culture. This Spanish culture, with its Catholicism, its Thomistic philosophy and science, is manifested by the Spanish Baroque cathedrals and other buildings, in the Catholic cult, in the remnants of the hierarchical order of values and social ranks, and in many other details. A careful study of the Spanish colonial culture, however, shows how it was modified by the impact of the precolonial Mexican culture. For instance, the painting of the angel at the Tepotzotlan Jesuit Monastery, and especially the beloved patron saint of Mexico, the Virgin of Guadalupe, as well as the style of some of the chapels, display a distinctly Indian influence.

The third cultural system of Mexico is a French, positivistic, and democratic culture that lasted for some sixty years during the nineteenth century and to a large extent supplanted the Spanish colonial culture. This French culture, based mainly upon the philosophy of Auguste Comte, has manifested itself in a thousand ways, beginning with the nationalization of church property and the secularization of religion and ending with the rise of democratic and "enlightened" dictatorial political regimes.

The fourth component system of the total Mexican culture is that manifested by the Anglo-American system of economic and cultural values, which modified the French and other cultural systems and was articulated especially in the forms of economic organization and the material aspects of living. In the colonial period, Mexico was dominated by the "Spanish-Catholic religious passion," in the nineteenth century by the French "political passion," and at the end of that century by the "economic passion" and the "economic democracy" of Bentham, Mill, Jevons, Marshall, Taussig, and others. The period of the Diaz dictatorship was the golden age of American and British capitalists and of industrial progress as the main instrument of social progress.

Finally, the fifth component of the total Mexican culture is contemporary Mexican culture. It represents a sort of combination of the intuitive (Bergson), phenomenological, and axiological philosophy of Husserl, Max Scheler, and Hartmann—as well as Mexico's own notable nonpositivistic philosophers—Anglo-American democracy and technology, and Soviet and Marxian economic, political, and social values. The fusion of these elements into the passionate, thoroughly "aesthetic," deeply religious—and at the same time Marxian—scientific and economic culture is clearly expressed in the frescoes of Orosco and Rivera. This fifth new culture is not quite integrated as yet; it is still in the process of becoming, but it is already the most important component of the total Mexican culture. (*Ibid.*, pp. 17–28.)

In a similar manner, Northrop analyzes the "free culture" of the United States. Concretely diverse, the "soul of the United States is basically Anglo-American, just as the soul of Mexico is Spanish-American in character," he says. In the total complex and diverse culture of the United States, this dominant Anglo-American cultural system is based largely upon the philosophy of John Locke (supplemented by that of David Hume, Bishop Berkeley, and other English empiricists), a philosophy grounded in turn in the science of Galileo, Huygens, and, especially, Newton's *Principia*. The Declaration of Independence, the Constitution of the United States, the main legal statutes concerning property and other rights, the prevalent conception of the role of government and of the rights of man, all these and many other basic traits and values of the United States culture are almost a verbatim articulation of the principles of Locke's philosophy. So also, essentially, is the economic organization of this country as the "businessman's world." Its economy and ethics are, in a broad sense, the economy of Smith, Malthus, Ricardo, and Jevons, in addition to the utilitarian ethics of Bentham and Mill, which are a sort of application of Locke's principles to the field of economics and ethics. Again, the predominant religion of the country, Protestantism, is largely an enunciation of Locke's principles in the realm of religion.

Even such a detail as the policy of this country toward Mexico has consistently been an articulation of Locke's idea that the main function of government is the protection of private property. In accordance with this principle, the United States tried to protect the rights of American corporations that owned almost all of Mexico's oil and other natural resources by sending a military force into Mexico and protesting against the nationalization of these resources by the Mexican Government. The main argument of our Secretaries of State from Woodrow Wilson's administration through Franklin Roosevelt's has been that the rights of property are sacred and inviolable, even when such rights rob Mexico's native population of the necessary minimum means of subsistence and of the elementary rights of man and citizen. In brief, the central and largest part of the total culture of the United States has been but a consistent articulation of Galileo's and Newton's mathematics and physics as the foundation of the Lockean philosophy and the philosophical, economic, and ethical principles of Hume, Bishop Berkeley, Smith, Bentham, Mill, and others.

The total culture of the United States also contains several other systems: remnants of Indian precolonial culture, the culture of the Aristotelian-Thomist Catholic Church, and the emerging new culture that transcends the Galilean-Newtonian-Lockean culture. It is based on up-to-date natural science and a philosophy grounded in this modern science. So far, however, these have been minor cultural systems, the major one being the Lockean-Protestant-Individualistic-Businessman-Atomistic-Operational. This cultural system is articulated in all compartments of American culture. Grant Wood's picture entitled "Daughters of the Revolution" is an example of Locke's *tabula rasa* of the human soul or personality. (*Ibid.*, pp. 66–164.)

Northrop also analyzes the total cultures of England, Germany, Soviet Russia, and the Roman Catholic Church.

In the case of Soviet Russia, he shows the decisive role of Marxian philosophy in establishing the basis of the contemporary Soviet Russian culture. "Russia is what it is today not because there was any necessity that it be that way, but largely because, for the reasons indicated [in the analysis], the leaders of the Russian revolution took the speculative philosophical theory of Marx, and by persuasive and forceful means brought others to its acceptance, and built political action and cultural institutions in terms of it." Marxian-Hegelian philosophy (and the natural science in which it is grounded) is the main premise that is now articulated by thousands of ideological, philosophical, religious, political, economic, artistic, and other cultural phenomena of Russia's main cultural system. This Marxian philosophy is the master key to a comprehensive explanation of millions of small and large enigmas of the total Soviet culture. (*Ibid.*, pp. 246, and ch. 6.)

Having shown the existence of comparatively vast cultural systems in the total cultures of separate nations or in the Roman

Catholic Church, Northrop goes further and "unearths" the two vastest cultural supersystems: one based upon "scientific" or "theoretic," the other upon "aesthetic" or "intuitional," components. The first is dominant in the West's culture; the second in that of the East.

Aesthetic or intuitional cognition or knowledge is derived from, and refers to, objects directly arrived at through experience, the "pure facts" like "blue" or "love" or any other "pure experience" unmediated by any concepts, and properly knowable only to a person who has such an experience. "Blue" is inaccessible to the blind; the music of Beethoven remains unknown to the deaf; at best they can only have a substitute diagram for these. A person who never experiences love or hate remains ignorant of these emotions. All phenomena belonging to this category of the immediately sensed, perceived, apprehended, experienced phenomena make up the aesthetic continuum or aesthetic component in the nature of things or reality. Any knowledge or notion derived in this direct, intuitive way is the aesthetic or intuitive component in knowledge or cognition. The aesthetic continuum itself has two main forms: (a) the *differentiated*, like "blue," "soft," "lovely," "warm," or "cheerful," when some of the infinite properties of the undifferentiated continuum are specifically distinguished, "picked up," or differentiated by direct intuition as "pure fact"; (b) *undifferentiated* aesthetic continuum, meaning the primeval aesthetic continuum out of which arises any directly sensed differentiation. It pervades all the differentiated "aesthetic phenomena." It is neither A nor non-A, neither this nor that; at the same time it is the *coincidentia oppositorum* that potentially embraces A as well as non-A. This undifferentiated aesthetic continuum is the Jen in Confucianism, Tao in Taoism, Nirvana in Buddhism, Brahman or Chit in Hinduism, the "Divine Nothing" of true mystics, the "Infinite Manifold," the *coincidentia oppositorum* and the Supraessence of St. Augustine, Pseudo-Dionysius, J. S. Erigena, Nicolas of Cusa, and of all true mystics. It cannot be expressed in words. It cannot be described by any concepts or terms. It is truly ineffable. It can be experienced directly only as a "pure fact" through the specific technique of the Yogi or of the true mystics. It cannot be conceptualized and analyzed scientifically.

In this undifferentiated form the aesthetic aspect of the nature of things has been intuited or immediately apprehended in all its all-embracing indeterminateness, mainly in the Oriental cultures of China, India, and other Buddhist or Jainist cultures. And these cultures have been largely built on this aesthetic—differentiated and undifferentiated—continuum and the aesthetic component of human knowledge.

"Theoretic" or scientific knowledge, concept, or cognition is indirectly derived from, and refers to, the component in the nature of things that is never presented as "pure experience." It is postulated as an *a priori* hypothesis and is in part and indirectly verified *a posteriori* through experimentally checked deductive consequences. The theoretic or scientific component in reality or in the nature of things is therefore quite different from the aesthetic component; the theoretic component is never immediately sensed, perceived, intuited, or apprehended, but is always postulated, mathematically designated, and indirectly verified through its experimentally checked deductive inferences. Chairs, tables, or any three-dimensional objects, electrons, molecules, universals—everything up to God the Father—belong to the theoretical component in the nature of things. Not one of them is immediately sensed, perceived, or apprehended.

The two components of the nature of things or of reality are thus quite different from one another, but they are mutually supplementary. Each presents its own "aspect" of the nature of things, quite different from the other, but equally real and mutually complementary. As a matter of fact, an adequate knowledge of anything requires its "epistemic correlation"—namely, a valid correlation between the aesthetic component and the respective theoretic component. Together they give an adequate knowledge of the nature of things. Separately they give at best only a one-sided comprehension or apprehension of things, either purely "aesthetic" or purely "theoretic." Thus, what is "aesthetically" sensed as "sound" is theoretically a "vibration of air waves"; the "aesthetically perceived" color "blue" is theoretically either a vibration of ether waves of a certain length or of light waves of a certain spectral composition. An electron cannot be immediately observed. It is an *a priori*, postulated hypothesis. However, its reality and postulated properties can be experimentally verified through the Wilson cloud chamber where, on the chamber's fuzzy aesthetic continuum, the electrons appear as "flashes." Aesthetic "flashes" and theoretic "electrons" thus are epistemically correlated and together give a "two-sided," adequate cognition of the nature of electrons.

Having elucidated the aesthetic and theoretic kinds of knowledge and components in the nature of things and their epistemic correlation, Northrop proceeds to show that the Orient's total culture, especially that of China and India, has been dominated mainly by the vast aesthetic cultural supersystem that is based upon aesthetic or intuitional apprehension. On the other hand, the total Western culture has been dominated by the vastest scientific cultural supersystem, based upon theoretic or scientific (postulational) knowledge. Several theoretic cultural systems have played the role of minor systems in the culture of the East, and several minor aesthetic cultural systems have existed in the West's culture; but they are minor currents in these predominantly aesthetic and theoretic cultures.

The main Oriental religions and ethics, such as Confucianism, Taoism, Hinduism, Jainism, with their absolutely indeterminate "aesthetic continuum" of Jen, Tao, Brahman, or "empty Nirvana"; the Chinese, Hindu, and Buddhist fine arts, especially painting; their psychology, with its indeterminate "perhaps" or "maybe"; the tolerance of these religions and ethics toward other religions and ethics as "differentiations" of the undifferentiated aesthetic continuum; their laws and even many forms of their economic and political processes—these and thousands of other phenomena are but articulations of the basic "aesthetic component" that lies at the foundation of these cultures. (*Ibid.*, chs. 7, 12.)

On the other hand, the remarkable progress of Western science and technology; the determinate, theistic, and deistic Catholic and Protestant religions, supplemented by the Jewish and the Mohammedan, all claiming the monopolistic truth and all being theoretically postulated and indirectly rationalized; the Western determinate—rational—ethics and law; the Western fine arts, which are mainly a means to convey some theoretically conceived ideas and values; the predominant Western philosophy

—Thomistic Aristolelianism, Cartesian rationalism, Lockean-Humean empiricism, Kantian criticism, Fichtean ethical idealism, Comtian-Spencerian positivism, Hegelian-Marxian dialectic —these and thousands of other cultural phenomena of the West are but the articulations of the theoretic component on which they are based.

Northrop's development and demonstration of this thesis, especially in the field of Western and Eastern fine arts, is brilliant. He does not deny that the total Eastern and the total Western cultures each exhibit enormous diversity and self-evident contrasts. Nevertheless, the more contrasting the various parts of each culture are, the more similar and congenial they are in the basic aesthetic or theoretic components that permeate all parts of each culture.

The purpose of developing these theories is to find out whether diverse cultures are only diverse or mutually contradictory; and, if they are conflicting, what is the scientific way of resolving the conflicts between the Anglo-American and the Latin American (especially Mexican) cultures; between the "capitalist" and "communist" societies; between the Lockean liberal, political democracies and the Marxian socioeconomic democracies; between Roman Catholicism and Protestantism; and especially, and most of all, between East and West?

Since all the main cultural systems and social institutions are based upon their respective philosophies, which in their turn are grounded in their respective states of science (and/or aesthetic apprehension), the most effective way of solving the conflicts, according to Northrop, is to eliminate first the apparent or real contradiction between the mathematical and natural science of conflicting cultures and societies, and then the conflict between the basic philosophies, grounded in the different natural science of the conflicting cultural systems and institutions. When the conflict between these true foundations of the antagonistic cultural systems is removed, these cultures and institutions become mutually compatible and harmonious. Then peaceful coexistence, cooperation, and mutual supplementation replace the conflict and struggle between the cultural systems and their human societies.

A philosophy and culture built on the epistemic correlation of both components removes the contradiction of East and West, and Soviet Russia and the Lockean democracies, of the United States and the Latin American cultures. Each culture and society gains immeasurably and enriches itself by being supplemented by the harmoniously infused different cultural values.

The author elucidates these ideas in considerable detail and applies them to the concrete solution of most of the important conflicts of our time.

CRITICISM

Since Northrop's cultural unities are real meaningful-causal systems and since most of his other propositions appear to be correct, they do not need any criticism on my part. There are, however, certain points in his theory that need a close examination, namely, his "aesthetic-intuitional" cognition, component of reality, and cultural supersystem dominant in the East, and his "theoretic-scientific" knowledge, component of reality (of "the nature of things"), and supersystem dominant in the West; and his insistence that the philosophical presuppositions of cultural systems are dependent upon the existing state of, particularly, physicomathematical sciences.

The "aesthetic" and "theoretic" cultural systems are the vastest among Northrop's cultural *Ganzheiten*. They can therefore be called "supersystems," though he does not use this term.

The main shortcoming of this dyadic theory of cognition, forms of reality, and cultural supersystems is that each of Northrop's classes, especially his "aesthetic" one, represents a unification of two basically different forms of cognition, of "the nature of things" and of cultural supersystems. In order to explain this statement I have to outline my "triadic" theory in these fields:

1. The total reality or, in Northrop's terms, the total "nature of things" is infinitely many-dimensional and in its inexhaustible plenitude can hardly be fully known by the finite human mind.

2. Being ourselves an important part of this total reality, we can and do grasp some of its basic differentiations. Of its

innumerable modes of being, three basic forms of the total reality appear to be essential and cognizable: empirical-sensory, rational, and "superrational-supersensory" (but not "supernatural"), representing the deepest, the highest, and the most "hidden" forms of the total reality. It is different from the sensory and rational forms and inaccessible to sensory and rational cognition. This conception does not deny the sensory-empirical form of the total reality but it makes it only one of its three aspects. Though this "three-dimensional" or integral conception of the total reality is only a rough approximation to its innumerable aspects, nevertheless it is a more adequate approximation than any of the philosophies that reduce the total reality either to purely sensory-empirical or consciously rational or "superrational" modes of being.

3. In accordance with this three-dimensional cognizable reality stands the three-channeled integral theory of cognition of this reality. In contrast to one-sided theories of cognition which claim that we cognize the reality only through sense-perception and observation (sensate system of truth), or only through rational, logicomathematical reasoning (rational system of truth), or only through "superrational" intuition (ideational system of truth), the integral theory of cognition contends that we have not one but many ways of cognition and, among these, three basic channels of acquiring knowledge of the total reality: sensory, rational, and "supersensory-superrational." The empirical aspect of the total reality is perceived by us through our sense organs and their extensions: microscopes, telescopes, radars, masors, etc. The rational aspect or differentiation of the reality is comprehended by us mainly through our reason: mathematical and logical thought in all its rational forms. Finally, the glimpses of the "superrational-supersensory" modes of being are given to us by the true "superrational-supersensory" "intuition," "insight," "inspiration," or "flash of enlightenment" of all creative geniuses: founders of great religions, sages and giants of philosophy and ethics, great scientists, artists, and other preeminent creators in all fields of culture. This superconscious "intuition" or "insight" is different from the sensory and rational ways of cognition and creativity. It should not be mixed with

Freud's or Jung's or E. von Hartmann's "unconscious," "sub-conscious," or "racial memory," as is usually done. While the "superconscious" lies above the conscious and rational, the unconscious is below the conscious level of mental activity. Though the superconscious-intuitional mode of cognition and creativity is still doubted by many sensate psychologists and epistemologists, at the present time we have a sufficient body of empirical and logical evidence ascertaining its existence and functionings.[5] Its main function is that of a revealer, starter, and supreme guide in the *great* discoveries, inventions, and creative achievements (small ones are achieved by cooperation of sensory and rational cognition). In this capacity it cooperates with sensory and rational ways of cognition and creation, whose main functions seem to consist in developing and empirically testing the illuminating idea flashed by the superconscious intuition of genius. All great achievements and discoveries are always the result of the unified work of all three ways of cognition and creativity. The truth obtained through the integral use of all three modes of cognition ("triple epistemic correlation") is fuller and greater than that achieved through one of the three channels alone. The history of human knowledge and creativity is a cemetery filled with wrong empirical observations, false reasonings, and cockeyed pseudointuitions. In the integral use of all three ways, they supplement, correct, and balance one another. Integral cognition means that we learn about the total reality not only from empirical scientists, logicians, and mathematicians, but also from great religious and ethical leaders like

---

[5] See an analysis, evidence, and literature on this in P. Sorokin, *The Ways and Power of Love*, chs. 5, 6; *Social and Cultural Dynamics*, Vol. IV, ch. 16; and Allen, *P. A. Sorokin in Review*. As "spiritual insight," it is discussed by E. W. Sinnott in his *Two Roads to Truth* (New York, 1953); as "intuition" in F. S. C. Northrop's *The Meeting of East and West* (New York, 1946); as "inductive leap" in H. Margeneau's *Open Vistas* (New Haven, 1961); as the supreme form of mental activity by Björn Sjövall in his *Höjdpsykologi* (Stockholm, 1959); by Arthur Koestler in his *The Act of Creation* (New York, 1964); as the Taoist "no knowledge" by R. G. H. Siu in his *The Tao of the Sciences* (New York, 1957); and as "mystical experience" in R. G. Johnson's *Watcher on the Hills* (London, 1959). Under different terms the superconscious is acknowledged by V. Frankl, G. Allport, Saint John Perse, C. Gattegno, R. Assagioli, and many other investigators of human personality, human mind, and methods of cognition and creativity.

Buddha, Lao-tse, Jesus, and from creative geniuses like Beethoven and Mozart, Phidias and Michelangelo, Homer and Shakespeare.

The integral cognition is particularly necessary in the cognition of man and of psychosocial and cultural phenomena, because the superorganic human world is made up not only of physical and biological forms of being but also of the "immaterial"—unconscious, conscious-rational, and superconscious-superrational forms and energies of the total reality, and because man is not only physical object and biological organism but a rational thinker and doer, and, particularly, a "supersensory and superrational" creator, an eminent participant in creative processes of the cosmos. So also is the sociocultural, human universe created by man. Franz Kafka's *des Menschen Tiefe ist seine Höhe* (the deepest in man is his highest) beautifully sums up this point.

4. In the history of human thought, creativity, and culture, there have been cultures and periods in which each of three ways of cognition has been dominant: the *sensory*, giving sensate system of truth, sensate conception of reality, and sensate cultural supersystem; the *rational* (logicomathematical), giving idealistic system of truth, reality, and cultural supersystem; and the *supersensory-superrational cognition*, producing the ideational system of truth, conception of reality, and cultural supersystem. Side by side with these three cognitive and cultural orders, there have been a few periods and cultures dominated by the integral cognition system of truth, reality and cultural supersystems; and there have been also a multitude of poorly unified, eclectic cultures and periods. My *Dynamics* deals in a detailed and systematic way with the sensate, rational (idealistic), and ideational systems of cognition, truth, reality, and sociocultural orders or supersystems and investigates again in the most detailed and empirical way the fluctuation of these three orders in history of the Greco-Roman and Western cultures—and more concisely— in that of the Egyptian, Chinese, Indian, and some other total cultures.[6]

5. In the light of this integral theory, the main shortcoming

---

[6] See all four volumes of the *Dynamics*.

of Northrop's dyad is that in his "aesthetic" form he unites two fundamentally different forms of cognition, truth, aspects of reality, and cultural supersystems—sensate and ideational. These two forms in no way can be identified with each other and treated as one "aesthetic" form.

Northrop seemingly puts them together for the reason that they are both "immediately intuited," "directly sensed," "immediately apprehended," and "immediately perceived."

Here lies the weak point of his dyadic division and of a number of conclusions he draws from it. To begin with, the undifferentiated continuum—God, Tao, Chit, Nirvana, Jen, Brahman, Atman—is certainly neither "directly observable" nor "immediately inspected" and "sensed" in the same manner in which we sense, observe, and inspect "blue." "Blue" is perceived by all (except the blind), but the "undifferentiated continuum" and its deepest aspects are intuited only by a few, and only after long training, endeavor, and the peculiar grace of genius.

Otherwise, there would hardly be any difference between a great genius and an ordinary mind perfectly capable of immediate sense perception, of even good logic, and perfectly incapable of discovering a great verity or of creating a great value.

In brief, to identify sensory perception with supersensory-superrational intuition, the sensory with the ideational, is impossible; they are much more different from each other than even Northrop's "aesthetic" and "theoretic" categories.

The same error is responsible for the kind of things Northrop puts into each of his two classes, especially into the aesthetic category. To the aesthetic component he attributes all sense data, emotions, pains, and pleasures; Nirvana, Tao, Chit, Jen, Atman, Supraessence, even the essentials of the Russian Orthodox religion, the frenzy of the Mexican or Spanish soul, practically all the Oriental religions (except Judaism, Mohammedanism, and Shintoism), a yogi in the state of *samadhi*, or a Zen Buddhist in the state of *zatori*, or a Christian mystic who forgets in his state of ecstasy about God the Father and possibly about the whole "theoretic" Christian credo; all the fine art for the sake of art that symbolically and impressionistically conveys to us the undifferentiated continuum, beginning with almost all the art of the East—but not the religious, symbolic art of the West—and ending with the work of the French Impressionists and the abstract paintings of Georgia O'Keefe; most of the Eastern cultural phenomena; and a legion of other things that are immediately perceived, apprehended, sensed, intuited, grasped, without any theoretical ideas and concepts by postulation.

To the "theoretic" component belong almost any theoretical construction, beginning with all scientific hypotheses and ending with the theory of the Trinity and God the Father and the Christian, Mohammedan, Shintoist theologies; almost all "rational" philosophies; the bulk of the ideology of the Roman Catholic Church but for some reason not that of the Russian Orthodox Church; all the fine arts that function as a mere means for conveying various conceptual constructions of a theoretical sort; all the empirical tables, stoves, three-dimensional objects; universals, postulational concepts, electrons, molecules, protons; the bulk of Western cultural phenomena; and all the other things that are not immediately intuited, perceived, sensed, and apprehended.

One immediately perceives an utterly odd assortment in the contents of each class. For instance, one cannot understand why the bulk of Eastern art should belong to the aesthetic and the bulk of Western to the theoretic category. In both arts, a part has been "art for art's sake" and not a means for communication of this or that theory. In both arts, a part of the content represents a symbolic communication concerning the undifferentiated as well as the differentiated aesthetic continuum. A great deal in Western Christian medieval art represents "a visible and audible sign of the invisible world" of the Kingdom of God in its differentiated and undifferentiated forms. So also does a large portion of Eastern religious art. It symbolizes not only the "undifferentiated continuum" but no less, and even perhaps more, its differentiated forms and respective "theories" and beliefs. Finally, both arts have a secular, sensate form as a means for hedonistic, eudemonistic, or utilitarian enjoyment, relaxation, happiness, invigoration of the jaded nerves, and just pleasurable time-passing.[7]

[7] See the empirical evidence for these statements in my *Modern Historical and Social Philosophies*, pp. 250–254.

Still more odd is Northrop's classification of the cultures of the Catholic, Protestant, Judaist, Mohammedan, and Shinto religions as theoretic, and the cultures of the Russian Orthodox, Confucianist, Taoist, Jainist, Hinduist, and Buddhist religions as aesthetic. The reason for this classification is the supposition that the theoretic religions arose from theorizing (through concepts by postulation) about some of the differentiated properties of the undifferentiated continuum, whereas the aesthetic religions are based on an immediate intuition of the undifferentiated continuum.

This division is questionable. All his theoretic religions, except perhaps Shintoism, certainly contain an undifferentiated continuum—about as much as his aesthetic religions. All the theoretic religions have their mystical aspect, which by its very nature is a supersensory and superrational intuition of the ineffable.

There is a strong mystic current in the Greco-Roman world (Plato, Xenocrates, Apollonius, Theon, Plotinus, etc.) and in Judaism (Philo, etc.). The Suffist current in Mohammedanism is apparent in the writings of such great mystics as al-Ghazali and al-Hallaj. An uninterruptedly strong mystic current is apparent in all denominations of the Christian faith. One has only to look into the Gospel of St. John and the works of Pseudo-Dionysius, Basil the Great, Gregory of Nyssa, St. Augustine, Maximus the Confessor, Erigena, St. Anselm, Hugh of St. Victor, Thierry, Joachim of Floris, St. Francis of Assisi, Nicholas of Cusa, and of the "practical mystics" like John of the Cross, Teresa, Eckhart, Ruysbroeck, and thousands of others. They and their "*docta ignorantia*" are the Christian "mouthpieces" of the ineffable, the "Supra-essence," the "Divine Nothing," the "*coincidentia oppositorum.*"

Mysticism, as one of the main religious and secular philosophies of the Greco-Roman culture and of the Western world, gives an "indicator" of 1039, much stronger than those of fideism (369), scepticism (279), and criticism (197); it is exceeded only by empiricism (1338) and rationalism (1534). At some periods of Western thought and culture, such as the fourth century B.C., around the beginning of our era, in the second to the fourth centuries A.D., and in the twelfth and in the fifteenth centuries, the tide of mysticism was very high in the Greco-Roman and Christian West. It became low only during the last five centuries of our predominantly sensate culture.[8] Even more, ideational truth and cognition (in its religious form similar to the dominant ideational truth and cognition of the Hindu, Chinese, Mohammedan, and other Asiatic cultures) has also been dominant in Western culture: its index of 1650 is higher than that for the system of truth of rational reason (1292) and the system of truth of the senses (1338), not to mention the index of 476 for scepticism and criticism.

On the other hand, an ideology or theoretical creed based on concepts by postulation is not confined to the Catholic and Protestant branches of Christianity or to Judaism, Moham-medanism, and Shintoism. It is present to hardly a lesser degree in Russian Orthodox and Eastern Christianity generally, in Con-fucianism and Taoism, and in all denominations of Hinduism. It exists in all Buddhist denominations as well as in Jainism, Zoroastrianism, and practically all Eastern religions and philoso-phies.

The predominantly theoretic, scientific, and technological character ascribed to Western culture, in contrast to the pre-eminently aesthetic, nonscientific culture of the East, also needs serious qualification. Western culture became such only after the thirteenth—or even the fifteenth—century. Before that, the dominant culture of Europe was predominantly ideational. It centered mainly around the supersensory and superrational Kingdom of God and was little interested in science and tech-nology. Certainly it lagged far behind the science and technology of the Eastern cultures of India, China, and of Arabia. Here again, instead of a perennial contrast between the allegedly "aesthetic" East and the "theoretic" West, we really have a shifting picture: the West (up to the fifteenth century) lagging behind the East in theoretic science and technology and for the last five centuries leading the East.[9]

---

[8] See the list of Greco-Roman and Western mystics in the *Dynamics,* Vol. II, pp. 639 ff.

[9] See the movement of scientific discoveries and inventions in the *Dynamics,* Vol. II, chs. 1, 2.

Northrop's aesthetic and theoretic categories are defective because into the aesthetic category are put two basically different classes—the strictly sensory and the supersensory-superrational. These should not be united, for such a unification leads to a series of errors. The two categories being defective, the two cultural supersystems built upon them cannot be and are not real meaningful-causal unities; correspondingly, the geographical allocation of these supersystems—the aesthetic to the East and the theoretic to the West—is also somewhat incorrect. A translation of Northrop's dyadic statements into the language of my triadic propositions and of Northrop's double "epistemic correlation" into my triple "epistemic correlation," where sensory, rational, and supersensory cognitions and components mutually check and fruitfully supplement one another, may eliminate most of the shortcomings of Northrop's theory in this respect.

In many passages of his work Northrop states, without reservation, that cultural systems are based upon philosophical presuppositions and that these in turn are determined by mathematical and natural sciences existing in a given culture. For many logical and empirical reasons, the relationship between science and philosophy in actual human behavior and culture is not so uniform and one-sided as Northrop and E. de Roberty claim. Now science emerges first and determines the prevalent philosophical presuppositions of cultural systems; now the existing philosophical presuppositions—beliefs, general ideas, and philosophies—emerge first and determine the state of science. Sometimes these presuppositions can become the foundations of cultural systems in spite of being contradictory to the existing science and can even suppress science or give to its development a different direction from that dictated by science itself. At other times, science and philosophy emerge together and mutually condition each other. The theory of a one-sided dependence of philosophy or religion upon physical and mathematical science has to be viewed as a partial and limited case rather than as a universal and invariable uniformity.[10]

[10] See the reasons and empirical evidence in the *Dynamics*, Vol. IV, chs. 6, 7, and pp. 167, 196, and 292–302. This conclusion agrees with Kroeber's finding, outlined further.

The foregoing criticisms exhaust the important points of disagreement between Northrop's views and my own. Except for several unimportant details, the rest of our readings of historical events are essentially similar and often complementary.

ALFRED L. KROEBER (1876–1960)[11]

Of Kroeber's works, most important for our purposes are *Configurations of Culture Growth* (Berkeley, 1944), *The Nature of Culture* (Chicago, 1952), *Culture: A Critical Review of Concepts and Definitions* (in cooperation with C. Kluckhohn; Cambridge, Mass., 1952), and *Style and Civilization* (Ithaca, N.Y., 1957).

These works, especially the *Configurations of Culture Growth*, deal with the basic problems of change of the high-level cultures and their main systems: science, philosophy, philology, sculpture, painting, drama, literature, music, and the state organization and power of ancient Egypt, India, China, Japan, Iran, of the Arab-Muslim, Greco-Roman, Byzantine, and Hebrew cultures, and of the cultures of France, Germany, Italy, Spain, England, the Netherlands, Switzerland, the Scandinavian countries, Russia, Poland, and, finally, of the United States.

The specific procedure Kroeber uses to note and "measure" the changes in culture patterns for each country is to study the number and rank of men of creative genius. Insofar as an important pattern in any field of culture is most fully expressed through its men of genius, the appearance of a galaxy of creative geniuses of the first rank at one period, and their quantitative and qualitative decline at another period, can be taken as a good index of the flowering and decline of creativity in a given cultural compartment for the periods considered.

In accordance with this material and procedure, Kroeber's analysis opens with "philosophy," beginning with the Greeks.

---

[11] A more detailed analysis and criticism of Kroeber's theory is given in my *Modern Historical and Social Philosophies*, chs. 9, 13.

He compiles a list of all the main Greek philosophers, carefully noting the years of their life-spans and the places of their births. He accepts the prevalent evaluation of the philosophers and sums up the main creative movements in Greek philosophy as follows:

> In Greek philosophy, two grand divisions must be distinguished: a productive period, little more than three centuries long; and a period of essentially non-productive continuation, which is of indefinite duration. The productive period . . . runs from 585 to about 270, when the Stoic, Epicurean, and Sceptic doctrines had taken shape. The culmination is universally set with Plato and Aristotle, and may for convenience be put at 350, when both were alive and adult. Within fifty years of Aristotle's death, nothing new was any longer being produced in Greek philosophy, even by able men. The patterns which it had developed were evidently exhausted. . . . They merely continued to be refilled, in more or less new combinations, thereafter [until the last school of philosophy at Athens was closed by Justinian in A.D. 529].

Thus we have here one of the skew curves fairly typical of many creative movements; three centuries of rising development followed by eight of decline and final extinction. "An activity begins, develops, reaches a peak, begins to decline and there freezes. Thereafter it may continue indefinitely with imitation, repetition, or reduction" [in an institutionalized form, or, otherwise, as long as the culture that produced it survives]. (*Configurations of Culture Growth*, pp. 32–34.)

Kroeber goes on to note several details of this process, up to its overlapping with the "reorientation movement" of the Neo-Pythagoreans, Gnostics, and Neo-Platonists, which eventually merges into the cosmopolitan Christian medieval philosophy.

In a similar manner, Kroeber follows the configurations of growth, fluctuation, and decline of Christian, Arab-Muslim, Occidental—medieval and modern—philosophy (German, French, Italian, English, Dutch), and of the Indian and Chinese philosophies. At the end of these explorations, he sums up the significant conclusions concerning the configurations of the growth and decline of philosophical systems and creativity generally, and

its particular forms specifically. Here are some of these conclusions:

The contents of no two philosophic growths are ever the
same. Most of the cultures under consideration have produced
their important philosophies in two growths or in separate movements. In some of these cultures (the Greek and Chinese, for
instance), the first blossoming of philosophy was the greater,
whereas in others (the Occidental and Arabic, for instance), the
second wave was more creative.

In some cultures philosophy was born and moved within
the main religion; in others, philosophy grew up without a close
tie with religion or with very loose ties.

Equally diverse is the relation of philosophy to science. In
some cultures, for instance the Arabic-Muslim, a philosopher
was at the same time a scientist and vice versa; in other cultures, like the Chinese, Indian, and the medieval Occidental,
philosophy emerged and grew without a close tie with science,
because science was still undeveloped.[12]

As to the duration of the creative pulse, it also varies, according to Kroeber, from 150 to 400 years, with 300 the most
common. The culmination of the growth sometimes falls near
the end of the growth period, sometimes early in the second half.

The data show the rarity and spottiness of philosophical
creativity; the spottiness is not random but highly concentrated.
Philosophical creativity in the five main cultures studied flourished during little more than a third of the duration of the
civilizations in which it had become established as an activity.
And it occurred in only a small area of these civilizations: Early
Chinese philosophy flourished only in northeastern China; the
Hindu in the Ganges Valley and later on in southern India; the
Greek mainly in Ionia. Considering that many great cultures such
as those of Egypt, Mesopotamia, Persia, and Japan, as well as a
multitude of lesser cultures or civilizations, have not produced
any truly significant philosophy, the rarity and spottiness of
philosophical creativity become striking.

---

[12] This contradicts E. De Roberty's and Northrop's theories of the
uniform determination of philosophy by science.

It is significant that the great philosophies emerged simultaneously, about 600 B.C. in three of the five cultures—the Chinese, Indian, and Greek. Another moment of philosophical creativity occurred at about the same time, from A.D. 1050 to 1200, in three cultures—the Chinese Neo-Confucian, the Christian Scholastic, and the Arabic.

Why this is so, and what the factors are that determine philosophical creativity, remains an enigma. Negatively, we can assert that neither a certain civilization's general flourishing, nor its political power and economic prosperity, is enough to produce a great philosophy. The same is true of the flourishing of religion or science.

In a similar way, Kroeber proceeds to study the dynamics of creativity in science, philology, sculpture, painting, drama, literature, and music in the same main cultures. Finally, he studies separately the movement of creativity in all these cultural systems in each of the nations studied. This last investigation gives us the dynamics of the intellectual, philosophic, and aesthetic creativity of Egypt, China, Japan, India, Greece, Rome, the Near East, Islam, and the main Western countries, including Russia and Scandinavia, the Jews, and the West as a whole. A study of the cultural growth of nations permits us to grasp the typical constellations of these systems within one nation, and their change in the course of time.

Egyptian civilization uniquely rose and fell at least four times within the same patterned frame before it exhausted itself. This shows, among other things (and contrary to Danilevsky and Spengler), that a given civilization can have more than one period of blossoming and decline. In a total of 2,790 years, about 64 percent of the years were reasonably successful—prosperous and politically satisfactory. In many cases, creativity paralleled political and economic prosperity in several fields of culture; but this did not always happen, and in the case of science and literature the nonsynchronicity of economico-political progress and the flare-ups of scientific-literary creativity are fairly conspicuous.

China had two big creative pulses; Japan had four; India two; the Greco-Roman-Byzantine culture had several; the Arabic one big one; France three; England three; and Germany four. In most of these instances, the economico-political prosperity peaks did not notably coincide with the peaks of cultural creativity.[13]

We must now sum up the main results of Kroeber's extensive and scholarly analysis of the hows and whys of change in culture or civilization:

1. There is no universal uniformity dictating that every culture must develop into a high-level culture with master patterns of this or that cultural value. Only a very limited number of cultures have developed such patterns.

2. There is not sufficient evidence "of any true law in the phenomena dealt with; nothing cyclical, regularly repetitive, or necessary."

3. There is no uniformity decreeing that every culture, having once flowered, must wither without chance of revival.

4. Each major culture displays "the existence of certain fundamental patterns (supersystems) characteristic" to it. The number of such "high-value culture patterns" is very limited. They occur rarely, in a few cultures only, have a limited life-span, and are concentrated in time and space.

5. The life-span or duration of these "high-value culture patterns" seems to be shorter than that of "low-grade culture patterns," which can go on with much less change and for a much longer time.

6. The average duration of the growth and blossoming of these patterns fluctuates greatly, from a few decades to a few centuries, depending upon the class of cultural phenomena and their constellation.

7. The duration of a vaster (embracing) pattern tends to be longer and more continuous than that of a narrower sub-pattern, a part of the vaster one.

8. Though all the reasons for this transience of the high-value culture patterns are far from clear, one is patent: It is inherent in or immanent to the pattern. Having run through all

[13] This contradicts the claims of the Marxian and dichotomic theories examined in Chapter 11.

its possible variations, the pattern exhausts its potentialities and either dies or becomes aridly repetitive and ossified.

9. As a detail, the high-value patterns of contemporary Western philosophy and fine arts have, since 1880 and more strongly since 1900, displayed signs of the creative exhaustion of their possibilities and the growing dissolution of their patterns: "Jagged rhythms and dissonance in music, free verse in poetry, plotless novels, cubism, abstractionism, and surrealism in sculpture and painting [indicate exhaustion]. . . . Only science and wealth-production probably are holding up their heads."[14] However, until science becomes sterile and wealth-production shrinks, it would be rash to predict the impending death of Western culture.

10. In the life-course of a high-value pattern (supersystem) there is now only one "pulse" or blossoming, now two, now three, and once in a while even a greater number of pulses or flowerings, with lulls or creative rests in between. Sometimes the first pulse is the greatest creatively, sometimes the second is, sometimes even the third. In brief, there is no uniform evidence that all master patterns of culture blossom only once, or that they all have the same number of creative pulses.

11. Practically all national cultures studied are deficient in creativity in one or more fields of culture; none is encyclopedically creative. Thus the cultures of Egypt, Mesopotamia, Rome, Japan, and Renaissance Europe were uncreative in philosophy. So was Arabic civilization in sculpture. Rome, Medieval Europe, Japan (excepting in algebra), and largely China were uncreative in science. The economic and political blossoming of Greece, Germany, and Italy was absent during most of the cultural florescences of these countries; and so on.

Since cultural florescence occurs in some fields of culture, while creativity in other fields is absent, this means that cultural creativities in two different fields are hardly causally or functionally connected with one another. Such a conclusion

---

[14] This somewhat agrees with F. Petrie's uniform time-sequence of blossoming of various systems in all civilizations, namely: architecture, sculpture, painting, literature, music, mechanics, theoretic science, and, lastly, wealth.

openly contradicts the theories of the total integration of each culture, explicitly and implicitly claimed by the so-called functional sociologists and anthropologists and the totalitarian integralists of culture.

12. In studying the relationship of the florescence of sculpture and painting—generally considered particularly close to each other—Kroeber finds that, out of thirteen instances, sculpture develops (in the same nation) earlier than painting five times, simultaneously twice, later twice; four times one or the other is lacking.[15] Similarly, the relationship between philosophical and scientific florescences also happens to be far from close. Twice—in China and India—great philosophical systems appeared before any tangible scientific progress was made; subsequently, scientific progress lagged behind that of philosophical creativity in these cultures. In Greece, and in a few other instances, philosophy and science emerged together, flourished together for some time, and eventually separated and followed different courses in their creative pulsations. In most of these cases, the course of scientific creativity happened to be more continuous and of a longer duration than that of philosophical creativity.

13. A similar lack of close interdependence is shown between political-economic growth and the florescence of other cultural activities. First, there were nations (the Mongols, Turks, Lithuanians, Macedonians, Achaemenians, and Sassanian Iranians—except for the Iranian creativity in religion) that built powerful empires without either simultaneously or generally contributing much to most fields of culture. They represent what Danilevsky calls the "negative agencies of history." On the other hand, several nations, like Germany in its earlier cultural florescences, or Renaissance Italy, or even Greece, had creative periods when in a state of political weakness, distintegration, or unintegration. Some others showed their cultural creativity in certain fields even after losing their political independence.

---

[15] This contradicts F. Petrie's and P. Ligeti's uniform time-sequence of the blossoming of these arts. See on their theories my *Modern Historical and Social Philosophies*, ch. 2.

14. Other conditions being equal, the richer the item-content of a culture the greater the chance of creating a more important cultural system. Cultures that are poor in content have a lesser chance of such creativity. Hence, the importance of cross-fertilization of one culture by another.

15. Kroeber does not study religious creativity as he does the fine arts, science, philosophy, and to some extent politico-economic creativities, but in passing he does make several observations. One is that, within the same national culture, "It seems normally to be religion which first reaches its chief climax, and then the aesthetic and intellectual (scientific and philosophical) activities as they free themselves from religion. . . ." Thus a definite time order of the blossoming of these cultural classes is stated here: first come religious, then aesthetic-scientific-philosophical florescences. This "uniformity" does not preclude the development first of a scientific, aesthetic, or philosophical creativity in the peoples who do not develop any important religion afterwards; such cases, however, are comparatively rare.

Another of Kroeber's observations is that religion often produces its own philosophy and its own fine arts. A third observation is that a philosophy or art completely dominated by religion is not likely to be the highest or greatest form of philosophical or aesthetic creativity. Only when these acquire some degree of autonomy from religious control and become secular to some extent do they seemingly reach the culmination point. However, when this liberation is complete and the art (or philosophy) becomes completely secular and usually quite profane, the decline of creativity sets in. "Room is made for the shallow and the frivolous, for the purely formal and precious, and decline sets in." The same is true of philosophy and, in a few cultures, even of science.

16. As to the tempo of the change, or of the progress of growth of cultural systems, Kroeber's data indicate "rather conclusively that the rate has not gained in speed" (contrary to the prevalent opinion of its acceleration). "So far as high quality growths are concerned, they seem to take about as long now as they did one or two thousand years ago." Perhaps in regard to content-items the belief in acceleration is valid—"information

material" may now be produced faster—but it is wrong insofar as the high forms or great cultural patterns are concerned.

17. "Owing to the accidents of where and on whom civilizations alight" there have been many areas or peoples uncreative in culture generally, or creative only in regard to the lesser values, or actually retarded in cultural creativity. From the standpoint of total culture-history all the populations of Europe belong to the retarded group: Most, except the Greeks and Romans, entered the stage of cultural creativity much later, only from 1,500 to 1,000 years ago; finally, the marginal peoples of the north and east of Europe began to contribute the highest cultural values only some two or three centuries ago.

18. The insular cultures of the East Indies, Japan, and Great Britain show some peculiarities of culture growth common to all three cultures: They are all somewhat backward or late in becoming civilized, and their cultures are dependent upon and derived from the continental cultures of India (in the case of the East Indies), China (for Japan), and Europe (for Britain).

19. By studying the culture growth in space, its two different types of expansion or diffusion are noticeable: one from the center onward, the other from the periphery toward the center.

20. Culture as such does not and cannot die. But specific cultures, geographically limited, can and do die, not so much through the death of their populations as through their replacement by different cultures. Today there is still a Mohican population, but Mohican culture is already extinct. Language as such does not die, but specific languages do die. Ordinarily the cultures die through being replaced by a "superior" (under the circumstances) culture, regardless of whether this superiority is real or apparent.

21. Kroeber does not share Spengler's organismic conception of culture with all its parts tightly integrated around the prime symbol, nor does he fully share Spengler's thesis that great cultures can never blend or be transmitted, and that they must die and be superseded by other cultures. Culture material is surely borrowed or transmitted; with it some patterns are also

passed from one culture to another. However, in regard to larger master patterns the situation may be different.

22. Kroeber also finds it impossible to accept, without further evidence, the Spenglerian view that all great cultures pass through the same states.

23. He admits that as an infrequent phenomenon, a high-value cultural pattern (supersystem) can be and is once in a while fundamentally reconstituted. Having reached a point of saturation along its previous line of growth, after a pause and through certain efforts, it resumes its growth along somewhat new lines. In other words, it transforms itself into something very different from what it was, without losing its sameness or identity. (*Ibid.*, pp. 663–834.)

Kroeber's other works in this field, including his latest *Style and Civilization*, did not add substantially to these conclusions. *Style and Civilization* contains several interesting observations concerning Spengler's, Toynbee's and my own theories. Some of these are correct, some are questionable, while some are ambivalent and somewhat contradictory. For instance, he says that civilizations or *Hochkulturen* are real *Ganzheiten* unified by their "superstyle" (though his conception of "style" and "superstyle" remains fairly vague). "I do believe absolutely in the reality and significance of the particular styles. . . . I also believe that Egyptian and Chinese and Hellenic civilizations existed. . . . Their reality is undeniable. . . . Civilizations are certainly significant macro-phenomena." On the other hand, he asserts that he has "never claimed complete integration (of civilizations or total cultures), either of significance or through causality."[16]

Kroeber ascribes to me a radical and "total denial" of reality and unity of civilizations or the total cultures, and criticizes me for this alleged denial.[17] On the other hand, he states: "I agree with Sorokin unreservedly that no civilization can be completely integrated."[18] On my part, I can only say that I have never denied either the *reality* of civilizations or of any total culture. Nor have I denied their *partial* unity and integra-

[16] *Style and Civilization*, pp. 174–175.
[17] *Ibid.*, pp. 173, 174, ff.
[18] *Ibid.*, p. 182.

tion. I have criticized all "cultural atomists" who view total cultures or civilizations as a pile of incidental, contingent, singular congeries—persons, events, ideas, values, and material things—and who do not see there a legion of unified systems and supersystems.[19]

Kroeber's division of the total culture into "reality culture" and "value culture" represents a variety of Weber, Merton, and MacIver's "dichotomic theory of cultural systems." In a subsequent chapter on "dichotomic theories," Kroeber's variation of these will be mentioned.[20]

Kroeber's conclusions have been delineated in some detail because they are fairly definite and important, and because they are based upon substantial empirical evidence. Most of them happen to be similar to my own conclusions. The similarity of the conclusions reached independently by both of us reinforces their validity.

CRITICISM

Kroeber's theory has three shortcomings: first, the vagueness of such of his concepts as the "master pattern," "high-value culture pattern," "civilization," and the like; second, his use of the number and quality of talented persons as a measure of cultural creativity; and third, the sensate bias underlying his conception of cultural creativity.

Anthropologists and sociologists regularly use the term culture pattern and its derivatives just as they regularly use the terms culture integration, functional system, and their derivatives. Unfortunately, they rarely define these terms clearly. An overwhelming majority of functional and integrating anthropologists and sociologists have not as yet discriminated between congeries and systems as basically different phenomena.[21]

---

[19] See my substantial—and so far not discredited—criticism of "the totalitarian integrators of culture" as well as of the "cultural atomists" in my *Dynamics*, Vol. I, chs. 1, 2, and pp. 167 ff.; and Vol. IV, pp. 128–142. An abridged criticism of both is given in the preceding chapters of this work.

[20] See Kroeber, "Reality Culture and Value Culture" in his *The Nature of Culture*, pp. 152–166.

[21] On this confusion see the *Dynamics*, Vol. I, ch. 4, and Vol. IV, chs. 1–3. See also *SCP*, pp. 337 ff.

Though Kroeber has been careful to distinguish between various combinations of culture traits, his analysis seemingly has not gone far enough to make clear what he means by the terms culture patterns, master patterns, reality-culture, and value culture. Do these terms refer to congeries, indirect causal ensembles, or causal, meaningful, meaningful-causal systems? Implicitly, and here and there explicitly, he seems to mean something close to my "causal" and "meaningful-causal systems." He does not clarify this point, however.

Like myself, Kroeber uses the occurrence of persons of genius as a measure of cultural creativity. I have also used this method systematically for studying the rise and decline of materialism, idealism, empiricism, rationalism, the movement of discoveries and inventions, and other cultural currents.

For example, to establish a rough estimate of when, in the period from 600 B.C. to A.D. 1920, the influence of materialistic philosophy was growing and when it was declining, we took all the Greco-Roman and Western philosophers and made a separate listing of all the materialistic philosophers. Then, taking the total number of philosophers (materialistic and nonmaterialistic) as 100 percent for each period of 25, 50, and 100 years, we computed for each period the percentage of materialistic philosophers in the total. These percentages of materialistic philosophers gave us a rough measure of the comparative influence of materialistic philosophy in the total philosophy of each period. In one computation of these percentages all listed philosophers were given 1 to 12 points of "weight" (according to their magnitude as measured by editions and re-editions of their works, by translations of their works, by the number of monographs about their philosophies, by the size of their followings, and so on). The curve of the percentages of materialist philosophers obtained in this way runs roughly parallel to that based on giving equal value to each philosopher. Possibly in a more systematic manner, and with a fuller list of men and women of genius in each cultural field than the samples by Kroeber, I used a procedure similar to Kroeber's.

If I raise the subsequent questions, I do it not for the sake of criticizing Kroeber, but rather to elucidate the danger points in this procedure. To begin with, it is heavily loaded in favor of all sensate cultures and periods and against all ideational cultures and periods. The point is that sensate cultures are individualistic and singularistic, whereas ideational cultures are collective and anonymous. In sensate cultures, each creative person passionately strives to immortalize, glorify, or publicize his individual name and achievement. Anything of importance created in such a culture bears the name of its creator and is registered carefully in the annals of its history. In this sense, sensate cultures are good publicity cultures for each individual creator.

Ideational culture and man are not interested in advertising the individual creators. Creators in such a culture create for the greater glory of God, not for mortal fame. Creations are done collectively. They remain, as a rule, anonymous. We do not know who created many of the architectual glories of India, or Taoist China, or the great medieval cathedrals and sculptures of Europe. Except for a very few names, nothing is known of their creators. This is even more true of examples of great art on a smaller scale. This difference leads directly to an enormous deflation of ideational creativity and a great inflation of sensate creativity when it is measured by the number of individual creators mentioned in sensate and ideational cultures or periods. As a matter of fact, the commonly accepted lack of creativity in either our ideational Middle Ages or the ideational Hindu or Taoist cultures is largely due to the "deflations" of such cultures.[22]

Kroeber makes no distinction between ideational and sensate cultures and periods. Therefore, the results of his procedure are tangibly biased, calling for correction by a relative increase of the creativity of ideational cultures and periods and a decrease of sensate creativity. With such a correction, the creativity curves are likely to be tangibly different from Kroeber's curves.

Another shortcoming of this procedure is that it gives a less accurate curve of creativity in a given field than the curve based not on the number of creative persons but on that of the dis-

---

[22] See, on this difference, the *Dynamics, passim.*

covered, invented, or created values. In my study of the movement of scientific discoveries and inventions, I made two numerical series: one giving all the known scientific discoveries and inventions and another giving all the names of scientists and inventors mentioned in the *Encyclopaedia Britannica*. Compared with each other, the series of discoveries and inventions is much more complete and accurate than that of the scientists and inventors; in some periods and countries there was a tangible deviation of the two series from each other.

The discussion of the biased character of Kroeber's procedure leads us to the point of his study that is most doubtful, that is, the somewhat biased and subjective character of his concept of creativity (or florescence or blossoming) and of the results obtained. By this biased character I mean not only the procedure discussed but the very criteria of what is and what is not creative in a sociocultural field. Kroeber does not distinguish various types of creativity like ideational, idealistic, sensate, classic and romantic, religious and secular, and so on. Instead, without any distinction in typology, he simply takes the names given in a good text in a certain field together with the judgment of the text about the comparative magnitude of some of the names and in this way builds his periods of greater or lesser creativity. I have already pointed out how such a procedure inflates the creativity of sensate and deflates that of ideational cultures or periods. Now it can be asserted that a nondistinction of ideational, sensate, and idealistic forms of creativity makes these inflations and deflations incomparably greater than the procedure itself does. The point is that what is creative depends upon our criteria. The criteria of great creativity of ideational and sensate cultures are strikingly different, often opposite. What is a great creation for an ideational man and culture (say, a Gregorian chant, a symbolic sculpture or fresco, a religious belief, a theological treatise, the life of a saint, a religious ceremony or ritual, an ascetic hermitage, a poor monastic community, meditation and contemplation) is often mere dirt, superstition, ignorance, and ugliness for a sensate man and culture. And, vice versa, most of the great sensate creations are negative to ideational man. As "the devil's temptations, empty, valueless, transitory toys fit for the fools, the sinners, and the condemned"; "No one who loves Christ cares for this world"; "Lay not up for yourselves treasures upon earth. . . . But lay up for yourselves treasures in heaven. . . . Seek ye first the kingdom of God." Such are the typical ideational reactions to practically all sensate values and creations.

In practically all the books used by Kroeber, the criteria of creativity of their authors, which Kroeber accepts, are almost entirely sensate. An overwhelmingly greater part of the historical books written over the last three centuries have been written by predominantly sensate historians, with sensate criteria of what is creative and what is not. These authors and Kroeber who follows them give to us the movement of creativity of cultures and periods mainly as it appears from the sensate standpoint. More, Kroeber has omitted practically the whole field of religious and ethical creativity, which are the main areas of ideational creativity. For this reason his total creativity of many periods and cultures is inadequate. If the creativity of the same cultures and periods are studied from ideational or idealistic positions and religious and ethical creativity are not omitted, the movements of creativity would differ greatly from those seen from the sensate standpoint.

The only way to avoid this one-sidedness is to distinguish ideational, idealistic, and sensate systems of values and types of creativity, and, assuming a neutral position for each system, to try to find out what kind of values are created in each of these types of culture. When this is done—as I did in my *Dynamics*—ideational culture will be found to be creative in the field of religion and uncreative in the field of science and technology; it is creative in ideational music, painting, sculpture, architecture, drama, ethics, and law and uncreative in the sensate forms of these cultural phenomena. Sensate culture will be found to be creative in science, technology, utilitarian economics, but little creative in religion or in ideational forms of all classes of cultural phenomena.

This explains the inevitably one-sided character of the curves of creativity in Kroeber's work, as well as of the bulk of historical, humanistic, and social-science works of the last three centuries, with their predominantly sensate standpoint. The bulk of these works still view everything from the sensate standpoint as the only one possible and absolute, not admitting any other standpoint. It is high time that this Ptolemaic standpoint be replaced by at least a Copernican or a contemporary-astrophysical and relativity standpoint. From such a position, ideational, idealistic, and sensate systems and criteria of values and creativity are equally important.

The scientific competence and wisdom of Kroeber helped him to avoid this pitfall to a considerable degree. However, he could not escape it completely, and this sensate bias tangibly vitiates his conclusions and results.

With the suggested correction, the bulk of Kroeber's procedures and results appear to be sound and in essentials coincide with the results of my own study of these problems.

FLORIAN ZNANIECKI (1882–1958)

The next work seriously concerned with the problems of cultural and social systems is Florian Znaniecki's *Cultural Sciences: Their Origin and Development.*[23] Perhaps the best and shortest way to outline Znaniecki's views in these problems is to start with his evaluation and criticisms of my theories. His criticisms pointedly indicate similarities and disagreements between our conceptions. In discussing various "attempts to develop a general theory of culture" (theories of Vico, Herder, Hegel, Marx, Spengler, and Toynbee) he says:

> As yet the only thorough and consistent effort to integrate all specialized nomothetic cultural sciences into a general theory of culture is that of Sorokin. . . . Sorokin is the first cultural scientist to apply the same approach to every realm or, as he calls it, "compartment" of culture and to relationships between the cultural phenomena of different compartments. His basic concept is that of *system.* Although this concept has been used by specialists in various realms—students of philosophy and of science, economists, political theorists, sociologists—yet

[23] (Urbana, Ill., 1952).

nobody before him extended it to all categories of cultural phenomena. The number and diversity of particular cultural systems he includes in his investigation are unequalled. Moreover, his study covers systems ranging from the very simple to the very complex. He takes into account differences in their integration, ranging from congeries to highly organized systems, and compares their relative duration and the range of their extension. He emphasizes the need of studying changes in systems, those which are immanent and those which are caused by extraneous influences. And throughout his study the problem of relationships between the systems included in various realms of culture is taken fully into consideration. Generally these relationships are of two kinds: (1) logico-meaningful connections, those between contemporary systems belonging to different compartments—religion, philosophy, art, technique, economic organization, political organization; and (2) causal-functional relations between changes which occur within these different compartments.

No doubt quite a few of (Sorokin's) generalizations are scientifically defective, but these defects are of minor significance; for no methodologist or historian of science would expect that such an original attempt by an individual thinker to cover every realm of cultural phenomena to which many specialists have devoted their whole life could be immediately and fully successful. It should be judged as a creative effort intended to open a new way for future intellectual progress.[24]

Znaniecki's main objection to my theory of social systems is that my "social systems—such as the state, the family, a political party, or a university—are not cultural systems like language, science, religion, and the fine arts, although they are integrally connected with the latter. If he [Sorokin] had applied the humanistic coefficient in his studies of social systems, he would have realized that a social group, as experienced and evaluated by its members, has the essential characteristics which he ascribes to other cultural systems."[25]

I already answered this objection in my reply to O. Anderle's similar criticism. Although each social system (organized group) in its total culture has its own system of culture as its *raison d'être* as well as several additional cultural systems and con-

---

[24] Znaniecki, *op. cit.*, pp. 377–378.
[25] *Ibid.*, p. 378.

geries, and although each cultural system has its own social group that operates, uses, and realizes it, nevertheless the cultural and the social systems are neither identical nor coterminal *Ganzheiten.* Their difference can be summed up as follows:

> A given cultural system—and especially a vast one—does not localize and delimit itself within one social system (group) but like an ocean current, washing many shores and islands, spreads over many different groups, sometimes an enormous multitude of these. Beginning with the simplest systems of meanings and norms like the table of multiplication, "love your neighbors," the rudiments of science, a belief in God, this or that poetry or fairy tale, this or that language, and ending with vast cultural system of science, of Christianity or Buddhism, of widely diffused language (like English), idealistic or materialistic philosophy, Beethoven's music or jazz crooning, democratic political system or communism, capitalism, socialism or totalitarianism, these cultural systems in their ideological, behavioral, and material forms spread and root themselves in the total culture of various occupational, national, ethnic, racial, economic, political, religious, sex-age groups, in various classes, castes, families, tribes and state-groups. . . . The boundaries of diffusion and entrenchment of cultural systems do not coincide with the boundaries of organized groups. If mapped, they would give very different trajectories. *Only the specific cultural system*, which is the reason for the existence of a given organized group, is somewhat confined within it as its *accepted* ideological, behavioral, and material cultural system. The *approved* ideological, behavioral, and material cultural system of the Roman Catholic Church is loosely confined within it as an organized social system. But even it embraces not one but a multitude of the rich and the poor organized groups, the European, the Asiatic and the American collectivities, the white-yellow-and-black racial groups and persons, the young and the old, the male and female societies and associations. Moreover, the ideological system of the Catholic Church is diffused not only among the members of the Church but, as an ideological cultural system, it is known and present in the minds of many non-Catholics and even of the opponents of the Catholic Church. Thus the ideological part of a cultural system, specific for a given organized group, is not ordinarily confined to it. (*SCP*, pp. 335–337.)

Some cultural systems, like elementary mathematics and the rudiments of science or such languages as English or such religions as Buddhism, are spread and function in their ideo-logical-behavioral-material forms among thousands of different social systems (organized groups).[26]

The general reason for this nonidentity and noncoterminality of organized groups and cultural systems is at hand: Any organized group or individual in order to live must have at least a basic elementary scientific system (beginning with rudimentary arithmetics and an elementary knowledge of physical and biological phenomena), a common language and art-values, common mores and a moral code, common beliefs, recreation, techniques, and several other cultural systems and congeries shared by many social groups and persons. For this reason some of the cultural systems, like scientific, language, moral, and others, make an important part of the total culture of many social systems (groups). On the other hand, practically none of the cultural systems, and none of the *specific* culture systems morphologically confined to a single social group as its *raison d'être*, covers the whole realm of inorganic, organic, and superorganic reality and none meets all the needs of the living, thinking, and acting groups and individuals. In order to live and to satisfy their basic needs, any individual or group has to deal with many

---

[26] At least, in regard to many cultural systems, their nonlocalization and nonconfinement within one social system (group) was stressed by Durkheim and Mauss: "There are [social phenomena] which [in contrast to political society, which occupies a definite territory and is capable of being geographically represented] have no clearly defined frames; they pass above political frontiers and extend over spaces which cannot be easily determined. . . . Political and juridical institutions, phenomena of social morphology, are parts of the constitution belonging to each people. On the contrary, myths, stories, money, trade, fine arts, techniques, instruments, languages, words, scientific knowledge, literary forms and ideals, all these travel. . . . There are not only isolated facts (congeries), but complex solidary systems which are not limited to a determined political organism (or to any single social group). . . .

To these systems of facts, which have their own unity, their own way of being, it is convenient to have a special name: the name *civilization* seems to be the most appropriate." E. Durkheim and M. Mauss, "Civilisation et types de civilisation," *L'Année sociologique*, XII (1913), 47 ff. Even cultural political systems are often not confined to any single political society or state, but are spread among several states or political groups.

aspects of the total reality and has to have a minimum of scientific, religious, artistic, ethical, and technical ways and instrumentalities of satisfying these needs. For this simple reason, an individual or group cannot limit its total—ideological, behavioral, and material—culture to one cultural system. It has to have, in a rude or refined form, most of the main cultural systems: scientific, religious, moral, technological, and aesthetic, as well as many practical systems of how to do this or that and how to satisfy this or that need. Hence the pluralism of cultural systems and congeries of any organized group.[27]

The nonidentity and noncoterminality of social and cultural systems is demonstrated also by the different longevity of these systems. In a somewhat modified form, Christianity as a religious cultural system still lives a vigorous life, although hundreds, even thousands of Christian political, occupational, economic, ethnic, sex-and-age-organized groups have died and disappeared from the living stage of history. Any decennial census of religious bodies informs us that several denominational groups have become extinct during the ten-year period since the previous census. On the other hand, political nations, like China, England, Russia, and the United States, are still living, although hundreds of various religious, aesthetic, political, philosophical, and other cultural systems in the total culture of each of these nations has appeared, lived, and died—especially those systems that are but temporary fads and fashions. The life-span and mortality of social and cultural systems are essentially different from each other.[28]

Since the same cultural system is found to be a part of the total culture of many social systems (groups), since each organized social group has not one but many different cultural systems in its total culture, and since the tempo and direction of change as well as the life-span of the cultural and social systems are quite different from each other, these unquestionable facts quite firmly testify to their essential difference. This difference pro-

[27] *SCP*, pp. 335–341. In this work, this point is carried factually through the whole volume.

[28] See the typical longevities of various cultural and social systems in my *SCP*, chs. 34 and 47.

hibits regarding social and cultural systems as identical *Ganzheiten* and treating them as identical unities.[29]

This erroneous identification is an important shortcoming of Znaniecki's and many other theories. It is responsible for several vague points in his otherwise significant theory of social action and social systems. Before outlining it, I shall briefly comment on Znaniecki's other criticisms of my theory.

His next objection is directed against my theory of cognition. "[Sorokin] considers that full knowledge of the cultural universe can be attained only by combining three methods: those of empiricism, rationalism and mystical intuition. While the first two methods are actually combined in every science, the third has been unanimously rejected by all scientists."[30] This is entirely incorrect. First, superconscious or metalogical intuition as the way of cognition and creativity, and as opposed to sensory perception and rational, logicomathematical reasoning, has been fairly generally recognized by enormous numbers of great mathematicians, like Gauss, Arago, Poincaré, Birkhoff, the whole "intuitional school" in mathematics, and by almost all eminent mathematicians of our time. It has also been recognized by great physicists and natural scientists, like Pascal, Kepler, Newton, Galileo, Haller, Black, Ampère, Liebig, Davy, Berthelot, Humphreys, Faraday, Moore, Planck, Einstein, Bernard, and by 83 percent of 232 natural scientists queried by the American Chemical Society.

Most of the great philosophers and epistemologists stress the paramount importance of this intuitional way of cognition and creativity, beginning with the Upanishads in India and Taoism in China and passing through Plato, Aristotle, the Neo-Platonists, the Neo-Pythagoreans and Gnostics, Clement of Alexandria, Plotinus, St. Augustine, Pseudo-Dionysius, J. S.

[29] This means that cultural and social systems differ from each other not only "analytically," as correctly stated by A. Kroeber and T. Parsons, but substantively. Cf. A. Kroeber and T. Parsons, "The Concept of Culture and of Social System," *ASR*, October, 1958, pp. 582–583.

[30] *Ibid.*, p. 378. A similar statement on this method is made by D. Martindale, *The Nature and Types of Sociological Theory* (Boston, 1960), pp. 116–117, and by other sociologists.

Erigena, Albertus Magnus, St. Thomas Aquinas, Nicolas of Cusa, and by most of the great scholastics of the late Middle Ages. This list can be extended to include even such apparent rationalists as Descartes and Spinoza, even such sceptical—critical—thinkers as Hume and Kant, not mentioning Schopenhauer, Fichte, Schelling, and Nietzsche, such objective idealists as Hegel, modern philosophers like Soloviev, Tolstoi, Bergson, Lossky, James, Whitehead, Husserl, Berdyaev, Kierkegaard, Maritain, Scheler, Jaspers, and Heidegger.[31]

Finally, almost all great artists, including Mozart, Beethoven, Brahms, Tchaikovsky, and Michelangelo, and all great religious and moral leaders, including Lao-tse, Buddha, Zoroaster, Moses, the Hebrew prophets, Mahavira, Jesus, St. Paul, al-Hallaj, al-Ghazali, and Mohammed, unanimously acknowledge the important role of the metalogical intuition (or "jnana" or "no-knowledge" or "inner light" or "enlightenment" or "genius" or "inspiration" or "divine revelation") in cognition and creativity.[32]

My eminent friend's criticism is entirely baseless, due to his traditional, largely obsolescent, positivistic theory of cognition and scientific method. This antiquated epistemology of inflated empiricism—still maintained by many sociologists—is also responsible for a number of shortcomings in Znaniecki's *Cultural Sciences* and for his objections to my conceptions of social time, social space, and cultural supersystems. Znaniecki's purely dogmatic criticism of my theory of social time and social space testifies again to his unawareness of the fact that his empirical "watch-time" and three-dimensional geometric space are only one of several sociocultural concepts of time and space. He seems to have failed to follow recent investigations of these problems by Durkheim, Gurvitch, myself, and several others.[33]

[31] It is a curious fact that most of the "positivists" use the terms "intuition," "insight," "genius," and "inspiration" without explaining what these terms mean.

[32] See the detailed logical and empirical evidence and literature on this problem in the *Dynamics*, Vol. IV, ch. 16; *The Ways and Power of Love*, chs. 5, 6, 19; and in Allen, *P. A. Sorokin in Review*, pp. 383–408.

[33] This is not the place to enter into a discussion of the various theories of social time and social space. Since Znaniecki does not give

Furthermore, his interpretation of my concept of supersystem is incorrect. My sensate, ideational, and idealistic supersystems are not mere "ideal-typical generalizations," or schema, but unquestionable realities or facts solidly demonstrated by a vast body of logical, empirical, and quantitative evidence so vast and so complete as to make the fact of the integration of some cultures into these supersystems undeniable. Znaniecki himself in other parts of his work acknowledges the reality of the sociocultural supersystems.[34]

Finally, I do not have any objection to Znaniecki's conclusion that my theory "transcends the limits of scientific research" and becomes a sort of philosophy of history—"superior to all philosophies of culture developed by his predecessors. Compare it, for instance, with the philosophy of Hegel and the neo-Hegelians and with that of the biological evolutionist."[35]

If by "scientific research" Znaniecki means pedestrian, one-sided, superficial empiricism, then my integral theory of cognition, and my methods, transgress such a pseudoscientific research, and I am glad it does so.

As to my sociological theory of culture being a mere philosophy of history and culture—albeit one "superior to all [pre-

---

any evidence to support his criticism, I can simply refer to my and Gurvitch's works where these problems are comprehensively treated and the relevant literature is indicated. Cf. P. Sorokin, *Sociocultural Causality, Space, Time* (New York, 1964); and the *Dynamics*, Vol. IV, chs. 9, 10. See G. Gurvitch, *Déterminismes sociaux et Liberté humaine* (Paris, 1955), ch. 1, and *passim*; R. M. MacIver, *The Challenge of the Passing Years* (New York, 1962); W. E. Moore, *Man, Time, and Society* (New York, 1963); and articles of C. Kluckhohn, W. Firey, W. E. Moore, and G. Gurvitch in E. Tiryakian's volume, *Sociological Theory, Values, and Sociocultural Change* (New York, 1963).

[34] "Many limited systems, repeatedly performed, can be integrated into a much more comprehensive system. . . . A plurality of special ideational models . . . may become subordinated to some general model and more or less consistently integrated into (vaster and vaster) ideological system of standards and norms." His further description of the medieval Roman Catholic Church represents but a replication of my description of the medieval Christian Church and culture as an example of the ideational supersystem. In other words, Znaniecki himself operates with vast cultural systems corresponding to my "supersystem." Znaniecki, *Cultural Sciences*, pp. 271 ff., 327 ff.

[35] *Ibid.*, p. 379.

ceding] philosophies of culture"—I take this sort of criticism as the highest of compliments. In the Preface to Volume I of my *Dynamics* I say: "Since almost all great sociological systems are a brand of philosophy of history, and since most of the great philosophies of history are a sort of sociology of cultural change, I do not have any objection to the use of this name by anyone who fancies it to describe the present work."[36]

The main body of Znaniecki's theory of social and cultural systems is congenial and similar to my own theory. Like myself, he regards the world of culture as "essentially different from the natural universe" and biophysical order and the cultural sciences as different "from those sciences which are popularly called natural."[37] Like myself, he sees the difference between the cultural and the natural (biophysical) phenomena in the conscious and axionormative character of sociocultural realities. This characteristic is fairly similar to my component of meanings-values-norms as the *differentia specifica* of sociocultural or superorganic phenomena distinguishing them from the inorganic and the organic realities.[38]

I do not have any objection to Znaniecki's definition of cultural actions as a "limited, dynamic system of interdependent, changing values" that may be "organized and combined into (vaster and vaster) complex systems of actions . . . with the same central or dominant value to which the other values included in them are subordinated. It is this dominant value which gives such a complex action its unity."[39]

The essentials of his theory of cultural systems and of systems of social actions are notably similar and congenial to my theory of cultural and social systems. The main points of difference between our sociological frameworks are—besides those which have been discussed above—first, Znaniecki's failure to develop his outline into a detailed, systematic theory, and, second, his failure to apply to, and to test, his conceptions and conclusions by systematic, relevant, empirical facts. His con-

36 The *Dynamics*, Vol. I, p. x.
37 Znaniecki, *op. cit.*, pp. viii, 9–10.
38 *Ibid.*, pp. 187, 388–389.
39 *Ibid.*, pp. 192 ff.

ceptual framework remains in the blueprint stage, although he makes a slight attempt to build on the blueprinted social and cultural structures and to follow their change in actual historical processes and social life.[40] In the whole volume, there is hardly any statistical or experimental or other empirical data to confirm his hypotheses, deductions, and conclusions. My third objection is to his differentiation of "social actions" from "nonsocial actions," by which he means all scientific, religious, philosophical, artistic, political, economic, ethical, and other specified actions. This differentiation is hardly tenable: If we exclude all these nonsocial actions from the realm of cultural and social actions, what remains of "conscious axionormative social actions"? Hardly anything more than "physical motion" of the type studied by and belonging to the physical and biological sciences. The distinction is further untenable because "nonsocial" cultural values are installed by Znaniecki into his very definition of "conscious actions" as a dynamic system of interdependent, changing values, and into his conception of "social action" and "social system," in the form of legal and ethical norms and standards that regulate and define these actions and systems. If these values, consciousness, and norms are canceled, there remains nothing but physical motions studied by physical sciences.

Finally, his very reduction of social systems to systems of "social action" does not adequately define the componential structure of sociocultural phenomena: No scholar can adequately study social actions without studying the conscious individuals who perform these actions; the meanings-values-norms objectified, exchanged, and realized by these actions; and the material media or vehicles involved in these actions.[41] No playwright can produce a good play without delineating the individuals who are performing the actions and without having the plot or central idea of the play unfolded by the specific characters of the actors.

---

[40] In a purely descriptive way, he and W. I. Thomas gave a brilliant analysis of a specific social system in their *Polish Peasant* (New York, 1927).

[41] See *Cultural Sciences*, chs. 10–14. Social relation and interaction "is not really a relation (and interaction) between individuals as such but between their *actions*." *Ibid.*, p. 388.

In brief, my theory of the componential structure of sociocultural phenomena appears to be more adequate and correct than Znaniecki's and other theories of "social action" that indicate only one of the components of sociocultural phenomena.[42] Later on, in analyzing Znaniecki's and T. Parson's theory of social systems, this matter will be discussed more fully.

[42] In other places in his book, Znaniecki clearly stresses the "ideological models," "standards and norms," human beings and vehicles as unavoidable components of cultural phenomena. See chs. 10, 11, and *passim*. However, he hardly ever gives any analysis of these components.

CHAPTER 10

Dichotomic Theories of

Cultural Supersystems[1]

RECENT VARIATIONS IN THE DICHOTOMIC THEORIES

Among the modern theories of cultural systems and super-systems the dichotomic models occupy one of the most important places. Some of the ideas behind these theories are found in the teaching of Confucius and Mencius, of Hindu and Buddhist thinkers, and in the works of Plato, Aristotle, Polybius, and other Greco-Roman scholars. In a more developed form, they are found in the writings of several social thinkers of the seventeenth, eighteenth, and first half of the nineteenth centuries.[2] Karl Marx and Friedrich Engels, by their division of sociocultural relations into two main classes, the "relations of production [which] constitute the economic structure of society," and the "ideological superstructure," consisting of "juridical, political, religious, artistic or philosophical forms and relationships," gave a new life and full development to the economic variation of the dichotomic theories.[3] Almost all recent theories of this kind represent variations and elaborations on the Marx-Engels' division. Most important of these theories are those of A. Coste, L. Weber, A. Weber, R. M. MacIver, W. Ogburn, F. S. Chapin, T. Veblen, M. Tugan-Baranovsky, and others.

---

[1] See the more comprehensive analysis and criticism of these theories in the *Dynamics*, Vol. IV, pp. 155–196, 302–321.

[2] See, on the predecessors of Marx-Engels' theories, *CST*, pp. 514–523.

[3] See a detailed analysis of Marx-Engels' theories in *CST*, pp. 523–546; for a comparison of the early sketch of Marx's theory with his later version of it, cf. G. Gurvitch, *La vocation actuelle de la sociologie* (Paris, 1963), pp. 220–332.

The common characteristic of all the dichotomic theories is that, without any explicit distinction between sociocultural systems and congeries, they divide the total culture of all societies into two different classes, and claim that all the phenomena within each class are interdependent and change along the same pattern, whereas the patterns of the change of each class are fundamentally different.

Coste divides all sociocultural phenomena into two classes, "social" and "ideological." He does not distinguish, however, between systems and congeries. By "social" facts, Coste means the phenomena of government, the production and distribution of economic or useful things, beliefs, and solidarity. By "ideological" facts, he means the phenomena of nonpractical or nonuseful arts, such as poetry, philosophy, and various ideologies, including those of the theoretical and nonapplied sciences, that do not have a useful or utilitarian character. While the "social" phenomena of government, of economics, and of belief and solidarity are closely united and correlated with one another in their change, fluctuation, and evolution, the "ideological" phenomena do not show any close correlation with the "social" phenomena. In other words, "sociality" and "ideological mentality" are independent of one another.[4]

Changes in the "ideological" phenomena proceed sporadically, irregularly, and without continuity, consistent direction, or accumulation. They rise and decline. The "socially" most powerful societies are often inconspicuous, so far as their ideological achievements and ideological men of genius are concerned, whereas the "socially" weak societies often have an abundance of great ideological creations—in art, in a theological system of religion, in literature, and in theoretical science or philosophy. The "social system" with its elements, on the contrary, shows continuity, regularity, accumulation, and a linear direction of progress. In this linear trend, the "social system" has passed, in all its compartments—economic, government,

    [4] P. Sorokin, *CST*, p. 360. See there a more substantial outline of Coste's theory. See A. Coste, *L'expérience des peuples et les prévisions qu'elle autorise* (Paris, 1900), chs. I, II; and *Les principes d'une sociologie objective* (Paris, 1899), chs. II, III, IV, XXII.

beliefs, and solidarity—through five stages, from "burg" to "Federation of Metropolises." In each stage, each of these compartments or subsystems is integrated with the others and changes with them.

Similar to Coste's theory in relevant points are the theories of L. Weber, A. Weber, W. Ogburn, R. MacIver, and many others.[5]

According to Louis Weber, man and his mind are double in nature: *homo faber*, technical and fabricating man, on the one hand, and *homo socius*, social man, on the other.[6] In order to live and survive, man had to be and has to be homo faber, manipulating and controlling the external, material objects of nature. As a social animal, he had to develop social instincts and respective proclivities of his mind. These two aspects of human nature and intelligence manifest themselves now in his technical preoccupations and activities, now in his social and speculative activities and preoccupations.

> Between these two tendencies, the geometrico-mechanical comprehension of the external world, and a speculative conception of this world which forms in us when we become aware of it through the looking-glass of the social categories, there is neither harmony, nor any rational correspondence; rather there is a discordance and almost antinomy. It is said when man thinks about nature and its conditions, he thinks with the brain of another age, and, though possessing the technical knowledge of the adult, he philosophizes, nevertheless, as a child. (L. Weber, *Le rythme du progrès*, pp. xi–xiii.)

[5] With a reservation, to this group of theories belongs also the theory of W. G. Sumner and A. G. Keller, so far as it distinguishes the "maintenance mores" (concerned with the ways of getting a living) from the secondary or superstructure or derivative mores of ethics, religion, art, and other non-"maintenance mores." See especially A. G. Keller, *Societal Evolution* (New York, 1931), pp. 208, 218 ff., 225–226, 246–250. A. Kroeber's theory of "reality culture" and "value culture" gives his variation of the dichotomic theories. See A. Kroeber, *The Nature of Culture*, pp. 152–166. Another variation of these theories is given by R. Merton in his "Civilization and Culture," *Sociology and Social Research*, XXI (1936), 105–113.

[6] Louis Weber, *Le rythme du progrès* (Paris, 1913). See also his "Civilisation et technique," in *Civilisation: Le mot et l'idée* (Paris, 1930), pp. 131–143.

In any society and culture, there are always these two different supersystems, each of which unites a large number of subsystems. The technical supersystem embraces technology, practical and applied sciences, economic processes of production and modification of material things, practical inventions, practical language, and other sectors of culture. The speculative and reflective systems consists of religion, magic, ethics, law, arts, philosophy, and the theoretical sciences. At one moment one of these supersystems predominates in a given society ("reflective or speculative" in the Middle Ages, for instance), at another its competitor (the technical, in the modern age). Each of them, when dominating, imprints its respective culture with a definite stamp.

Of these, the homo faber technical system (and thought and activities) appeared earlier than the speculative, reflective, or social. Changes in these systems and in all the elements of each system proceed in different ways. The technical supersystem changes gradually, continuously, and accumulatively. Change in the reflective supersystem proceeds sporadically and nonaccumulatively. Since the technical progress or change is accumulative and continuous, it influences the change of the speculative system in the total culture much more than the latter does the former.

Such is the essential framework of this theory. Not much different is the theory offered by A. Weber, R. MacIver, and T. Veblen. Alfred Weber rightly points out that if sociology does not want to be sterile and pedantic, it must deal not only and not so much with the pure study of forms and the description of little facts (however precise), but must attack the central problems of social and cultural life, and try to understand the historical processes, their meanings, and the how and why in their totality.[7]

Following this objective, he finds that the total sociocultural world of any given society or area (social system), and the

---

[7] Alfred Weber, *Ideen zur Staats-und Kultursoziologie* (Karlsruhe, 1927), pp. 5–6. His later work, *Kulturgeschichte als Kultursoziologie* (Leyden, 1935), does not advance much the theory set forth in the *Ideen*.

total change in it (*Gesellschaftsprozess*), consist of two different systems—civilization and culture—and two different processes—the process of civilization (*Zivilizationsprozess*) and cultural change (*Kulturbewegung*). By civilization, A. Weber means something similar to F. Bacon's "mechanical arts," to L. Weber's technical system, and, in a generic form (though not in concrete content), to Coste's "social category." It is a world of scientific, technological, economic, material, utilitarian, sociocultural phenomena. By culture, he means reflective, spiritual, nonutilitarian values and phenomena—religious, philosophical, artistic, ethical and the like.[8]

The total sociocultural change (*Gesellschaftsprozess*) is composed of these two main processes, *Zivilizationsprozess* and *Kulturbewegung*. The manner of change of each of these processes is different: *Zivilizationsprozess* is universal, ever diffusing itself over larger and larger sections of humanity, regular, accumulative, linear in its expansion and perfectibility; it is a line of progress. *Kulturbewegung* is irregular, nonaccumulative, having no linear trend, bounded by a certain historical culture area, or society, beyond which it does not diffuse, in spite of cultural contact; it is nontransferable to other cultures.

From these brief descriptions, we can easily recognize the essential similarity of the schemes of Coste, Louis Weber, and Alfred Weber.

Quite similar in essential points is the scheme of R. MacIver. He attributes the inadequacy of the present haphazard description of historical change to the scholars' failure to recognize the basic unity of the phenomena they describe. Without any real unity, no real change can take place, because any real change presupposes continuity, and continuity exists only in a certain unity. He aptly says: "Without this concept of unity, historical research is only cutting separate trails through the jungle of events."[9] In brief, he realizes clearly the necessity of distinguishing between a unity of systems and a unity of congeries. As

---

[8] A. Weber, *Ideen*, pp. 2 ff.
[9] R. MacIver, "The Historical Pattern of Social Change," *Journal of Social Philosophy*, October, 1936, p. 36.

congeries are infinite in their number, no mere description of a change or shift in congeries allows us adequately to comprehend the how and why of the general patterns of change. Hence, MacIver's search for the main systems or unities in the jungle of the sociocultural phenomena. His solution boils down to the recognition in the total sociocultural world of two different fundamental classes or systems, namely, a civilization system and a culture system. The first is made up of all the sociocultural "elements" that have a utilitarian character, that serve as means rather than as ends or self-values; such are the technological, scientific, economic, and political systems. The culture system is composed of sociocultural elements that are "values-as-ends": "The family, the church, the club, the discussion group, the gossip party, the sport organization, the association of the fine arts and of the sciences, the alumni association, and certain forms of educational institutions, are typical embodiments of values-as-ends."[10]

The patterns of change of each of these systems are different: Civilization or technological change is gradual, accumulative, linear, and progressive along the line of better and better civilizational means. Cultural change is intermittent, hardly accumulative, nonlinear, progressing in wave-like lines or in "cycles and rhythms." Civilization—the latest and most perfect machinery, cars, and airplanes,—is universal in its nature; it diffuses among all the different peoples with different cultures. Culture, on the contrary, is something most intimate; it can belong only to a given group, and to no other. It does not have universality; does not penetrate beyond a certain group; does not diffuse *urbi et orbi*, and is confined to a limited social area.[11]

---

[10] See also MacIver, *Society* (New York, 1937), ch. XII. These criteria have been used by many economists for separating economic activities from other ones. "Economic activity is characterized by two specific marks: objective: nature but not man being an immediate object of it; subjective: economic activity is always a means and not an end in itself." M. I. Tugan-Baranovsky, *Foundations of Political Economy* (6th ed.; Riga, 1924, in Russian), p. 9. See ch. I. This, perhaps, is the best formulation of what A. Weber and MacIver mean by civilization.

[11] In his *Social Causation* (New York, 1942), he somewhat restated his theory by dividing the total "conscious form of Being" into

Both these systems coexist in any society and mutually influence one another. But as the progress of the civilizational order is relentless, accumulative, and unobstructable, the technological order seems to condition the cultural order notably more than is true of the reverse.[12]

The theories of W. Ogburn and F. S. Chapin are constructed along the same lines. According to Ogburn, sociocultural phenomena fall into two main classes: material culture and nonmaterial culture. Material culture is not defined clearly by the author.[13] But from the context of his writings, it is evident that material culture embraces technological inventions, economic, and a few other classes of sociocultural phenomena. Nonmaterial culture consists of nonmaterial sociocultural phenomena, such as art, philosophy, religion, partly social, political, and other forms of organization, and other sectors of the sociocultural world.

Ogburn's two systems of culture are different, and being so, change in different ways. Material culture changes along a linear trend of a selective accumulation; in the course of time it progressively grows and becomes more perfect; the change in it is continuous (though not at the same rate and tempo all the time); the tempo of change is faster than in the nonmaterial culture. In the process of change, the material culture, as a rule, leads, while the nonmaterial culture lags. This means that the material culture is more powerful than the nonmaterial—again a thesis shared by all the preceding theories. Nonmaterial culture

---

the social, technological, and the cultural orders, indicating roughly the main sectors of each order. However, the essential principles of the earlier version of his theory are retained in this latest version.

[12] On this point, an ambiguity runs throughout both works of MacIver. On the one hand, he emphatically stresses the mutuality of influence, and even that culture controls the ship of technology or civilization and determines for what it is used. See *Society*, pp. 462–464 and 470–473. This ambiguity, inevitable in such a setting, runs throughout the whole theory of MacIver.

[13] In his *Social Change* (New York, 1922), he introduces the term without any definition or specification, pp. 60 ff. See also his *Recent Social Trends in the United States* (New York, 1933), pp. xiii ff., where the whole theory is newly stated. Specific definitions given do not clear up the vagueness.

changes sporadically; it is neither accumulative nor universal.

Finally, a number of other theories, like those of Karl Marx and Thorstein Veblen,[14] run along somewhat similar lines, with one difference: They stress clearly the economic or technological system in the total sociocultural world ("material power" and "material forces of production," of Marx and the technological system of Veblen), but do not group the rest of the sociocultural traits into another definite system. They leave them as a kind of residual category, in which they sometimes distinguish such subsystems as Marx's "legal and political superstructure" and "ideology"; but this is done *en passant*, so to speak. Another difference is that Marx's and Veblen's theories implicitly assume that the whole sociocultural world is integrated tangibly around their "economico-technological" system, into one whole system, and that, therefore, when the axis changes, the rest of the sectors of the sociocultural world change also. But this difference— important at first glance—is not so important in reality, because, after all, L. Weber, Ogburn, and MacIver also claim that the technologico-material system changes continually and is irresistible in its effects upon the cultural nonmaterial system, which means, in fact, that both their systems are somehow integrated into one causal system, dominated by the civilizational or material system. Marx's theory is in fact a prototype of all the other—later—theories surveyed.

CRITICISM

The main defect of these theories is that none of them has gone beyond some more or less general statements as to the nature of their sociocultural system or unity. Is the system one of causally united elements, or one of meaningfully united elements, or is it just a formal class-concept, a mere sum of similar congeries? If so, how does it differ from congeries? None

---

[14] See K. Marx, *A Contribution to the Critique of Political Economy* (New York, 1904), pp. 11–13 and *passim*. For a general outline and analysis of Marxian sociology, see *CST*, ch. 10; G. Gurvitch, *Dialectique et sociologie* (Paris, 1962), ch. VIII; T. Veblen, *The Instinct of Workmanship* (New York, 1914); *The Theory of the Leisure Class* (New York, 1899); *The Place of Science in Modern Civilization* (New York, 1919); and *The Higher Learning in America* (New York, 1918).

of the authors, except MacIver, even attempts to define his system. Still less do we know whether a certain class of social phenomena, for instance, art or religion, in *all* its forms, always belongs to one of the two systems, or if it belongs to it only in a certain form. For example, when art is visual or sensate or when religion is "scientific" they belong to one class; they belong to the other system when art is ideational or when religion is superrational. The theories are indeed foggy.

So far as one must assume that they really mean something definite one finds that the dichotomic divisions of these theories are fictitious rather than real, logically defective, and factually fallacious. Let us take, from that standpoint, one variant after another.

● Material versus Nonmaterial Culture

What is material culture? In one place we are told that the materiality of the culture-trait "lies not in the life (or physical properties) of a particular object, but in the perpetuation of the *knowledge* of the making of the object."[15] Further on, we are told again and again that material culture "grows through inventions," "because of inventions," or "because of mental ability."[16] This means that material culture itself is a form of knowledge, because invention or mental ability is neither a physicochemical process as such, nor a biological process as such (many organisms do not invent), but a mental process or thought. As such, it has to be classed by Ogburn with the nonmaterial culture, because science is regarded by him as a form of the nonmaterial culture. Thus we have two propositions: "Knowledge is material culture"; and "knowledge [science] is nonmaterial culture."

As R. Merton rightly remarks,

The same cultural trait is at times classified [by Ogburn] as material, at others as nonmaterial. For example, the use of objects and substances is a part of material culture (*Social*

[15] Ogburn, *Social Change*, p. 74.
[16] *Ibid.*, pp. 36, 103, 269, and *passim*.

Change, 72), while ways of doing things and rules involved in handling technical appliances are nonmaterial (*ibid.*, 28, 44, 271). Again, the methods of making objects are both material and nonmaterial (*ibid.*, 12, 105, 106). And so on.[17]

All this means that the fundamental premise of Ogburn's theory is defined poorly, even self-contradictorily; for this reason alone it can hardly serve as a foundation for the subsequent propositions based upon it.

The same is true of Marxian and similar theories of the "economic interpretation of history." Their "means and instruments of production," "material power of production," "relations of production," and "economic structure [or system] of society as the real foundation on which rise legal and political [and other ideological] superstructures" are poorly defined. These theories completely overlook the fundamental fact of the composite and derivative nature of any economic system as clearly determined by the available scientific knowledge and technology and by the character of ethical and legal norms prevalent in the society, as well as by the tangible influence of religious, philosophical, political, and even aesthetic factors. In its phases of production, distribution, and even consumption the economic system of a social group incorporates scientific (including technological) knowledge and the legal and moral norms prevalent in it. The economy of the Bronze Age was only as advanced as its knowledge, technology, and legal norms. Before acquiring a knowledge of the properties of fire, wind, the wheel, or, later on, of steam, electricity, and atomic fission, and before inventing instruments using these energies, no Stone, Copper, Bronze, or Machine Age system of economy could be established: The available knowledge determined the kind of economy for each society in the past and it is still determining it at the present. Likewise, the kind of law norms prevalent in a given society definitely condition the main forms of economic relationships in it—whether there will be communal or private property and what the legal ways of acquiring, utilizing, possess-

---

[17] See R. K. Merton, "Civilization and Culture," *Sociology and Social Research*, XXI (1936), 104.

ing, managing, exchanging, and disposing of economic goods
will be. This derivative nature of economic system can be
expressed by the equation

$$ES = f(ST + LE)$$

(The economic system of any society is largely a function of its
science and technology plus its laws and ethics.) Less important
but nevertheless significant is the conditioning role of the
society's religious, political, philosophical, and aesthetic values
and norms. A considerable power of economic forces is due to
the power of the scientific-technological and ethical-legal forces
that the economic system incorporates. With a change in its
scientific-technological knowledge and ethical-legal norms, the
society's economic system undergoes a corresponding change.[18]

This composite-derivative nature of the economic system
does not mean that it should be regarded as some sort of "prime
mover" in sociocultural change or as "real foundation" for the
noneconomic superstructure, as Marxian theory contends. If we
subtract from any economic system its scientific-technological
and ethical-legal components, little would remain, just as if we
subtract hydrogen and oxygen from water, little remains.

The second fundamental error of both Marxian and Og-
burnian theories is in viewing the material and nonmaterial as
two separate entities or different classes of phenomena. It is
an error, because, as we have seen, any object or trait or
element of culture always has two aspects: the inner, sociocultural meaning, which is its nonmaterial (symbolic) aspect;
and the external or material aspect, consisting of vehicles and
agents composed of inorganic and organic phenomena that
incarnate, objectify, externalize, or socialize the inner aspect,
or sociocultural meaning. In my *Dynamics,* I point out that:

> These external vehicles belong to a culture only so far as they
> are the manifestation of the internal aspect. . . . Deprived of
> its inner meaning, the Venus of Milo becomes a mere piece of
> marble . . . a Beethoven symphony turns into a mere combina-

[18] See a development of this proposition in the *Dynamics,* Vol. IV,
pp. 122 ff.; R. Stammler, *Wirtschaft und Recht nach der materialist
Geschichtsfassung* (Leipzig, 1896); and in L. Petrazycki, *Die Lehre vom
Einkomenn* (Leipzig, 1893).

tion of sounds, or even into vibrations of air waves of certain length to be studied by physics.[19]

Deprived of their inner meaning, a tool, knife, hatchet, automobile, dredging apparatus, radio set, and national flag all cease to be objects of culture and become merely physical, chemical, or biological articles. A scientific idea when it becomes social and emerges from the mind of the person who conceived it into the social world, always objectifies itself in some "material" vehicles: in a speech (sound, air waves), in a book, in a phonograph record, in a film, manuscript, instrument, apparatus, laboratory, scientific lecture, meeting, classroom, university, academy, institute, and in a hundred other—perfectly material—forms. A technical idea externalizes itself in the form of the machinery or instruments invented, and in the material possessions of the corporation that exploits the invention.

Similarly, a religious belief, on becoming sociocultural (that is, accessible to others), inevitably externalizes itself in the vehicles of sermon, pulpit, manuscript, book, printing press, music, ceremonies, religious statues, pictures, icons, in the building of chapels, temples, cathedrals, and in the formation of religious organizations with all their material properties and complexes.

An aesthetic idea, becoming social, incarnates itself in pictures, statues, ornamentations, buildings, musical scores and instruments, conservatories of music, auditoriums, a symphony hall, an exhibition palace, and in numerous other perfectly material forms.

The heavy volumes of law codes and statutes, policemen, judges, courtrooms, prisons, gallows, electric chairs, and other material instruments of punishment are the "material" vehicles of juridical and ethical ideas and values.

The same is true of political or economic or social ideas, values, and norms. Each of them, if conceived by an individual, cannot become social—that is, accessible to others—without some form of externalization or materialization, because (ex-

---

[19] See the *Dynamics*, Vol. I, pp. 55 ff.

cluding telepathy and clairvoyance) we cannot convey to anybody anything of our inner experience—ideas, feelings, emotions, volitions—without externalizing it. Externalization means "materialization." It requires physical vehicles and agents. We know that any empirical sociocultural system has the "material" components of vehicles and agents. On the other hand, no object or phenomenon, no matter what its physical or chemical properties, can become an object or phenomenon of culture without having the inner aspect of meanings. When this axiom is understood, all the absurdity of the contrast of material (vehicles) to nonmaterial culture (meanings) as separate entities and classes or objects becomes evident.

For this reason also, the dichotomy of Marx-Ogburn, taken in this form, is not acceptable.

● Technological versus Socioreflective Culture

Does the dichotomy of Louis Weber, and partly of Marx and Veblen, fare better than the material-nonmaterial dichotomy? Hardly, and for similar reasons. These theories like to start with the old statement *Primum vivere deinde philosophare,* or, as Goethe put it, "At the beginning was action,"[20] and, as W. G. Sumner put it, "The first task of life is to live; men begin with acts, not thoughts."[21] These theories claim that man was first homo faber, and not homo socius or thinking homo sapiens, and that action, practice, ways of doing things, or techniques, preceded and do precede any thought and are phenomena distinctly different from thought. Hence, the separation of technique, or the technical class of sociocultural phenomena, from the nontechnical class. Is all this logically sound? No, it is not. First of all, there is not a scintilla of factual or logical evidence to indicate that homo faber preceded homo sapiens or homo socius. Logically, in order to be even the most primitive homo faber, man had to be, to some extent, a thinking—in the primi-

---

[20] See L. Weber, *Le rythme du progrès,* p. 123.
[21] W. G. Sumner, *Folkways* (New York, 1906), pp. 1, 2, 25, and *passim*; and A. Keller, *Societal Evolution* (New York, 1931), pp. 208 ff.

tive manner—homo sapiens; otherwise, he could not make or manufacture anything (since he is not considered to be guided by instinct. If he is guided by instinct only, then he is just an animal, an object of biology and not a bearer of culture). Some thought was needed on his part to make even the simplest stone weapon to throw at an animal, not to mention more complex operations.

Putting aside the priority of the emergence of *homo faber,* and turning our attention to the actual and known behavior of man, we can certainly claim that men do not always begin with actions: In all their rational or semirational behavior, in all their conscious actions, they either think before acting, or think simultaneously with the action. The portion of such rational, semirational, conscious, purposive actions is enormous in the total human behavior.

In its claim of universality, the discussed pragmatic argument is evidently fallacious. It elevates a partial class into universal rule. A blind and thoughtless action is not sufficient to become a real power of sociocultural change, to be "accumulative," and to influence increasingly all the other sectors of the sociocultural phenomena. A blind and erroneous action leads only to the perdition of the actors, and not to the accumulation of culture, experience, and knowledge. If the thoughtless action, like an instinct, happens to be adequate, to meet the need, the result will be a development of instinct, a stagnation of the instinctively correct responses, and the eventual stagnation of the whole sociocultural life. The result will not be an ever-changing culture, or any social technique as distinct from the instinctive technique of animals. In brief, the argument kills itself with its self-contradictions, and can be left at that, to rest in peace.

The dichotomic classification of sociocultural phenomena into technical (or technological) and nontechnical (nontechnological) is hopelessly untenable. Any class of sociocultural phenomena, including the class of supposedly nontechnical phenomena, has its technical and nontechnical aspects, just as any class of sociocultural phenomena has its "material" vehicles and its "nonmaterial" meanings and aspects. Technique means the way of doing things—the way of using instruments and tools, and the means for consciously and unconsciously realizing certain objectives. Painting, sculpture, architecture, music, literature, drama, religion, science, law, ethics, economic, political, and social organizations all have their own technique and cannot help having it. In brief, any class of sociocultural phenomena has its technique, up to the technique of "technology."

Any scientific system, be it physics or chemistry, history or biology, has its technique of research, of study, of training, of conservation, and of propagation. In most cases, it is a very intricate, difficult, and complicated technique requiring years of training. Meanwhile, science generally, and the social sciences in particular, are, according to the criticized theory, supposedly nontechnical or nontechnological phenomena.

Any religion has a vast technical element: the techniques of its prayers, its rituals, its meetings, its inculcation, and its propagation. It also has an enormous number of "material" vehicles, instruments, tools, and a very rigid and intricate code of hieratic rules and norms of technical procedure to achieve its ends. And religion is supposed to be a nontechnical phenomenon!

Any art, be it music, painting, architecture, theater, literature, has its own technique. Each artist often has his own special method of creating and years and years of training are necessary to master even a small part of this technique. Art also is allegedly a nontechnical phenomenon.

To contrast technical with nontechnical phenomena as separate classes is no more sound than to contrast one side of my hand with the other, or one side of a cloth with the other (the objectifying vehicle to the meaning). To say that one side of the cloth is leading in change, the other lagging, or that one side appeared earlier than the other, is also untenable.

Put in such a form, the theory is certainly wrong. It may, however, be put in a different form, namely, that certain classes of sociocultural phenomena (with their technical and nontechnical aspects) are united into one system—for instance, an economic and technological system—while other classes of sociocultural phenomena—for instance, art, religion, science, ethics, and law—are united into another system and these systems change differently. This leads us to the third variety of the dichotomic theories—civilization versus culture.

● Civilization versus Culture; Sociality versus Ideology

Here we are confronted with considerable vagueness as to exactly what is meant by each class and of what "strains"—elements, components, subsystems—of sociocultural phenomena each class is made up. A. Weber does not give any clear *fundamentum divisionis.* A. Coste, M. Tugan-Baranovsky, and R. MacIver do: It is the *principle of utility* or that of *values-as-means and as ends.* Is the principle valid? Does it serve as a reliable guide in the distinction as to which is which? I am afraid not. First, because each of these authors puts the same class of phenomena now in one, now in the other of their dichotomic classes. For instance, Coste puts beliefs and religion now in one, now in the other of his classes. So also does MacIver. Science is put by him now into civilization,[22] now into culture.[23]

Then, on the same utilitarian principle, Coste puts beliefs into his sociality class (corresponding to MacIver's civilization); MacIver and A. Weber put religion generally into the class of culture, or what Coste calls ideology. Thus, though guided by the same principle, the authors use quite different methods of "pigeonholing" sociocultural phenomena. Such inconsistencies and contradictions are numerous throughout their works. This shortcoming is not surprising, considering the nature of their criteria. The principle of utility or usefulness, by its very nature, cannot serve the purpose satisfactorily. If it is taken psychologically, or as what each man thinks is useful and what is not, we are swamped in a maze of individual fancies, differences, and contradictions. Psychologically, an atheist regards religious functions as perfectly useless; a believer,

---

[22] See MacIver, *Society*, pp. 403–404.
[23] MacIver, "The Historical Pattern of Social Change," p. 41.

on the contrary, considers them most useful and vitally necessary, and helpful even in his business.

Psychologically, Coste and MacIver regard all theoretical
science (natural, social, and humanistic)[24] and all the fine arts
as devoid of utility, or as "values-as-ends." There are thousands
of persons—scientists, artists, plain people—who, psychologically, decidedly disagree with such a diagnosis; in their opinion,
the sciences and arts are highly useful, in the narrowest sense
of the term. Coste, Weber, and MacIver regard technology as
useful and put it into the class of sociality or civilization but
there are many writers, thinkers, and ordinary people who
deplore technological progress, find it harmful and poisonous,
and believe that it deprives culture of beauty and health, and
saps the very vigor and vital force of mankind.[25] And so on.

Psychologically, there exists no uniformity or judgment
as to what sociocultural phenomena are useful and what are not,
what are values-as-means and what are values-as-ends.

That these statements are not mere conjectures is shown
by an actual study of the relationships between the overt activities of individuals and groups and the motivation for these
activities. Our study of the actual motivation for 55 overt
activities by 103 persons, shows, first, that there is no close
and specific relationship between a given overt activity and a
given motive, including whether the activity is regarded as a

---

[24] MacIver regards the association of the fine arts and sciences as a
"typical embodiment of values-as-ends." See "The Historical Pattern of
Social Change," p. 41.

[25] See, for instance, Tolstoi's, Gandhi's, Ruskin's, and Inge's utterances about it; or such works as those of G. Lombroso, *La rançon du
machinisme* (Paris, 1931); R. A. Freeman, *Social Decay and Regeneration* (Boston, 1921); H. Adams, *The Degradation of the Democratic
Dogma* (New York, 1919); J. L. Duplan, *Sa Majesté la machine* (Paris,
1930); D. Rops, *La monde sans âme* (Paris, 1932); H. Dubreuil, *Standards* (Paris, 1929); H. de Man, *Au delà du Marxisme* (Paris, 1929);
G. Duhamel, *L'humaniste et l'automate* (Paris, 1933); H. Bergson, *Les
deux sources de la morale et de la religion* (Paris, 1932); O. Spengler,
Der Mensch und die Technik (Munich, 1933); A. J. Toynbee, *A Study
of History*, Vol. III, pp. 154–174; Vol. IV, pp. 39–56, and *passim* in all
six volumes; L. Mumford's *Technics and Civilization* (New York, 1935),
and *The Culture of the Cities* (New York, 1938); and P. M. Schuhl's
Machinisme et philosophie (Paris, 1938).

means or end. Here are examples of the main motives of various activities: Religious activity has as its motives (with different persons and with the same individual at various times): physical need, personal comfort, habit, custom, utilitarian and economic reasons, coercion, force of circumstances, curiosity, change, and so on. Dancing has as its motives personal amusement "social," "custom," preparatory, exercise, etc. Eating is motivated by physical need, habit, curiosity, force of circumstances, and so on. These responses indicate a much more complex picture of motivation and its changing character than is usually realized. Likewise, they show that the same activity, even that of eating, now appears to be a mere means, now an end in itself. Religious activity for some is an end-value, for others a means-value. Even for the same individual it is now means, now end.[26]

There is no possibility of maintaining the dichotomy criticized on a psychological basis. MacIver realizes this; therefore he tries to shift the problem from the subjective-psychological plane to the objective-sociological one. He claims that such a dichotomy, with the compartments of culture mentioned in each dichotomic class, is given sociologically, as an objective, superindividual, social reality.

Is the claim valid? One seriously doubts it, considering that the author himself placed science, for instance, now in one, now in other groups. One can also question whether the "family, the church, the club, the discussion group, the gossip party, the sports organization, the associations of the fine arts and of the sciences, the alumni associations, and certain forms of educational institutions, are typical embodiments of values-as-ends," while the technological, economic, and political systems are "typical values-as-means." We know that for many ordinary people and thinkers,[27] from the Sophists, Sextus Empiricus, Lucian, Marsilio of Padua, Machiavelli, Pierre du Bois to a legion of sceptics, liberals, and radicals, the only justifying reason for religion and church is that they are socially useful: are good means to certain ends. We know many people who

[26] See detailed data in P. Sorokin and C. Berger, *Time-Budgets of Human Behavior* (Cambridge, Mass., 1939), part III.

[27] See the evidence for that in our *Time-Budgets of Human Behavior*, part III.

marry (especially a rich partner) and start a family as a mere means to ends entirely outside the family.[28] A large number of persons regard exercise and sports as a nuisance,[29] but as necessary means for maintaining their health. On the other hand, for many technological inventors, and possibly for the majority of the great inventors, invention itself has been the end, the self-value, and not a means to something else.[30] This is even truer of many scientists and scholars and their organizations. There have been many money-makers, businessmen, and builders of empires who took business and money-making as an end in itself.[31] As for political systems, one has to discount Plato, Aristotle, Hegel, and a host of the greatest writers on the state and government, who have taken the state and government as the end-value, as the condition and at the same time as the realization of the highest value—certainly much higher and of much more value-as-end than MacIver's gossip-sports-alumni associations and the like.

These facts cannot be doubted, but it may be argued that they present the situation from a psychological rather than from a sociological standpoint. If so, we may ask what the evidences are that sociologically it is as claimed by MacIver. Unfortunately, he does not give any evidence at all. The only course open to him is to demonstrate that an objective investigation of the enumerated classes of sociocultural phenomena shows that technological, economic, and political activities are always and everywhere utilitarian, while the family, religion, arts, science, and philosophy are uniformly and perennially devoid of a utilitarian character. To prove such a contention is hardly possible. First, if the alleged useless or nonutilitarian classes of sociocultural phenomena were such, how have they survived

---

[28] See the data, *ibid.*

[29] See diversity of motivation, *ibid.*

[30] See F. Taussig, *Inventors and Money-Makers* (New York, 1915), where the real psychology of the inventors and their passion for their work is excellently documented. J. Rossman, *The Psychology of the Inventor* (Washington, 1931), ch. X. Of 710 inventors asked about the motives for their inventing, 193 indicate love of inventing; 167, financial gain; 118, necessity; 73, desire to achieve; 27, prestige; 22, altruism; 6, laziness; and so on.

[31] See Taussig, *ibid.*, for the businessman.

through all the long ages of human history? Second, there are enough studies of even the most primitive religion and magic to show their exceptionally great utility in a number of ways: Plato, Aristotle, ibn-Khaldun, Vico, St. Thomas Aquinas, and other idealistic thinkers, as well as such sceptical or scientific investigators as Marsilio of Padua, Machiavelli, E. Durkheim, J. Frazer, G. LeBon, B. Kidd, G. Sorel, V. Pareto, C. Ellwood, Max Weber, and F. de Coulanges, have proved the utilitarian functions of religion unquestionably.[32] The same can be said, with a slight variation, of the arts, and especially of the sciences, of ethics, law, and of any class of the "culture" phenomena. And vice versa, not every form of technological, economic, or political activity has been always and everywhere useful. If it were so, no "bad economics," "poisonous politics," and "detrimental technology" would ever have existed.[33]

From the standpoint of ideational ethics, all the sensate utilities lead but to perdition; union with the Absolute and all that leads to it is the only real value. From the standpoint of sensate ethics, ideational ethics and values are but superstition and obscurantism. In brief, any objective examination would show that sociologically there are no such things as useful and nonuseful classes of sociocultural phenomena as such, or values-as-means and values-as-end as such. Still less is it an objective sociological fact that economic, political, technological, and other classes are sociologically "means," while the gossip party and the sports organization are "ends."

Sociologically there is no class of sociocultural objects which for all people, at all times, in all cultures, is always end-value or always means-value. Even within the same culture, say, sensate, practically each and all of its main systems divide (sociologically) their own values into end-values and means-

[32] See especially such works as J. G. Frazer, *Psyche's Task* (London, 1913); and G. Sorel, *Reflection on Violence* (New York, 1912), pp. 133 ff., where he shows the usefulness of mythology. For other works, see my *CST*, pp. 54 ff. and ch. 12.

[33] Toynbee shows clearly that, if anything, technological progress has been associated with a decline of civilization, but not with its growth and improvement. See his *A Study of History*, Vol. III, pp. 154 ff.; Vol. IV, pp. 39–56, and *passim*.

values, into positive and negative, resulting in a pyramid of values. Religion has its end-value: God, union with Him, salvation of the soul. It also has its means-values: fasting, a pious life, donations to the church and to the poor, regular attendance at services, a decent church building, and so on. Science similarly has its end-value: truth and real knowledge, and its means-values: obtaining a good endowment for a university, good laboratories, libraries, instruments, and techniques of study. Art has its end-value: beauty, and its means-values: brushes, canvas, piano, etc. The end-value of business is to carry on the enterprise successfully and along the line of social service; its means-values are advertising, salesmen, organizers, workers, successful competition, etc. So also with politics and government.

In each class of sociocultural phenomena, all its values are held not as equal, but as stratified into a heirarchical pyramid, beginning with the negative and meanest of the means-values and ending with the final, supreme end-value. There is hardly an important sector of culture and society that regards all its values as equal, either all as mere means or all as mere ends, or which puts all of them on the same level.

Such is the real sociological situation, not the imaginary one postulated by our authors. These authors have no real basis on which to claim that sociologically their dichotomy is well grounded. Their dichotomic division of the total sociocultural world into two different supersystems is fallacious. No less fallacious, therefore, is the imputation to each of these divisions of a series of different characteristics.

We have seen that all the dichotomists claim a series of differences in the functions and mode of change of each of their two systems. They assure us that the technological, societal, material, civilizational system changes more regularly, is accumulative, is linear in its progressive "biggerness and betterness," diffuses earlier, easier, and over all cultures and leads in change; and that the other system, ideological, nonmaterial, cultural, is neither accumulative nor linear in its development, nor is it universal in its diffusion; it is "local," limited to a given society or area, and lags in change.

Are such statements valid? Logically, if the dichotomies themselves are questionable, these conclusions must be expected to be doubtful also. Factually, too, they appear to be inadequate.

The claim that material culture (or civilization or sociality) is universal in its character, more easily diffuses among all kinds of societies and culture, and is adopted and accepted by all of them, while the nonmaterial culture remains, and is bound to remain, a purely local phenomenon, incapable of diffusion over different cultures, is also quite doubtful. Yes, since the end of the nineteenth century, many a new technological invention has spread over the whole planet: automobiles, airplanes, radio, and so on. But, since World War I, such "quantities" of nonmaterial culture as communism, fascism, totalitarianism, jazz music, and certain forms of dancing have also diffused over the whole planet; and if we measure the spread and universality of the diffusion by the number of individuals and groups who accepted and who use the above material and nonmaterial complexes, it is likely that communism, fascism, and totalitarianism spread more widely and in a shorter period of time than the automobile or the airplane. In other words, the supposed nonuniversal "cultural" traits are at least as universal as the supposed universal "civilization" traits. The Bible is evidently nonmaterial culture; and yet it is hard to find any technological invention that is diffused *urbi et orbi* as much as the Bible. So also with the works of Shakespeare and Beethoven; the Confucianist and Platonic philosophies; the use of lipstick and the bobbing of hair; monarchy and republic; socialism and progressivism; monogamic and polygamic family life; styles in fashion, art, and parliamentarism; evening dress and theosophy. The spread of Hinduism, Buddhism, Christianity, and Mohammedanism is a further example of the wide diffusion of nonmaterial culture in the past. The progress of the Syriac alphabet from Syria to the Mongols and Manchus of Asia; of the Hellenic patterns of art from the Greco-Roman to the Hindu world; the diffusion, adoption or independent invention of very similar moral codes among an enormous number of primitive and historical societies of the past and present;[34] the presence of an enormous number of similar political institutions, similar forms of marriage and family life, religious beliefs, forms of social organizations, mores and manners among a large number of societies of the past and present, often separated from one another by vast areas[35]—all these instances of the widespread or independent invention of similar values of nonmaterial culture among hundreds and thousands of different tribes, societies, and nations are eloquent evidence of the ability of the nonmaterial values to diffuse or to ground themselves among the most different cultures and peoples. This fact alone makes the claims of the dichotomist theories entirely invalid.

On the other hand, many a purely technological invention does not spread beyond the society that invents it and needs it. The Polynesians and the Eskimos invented the ingenious tech-

[34] With reference to the members of the same society, the main moral commandments and also the main crimes are similar, almost identical, in the codes of Judaism, Hinduism, Buddhism, Christianity, Confucianism, Taoism, Mohammedanism, and almost all the historical and primitive societies. In regard to crime, see *Dynamics*, Vol. II, ch. 15, especially pp. 576 ff. See also, regarding the similarity of the moral codes, *ibid.*, chs. 13 and 14. See also L. Hobhouse, *Morals in Evolution* (London, 1923); and E. Westermarck, *The Origin and Development of Moral Ideas* (2 vols.; London, 1906).

[35] For instance, such a culture trait as "hereditary government" is found among 90 different primitive societies, in the sample of Hobhouse-Wheeler-Ginsberg; as "personal government" among 80 societies; as "matrilineal descent" among 75; as "patrilineal descent" among 84 different tribes and societies; as "slaying the vanquished prisoners" among 105; and so on. See L. T. Hobhouse, G. C. Wheeler, and M. Ginsberg, *The Material Culture and Social Institutions of the Simpler Peoples* (London, 1915). See many instances of such similarity in the nonmaterial traits of the cultures of different peoples and societies in J. Mazzarella, *Les types sociaux et le droit* (Paris, 1908), and in the volumes of his *Studi di etnologia giuridica* (Catania, 1903). Examples of such wide diffusion or invention of similar cultural systems or traits are found in practically any competent text on cultural anthropology, ethnology, and sociology; and they are found in the beliefs, myths, poetry; in forms of family life and marriage; in forms of political organization; war and peace; magic and rituals; patterns of arts and ceremonies; ethical norms and mores; in practically any field of so-called nonmaterial culture. In view of this undeniable fact, one can only wonder that the dichotomist theorists set forth their claim seriously. See also M. Mauss, "Civilisation: Éléments et formes" in *Civilisations: Le mot et l'idée* (Paris, 1910), 84 ff.

niques of navigation perfectly fitted to their conditions. Societies in a mountainous region did not adopt it and remained untouched by it. Assyrians and Spartans invented (or adopted) an excellent technique of military organization. Many societies that did not need such a technique were untouched by it and did not adopt it. The technique of heating buildings by electricity, oil, or gas, or of constructing buildings capable of retaining warmth has not spread into tropical and subtropical regions. The technique of fishing has not been adopted by societies living in regions that do not have streams or lakes, or water with fish in it. Material values in no way monopolize the privilege of being more needed than nonmaterial values. The facts testify against the theory that *all* material values are needed by *all* societies, while *all* nonmaterial values are not needed by any except the society in which they were created. The real situation is that among both kinds of values—material and nonmaterial—there are some that are needed by a large number of societies, therefore they are widely adopted (or independently created in various societies); and there are material and nonmaterial values that meet only the local need of a given or of a few particular societies. As such, they remain "parochial" values and do not spread to different societies and areas.

The defenders of the criticized theories say that though the nonmaterial culture may diffuse as widely and speedily as the material, its diffusion is much less real. The Communism and the Christianity of the Russians, the Chinese, the Negroes, the Hindus, the Abyssinians, the French, and the Americans are similar only in name, they point out; in their real character these ideologies represent something very different to each of these groups. True. But the same is true of the diffusing material objects. Why? Because trait (or system), no matter whether it is material or nonmaterial, when it diffuses from one group to another undergoes a transformation in its use, meaning, value, and character (when the groups are different in their culture). The greater the difference, the greater the change the trait must undergo.[36] Only in passing between similar groups can the

[36] One can easily see that the proposition is a partial case of the general principle of selectivity of any sociocultural system. If any system is selective, it accepts some and does not accept other traits. Those which

migrating congeries or systems continue without a modification in its qualities, functions, use, and so on. An automobile seems to be the same automobile in New York as it is in the African bush. The most superfluous test indicates, however, that it is different: It is operated differently (in some cases outrageously); it is used for different purposes; its value and meanings are different; its troubles and repairs are different.

The dichotomic claim about the lead and lag of material and nonmaterial cultures is also untenable. If the theory means that in the emergence or change of any cultural system its material and behavioral forms emerge and change first, the theory is fallacious. As a rule, ideas, concepts within a system, including technological invention, precede their material objectification and socialization. Similarly, a change in the system's component of meanings precedes as a rule a change in its other components.[37]

If the theory means that practical technological invention precedes in time theorical discoveries in the corresponding pure science, as, for instance, that physicochemical technology precedes the development of mathematics, physics, and chemistry, or that medicine and agronomy precede the discoveries and development of theoretical biology, then the theory is equally untenable.

Sometimes the technological inventor in the process of his work discovers an essential theoretical principle, but even then it can be only one of the many theoretical discoveries that must have been known before his invention was possible. The tables in my *Dynamics* (Vol. II, ch. 3, and Vol. IV, ch. 7) show clearly that discoveries and inventions go hand in hand in their major movements, although in minor fluctuations now one and now the other may seem to lead.

If the theory means that in the life history of a given total culture the scientific, technological, and economic discoveries emerge, blossom, and change first, whereas religious, artistic,

---

it accepts must be changed if they are notably heterogeneous in relation to the system; and the greater the heterogeneity, the greater must be the modification. When it is too great, the system does not ingest it at all. Cf., on the uniformities in this field, the *Dynamics*, Vol. IV, ch. 5.

[37] See, on this uniformity, *SCP*, ch. 35.

sociopolitical, philosophical and ideological discoveries emerge, blossom, and change later, the theory is again untenable, both logically and factually. Again, the data of the *Dynamics* referred to explicitly contradict such a generalization.

In the annals of history, persons who created important religious and political systems emerged several centuries before the scientific, technological, and economic discoveries, creators, and inventors. This is true of all countries studied.

If the theory means that natural-science disciplines and technologies emerge, develop, and change earlier than social, humanistic, religious, artistic, philosophical, and ethical ones (in the sequence mathematics and mathematical technology; astronomy, physics, chemistry, and their technologies; biology and its technologies), the theory becomes essentially similar to Comte's theory and, like it, is untenable. Data on discoveries in science and humanities in Arabia, as well as in various natural sciences throughout the world, and data on historical persons creative in specified fields in no way corroborate such a claim. They show, rather, that the invention or creation of a new system in religion, politics, social science, the humanistic disciplines, philosophy, or the fine arts occurred either before or at the same time as discoveries in the mathematico-physicochemical and technological fields.[38]

This is corroborated by data on the paleolithic and neolithic cultures. In all primitive tribes we meet not only the rudiments of physicochemical sciences and their technologies but often much better developed systems of religion and magic, the fine arts,[39] family and political organizations, and laws and mores.

Furthermore, until comparatively recently, no sharp divisions existed between science, philosophy, religion, and technology. Almost all of the eminent thinkers of Greece and Rome

[38] Cf. A. Kroeber, *Configurations of Culture Growth*, pp. 779 ff. He does not find any single people in whose culture science emerges first, followed by religion. The rule is that religion reaches first a high degree of integration and then science, arts, etc., develop. See especially *Dynamics,* Vol. IV, ch. 7.

[39] See especially F. Boas, *Primitive Art* (Oslo, 1927); H. Read, *Art and Society* (New York, 1937); and R. H. Lowie, *Primitive Religion* (New York, 1925). See other references in the *Dynamics, passim.*

and medieval Europe were at once scientists, philosophers, moralists, and political and social ideologists; many were also technological inventors, like Thales of Milet, Pythagoras, Architas, Anaximander, Archimedes, and Democritus.[40] A host of others, Hesiod, Homer, Pythagoras, Philolaus, Thales, Heraclitus, Empedocles, Zeno, Anaxagoras, Leukippos, Socrates, Protagoras, Georgias, Plato, Aristotle, Erigena, St. Thomas Aquinas, Albertus Magnus, Duns Scotus, Nicholaus Cusanus, Roger Bacon, and others, were simultaneously philosophers, theologians, scientists, social, political, juridical, and ethical thinkers and artists. One could not expect that the scientist in these men would change earlier and faster than the philosopher, the theologian, the law-giver, or the political thinker. If each of these individual thinkers is assumed to be logical, his total ideology must have changed more or less consistently, in togetherness. On the other hand, if each is assumed to be illogical, the very fact of illogicality precludes the possibility of any uniform change that would give consistent precedence to the change of his scientific and technologic thoughts.

As to the seemingly convincing argument that the rate of change in material culture is faster than in nonmaterial, the argument breaks down in its failure to adduce any unit of the velocity of change. Without such a unit, comparison of the amount or rate of change between material and nonmaterial phenomena becomes impossible. Which change is larger or faster: from Paganism and Judaism to Christianity, or from horse-drawn transportation to the horseless car? From polygamy to monogamy or from pastoral economy to agricultural? From Classic architecture to Gothic or from a "natural" economy to a money economy? From capitalism to communism or from steam to electricity? From gunpowder to atomic fission or from national sovereign states to a world-state? Which of these changes covers the greatest sociocultural distance in the smallest

---

[40] See P. M. Schuhl, *Machinisme et philosophie* (Paris, 1908), ch. I; H. Diels, *Antike Technik* (Leipzig-Berlin, 1924), pp. 98 ff.; L. Robin, *Platon* (Paris, 1935); F. M. Feldhaus, *Die Technik der Antike und des Mittelalters* (Potsdam, 1931); and A. Rey, *La science dans l'antiquité* (2 vols.; Paris, 1930–1933).

periods of time? Without yardsticks to measure by, the question is unanswerable.[41] The argument of the dichotomists becomes entirely void.

No less void is their argument that while the material culture of the last few decades has changed enormously, the nonmaterial culture lagged and is now hopelessly obsolete. The argument is purely subjective and arbitrary in the choice of criteria. The sublimest norms of ethical conduct, the Golden Rule, the ethical systems of practically all the great religions, and especially the norms of the Sermon on the Mount, were discovered and formulated in the ethical or nonmaterial culture of thousands of years ago. The behavioral and material realization of these norms have hopelessly lagged up to the present time. Science and technology have not yet objectified in their own or in the total material culture these nonmaterial discoveries. Similarly, the just "familistic" economic and political systems were formulated by religious, ethical, political, and social thinkers long ago, by thinkers like Ipuver, Moses, Confucius, Lao-tse, Hesiod, and Plato, to mention only a few. And yet the respective material and technological economies and political regimes have been unable up to the present time to realize these ideological systems. Some of the greatest aesthetic values in literature and painting, sculpture and architecture, music and drama were developed long ago in ancient Egypt and China, India and Greece, Rome and Persia. The material, technological, and economic culture contemporary with these creations was, by comparison, infinitely more primitive, imperfect, and inefficient; even today's material culture cannot boast any comparable perfection in its own field. These nonmaterial creations have already waited a few thousands of years for corresponding achievement in the material culture and they are still waiting. Nonmaterial "utopias" of beautiful garden cities; of flying carpets and machines, even of intra-atomic fission, dissolution, and re-creation emerged several thousands of years ago; many of these dreams have not been realized at all.

---

[41] See a development of this in my "Recent Social Trends," *Journal of Political Economy*, April, 1933.

Actually, the argument on either side is equally fallacious since it makes the two basically false assumptions discussed above: first, that the ideologies and material vehicles of cultural systems may be separated, and, second, that all material components and all nonmaterial components may be combined in two pseudosupersystems. We have already seen that such a procedure ignores the true togetherness of cultural systems and assumes, on the other hand, a wholly spurious togetherness of the artificial material and nonmaterial cultural dumps.

Meaningless also is the statement that while the material culture of the last century has enormously changed, our family, political, artistic, ethical, and religious cultures have remained unchanged and obsolete. First, it is untrue to say that in the last century or decades or even years our nonmaterial culture has not changed; it has enormously changed in all its compartments. Second, even if it had not changed, what grounds would there be for calling it obsolete or antiquated? Suppose the family had remained strong, truly familistic, divorce-free, with generally sound and healthy domestic conditions and relationships ensuring good education for the children and minimizing juvenile delinquency. Would such an institution need to change to avoid obsolescence? If it did and the change took the form of an enormous increase in divorces, separations, sex scandals, and juvenile delinquency, could it then be said to be keeping up with material changes and becoming "modern?" Is the music of Bach, Mozart, and Beethoven obsolete? Do jazz and rock 'n' roll represent a progress in music that corresponds to the change in material culture? Is Shakespeare obsolete and only the latest best seller the representative of modern literature?

It is meaningless to talk about the enormous change in the material culture and obsolescence of the "lagging" nonmaterial culture. The fact that the Beethovens and Shakespeares emerged several centuries ago is evidence of the leading role of the nonmaterial fine arts rather than their lag in comparison with the material culture.

In all their deploring of the supposed lag of nonmaterial culture, the dichotomic theorists never pause to reflect exactly what kind of nonmaterial culture would correspond with each stage of material development. What sort of family institution, music, philosophy, law, painting, or sociology would be appropriate to "atomic material culture?" Is the "obsolescence" of the family in such a culture to be avoided by a change in the polygamic, monogamic, patriarchal, or matriarchal form? Should the birth rate be higher, the divorce rate lower, or vice versa? What kind of music should accompany atomic fission? What religion, if any? What ethics?

These questions have never been answered because technology itself could never supply criteria for judging the level of nonmaterial culture. Criteria of obsolescence in music, religion, family, law, and philosophy must be drawn respectively from music, religion, family, law, and philosophy. No other judgments can have any meaning because, lacking any appropriate standard, they must break down in vague generalizations.

If the theories claim that technology changing itself always forces a change in nonmaterial culture, the statement is again largely fallacious. We know a large number of cases where an existing technology decayed not through technology but through the impact of nonmaterial culture. Toynbee cites how the splendid Roman roads, magnificent irrigation systems of the Tigris and Euphrates valleys, Ceylon, the Pontine marshes, and China went to pieces not because of a decay in technical skill but because of the incidence of social, political, and moral anarchy among the respective peoples. We have witnessed gigantic destruction of technological culture on the surface of this planet in the wars and revolutions of this century.[42] Contemporary historians have found that the economic and technological decline of the Greco-Roman world was "not the cause, but one of the aspects of the more general phenomenon of social disorganization."[43] On the other hand, the development of modern technology, modern capitalism, and modern material culture came not before but partly later than, partly simultaneously with, the development of sensate fine arts, and of materialistic

[42] See Toynbee, *A Study of History*, Vol. IV, pp. 40 ff.
[43] M. L. Rostovtzeff, *The Social and Economic History of the Roman Empire* (New York, 1926), pp. 302 ff., 432 ff.

and utilitarian philosophy, utilitarian and hedonistic ethics, secular law, new forms of political and social thought, individualism, singularism, nominalism, the Renaissance, the Reformation, and a host of other nonmaterial cultural systems.[44]

The fallaciousness of the theory of the unilateral effectiveness of material culture may also be demonstrated by examining primitive societies where different forms of nonmaterial culture are found to exist among peoples with similar technological and material cultures. On the other hand, similar religion, fine arts, literature, marriage customs, family organization, and political and judicial institutions are found among populations with dissimilar technological and material cultures.[45]

Finally, it is false to contend that material culture is accumulative while the nonmaterial is not. This statement is again so ambiguous and vague that several possible meanings of it must be considered. If it means literally what it says, then it is obviously wrong; as time goes on nonmaterial culture accumulates in all its forms. At the present time we have much a greater mass and diversity of musical compositions, literary works, sculpture, pictures, buildings, philosophies, religions, ethical systems, law codes, and social and political theories than we had 100, 500, or 5,000 years ago. Tables in the *Dynamics* show that religious and political series of historical persons are the longest, the most continuous, and accumulate the fastest, and that the business series of historical persons is the shortest, the most discontinuous, and the least accumulative.

If the statement means that only in science and technology do new discoveries or inventions actually produce new things, it is also wrong. Important religious, aesthetic, or philosophical innovations are no less new. Confucianism, Taoism, Judaism, Christianity, and Mohammedanism are each as novel as any

---

[44] See the *Dynamics*, all 4 volumes, for corroboration of these statements. See also M. Weber, *Gesammelte Aufsätze zur Religionssoziologie* (3 vols.; Tübingen, 1922–1923), though he enormously exaggerates the role of Protestantism. See also A. Fanfani, *Catholicism, Protestantism, and Capitalism* (New York, 1936).

[45] See Hobhouse, Wheeler and Ginsberg, *Material Culture and Social Institutions*. See other relevant facts in my *CST*, ch. 10; *Dynamics*, Vol. IV, ch. 7.

new gadget in comparison with its predecessors. The same is true of important philosophical, literary, architectural, musical, or legal creations. Actually the novelty is not absolute in either nonmaterial or material fields. The "new" technological invention or scientific discovery is generally a combination of old elements or a variation of an old principle. The basic principles even of atomic structure, fission, and destruction are very old, dating back to Democritus and Leukippos and still older thinkers of ancient India. Principles of atomic structure, fission, and destruction are fairly accurately formulated in several old Hindu sources that suppose a cycle of elemental dissolution of all material elements—space, smell, color, form, flavor, sound, ether, and matter with all their properties—to occur periodically every 311,040,000,000,000 mortal years.[46]

Creation in nonmaterial cultures similarly involves the combination and variation of older systems. Bach's music in comparison with its predecessors is as new as a locomotive in comparison with a horse and wagon; but both Bach's music and the locomotive represented a lucky marriage of two or more ideas existing before. Both combined in a new way existing elements. There is no basis for claiming a distinction between the material and nonmaterial culture systems in respect to the novelty of their creations. In both cases accumulation means replacement of the old with the new, which is itself compounded of old.

If, finally, this thesis means that only in material culture is there a progression of change toward perfection, the proposition is again very questionable. Is German beer a more perfect sample of material culture than Roman wine? The answer is purely a matter of personal taste—it cannot be decided objectively and scientifically. The same must be said of the latest fashion in dress, food, and fuel in comparison with the old. If we had the courage of our convictions, many of us would

---

[46] See among many Hindu sources *The Vishnu Puránà*, tr. by H. H. Wilson (5 vols.; London, 1864–1877), Vol. V, pp. 55, 162, 195 ff.; and Vol. I, pp. 114 ff. See other sources and quotations in my *Dynamics*, Vol. II, pp. 353 ff.; and Vol. IV, pp. 442 ff. On variations of atomic theories, see Vol. II, pp. 439–446.

prefer old-fashioned dress, our mother's cooking, and wood fires to many modern forms of these material cultures.

This is true even of more complex gadgets. Many of our contemporaries, including a number of scientists, wish that the atomic bomb had never been invented; many of us would prefer to dispense with the disturbing, threatening, noise-making planes and rockets if we could. Because in an increasingly complex life they became all but inevitable it does not follow that we must make a virtue out of the necessity. Still, a large number of city dwellers see no virtue in the necessity for living in crowded tenements in big cities with all their bustle and hustle, dirt and glitter, excitement and killing monotony. Similarly, many people do not feel they are better off in the deadly monotonous life of a modern factory than their grandfathers were on the farm.

All this means that as soon as an investigator introduces the principle of "more perfect" and "better," he abandons the ground of scientific objectivity and begins to evaluate his personal preferences.

From the standpoint of a killer and perhaps of an inventor the atomic bomb is a better instrument of destruction than its predecessors; from the standpoint of humanity, and especially the victims, it is a hellish invention. The position of the "objectors" is at least as defensible as that of its proponents. The same can be said of other gadgets. Judging by the rapidly increasing suicide rate, mental disorders, and destructive wars of this century, it would seem that this century of great technological progress has not made humanity happier or better satisfied with life.

On the other hand, on the ground of this subjective preference, a better case for "progress" could be made out for advances of nonmaterial culture. There are few people who desire to reject the latest astrophysical cosmologies and return to the Ptolemaic system. After the emergence of the great religions and ethical systems few wish to return to religiously primitive animism, fetishism, totemism. After the great philosophical systems we do not aspire to return to primitive philosophies. After Bach, Mozart, and Beethoven we can hardly go back to the mere plain chant. After great historical works we can no longer accept primitive fantastic histories.

If such reversions to the more primitive occur, they happen in both material and nonmaterial cultures. War destroyed many parts of Europe, Asia, and Africa and returned them to a material culture even worse than that of many primitive tribes. Somewhat similar relapses in nonmaterial culture now and then also occur.

The totality of these considerations and of empirical evidence shows the untenability of the dichotomic lead and lag theories. At best they fall into the familiar error of elevation of a partial fact into a universal rule.[47]

GENERAL CONCLUSION

Despite my criticism of them, the dichotomic theories, in analyzing several basic problems of sociocultural reality, have greatly contributed to our knowledge of this reality by their valid clarifications of these problems as well as by their "enlightening errors."

[47] See a further criticism and the literature in my *Dynamics*, Vol. IV, chs. 4, 6, and 7.

CHAPTER 11

Recent Typologies of Cultural

Systems and Supersystems

EXAMPLES OF CULTURAL TYPOLOGIES

The examined theories of cultural systems and supersystems do not exhaust the rich variety of the current typological interpretations of cultural phenomena. To round out our survey of partly systemic, partly eclectic typologies of culture, several of such theories are outlined in this chapter. Each brings out some features of cultural reality worthy of our attention. W. Schubart's and H. Becker's theories portray different types of systems of culture; N. Berdyaev and J. Ortega y Gasset depict the types of historical culture of the West, their succession and their crises. A. Schweitzer and F. R. Cowell give to us a recent variation of the idealized conception of civilization and *Kultur* and interpret from this standpoint today's crisis of civilization. Finally, the theories of aesthetic systems and their change inform us about some uniformities in the field of art phenomena. Taken together these theories throw a light upon several dark points of the cultural world and its important processes.

WALTER SCHUBART: FOUR TYPES OF CULTURE

In any discussion of the recent "rhythmic"[1] philosophies of history, which are concerned with the present state and inter-relationship of the European and Russian cultures, Walter

---

[1] A systematic history of rhythmic and cyclic theories of historical processes can be found in the *Dynamics*, Vol. II, ch. 10, and Vol. IV, chs. 8–16. See also G. E. Cairns, *Philosophies of History* (New York, 1962).

Schubart's *Europa und die Seele des Ostens* should be mentioned.[2] Its author is a German philosopher and historian who spent a considerable amount of time in Russia. Its publication in Switzerland in 1938 was little noticed at the time. A few years later it appeared in an abbreviated Russian translation (outside the Soviet Union); recently it has been translated into French and English. Much attention has been paid to it and to his *Dostojewski und Nietzsche* (1939) and *Geistige Wandlung* (1940) in the last few years.

The essential points of Schubart's "philosophy of history" are as follows:

1. Historical processes are rhythmic. The old Hindu, Persian, Jewish (the book of Daniel), Mexican, Empedoclian, Heraclitian, and more recently Goethe's, Nietzsche's, and Spengler's "cyclic" interpretations of sociocultural processes are essentially correct in their central ideas.

2. The most important historical rhythm consists in a succession of four aeonic prototypes of culture and of personality. The unfolding of each prototype in the course of time and its struggle against its predecessors and its successors constitutes the central process of cultural history and endows it with epochal rhythm, tension, and conflict.

3. Each aeonic prototype of culture transcends the boundaries of nation or race. Its area may cover the whole continent. Within its domination-area each cultural prototype permeates the whole culture and every human being in the area with its specific character. Without losing his moral freedom, each person is forced to reckon with the dominant cultural prototype, either actualizing it or opposing it, but never ignoring it. After all, opposition is but a form of recognition.

4. Each time mankind is "fertilized" by a new prototype, a great creative process repeats itself anew. A feeling of youthfulness sweeps over the respective culture. All that preceded the new prototype appears "antiquated" and obsolete. The new prototype is experienced as the supreme value, the end toward which all preceding history has been a mere preparation. The

2 (*Lucerne*, 1938).

"new epoch" or the "modern period" begins. The emerged prototype in time unfolds itself, and the values it was pregnant with are delivered. Having exhausted its creative mission, it ages and in its turn gives way to a new prototype. Thus the epochal rhythm continues:

> Behind this change of the prototypes some unknown law is probably hidden—the law according to which the divine creative forces now pour themselves into the given empirical world of things, now withdraw from it. Not being able to explain them rationally in all their details, we can only guess at these uniformities; we can either intuit them silently or hint at them by parables and symbols. (*Europa und die Seele des Ostens*, pp. 13 ff.)

5. The four main prototypes of culture and personality, or "soul," that replace one another in the course of time are the Harmonious, the Heroic, the Ascetic, and the Messianic.

The Harmonious culture mentality and Harmonious man experience the cosmos as animated by inner harmony, as perfect, as not requiring any human leadership or reconstruction. The idea of evolution or progress does not exist in such a cosmos because Harmonious man regards the purpose of history as achieved. The cosmos, being perfect, is viewed as eternally static and not dynamic. The Harmonious person lives peacefully in and with the whole world, as an inseparable part of it. The Homeric Greeks, the Confucian Chinese, and the Gothic Christians of the West from the eleventh to the sixteenth centuries are examples of this Harmonious prototype. Permeated by the feeling of eternity, the Gothic Christian trustfully looked up to heaven. His temples piously surged higher and higher into the sky. The earthly landscape was largely forgotten, and Gothic man busied himself mainly with the salvation of his soul, the grace of God, and *requiem eternam* in God's Kingdom.

The Heroic culture mentality and man view the world as a chaos which they must put in order by their organizational effort. The Heroic man does not live peacefully with the world but is set against it in its existing form. He is full of self-confidence, self-pride, and lust for power. He looks at the world as at a slave; he wants to master and mold it according to his own plans. He does not look up to heaven reverently; instead, being full of lust for power and pride, he looks down at earth with inimical and jealous eyes. He goes progressively further away from God and sinks deeper and deeper into the world of empirical things. Secularization is his destiny; heroism his main life feeling; tragedy his end.

In such a world, especially in such a culture and man, everything is dynamic. Nothing is static in the Heroic universe. Like Prometheus, the Heroic man challenges any power and any god. He is active, tense, and maximally energetic. Accordingly, the Heroic or Promethean epochs are especially dynamic, mobile, and active. The Roman world at the zenith of Roman power felt itself to be thus, and in the Germano-Romanic West after the sixteenth century this prototype has also been dominant. The Promethean Western culture and man of the last four centuries are good examples of this prototype.

The Ascetic culture mentality and man experience the empirical existence as an error, the sensory world as a mirage and evil temptation. They run away from both into the mystic realm of supra-essence or suprareality. The Ascetic person leaves the sensory world without regret. He has neither desire nor hope for its improvement. He does not try to change it at all. Therefore the epochs of the Ascetic prototype's domination are even more static than those of the Harmonious culture and man.

The Hindu of Hinduism and Buddhism, the Neo-Platonists, and most of the truly ascetic groups and sects are examples of the Ascetic prototype of culture mentality and man.

Finally, the Messianic culture mentality and man feel themselves called upon to establish on earth the supreme divine order, whose idea they ineffably bear in themselves. The Messianic man wants to re-establish around himself the harmony that he feels in himself. He does not accept the world as it is. Like the Heroic man, he too wants to change it—not for his own self-will or self-satisfaction, but in order to fulfill the mission assigned to him by God. Like the Harmonious man he also loves the world—not as it is, but as it ought to be.

The goal of the Harmonious man is reached; that of the Messianic man is far away, in the future. In contrast to the Ascetic man, however, he firmly believes that this goal can be reached. The Messianic man is inspired not by the lust for power, but by the mood of reconciliation and love. He does not divide in order to rule, but looks for the divided in order to unite it into one whole. He is not moved by suspicion and hate, but by deep trust in the true reality. He sees brothers, not enemies, in human beings. He views the world not as booty to be grabbed, but as rough stuff in need of enlightenment, ennoblement, and consecration. He is possessed by a sort of cosmic passion to unify what is separated, to harmonize what is discordant, to make visible on this planet the Kingdom of God or his highest ideal. He works for a realization of this highest ideal here on earth.

Like the Heroic man he is full of energy, activity, and dynamism. Accordingly, the Messianic epochs are dynamic too. The early Christians and most of the Slavs are examples of this prototype.

These four prototypes can be summed up in the following phrases: consonance with the world (Harmonious); domination over the world (Heroic); running away from the world (Ascetic); and consecration of the world (Messianic).[3]

6. Like Danilevsky, Spengler, and Toynbee, Schubart rejects the linear interpretation of historical process and the "justification" of all history by some future and final goal of progress. He states, as do all partisans of the rhythmical conception of sociocultural change, that "before God all times are equal," even the Heroic epochs, which do not care for God at all. Each aeonic epoch contains its own value and justification, as great as those of any other epoch. Like a pause in a melody, even the godless periods have their own *raison d'être*. An incessant unfolding of the creative, divine forces occurs in each time-moment; therefore each moment bears in itself the justifying reason for its existence, for otherwise no future goal can justify any past moment of history.

[3] W. Schubart, *Europa*, pp. 13–16.

7. Especially breath-taking are the periods when one proto-type dies out and a new one begins to emerge. These periods are the intermediary, apocalyptic moments of humanity. In such periods people feel that everything is crumbling and the end of the world is coming. In fact, such moments have been repeated many times and will be repeated many more times in the future.

8. The twentieth century is one of these intermediary, apocalyptic periods. For several decades now, a few seers have foreseen that something important was ending: the post-Atlantis humanity, according to Merejkovsky; Christianity, according to Unamuno; the thousand-year-long Western culture, according to Spengler; capitalism, according to Marx; the epoch of the Renaissance, according to Berdyaev. It is precisely this transitory character of our age that makes it so dynamic and so self-contradictory. It is full of sadness and full of hope, of dark forebodings and of cheerful prospects. Before our eyes, we see dying not a single race or nation nor a single culture, but a whole preceding cultural epoch. Which epoch?

9. During the last thousand years two epochal prototypes have grown on European soil: the Harmonious-Gothic and the Heroic-Promethean. The Gothic prototype was born of the catastrophes of the eleventh century and lasted up to the sixteenth century. It was a Harmonious culture with all its earmarks. It was creative and fruitful in its own way. Between 1450 and 1550, however, a transition from the Gothic-Harmonious to the Heroic-Promethean prototype took place. This Promethean-Western man cared little for God or for the salvation of his soul and much for the conquest of the world. In the course of some 500 years the Promethean man, through his most intense activities, has indeed succeeded in changing the surface of the earth and in pushing his ambitious plans far and high. He has indeed created a new sociocultural world in his own image.

After 500 years of the Heroic-Promethean epoch we are now at the threshold of a new epoch. The heavy clouds of destiny are hanging over the Promethean culture. Lightnings and deadly tornadoes are sweeping over it. Europe is fatally sliding into her most bloody catastrophe; she is approaching the end that was inherent in the birth of her Promethean culture. Nothing can stop its death. On the horizon, however, the dawn of a new epochal prototype, the Messianic-Johannian (St. John of the Gospel), is beginning to loom. This Messianic-Johannian epoch will be congenial to the Gothic-Harmonious. While the Promethean man and culture hated and disdained the Gothic culture and man, the coming Messianic culture and man will admire them and love the Middle Ages of Europe. This Johannian epoch will be animated by the spirit of solidarity, reconciliation, love, and unity. The realization of a truly creative and friendly one-world will be the chief mission of the Johannian man.

10. Which human groups will be the leaders or instrumentalities of the new prototype, and which are going to oppose it, depend upon the specific characteristics of these groups at the moment of the emergence of the prototype. The combination of two factors—the relatively constant geographic environment and the ever-dynamic immanent change of the prototypes—determines the essentials of historical process and the "physiognomy" of each group, including the racial and national groups, at any moment of history.

11. When these relatively constant national traits coincide with, or are congenial to, the emerging cultural prototype, the nation in question becomes the leader in the rising culture and reaches the zenith of its cultural creativity, which may or may not coincide with the zenith of its political power. Thus, with the emergence of the Western Promethean man and culture, Prussia and the Prussians became the leaders among the Germans and the German states because their ethnic national traits were most congenial to those of the Promethean prototype. Among the European nations the Prussians and the Anglo-Saxons became the leaders and the examples of this epoch. For the same reason the Jews have become increasingly influential during the last 150 years; their relatively constant traits happened to be congenial to those of the Promethean man.

With the development of the Promethean culture the initiative progressively comes from the north and the main historical stage shifts to the north. The leadership of the sixteenth century belonged to the Italians and the Spaniards, of the seventeenth century to the French, passing in subsequent centuries to the Prussians, then to the Anglo-Saxons and the Scandinavians. The Lower-Germans (*Niederdeutsche*), the Anglo-Saxons, the Prussians, and the Puritans (Americans) are the titans of the Promethean technological epoch. Parallel with this change in leadership the main arena of the Promethean culture has also shifted northward, from Italy and Spain to Northern Germany, England, and North America.

12. In the emerging Messianic-Johannian epoch the central stage of history again shifts and the leadership passes from the Promethean nations to those whose national character is best suited to the Johannian prototype:

> The most important event in the making is the rise of the Slavs as the emerging cultural leader. However unpleasant this is for many, such is historical destiny; nobody can stop it; the next centuries belong to the Slavs. The Nordic Promethean culture is dying; its place is being taken by an Oriental Culture. [The] Johannian epoch is [a] Slavic aeon. . . .
> The Promethean West enriched humanity through the most perfect forms of technics, statehood and communication, but it deprived mankind of its soul. Russia's mission consists of returning this soul to humanity. Russia possesses exactly those spiritual forces which Europe either lost or destroyed. Russia is a part of Asia, and at the same time a member of the Christian Commonwealth of nations. She is a Christian part of Asia. In this lies the specific peculiarity of Russia and the uniqueness of her mission. Only Russia can spiritualize a humanity that is drowned in the swamp of material things and spoiled by the lust for power; and this in spite of the Bolshevist agony that Russia is experiencing at the present time. The horrors of the Communist regime will pass, just as the night of the Tartar yoke passed, and the old motto, "*Ex oriente lux*," will come through. By this I do not want to say that the European nations will lose their importance; they will only lose the spiritual leadership. They would no longer represent the dominant human type, and this would be a real blessing for humanity. An enormous multitude, and especially many of the finest minds, long for the end of the worn-out Promethean culture. They feel its present poverty and look for a new possibility. However reckless it may sound to many, it should be stated definitely that Russia is the only country which can

and will free Europe. From the unfathomed depths of her own crucifixion Russia is obtaining the deepest understanding of human beings and of their life values, in order to communicate it to all nations of the earth. (*Ibid.*, pp. 16–27.)

13. The realization of this goal will not be achieved peacefully, according to Schubart. Politically, the West-East problem signifies conflict and war. Some 500 years would be required for its solution, a period similar to the one that was necessary to achieve a balance between the Germanic peoples and ancient Rome. A grand reconciliation is often preceded by intensive political and military conflicts. Viewed in this light, the Russian-European relationship has grown increasingly tense.

This "mutually interpenetrating" political conflict between Russia and the West has continued *crescendo* since 1812. Europe has incessantly tried to weaken, stop, suppress, and crush Russia economically, culturally, diplomatically, and militarily. Besides invasion by separate European states, Europe as a whole invaded Russia in 1854 (the Crimean War), threatened to do so several times later on, and then invaded again in 1914. After being repulsed and answered by the Russian Revolution, the West once more, in 1918, sent its combined expeditionary forces to crush the Revolution, suffocate Russia by the *cordon sanitaire,* and destroy Russia by shearing from her as many of her Asiatic, Caucasian, Pre-Baltic, Western, and Eastern parts as it could. Failing in this, the West organized the Fascist, Nazi, and other anti-Russian forces and created a new gigantic military power for a new invasion. (Schubart's book was published in 1938, before World War II.) In brief, the war of 1914 opened a new Hundred Years' War between the Promethean West and Russia, or rather the East organized and led by Russia.

14. In a subsequent part of his book Schubart gives a comparative analysis of the Promethean and Russian souls, and outlines the comparative psychology of various Western nations, specifically the German, French, Anglo-Saxon, and Spanish.[4]

[4] See on this my *Modern Historical and Social Philosophies,* pp. 132–136.

Schubart concludes his book by reiterating that the Promethean prototype of the West is coming to an end and a new Messianic soul is being born in Russia:

> The coming Russia is that refreshing wine which will revitalize the dried up life-stream of today's humanity. The West is that strong container in which we can keep the wine. Without a strong, holding form the wine will be spilt and lost; without the wine the precious container will only remain an empty and useless toy. Contemporary Europe is a form without life. Russia is the life without form. . . . The Englishman wants to see the world as a factory; the Frenchman as a salon; the German as a military barrack; the Russian as a Church. The Englishman seeks for profit; the Frenchman wants glory; the German power; the Russian sacrifice. The Russian wants nothing from his neighbor except brotherhood. . . . This is the essence of the Russian brotherhood and of the Gospel of the future. (*Ibid.*, pp. 313–318.)

CRITICISM

Schubart's thesis that the Russian soul and culture are Messianic and are destined to take the leading role in the coming Messianic period of human history remains largely a matter of belief, supported by scant evidence on Schubart's part. It contains only a grain of truth in the sense that the European phase of human history is over, and the center of history is now shifting to the region of the Pacific, where, besides the Americas, India, Japan, Indonesia, and China, Russia will also be playing a leading part.[5] Schubart's prototypes of culture and personality are suggestive but require marked modification. His prototypes are somewhat congenial to my Ideational, Idealistic, and Sensate prototypes of culture and personality: his Heroic-Promethean type is similar to my Active Sensate type, his Ascetic type to my Ascetic Ideational, and his Harmonious-Messianic to my Idealistic or Integral type. But his types do not include the Active Ideational, Passive and Cynical Sensate, Pseudo-Ideational, and Eclectic types;[6] nor

---

[5] See on this trend my *Basic Trends of Our Time* (New Haven, 1964).

[6] See, on my taxonomy of cultural supersystems and types of personality, the *Dynamics*, Vol. I, pp. 67–101.

does he delienate his prototypes clearly and in sufficient detail. He fails also to systematically demonstrate the existence of his types or supersystems in historical cultures of mankind; he does not tell us in what cultures, when, and to what extent each of his prototypes existed as a dominant supersystem. He merely says that the Harmonious culture and man are exemplified by the Homeric Greeks and the Confucian Chinese; the Ascetic by the Neo-Platonists and the Hindu of Hinduism; and the Heroic by the Western culture and man of the last few centuries. This sort of illustration is quite insufficient to prove his thesis. The same can be said for his contrasting characterization of the Western and Russian personality types: It is impressionistic rather than accurate. Despite these defects, his typologies of personality are more penetrating, more real, and therefore more scientific than most of the so-called scientific classifications of personality types.

HOWARD BECKER (1899–1960): SACRED-SECULAR TYPES

Becker's Sacred-Secular theory represents his main contribution to macrosociologies of cultural and social systems.[7] In his earlier work he occupied a nominalistic-singularistic position,[8] a position considerably neutralized in his later works where he introduces such concepts as plurality patterns, interhuman structures, groups, abstract collectivities, institution, continuum, and even society types[9] that are hardly less reified substitutes for the terms and concepts previously rejected by him. Despite this shift toward the systemic position, Becker never adopted it fully. This explains why he prefers to call his

[7] A detailed analysis of Becker's sociology is given in C. P. and Z. K. Loomis, *Modern Social Theories*, ch. 2.

[8] See, on Becker's nominalistic-singularistic standpoint, his *Systematic Sociology* (New York, 1932), pp. 56 ff., 80 ff., and *passim*.

[9] "Functioning institutions and functioning society amount to the same thing. . . . As long as a society is in some sense a 'whole' it has working 'parts'; these parts are reciprocally connected or there would be no 'whole'." H. Becker, *Man in Reciprocity: Introductory Lectures on Culture, Society, and Personality* (New York, 1956), p. 239.

theory of Sacred, Secular, and Intermediary types of sociocultural formations Sacred-Secular-Continuum and not a Sacred-Secular System. The essentials of this theory can be summed up as follows:

1. The categories of Sacred and Secular societies represent the central "constructed types" in Becker's sense of these terms.

2. His terms are defined as follows:

> Sacred, sacredness and sacralization . . . all designate . . . orientation on the part of members of a society toward values . . . held to be worthy of being made or kept inviolate. . . . Secular, secularity and secularization . . . designate orientation on the part of members of a society toward certain values . . . held to be worth pursuing regardless of entailed changes in the values themselves . . . or other changes. A sacred society is one bringing its members to be unwilling or unable, in whatever measure, to accept the new *as the new is defined in that society.* A secular society is one bringing its members to be willing and able, in whatever measure, to accept or pursue the new *as the new is defined in that society.*[10]

3. These two types represent two opposite poles of a "continuum" of many intermediary types of concrete societies situated between its extreme Sacred-Secular poles. Moving from the Sacred pole to the Secular, these intermediary types give four distinct subtypes: the *Proverbial*, closest to the Sacred, is marked by the "holy" and inviolable character of its "traditionally nonrational" values, reluctant to change, hieratic and ritualistic in realization, manifestation, and reinforcement of its "holy" values. The members of the Proverbial society are capable of being martyrs in defending their Sacred values and their penal code imposes the death penalty or severe sanctions for violation of their holy norms of conduct. Such social groups tend to be static and change little in the process of their historical existence. The next subtype is the *Prescriptive*. It is stamped by "sanctioned rationality," "intimate, moralistic and conventional" character of its values, "commemorative and ceremonial" ways of affirmation, reinforcement, and practice of

---

[10] H. Becker, "Sacred Society," UNESCO, *Dictionary of Social Science*, also his "Current Sacred-Secular Theory" in H. Becker and A. Boskoff, *Modern Sociological Theory* (New York, 1957).

these values, by a lesser reluctance to change, a lesser willingness to die for its values, and less severe sanctions for their violations. It is less absolutistic and more relative than the Proverbial type. The next type, closer to the Secular pole, is the *Principial.* Its values are embodied in general principles less rigid and more elastic, more relativistic, expedient, rational, and changeable than the values and norms of the Proverbial and the Prescriptive types. Finally, the *Pronormless* subtype is a main form of the Secular sociocultural type. Its values are quite relativistic, changeable, favoring an extremely free-and-easy state of affairs, leaving a wide margin for a free choice of the relativized and atomized values. In this extreme "normlessness," such a society tends to be nonrational, largely motivated by hedonistic, emotional values of "comfort and thrill." Individual whim ("I like it because I like it, and what is to stop me?") largely replaces most moral and obligatory norms of conduct. Such a society is in a state of incessant, now orderly, now disorderly flux.[11]

4. In the process of historical existence each of these types changes. "The path from one polar societal type is not a one-way street, all around us can be seen evidence of the fact that societies, even 'modern societies' can journey from secular to sacred as illustrated by the Germans 'turning back the clock' from the Weimer secularity to Nazi sacredness."[12]

5. The factors of the change are partly internal, like inventions, class-struggle, etc., partly external to each society, like defeat in battle, floods, drought, pestilence, and famine. Becker stresses, particularly, the role of diverse internal and external conflicts and crises, and does not give a systematic theory of the forces of change. He indicates, however, that any society, including even "the most isolated sacred society is empirically but a moving equilibrium maintained by the equal action of . . . processes of disorganization and reorganization." When the change is fundamental and rapid, the society experiences a crisis, and "in crisis situations we regress to

[11] H. Becker, "Current Sacred-Secular Theory," pp. 145 ff.
[12] H. Becker and R. Hill, *Family, Marriage and Parenthood* (Boston, 1955), p. 45; H. Becker, *Man in Reciprocity,* pp. 171, 373, 441–442.

earlier types of societal organization (to the Sacred type)." In any rapid change "there are costs of change"—namely, greater or lesser disorganization of the society's members, its institutions, values, and orderly way of life.[13]

Such is the skeleton of Becker's Sacred-Secular typology. In his works it is considerably developed and accompanied by classifications of types of rationality into "expedient and sanctioned," of types of nonrationality into "traditional and emotional," of types of isolation into "vicinal, social, and mental," of personality types into "the unmoral, the demoralized, the segmental, the marginal, the regulated, the decadent and the liberated man."[14]

CRITICISM

Since Becker's Sacred-Secular typological continuum is based upon the major premise of either "reluctance or acceptance of change," and since other characteristics of the Proverbial, Prescriptive, Principial, and Pronormless types are logically and factually associated, these types can be regarded as vast meaningful-causal systems and the Sacred and the Secular types as two vast supersystems. Viewed either as systems and supersystems or merely as constructed types, Becker's theory has some cognitive significance. Its importance might have been still greater if it were not marred by serious defects due largely to his ambiguous position between the singularistic-nominalistic and systemic viewpoints.

The first of these defects is the unclear meaning of the continuum and its four constructed types. Are these abstract, semifictitious—"*als ob*," or "*as if*"—constructions that have a remote, if any, relationship to *empirical* sociocultural realities or groups? Or are they generalized types of a multitude of *empirical* collectivities repeated in time and space? Or are they meaningful or meaningful-causal sociocultural systems and supersystems really functioning and living in the human sociocultural world? If they signify just abstract, fictional, "as if," or *als ob*

---

[13] H. Becker, *Man in Reciprocity*, pp. 441–442, and *Through Values to Social Interpretation*, p. 185.

[14] H. Becker, *Man in Reciprocity*, pp. 198–199.

constructions, they are useless for our cognition of the empirical sociocultural world.[15]

If they are generalized types of frequently given *empirical* sociocultural complexes, then this meaning of these types should have been developed, clearly defined, and systematically demonstrated by indicating a multitude of historico-empirical societies corresponding to each of these types. All Becker furnishes along this line are a few incidental illustrations of each type.

If these types mean either cultural or social systems and supersystems, then again their reality and unity had to be corroborated logically and empirically. No such corroboration is given by Becker.

From this initial defect, several other shortcomings follow. The basic Sacred and Secular types appear to be a variation of F. Tönnies' *Gemeinschaft* and *Gesellschaft* types of organized social systems. While Becker justifiably rejects some of the shortcomings of Tönnies' types of community and society, his own variation of these types introduces other factual and logical errors.

For instance, most of the characteristics of the Sacred— Proverbial and Prescriptive—types that he infers from, and builds upon, the major premise of "reluctance to change" hardly follow logically from this premise and hardly are causally connected with it. The same is true about the characteristics of the Secular Pronormless and Principial types, which Becker deduces from, and correlates with, the major premise of "readiness and acceptance of change" of the Secular type. Logically, from the "philosophy of unchangeable Being" (the values and value-orientation) of the Sacred societies it does not follow at all that such societies have to be "traditionally nonrational," loyalistic, intimate, moralistic, ready for martyrdom, and inflicting liberally the death penalty for violation of their values and norms of conduct. Logically, the eternalistic philosophy of unchangeable

---

[15] In subsequent chapters, the preoccupation of contemporary American sociologists with "theoretical constructions" of all sorts of fictitious "conceptual frameworks," and with "abstract paradigms" that help us little to understand the what, how, and why of the empirical sociocultural universe we live in, will be discussed in some detail.

Being from Taoism, the Upanishads, Parmenides, Zeno, and Euclid to von Hartmann, Heidegger, and Jaspers is as rational and nontraditional as the temporalistic philosophy of Incessant Becoming of Heraclitus, Epicurus, Nietzsche, Mill, James, and other partisans of such a philosophy. Empirically, both kinds of philosophy and respective attitudes, together with the philosophy of the integrated "temporalism-eternalism," have been given in the past as well as in modern time: Even for the period 1800–1900, in the total philosophy of the West, the eternalistic philosophy of Being still gives 51 percent, whereas the temporalistic philosophy of Becoming gives 33 percent and the integral synthesis of both 16 percent.[16]

If instead of these systematic data we take the Zuni or the Hopi Indian tribes, whose total cultures and mentalities are closer to Becker's Sacred type, we hardly can call them more "traditionally nonrational" than the culture and mentality of the Dobu, which are closer to Becker's Secular Pronormless type. The same can be said of the culture, mentality, and conduct of many historical societies that are closer to the Sacred type compared with those of historical groups closer to the Secular type. Becker's correlation of his major premise of "reluctance to change" with "traditional nonrationality" is neither logically nor empirically warranted.[17]

The same is true of his correlations of other characteristics of his Secular and Sacred types with their major premises. "Reluctance to change" neither logically requires nor is empirically

[16] See the movement and fluctuation of these currents of philosophical thought in Greco-Roman and Western history from 600 B.C. to A.D. 1920 in the *Dynamics*, Vol. II, ch. 5, and the detailed list of the representatives of each of these currents on pp. 663–675.

[17] One of the reasons for Becker's error is his uncritical acceptance of Max Weber's ideas about rationality and nonrationality. As Weber uses these terms, at least six different meanings can be detected. As a result, these concepts remain very poorly, sometimes even contradictorily, defined by Weber. The same is true of Becker's use of these terms. In my *Dynamics*, I have shown (logically and empirically) that the ideational (Becker's Sacred) mentality is as rational and logically consistent with the ideational major premise about the nature of the true reality-value as the sensate (Becker's Secular) mentality built on the sensate major premise. The difference between these mentalities is due not to their rationality or nonrationality, but to the basic difference of their major premises concerning the nature of the true reality-value.

(causally) connected with such features of the Sacred types as: "loyalistic, intimate, moralistic, fitting, appropriate value-orientation," and of the severe character of the sanctions for violating norms of conduct. Logically, these features can be associated with the premises of "acceptance and readiness to change" and, empirically, they can be found about as frequently in the Secular type of society as in the Sacred. The same is true of the major postulate "approval of and readiness to change" and such characteristics of the Secular type as "expedient, unlimited rationality, affective nonrationality, anticeremonialism, normlessness," and the mild penal sanctions for violating norms of conduct. Becker does not demonstrate empirically that any of these traits are causally connected with "philosophy of Becoming" implied in the "readiness to change." For instance, the overabundance of parades and ceremonials, the election of endless queens, beauties, and champions, and the plethora of annual academic ceremonies hardly support the characteristic of "anticeremonialism" ascribed to our supposedly Secular society.

Still more questionable is the severe punitive sanctions ascribed to the Sacred and the mild sanctions attributed to the Secular societies. In this point, Becker again uncritically accepted E. Durkheim's theory that penal sanctions in Sacred societies, especially for the violation of religious norms, are much severer than those in Secular societies. Durkheim's reason for this uniformity is that crimes in Sacred societies offend the whole group, whereas crimes in Secular groups insult only individuals. Severe sanctions in Sacred collectivities also serve the purpose of reinforcing their collective system of values.[18]

When Durkheim's and Becker's generalization is systematically tested by a detailed study of the penal systems and criminal codes of various preliterate and historical peoples, the generalization is not supported at all by the relevant facts.[19] Still less convincing is Durkheim's *logical* argument that severe sanctions

[18] See on this theory Durkheim's *De la division du travail social* (Paris, 1893), and his "Deux lois de l'évolution pénale," *L'Année Sociologique,* IV 63 ff.

[19] See the literature and a systematic, detailed study of the criminal codes of Greece, Rome, and the West, ranging from the Barbaric codes of the fifth century to the modern criminal codes of Soviét Russia, Nazi Germany, and Fascist Italy, in the *Dynamics,* Vol. II, pp. 523–627.

are necessary for reinforcing the collective values of the Sacred society. The strong, unanimously accepted, deeply interiorized, holy character of the values of the Sacred society effectively control the behavior of its members from within; thus the Sacred society does not need severe sanctions as much as the Secular society with its atomized and conflicting values, its moral anomie, and the widespread search for maximum pleasures, comforts, and thrills. For maintaining elementary order, the Secular society needs the executioner and the policeman much more than does the Sacred society. The available body of empirical evidence fairly definitely supports this conclusion.[20]

Not quite correct either is Becker's description of the effects of crises and calamities upon the religious and moral behavior of the members of a society in crisis. He mentions only the demoralizing and disintegrating effects of crises instead of the two-sided, moral and religious polarization uniformly occurring in times of crises and catastrophies. Certain members of a society in crisis become more irreligious, demoralized, and criminal whereas others become more religious and morally ennobled.[21]

In a similar way it can be proved that several other conclusions of Becker are erroneous empirically and logically. His types are neither causal nor meaningful systems but logical and empirical congeries. Each type is made up by throwing together several variables unrelated to the main premise or to one another.[22]

Another shortcoming of Becker's theory is that it tells very little about the character of the values of Sacred or Secular culture—the character of their systems of truth and cognition, their science and philosophy, their ethics and law, their fine arts, their economics and politics.

---

[20] *Ibid.*, chs. 13, 14, 15.

[21] See my *Man and Society in Calamity* (New York, 1942), chs. 10, 11.

[22] This explains the surprising character of some of the concrete societies mentioned by Becker as examples of his Sacred or Secular types. For instance, he diagnoses Nazi Germany as a concrete example of the Sacred type. Considering that Becker's main criterion for the Sacred and the Secular type is either "great reluctance to change" or "great readiness to change," it is surprising that Nazi Germany, with its violent and radical changes, is put into the Sacred class.

Becker's theory hardly represents an improvement on the —somewhat similar—theories of Saint Augustine, Vico, ibn-Khaldun, F. de Coulanges, Northrop, Schubart, or even my own. Its real contribution consists in its insights, sharp observations, and thoughtful analyses of several secondary problems.

NIKOLAI BERDYAEV (1874–1948): CULTUROLOGY

Berdyaev is the author of many works in philosophy, social science, political economy, and ethics, among them *The Meaning of Creativeness* (1916), *Philosophy of Inequality* (1922), *The Meaning of History* (1923), *The New Middle Ages* (1924), *Solitude and Society* (1930), and *Christianity and Class Struggle* (1931). Most of his books have been translated into several languages.

We shall omit the metaphysical part of Berdyaev's culturology and philosophy of history, but the following empirical points of his reading of historical events should be mentioned:

1. A mere description of singularistic historical events, persons, and objects only results in an historical corpse. "When one reads a scientific book on, say, ancient peoples, one clearly feels that from the history of cultures of these peoples their soul, their inner life are removed and one gets instead only a sort of external photograph or picture" that does not in the least explain the why, wherefore, or even the how of all these events and persons. In order to understand these whys and wherefores, the soul, and the inner logic of history, it is necessary "not only that the object matter of history be historical, but also that the cognizing subject of historical study experience and unfold in himself 'the historical.' " On this point Berdyaev, like Spengler and Northrop, insists on a direct intuitional identification of the cognizing subject with the cognized object, without which no adequate understanding of anything, especially of historical and sociocultural processes, is possible.[23]

---

[23] N. Berdyaev, *The Meaning of History* (U.S. ed,; New York, 1936), pp. 30–34. See also *Solitude and Society* (London, 1930), pp. 48 ff. See also, besides the cited works of H. Lefebvre, F. Dumont,

2. Like all the other authors under consideration, Berdyaev rejects all forms of the linear interpretation of historical process and all linear theories of progress. Theories of progress are not tenable either metaphysically, logically, factually, or ethically.

3. All great cultures are simultaneously mortal and immortal in their existence within the limits of empirical history itself. They contain temporal as well as eternal principles. Each culture emerges, flowers, has its ups and downs, and eventually declines as a unity; at the same time, each survives in its perennial, eternal values. Greco-Roman culture did not disappear entirely at the time of its fall. Its perennial values, such as Roman law, Greek art, Greek philosophy, and so on, did not die; they were incorporated into the culture of the Middle Ages and of Arabia and are still living a vigorous life. In other words, the temporal elements or values of a culture die; the perennial ones persist and live as long as human history goes on. Even after its empirical end the transfigured perennial values will, in some transcendental, mystical way, pass beyond the empirical end of history into the "transcendental great beyond."

Here Berdyaev points, in general terms, to what I call the lasting and dying elements in culture, with their indefinitely long and limited life-durations, a point that has so far been overlooked by social scientists and philosophers of history.[24]

4. Independently of—and possibly even earlier than—Spengler, Berdyaev regarded Western culture as already having passed its barbaric, medieval Christian, and modern humanist secular phases. Its medieval Christian phase was over in the thirteenth century, and its humanist phase ended in about the nineteenth century. To Berdyaev the twentieth century is the transitory period from the dying humanist phase to the emerging phase of the "new Middle Ages."

The main task of the medieval phase of Christian Western

H. Marrou, C. Lévy-Strauss, and L. Goldman, H. Heimpel, *Über Geshichte und Geshichtswissenschaft in unserer Zeit* (Göttingen, 1959); and F. Wagner, *Moderne Geshichtsschreibung* (Berlin, 1960).

[24] See my "Lasting and Dying Factors in the World's Culture," in F. S. C. Northrop (ed.), *Ideological Differences and World Order* (New Haven, 1949).

culture, according to Berdyaev, was to discipline, manifoldly develop, and spiritualize man, or to accumulate the "spiritual fission forces" in the developed personality and the Western culture. Monkhood and knighthood fulfilled this function by disciplining and spiritualizing man. The images of a monk and a knight are veritable types of a disciplined, integrated, and manifold personality, spiritually free, unafraid of anything external, with enormous concentration on the inward through tense "fission forces" centered around the Kingdom of God. This medieval phase had to end and did end, because it did not supply a sufficient channel for releasing the enormously concentrated forces for a free, creative transformation of the empirical reality. The Middle Ages end with the marvelous Christian mystical Renaissance of the thirteenth century that serves as a bridge to the subsequent humanist phase. Joachim of Floris, St. Francis of Assisi, Dante, Giotto, and St. Thomas Aquinas are the brilliant stars of this wonderful Renaissance, which is the summit and the end of the medieval phase.

Then follows the largely non-Christian, even increasingly anti-Christian, phase of Western culture's secular humanism. Humanism puts man in the center of the universe, makes him the measure of all things and the highest value. Its main function was to release and develop the free, creative forces of man: man's trial and test in freedom, unhampered by anything except man's own sense, reason, and self-control. It was, therefore, the period of man's liberation from all "superhuman" controls. These tasks were accomplished in the course of some six centuries. Humanist culture spent most of the funds accumulated in the previous periods and exhausted its creative power. As a result, in the nineteenth century, this humanist culture immanently produced the ever-increasing germs of its own destruction. The medieval Christian and the humanist modern phases both dialectically led to their own decay.

The medieval Christian culture, instead of becoming absorbed in the aspired City of God, ended—dialectically—by becoming enmeshed in the City of Man. The Christian Church itself grew into the most powerful empirical organization in entire medieval Europe. Humanist culture aspired to man's glory, power, and creativity. It finished instead by the utter demoralization of man, the disintegration of the manmade universe, and the exhaustion of man's creative forces: "Here the dialectics of history consist of the self-affirmation of man that has led to his self-extermination." The humanist period opens with man full of joy and self-confidence. It ends with him disillusioned in all his dreams and strivings. None of his great expectations was realized.

5. In discussing the reason why all great cultures eventually disintegrate as unities (surviving, however, in their perennial values), and why their creative power eventually declines, Berdyaev makes a highly suggestive generalization: "Culture is not a realization of a new *life*, of a new way of existence, but a realization of new *values*. All achievements of culture are symbolic rather than realistic."

In its creative period, culture creates not for the practical purpose of a utilitarian or hedonistic improvement of the empirical life, but for the sake of the values themselves. It creates truth for the sake of truth and cognition, beauty for the sake of beauty, goodness for the sake of goodness. In all this there is little of "real, practical life," of the passionate "will to live," of the intense desire to organize "life," to enjoy "life."

Having created the values, however, culture dialectically and immanently changes its direction and passes beyond culture into the Spenglerian "civilization." Created values cannot help entering real life and changing it; with the change the culture itself changes. It now tends toward a practical realization of its power, toward a practical organization of life. A period of cultural blossoming presupposes a severe limitation of the will to "live"; it demands an unselfish, somewhat ascetic transcendence over the passionate "gluttony for life." When such a gluttony for life develops in the masses, then this life, and not the cultural creativity, becomes the supreme end. Since they are always aristocratic, cultural creativity and culture cease to be the supreme self-values and become mere means for the "practical improvement of life," for "prosperity and happiness." With the degradation of culture and of pure creativity to the level of third-class means-values, the will for culture and disinterested creativeness weakens and eventually dies. Under these conditions culture cannot stay at its high level; it is bound to deteriorate. Its quality tends to be replaced by quantity. A sort of social entropy develops and culture turns into an uncreative "civilization."

This explains why the highest cultural blossoming of Germany at the end of the eighteenth and beginning of the nineteenth centuries—when within a period of a few decades the world saw Lessing, Herder, Goethe, Schiller, Kant, Fichte, Hegel, Schelling, Schleiermacher, Schopenhauer, Novalis, Mozart, Handel, Haydn, Beethoven, and dozens of other first-class "stars"—occurred in the period when the real life of Germany was poor, difficult, depressing, and bourgeois. Similarly, the real life of Italy's Renaissance period was miserable and unenviable. Even the practical life of the great creators themselves —be it Mozart or Beethoven, Leonardo or Michelangelo—was painful and tragic. "Culture has always been a great failure with respect to life." There is a kind of oppositeness between culture and life. When life becomes civilized, happy, and prosperous, then the creativity of culture declines and culture is replaced by "civilization." Such is the dialectic of the decline of creative culture into uncreative civilizations.

Although it is fairly general, this degradation of culture into civilization is not a creative culture's only destiny. Culture can take another way—the way of religious transfiguration of life, and through that the realization of genuine existence (being). Such was the course that the declining Greco-Roman culture followed. It resulted in the emergence and growth of Christianity. At its heroic and truly Christian period, Christianity led to the religious transfiguration of life and the creation of a great Christian medieval culture. Eventually, Christianity ceased to be solely religious and became largely verbal and ritualistic, with much economic and political machinery; as such it lost its transfiguring power. It is possible that the West's transitional culture will choose this religious way of transfiguring life in order to perpetuate its perennial values and bring humanity closer to a genuine creative life.

Russia may play an important role in this pilgrimage of culture; however, this role still remains problematic and uncertain. Berdyaev is much less complimentary toward Russia than are Schubart, Danilevsky, and Spengler: "The traditions of culture have always been weak in Russia," he says. "We have built a rather ugly civilization. Barbarian forces have always been strong with us. Even our will towards a religious transfiguration of life has been infected by a sort of sickly daydreaming." Under these conditions only Russia's potential religiosity, together with the most intense suffering and a consciousness of the epochal crisis, may help her to find the way of religious transfiguration of life instead of decaying into an uncreative civilization or barbarism.

CRITICISM

Since the metaphysical meaning of history in Berdyaev's philosophy and most doubtful points of his empirical culturology are intentionally omitted in this outline, the delineated features of his theory of culture and of its dynamics are essentially correct. They contain only minor errors that can be passed by without a special examination.

JOSÉ ORTEGA Y GASSET (1883–1955): THEORY OF HISTORY

Of other significant works dealing with the structure and dynamics of social and cultural systems, José Ortega y Gasset's *Man and People, History as a System*, and, especially, his *Man and Crisis* and the *Revolt of the Masses* need to be mentioned. Though the eminent Spanish philosopher did not develop an empirical theory of cultural and social systems, nevertheless he gave an outline of such a theory in his interpretation of the crisis of our age and of the basic historical processes.

In *What Is Philosophy?*, Ortega defines philosophy as "knowledge of the Universe, or everything there is [without knowing] what there is, [or] if what there is forms a Universe or a Multi-verse, [or] whether Universe or Multi-verse will be knowable."[25] He goes on to say:

[25] J. Ortega y Gasset, *What Is Philosophy?* (New York, 1961), pp. 90–91, and chs. 1–4.

On searching carefully for the basic data of the Universe I find that there is one primary and fundamental fact which carries its own assurance. This fact is the joint existence of a self, a subjectivity, and of its world. The one does not exist without the other. . . . Therefore the basic and undeniable fact is not my existence, but my coexistence with the world. . . . The primordial reality, the fact of all facts, that which is given to me is . . . "my life" . . . and my life is primarily a finding of myself in the world.[26]

On this axiom of the "radical reality" Ortega builds his system of philosophy as well as his theory of the "social," "social relations," "society," "culture," and their transformations and fluctuations. He makes a series of significant observations concerning scientific and philosophical methods of cognition—including the all-important role of intuition "as a mental state in which an object is present before us," sometimes sensorily, sometimes without touching our senses—and several other problems.[27] Since these do not directly concern us we can pass them by without further discussion.

Ortega's *Man and People* is an inquiry into the basic problems of sociology—of "what the social is, what society is." According to Ortega the reason for such an inquiry is the fact that sociology, which supposedly deals with these problems, "has nothing clear to say about what the social is, about what society is. . . ."[28] Such a criticism disposes the readers to expect a new, deep, and enlightening analysis of these and other sociological problems.[29] Regretfully this sort of expectation is not justified by the book.

Ortega merely repeats what is more precisely said in many competent sociology texts. *Man and People* contributes hardly

---

[26] *Ibid.*, pp. 200–212.

[27] *Ibid.*, pp. 50–59, 126–132.

[28] J. Ortega y Gasset, *Man and People* (New York, 1957), pp. 12–13; the book is interspersed with similar critical remarks about the ineptitude of sociologists to cope with their basic problems; see pp. 139, 140, 147, 176, 178–179, 229–230.

[29] Similar critical remarks about sociology have been made by several recent scholars like A. Toynbee, K. Popper, and V. Pareto, who themselves have become—explicitly or implicitly—sociologists. See J. B. Ford, "Toynbee versus Sociology," *Communicaciones al XX Congresa Internat. de Sociologia*, V (Cordoba, 1963), 157–184.

anything new to sociological theory of the "social" and "society"; as such, it can be dismissed without further analysis.[30]

Much more significant for our purposes is Ortega's *Man and Crisis*.[31] The book opens with a criticism of the traditional conception of history as a mere chronological recital of so-called historical facts and events. The author correctly challenges L. von Ranke's famous contention that, through a mere chronological description of these facts, historians can find out *"wie es eigentlich gewesen ist"*—"how things actually happened." Ortega y Gasset rightly indicates that history is not a mere collection of raw facts and data and that the "correct interpretation of facts" is necessary to adequately comprehend it:

> By themselves, facts [like hieroglyphics] do not give us reality; on the contrary, they hide it, which is to say that they present us with the problem of reality. If there were no facts, there would be no problem, no enigma, there would be nothing hidden which is necessary to de-hide, to dis-cover. . . . Facts cover up reality; while we are in the midst of their innumerable swarmings we are in chaos and confusion. In order to discover reality we must for a moment lay aside the facts that surge around us, and remain alone with our minds. Then, like all great scientists do, we must build a postulational hypothesis or "an imaginary reality, a pure invention of our own." After thinking through all the facts of this imaginary reality [that is, after deducing all the consequences of our postulational hypothesis], we must compare them with the facts which surround us. If they mate happily with one another, this means that we have deciphered the hieroglyph, that we have discovered the reality which the facts covered and kept secret. That labor is what science is.[32]

In accordance with this understanding of the science of history, the author gives to us his theory of historical crises, particularly his analysis of the "what, how and why" of the crisis of our age, and of the long-time fluctuations of the basic

---

[30] Even its "philosophical-psychological" hypothesis concerning the emergence in human individuals of consciousness does not differ much from similar theories of J. M. Baldwin, C. H. Cooley, J. Royce, E. Husserl, G. H. Mead, J. Piaget, M. Buber, and M. Scheler.

[31] J. Ortega y Gasset, *Man and Crisis* (New York, 1958).

[32] *Man and Crisis*, pp. 13–17.

types of culture and the ways of historical life. The gist of his ideas can be gleaned from the following quotations.

> There are many reasons for surmising that European man is lifting his tent from off that modern soil where he has camped these three hundred years and is beginning a new exodus toward another historic ambit, another manner of existence. This would mean that the ground of the modern age which begins beneath the feet of Galileo is coming to an end beneath our own. Our feet have already moved away from it. . . . [For this reason] it becomes very important for us first, to understand precisely just what is the system of life which we are abandoning; second, to know what it means to live in the midst of an historic crisis; third, to inquire how an historic crisis comes to an end and how we enter into a new age.[33]

The ultimate task "in which man is irremediably engaged and which defines his destiny is living," says Ortega. "All the other things that occur to us do so because one single thing is happening to us—the act of living." But in order to satisfy this "hunger to be," man needs first to find out what he is and to ask himself what are the things around him and what, there in the midst of them, is he:

> Every man's life starts with certain basic convictions about what the world is and what man's place in it is. . . . This "world" or "environment" or "reality" is not given to us (ready made), nor is it simply there; it is created by our convictions . . . by our interpretations of the chaotic mass of endless things and happenings in our life and in our surroundings.[34]

Whether or not man wants it, he has "to frame a general interpretation of his surroundings, a system of convictions about it in order that he can move about among things and act upon them."

Man's culture, he says, "is only the interpretation which man gives to his life":

> [It is] the series of more or less satisfactory solutions which he invents in order to handle his problems and the needs of his

[33] *Ibid.*, p. 10.
[34] *Ibid.*, pp. 20–24, 27, 73–74.

life. These include the material order of things as well as the so-called spiritual. When these solutions are created for genuine needs, they too are genuine solutions; they are concepts, evaluations, enthusiasms, styles of thought, of art, of law, which really emanate from the deep heart of man. . . . He who creates an idea does not have the impression that it is any thought of his; but rather he seems to see reality itself in immediate contact with himself. There, then, are man and reality, both naked, one confronting the other with neither screen nor intermediary between them.[35]

Though Ortega does not use the terms "cultural system" or "supersystem," he asserts that at some of the periods their "basic interpretations"—"concepts, evaluations, enthusiasms, styles of thought, of art, of law"—are unified into one dominant order that satisfactorily answers man's questions about what he is and the nature of the reality he lives and acts in. It meets man's genuine needs and guides his conduct and way of life. Such periods and cultures Ortega calls the "classic age" or "golden age" of culture: "In the classic age, in the golden age, man believes he knows on what he can depend in regard to his surrounding; he has a system of convictions which are genuine and strong. . . . The world in which the man of the golden age finds himself contains a minimum of unresolved problems."[36] In such periods man has, and lives on, *faith*—whether it be faith in science or in reason or in God.

Greece and Rome had such a "classic age" of their culture and social life; but, like any empirical cultural order, after it had exhausted its creative fund, it disintegrated, and the Greco-Roman world found itself in sharpest crisis from the second century B.C. to the fifth century A.D. During these centuries a new Christian order, based on faith in God, emerged, grew, and became dominant in the centuries from the fifth to the thirteenth. Then this Christian order began to disintegrate and, after the fourteenth and fifteenth centuries of transition and crisis, it was replaced by a new cultural order based on faith in science and humanist rationalism. In its turn, this secular, scientific, humanist

---

[35] *Ibid.*, p. 97.
[36] *Ibid.*, pp. 102 ff.

order, after delivering its creative achievements, began to disintegrate. Its disintegration ushered the Western world into the new great crisis that we face now.

In *The Revolt of the Masses,* Ortega noted that there was beginning to rise on the European horizon groups of men who do not want to have reason: "a new type of man and of life disposed to live on unreason." As in all similar crises, modern man finds himself in a state of utter confusion, amidst the debris of the preceding cultural order—now obsolescent and moribund —and without a new cultural order. This transitional crisis is responsible for a legion of the mental, moral, and social happenings of our time. A large part of Ortega's work is devoted to a penetrating analysis of the essential cultural, social, and personal characteristics of the crisis periods, fairly uniformly recurrent in the past as well as in the present crisis. In *The Revolt of the Masses,* he boldly sketches some of the conspicuous characteristics of the type of personality and of the collectivities ("masses") of our age of crisis:

> The characteristic of the hour is that the commonplace mind, knowing itself to be commonplace, has the assurance to proclaim the rights of the commonplace and to impose them wherever it will. . . . As they say in the United States: "to be different (in our age) is to be indecent." The mass crushes beneath it everything that is different, everything that is excellent, qualified, and select. . . . Here we have a formidable fact of our times.[37]

By his "commonplace" man, Ortega means not only the poor laborer, but the dominant man of our age. Produced immanently by the sociocultural milieu of past centuries, this mass-man neither knows of the efforts of the creative minority of those centuries to obtain his Bills of Rights and to enormously improve his economic and social conditions, nor does he feel any obligation to his own society or recognize any authority besides himself. He takes all the achievements of the nineteenth century for granted. He is self-satisfied. He does not know much about the past, about traditions, about continuities. In this sense

---

[37] Ortega, *The Revolt of the Masses* (New York, 1932), p. 18.

he is rootless. "Any remains of the traditional spirit have evaporated. Models, norms, standards are of no use to us. We have to solve our problems without any active collaboration of the past."[38] Hence, the uncertainty and confusion of our times.

Our masses, Ortega says, "are only concerned with their well-being and at the same time they . . . do not see, behind the benefits of civilization, marvels of invention and construction which can only be maintained by great efforts and foresight. They imagine that their role is limited to demanding these benefits peremptorily, as if they were natural rights."[39]

Confused, rootless, and self-assured, mass-man violently interferes—by direct action—in everything: "The type of man dominant today is a primitive one, a *Naturmensch* rising up in the midst of a civilized world. The world is a civilized one, its inhabitant is not." He wants his car, luxuries, pleasures, fun, and other benefits of civilization, but he believes that all these are natural gifts somehow coming by themselves from the Garden of Eden.

Mass-man is joined in our times by another type of sophisticated barbarian, the technician. The technician competently carries out his specialized work, but he is semi-ignorant of science, culture, and history:

> In politics, in art, in other sciences he adopts the attitudes of primitive, ignorant man; but he adopts them forcefully and with self-sufficiency. . . . By specializing him, civilization has made him hermetic and self-satisfied within his limitations; but this very inner feeling of dominance induces him to predominate outside of his specialty. Therefore he behaves in almost all spheres of life as does the unqualified, the mass-man.

These two types of the contemporary mass-man dominate politics and government. For this reason the greatest danger today is the state, for it has become the mechanism of violence and direct action. Today's power-elite forgets that Talleyrand said to Napoleon: "You can do everything with bayonets, Sire, except sit on them." Real ruling is the quiet exercise of func-

---

[38] *Ibid.*, pp. 19 ff., 36.
[39] *Ibid.*, pp. 60–68.

tions approved by public opinion, not an aggression of violence. Now, there is no public opinion; instead there is a multitude of discordant voices. The result is an extraordinary explosion of bloody violence—wars, revolutions, crimes—and the end of the European leadership in human history: "The European commandments have lost their force. . . . Europe is ceasing to rule, and no one sees who is going to take her place."[40]

Such is the skeleton of Ortega's theory of cultural orders and their dynamics and of today's crisis in Western society and culture.[41] Despite their somewhat impressionistic character, his books give a thoughtful interpretation of a chaotic mass of concrete historical facts and events. Ortega's macrosociology of cultures does not need any particular criticism from me because of an essential congeniality between many important points of his theory and my own. Independently from each other we seem to have come to a number of similar conclusions.

IDEALIZED OR "NORMATIVE" CONCEPTIONS OF CIVILIZATION AND CULTURE

● Evolution of the Meanings of the Terms "Civilization" and "Kultur"

Lucien Febvre and E. Tonnelat in their painstaking studies show that the terms "civilization" and "*Kultur*" appeared in the French, English, and German languages comparatively late: The word *civilization* was used for the first time in French texts in 1766, in English texts in 1773; the term *Kultur* emerged in German texts toward the end of the eighteenth century, probably in 1774 or 1793.[42] The earliest meanings of both terms were

---

[40] *Ibid.*, pp. 112–113, 135.

[41] A much more detailed analysis of Ortega's sociology and philosophy of history is given in R. Agramonte's *Estudios de Sociologia Contemporanea* (Mexico City, 1963), ch. 7.

[42] L. Febvre, "Civilisation, Evolution d'un mot et d'un group d'idées," and E. Tonnelat, "Kultur, Histoire d'un mot, evolution du sense," in L. Febvre, M. Mauss, E. Tonnelat, A. Niceforo, and L. Weber, *Civilisations: Le mot et l'idée* (Paris, 1930), pp. 1–73. See also

highly idealized. Civilization meant "a triumph and expansion of reason, not only in the constitutional and political domains but also in moral, religious, and intellectual fields," a refined and enlightened society in contrast to savagery and barbarism; the progress of science and arts and freedom and justice, and the elimination of war, slavery, and misery. "Civilization meant, first of all, an ideal, and in a large measure a moral ideal."[43]

Similar was the early meaning of *Kultur*. It signified "enlightenment," "mental and spiritual refinement," the vital, moral, and intellectual ennoblement of individuals and peoples, the refinement of manners and mores, the liberation of the human spirit, and the progress of arts and sciences.[44]

Both words were born in their destined hour. "Both rapidly expanded, grew, and had a most fortunate destiny."

Subsequently, these terms began to be used in a less idealized, more prosaic sense: They were coming to be used to mean the totality of acquired characteristics of an individual or group, and, by Rousseau, Fourier, and others, to mean a destructive force or the phase of degeneration, demoralization, and decay of a society and its culture.

Despite this, the initial, idealized conception of these terms has continued to run as a minor stream throughout the nineteenth and the twentieth centuries up to the present time. The theories of A. Schweitzer and F. R. Cowell can serve as recent variations of this "normative" idealized, moralized, and spiritualized interpretation of cultural phenomena.[45] A brief outline of these theories follows.

H. Levin, "Semantics of Culture," in *Daedalus*, Winter, 1965, pp. 1–13. The papers of G. Holton, J. Ackerman, E. Leach, H. Brooks, G. Kepes, H. Marcuse, E. Weil, and others discuss the "normative elements" of culture vs. the actual reality of cultural phenomena." The "normative" aspects of culture are also stressed in C. W. Mills, *The Sociological Imagination* (New York, 1959), and in D. Martindale, *Social Life and Cultural Change* (Princeton, N.J., 1962), chs. 17, 18.

43 Febvre, Mauss, Tonnelat, *et al.*, *Civilisation*.

44 *Ibid.*, pp. 62 ff.

45 Idealized and "normative" also is the concept of culture adopted by the Societé Européenne de Culture. See its *Statuts* (Venice, 1962), pp. 62–100; cf. also G. Jaeger and P. Selznick, "A Normative Theory of Culture," *ASR*, October, 1964, pp. 653–669.

ALBERT SCHWEITZER (1875–1965): THE DECAY AND RESTORATION OF CIVILIZATION

Only a few points in Schweitzer's interpretation of the decay and restoration of civilization or culture (in contrast to Spengler, he uses these terms synonymously) directly concern us.[46]

1. Schweitzer's idealized conception of civilization is preeminently ethical. "Civilization is twofold in its nature: it realizes itself in the supremacy of reason, first, over the forces of nature, and, secondly, over the dispositions of men. . . ." Moral control over men's dispositions is much more important than control over nature. Mastery over human disposition means ethical mastery in the sense of willing material and spiritual good to mankind, to every individual, even to every living organism. Reverence for life is the essence of this ethical mastery. Such an ethics of unconditional will to live and reverence for life is "the essence of civilization." Its progress is much more important than the material progress of humanity. In its integral sense, civilization means the sum total of all progress in all fields of man's creative activity, insofar as it leads to ethically perfecting the individual and the community.[47]

2. Understood in this sense, contemporary Western civilization is in a state of deep (though not hopeless) decay. The decline began around the middle of the nineteenth century and has progressed steadily from that time up to the present. In the present crisis it is not just the civilization of this or that people that must be given up as lost, but that of mankind, present and future, if no rebirth takes place within the present civilization.[48]

3. The main reason for this, as well as for previous decays of civilizations, is ethical: "If the ethical foundation is lacking, then civilization collapses, even when in other directions crea-

---

[46] A more detailed analysis of Schweitzer's theory is given in my *Modern Historical and Social Philosophies*, pp. 267–272.

[47] A. Schweitzer, *The Philosophy of Civilization* (New York, 1949), pp. 22–23, 38, 91.

[48] *Ibid.*, pp. xii–xv, 2–6, 39.

tive and intellectual forces of the strongest nature are at work." The indispensable conditions for the florescence of a civilization are an approximation to the ethics of a reverence for life, preached and practiced by the respective society, and a corresponding world-philosophy that rationalizes, develops, justifies, demands, and affirms such an ethics in the mentality, behavior, social institutions, and culture of social groups.

Each time in the past when such a world-view and ethics were operative, the society or period flourished. Each time these forces were weak, or were altogether absent, or the world-view was of a wrong kind, the civilization or culture passed through a crisis. Of the past world-philosophies, Taoism, Confucianism, Hinduism, Buddhism in the Orient, and some of the Greek and subsequently European philosophies, only partly met the demand of the ethical world-view; the Stoic philosophy, and especially the rationalist and empirical philosophies of the illuminati and the empirical rationalists of the eighteenth century, met the demand much better than did other world-views. As a result, the Greco-Roman or Western civilizations of these periods were in comparatively satisfactory shape. Around the middle of the nineteenth century this creative *élan* came to an abrupt end.

The reason for this and for the subsequent "suicide of civilization in progress" was the abandonment of the ethics of life-affirmation and modern "philosophy's renunciation of her duty." The philosophy of the eighteenth century put forward ethical ideals and tried to embody them in practice but in spite of its considerable success this philosophy could not meet acid criticism and succumbed because it too was vulnerable and inadequate. Attempts by Kant, Goethe, Schiller, Fichte, Hegel, and others to provide this tottering building with a new foundation were unsuccessful because their world-views were also vulnerable.

Several secondary factors, derived from the lack of an ethico-philosophical foundation, have furthered the decay of Western civilization. These are modern man's fettered economic position; his being overworked and incapable of self-collectedness; his increasing inability to concentrate on meditation; a decrease in creative thinking and an increase in superficial "mob-mindedness," patterned by various "manufacturers of public opinion" (newspapers, etc.); a lack of spiritual independence and humanity; the development of ethical nihilism and an unethical conception of civilization; the greater development of the material, rather than spiritual, part of our civilization; and a rapid advance in ethically indifferent knowledge and technology. All these are by-products of the main cause of the decline; but after their emergence they, in their turn, contributed to the suicidal drift of our civilization.

4. This drift, however, is not absolutely hopeless. It can be stopped and reversed, but this will require building up a new ethico-philosophical foundation for our civilization that can stand any criticism, is "full-proved," logically impeccable, and factually unassailable. Schweitzer's ethics and philosophy of life affirmation is such a foundation.

In surveying the history of ethics and philosophy, beginning with the Taoist, Confucianist, Hinduist, and Buddhist world-views and ethics, and ending with the modern European-American ones, he finds that all these ethics and world-views were inadequate to different degrees. They all suffered from a dualism between knowing and willing; between ethical aspirations and the physical world as it is. They all tried to root their ethical values and imperatives in the external world as it is presented by science. They all failed in this task because if we take the world as it is we cannot discover in it anything ethical, any evolution toward ethics, or any value precious for us. Any ascription of such values, ethics, and purposes to the world as it is is just an anthropomorphism based on nothing and rejected by science. The world as it is cannot serve as a basis or support for an ethics of life-affirmation or for any ethics whatsoever.

Instead of engaging in this hopeless enterprise, Schweitzer proceeds to build his ethics and world-views from the opposite end. He starts with the most self-evident *will to live* as the ultimate, unquestionable, unmediated, axiomatic experience of everyone living, more axiomatic even than the Cartesian *cogito ergo sum* ("I think, therefore I exist"). "The knowledge which I acquire from my will-to-live is richer than that which I win by observation of the world. . . ."

Our knowledge of the external world is knowledge from the outside, mediated, always incomplete and uncertain. "The knowledge derived from my will-to-live is direct, and takes me back to the mysterious movements of life as it is in itself."

Schweitzer's interpretation of reverence for life is "to be in the grasp of the infinite, inexplicable, forward-urging Will in which All Being is grounded. It rises above all knowledge of things." It leads to a union with the ultimate reality which is "the infinite Being in infinite manifestations." Thus, this voluntaristic theory starts with a self-evident, voluntaristic will-to-live; from this premise rationally develops the world-and-life-affirmation world-view; and ends in a nonrational mysticism, because "the rational, when it thinks itself out to a conclusion, passes necessarily over into the nonrational. World-and-life-affirmation and ethics are nonrational."

It is, therefore, comprehensible why Schweitzer views science and a "scientific philosophy" that studies the world from outside as superfluous for the ethics and philosophy of life-affirmation:

> Ethics and aesthetics are not sciences. . . . There is therefore no such thing as a scientific system of ethics; there can only be a thinking one. Ethics have nothing to expect from any theory of knowledge. All attempts to bring ethical and epistemological idealism (or materialism) into connection with one another must be recognized as useless for ethics. Ethics can let space and time go to the devil. (*The Philosophy of Civilization*, p. 289.)

On this point, Schweitzer agrees with Spengler, Schubart, Koneczny, Berdyaev, and to some extent Northrop, in stressing the primacy of the living, intuitive, unmediated, direct cognition of the all-pervading infinite Being in its infinite manifestations or "differentiations" versus the mediated, uncertain knowledge from outside, where, as in science, the cognizing subject and cognized object are outside one another. On the other hand, he disagrees with de Roberty, Northrop, and Kroeber, who consider scientific knowledge and the philosophy grounded in it as the indispensable foundation of civilization and its ethics.

5. Having cleared the way, Schweitzer, from his axiomatic will to live, deduces the detailed ethics of life-affirmation, life-

reverence, love, altruism, and the concrete "imperatives" for ethical conduct and social relationships. He uncompromisingly affirms the ethical protection of any life and any organism, up to the smallest and perhaps even injurious one, resembling the Buddhist ethics in this point.

6. Since "of all the forces that mould reality, morality is the first and foremost," Schweitzer's "prescription" for a creative rebirth of the civilization of the West and of mankind consists of elaborating, diffusing, and rooting the ethics and world-view of life-affirmation—first in individual mentality and conduct and then in social institutions and culture. The ethical transfiguration of mankind, individuals, and civilization itself is a condition without which no rebirth is possible. On this point, Schweitzer was the most eminent theoretical, and especially practical, advocate of ethical value as the paramount factor in humanity and civilization. He practiced what he preached.

CRITICISM

As to the shortcomings of Schweitzer's philosophy of civilization, the following deficiencies can be noted here. Schweitzer's contentions that each flourishing civilization has a minimum of ethical values vigorously functioning and that a decay of ethical values is part and parcel of the decay of civilization are correct. However, his theses that the ethical factor is the main foundation of every great civilization and the main factor of its decay are dogmatically asserted rather than adequately proved. In addition, Schweitzer seems to assume that the ethical compartment of a civilization lives and functions by itself, in isolation, depending little upon the civilization's science, religion and philosophy, fine arts, law, economics, and politics. Such a supposition is somewhat fallacious for at least most of the civilizations. Many a scholarly work, including my own *Dynamics*, has shown rather conclusively that the ethical values of a given culture or cultural supersystem are closely connected with other cultural systems of a certain society. Thus, in a predominantly Ideational culture, the dominant ethics and law are Ideational also; in a predominantly Sensate society, the dominant ethics and law are Sensate. Further, a society's ethical values change along with its other values and in the same direction. Thus, the ethical decay of the contemporary West is but a part of a decline of the whole Sensate supersystem of the West and can be understood only in this context.

The same is to be said of the "world-view" or the *Weltanschauung*. It also does not arise by itself as a *deus ex machina* and does not become dominant in a given society by its own force only, but is tangibly conditioned by the character of the prevailing culture and its dominant supersystem. In a predominantly Ideational society only Ideational world-views can become dominant (mysticism, idealism, religious rationalism, fideism, eternalism, unconditional ethics of love, the sacral law, etc.); in a predominantly Sensate society only Sensate philosophies can become dominant (materialism, scepticism, empiricism, positivism, temporalism, manmade relativistic, utilitarian, and hedonistic ethics and laws, etc.) When an Ideational supersystem is being replaced by a Sensate, Ideational world-views tend to decline while Sensate philosophies increase at their expense. And vice versa. Schweitzer somehow fails to see this connection between ethics, together with world-views, and the dominant character of a given culture; therefore, he contributes little to our understanding of what civilizations really are and why and how they rise, live, and decay. Out of these complex problems he selects only one of many subsystems, or factors or values—the ethical—and asserts that it plays an important role in all these complex processes—a correct assertion made many times before.

Another serious shortcoming of Schweitzer is his history of the ethical philosophies (world-views). However thoughtful, his interpretations would be questioned as to accuracy by many scholars. Thus his interpretation of the Taoist, Hinduist, Buddhist, and other mystic philosophies of the ultimate reality—of Northrop's "undifferentiated continuum"—as a pure negativity or a pure emptiness would be vigorously criticized as inaccurate by most Taoist, Hinduist, and Buddhist thinkers.

I find peculiar Schweitzer's particularly high estimate of the *Stoic Weltanschauungen* and the philosophical, ethical, political, economic, and social theories of the seventeenth and especially the eighteenth centuries—those of Locke, Helvetius,

Hume, Bentham, Smith, Condorcet, Herder, Lessing, and others. Schweitzer views these theories and philosophies as especially conducive to the ethical reverence for life, and through that to an invigoration and growth of civilization. He seems to be quite unaware of the fact that most of these theories were Sensate and as such gave rise to, among other things, the relativistic, manmade, utilitarian, and hedonistic ethics that were bound to become increasingly relativistic and hedonistic until, in the course of two hundred years or so, all these values have been ground into dust and have lost most of their binding power and even moral prestige. Ethical values and norms have become "mere ideological smoke screens," "opiates of the people's mind," Freudian "rationalizations," Marxian "ideologies," and Paretian "derivations" supposedly used by a clever minority to fool and exploit a stupid majority, and serving as a beautifying screen for the ugly vested interests of the powers that be.

In other words, Schweitzer extols exactly those Sensate philosophies which, if they did not initiate (because European Sensate ethics and philosophies had already emerged in the fourteenth century), at least gave a great impetus to, an ethical and civilizational decay that became catastrophic, according to Schweitzer, at the middle of the nineteenth century.

The next important point is Schweitzer's position in regard to the role of science in the ethical regeneration of civilization. In contrast to Northrop, who seemingly overvalues this role in regard to philosophy and ethics, religion, and the fine arts, Schweitzer rather greatly underestimates it.

His position is very vulnerable. Here again we meet Schweitzer's separation of ethical values and principles from others—in this case, scientific ones. Ethical goodness (reverence for life) is made independent from, and unrelated to truth and beauty. On metaphysical as well as empirical bases such a separation is untenable. Metaphysically, truth (science, religion, philosophy), beauty (the fine arts), and goodness (ethics) are three main value-aspects of one undivided *summum bonum*. Empirically, each "energy" of this trinity can be transformed into other two energies: Truth is transformable into beauty and goodness, goodness into truth and beauty, and beauty into truth and goodness. Real truth is beautiful and good; real beauty is true and good; and real goodness is true and beautiful. On these grounds Schweitzer's position is untenable.

His position is also untenable pragmatically. We can agree with Schweitzer that the ethical axiom or basic principle is a sort of postulate, independent of science. One can indeed postulate, as Schweitzer does, the supreme principle of unconditional reverence for life, or other ethical principles, up to the postulate "Hate is the supreme ethical value," and build upon it the ethics of hate exemplified by the ethics of Shakespeare's *Timon of Athens*. When, however, the postulated ethics are to be built and to become effective in human conduct and social institutions and culture, science enters as the most efficient, necessary, and best expert counselor on the ways and means of grounding ethics in empirical social reality and a realization of it in the ideological, behavioral, and material culture and population. Without scientific help in these tasks the ethics chosen and postulated have hardly any means being realized. (See on this point H. Margenau, *Ethics and Science* [New York, 1964].) In medicine, the preservation of health and life are also postulated as the main value. But after this postulation has been made, science is the indispensable and best agent for the maintenance and improvement of health and the preservation of life, and it teaches what are the best ways and means for realizing these goals. Even in aesthetics, the relationship between beauty and science is similar.

These considerations show why Schweitzer's position here is untenable and why, among other things, I myself found it necessary to mobilize scientific forces and establish the Harvard Research Center in Creative Altruism for the accomplishment of an ethical task identical to Schweitzer's. If we knew more about how to make human beings and groups, social institutions and culture less egocentric, less selfish, more altruistic, and more creative, the realization of this ethical ideal would be helped along enormously, and future wars and catastrophes would be eliminated. Without the scientific knowledge provided by this know-how, the ethical ideals are doomed to remain unrealized or will be realized at an enormous cost in blood and suffering.

Schweitzer's position here explains why he has given us hardly any promising and effective prescription for how to root his "reverence for life" in the sociocultural soil and make it an actual practice in human behavior and interrelationships. The few statements that Schweitzer makes on this point are platitudinous rather than helpful.

Such are the main shortcomings of the work of this eminent moral leader. This criticism in no way denies the great services he has rendered humanity by his teaching and especially by his practice. By stressing the importance of the ethical element in civilization he put his finger on the most urgent need of humanity at the present time. But these and other virtues of Schweitzer and his work do not override the shortcomings that have been pointed out. (See P. Sorokin, *The Ways and Power of Love.*)

F. R. COWELL (1897–   ): THEORY OF GENUINE CULTURE

Among the theories of culture that distinguish between cultural congeries and systems and that view the realm of cultural phenomena as different from that of physical and biological realities, F. R. Cowell's theory deserves to be mentioned. It is given mainly in his *Culture in Private and Public Life*.[49] His distinction between cultural systems and congeries is clearly expressed in this book. Despite an enormous collection of factual fragmentary data about the cultures of different peoples, such a collection, he says, is insufficient for a real knowledge of the structural and dynamic essentials of cultural realities:

> The need becomes great for some all-inclusive scheme whereby the myriad findings of the explorers and cultural anthropologists can be analyzed and classified, some fertile generalization or generative *idée mère*, in de Tocqueville's phrase, capable of

[49] (London and New York, 1959). See also Cowell's *History, Civilization and Culture: An Introduction to the Historical and Social Philosophy of P. A. Sorokin* (Boston, 1952). Besides these works, Cowell has published *Cicero and the Roman Republic, Everyday Life in Ancient Rome*, and other works on Roman history.

introducing some order and system into what would otherwise remain mere anecdotes or travellers' tales. . . . Not merely does the idea of a culture as a system of meanings and values provide tourism (and anthropological factfinding) with a . . . rational justification, but it furnishes also the framework of ideas about truth, beauty and moral worth which are the foundation of any serious coordinated study of comparative culture both in space and in time.[50]

After a careful analysis and criticism of the main conceptions of culture, Cowell defines culture as "that which, being transmitted orally by tradition and objectively through writing and other means of expression, enhances the quality of life with meaning and value by making possible the formulation, progressive realization, appreciation and the achievement of truth, beauty and moral worth." Culture includes the "stream of traditional beliefs, habits and practices by which the lives of the great majority of mankind are mostly directed and by which the continuity of social life is assured." It also includes the new meanings, values, and practices introduced by the creative few:[51] "There are different levels of culture and . . . there are wide differences in human attainments and by no means everybody succeeds in reaching the higher levels as they would need to do if they are to live 'at the height of their times.' "[52] Understood in this sense cultural forces are the main determinants of human sociocultural life:

> Cultural determination [of this life] therefore is no empty formula but a short-hand expression for the immense force of the traditional stream of cultural values and practical human energies of the creative few. This interpretation of history is the belief that the ideas upon truth, beauty and moral worth guiding the dominant sector of society are significant operative factors giving character to the different eras of mankind.
> The theory of cultural determination has the merit of providing a more realistic picture of the great variety of forces and influences at work in any community at any one time than [do] the relatively static, monolithic unitary views of

[50] Cowell, *Culture in Private and Public Life*, pp. 37–38.
[51] *Ibid.*, pp. 105, 221.
[52] *Ibid.*, p. 105.

political theory . . . of the "political man" who has sometimes been supposed to correspond to the equally fictitious "economic man" of economic theory. The cultural approach, on the contrary, brings out the rich complexity of the real world.[53]

These leading ideas are well developed and documented in Cowell's work, side by side with his pointed criticism of many other theories of culture and of the factors of sociocultural change. In essentials most of his conclusions are in agreement with my own. For this reason, there is no need, on my part, to criticize the basic points of his theory.

SOCIOLOGY OF AESTHETIC SYSTEMS[54]

One of the earliest and most stimulating currents in the recent upsurge of intelligible readings of historical events appeared in works dealing with art phenomena. A number of thoughtful investigators of these phenomena discovered several uniformities in the change, development, and cycles of art systems, and of sociocultural processes in general. A considerable fraction of these generalizations "scooped" many formulations made later by various sociologists and philosophers of history.

We shall begin our analysis with those that attempt to explain uniform sequences in the development and florescence of art phenomena and—through those—uniform sequences in the change of sociocultural phenomena generally.

Of several works that deal with these questions, two representative volumes are *The Revolutions of Civilization* by Sir Flinders Petrie[55] (whose contentions were reiterated in his article "History in Art")[56] and Paul Ligeti's *Der Weg aus dem Chaos*.[57]

---

[53] *Ibid.*, p. 144.

[54] For a more detailed treatment of these theories, see my *Modern Historical and Social Philosophies*, ch. II; and the *Dynamics*, Vol. I, chs. 5–13.

[55] (London, 1912).

[56] *Antiquity*, September, 1931. See also O. G. S. Crawford, "Historical Cycles," *Antiquity*, March, 1931, pp. 5–21.

[57] (Munich, 1931).

According to Petrie not all forms of art in a given culture, or in its great period, blossom simultaneously. Some branches of art always reach the stage of liberation from the archaic and advance into free and finer forms earlier than others. Generally, a uniform and regular sequence is established. The turning point appears first in architecture and sculpture; "next comes Painting, then Literature, Music, Mechanics, Theoretic Science, and lastly Wealth. When there is no survival of useful abilities, then the race is doomed, and only lives on its prestige and savings, until its wealth attracts a more vigorous people. Mene, Tekel, Up-harsin may be seen written on every full-blown civilization." (Petrie, "History in Art," pp. 288–289.)

Having studied from this standpoint the eight periods of Egyptian culture and several periods of the Greco-Roman and European civilizations, he finds that this order has been uniformly recurrent. For instance, for the European period corresponding to the eighth in his classification, he gives the following dates for the turning of the various branches of art and other kinds of creative activity from "archaic" forms to "freedom":

European sculpture	in	A.D.	1240
European painting	in		1400
European literature	in		1600
European music	in		1790
European mechanics	in		1890
European science	after		1910
European wealth	after		1910

Thus, in this great cultural period, if we take advanced sculpture (and architecture) as the standard of comparison, the turning point from archaism to freedom, which is near the culmination point, lagged in painting by about 160 years, in literature by about 360 years, in music by 550 years, and in science and wealth by some 650 years.

A similar uniformity of sequence is shown, according to Petrie, in the development of all civilizations. The sequence is always the same. The lag may vary, however, tending to become longer as time advances.

The theory of the eminent Egyptologist, though stimulating and suggestive, when tested is found to be doubtful.[58] Petrie, like many others, ascribes to social and historical processes a uniformity they do not have.

In contradistinction to Petrie, Ligeti does not think that sculpture and architecture go closely together in all ages, but that in all cultures architecture always blossoms before sculpture. The essence of Ligeti's theory of the art sequence is as follows: In any great culture, architecture is the first and earliest form of art to flower; then, when the culture reaches the point of maturity, sculpture flowers; finally, as the culture begins to decline, painting reaches a high level of art. This order is invariable and uniform in the development of all great cultures. In European culture the Middle Ages are marked by the greatest development of architecture, sculpture and painting remaining primitive. The Renaissance is the period that sees the triumph of sculpture as the synthesis of architecture and painting. Finally, in the present modern age nothing remarkable has been achieved in sculpture or architecture, but in painting an incomparable level has been reached. Similarly, the first centuries of Greek art produced architectural triumphs; the sculptural or plastic age, represented by the statues of Harmodius and Aristogiton (c. 510 B.C.), culminates in the art of the Age of Pericles and ends in about 390 B.C. with the work of Myron, Phydias, Polycleitus, and others. After 390 B.C. came the age of painting, the *malerisch* age. Likewise in Egypt the art of the Old Kingdom was architectonic, and its greatest achievement was in architecture; the art of the Middle Kingdom was plastic; the New Kingdom was marked predominantly by great achievement in the field of painting. We find the same sequence in the history of China, Japan, and other countries. Ligeti points out that "Behind the rhythm of these arts there is a law, or uniformity which operates everywhere that human culture is given. . . . Each culture begins with the architectonic period and ends with the period of painting." (*Der Weg aus dem Chaos*, p. 34.)

---

[58] See the criticism in the *Dynamics* and in *Modern Historical and Social Philosophies*.

Side by side with these long waves, on which Ligeti's "law of the three states" in the development of art and culture is based, are waves of a still longer duration, as well as other, shorter waves. Thus, with regard to the longer waves, not only does every culture pass through these three states enumerated by Ligeti, but all cultures, considered together, show the same uniformity in their time sequence. The great ancient cultures, like the Egyptian, are predominately architectural; later cultures, like those of Greece and Rome, are predominantly plastic; modern cultures, like the European, are predominantly *malerisch*. Such is the long rhythm of the development of human art generally and human culture as a whole.

As to the shorter waves, there are periods about 130 years long, in which the same architecture-sculpture-painting sequence occurs.

It goes without saying that such a construction involves a value judgment of the highest achievement in each of these arts, and, as is the case with all such evaluations, an element of subjectivity must enter. For one investigator, the highest achievement in a given art may be of one kind; for another, a different kind. The periods of highest accomplishment would be correspondingly different for each investigator. When we consider Ligeti's statements in the light of the timing indicated by other authorities, Ligeti's "uniform law" does not appear to be uniform for all cultures, and thus ceases to be a general law.

The theories of Ligeti, as well as several others of this type, are possibly influenced by the theory of Hegel's *Aesthetik*.[59] In any case, there are several resemblances between Hegelian theories and the theories of these men. The essentials of Hegel's theory relevant to this problem are as follows: In conformity with the chief principle of his philosophy, Hegel views the evolution of art as the process of self-realization in the course of time, or of an unfolding of the Idea or Spirit. In this process of unfolding there are three stages (*Hauptstufen*), each with its characteristic type of art: the symbolic, the classical, and the romantic.

[59] G. W. F. Hegel, *The Philosophy of Fine Arts* (3 vols.; London, 1921)

In the symbolic state and type of art, the Idea is inadequately expressed and is dominated by external form; in the classic stage there is unity of content and form in art; in the romantic stage the balance is again disrupted, because here the Idea, being infinite, strives to be free from the finite forms of external sensate expression, and therefore soars in all its infiniteness, demoting the external form to a place of secondary importance.

The most adequate objectivization of the symbolic stage and type is architecture; of the classical type and stage, sculpture; of the romantic, painting and, especially, music and poetry. This is not all. Each of the arts, in the process of its evolution, passes through these three stages; for instance, architecture evolves through symbolic, classical, and romantic periods. The same is true of sculpture, painting, music, and poetry.

From this outline one can see the points of similarity between Hegel's concept and Ligeti's.

Since the sequential uniformity postulated by Ligeti and others is not a universal law at all, the bottom drops out of their sociological generalizations, and the validity of these now becomes highly questionable. Let us look more closely at Ligeti's sociological correlations. If they are not always accurate, they are for the most part suggestive and ingenious. The chief generalizations may be summed up briefly as follows:

1. Any culture (or great period in a culture or even the whole history of mankind) passes through three main stages: architectural, plastic, and *malerisch*.

2. At each of these stages the culture is characterized by several important traits, common to all cultures at the same stage of development. (See the table on culture characteristics.)

These culture characteristics represent the chief sociological correlations between the predominant art and other aspects of a culture. If we ask why these correlations occur, Ligeti's answer is interesting. Like almost all investigators of art, he rightly says that art is one of the best barometers of culture. What are the reasons for this association? They become comprehensible if we study the culture in which a given painting, piece of sculpture, or specimen of architecture was produced. We must consider to whom these objects were addressed and for

Culture Characteristics

Architectural	*Plastic*	*Malerisch*
1. The beginning of an upswing of culture. It is virile and stern. It is marked by a collective state of mind and discipline.	Intermediate between the characteristics of the architectural and *malerisch* stages; their harmonious synthesis.	1. Decline of the culture or a great cultural period. It is stamped by femininity, sensate mentality, and individualism.
2. It is a culture of volition and strong determination to achieve an ideal.	*"*	2. It is a culture of enjoyment of what has already been achieved before, a culture of waste and sensual indulgence.
3. It is stamped by strong ethical idealism and morality (antisensate, antihedonistic, and antiutilitarian).	*"*	3. Such terms as materialistic, sceptical, critical, "scientific," erotic, Epicurean, and utilitarian characterize such a culture.
4. It is dominated by religion, by belief, faith, and religious dogmatism. Its leaders are great religious and moral teachers.	*"*	4. There is a predominance of reason over belief. Intellectualism and the "scientific" attitude come to the fore.
5. Order and stability predominate over dynamic progress and change.	*"*	5. Freedom and progress predominate instead of order. There is variety, revolution, disorder, and mobility.
6. Its aristocracy is theocratic and noble,	*"*	6. Bureaucrats, moneymakers, imperialists,

Culture Characteristics—Continued

Architectural	Plastic	Malerisch
because of its religious, moral, and social achievements but not because of wealth.		and "liberal" thinkers are the leaders.
7. There is a predominance of agriculture and handicraft.	`"`	7. There is a predominance of commerce, manufacture, "business," and machinery.
8. There is a mobilization and integration of mentality and an awakening of the spiritual *Geist*.	`"`	8. There is a disintegration of mentality and decline of spiritual *Geist*.

whom they were created, and we must inquire into the very essence of architecture, sculpture, and painting. A painting is usually the work of one man and of one lifetime. A great building is always the work of many men, of a collectivity, and sometimes of several generations as, for example, most of the cathedrals of the Middle Ages. He who is an individualist and wants to create alone is attracted by painting; those who want to create great things together, in a cooperative association, turn to architecture. "A picture is the message of one man, a building is that of many." Hence the connection of the *malerisch* stage with individualism and freedom, and the architectural stage with cordial, familistic collectivism, and collective discipline.

Further, a painter addresses only a few people through his painting, and sometimes he paints for only one person. Pictures are always secluded in a building, and are accessible only to a few. Architecture addresses itself to the masses, because any great architectural creation, whether it be cathedral, pyramid, castle, palace, public hall, or government seat, is seen and can be seen by many, by unlimited masses of people. Architecture is unwieldy, heavy, immobile, but always real. Its material is hard and rough: earth, stone, steel, and the like. It is little suited to express lightness, movement, change, or anything merely showy. It is an expression of will, determination, and effort. There is nothing deceitful about it. It is the reality of the three dimensions, and it creates that reality itself. It is by nature somewhat ascetic and idealistic. It is the *Sein,* Existence, Being (in contradistinction to Becoming). Painting, on the contrary, is Show, Illusion, Deceit, mere Appearance. Its essence is the representation of three-dimensional reality upon a two-dimensional surface, through light and shadow. It is *Schein,* not *Sein.* In this sense it is not real. Architecture must be orderly, disciplined, systematic, and free from mere fancifulness or whim, because otherwise it cannot produce anything lasting. It is Order, System, Effort, Law, and Discipline. Painting can be and is fanciful, individualistic, impressionistic, irregular, anarchistic, free, and liberating, because it deals with the world of shadows, and passing and momentary impressions. It is Fancifulness, Freedom, Life, and Impression.

When these properties of architecture and painting are considered, it becomes at once comprehensible why a culture at the architectural stage has the characteristics of order and stability, and at its *Malerisch* stage is stamped by individualism, freedom, intellectualism, impressionism, light-mindedness, momentary Epicureanism, a *carpe diem* attitude, irreligiosity, revolution, disorder, and other such traits. It is stamped by these not because of painting, but because painting is the form of art best suited to such a cultural *Gestalt.* It is structurally, logically, and causally a part, a symptom, and a quality of such cultural status.

Such is the explanation for the association of the predominant form of art with other important aspects of a culture. Though many of these ideas are not new, the pages of Ligeti's work dealing with this aspect of his theory are suggestive and even profound. Even though one rejects his main theory that a uniform sequence exists in the development of art and, consequently, his main sociological conclusions about the future of our culture or other cultures, one must nevertheless agree that his discussion contains a great deal that is valid—if not universally, then at least for some cultures and some periods. Ligeti has shown beyond the possibility of doubt that there does exist a close connection between the dominant form of a culture and the dominant forms of its art.

Another group of studies of art phenomena tries to establish to what extent the development of art generally and of a specific art particularly is uniform in various cultures, and to what extent art serves as a barometer of a society and culture.

Waldemar Deonna, in the three large volumes of his *L'archéologie, sa valeur, ses méthodes,* takes four great art systems in sculpture and, in part, painting—the paleolithic, the neolithic, the Greco-Roman, and the Christian—and tries to show that each of these systems has passed through similar fundamental periods of archaism, classicism, and finally decadence.[60] In each of these phases the traits and style of all four systems of art are strikingly homogeneous. The similarity is so great that statues of early medieval Europe (before the twelfth century) can easily be mistaken for those of archaic Greece (before the sixth century B.C.), and vice versa. In comparing the geometric statues of the archaic paleolithic with those of the archaic neolithic period, and with archaic Greek, archaic medieval, and so on, one cannot fail to see a striking similarity between them, even though they be separated from one another by centuries, even by thousands of years.

Deonna shows that each of these four systems of art starts, mainly because of inexperience and a lack of skill in the artists, with the archaic form. Then each progresses, becomes perfected, and reaches its climax, or classical period, after which each begins to decline. Deonna, not content merely with vague generalizations, presents a vast amount of factual material to substantiate and verify his theory.

Another theory of the same type is given by Frank Chambers who also tries to prove that the curve of art evolution and its essential stages are very similar in ancient Greece and Europe.[61] Both arts have passed through two similar stages. The first stage is characterized by a nonaesthetic estimation of

[60] (Paris, 1912).
[61] F. Chambers, *Cycles of Taste* (Cambridge, 1928); *The History of Taste* (New York, 1932).

beauty and the fine arts. In this stage all great art creations are produced, not for art's or beauty's sake, but for the sake of religion, morals, patriotism, civic virtue, and other nonaesthetic ends. The fine arts as such, and beauty as beauty, are viewed negatively and resisted. However, this does not hinder the creation of the greatest art values. Such was the case in Greece up to the fourth century B.C., and in Europe up to the Renaissance and the fall of classicism—i.e., the Academies. In the second stage there appears an appreciation of the fine arts for art's sake, and beauty for beauty's sake. At this stage the arts become free from their duties as the handmaid of religion or of other nonaesthetic values. "Aestheticism," art collecting, the connoisseur, art education, art criticism, and so on, now make their appearance. In spite of this, the art of the second stage hardly achieves the summits that were reached during the first stage, and it is soon destined to disintegration and decline:

> Both ancient and modern, both the Pagan and Christian eras, seem to have had a parallel aesthetic history. In both eras two esthetic states of mind have existed successively. It was the first state which caused the Parthenon to be built; it is the second state which now ponders its ruins, argues about its reconstruction, and sees passionate and romantic visions. The like of Homer, the Lyric poets, Herodotus, Thucydides, belong to the first state; the like of Strabo, Plutarch, Lucian, Athenaeus, Plotinus, to the second; Aristotle and, to a less extent, Plato are the links between the two. (*Cycles of Taste*, pp. 119–120.)

In his later work, where he analyzes the development of European art, Chambers repeats the same conclusions in a somewhat modified form. At this hour we live in a world not unlike that of Lucian, Philostratus, Athenaeus, and Plotinus, and in a few generations our civilization and its art will have run its appointed course.

While the theories of Deonna and Chambers deal mainly with the fields of sculpture and painting, other theories, making similar contentions concerning the uniformity of the main phases of art in various cultures, try to establish their claim with regard to literature and music. The theories of Bovet, Lalo, Verworn, Coellen, Riegl, Panofsky, Cohn-Wiener,

Schmarsow, Dvorak, Worringer, Wölfflin, and myself give us many generalizations in all fields of fine arts.[62] Almost all these authors view the likenesses in different art systems as the result not so much, if at all, of diffusion and imitation, as of independent invention free from imitation and copying. It is due partly to the similarity of human nature, partly to identical technical conditions (for instance, a lack of skill in archaic periods), partly to similar cultural configurations, and partly to the inner immanent logic of each art-system, the organization of which tends to create its own inner milieu in which, being isolated from the rest of the world, it lives its own life according to its own nature.

Some of the uniformities claimed by these theories are quite doubtful; some others, like Merton's "middle-range generalizations," appear to be correct if they are not overstated and overgeneralized. To a considerable degree they make intelligible an otherwise incomprehensible jungle of chaotic historical events. Without these generalizations, we are entirely lost in the jungle, and its endless facts make little sense in their how and why. With a few main rules to guide us, we can orient ourselves in the unmapped darkness of the jungle. Such is the cognitive role of these limited, approximate, prevalent rules and uniformities.

Such also is the cognitive value of the four main types of art phenomena and their fluctuations discussed in my *Dynamics*. The theory presented there is not irreconcilable with other theories mentioned above.

There is no need to outline here my rather extensive study of the painting, sculpture, architecture, music, literature, and drama of the Greco-Roman and Western cultures, or my much more cursory study of paleolithic, neolithic, primitive, Chinese, Hindu, and ancient Egyptian art forms.[63] But some of the most general conclusions may be briefly mentioned.

First, from the standpoint of art's inner content, external style, and objective or functions, all art phenomena easily fall

[62] See the *Dynamics*, Vols. I and II, and *Modern Historical and Social Philosophies*, ch. 2.
[63] See the *Dynamics*, Vol. I, pp. 195–730.

into four main types: *Sensate* art chooses sensory topics (house-wife, plant, animal, fight, kiss, etc.); its style is naturalistic or realistic, and the main purpose is to give sensory enjoyment and pleasure. *Ideational* art chooses supersensory and super-rational topics (the Kingdom of God, angels, devils, and the mysteries of salvation and redemption); its style is necessarily symbolic—"a visible sign of the invisible world"—because supersensory phenomena do not have any sensory forms, and its objective is to bring the human soul closer to God or to itself or to Tao, Nirvana, Brahma, etc. *Idealistic* art has for its topics partly the supersensory, partly the noblest sensory phenomena; the style is partly idealized naturalism, partly symbolic and allegoric, and the objective is an ennoblement and beautification of the sensory world and man and the bringing of man's soul closer to God, Tao, Nirvana, etc. *Unintegrated eclectic* art shows no unity of topic, style, and objective. It is an incoherent potpourri or hash of all sorts of topics, styles, and objectives.

Second, though all four forms of art are found in virtually all cultures and at all periods of the same culture, one of these different art supersystems is often dominant in a given culture at a given period and the dominant forms are often different in different civilizations. Thus Hindu, ancient Egyptian, or Taoist-Chinese art has been preponderantly ideational; the known Creto-Minoan and Creto-Mycenaean art was predominantly sensate. The dominant art of some preliterate tribes and paleo-lithic art is sensate; neolithic art is mainly ideational or idealis-tic. Finally, the art of many groups and cultures has been predominantly eclectic and incoherent.

Third, in practically all great cultures the dominance shifts from one art form to another in the course of time. For instance, the dominant art of Greece between the ninth and the sixth centuries B.C. was ideational, but in the fifth and fourth centuries B.C. became idealistic; from the fourth century B.C. to the fourth century A.D. Greco-Roman art was predominantly sensate; from the fifth to the twelfth centuries A.D., the ideational form dominated Western art; in the thirteenth and fourteenth centuries idealistic art was dominant in Europe; from the fifteenth to the twentieth centuries, Western art has been mainly sensate. At the present time, this sensate art is disintegrating and Western art is in a transitional, eclectic, incoherent state, manifested in pointillism, cubism, futurism, dadaism, surrealism, pop art, and, most recently, op art.[64] Though not so sharp, somewhat similar dominant waves can be observed in the art of India, ancient Egypt, China, and several other countries.

Fourth, each form of art expresses a certain mentality or "soul" and is inseparably connected in each instance with a specific type of personality and culture. Cultures as well as types of personalities display the same four forms: sensate, ideational, idealistic (or integral), and eclectic. Sensate art occurs in a predominantly sensate culture and in a society made up of mainly sensate personalities; ideational art occurs in a predominantly ideational culture and society; and so on. When a culture or civilization passes from one dominant type to another its art undergoes a similar change. When the medieval European culture, dominated by an ideational supersystem, passed after the fourteenth century into a predominantly sensate form, what had been predominantly ideational in medieval art became predominantly sensate. In other words, a given type of dominant art does not exist and change by itself, independent of the culture and the type of human personality that predominates in the society in which it appears and functions. Art is flesh of the flesh of the society, culture, and prevalent type of personality that has produced it. Each type of art emerges, grows, changes, and declines with the emergence, growth, change, and decline of the given type of culture, society, and personality.

Fifth, at the present time, the sensate culture, society, and personality that have been dominant for the last five centuries in the West are disintegrating; crumbling also is the sensate Western art that has been dominant for these five centuries.

Sixth, when studied in detail these patterns of the fluctua-

---

[64] A reflection of these changes in the style of reproduction of masculine and feminine types in sculpture and painting is studied in E. Werner Klimowsky, *Geschlecht und Geschichte: Sexuallität in ihrer Beziehung zu Kultur und Kunst* (Vienna, 1956).

tions of art do not fundamentally disagree with what some of the forementioned theorists have had to say about types of art and their cycles or rhythms.

Such in brief are the most general conclusions concerning art phenomena reached in the course of an investigation of the main types of culture and of their dynamics. The foregoing outlines the main types of sociologies of art phenomena and their dynamics. It shows that many general theories of culture or civilization have been preceded by similar theories about art systems and their change. The total contribution of these art theories to the recent "intelligible reading of historical events" is enormous.

GENERAL CONCLUSIONS ABOUT THE SYSTEMIC MACROSOCIOLOGIES OF CULTURE

Despite their differences most of the theories examined agree in several important points.[65] Their first agreement is that in the boundless ocean of sociocultural phenomena there exist vast cultural systems, supersystems, or civilizations that live and function as real unities. They are not identical with the state or the nation or with any social group. As a rule they transcend the boundaries of any social system. On the other hand, the total culture of any social group consists of several cultural systems coexisting side by side with the supersystem (if a given total culture reaches the supersystem level of integration). Danilevsky calls these supersystems "cultural-historical types"; Spengler calls them "high cultures"; Toynbee refers to them as "civilizations"; Kroeber as "high-value patterns"; Schubart, as the "prototypes of culture"; Northrop as "world cultures"; Berdyaev, as "great cultures"; I call them "cultural supersystems."

The second point of agreement of these theories is that, due to the triple interdependence of the whole system and its

---

[65] See a more substantial analysis of these agreements in my *Modern Historical and Social Philosophies*, pp. 275–320.

parts, these vast supersystems tangibly condition most of the surface ripplings of the sociocultural ocean, including the historical events and life-processes of smaller sociocultural systems and the actions of individuals and groups living a given cultural supersystem: Their ideological, behavioral, and material culture, their life-course and destiny are tangibly influenced by it. Due to the triple interdependence a change of a supersystem and of its important parts is mutually conditioned.

The third point of agreement contends that without an adequate knowledge of the supersystem we can hardly understand the structural and dynamic properties of all its important parts—of all its subsystems, sub-subsystems, and congeries—just as without a sufficient knowledge of a whole organism, of its gross anatomy and gross physiology, we cannot understand the anatomy and physiology of its organs, tissues, and cells.

Fourth, the macrosociological theories give to us, speaking figuratively, a gross anatomy and physiology of the whole cultural universe. A substantial knowledge of all the main cultural systems and supersystems equips us with a knowledge of all the macroscopic aspects of the whole cultural cosmos. This knowledge greatly complements the knowledge of microscopic cultural phenomena obtained through microsociological research. By its very nature, microsociological research cannot successfully study macrocultural realities: They are too big to be examined microscopically—not microscopes but powerful telescopes are needed for their investigations. For a fuller knowledge of sociocultural realities both macrosociological as well as microsociological studies are indispensable.

Fifth, the theories agree that the total number of vast cultural supersystems has in the whole human culture been small (while the number of small cultural systems has been practically innumerable). The total number of Danilevsky-Spengler-Toynbee's "civilizations" does not exceed some 30; R. Wescott gives to us a list of about 300, but the list includes not only world civilizations but also continental, national, provincial, and local civilizations. The world civilizations in this list do not exceed 15. If we take the vastest cultural supersystems or prototypes, most of the examined theories offer to us only two:

Northrop's aesthetic-theoretic; Becker's sacral-secular; Ortega's classic-crisis; the dichtomists' material-nonmaterial, civilization-culture, technological-ideological; Kroeber's reality-culture and value-culture; Sorokin's ideational, idealistic, and sensate (plus eclectic); and Schubart's harmonious, heroic, ascetic and messianic. If instead we take other classifications of vast cultural formations, such as paleolithic-neolithic-copper-bronze-iron-machine civilizations or hunting-pastoral-agricultural-industrial or "rural-urban" or any other classification based either upon main types of religion or of economy or of the type of family and kinship or of government or of solidarity (*Gemein-schaft-Gesellschaft,* "mechanical-organic") or Saint-Simon's critical-organic or Comte's theological-metaphysical-positive or Vico's civilizations "of the age of gods, of heroes, and of man," the number of the basic types still remains very small.

Sixth, the theories agree, explicitly or implicitly, that each of the vast cultural systems and supersystems is based upon some major premise or philosophical presupposition or prime symbol or ultimate value that the supersystem or civilization articulates, develops, and realizes in the process of its life-career in all its main parts or subsystems. Each of the great cultural unities is therefore either logically or aesthetically consistent or complementary in the meaningful aspects of its parts and compartments.

Seventh, each of these supersystems, after its grounding (objectification and socialization) in empirical reality, becomes a meaningful-causal unity. If it were a mere biocausal system, devoid of the component of meaning, it would not have been a sociocultural phenomenon at all. If its important parts were not united by causal interdependence, it would have been a conglomeration of vast congeries and not a unified system.

Eighth, the theories agree on the general characteristics of systems, supersystems, and civilizations. Explicitly or implicitly almost all the examined theories ascribe to it the following properties: a reality different from that of its parts; individuality; triple (general and differential) interdependence of parts upon one another and upon the whole system and of the whole system upon its parts; the preservation of its individuality or its "sameness" in spite of a change of its parts; the change in togetherness of all important parts; the self-directing (immanent) change and self-determination of its life-career with external forces either accelerating or slowing up, facilitating or hindering the unfolding and realization of the potentialities of a system or supersystem, sometimes even destroying it, but hardly ever transforming it into something radically different from its inherent potentialities; the selectivity of a system or supersystem in taking in the congenial and in rejecting the uncongenial elements of the external world; and the limited variability of a system or supersystem.

Ninth, the theories agree in their rejection of the linear conception of the life-course of systems and supersystems and of historical processes generally in favor of either cyclical or rhythmical or continuously varying conceptions. The theories contend that the historical life-course of systems, supersystems, and of mankind is ever new and ever old at any given moment. Incessantly changing, the life-course of a cultural unity is made up of uniform repeated activities, rhythms, relationships, processes, and components. The discovery of repeated structural or dynamic uniformities has been the main task of the systemic theories of culture and civilization.

Tenth, the theories all have a tangible similarity of the "phases" or "prototypes" of cultural supersystems or civilizations surveyed. The phase of growth or "spring" of Danilevsky-Spengler-Toynbee's civilizations is similar in several traits with Sorokin's ideational, Schubart's ascetic-messianic, Kroeber's "religiously dominated," Northrop's dominantly aesthetic, Berdyaev's barbaric-religious, and Becker's sacral prototypes. The phase of decline of civilizations in Danilevsky-Spengler-Toynbee-Koneczny's theory resembles Sorokin's overripe sensate, Schubart's heroic, Northrop's theoretic, Kroeber's secular, Berdyaev's humanistic-secular, Schweitzer's decline of civilizations, and Ortega's crisis civilization.

The eleventh similarity consists in an affirmation by most of the theories examined (with the exception of Danilevsky's and Spengler's) that the whole life-process of various civilizations, supersystems, or prototypes follows different courses in their genesis, growth, life-patterns, life-span, blossoming and withering, decline, and resurrection. Danilevsky's and Spengler's big organismic model of the life-cycle of these vast unities is applicable only to a few civilizations or supersystems. Most of them have different, more complex, and more original life-courses.

Twelfth, the theories examined unanimously diagnose our time as the time of the greatest crisis, as the end of the epoch of domination of the sensate-theoretic-secular-Promethean-scientific-technological culture dominant during the last four or five centuries and as a transition period toward a now emerging messianic-integral-new medieval-aesthetic-theoretic prototype of civilization or culture. Although they differ in detail, all the theories are in perfect agreement on this point. They all assert that we live between two epochs: one dying, the other emerging.

Thirteenth, all stress the coming revaluation of all hitherto dominant values, including a radical reconsideration of methods and ways of cognition. Practically all the theories expect, in the culture to come, a reunification of the supreme values of Truth, Beauty, and Goodness—hitherto separated from one another—into one *summum bonum.*

Agreement in these thirteen items strongly suggests the rough validity of these conclusions: Otherwise, a concordance could hardly be achieved on the part of distinguished scholars so different from one another in their philosophical background and their methods, in the starting points and the materials of their study, in their mentality, personal preferences, and life-history.

Despite the shortcomings of these theories, each of them brings into the open one or more important aspects of cultural realities; each of them enriches our understanding of the structure and nature, relationships, and processes of macrocultural unities and, consequently, of the whole cultural universe, including our own personality and behavior. Probably just because these theories deal with important cultural realities and earnestly try to understand their what, how, and why, a careful reader of the examined macrosociological works cannot help feeling the theories endeavor, and succeed to some extent, to unravel important "mysteries" of the "mysterious" sociocultural world. This feeling remains even when some of their conclusions appear to be doubtful. The surveyed macrosociologies increase our knowledge not only by their true discoveries but also by their errors—which cannot be said of all theories that deal with pseudorealities or pseudoproblems. For these reasons the examined theories represent possibly the most significant cognitive achievement among all the recent theories of general sociology.

PART FOUR

THEORIES OF SOCIAL SYSTEMS

CHAPTER 12

Recent Theories of Social Systems

INTERRELATIONSHIP OF CULTURAL AND SOCIAL SYSTEMS[1]

In Chapters 2 and 9, a preliminary definition of social system (organized group) and its relationship to cultural system was outlined. According to this outline, cultural systems and congeries and social systems and congeries (unorganized and disorganized groups) and integrated and unintegrated personalities of interacting individuals represent three inseparable but different dimensions of the multidimensional superorganic reality. Its cultural dimension consists of meanings, values, norms,[2] their integrated systems and unintegrated congeries given either in their ideological and/or behavioral and material forms—if and when these are objectified through overt actions and other biophysical media (vehicles). In a study of this dimension, the individuals and groups function mainly as creators, users, and operators of meanings, values, and norms.

---

[1] A detailed analysis of social systems and their relationship to cultural systems is given in the *Dynamics*, Vol. III, pp. 3–256, and in *SCP*, pp. 39–181.

[2] "Meanings may be classified as follows: (1) *cognitive meanings*, in the narrow sense of the term, such as the meaning of Plato's philosophy, mathematical formula, or the Marxian theory of surplus value; (2) meaningful *values* such as the value of religion or science or education or property or health or democracy; (3) *norms*, referred to as standard, like the norms of law, ethics, etiquettes, and technical norms, for the construction of machinery, writing a poem, growing vegetables, etc. These three classes of meanings are three main forms of the general concept of meaning. Any meaning is a value. Any value presupposes a norm of conduct with reference to its acceptance or rejection. Any norm is necessarily a meaning and a positive or negative value. Hence the terms 'meaning,' 'value' and 'norm' are used interchangeably to denote a general class of meaningful phenomena superimposed upon the biophysical phenomena, properties of persons and objects, actions and events." *SCP*, pp. 47 ff.

The social dimension of the superorganic reality is made up of the meaningfully interacting individuals, their meaningful actions and reactions, of unorganized and organized groups (social systems), and of interindividual and intergroup relationships. Meanings-values-norms enter and function here in three forms: as components making and defining the specific meaningful nature of social actions and interactions and of social relationships and groups (because the purely biophysical nature of these phenomena does not belong to the realm of superorganic reality and is not an object-matter of sociology but of biophysical sciences); as a set of economic, religious, political, or other meanings-values for whose realization, enjoyment, maintenance, and development the individuals interact and band together into an organized group (or social system); and as a set of law norms defining, regulating, guiding, and prescribing obligatory forms of all meaningful actions-reactions of interacting indiviudals and of the organization of social systems.

In the personality dimension of sociocultural reality, our attention is focused at the interacting individuals as psychosocial beings: at the general and special structure of their unconscious, conscious, and superconscious mentality, at their sociocultural ideology and behavior, at their position in the universe, and at their status, *caput,* functions, rights, and duties within each stratified and differentiated social system with which they are affiliated. This means that the componential structure of cultural, social, and personality systems is the same, but in each of these systems one of the components occupies the central place and becomes the focus of our attention and our study. (In this respect, three-dimensional sociocultural reality is similar to the Christian Trinity of God the Father, God the Son, and God the Holy Ghost: inseparable but different from one another.)

Analytically, we can study each dimension separately (as we did the cultural dimension in the preceding chapters), but even such a concentrated study of each dimension cannot be fruitfully accomplished without keeping in the background continuous references to and interplay with, the other two dimensions as well as the whole inseparable three-dimensional superorganic reality in which it exists. If it is completely isolated from it, it looses its specific properties and becomes a meaningless, empty shell. The same is true of the superorganic reality itself: A complete separation from it of one of its three dimensions or components destroys its unity and properties and turns it into different two-dimensional reality or even into a mere biophysical phenomenon.

For this reason all the theories that claim that the social and the cultural phenomena are quite different from each other and as such can and should be studied independently from each other—the cultural reality by the science of culturology and the social phenomena by sociology—go too far in their contentions. Earlier examples of such theories are given by the formal school in sociology (Simmel, Richard, Vierkandt, von Wiese).[3] Recent theories of this sort are exemplified by the conceptions of social and cultural phenomena of Becker,[4] Znaniecki,[5] White,[6] Wen-shan Huang,[7] Dollard,[8] C. Kluckhohn and O. Mowrer,[9] and Bidney.[10]

In the preceding discussion of Znaniecki's theory of cultural system we already met with this contention and found it wanting. Somewhat more cogent reasons for a separate study of cultural systems by the science of culturology and of social

[3] See on these theories *CST*, ch. 9.

[4] See L. von Wiese and H. Becker, *Systematic Sociology* (New York, 1932).

[5] Besides Znaniecki's *Cultural Sciences,* see his *The Method of Sociology* (New York, 1934), *The Social Role of the Man of Science* (New York, 1940), and *Social Actions* (New York, 1936).

[6] L. White, "Culturological vs. Psychological Interpretation of Human Behavior," *American Anthropologist, 48*; *The Science of Culture* (New York, 1949).

[7] Wen-shan Huang, *Collected Essays in Culturology* (Canton, 1939); *Culturology and Its Place in the System of Science,* Lingnam University, 1949.

[8] J. Dollard, "Culture, Society, Impulse and Socialization," *AJS,* XLV, 50–63.

[9] C. Kluckhohn and O. Mowrer, "Culture and Personality," *American Anthropologist,* XLVI (1944), 1–29.

[10] D. Bidney, "On the Concept of Culture," *American Anthropologist,* XLVI (1944), 30–44.

systems by sociology are given by Wen-shan Huang.[11] In his own formulation these reasons are as follows:[12]

1. Culturology is a new science that has emerged from sociology.

2. The greatest reason for that is that the structure of the cultural system is different from that of the social system. Cultural system is content. Social system is form. The total culture (content) of any family, state, political party, university, corporation is constructed by the values and meanings of language, science, religion, aesthetics, ethics, politics, economics, philosophy, law, and technology. One or many parts of cultural values are in the possession of all groups and becomes the dynamic agency or medium of their existence. Social systems or groups, such as the state or corporation, are the forms of organizations determined by law or ethics.

3. The social system is the continuator or agent and not the creator of the cultural system. Social systems or groups can be linked logically with certain cultural systems that are not created by social systems.

4. As agencies of cultural systems two types of social systems can be mentioned: one is a continuator of a *special* kind of cultural value, such as religious or philosophical or political value; the other includes all kinds of cultural values, such as the family or the state.

5. The nature of social and cultural systems is not identical. A cultural system is a value system, whereas a social system is a system of interacting human beings. A social system, in its organizational aspect, is mainly determined by legal and ethical cultural systems.

6. Cultural system and cultural process has its own life determined by its own laws. Hence the study of culture inevitably becomes an independent science with its own aim, level, scope, and laws.

7. Culture is not only superorganic, but also superpsychological, supersocial. It has its own mode of being.

[11] Cf. Wen-shan Huang, "Cultural System and Social System," *Social Science Journal*, Vol. I, No. 1, in Chinese.

[12] In a special memorandum kindly prepared for me.

8. A system of culturology should include at least the life of culture, the nature of culture, the structure of culture, the dynamics of culture, the types of culture, and cultural laws.

Practically all these propositions are in an essential agreement with my own theory in this field, with the exception of one point—Wen-shan Huang's overemphasis of the differences and separateness of cultural and social systems and his preference for a study of each of these systems by different sciences of sociology and culturology. A careful reading of his theory at once shows that he himself does not carry on this contention. Indeed, his very definition of these systems as "form" and "content" of the same superorganic reality (separated from its content its form becomes formless and separated from its form its content becomes largely empty); his proposition that the social system in its organizational aspect is determined by legal and ethical cultural systems; and his delineation of the properties of each system by comparing them with those of the other, demonstrate clearly the inseparability of these systems or dimensions from each other. His stressing their difference is correct, like stressing the difference of one side of a hand from the other side. But just as an adequate knowledge of the whole hand is impossible without knowledge of both of its sides, and knowledge of either side is hardly possible without that of the other side, so also an adequate cognition of any sociocultural phenomenon requires a cognition of all its three dimensions and their interrelationship with one another.

If my interpretation of Wen-shan Huang's theory is correct, he is making the same mistake that Znaniecki and several others have made.

With a corresponding variation this criticism equally applies to all the other theories that try to separate completely the social and cultural systems from each other or treat these dimensions-systems as identical with each other, or completely submerge one system in the other.[13] To sum up, for greater cognitive fruitfulness we can and should concentrate our study

[13] Cf., for details and samples of such theories, *SCP*, pp. 62–65, 85–88.

on each of these dimensions while always keeping in the back of our minds the fact of its inseparability from the other dimensions and from the whole superorganic reality of which it is a part. "The sociocultural reality is indivisible, and no one can make a special science of one aspect of it, ignoring the other aspects."[14]

SYSTEMS OF LAW AND RECENT THEORIES OF SOCIAL SYSTEMS

Recent theories of social systems have been less fruitful than those of cultural systems. Hardly any of the new theories gives to us anything significantly new or any important improvement on the theories of the preceding periods. In comparison with their predecessors many new theories appear more primitive and shallow than adequate and precise.

One of the reasons for this is that the realm of social actions, social relationships, social groups and institutions, and of other object-matters of the theories of social systems has been for centuries carefully studied, analyzed, and classified by the known and unknown jurisconsults and law-givers. The great ones, like Papinianus or Gaius, can be called great sociologists of law, social systems, and legal behavior. The results of their study have been precisely formulated in the form of law norms tested daily for their adequacy and preciseness in regulating all the important forms of social behavior and relationships and for organizing all social groups and institutions. The totality of such norms (with their corresponding commentaries and theories), unified, classified, and codified into one law system (subdivided into constitutional, administrative, criminal, civil, and international law), represent the fullest, most detailed, and most precise epitome of all important social actions-reactions, social relationships, and organized social groups and institutions as each is defined and analyzed in its genus and *differentia specifica*. All fully developed law systems like the Corpus Juris Civilis or the total law codes of many nations

14 *Ibid.*, p. 65.

determine in exact detail the rights and duties of each member: what, in regard to whom, when, how much, and under what conditions each member is entitled or obliged to do or not to do, to tolerate or not to tolerate; what the exact actions or functions are that he has to discharge in important specified circumstances; what his status, *caput*, role, or position is in each of the social groups he belongs to. In brief, the fully developed law codes precisely define practically all the important forms of social actions and relationships of each member of a given group of interacting individuals and prescribe a detailed "blueprint" for all socially significant behavior. Only actions and relationships that are socially unimportant are not included and not defined in the law codes. (*De minimis non curat lex*: "Law does not care about insignificant matters.")

Similarly, fully developed law codes define, analyze, and classify all important social groups and institutions: their sociocultural nature, the specific meanings-values they serve and maintain, their "constitution and organization," their objectives and functions, the conditions of their establishment, continuity, and dissolution—in brief, their "histology, anatomy, and taxonomy" with an "inch-map of their conduct." Only the groups and institutions that are socially unimportant are passed by undefined and unregulated by the law systems.

What is still more important, the definitions and formulas of the law codes had to be and usually are precise and clear; otherwise the law norms could not successfully regulate all important interindividual and intergroup relationships, nor could they authoritatively resolve innumerable and continuously arising interindividual and intergroup conflicts, nor could they constitute social groups and institutions.

A careful study of such great law codes as the Corpus Juris Civilis as well as of all the fully developed codes of law of many modern nations well confirms these statements. As *lex generalis omnium*, the Corpus Juris Civilis gives to us precise definitions, analyses, and classifications of all important social actions-reactions and relationships and of all significant social systems and institutions. Examples are: *jus publicum et privatum lex, civitas, potestas, imperium, majestas, princeps, dignitates, sub-*

jecti, manus, persona, status, caput, crimen, delicta, capitis deminutio, dominium, possessio, proprietas, beneficium, contractus, actio, obligatio, commercium, consensus, cessio, stipulatio, aequitas, injuria, familia, matrimonium, institutio, societas, universitas personarum et bonorum, and other important social relationships and social systems.

No wonder, therefore, that the definitions and classifications of the Corpus Juris Civilis were accepted and applied for several centuries in the Roman and Byzantine social life and, since the tenth century, have been incorporated in practically all law codes of the Western countries and Russia. As *lex generalis omnium,* they still live and function in today's law codes of the West and to a lesser degree in those of the East.[15]

Similar epitomes of social actions, relationships, and systems occur in all fully developed law codes. Compared with their conceptions and classifications of forms of social actions, relationships, and systems, recent theories of social systems are less precise, less detailed, and more incomplete than the formulas of law codes and of theories from which law norms are derived and on which are based the great and fully developed law systems.

One of the main reasons for the shortcomings of recent theories of social systems is the fact that almost all of these theories substantially ignore—deliberately or through ignorance —the invaluable scientific knowledge accumulated and incorporated in these law codes and in the theoretical science of law. Instead of utilizing this splendid legal histology, anatomy, and taxonomy of social actions, relationships, and systems (groups and institutions), they operate with homemade, often clumsy and poorly defined notions and concepts that vitiate all the theories constructed out of such defective conceptual building material.[16]

---

[15] See, on the diffusion, renaissance, and incorporation of formulas and conceptions of the Corpus Juris Civilis as the *lex generalis omnium,* I. A. Pokrovsky, *Istoria Rimskago Prava* (*History of the Roman Law*) (Riga, 1924), pp. 1–16, 244–281.

[16] These statements explain why in my theory of social systems (organized groups) the law norms are used as the main criterion and *differentia specifica* of social systems, of their componential organization, of their essential properties, and of their taxonomy. Cf. my *SCP,* ch. 9.

I realize fully the gravity of this criticism. I hope, however, in subsequent concise examination of the theories of social systems of F. Znaniecki, R. MacIver, R. Bierstedt, L. Mendieta y Nunez, C. Loomis, T. Parsons, G. Homans, O. Kühne, G. Gurvitch, and a few others to vindicate it to a considerable extent. For the sake of economy and clarity, this examination will be carried out "analytically." First, I shall examine the conceptions of social systems, their components and properties, as defined by these distinguished sociologists; second, their taxonomy of social systems; third, their dynamics (or physiology) of social systems. If competently done, such an analysis should provide a fairly adequate summary of today's theories in this field.

"SOCIAL ACTION" THEORIES OF SOCIAL SYSTEMS

F. Znaniecki's and T. Parsons' theories represent this brand. Both theories start with and are centered around the concept of "social action" as an elementary model and at the same time as the central component of the social system.

● Znaniecki's Theory

The general character of Znaniecki's theory and his concept of social and cultural systems were outlined in Chapter 9. Our main inquiry at this point concerns his concept of "social action" as the simplest model of a "closed" or "limited" social system,[17] which is but a "dynamic axionormatively organized system of social actions."[18] Are these concepts sufficiently analyzed and adequately defined by Znaniecki to give a significant theory of social systems? In their present form they are not. They need a great deal of clarification, modification, and

---

[17] See Znaniecki's meaning of the term "closed system," later on replaced by that of "a limited system," in his *The Method of Sociology*, pp. 11 ff., and in *Cultural Sciences*, pp. 163–164.

[18] *Cultural Sciences*, pp. 327 ff.

cleansing of their many ambiguities and errors before they can be considered satisfactory and correct.

Their first and most serious defect is a vague and fallacious differentiation between "social" actions and "nonsocial" cultural actions. According to Znaniecki, not all axionormative cultural actions and interactions between conscious individuals[19] are social actions—or social systems—but only those "bearing upon men as their objects and intending to provoke definite reactions on their part":

> They are *social actions,* clearly different from other actions which bear not upon men but upon material things, economic values, sacred objects and mystical powers, objects of aesthetic appreciation, linguistic symbols, or scientific theories, and which intend to produce not human reactions but technical, economic, religious, literary, scientific results. . . .[20]
>
> If sociology is essentially the science of human or social relations, then the primary phenomena which sociologists have to investigate are social actions, just as the primary phenomena investigated by religionists, students of material technique, economists, and theorists of arts are religious, technical, economic, artistic actions.
>
> We include in this category [of social actions] all those and only those human actions [individual or collective] which have as main values other human individuals as living and conscious beings, and which tend to produce some changes in these main values . . . as social objects. . . .[21]
>
> Social actions are axionormatively ordered [and regulated] by moral rules. . . . Every norm recognized by a social agent [consciously interacting individual] as his duty towards somebody else is a component of a social system in which this agent and the object of his duty [interacting persons] are bound together as partners. We call such a system a *social relation,*

---

[19] To the credit of Znaniecki, it is to be mentioned that, although he concentrates his analysis at a broad class of "creative actions," he does not reduce all axionormative, conscious actions to either "teleological" or "rational" or "logical" (conforming to the schema of "means" and "end," as Parsons and others do). Besides these forms, he acknowledges "the deterministic," "the habitual," "the imitative," and other forms of action that do not conform to the "means-ends" schema. His class of "creative actions" covers a much larger class of actions ordinarily called "creative." See his *Cultural Sciences,* chs. 7, 8, 9.

[20] *The Method of Sociology,* pp. 107 ff.

[21] *Cultural Sciences,* pp. 389 ff.

and this whole branch of sociology dealing with moral data might be termed the *theory of social relations.*[22]

If to these definitions we add Znaniecki's general concept of every (conscious) human action as a "limited, dynamic system of interdependent, changing values"[23] and of social relation as not really a relation between two (interacting) individuals as such, but between their actions,"[24] then we have a correct account of Znaniecki's concepts of social action, social relations, and social system.

CRITICISM

The first fatal defect of his definition is its vagueness and the fallacy of his criterion differentiating "social" action from other cultural "nonsocial" actions. We are told that social actions are those "bearing upon men as their objects and intending to provoke definite reactions on their part," whereas nonsocial—scientific, artistic, religious, political, and economic actions—"bear not upon men but upon material things . . . and intend to produce not human reactions but technical, economic, religious, literary, scientific results." If we have to believe this statement then neither the actions of a preacher delivering his sermon, nor of a scientist addressing his audience, nor of a politician speaking to his voters, nor of a businessman advertising his product, nor of a novelist writing and publishing his novel, nor of an inventor patenting his invention, nor of a judge presiding at his court are "social actions" and none of these persons intends to "bear their actions upon men" and to try to influence their mentality and behavior. According to Znaniecki, they address these activities just to "material objects" and values: The preacher, in other words, is preaching to the walls and columns of his church, the scientist is lecturing to the blackboard, and so on. The fallacy in Znaniecki's differentiation between the "social" and "nonsocial" actions is so obvious that hardly any criticism is necessary to show its inadequacy.

[22] *The Method of Sociology*, pp. 113 ff.
[23] *Cultural Sciences*, p. 192; *Social Relations and Social Roles* (San Francisco, 1965), pp. 16 ff.
[24] *Ibid.*, pp. 388 ff.

If we empty his "social actions-relations-systems" of all scientific, philosophical, religious, economic, and political meanings and values, there remains hardly anything sociocultural in these actions and motions: They become purely biophysical motions-relations-systems studied by the biophysical sciences. At best, there remain only moral and legal norms that, according to Znaniecki, axionormatively regulate social actions. But no moral or legal norm can regulate the sociocultural emptiness of motions stripped of all cultural values and meanings. Any moral or legal norm from "Thou shalt not kill" to "Citizens must pay their taxes" defines, regulates, and prescribes not just empty "rights and duties" and undefined actions-reactions, but, rather, specified political or economic or religious or scientific or artistic or matrimonial rights and duties. A mere "Thou shalt not," without any further specification of what one must not do or what sort of value one is obliged to give up, is completely meaningless. By the same token, Znaniecki's "social actions-relations-systems," emptied of all cultural meanings-values-norms also lose their "axionormative (moral and legal) component" and become biophysical phenomena studied by physicists and biologists.

If Znaniecki did not arrive at this conclusion and thus did not turn into a physicalistic sociologist, this is due to the fact that he did not follow his own concepts of social actions-relations-systems; he systematically transgressed them by filling the "sociocultural void" of his social actions-relations now by religious, now by medical, now by military, now by scientific, now by economic "cultural and psychological content." Only through this violation of his concepts has he, like the "formal" sociologists,[25] been able to mention a few examples of social actions and relations, such as cooperation and conflict, association and dissociation, antagonism and solidarity, and a few others. But even here to make these social actions-relations meaningful he, like G. Simmel, L. von Wiese, H. Becker, and other "formal" sociologists, had to define them by giving to

[25] See my analysis and criticism of the formal school in *CST*, ch. 9; cf. also A. Cuvillier, *Manuel de Sociologie*, pp. 182 ff.

them some cultural and psychological "content," without which they are devoid of any superorganic or sociocultural character.

His "moral rules," which "axionormatively regulate social actions" and which "have a distinctive character different from all other rules—religious, economic, technical, intellectual, and aesthetic"—are left undefined by Znaniecki, although he does say that they contain "a duty which binds" interacting individuals.[26]

Such a definition of moral and legal rules is quite inadequate: It does not specify and differentiate ethical, one-sided, imperative rules from the two-sided, imperative-attributive law rules, or from a multitude of religious, technical, aesthetic, and other rules.[27] Since "moral rules" are one of the important components of Znaniecki's "social actions-relations" this vague characterization contributes to the total vagueness of his "social action-relation-system."

Znaniecki's theory does not give an even remotely adequate analysis of the componential structure of his "social actions, social relations, and social system," their "anatomy and histology." Nowhere in his works does one find an exact formula of the necessary but sufficient components of any "axionormative interaction of conscious human beings" like my componential formula of meanings-values-norms; of conscious human beings tangibly influencing through their actions and vehicles the mentality and/or overt behavior of one another; and of the biophysical media (vehicles or conductors of interaction) through which interacting persons objectify their meanings-values-norms and convey and transmit them to the interacting partners. Nor does Znaniecki specify that in any axionormative social action-interaction there are always given among these individuals the subject of the right; the subject of the duty; the object of the right; the object of the duty; reference to the source or authority of the law norm they follow or violate;

---

[26] *The Methods of Sociology*, pp. 113–116.

[27] See a precise definition of law norms and a description of the way they differ from purely ethical or moral norms in my *SCP*, ch. 4. In aggravated form, this shortcoming vitiates other theories of social action, social behavior, and social systems, as we shall see later on.

additional specifications of time, place, conditions, ways of acting, etc.; the addressees of the law-activities. Nor does he specify and classify the actions of the subjects and objects of rights and duties. (The subject of a right is entitled to *accept* [objects or services], *do* [issue a command, marry, accept a property], or *not tolerate* [violence, attack, insults]; the subject of a duty is obliged to *do* [work, deliver goods, pay his debts] *tolerate* [reprimand, imprisonment, foreclosing his property]; or *not do* [kill, steal, violate law-norms].) Nor does Znaniecki's theory give an analysis of the psychological experience involved in, and motivated by the law norms, or the "distributive and organizational functions" of law norms in forming and constituting any and all organized social systems or groups.[28]

All we find in Znaniecki's theory of social action is a somewhat incidental mentioning of "conscious individuals," vague "social actions" emptied of their psychosocial content, "moral rules," "humanistic coefficients," "roles," and "values" —all poorly defined. In brief, Znaniecki's theory of social actions-relations-systems stops in its analysis at an initial point in its development. The result is that it does not give to us any roughly adequate "anatomy or histology" of social actions.[29]

Furthermore, he gives no taxonomy or systematic theory of change for these actions-relations-systems. Nor does he analyze systematically the basic properties of social systems as systems. Paraphrasing Kroeber's facetious remark about Toynbee's study of civilization and culture as dealing really little with these problems, we can say that Znaniecki's theory of social systems never gets to a systematic study of these phenomena.

Likewise, his theory says very little of the structure and types of the other two components of social actions-relations-systems: the consciously interacting individuals and biophysical

---

[28] For an analysis of these "histological" elements of the axio-normative interaction of individuals and of the cardinal importance of the "histology and anatomy" of social actions-relations-systems, see my *SCP*, pp. 69–92.

[29] This shortcoming is common to almost all theories of "social actions" and "social behavior."

media of objectification and socialization of the meanings-values-norms because of which and for the sake of which the individuals interact and exchange their "social actions" (vehicles and conductors of interaction and objectified "material culture" or, in a happy term of Moreno, the "sociocultural conserves"). In the examined works of Znaniecki one finds no systematic theory of sociocultural structure and types of personality, nor any classification of these types in their relationships with the social groups and cultural systems among which they live and interact. (In Znaniecki-Thomas' *Polish Peasant* there are outlines of these types not used in the general sociology of Znaniecki.)

Biophysical media (vehicles and sociocultural "conserves") in which the meanings-values-norms are externalized and objectified and through which the interacting individuals convey and transmit these meanings to their face-to-face or separated-in-space-partners of interaction are casually mentioned only in a few places and are passed by without any comments or analysis. Interacting individuals are frequently eliminated as components of interaction because "social relation is not really a relation between two (interacting) individuals as such, but between their actions."[30]

So, we are left with social actions and relations void of all cultural meanings-values-norms and separated even from the individuals who perform them. This separation turns these actions-relations into formless, foggy ghosts floating somewhere in a mysterious universe and existing mysteriously by themselves without any human individuals to perform them. Even physical mechanics in studying physical motions always says that they are the motions of either physical "particles" or "material bodies" or waves of certain physical energies. But Znaniecki outmechanics even physical mechanics. He constructs social actions and relations unattached to any subject who performs them. Durkheim's criticism of Simmel's formalism well sums up our reaction to Znaniecki's fogginess: "Sociology certainly has a right to constitute itself with an aid of abstractions; however

[30] *Cultural Sciences,* pp. 388 ff.

it is necessary that these abstractions were established according to the natural division of facts, without which the abstractions degenerate into fantastic constructions, into a vain mythology."[31]

Insofar as Znaniecki sees the general model of social systems in "social actions," and insofar as these actions turn, at best, into either poorly defined, superficially analyzed, and practically unclassified sociocultural phenomena or, at worst, into purely biophysical motions, even into transempirical ghosts unattached to their performers, it is inevitable that no scientific theory of social systems can be constructed of this sort of building material. This kind of "social actions" can in no way be identified with or be a general model of a social system. Even if social actions were not dehydrated by Znaniecki into ghostly abstractions and were studied in their living empirical reality, even then they could not be taken for a general model of social systems, for the same reason that the elements H and O separated from each other cannot serve as a model of water (H_2O). Meaningful or sociocultural actions are only a part of one of the three main components of social systems—an important property of the interacting individuals. Besides the component of individuals, any cultural interaction, especially its organized forms (social system), has the components of meanings-values-norms and of objectifying biophysical media as "materialized conserves" and as vehicles conveying the meaningful actions-reactions to the interacting partners.[32] Meaningful social actions, being a mere element of one of these three components, cannot, obviously, represent the whole social or cultural system.

[31] E. Durkheim, "La sociologie et son domaine scientifique," *L'année sociologique*, IV (1900), 181. This criticism of Durkheim is equally applicable to all theories of "social actions" and social behavior that have the deficiencies of Znaniecki's theory or that are heavily infected by similar diseases.

[32] This component of "sociocultural conserves" and conductors of interaction is almost completely neglected by most of the theories of social actions, relations, and systems. On the other hand, in the form of "material culture," torn from the other two components, it is "reified" and elevated into "the prime mover" of sociocultural change by the dichotomic and other theories. Both kinds of treatment of this component are certainly defective and need serious correction.

Without pointing here to additional defects and self-contradictions of Znaniecki's theory, we can conclude that he has not given to us an adequate theory of social systems. He started in the right direction with his concept of sociocultural reality as different from biophysical reality; he correctly defined the general class of "limited systems" and began his analysis of social systems. But in this analysis he was unfortunately deflected from the right path by his previous theory of social actions, which prevented him from a fruitful development of his concept of social systems and at the same time infected this concept with the diseases of his theory of social actions.[33] Although he correctly outlined the general direction and main lines of his theory of social systems, and supplied us with significant ideas and observations for building it, he failed in developing an adequate histology, or anatomy, or physiology or taxonomy of social systems.

● **Parsons' Theory**

The earliest version of Talcott Parsons' theory of social actions and systems, published in his *The Structure of Social Actions*,[34] has undergone considerable change in his later works, *The Social System*,[35] *Toward a General Theory of Action* (edited by T. Parsons and E. A. Shils),[36] and "An Outline of the Social System," and other articles and books published in recent years.[37]

Parsons' concept of social action as developed in *The*

---

[33] As we shall see, this has happened with other theories of social actions that were inflated into theories of social systems.

[34] (New York, 1937.)

[35] (Glencoe, Ill., 1951.)

[36] (Cambridge, Mass., 1951.)

[37] T. Parsons, E. Shils, K. Naegele, J. Pitts, *Theories of Society*, Vol. I (New York, 1961). See J. F. Scott, "The Changing Foundations of the Parsonian Action Scheme," *ASR*, October, 1963, pp. 716–735; see also his "The Impossible Theory of Action," *Berkeley Journal of Sociology*, 7(1962), 51–62; and C. and Z. Loomis, *Modern Social Theories*, ch. 6. About the American predecessors of the social action theory, cf. R. C. Hinkle, "Antecedents of the Action Orientation," *ASR*, October, 1963, pp. 705–715.

Structure of Social Action needs a careful examination: Though modified in his subsequent works, it continues to be the axis on which his theory of social systems is built. A large part of this volume is devoted to a thoughtful analysis of the sociological and economic theories of A. Marshall, V. Pareto, E. Durkheim, M. Weber, F. Tönnies, and K. Marx with particular attention to their theories of social action. Parsons' examination of these theories is done not so much for their own sake as to prove his point that all these theories were converging to one central voluntaristic theory of social action put forth in its "definitive" form by Parsons himself. In other words, these sociological theories are empirical proofs, according to Parsons, of the scientific adequacy of Parsons' theory. Throughout the volume Parsons emphasizes again and again that "this study has attempted throughout to be an *empirical* monograph. It has been concerned with facts and the understanding of facts. The propositions set forth have been based upon facts and direct references to the sources for these facts have been given throughout in footnotes."[38]

CRITICISM

We can dispense with this part of the work by the following observations:

1. It is somewhat presumptuous to treat the theories of the eminent sociologists as predecessors of, and the "means" theories for, Parsons' own voluntaristic theory of action.

2. Parsons' contention that these theories are converging to a common voluntaristic theory of action, and his ascription of a voluntaristic character to Marshall's, Pareto's, and Durkheim's sociological theories are largely baseless. A microscopic examination of these theories reveals hardly any traces of

---

[38] *The Structure of Social Action* (2d ed.; Glencoe, Ill., 1958), p. 697, and all of Chapter 18. E. Faris and a number of other sociologists noted Parsons' overestimation of his works: "He confidently believes that new knowledge has come into the world (with his work). Unfortunately, he does not spell out clearly these revelations." Faris further shows that all Parsons' revelations were revealed by many sociologists many years before Parsons. See Faris' review of Parsons' *Social System* in *ASR*, *18*(1953), 18.

"voluntarism" in Marshall's, Pareto's, or Durkheim's sociological as well as psychological and philosophical theories. Only Tönnies' and, to a lesser degree, Max Weber's theories can be called voluntaristic to some extent. This verdict is confirmed by Parsons himself: In his later works his "voluntarism" almost completely disappears and is largely replaced by Freudian biopsychology.[39]

3. His claim that his work is an *"empirical* monograph," that his theory consists of "empirically verified conclusions," and that his "propositions have been based upon facts" is also baseless. In all 817 arid pages of his volume one meets hardly one "oasis" of statistical, experimental, clinical, or historical facts. The most striking feature of this allegedly "empirical monograph" is, rather, a complete absence of empirical facts. His examination of the theories of Weber, Pareto, Durkheim, and Marshall—which examination he regards as empirical confirmation of his theory—does not confirm Parsons' propositions on the basis of the relevant facts investigated by Parsons himself. His examination of these theories, like any such examination, merely outlines (rightly or wrongly) these theories and the empirical facts in them dug out by their authors to corroborate *their* theories and not those of Parsons. He can accept or reject, as he does, some portions of these theories, but such an acceptance or rejection has nothing to do with empirically verifying his propositions or with "basing them upon facts"; it is simply an expression of his agreement or disagreement with these theories and *their* facts or as assertion of his belief as to *their* adequacy or inadequacy. This is something entirely different from Parsons' contention that his theory is empirically verified and confirmed by facts. A more accurate statement would be that, in his opinion, some portions of the theories of these scholars appear to him correct and confirmed by their empirical evidence.

4. Another general characteristic of Parsons' theory is the peculiar dualism and contradictoriness between, on the one

---

[39] At the end of *The Structure of Social Action* (p. 762), Parsons drops this term from his "three great classes of theoretical systems."

hand, his criticisms of positivism, utilitarianism, empiricism, and naturalistic and physicalistic sociology, economics, and social science—in their substantive theories, methods, and philosophical presuppositions—and, on the other, his own methods, concepts, and philosophical premises. Despite his criticisms, he himself, in constructing his model and in his conceptual definition of social action, systematically imitates the models, the concepts, and the definitions of mechanics and other branches of physics, not to mention his imitation of the models, concepts, and propositions of positivism, empiricism, naturalism, and utilitarianism that otherwise are severely attacked by him. A few examples of his imitation of the concepts, models, and propositions of classical mechanics were given in Chapter 3 (his "principles of inertia," of "action and reaction," of "equilibrium," and his formula of social action). In the subsequent analysis of his theory, further examples of this peculiar contradiction between his critical observations and his own practice will be given. Here it is enough to point out the contradiction, for it is bound to vitiate his whole theory since this theory is built on *imitative* conceptual material and methodological procedures of natural science, which, according to Parsons himself, are unsuitable, insufficient, and often inapplicable to the study of social phenomena.

5. One more remark is in order concerning this expository part of Parsons' work. Though, all in all, his analysis of the theories of Durkheim, Weber, Pareto, Marshall, Tönnies, and Marx is discerning and insightful, his concept of the criticized "positivism" has little to do with the positivism of Comte, Spencer, Littré, and of other leaders of positivistic sociology and philosophy. Parsons' "positivism" is a straw man created by Parsons and easily knocked down (see I. S. Kon, *Positivism in Sociology,* Leningrad, 1964). The same is true of Parsons' utilitarianism: It has little in common with the utilitarianism of Bentham, Mill, Spencer, and other leaders of utilitarian ethics, politics, and psychosocial sciences. Similar shortcomings mar Parsons' criticism of "empiricism" and his characterization of science and scientific methods as well as of idealistic, rationalistic, materialistic, and other types of philosophy. As he rambles over these vast fields, he drops here and

there observations that are, at best, questionable, at worst, incorrect.

6. This feature leads to another characteristic of Parsonian thinking and writing: a most complicated, sometimes unintelligible formulation of his ideas, expecially those concerned with his "analytical" propositions. A typical example of Parsonian abracadabra is given by his analytical definitions of *unit* and *element*:

> A *unit* in a concrete system is an entity which constitutes the common reference of a combination of statements of fact made within a frame of reference in such a way that the combination may, for purposes of the theoretical system in question, be considered an adequate description of an entity which, within the frame of reference, conceivably exists independently. The theoretical unit is the specific combination of logical universals in specific logical relations to each other into which these statements of facts are fitted. . . . An analytical *element* is any universal (or combination of universals) of which the corresponding values (or combination of values) may be stated as facts which in part determine a class of concrete phenomena. "Determine" here means that a change in these values within the framework of the same universal(s) involves a corresponding change in the concrete phenomena in respects important to the theoretical system.[40]

I must frankly confess that these definitions appear to me completely meaningless. If I had not had an idea of the meaning of unit and element, I would never have guessed that these lines defined them. For experimental verification of this conclusion I read these lines to a physicist, a biologist, and a sociologist (omitting the words unit and element) and asked them to guess what phenomenon or concept they defined. After a second reading, all three failed to guess correctly, and all declared that the words had no meaning at all. I am reasonably certain that if this experiment is repeated by other sociologists, the results are likely to be quite similar. Parsons' predilection for expressing platitudinous ideas in a ponderously complicated form—and his bent for unintelligible "analytical theorizing"— vitiate greatly the clarity of his ideas, the exact meanings of his

[40] *Structure of Social Action*, p. 35.

terms, and the adequacy of his definitions and theories.[41] It also makes exceedingly difficult a correct outlining of his concepts in a concise form. In the subsequent examination of Parsons' theory, attention will be paid only to those parts of his action schema that are intelligible—that is, amenable to analysis and verification.

7. As Parsons correctly remarks, "the origin of the mode of thinking in terms of the action schema is so old and so obscure that it is fruitless to inquire into it here."[42] Particularly strong have been the interpretations of all conscious human actions in teleological terms of "means and end" in the nineteenth and at the beginning of the twentieth century. Many psychologists, theorizers of law, sociologists, and educators have viewed all social action as oriented to the achievement of an end, purpose, or goal.[43] Parsons' theory of social action is

---

[41] This serious defect has been stated and severely criticized by many distinguished sociologists, including G. Gurvitch, L. von Wiese, E. Faris, C. Wright Mills, and others. It is largely responsible for such assessments of Parsons' theories as being mainly "vicious circles and empty and pretentious verbal formulae" (Gurvitch); as arid vagueness "often taken for wisdom" (von Wiese); as "about 50 percent verbiage, 40 percent well-known textbook sociology, and only 10 percent of possible—although rather vague—ideological use" (C. W. Mills); as pretentious "revelations" that Parsons "does not spell out clearly and the reader is left to discover for himself" (J. F. Scott), and so on. See Gurvitch, "Le concept de structure sociale," *Cahiers Internationale de Sociologie*, XIX (1955), 21–31; L. von Wiese, "Ein Neues Amerikanisches Sammelwerk," *Kölner Zeitschrift fur Soziologie*, 5(1952–1953), 87–98; C. W. Mills, *The Sociological Imagination* (New York, 1959), p. 49; E. Faris, his review of Parsons' *Social System*, *ASR*, *18*(1953), 18; and J. F. Scott, "The Changing Foundations." This kind of "analytical thinking" has probably been partly responsible for the recent proliferation of "analytical verbiage" in American sociology. Many American sociologists have become engaged in producing hundreds of senseless, fantasmagoric, and illogical "analytical theories" of all sorts. It is regretful that this part of Parsons' theorizing has been imitated more than the correct part, which is the valuable part.

[42] *Structure of Social Action*, p. 51.

[43] See on the earlier adherents of this sort of action schema R. C. Hinkle's article "Antecedents of the Action Orientation." Among special monographs dealing with social actions see R. Ihering's *Der Zweck im Recht* (2 vols.; Leipzig, 1877–1883), E. de Roberty's *Sociologie de l'action* (Paris, 1908), and D. Draghicesco's *L'ideal createur* (Paris, 1914). This last work is one of the best studies of purposeful action and motivation and of their role in human conduct and social life.

just one of the variations of this powerful, teleological stream of psychosocial thought. Of many theories that shaped Parsons' action schema, Max Weber's theory seems to have exerted a particularly strong influence. Of all the recent theories of social action Znaniecki's theory is possibly most similar to Parsons' action schema. Stripped of their secondary differences and the peculiarities of Parsons' style, the essential framework of both theories is quite similar.[44]

After these preliminaries we can now turn to examination of the main framework of Parsons' study, which is an analysis of the "structural aspect of systems of action, in a certain sense their 'anatomy.' "[45]

● Parsons' Concept of Unit Act and Action System

Parsons, imitating the "units of a mechanical system in the classical sense," defines, first of all, the smallest "unit act" of the action system:[46]

[This "unit act"] involves logically the following: (1) It implies agent, an "actor." (2) For purposes of definition the act must have an "end," a future state of affairs toward which the process of action is oriented. [In this sense, the schema of action is teleological.] (3) It must be initiated in a "situation" of which the trend of development differs . . . from the state

---

[44] Whether this similarity is due entirely to independent development of their theory by both sociologists or whether Parsons was influenced by Znaniecki's *Method of Sociology*, which he approvingly mentions twice in his volume (pp. 30 and 773), can be answered only by Parsons himself.

[45] *Structure of Social Action*, p. 39.

[46] These imitative mechanistic-physicalistic analogies are used throughout Parson's treatise much as organismic analogies were used by the organismic sociologists. Unfortunately, they help to clarify Parsons' concepts as little as organismic analogies helped to clarify organismic theories. By this feature, Parsons' theories can be classified as a variety of physicalistic-mechanistic theories. Some of his analogies, like the comparison of Weber-Parsons' (very doubtful) "law of increasing rationality" with the second law of thermodynamics,˙ are amusing rather than enlightening. *Structure of Social Action*, pp. 751–752.

of affairs to which the action is oriented, the end. This "situation" is in turn analyzable into two elements: "the conditions" over which the actor has no control and "the means" over which he has a control. Finally, (4) . . . there is a "normative" orientation of action [meaning by it "the choice of alternative means to the end" by the actor].

Further on we are informed that "an end is a future state of affairs to which action is oriented" and "a norm is a verbal description of the concrete course of action regarded as desirable." Parsons goes to define act as a "process in time. . . . The time category is basic to the scheme. The concept end always implies a future reference. . . . A normative orientation of action implies the possibility of 'error' in the choice of the means to the end:"

> The frame of reference of the schema is subjective. . . . It deals with phenomena as they appear from the point of view of the actor whose action is being considered. . . . Action is rational insofar as it pursues ends possible within the conditions of the situation, and by the means which, among those available to the actor, are intrinsically best adapted to the end for reasons understandable and verifiable by positive empirical science.

The main difference between the voluntaristic theory of action and the positivistic, empiricistic, and utilitarian ones is that, according to Parsons, "a voluntaristic system involves elements of a normative character" that are either completely or partially ignored by the positivistic and utilitarian theories.[47] To complete Parsons' "action frame of reference," his distinction of "unit" from "element," "emergent" from "elementary properties," "the descriptive" from the "analytical" levels of this schema need to be mentioned.[48] In an "analytical" sense, these elements of the unit act are neither concrete components nor phenomena in the empirical sense, nor are they subject to change. They are "analogous to the space-time framework of

---

[47] *Ibid.*, pp. 43–86.
[48] *Ibid.*, pp. 748–753. I leave to the reader of Parsons' volume the pleasure of deciphering the exact meanings of these crossword puzzles.

physics," so they represent a bunch of concepts each of which is necessary for the concept of action, and none of which can be "thought away" without making the concept of action unthinkable. (This is like saying that a concept of three straight lines meeting two by two in three points is necessary for the geometrical concept of the triangle.)[49]

CRITICISM

Parson's theory of action has all the defects of Znaniecki's theory and several additional ones.

1. Its first shortcoming is the extremely equivocal character of almost all the componential concepts of his action schema. Its "smallest unit act" is undefined or, as we have seen, is given the meaningless "abracadabra" definition of unit. In no way can this unit be compared with the particle or atom in physics; with the units of force, work, power, and energy in mechanics; with element in chemistry; or with the cell in biology. All Parsons' analogies with the "units" of physical and biological sciences are entirely baseless. His unit act cannot even be a generic form or element or prototype of all conscious actions. It is even more indeterminate than Bales' unit act or Moreno's social atom discussed before.

Parsons unit act, consisting of situation plus actor, plus conditions, plus means-end, plus norm, plus symbolic expression of Normative Elements,[50] plus time, plus additional F, L constituents, represents a complex compound of various actions similar to a chemical compound, like H_2SO or HCO_2H, or even a more complex compound, none of which can be taken for the simplest or generic "unit" or common constituent of all chemical bodies. In biological terms, his unit act is comparable not to a cell as the simplest generic model of organisms but to one of the multicellular species. To sum up, Parsons' unit act is neither the smallest nor the simplest constituent; it is a complex bunch of properties of different actions (purposeful,

---

[49] *Ibid.*, pp. 731–737.
[50] See Parsons' shorthand formulas of his unit act, *ibid.*, pp. 77–79.

normative, voluntary, and fundamental, complicated by the addition of two kinds of situational conditions, temporal and emergent, each of which, as we shall see, is poorly defined). So much for the unit act at this point.[51]

Parsons' "means-end" schema is interpreted in different ways: now as a strictly purposeful and voluntaristic action in which the actor deliberately sets forth a future goal and selects the means for its achievement; now in the sense of preceding action and its consequent results, regardless of any purposeful motivation; now in the sense of preceding cause and subsequent effect; now as meaning rational or logical actions (in the Weberian and Paretian senses); now as the conditions over which the actor has a control. In brief, what it actually means is never specifically defined.

The same is true of Parsons' concept of "norm" and "normative" action. In some cases it is used in the sense of law norm (though Parsons nowhere tries to define law norm); in other cases norm is defined as "a verbal description of the concrete course of action regarded as *desirable*," and normative as "applicable to an aspect, part or element of a system of action if, and only insofar as, it may be held to manifest a sentiment attributable to one or more actors that something is an end in itself regardless of its status as a means to any other end (1) for the members of a collectivity, (2) for some members of it, or (3) for the collectivity as a unit."[52] In still other cases norm is used in the sense of any kind of rule: legal, ethical, aesthetic, technical, etiquette, and so on; in still other cases it is identified with "expectancy" and "expected kind of action" from the partners of interaction. In brief, Parsons' "norms" and "normative" enjoy the liberty of being completely undefined.

---

[51] F. Adler's valiant effort to define "a unit concept for sociology" is much better than Parsons'; nevertheless it still remains undefined by him in his challenging paper "A Unit Concept for Sociology," *AJS*, LXV (1960), 356–364. See also S. M. Greenfield, "A Unit Concept for Sociological Theory," *Indian Journal of Social Research*, December, 1964, pp. 252–260.

[52] *Structure of Social Action*, pp. 75–76. This is another example of Parsons' long-winded, abracadabra pseudo definitions.

His concepts of rationality and rational enjoy a similar freedom. Max Weber uses these terms in at least six different ways; Parsons' uses are no less diversified. Now Parsons vaguely speaks of the "intrinsic rationality of [all? or which kind of?] action" (p. 698); now he excludes rationality from the necessary elements of an action system; now it signifies only a rationality of means; now it covers rationality of ends as well; now it is used in a "subjective" sense different from its "objective" form; now it is identified with Pareto's "logical" actions, in the sense of the adequate means for achievement of an end; now it is used in the strictly "logical" sense of the meaningful consistency of the subject and predicate of a proposition, like two and two make four, or the logical conclusion of a syllogistic premise; now it is given one of the meanings of the rationalistic philosophy; and so on.

No more clearly defined are the "actor" and the "social relations" of the schema. Parsons views an individual or personality as "the totality of observable unit acts described in their context of relation to a single actor" and "social relations" as a "secondary schema" from which "it is quite possible to isolate (conceptually) unit acts" (pp. 745–748). That is about all Parsons says about an individual or personality and "social relations." Like Znaniecki he finally isolates these components or elements from the action system and leaves the disembodied ghost of the action system floating somewhere in a foggy time-space in its "mystical-analytical" form of being. The vagueness and multimeaningfulness of the basic concepts of his unit act doom his whole theoretical superstructure.

2. Its second shortcoming is still more serious: Parsons' "general action schema" in no way can be regarded as a general formula defining the componential structure of, and applicable to, all conscious or social actions. There exist many conscious or social actions that are neither teleological nor normative nor in compliance with the schema of "means-end" nor that combine all the constituents (actor, means-end, normative character, controlled and uncontrolled conditions of "situation," and all the other elements or components) of Parsons' allegedly "indivisible unit act." As a matter of fact, his unit act and action system

represent, and his action schema is applicable to, only a very small portion of conscious human action.

Parsons' claim that his action schema is the "general" action schema and his theory the "general" theory of action is as baseless and inadequate as the proposition: "All human organisms have black hair, blue eyes, weigh 120 pounds, and are 5 feet tall."[53] This proposition correctly describes the properties of a small fraction of the human population. Expanded over the whole human population the proposition becomes fallacious empirically and analytically.

In its extrapolated form Parsons' action system is neither a logical nor an analytic nor an empirical (causal-meaningful) unified system. In its overgeneralized form it is a logical (analytical) and empirical congeries: a pile of concepts or empirical properties, unrelated to one another either logically or causally, and thrown together into a conceptual or empirical hash. Empirically, these properties exist separate from each other (the purposeful means-end actions exist independently from the normative ones and both forms of actions exist independent of many other forms of conscious actions). Logically, teleological (purposeful) actions can exist without any involvement with normative actions, and vice versa. The conception of either class of these actions does not require the conception of the other.

In its limited application, Parsons' formula for the action system represents a correct *description* of a small portion of conscious human actions without any explanation on Parsons' part of how and why these elements of his unit act combined together to produce the actions that are simultaneously teleological plus "voluntaristic" plus normative plus rational (or nonrational) performed in a "situation" part of which is under the control of the actor and so on. Like all purely descriptive propositions, Parsons' descriptive formula cannot be regarded as either an analytical or an empirical "general action schema," nor can it have any heuristic significance. To sum up, in its overextended form, Parsons' action system is an inadequate analytical and

---

[53] See, for a discussion of the logical adequacy of propositions and theories, my *CST*, pp. 29–37.

empirical congeries; in its properly limited form it is a purely *descriptive* shorthand formula whose heuristic value is very limited.[54]

3. Parsons' action schema as a "general theory of action" is neither a correct formula of the structure and properties of all conscious human actions nor of their correct "anatomy and histology." It is but a fairly vague description of the features of a small fraction of conscious actions, without any adequate analytic or empirical explanation of why these features combined together into this variety of actions. The heuristic value of this descriptive schema is very limited—which is made clear by the fact that it is rarely used by Parsons and Parsonians in their studies of concrete empirical realities.

4. The descriptive schema of this particular bunch of actions contains neither phenomenological nor psychological nor

---

[54] At the basis of this and other shortcomings lies Parsons' acceptance of the prevalent teleological interpretations of all conscious actions as purposeful and following the means-end schema. In addition, he identifies such actions with the voluntaristic and normative ones. Leon Petrazycki has clearly demonstrated that not all conscious actions are teleological and that, besides purposeful actions performed "for the sake of achievement of a goal," there are normative and fundamental actions quite different from the purposeful, from each other, and from other forms of conscious actions. In contrast to purposeful actions performed "for the sake of achievement of a future goal," fundamental actions are performed *because* of certain previous events or stimuli, like blushing and mumbling *because* of embarrassment, momentarily reacting by insult *because* of preceding insult, becoming angry *because* of preceding irritation, and so on. "This 'because of' action is different from purposive and normative actions. In the actions of 'because of' there is ordinarily no idea of a future purpose or end." Here man often acts even contrary to his purpose or willed goal: For instance, irritated by the boss's impudence, an employee explodes and gives him a real piece of his mind instead of previously planned purposive action to obtain the boss's benevolence by flattery. Purposive actions often take a considerable time to think of the goal and the means for its realization; meanwhile, we quite often are compelled to act instantaneously to the preceding "stimuli" or events. In most of such situations, we act "impulsively," which is another term denoting the "because of" actions. As a matter of fact, these "fundamental" actions occupy as big a place in the totality of our conscious actions as purposive ones.

Both the purposive and the fundamental actions essentially differ from the *normative* ones. Normative actions, best represented by our law-actions of realizing our legal rights and fulfilling our legal "duties,"

sociocultural properties of this bunch, nor does it give to us a living portrait of this variety of actions. The bunch represents a semicongeries of heterogeneous actions rather than a real causal-meaningful action system. Its conceptual or empirical constituents can be easily separated from one another and empirically exist independently of one another. This particular class of action system is hardly more unified (empirically or meaningfully) into a real system than the class of "vegetables" in botanical taxonomy or class of "game" among the animal species.

5. Parsons' "anatomy and histology" of this particular variety of actions overlooks completely such a general component of all conscious actions as the biophysical media of objectification and transmission to interacting partners of the purposes, means and ends, norms and volitions, and other meanings-values of the actor. Are we to assume that the actors regularly carry on their meaningful interaction through extrasensory perception,

---

are self-sufficient in their motivation and performance in the sense that the deeply interiorized law conviction (norm) is a perfectly sufficient motive for a person's compliance with the norm in the realization of his right and in the discharge of his duty. No other motive or stimulus or purpose is necessary in such normative actions. The appropriate law conduct is performed or propelled entirely by our law convictions with their imperative: "The subject of right is entitled and the subject of duty is obliged" regardless of any purpose or "because of" reason. Frequently, the normative actions of discharging our duties run contrary to our purposive actions aimed at achieving various hedonistic and utilitarian goals. "Duty demands," "duty compels" to sacrifice many goals contradictory to it. Normative action differs from the fundamental ("because of") action by its self-sufficiency and by its definite pattern of compliance with the law norm defining this pattern. In contrast to it, "because of" actions do not have any definite norm or pattern; they may assume any form, depending upon the nature of the preceding stimuli. They are devoid of the specific experience of normativeness (imperative-attributive experience) and of the ascription of duty and right (to the subjects of duty and of right) inherent in the normative actions.

Nondiscrimination of the purposeful, the normative, and the fundamental actions from one another and dumping them all into one pile of teleological "means-end" actions are responsible for Parsons' errors and for the errors of other partisans of mistakenly generalized "means-end" action schema.

See a brilliant analysis of the normative, the purposeful, and the fundamental classes of actions in Leon Petrazycki, *Law and Morality* (Cambridge, Mass., 1955), chs. 2, 3, 4, 5. An abbreviated characterization of his theory of law and morality and of these three classes of actions can be found in my *SCP*, ch. 4, and pp. 44–47.

telepathy, and clairvoyance? Such an assumption can hardly be acceptable, even to Parsons. Yet, his complete neglect of this component makes his "anatomy" of the action system similar to an anatomy of the human organism that says nothing about the heart or lungs or digestive system.

6. Parsons' theory of action also says very little about the actor(s) in his action schema. The actor is merely mentioned as a constituent of unit act and is eventually disattached from the action system and dismissed.

> The concept of "personality" is to be regarded as a descriptive frame of reference for stating the facts of human action. In this sense a personality is nothing but the totality of observable unit acts described in their context of relation to a single actor. The personality schema is another secondary descriptive schema of action.[55]

That is practically all one finds out about the actors and their personalities, their types, their mentality, their behavior, and even their voluntaristic features, means, and ends.

7. Nor does Parsons' theory say much about its central point of study—conscious human actions, including their voluntaristic variety. There is no psychological or morphological or phenomenological or social analysis and classification of human actions and no careful examination of the properties of voluntaristic actions as distinctly different from conscious nonvoluntaristic actions. A taxonomy of actions is completely lacking in this "generalized" theory of action.

8. There is no systematic theory of social or cultural systems. Only tangentially is social group or social system touched on. It is defined as a "plurality of actors" and as a "larger aggregate made up of persons as their unit." The "group schema" is declared "secondary" to the action schema. We are told that "There are no group properties that are not reducible to the properties of a system of action and there is no analytical theory of groups which is not translatable into terms of the theory of action."[56]

---

[55] Petrazycki, *Law and Morality*, p. 746. Parsons' "atomistic" conception of human personality can be seen here.
[56] *Ibid.*, pp. 746–747.

These lines indicate the predominantly nominalistic and atomistic character of Parsons' theory of action. This standpoint naturally prevented Parsons from developing a systemic theory of social groups as well as from constructing a theory of social action. Though the volume is entitled *The Structure of Social Action*, its action schema deals little with social action and concerns itself mainly with the specified "voluntaristic" brand of actions of individual actors.

Parsons' nominalistic-atomistic position is largely responsible also for a lack of any theory of cultural systems in his work. Cultural systems are mentioned only incidentally as "nonspatial and temporal," as consisting of "eternal objects to which the category of time is not applicable," as "not involved in 'process.'" "Concrete spatial objects and temporal events may have a cultural aspect . . . as symbols," he says.[57] We shall not enter here into a discussion of these highly equivocal and somewhat contradictory propositions. These lines sum up about all that is said of cultural systems in this volume.

The most valuable part of the whole volume consists in Parsons' thoughtful examination of Marshall's, Weber's, Pareto's, Durkheim's, and Tönnies' theories and in his criticism of what he calls "positivism," "empiricism," "utilitarianism," "naturalism," and a few other currents of sociological and philosophical thought. Though not new, most of his criticisms disclose the important shortcomings, inadequacies, and errors of these theories.

Parsons' own theory of action systems (or, rather, action congeries) contributes little to the extant knowledge of meaningful human actions, including the social, the voluntaristic, the normative, the purposeful, the rational, and other classes of conscious actions. His action schema is neither a generalized analytical schema nor a generalized empirical formula of any of these classes. It is but a vague description of a particular fraction of meaningful actions in which some of the characteristics of the purposeful, the normative, the voluntaristic, and other classes of actions are combined together into a super-

[57] *Ibid.*, pp. 763–764.

ficially unified bunch or into a congeries of action. Its limited heuristic value is still further decreased by the "analytical abstractions" in which Parsons' presents his ideas. Parsons' *intelligible* abstract propositions rarely touch the prosaic empirical realities of human actions. As a result, his monograph hardly enriches our knowledge of empirical human actions generally and voluntaristic actions particularly in their structural and especially in their dynamic aspects. One does not find any single empirical uniformity or even a "middle-range" empirical generalization concerning a correlation or covariation of action variables. We still have to wait for an adequate generalized theory of social action, its real "anatomy, histology, taxonomy, and physiology." Parsons' valiant effort does not fill this bill.

- ● **Parsons' Theory of Social Systems**

As mentioned, *The Structure of Social Action* hardly even attempts to give anything that can be called a theory of social systems. Fourteen years (from 1937 to 1951) separate the publication of Parsons' theory of social systems from that of his earlier work. During these years, Parsons' views on action systems, social action, and social systems seemingly changed. Just as his theory of action systems happened to be particularly similar to Znaniecki's theory of social action, so his theory of social, cultural, and personality systems turned out to be particularly reminiscent of the theories of earlier social thinkers as reformulated and developed in my works, beginning with the two volumes of my *Sistema soziologii* (Petrograd, 1920), and then, with some modifications and elaborations, my *Social and Cultural Dynamics* (1937), *Sociocultural Causality, Time, Space* (1943), and *Society, Culture, and Personality* (1947). In the period from 1937 to 1951 Parsons' ideas seem to have converged in the direction of mine. While there remains a multitude of dissimilarities between the two conceptual systems, their basic frameworks exhibit a notable resemblance. The table on pages 420–431 outlines the main concepts of both systems, their essentials and similarities. Their main differences will be pointed out later.

Similarities in the Two Conceptual Frameworks of Social Systems

Sorokin's Theory	Parsons' Theory

Meaningful Interaction as the Basic Process

1. "The most generic model of any sociocultural phenomenon is the meaningful (*symbolic*) interaction of two or more individuals. By 'interaction' is meant any event by which one party tangibly influences the overt actions or the state of mind of the other. In the absence of such an influence (unilateral or mutual) no sociocultural phenomenon is possible" [40]. "In its developed forms the superorganic (as personality, social system and cultural system) is found exclusively in the realm of interacting human beings and the products of their interaction" [4–5]. Meanings and values are superimposed upon the biophysical properties of interacting persons" [47].

"The interaction of ego and alter [make] a social system." [15] "In interaction we find the basic process which . . . provides the seed of what on the human level we call personality and the social system. Interaction makes possible the development of culture on the human level and gives culture its significance in determination of action" [17] [*SS* 3]. Interaction or "elementary orientation of action . . . on the human level involves . . . true symbolization. . . . A symbolic *system of meanings* is an element of order 'imposed' as it were on a realistic situation" [*SS* 10–11].

NOTE: The quotations are taken mainly from my *SCP* and *Dynamics*, from Parsons' *The Social System* (Glencoe, 1951), and T. Parsons and E. A. Shils (eds.), *Toward a General Theory of Action* (Cambridge, Mass., 1951). Quotations taken from *The Social System* are marked *SS*; quotations from *Toward a General Theory* indicate just the pages, without "*SS*."

Subjects of Interaction

2. "In homosociology the subjects of interaction are either human individuals (in interpersonal interaction) or organized groups of human beings (in intergroup interaction)" [42].

"Thus the actor-subject of interaction is either: (*a*) personality, or (*b*) a social system (collectivity)" [61, 247].

Trinity of Personality, Society, and Culture

3. "Sociology is a generalizing theory of the structure and dynamics of: (*a*) social systems and congeries; (*b*) cultural systems and congeries; (*c*) personalities in their structural aspect, main types, interrelationships and personality processes" [17]. "The componential structure of sociocultural interaction presents three aspects inseparable from one another, namely: (1) personality as the subject of interaction; (2) society as the totality of interacting personalities, with their sociocultural relationships and processes; (3) culture as the totality of the meanings, values, and norms possessed by the interacting persons and the totality of the vehicles which objectify, socialize, and convey these meanings. . . . None of the members of this indivisible trinity (personality, society, and culture) can exist without the other two. . . . For pedagogical purposes they may be studied separately; but when the analysis of each member of the trinity is concluded, this element must be referred to the triadic manifold, or matrix, in which it exists" [63–64].

"We are concerned with three systems, three modes of organization of the elements of actions; these elements are organized as social systems, as personalities, and as cultural systems. Though all three modes are conceptually abstracted from concrete social behavior, the empirical referents of the three abstractions are not on the same plane" [54].

Three Forms of Meaningful Culture Patterns

4. Cultural "meanings may be classified as follows: (1) *cognitive* meanings, in the narrow sense of the term, such as the meaning of Plato's philosophy or

"It is convenient to distinguish the following three major classes of culture patterns: (1) *Systems of ideas or beliefs.* Although cathexis and evaluation are al-of a mathematical formula . . .; (2) meaningful *values* such as the value of religion, science or health . . . with reference to its realization or rejection; (3) *norms* referred to as a standard, like the norms of law and ethics, norms of etiquette, technical norms, etc. These three classes of meanings are inherent aspects of meaningful (sociocultural) phenomena." [47].

ways present as orientational components, these cultural systems are characterized by a *primacy of cognitive interests.* (2) *Systems of expressive symbols*, for instance, art forms and styles. These systems are characterized by a primacy of *cathectic* interests. (3) Systems of *value orientations.* "Evaluation rests *on standards* which may be either cognitive standards of truthfulness, appreciative standards of appropriateness or moral standards of rightness." [8, 5].

The Concept of System

5. "The very definition of social interaction points out at once that any group of interacting individuals is first of all a causal-functional unity in which all components are mutually and tangibly interdependent. In any interaction system there is a triple interdependence of one part upon the other important parts, of the whole upon these parts, and of the parts upon the whole interaction system." [147–148].

"The most general and fundamental property of a system is the interdependence of parts or variables." [107].

Cultural System

6. "Cultural phenomena in their relationship to one another can be either integrated (solidary), unintegrated (neutral), or contradictory (antagonistic). They are integrated (solidary) when two or more interacting, that is, causally connected cultural phenomena stand in a *logical or, for art phenomena, aesthetic*

"Cultural patterns tend to become organized into systems. The peculiar feature of this systematization is a type of integration which we may call *consistency* of pattern. Whether it be the *logical* consistency of belief system, the *stylistic* harmony of art form, or the *rational compatibility* of a body of moral rules,

Similarities Table—Continued

consistency with one another. These make cultural systems. Cultural phenomena are *unintegrated when they* are *logically or aesthetically unrelated to one another.* They are *contradictory* (antagonistic) when they are *logically or aesthetically inconsistent* and *contradictory.* (The unintegrated and contradictory cultural phenomena make "cultural congeries.") The integration, lack of integration, and contradiction of cultural phenomena concerns alike all three levels of culture-ideological, behavioral, and material. Not only the meanings, values, and norms can stand to each other in the relationship of logical or aesthetic consistency, unrelatedness, and contradiction, but also the overt actions and the other material vehicles, as far as they articulate and express the respective meanings, values, and norms" [314]. (All four volumes of my *Dynamics,* and *Sociocultural Causality, Space, Time,* and *Society, Culture, and Personality* analyze in great detail—logically and empirically—the structure and change of all systems, supersystems, and congeries from this standpoint of the logical and aesthetic meaningful consistency and the causal-functional relationship.)

the *internal coherence* of a body of cultural patterns is always a crucial problem for the student of culture." "The determination of the extent of the consistency of pattern and deviations from it in a given culture presents serious difficulties for the analyst. The overt, or explicit culture almost always appears fragmentary at first, and its parts seem disconnected. Only under special conditions is explicit systematization carried out by the creators and bearers of the culture themselves" [21, 22, 55]. (As the authors of *Toward a General Theory* and *The Social System* did not go much beyond this general definition of the cultural system, there is no reason to continue the points of similarity in my and the authors' conception of cultural system. As a significant detail, many of the terms used by me, like the "creators and bearers of culture," "systems and subsystems," etc., cropped up in *Toward a General Theory* and *The Social System.*)

Social System and Its Properties

7. "Interaction processes between the parties may be either unorganized, organized, or disorganized" [70]. "Organized in-

"A social system is a system of interaction of a plurality of persons." ["Its characteristics are:]

Similarities Table—Continued

teraction system makes organized social group or social system" [79]. ["It's characteristics are:]

A. Any long existing organized group has to have a minimum of *solidarity* among its most powerful members. Its members interact because of or for the sake of certain meanings-norms-values. . . . In any durable interacting system it is necessary to have a *set of norms-values-meanings obligatory for all,* backed by *power and enforced"* [148]. "Any social system is a group integrated or logically *consistent* in its (main norms, values, and meanings). . . . This consistency is never perfect, but its minimum is found in any group as long as it remains an organized group" [148].

B. "A social group, or social system as a totality of interacting individuals, is organized when its *central set of meanings and values,* as the reason for their interaction, is somewhat *consistent* within itself and assumes the form of norms precisely defining all the relevant actions-reactions of the interacting individuals in their relationship toward one another, the outsiders, and the world at large; and when these law norms are *effective, obligatory,* and, if *need be, enforced* in the conduct of the interacting persons." "In an unfolded form the definition means (1) that these norms determine in detail what *the rights* and *duties* of each member are; what, in regard to whom, when, how much,

A. The value-orientation of the different actors in the same social system must be integrated in some measure in a *common* system. All ongoing social systems do actually show a tendency toward a general system of common cultural organization. The sharing of value-orientation is especially crucial, although consensus with respect to systems of ideas and expressive symbols are also very important determinants of stability in the social system" [23, 24]. "It is this integration by common values, manifested in the action of *solidary* groups or collectivities which characterizes . . . integrations of social systems" [203]. "The primary integration of the social system is based on an integrated system of generalized patterns of value-orientation" [203]. "A social system must be coherently organized and not merely random assortment of its components" [25]. It has "the inherent limitation on the compatibility of parts within the same system" [107].

B. "Cultural value-orientation . . . in the form of the *general moral consensus* regarding *rights and obligations,* constitutes therefore one fundamental component of the structure of the social system." "Social integration, however much, it depends on internalized norms, cannot be achieved by these alone. It requires some supplementary coordination provided by *explicit prescriptive* or *prohibitory role expectations (e.g., laws)* enunci-

Similarities Table—Continued

and under what conditions each *member* is *entitled* and *obliged* *to do* or *not to do*, *to tolerate* *or not to tolerate*; what are the exact *functions* or *roles* which a member has to play; what his *status* is in the system of interaction as determined by the totality of his rights-duties, functions, and roles. (2) The norms generate the *official law and* *government of the group with its* *legislative, executive, and judi-* *cial functions.* (*'organizational* *and distributive'* or *allocative* functions of meanings-values-norms). (3) By defining rights and duties, roles and functions the norms clearly indicate what relationships or forms of interaction *are to be expected* between the parties: as *obligatory*; as *prohibited*; as *recommended* (not required). (4) Through their definition of the rights-duties, functions (or roles) and status of every member, the norms make a group of interacting individuals into a clearly *differentiated and stratified body*. (5) The group has an economic complex of vehicles (material instrumentalities and values) possessed, used, and operated to carry on the functions of the group and, often, to give to it its means of subsistence. (6) The group ordinarily gets a name, sign, or symbol of its identity. These are the exact characteristics of organized interaction (or social system) in contradistinction from unorganized interaction" [70].

  C. "If any organized group is

ated by actors in specifically differentiated roles to which is attached responsibility in collective terms" [203]. "The most significant unit of social structures is the *role,* or *'status-role.'* The role is that organized sector of an actor's orientation which defines his participation in an interactive process. . . . It involves a set of complementary expectations concerning his own actions and those of others with whom he interacts. Roles are institutionalized when they are . . . organized *around expecta-* *tions of conformity with morally* *sanctioned patterns of value-* *orientation* shared by the members of the collectivity in which the role functions" [23]. "There is the positional aspect—that of where the actor is 'located' in the social system. This is what we call his *status* [*SS* 25]. "A social system is *differentiated system"* [*SS* 114]. "There is always a differentiation of functions within any action system. There must accordingly be an allocation of such functions to different classes of roles. . . . The regulation of all these allocative processes and the performance of the functions which keep the system going . . . is impossible without a *system of definitions* *of roles and sanctions for con-* *formity or deviation"* [25]. There is also "a large proportion of social roles" that are "not minutely prescribed. . . . Sanctions are not invoked against deviance within certain limits" [24]. [My "recommended" and "un-

Similarities Table—Continued

a causal-meaningful unity, this means that it is as a group a real unity different from a mere sum of its components" [149].

D. Social system is *selective*: "it takes only certain elements from the outside world into its components and rejects other elements" [156].

regulated" relationships.—P.S.] "There must also be special institutional mechanisms through which the allocative decisions are made and implemented. The institutional roles to which *power and prestige* are attached play a preponderant part in this process. . . . These *allocative and integrative roles* ["distributive and organizational" in my terminology.—P.S.] may be considered to be an important integrative mechanism of the society" [26]. "The allocation of the facilities necessary to perform functions and the rewards [of power and prestige] cannot be left to an unregulated competitive process" [201]. "They are regulated obligatorily" [25].

C. "The collectivity as an action system is not the simple sum of the actions of the individual actors involved. . . . To the individual actors the collectivity is . . . a social object (thus an alter)" [61]. "The social system in certain respects is independent of particular individual actors" [*SS* 497].

D. "The determination of functions . . . in a social system implies a *process of selection* in accordance with its standards of evaluation" [25, 101].

Change in Social Systems

8. "Any sociocultural system, being a 'going concern' incessantly functioning, inevitably changes as long as it continues

"The order [of a social system] must have a tendency to self-maintenance, which is very generally expressed in the con-

Similarities Table—Continued

to exist and function, even if it is placed in a wholly static environment. The cause of change in a social system is inherent in the system itself." "An additional reason for the change of a sociocultural system is its milieu, which is made up mainly of a multitude of other changing systems and forces" [696]. "From the moment of its emergence a social system is a self-changing and self-directing unity that bears in itself the essentials of its life-career. . . . As such it has always a margin of autonomy from the external forces. . . . The external forces exert the following influences: acceleration or retardation, facilitation or inhibition, sometimes even destruction of the social system." "Many investigators term the self-changing and self-directing property of the system equilibrium. While the term has very definite meaning in physical mechanics, it is devoid of meaning when applied to sociocultural phenomena" [154–155].

cept of equilibrium. It may be an ordered process of change. . . . A fundamental potentiality of instability, an *endemic possibility of change is inherent* in this approach to the analysis of social systems." "Changes in the *external* situation of a social system, in its environmental conditions . . . in the social situation of the system (as in its foreign relations) may be cited as the chief *exogenous* factor in change" [231–232]. "Inherent strains in a system result in its change" [*SS* 490 ff.].

9. "In the life process of an incessantly changing group, periods of orderly, lawful change are followed now and then by periods of disorderly, revolutionary sudden upheaval." "In virtually all extensive social groups there is a certain amount of maladjustment in the form of discrepancy between the official law (value-system) and the unofficial law—(value-system) of a part of the members. This mal-

"The present theory is equally concerned with slow cumulative change and with sudden or fluctuating change" [230–231].

"No one system of value orientation with perfect consistency in its patterns can be fully institutionalized in a concrete society. There will be uneven distributions among the different parts of the society. There will be value conflicts and role conflicts. The consequence of such

Similarities Table—Continued

adjustment calls forth the phenomenon of crime. In this sense, crime and punishment are immanent consequences of the existence of organized groups (social systems). . . . The widening discrepancy between the official and the unofficial law-convictions (value-systems) of some of its members now and then assumes extraordinary proportions. . . . An unbridgeable chasm appears between the system of values of the partisans of the official law and that of its opponents. . . . If the official system of values is not changed peacefully, its opponents strive to overthrow it by violent, unlawful, revolutionary methods" [481].

imperfect integration is a certain instability. . . . Any society in which the allocations create or maintain dissatisfactions will be open to change" [231–232].

10. "As much as a social system is a causal-functional and meaningful unity, so far an *essential change* in *one of its parts leads to a respective change in its other important parts*. A change in the parts alters the whole group and the change of the group as a whole alters its important elements" [154]. "The situation is analogous to a large number of anatomical, physiological, psychological and sociocultural changes experienced by an organism when it passes from childhood to maturity; weight and stature increase, muscles, glands and organs undergo important anatomical and physiological changes. All these proceed interdependently, in togetherness, as manifestations of

"There is no inherent reason why 'the *motive force*' of social change in *general* has to be sought in *any one sector* of the social system or its culture. The impetus to a given process of change may come from an evolution of 'ideas.' It may come from secular changes in climate. It may center in shifts in the distribution of power or in technological development. . . . The theoretical generalization of change will in all probability *not* take the form of a 'predominant factor theory,' such as an economic or an ideological interpretation, but of an analysis of the modes of interdependence of different parts of the social system. From such hypotheses it should be possible to predict

Similarities Table—Continued

the basic change of the whole organism. It is ridiculous to separate out of these interdependent changes one factor like the appearance of a mustache as the cause of all the other changes. . . . In biology the absurdity of this procedure is evident. Unfortunately, it seems not so evident in the similar change of sociocultural systems or super-systems. The Marxians persist in regarding 'the economic mustache' as the cause of all the other changes in the system, including the change of religion and ethics; while the Weberians find the cause of all the other changes in 'the religious weight' or 'the gland of the *Wirtschaftsethik.*' The same is true of all theories of the specific main factor of a change of social or cultural systems (in contrast to sociocultural congeries where such a mechanical use of the 'independent-dependent variables' is possible). Actually the fallacy of Marxian and Weberian theories is clearly demonstrable. The basic fallacy of these theories is that they do not distinguish between the change in systems and congeries. Both theories treat their 'economic' and 'religious' factors atomistically, as congeries in regard to one another. They naturally arrive at the 'mustache theory' of factors of change" [657–658].

"No generalization can be made as to the order of change among subsystems (of a larger

that a certain type of change . . . have specifiable types of consequences" [233]. [Several other generalities about the change of social systems, such as "the plurality of possible origins of change, due to interdependence of a plurality of variables," "cycles and rhythms" in change, "direction of change," "togetherness of change," "the limits in the direction of change," etc., developed in *The Social System* are but a vaguer delineation of what is systematically analyzed and empirically tested in my works in a fully developed form. Cf. *SS* 490 ff.—P.S.]

Similarities Table—Continued

system). It is unlikely that any subsystem uniformly leads or lags. In a complex system functioning in a dynamic environment, there seems to be no logical reason why change should always affect one and the same subsystem first or another last. The logical considerations are supported by observations of comparatively simple systems. A 'pathological' change in a car does not always begin with the same part, say, battery or spark plugs. Disease strikes some human organisms first in the lungs to spread later to other organs; in others a disease begins first in the digestive organs or heart or nervous system or other organs. Such a lack of uniformity (with their respective factors) must be expected still more in sociocultural systems which are more complex, more dynamic, and more subjected to the changing conditions of their milieu" [661–662].

"If and when it is ascertained that certain processes of a given social group or cultural system are rhythmic, and when the phase structure of the respective rhythms is known (whether it is a two-, or three-, or four-phase rhythm, whether it is periodical, etc.), it can be expected that the phase of rhythms and the rhythms themselves will continue to occur in their ascertained order, so long as the systems retain their essential character. . . . Respectively the oncoming phases can be predicted" [687].

Similarities Table—Continued

Personality-System

11. In my works there is laid down a systematic analysis of the mental (its unconscious, conscious, and superconscious forms) and sociocultural structure and dynamics of personality as a microcosm reflecting the sociocultural macrocosm. Specifically, (*a*) the structure of the "ideological and behavioral" culture of personality; (*b*) how much the total culture of the individual is integrated, unintegrated, and disintegrated; (*c*) plurality of the egos (roles) in the individual; (*d*) their harmony and conflict as a consequence of harmony or conflict of the groups the individual is affiliated with; (*e*) dynamics of personality and parallelism of social, cultural, and personality processes; and so on, [*SCP*, chs. 17, 18, 19, 48; *Dynamics* IV, ch. 16; *The Ways and Power of Love*, chs. 5, 6, 7.]

Parsons is rather parsimonious in his systematic analysis of mental and sociocultural structure and dynamics of personality. Besides a cursory analysis of the needs and psychological processes in the individual along somewhat eclectic—Freudian, utilitarian, hedonistic and other lines—the generalities he gives, as, for instance, that each individual is a member of several social systems, that he is a "bundle of a plurality of statuses and roles," that these statuses and roles may be in conflict with one another, and so on, are similar to the theory of personality as a sociocultural microcosm developed in my works.

12. There are several more detailed concordances. They follow from the basic similarity of the main framework of the inseparable trinity of the social, cultural, and personality systems in the sociocultural universe.

The similarity of the two conceptual frameworks is as great as that between Parsons' theory of social system and any recent —sociological, anthropological, or psychological—theory in this field. Parsons' new framework shows a very tangible departure from the seminominalistic and singularistic standpoint of his *Structure of Social Action* with its "unit act" and its voluntaristic "means-end schema." This standpoint and schema are now practically abandoned in favor of a more "generalized" level of analysis (*SS* 9), and the Weberian seminominalistic and singularistic framework of actions, actors, and roles is replaced by a more adequate "realistic" framework of social system, cultural systems, and personality system, or by the "whole play," of which roles, actions, and actors are but components.

● Dissimilarities in the Two Theories

Side by side with the basic similarities, there is a multitude of dissimilarities between the two sociological theories compared. One of the reasons for the dissimilarities is Parsons' uncompleted transition from his previous largely nominalistic position to the new systemic one. The "sins" of his earlier framework continue to visit upon, crop in, and vitiate the new version of his theory. The incompatible elements of his earlier and later theories clash and hinder their logical integration into one system. This eclecticism is the main defect of the later versions of his theories, which still remain in a state of flux, even after the publication of the discussed two volumes on social systems. Without following all the latest modifications of Parsons' theories (some of which show a regression to his earlier "schema"), the following defects of his theory of social systems can be briefly mentioned.

1. His theory is full of "analytical" abstractions little related to concrete sociocultural facts.[58] Only occasionally do his abstractions condescend to empirical social groups and cultural and personality systems, and then only for the purpose of illustrating his concepts and hardly ever for systematically verifying

---

[58] "We deliberately decided to forego documentation by references to relevant literature . . ." and—the authors could add—to relevant empirical facts. Parsons and Shils, *Toward a General Theory of Action*, pp. 51–52. This and subsequent criticisms apply also to Parsons' "Evolutionary Universals in Society," *ASR* (1964), 339–357, and to *An Outline of the Social System*, in which the already vague strategic concepts of previous works are still more confused by new rewordings of these concepts and by self-contradictory propositions, some of which are mentioned below and in Chapter 17 of this work.

his propositions. For this reason, his abstractions help little either in analyzing empirical sociocultural facts or in understanding their nature, structure, interrelationships, change, and uniformities. Parsons indefatigably piles his abstractions, classifications, paradigms, and figures one upon another; and yet, so far, their heuristic fruitfulness remains undemonstrated. One can study and memorize by heart his "set of five dichotomies," his "four different levels of systematization of conceptual schemes," his "several types of actions," his "cultural systems," "value orientations," and, still more detailed and numerous, his "figures and classifications" of "components of action," "pattern variables," "need-dispositions," "role-expectations," "object-systems," "primary mechanisms of adjustment," "instrumental complexes," and so on.[59] And yet, a knowledge of these terms hardly enriches one's understanding of the realities of empirical social groups, cultural configurations, and human personalities, simply because the logical nature of most of these abstractions is vague: The definitions of class phenomena often fail to indicate their genus and *differentia specifica*; classifications are haphazard and devoid of an adequate *fundamentum divisionis*. They overlap and crisscross one another. His "grouping of choice pattern variables" can serve as an example of these abstractions. It represents a logical hash of "value-orientations," "focus of social value systems," which are subdivided into "universalism-particularism" and "ascription-achievement" and are combined with "collective-self-orientation," "diffuseness-specificity," "neutrality-affectivity," "focus of personal value system," and "motivation-orientation."[60] A no less logical and empirical potpourri is Parsons' classification of the "integrative" and "allocative" mechanisms for solving external and internal problems. The accompanying vocabulary includes cognitive learning, reality testing, inhibition and evaluation, substitution, displacement, fixation, and cathectic learning.[61] These and similar tautological

---

[59] See a veritable orgy of abstractions, classifications, paradigms, and figures in Parsons and Shils, *Toward a General Theory of Action*, pp. 245–275.

[60] *Ibid.*, p. 253.

[61] *Ibid.*, p. 255.

classifications (Is there any "learning" that is not "cognitive"?) make the old Linnaean botanical taxonomy seem perfectly adequate.

These defects are increased by the vagueness of Parsons' basic concepts: "society," "role-expectation," "conformity with, and deviation from the normative patterns," "equilibrium," and so on.

Parsons defines society, as opposed to a collectivity, as a self-sufficient group. Aristotle's definitions of the family, the village, and the city-state point to self-sufficiency as the *differentia specifica* of the city-state.[62] Aristotle's concept of a self-sufficient society clearly indicated the specific empirical group (the Greek city-state) that it had in view. In the historical conditions of ancient Greece, his definition was empirically clear and correct. In contrast to this, Parsons' and Levy's definition of society as a self-sufficient group does not define clearly what kind of social group in the present historical conditions is a "self-sufficient society." Nothing, with the possible exception of an isolated primitive group, neither the present family nor village nor city nor state, is a self-sufficient body. All must satisfy their needs through economic, political, religious, scientific, educational, and cultural interchanges with other people, cities, regions, states, and nations. Until Parsons tells us which of the numerous empirical groups of our time are self-sufficient, his definition of society becomes void and so also does his definition of collectivity.

Still more indefinite are his "role expectations" and "deviations from normative patterns" of social systems. His category of "role expectations" does not differentiate clearly the role of "lawful" expectations, which are based upon the rights and duties of the parties prescribed by law norms, from all the other role expectations to which the parties are neither entitled nor obliged by the law norms. The psychological, the social, and the legal functions of these two kinds of role expectations are profoundly different from each other. Only the "legal" role expectations are obligatory and enforced, only their violation is pro-

---

[62] Aristotle, *Politics*, Bk. I, ch. 1.

hibited and punished, while all the other—comparatively un-important—role expectations are left to be handled by the parties themselves, or by chance, because *de minimis non curat lex.* The psychological experience of these two "expectations" is also profoundly different.

The fulfillment or violation of our "legal" role expectations basically differs from the fulfillment or violation of our "extra-legal" or "fanciful" role expectations. Parsons ascribes to the fanciful or extralegal expectations the properties of the legal ones on the one hand, and smothers these properties in the vague category of role expectations on the other. At any rate, his role expectations is a poor substitute for the incomparably clearer concept of law norms with rights and duties allotted by them to the parties involved, regardless of any "expectation." The term expectation is never mentioned in the codes of law norms, which remain obligatory regardless of whether the respective action is expected or not. There is no excuse for identifying the expected with the obligatory and the nonexpected with the reprehensible.

The same is true of Parsons' category of "deviation." Not every deviation from all the prevalent normative patterns in a given group is unlawful, prohibited, or criminal, as Parsons' concept of deviation seems to imply. Only deviation from or transgression of the obligatory patterns of the law norms is un-lawful. Each of us has a wide margin for deviating from many prevalent fashions, fads, tastes, sports, ideologies, philosophies, and other normative patterns popular or dominant in the United States. And neither law-enforcing agencies, nor public opinion, nor organizations, nor our neighbors regard such deviations as unlawful, criminal, or reprehensible. In any organized group there is always a wide margin for deviation.

Among the terms he borrows from the physical sciences, Parsons is especially fond of "equilibrium," which he takes to mean the stability, order, and continuity of the social system. Instead of adequately describing how and why social systems originate, become organized, differentiated, and stratified; how and why they change in orderly and disorderly ways; how they maintain their identity and sameness; how and why they fluctuate in their growth and decline; what their comparative life-span is—instead, in other words, of giving an adequate "physiology" of social systems, Parsons offers his doubtful manipulations with the term equilibrium.[63] One example of such an operation was given in Chapter 3. Other manipulations with equilibrium occur throughout Parsons' works and none is any more felicitous than the example discussed there. It remains poorly defined and its fruitful application to the study of social phenomena is never demonstrated.[64]

The shortcomings of Parsons' "*constructions fantaisistes*" (in Durkheim's term) are increased by the confusion of his ever-changing psychological theories: Voluntaristic, rational, Freudian, and behavioristic psychologies pop out one after another in his various schemas.

With his inquisitive and discerning mind Parsons himself seemingly understood the deficiencies of each new version of his theory. One of these new versions represents a scheme of four levels of structural organization: the primary, the managerial, the institutional, and the societal. Subsequently, these levels are transformed into four main dimensions of system structure and process: the external-consummatory (called "goal-attainment"); the external-instrumental (called "adaptation"); the internal-consummatory (called "integration"); the internal-instrumental (called "pattern-maintenance and tension-management").[65] There is no need to go into the details of this new schema. Logically, it makes "goal-attainment" something basically different from "adaptation," which consists in part of "goal-attainment activities" and has its own ends.

The schema's separation of the instrumental from the con-

---

[63] See an analysis of the main "physiological" processes of social systems in my *SCP*, chs. 21–34.

[64] See, on the five different meanings of this term and on the fruitlessness of its application in sociology, my presidential address at the Thirteenth International Congress of Sociology: "Le concept d'equilibre: est-il nécessaire aux sciences sociales?, *Revue Internationale de Sociologie*, September–October, 1936. In an abbreviated form, this address is reprinted in the *Dynamics*, Vol. IV, pp. 677–693.

[65] T. Parsons, "General Theory in Sociology," in R. Merton, L. Broom, and L. Cottrell, Jr. (eds.), *Sociology Today* (New York, 1959), pp. 3–38.

summatory similarly overlaps. It is but another variation on MacIver's dichotomic division of "values-as-ends" and "values-as-means." If one went along with this schema, then all the "pattern-maintenance" and "tension-management" activities of governments, corporation executives, and individuals would seemingly have no "goals" and have to be declared purposeless activities, and so on. Logically, the categories are overlapping; a subspecies is confronted with its species; some of the purposeful activities are classified as "goal-less" or put into a separate class of "integration," and vice versa. Empirically, the fruitlessness of this classification is well displayed by Parsons' illustrative application of it to the nuclear family. We are told that:

> The differentiation of familial roles by generation is a special case of the external-internal differentiation in its hierarchical version, with the paternal generation performing the "external" roles; differentiation by sex is a special case of the instrumental-consummatory line of differentiation. In this case the masculine role performs, for the family as a system, primarily instrumental functions, whereas the functions of the feminine role are primarily consummatory.[66]

The correct part of this ponderous statement is much better expressed in an old platitude: In the family the husband is ordinarily the "secretary of foreign affairs" while the wife is the "secretary of the interior." If the rest of the statement were correct we would express our sympathy for the unfortunate males allotted only the burdensome "instrumental roles" and "means-values" and would congratulate the happy females alloted mainly the pleasurable "consummatory roles" and "ends-values"! I doubt however that an overwhelming majority of males and females would agree with this statement. It is empirically incorrect and quite one-sided.

To sum up, this latest schema is hardly better in its cognitive fruitfulness than most of the preceding schemas. If, in the terms of E. Mach, a scientific theory is an adequate adaptation of its ideas to the respective empirical reality and of the ideas themselves to one another, these "schemas" hardly achieve either

[66] *Ibid.*, pp. 9–10.

one of these adaptations. This, perhaps, is the reason why the schemas are rarely or only superficially mentioned in the empirical studies of Parsons himself.

Parsons' essay on Christianity[67] is a good example of how little he uses his schemas to analyze concrete empirical problems and how his empirical theses disregard those facts that contradict his proposition. In this article, his hypothesis and arguments are formulated in the "ordinary" terms of historical and sociological studies, and his schemas and their terms are hardly used at all in his interpretation of the evolution of Christianity. In a genuine spirit of "creatively important differences of opinion," Parsons challenges my theory of the decline of institutionalized Christianity with the rise and domination of the sensate supersystem in European culture during the last four or five centuries. Parsons' challenging thesis is that the process of increasing "control, if not [the] shaping, of secular society in the interest of Christian ideals" has been and still is a basic process in the historical life of Christianity and of the Western world.

This is not the place to examine critically his thesis and his arguments.[68] It is enough to note here that the development of both Christianity and Western society is described by Parsons not in the terms of his "schemas," but in the ordinary terms of historical works that deal with these problems.

As to the substance of his challenging hypothesis, suffice it to say that he hardly succeeds in undermining either my theory of the decline of Christianity with the rise and domination of the sensate supersystem, or Nietzsche's, Weber's and Troeltsch's, or Spengler's, or Schubart's theories of the decline of Christianity after the seventeenth century. Logically, Parsons' argument is similar to the argument that the best way to eliminate crime is to declare all crimes legal.

By a similar logic, that is, by declaring many non-Christian

[67] T. Parsons, "Christianity and Modern Industrial Society," in E. A. Tiryakian (ed.), *Sociological Theory, Values, and Sociocultural Change: Essays in Honor of Pitirim A. Sorokin* (New York, 1963), pp. 33–70.
[68] This is done in my paper "The Western Religion and Morality of Today," in the *International Yearbook for the Sociology of Religion* (Cologne, 1966), Vol. II.

and anti-Christian secular phenomena the realizations of Christian ideals in modern times, Parsons tries to prove his thesis. Even such phenomena as the liberation of the individual from basic Christian dogmas and from the moral guidance of the Christian Church, the replacement of the Christian aspiration for the City of God by that for the secular City of Man, the increasing replacement of the Christian ethics of love and charity by utilitarian and hedonistic ethics, the decay of monastic ideals, and the establishment of the capitalist system signify, to Parsons, not a decline but a growing realization of Christian ideals and the Christian religion.[69]

His theory is decisively contradicted by a vast body of well-ascertained facts. He himself acknowledges that, in the process of the alleged expansion of the influence of Christian ideals in the secular society, Christianity has suffered many losses: A number of its dogmas, values, and institutions have decayed; others have lost their ethos and pathos; and still others have been replaced by non-Christian or anti-Christian ideals, values, ideologies, and institutions.

My criticism of Parsons' theory shows one additional shortcoming of his schemas: his somewhat cavalier treatment of empirical realities. Because he is so immersed in formulating his various schemas, he hardly ever pays much attention to empirical realities. He has not studied them as carefully and as systematically as they should be studied. The discussed essay displays this shortcoming.

The preceding analysis outlines the essentials of Parsons' theories, their cognitive nature, and their *differentia specifica*. My criticism shows their weak points and serious defects. The net result of this analysis and criticism is that Parsons' theories of social systems do not contribute much either to the physiology

---

[69] These interpretations by Parsons are possibly responsible for the qualification of Parsons' theory by the Soviet sociologists as "the right-wing conception of today's bourgeois ideology in the United States," "serving the vested interests of the power-elite," and propagandizing "unconditional loyalty of all Americans to the dominant economic and political order." H. B. Novikov, "Sovremmenny amerikanski kapitalism i teoria 'sozialnago deystvia' T. Parsonsa," *Voprosy Filosofii*, *3*(1963), 129.

or the taxonomy of social systems. Their contribution lies mainly in the anatomy and histology of social systems. But even in these fields the cognitive value of Parsons' theories is tangibly marred by his "*constructions fantaisistes*" and limited by the defects of his nominal schemas.

CRITICISM OF OTHER ANALYTICAL THEORIES OF SOCIAL SYSTEMS

Parsons' analytical theory is one of a multitude of analytical schemas that have flooded the field of sociology during the last few decades. With a proper modification, the preceding criticisms of Parsons' theories apply to most of the abstract, analytical constructions of social, cultural, and personality systems, of diverse sociocultural processes of dynamics and change, of various typologies of social structures, and, finally, to most of the theoretical schemes about all sorts of sociocultural phenomena that on a mass scale have been manufactured in recent times.

Almost without any important change the criticisms apply to Marion J. Levy's *The Structure of Society*.[70] Levy's conception of social action, social system, and society follows Parsons' conceptual framework. Here and there it adds something "analytical" to it, improves it in some points, and worsens it in other respects. All in all it is more intelligible in its definitions and less cumbersome. Despite this, Levy's conceptions represent definitions of abstractions by abstractions and for abstractions. Logically, they are not always clear, consistent, and adequate. Empirically, due to their vagueness, they are either difficult to apply to a proper empirical reality (social action, system, society) or, when they are applicable, they prove to be deficient. For instance, following Parsons, Levy defines society as:

> a system of action in operation that (a) involves a plurality of interacting individuals of a given species . . . who are re-

[70] (Princeton, N.J., 1952.) See also his "Some Problems for a Unified Theory of Human Nature," in E. A. Tiryakian's *Sociological Theory, Values, and Sociocultural Change*, pp. 9–31. The criticisms apply also to the articles of E. Shils, K. D. Naegele, and J. R. Pitts in Parsons-Shils-Naegele-Pitts, *Theories of Society* (2 vols.; New York, 1961).

cruited at least in part by the sexual reproduction of members of the plurality involved, (b) is . . . *self-sufficient* for the action of this plurality, and (c) is capable of existing longer than the life span of an individual.[71]

Since the trait of self-sufficiency distinguishes Levy's society from his social system, the question arises: Which of the existing social groups is society in Levy's sense? Neither the family, nor village, nor city, nor state, nor nation, nor any other important group is self-sufficient or autarkical in our time: They all have—and need to have—commercial, political, religious, scientific, linguistic, and cultural exchanges with other people and groups. With the exception of, perhaps, a few absolutely isolated primitive or stranded groups, if such groups still exist in today's human universe, 99.9 percent of all contemporary "social systems" are not self-sufficient; therefore, they are not "societies" in Levy's sense. His concept of society is thus largely meaningless in its application to empirical social realities.

On the other hand, according to this definition of society, the whole Roman Catholic hierarchical organization is not a society, because its members are not "recruited by sexual reproduction." No more satisfactory is Levy's definition of a social system, as "any system of social action involving a plurality of interacting individuals . . . ; as any patterned collection of elements." The definition obviously does not distinguish organized groups from nonorganized or disorganized ones or social systems from social congeries: Mob, crowd, and incidental gathering of individuals all are social systems, according to this definition. As a result, the term social system becomes largely meaningless.

Since these basic concepts are logically and empirically deficient, their defects vitiate all Levy's subconcepts that are logically dependent upon them. "Function" and "structure," "functional and structural requisites and prerequisites," "eufunction and dysfunction," "eustructure and dystructure" are all verbal abstractions hardly helpful either for the comprehension of empirical social systems or for the cognitive analysis of social realities. When some of these concepts are somewhat specified, like Levy's four conditions that may terminate a society or the

[71] M. J. Levy, Jr., *The Structure of Society*, p. 21.

"functional requisites" of any society, they are almost always either platitudes or tautologies, a condition aggravated by the fact that he often does not mention some of the important "conditions" and "requisites" or includes "requisites" that are not applicable to all societies. For instance, in discussing the four conditions that may terminate a society, Levy does not mention such common ways as terminating an organized group by the vote of its members or by the elapse of a pre-established time-span or by a radical change in its system of meanings-values-norms. Among the "functional requisites" of any society Levy lists a shared set of goals and a similar cognitive orientation. If we accept these requisites for the continued existence of any social group or system, we have to believe that the prisoners of all prisons share the goals and cognitive orientations of their imprisoners, that slaves share the goals and values of their masters, that the conquered agree with the objectives and values of their conquerors. Since prison societies and the social systems of slaves and masters and of the conquered and their conquerors have existed in many areas of the world for many centuries at a time, and since we are certain that the overwhelming majority of prisoners, slaves, and the conquered have not shared the goals and cognitive orientations of their rulers, this "requisite" is *not* a requisite for the existence and functioning of any and all societies, social systems, or groups. As a matter of fact, all coercive societies of the past and of the present have lived without it.

Similar criticism can be leveled at Levy's other requisites and prerequisites. Instead of analytical speculation about the requisites and prerequisites of the establishment, functions, and termination of a poorly defined abstract society and social system, instead of interpreting these processes in the terms of a mystical equilibrium and disequilibrium, adaptation and maladjustment, eufunction and dysfunction, Levy and other analytical and structural-functional investigators of organized and unorganized social groups could have solved these problems much more adequately by a careful study of the past and present empirical organized groups, particularly their written or unwritten codes of law. These codes, as a rule, clearly define all the relevant conditions, prerequisites, and requisites of their emergence and establishment, their functions, their continuity, and their termination.[72]

By a careful study of the empirical processes of empirical social groups, social scientists have delivered to us an incomparably better knowledge of society than the platitudinous fragments of knowledge delivered by all the analytical and functional theories taken together. Of course, this sort of empirical study requires much more labor, time, and energy than an "analytical" speculation, but the easy way is not always the most fruitful way.

Levy's concepts of "eufunction," "dysfunction," "eustructure" and "dystructure" are defined through their useful or harmful relationship to the society's "adaptation" or "adjustment" or to the "persistence of the (social) unit." No lengthy analysis is needed to understand the essentially subjective and evaluative character of these concepts. Whether the activities of Socrates, Jesus, Washington, and Marx are "eufunctional" or "dysfunctional," whether the movements of the early Christians, the Communists, or the civil-rights workers are the movements of "adaptation" or "maladaptation" of a "society" or "social system" or "social unit," depends upon with which side or with which party we identify ourselves in respective societies. Once we make such an identification, we merely demonstrate our subjective sympathy or bias with the chosen party—which fact hardly increases our knowledge of the sociocultural reality involved. If, on the other hand, we do not make such an identification with one of the parties involved and, generally, do not specify *from whose standpoint and for which party* a given state of affairs appears to be the "eufunction or dysfunction," an "adaptation" or a "maladjustment," these terms become meaningless. Whether we identify or do not identify with one of the parties involved, these inherently subjective and evaluative terms do not increase our knowledge of the "given state of affairs." In both cases they become either meaningless or even "dysfunctional" insofar as they infect by their arbitrariness and subjec-

---

[72] That is exactly the way in which these and related problems are analyzed and typologically generalized in my *SCP*, chs. 21–34 (for social systems) and chs. 35–47 (for cultural systems).

tivity the whole analytical schema in which they play the role of its basic concepts. When these schemas are carefully examined from this standpoint they are found indeed to be arbitrary and subjective despite the powder and rouge of such pseudoscientific terms as equilibrium, function, dysfunction, and the like with which the subjective evaluations of their authors are well covered and beautified for public inspection.

CHAPTER 13

Functional and Psychological ("Nomenclature") Theories of Social Systems

FUNCTIONAL THEORIES

With some modifications, the criticisms in the foregoing chapters apply also to so-called functional theories of social systems. In the chapters dealing with cultural systems, the inadequacies of various "functional" conceptions of cultural systems were discussed. At this point, we can briefly mention the defects of the functional analyses of social systems. R. Merton and M. J. Levy correctly state that "the functional orientation is of course neither new nor confined to the social sciences,"[1] and that "structural-functional analysis . . . has a pedigree that stretches indefinitely far back. . . . The only 'new' aspect of it is its formidable new name, 'structural-functional analysis!' "[2] No less correct is K. Davis' assertion that "for more than thirty years now functional analysis has been debated among sociologists and anthropologists. Perhaps the time has come for the debate to be either settled or abandoned. My view is that it should be abandoned, because it rests on the false assumption that there is a special method or body of theory called functional analysis which can be distinguished from other methods or theories *within* sociology and social anthropology."[3]

[1] R. K. Merton, *Social Theory and Social Structure* (rev. ed.; New York, 1957), p. 46.
[2] M. J. Levy, Jr., *The Structure of Society*, p. 27.
[3] K. Davis, "The Myth of Functional Analysis," *ASR, 24*(1959), 757–758.

The opposite view, which claims that modern functionalism is "a special method and body of theory," is held by some functionalists as well as by some nonfunctionalists, like D. Martindale and P. L. van den Berghe.[4] Whichever *differentia specifica* of functionalism we take—Merton's, Martindale's, Van den Berghe's, Barber's, or Bredemeier's—they all belong to various systemic, integral, organismic, sociologistic, even to some of the singularistic-atomistic currents of sociological thought. The history of the functionalism theories largely coincides with that of the systemic theories as they are outlined in Chapter 5 of this work. None of the specific characteristics, postulates, and elements of functionalism mentioned by Merton and Van den Berghe belongs exclusively to functionalism. Its only new traits are its name and its reformulations of some of the minor propositions of the systemic, the integral, the organismic, and of other centuries-old currents of social thought.

Robert Merton's analyses of the basic problems of functionalism and his theory of reference groups represent one of the best examples of the functionalist theory of social systems or structures. A concise critical examination of his theories in this field can show what is really new in the functionalist theories, whether what is new is scientific, and, if so, whether it significantly contributes to our knowledge of empirical sociocultural realities. Merton's studies of these problems are published in his volume *Social Theory and Social Structure*.[5]

The strongest point of his theory of functionalism consists in his critical examination of the main functional conceptions of recent sociologists and anthropologists. Almost all his criticisms are sound and to the point.[6] The main defects of his own concept of functionalism and of his theory of "reference groups" are the ambivalence of certain essential features of his functionalism; his numerous violations of his own rules of

---

[4] D. Martindale, *The Nature and Types of Sociological Theory*, pp. 446 ff.; P. L. van den Berghe, "Dialectic and Functionalism," *ASR*, 1963, pp. 695 ff. See also D. Martindale (ed.), *Functionalism in the Social Sciences* (Philadelphia, 1965).

[5] Merton published many papers not included in *Social Theory and Social Structure*. In the present volume, only his theory of functionalism and of social system are examined.

[6] Merton, *op. cit.*, pp. 19–50.

scientifically sound functional theory; the teleological and sub-jectively evaluative character of his functionalism; the heuris-tically doubtful nature of his "paradigms" and "codifications"; and the presence of platitudes dressed up as scientific proposi-tions.

1. The ambivalence of Merton's functionalism is well exemplified by his contradictory statements about functional theory as "neither new nor confined to the social sciences" on the one hand, and, on the other, as representing a new approach and as the best brand of scientific sociology today, for which "little of what the early forerunners [specifically A. Comte and H. Spencer] wrote remains pertinent."[7]

If functionalism is "neither new nor confined to the social

---

[7] This ambivalence conspicuously permeates most of Merton's theories. At different places in his volume, he dubs Comte's, Spencer's, and others' "grand systems of sociology" as "speculative systems" and justifiably pleads for "theories of the middle range." He himself formu-lates several theories, "paradigms," and "codifications" far transcending the "theories of the middle range." While his right hand asserts that any "middle-range theory" has to be empirically verified, his left hand writes propositions devoid of any empirical test and confirmation. He demotes Comte's and Spencer's sociological theories to the level of mere "specu-lations," and, at the same time, he extolls some recent "analytical con-jectures" as models of scientific theory—despite this model being devoid of any empirical corroboration and logical elegancy. On the one hand, he declares that the theories of the forerunners of sociology have little pertinency to sociology today; on the other hand, his best essays repre-sent only thoughtful variations on the themes of Durkheim ("anomie"), M. Weber (bureaucracy, science, pietism, and Protestantism), and Scheler, Marx, Mauss, and Freud (sociology of knowledge and person-ality). Despite his dislike of metaphysics, speculation, and nonempirical abstractions, at least one-third of his volume is devoted to *ad hoc* dis-cussions of logical, epistemological, metaphysical, and methodological problems belonging to the fields of logic, methaphysics, and philosophy rather than to the field of sociology. He demands maximal precision and empirical confirmation of a sociological theory, mentions many works (which in fact have neither precision nor empirical evidence) as excel-lent models of such a theory, and passes without mention several works that meet these requirements much better. He attributes several "dis-coveries" to recent sociologists (for instance, the concept of "status" and "role" to R. Linton) that were discovered, precisely formulated, and often incorporated in the codes of law or in social practice centuries ago (as exemplified by the Roman law's excellent formulas of *status libertatis, status civitatis,* and *status familiae*).

These examples illustrate what I mean when I say that a particularly conspicuous trait of Merton's theories is their ambivalence.

sciences," then we must ask why this not-new theory is given a new name, "functionalism," and why it is viewed as a new approach in sociology. If it is a new current of sociological thought, then why does Merton style it an old theory? This sort of contradiction stamps Merton's functionalism in other points.

2. The second defect of his functionalism is that Merton gives this term and its derivatives several different meanings, including meanings that he criticizes in other conceptions of functionalism. His clearest definition of it is as follows: "The central orientation of functionalism (consists) in the practice of interpreting data by establishing their consequences for larger structures in which they are implicated." His functional theory of reference groups "centers on the processes through which men relate themselves to groups and refer their behavior to the values of these groups," whereas his functional sociology "centers on the consequences of these processes, primarily for social structures but also for individuals and groups involved in these structures."[8] If these lines define the specific characteristics of functionalism, then certainly functionalism was born long ago, and Confucius, Lao-tse, Plato, Aristotle, St. Augustine, and almost all the eminent social thinkers of subsequent centuries have been "functionalists," because in their writings and teachings they have tried to interpret their data "by establishing their consequences for larger structures in which they are implicated" (Confucius, Plato, Aristotle for "the state" or their society, St. Augustine for the Roman Empire and the City of Man, and so on), and because their theories "centered" on the same processes and consequences on which Merton centers *his* functional theory of social systems. The trouble with Merton's functionalism is that he uses this term and its derivatives in several other senses: The concept of functional requirement in his writings now tends to be tautological or ex post facto; now tends to be confined to the conditions of "survival" of a given system"; now assumes an explicitly evaluative utilitarian and disutilitarian character in his "functions" and "dysfunctions"; and now is identified with purposeful or rational

---

[8] Merton, *op. cit.*, pp. 46–47, 226, 384.

actions.[9] By giving functional terms these different meanings he not only makes these concepts vague and indeterminate but contradicts his own criticisms of these varieties of functional interpretations.

3. Despite his own warnings against infecting functional theories with subjective evaluations, radical or conservative ideologies, and diverse teleologies, his introduction of the concepts of functions and dysfunctions explicitly makes his system of functionalism subjectively evaluative, arbitrarily ideological, and teleological:[10] "Functions are those observed consequences which make for *adaptation or adjustment* of a given system; and dysfunctions, those observed consequences which lessen the *adaptation or adjustment* of the system."[11] These definitions are evaluative, subjective, and teleological. Are the civil-rights demonstrations of Negroes functions or dysfunctions? Are American, Soviet, and Cuban foreign policies functions or dysfunctions? For what sort of adaptation? For what groups or individuals? For the realization of what sort of values and objectives? In which way can each of these processes be scientifically diagnosed as function or dysfunction? If these questions cannot be answered, then the terms are meaningless. If they can be answered, the terms inevitably become subjectively evaluative and arbitrary (which fact is clearly shown by the opposite evaluations of, say, the civil-rights movement by the Negro leaders of the movement and by Southern politicians). All the criticisms of this point in Levy's theory fully apply to Merton's functions and dysfunctions.

The subjectively evaluative character of Merton's conception of functionalism makes it inescapably teleological.[12] This teleology quite clearly comes out in the first step of functional analysis that he prescribes. According to him, this first step consists in setting "certain functional requirements of organisms

---

[9] *Ibid.*, pp. 52 ff.
[10] *Ibid.*, pp. 30–50.
[11] *Ibid.*, pp. 51.
[12] If Gunnar Myrdal's statement that functionalism "must lead to a conservative teleology" may be questioned in the "conservative" specification of teleology, it is quite correct in the characterization of functional theories as teleological. See Myrdal's *An American Dilemma* (New York, 1944), Vol. II, p. 1050.

(or social systems), requirements which must be satisfied if the organism (or social system) is to survive, or to operate with some degree of effectiveness."[13] So, according to this recipe, if we want to make a functional analysis of a bird, our first problem is to find out what the functional requirements are that enable a bird to survive and fly effectively. I am quite certain that biologists do not follow this recipe in their study of birds, for no biologist can list in advance all the fantastically numerous requirements for survival or effective performance of a single bird under all the different conditions of its life-course. Still less can he compile such a list of requirements applicable to *all* organisms of all species under all the infinitely diverse conditions of their lives. Instead, the biologist studies the anatomical, histochemical, physiological, and behavioral properties of birds and concludes that "Birds fly because they have wings."

Instead of making teleological speculations, biologists make their conclusions about the properties of organisms on the basis of an empirical study of living forms; they formulate their conclusions in matter-of-fact, empirical, and *causal* terms. The same is true of a study of the social system. No scholar can compile a scientifically adequate list of the functional requirements for survival or growth or effective operation of a state, church, family, business corporation, political party, or of any other group before these social systems are carefully investigated. If and when they are studied, then we can scientifically account for the ways, conditions, and means of their survival, growth, and effective operation. No wonder that the teleological speculations of our "functionalists" have yielded hardly any significant results—only tautologies and platitudes, like "in order to survive any social system has to have its members, must be able to defend itself against its enemies, and has to have a necessary minimum of material resources for the discharge of its functions."[14] So much for this defect.

---

[13] Merton, *op. cit.*, p. 49.

[14] In "analytical" and "functional" theories, the criticized sort of teleological inquiry is additionally aggravated by the theorists' quest for the functional requirements for "preserving the *equilibrium* of a system." As was shown before, the term "equilibrium," used in this sense, becomes

4. Although Merton recommends "middle-range" theories as the most promising and fruitful theories at the present state of sociology, he could not resist the temptation of formulating a "paradigm for and codification of functional analysis." He modestly styles this "initial and tentative step in the direction of codifying functional analysis in sociology"; nevertheless, he views his paradigm as "central to functional approach," factually going far beyond the "middle-range" theories.

What shall we say of these paradigms and codifications? About the same that we said of Parsons' paradigms and schemes. If an investigator wishes to be guided by Merton's paradigm, he must be an omniscient sociologist excellently versed in all branches, methods, and problems of general and special sociologies. A glance at just the first section of the paradigm confirms this statement. The section reads:

> 1. The item(s) to which functions are imputed: The basic requirement is that the object of analysis represent a *standardized* (i.e., patterned and repetitive) item, such as social roles, institutional patterns, social processes, cultural patterns, culturally patterned emotions, social norms, group organization, social structure, devices for social control, etc.[15]

Only an encyclopedically versed sociologist, who in addition is an expert psychologist, culturologist, historian, jurist, political scientist, and methodologist, can fruitfully cope with this first requirement of the paradigm. Only an omniscient doctor of all sciences can successfully meet all the other requirements of the paradigm. As a whole it reads like the table of contents of a compendium of general and special sociology. As such, it has nothing in common with the important methodological treatises of Plato or Aristotle, St. Thomas Aquinas or Ockham, Bacon or Locke, Kant or Hegel, Descartes or Leibnitz, Comte or Spengler, Marx or Durkheim. It does not give any specific method (or even a technique) of functional analysis,

---

either meaningless or acquires a bizarre connotation. As a result, the whole inquiry turns into a perfectly indefinite quest for some indeterminate requirements necessary for preserving the quite nebulous "equilibrium" of a poorly defined social system.

[15] Merton, *op. cit.*, p. 50.

nor does it sum up the main results of such an analysis of the important problems of sociology. If anything, like Parsons' paradigms, it represents a modern variation on Alexandrian or medieval scholasticism at its decaying period. Both are heuristically sterile, empirically useless, and logically cumbersome tables of contents.

5. Finally, a multitude of Merton's propositions, especially in his theory of reference groups (Chapters 8 and 9) represent a codification of trivialities dressed up as scientific generalizations. Here are a few examples of this sort of platitude: "Conformity to norms of an out-group is equivalent to what is ordinarily called non-conformity, that is, non-conformity to the norms of the in-group." "Those privates who accepted the official values of the Army hierarchy were more likely than others [especially those who did not accept these values] to be promoted." "Positive orientation toward the official mores [of the Army or large social system] would appear to be functional in supporting the legitimacy of the structure and in keeping the structure of authority [of these systems] intact." "Anticipatory socialization [an aspiration to become a member of a higher or desirable group] is functional for the individual only within a relatively open social structure providing for mobility." "What the individual experiences as estrangement from a group of which he is a member tends to be experienced by his associates as repudiation of the group, and this ordinarily evokes a hostile response." "Insofar as subordinate or prospective group members are motivated to affiliate themselves with a group, they will tend to assimilate the sentiments and conform with the values of the authoritative and prestigeful stratum in that group." "The person who identifies himself with a reference individual [as a role-model or hero] will seek to approximate the behavior and values of that individual in his several roles."[16] This sort of triviality goes on and on throughout Chapters 8 and 9, which deal with the centuries-old problems of social groups, called by Merton "reference groups."

Merton's theory of reference groups represents a thoughtful but fragmentary and incidental codification or recapitulation of

16 *Ibid.*, pp. 262–386.

several—more systematic—theories of social groups. Merton starts out by commenting favorably on the concept of "relative deprivation," briefly mentioned but never defined in S. A. Stouffer *et al., The American Soldier.*[17] Contrary to his sound rule of defining basic concepts as clearly as possible and to demand such definitions from other scholars, Merton in this case generously excuses his friends for failing to give practically any definition of "relative deprivation." He states that though this concept "nowhere finds formal definition in the pages of these volumes . . . this absence of a formal definition of relative deprivation is no great handicap."[18] Why does Merton make such an exception? Is it not a risky task to try to make such an undefined and nebulous concept the cornerstone for a whole theory of social groups? We would say that it was, especially since the hypothesis of relative deprivation is an almost tautological platitude: Among drafted American soldiers those soldiers who by the draft were deprived (or who thought they were unfairly deprived) of their civilian rights-values-privileges or who thought they were unfairly treated in the Army in regard to promotions, burdensome Army duties, etc., tended to be more dissatisfied with Army life than those who were not deprived (or who did not think they were unfairly deprived) of their civilian rights-values-comforts and who did not think they were unfairly treated in the Army. Did we not know before that not only in the Army but practically in any population those who do not feel they are unfairly deprived of their rights-privileges-values are less dissatisfied with the conditions of their life in their group(s) than those who feel they *are* unjustly deprived of their rights-values-privileges? We knew well that in any society those members whose "imperative-attributive" law convictions are not contradicted or violated by the obligatory norms of their group(s) tend to be more satisfied with their life in their group(s) than those whose "imperative-attributive" law convictions *are* contradicted by the official norms of their group(s).

Merton's taking this platitude for an important discovery

---

[17] Vols. I and II.
[18] Merton, *op. cit.,* pp. 227 ff.

and making it a starting point and cornerstone for his theory of reference groups is largely responsible for the many short-comings of his theory. With all his talent neither he nor anyone else could inflate this platitude into an important "middle-range generalization" or an original and significant theory of social systems.[19]

As a result, Merton's discussion of membership and non-membership groups, multiple-solidary and conflicting groups, and the "uniformities of behavior derived from reference-group theory" hardly provide new or real uniformity. The same is true of his analysis of the "functions of positive orientations to nonmembership groups," the "social processes sustaining or curbing these orientations," his list of "group properties," his criminal and noncriminal (ideological) types of nonconformist "deviant behavior," and, finally, his role-set, status-set, and status sequences. These basic problems of sociology are touched by Merton too cursorily, too fragmentarily to enrich us with a new knowledge in these fields.

Merton's theory of membership and nonmembership groups is greatly muddled by the too meager and incidental material from the American soldiers on whose replies he builds it, by a lack of a theory of subordinated, coordinated, and neutral relationship of various social groups to one another, and by a resulting arbitrariness as to which are the membership and which the nonmembership groups of an individual. Most of Merton's "uniformities" are exemplified by the trivialities already quoted and others like them. His list of "group proper-ties" cites only a few of the basic properties common to all organized groups and enumerates several unessential features possessed only by some specific groups. His long discussion of the essential difference between "ideological" and "criminal" nonconformists is a hardly needed elaboration of the obvious. The same is true of his analysis of the "functions of positive

---

[19] The interviews with a few units of the American Army were quite fragmentary, largely contradictory, and doubtful in the sincerity of the answers of the drafted soldiers. In brief, the material of *The Ameri-can Soldier* on which the hypothesis of relative deprivation is built is quite poor as the basis for any solid scientific theory. See my criticism of *The American Soldier* in my *Fads and Foibles*, pp. 122–130, 145–150.

orientation to nonmembership groups." His formulas of the role-set, status-set, and status consequences are a variation on the desiccated scholasticism of the Middle Ages. For a novitiate in sociology, his theory of reference groups is enlightening and instructive. It is formulated—in contrast to Parsons' jig-saw puzzles—in a comprehensive and elegant style. For an old hand in this discipline, however, it is a somewhat fragmented and cursory recapitulation of more adequate theories of social groups developed by several sociologists of the preceding and present generations.[20]

The positive contribution of Merton's theory discussed consists in (a) bringing to the attention of sociologists a number of basic points in a scientific theory of social groups that are often overlooked by many textbooks on sociology, and (b) in a series of psychosocial observations bridging the specified social realities with corresponding psychological experiences of the persons and groups involved.[21]

[20] A similar fragmentation of the "classic" theories of Tönnies, Durkheim, Comte, Spencer, Weber, Pareto, and others is a fairly common feature of many recent sociological theories. A number of contemporary sociologists—in trying to give a more precise version of these "classic" theories—divide, differentiate, classify, and modify them to such an extent that little remains of these generalizations except a pile of fragmentary propositions of minor cognitive significance and value. See on this fragmentation, A. Cuvillier, *Manuel de Sociologie*, pp. 140–241.

[21] The main contributions of Merton to sociology consist not so much in his theory of functionalism and of reference groups as in his thoughtful studies in the sociology of knowledge and science, psychosocial anomie, bureaucracy, radio and film propaganda, manifest and latent functions, and other empirical investigations with specific social theories involved. Most of these studies represent Merton's variations on the themes of earlier masters: on M. Weber's Protestantism, pietism, science, and bureaucracy, on Durkheim's anomie, on Scheler's, Mannheim's, and Sorokin's *Wissensoziologie*, and on the unanticipated—manifest and latent—consequences of human actions long ago formulated in the proverb, "Man proposes, but God disposes."

Nevertheless, like Beethoven's variation on Mozartian themes or Brahms' variation on the themes of Paganini, Merton's variations are admirable in many ways and certainly contribute a great deal to our knowledge of these problems. He has also contributed significantly by his thoughtful criticism of the theories of other sociologists, including my own "yarns." As an example of his critical analysis, Merton's and B. Barber's "Sorokin's Formulations in the Sociology of Science," in P. Allen, *P. A. Sorokin in Review*, pp. 332–370, can be mentioned here.

Despite these contributions, Merton has hardly succeeded in proving the existence of "functional sociology" as a *sui generis* system of sociological thought distinctly different—in methods and substantive theories—from other systems. Although his contributions in the field of social systems or "reference groups" have been important, they have been limited. He has not given to us a comprehensive theory of the social system—its componential structure and its basic properties. He has hardly even attempted to furnish a taxonomy and "physiology" of social systems—that is, a systematic theory of social and cultural change.[22] If he seriously engages himself in substantial studies in these fields, he can notably enrich our knowledge of these divisions of sociology.

PSYCHOLOGICAL "NOMENCLATURE" THEORIES

In between the analytical and functional theories of social systems and the empirical and dialectic theories, the nomenclature conceptions of social systems can be briefly mentioned. They represent a sort of intermediary—partly analytical and partly empirical, partly nominalistic and partly holistic, but mainly psychological—approach to the study of social *Ganzheiten.* Charles P. Loomis' theory of social systems is a typical example. His starting definition of social system is formulated in empirical terms:

> Interaction tends to develop certain uniformities over time, some of which tend to persist. As they are *orderly and syste-*

---

[22] While Merton's discussion of the mutual relationship of sociological theory and empirical research is essentially correct, in his own studies he does not always follow his own rules. In some studies, he gives a vast body of empirical facts, but applies for their interpretation an uncritically accepted, inadequate theory of Max Weber, which, later on, in his "Bibliographical Postscript" (pp. 595–606 of *Social Theory and Social Structure*), he had to amend and correct in the light of recent studies largely contradicting Weber's hypothesis. In other studies, like his theory of reference groups, he formulates several "middle-range" hypotheses, but gives for their confirmation only fragmentary, inadequate empirical evidence amounting to mere illustrative cases.

matic, they can be recognized as *social systems*. Because the *social system* is composed of identifiable and interdependent parts it is said to possess social structure. . . . The social system is composed of the patterned interaction of members.[23]

Following this definition Loomis gives a good empirical description of the "old-order Amish as a social system," of several rural social systems[24] (the rural family, the rural informal groups, the hamlet, the neighborhood, the trade center, and so on), and of other organized groups. In order to give a thorough analysis of empirical organized groups and of sociological theories, however, Loomis developed his own conceptual model of the social system, called the "Processually Articulated Structural Model," or PAS model. This model starts out with the nominalistic concept of purposive, motivated, and normatively regulated action, passes to reciprocal meaningful action or interaction of a plurality of actors, and then to a social system as an orderly and systematic symbolic (meaningful) interaction of actors or individuals. Several interlinked social systems make up society, or the "master system." In all so-defined social systems or society, the "elements that constitute it as a social system and the processes that articulate it remain the same."

Loomis's PAS model consists largely in enumerating the "persistent elements and processes [that] appear at all levels of orderly interaction . . . the constituent parts of some larger whole."[25] These elements are classified by Loomis as follows: belief (knowledge); sentiment; end, goal, or objective; norm; status-role (position); rank; power; sanction; and facility. To each of these elements corresponds a respective "elemental

[23] Charles P. Loomis, *Social Systems* (Princeton, N.J., 1960), pp. 3–4. See also C. P. Loomis and Z. K. Loomis, *Modern Social Theories* (Princeton, N.J., 1961), ch. 1.

[24] See C. P. Loomis and J. A. Beegle, *Rural Social Systems* (New York, 1950), chs. 2–8, and *passim*. A good analysis of rural social systems is given also in T. Lynn Smith, *The Sociology of Rural Life* (New York, 1947), and in Sorokin-Zimmerman-Galpin, *A Systematic Source Book in Rural Sociology* (3 vols.; Minneapolis, 1930–1931; New York, 1966).

[25] Loomis, *Social Systems*, pp. 1–5.

process" and "structural-functional category": To the "belief-element" corresponds the process of "cognitive mapping" and the structural category of "knowing"; to "sentiment" corresponds the process of "tension management and the communication of sentiment" and the structural category of "feeling"; and so on. These nine elements, processes, and functional categories are supplemented by "comprehensive or master processes (communication, boundary maintenance, systemic linkage, institutionalization, socialization, and social control) and by "conditions of social action: territoriality, size, time."[26] This schema is applied by Loomis and Loomis in their analysis of various empirical social groups and of the sociological theories of seven American sociologists.[27]

The PAS represents a nomenclature of the important points that an investigator of any social system has to study rather than a theory of social systems. This nomenclature is analogous to the *"nomenclature de la science sociale"* of the Le Play School[28] or to various guide-instruction schedules for anthropological investigation of various preliterate groups (like the *Questionnaire de sociologie et ethnographie* by the Paris Anthropological Society or the *Ethnographische Fragesammlung zur Erforschung des Sozialen Leben der F. Völker* (Leipzig, 1906). These nomenclatures and instruction schedules enumerate important points of either the family or society or of a primitive group that need to be carefully studied in order that the investigated family or group may be adequately understood and scientifically described. Such nomenclatures are helpful in a systematic study of social systems or groups but they hardly offer a comprehensive theory of social systems in a proper sense of this term. Guided by his PAS, Loomis gave a correct description of various empirical groups and a thorough analysis of several sociological theories, but this does not make the PAS a significant theory of social systems. Its "elements," like "believing, feeling, achieving, facilitating, and decision-making," occur in

---

26 *Ibid.*, pp. 6–11.
27 Loomis and Loomis, *Modern Social Theories.*
28 See *CST*, ch. 2.

practically all humans, members of organized groups as well as participants in unorganized and disorganized groups. These "elements," "processes," or "structural categories" do not contain the criteria distinguishing social systems (organized "orderly" groups) from social congeries (unorganized and disorganized gatherings). The PAS is essentially nominalistic-singularistic in character, as are all theories of social actions; as such, it provides a helpful nomenclature for the study of social and cultural systems and congeries, but it is not a systematic theory of sociocultural systems.

The PAS "elements," "processes," and "structural-functional" categories are psychological features of human individuals rather than anatomical (structural) and physiological (dynamic) properties of social and cultural systems. Loomis's nine "elements" and their corresponding "structural categories" do not give to us a real "anatomy" or morphology or structure of social systems for the same reason that an enumeration of such functions of organisms as breathing, eating, sleeping, and running do not give us a knowledge of the organisms' anatomical or morphological structure. Neither Loomis nor any sociologist can construct a scientific theory of the structure of social or cultural systems by merely enumerating some of the psychological experiences of individuals.

The PAS "process"—"cognitive-mapping," "tension-management," "goal-attending," "decision-making," and so on—is again not a list of the basic, generic, recurrent processes of social or cultural systems but rather a list of mental processes of individuals (regardless of whether they are members of an organized or unorganized or disorganized social group). These psychological processes are quite different from the recurrent processes of social or cultural systems, such as how and why such systems originate and become organized, how and why they become differentiated and stratified, how and why they maintain their identity and continuity, how they acquire, exchange, distribute, and lose their members, how and why they change, how and why they organize their systems of values, relationships, and institutions, how and why they grow or deteriorate, and, finally, how and why they die and, once in a while, resurrect themselves.[29] These recurrent processes of social systems are quite different from Loomis' psychological processes of individuals: The former but not the latter make up the "physiology" of social and cultural systems. These systems' processes are hardly touched in the PAS classification of "processes." In brief, PAS does not contribute much to the anatomy or dynamics of social and cultural systems.[30] Nor does PAS supply any systematic taxonomy of social systems. Loomis analyzes religious, educational, welfare, and health social systems, the Amish community, and some of the rural communities of Latin America, but he does not give any comprehensive taxonomy of social systems. In this respect, his PAS schema shares the deficiency of other analytical and functional theories of social systems.

More significant is Loomis's contribution to the typology of social systems.[31] He and John C. McKinney have published an able survey and analysis of the basic typologies of the social systems of Tönnies, Durkheim, M. Weber, Cooley, Redfield, Becker, Sorokin, Parsons, and others.[32] These typologies together with their empirical studies of several social systems, though hampered by the PAS psychological pigeonholes, are,

---

[29] See a systematic analysis of the basic recurrent processes in social and cultural systems in my *SCP*, chs. 21, 47.

[30] These defects are common for almost all sociological theories of "social action" and "social behaviorism." Hardly any of these has contributed notably to the "anatomy and physiology" or to the theory of structure and dynamics of social and cultural systems.

[31] Ordinarily, mixed taxonomy and typology of social and cultural systems study different dimensions of these systems. See on this Chapter 16 of this work.

[32] Cf. J. C. McKinney and C. P. Loomis, "The Typological Tradition," in J. S. Rouček, *Contemporary Sociology* (New York, 1958), pp. 557–582; and J. C. McKinney, "The Role of Constructive Typology in Scientific Sociological Analysis," *Social Forces*, March, 1950. (See in these articles the relevant literature on typologies of social systems.) Cf. also W. Heinrich, "Dualistische Lehrgebäude in den Sozialwissenschaften: Zur Frage des Polaritätdenkens in Soziologie und Nationalökonomie," *Österreichische Akademie der Wissenschaften* (Vienna, 1964). A. Cuvillier, *Manuel de Sociologie*, Vol. I, chs. IV–V. W. Heinrich's and A. Cuvillier's surveys and analyses of dualistic or polarized typologies of social systems deal with many theories in this field not mentioned in the studies of Loomis and McKinney.

nevertheless, a careful analysis of sociological theories and a significant contribution to rural sociology, general sociology, and to the theory of social systems.[33]

[33] The psychological-singularistic character of my "elements-processes-structural categories," aggravated by acceptance of some of Parsons' "scholastic pattern variables of action orientation," is largely responsible for the Loomises' failure to analyze the bases, criteria, and conception of social and cultural systems in their otherwise careful examination of seven sociological theories in *Modern Social Theories*. The authors correctly pigeonhole each theory into each of their "elements" of believing, feeling, achieving, norming, and so on, but fail to establish whether each of these theories has a clear conception of social and cultural systems, and, if it has, what the criteria are of the system and to what extent each conception of a system is exemplified and tested by the relevant empirical facts and how much it helps in the comprehension of the empirical realities of the superorganic world. On this point, I agree with the criticism of the Loomises' work by Alvin Boskoff, in his review published in *Social Forces* (1963), 249–250.

CHAPTER 14

Dialectic Theories of Social
and Cultural Systems

SKETCH OF THE HISTORY OF DIALECTIC

Dialectical logic, method, philosophy, and social theories have had a long, venerable, and fruitful life-course in the history of human thought.

Indeed, we find a skillful use of dialectic by the early Taoists, Hindus, and Buddhists,[1] by the Greek pre-Socratic thinkers, like Heraclitus, and by Plato, Aristotle, Plotinus, and other neo-Platonists.[2] Dialectical logic finds a magnificent development in the work of the Mahayana Buddhists: Nagarjuna, Asanga, Vasubandhu, Gotama, Dignaga, and Dharmakirti.[3] Dialectical logic is well exemplified by Damascius and by some of the Church Fathers, like Clement of Alexandria, Origen, Tertullian, St. Augustine, Pseudo-Dionysius,[4] Maximus the Confessor, Erigena, and so on. Despite a repudiation of dialectic as the "art of sterile discussion" by St. Thomas Aquinas and as the "art of talking of everything and nothing" by Duns Scotus, the dialectic logic of complementarity and polarity was nevertheless partially used by these and other great scholastics (Hugh of St. Victor, Albertus Magnus, and

---

[1] See a brief sketch of the history of dialectical logic in *The Ways and Power of Love*, pp. 364 ff.

[2] See an outline of the dialectics of Plato and Plotinus in G. Gurvitch, *Dialectique et Sociologie* (Paris, 1962), pp. 30–44.

[3] See on this the excellent works of T. Stcherbatsky, *Buddhist Logic* (2 vols.; Leningrad, 1932), and *The Central Conceptions of Buddhism* (London, 1923). See also R. G. H. Siu, *The Tao of Science* (New York, 1957).

[4] See Gurvitch, *Dialectique et Sociologie*, pp. 44–49, on the dialectics of Damascius and Pseudo-Dionysius.

some of the medieval mystics—Eckhart, for example). Subsequently, it finds its development in the dialectic of the *"docta ignorantia"* of Nicholas of Cusa and in the reasonings of mystics like St. John of the Cross and Boehme. Later on, in various forms, including Kant's "dialectic of a radical negation of dialectic," this method and logic have been artfully utilized by many eminent philosophers, natural scientists, and social thinkers, Fichte, Hegel, Marx, and Proudhon, to mention but a few.[5] In its "polarity" form, dialectic has been widely used by a large number of "typological" sociologists and economists who, like Tönnies, Spengler, Oppenheimer, Rüstow, and many others, constructed "dualistic polarity concepts" of two opposite or contrasting types of social and cultural systems. Tönnies' *Gemeinschaft-Gesellschaft,* Spengler's *Dasein-Wachsein,* and Rüstow's *Herschaft-Freiheit* are examples of these dualistic pairs of opposite types.[6]

Finally, there has been a conspicuous renaissance of dialectic in recent years in the natural and social sciences. A galaxy of eminent physicists and mathematicians, such as Niels Bohr, Louis de Broglie, F. Gonseth, J. L. Destouches, W. Heisenberg, and others,[7] have introduced it, in the form of "dialectic complementarity," into microphysics, nuclear physics, the mathematics of the infinitely great and the infinitely small, and for reconciling opposite theories in these fields. A special international review, *Dialectica,* was established in 1947. In *Dialectica* scientists of various exact sciences endeavor to find, through the dialectic method, a solution to various (conceptual and experimental) difficulties confronting them in their research.

In recent years, we have observed an increasing number

[5] See Gurvitch, *Dialectique et Sociologie,* pp. 50, 156.

[6] See, on this variety of dialectic, W. Heinrich, *"Dualistische Lehrgebäude in den Sozialwissenschaften."*

[7] See, for example, Niels Bohr's article in the *Revue de Methaphysique et de Morale,* Nos. 1–2 (1961), 1–34; L. De Broglie, *La Physique nouvelle et les Quanta* (Paris, 1937); F. Gonseth, *Le Problème du Temps: Essai sur la Methodologie de la Recherche* (La Neuveville, Switzerland, 1964); and G. Bachelard, *L'activité rationnelle de la physique contemporaine* (Paris, 1951).

of works devoted to the dialectic in philosophy and the social sciences and a still more rapidly increasing use of this method in the research of social, cultural, and psychological phenomena by the Soviet Marxist scholars[8] as well as by Western philosophers, sociologists, and psychosocial investigators. Representative examples of recent Western works on dialectic include the monographs of Merleau-Ponti, Sartre, Gurvitch, and Kühne; others will be mentioned in subsequent sections of this chapter.[9] It is likely that this renaissance of dialectic will continue in the years to come. The dialectical current of sociological thought is so significant that no survey of today's sociology can afford to pass it by (as has been done by many American and, to a lesser degree, European sociologists). The most eminent leader of the "empirico-realist dialectic sociology" of our time is undoubtedly George Gurvitch (who christens his system of sociology the "*hyper-empirisme dialectique*" or "empirico-realist dialectic"). For this reason our analysis of dialectical sociology and the dialectical theory of social and cultural systems centers around an examination of Gurvitch's empirico-realist dialectic sociology.

GURVITCH'S EMPIRICO-REALIST DIALECTIC SOCIOLOGY

A scholar of extraordinary erudition, the author of numerous important works in philosophy and in general and special

---

[8] See the Soviet journal *Voprosy Filosofil*, each copy of which contains several studies devoted to dialectic. V. I. Cherkesov, *Materialist Dialectic as Logic and as a Theory of Knowledge* [*Materialisticheskaya dialektika kak logika i teoria poznania*] (Moscow, 1962); G. V. Platonov and M. N. Rutkevitch, "The Dialectic of Nature as a Philosophical Science" ["O dialektike prirody kak filosofskoy nauke"], *Voprosy Filosofii*, No. 3 (1963), 134–145; and M. Rosental, *The Principles of Dialectic Logic* [*Prinzipi dialekticheskoy logiki*] (Moscow, 1960). A large number of special monographs devoted to dialectic has been published by Soviet scholars, not to mention hundreds of articles.

[9] M. Merleau-Ponti, *Les aventures de la dialectique* (Paris, 1955); J. P. Sartre, *Critique de la raison dialectique*, Vol. I (Paris, 1960); G. Gurvitch, *Dialectique et Sociologie*; and O. Kühne, *Allgemeine Soziologie* (Berlin, 1958); P. M. Blau, *Exchange and Power in Social Life* (New York, 1964).

sociologies,[10] and a successor to Durkheim's chair at the Sorbonne, Gurvitch (1894–1965) developed his empirico-realist dialectic sociology into one of the most original and significant sociological systems of our time. Its complexity, peculiarities, and abundant classifications do not allow it to be adequately summarized in a few pages.[11] All I can do in these pages is to give an idea of the essential character of his system—its dialectical method, its conceptual framework, the ways in which the method is applied to the study of the total social reality, and the cognitive results of Gurvitch's study.

● Features and Forms of Gurvitch's Dialectic

In its long history, the term dialectic has been given so many different meanings that, unless it is clearly defined, it may mean anything and nothing. Gurvitch gives an extended analysis, specifications, and classifications of the main forms of dialectic method as well as of dialectic processes in objective social reality. Here are the essential features of Gurvitch's dialectic:

1. He distinguishes dialectic as a method of study of dialectic movements in the total social reality, as the real dialectic movements continuously going on in this reality, and as dialectic relationships between the dialectic method and real social movements. A unification of all these three forms of dialectic,

---

[10] Of the numerous works of Gurvitch, the following ones can be mentioned here: *Traité de Sociologie,* in collaboration with 27 specialists (2 vols.; Paris, 1958 and 1960); *La vocation actuelle de la Sociologie* (Paris, 1957); *Déterminismes sociaux et liberté humaine* (Paris, 1955); *Sociology of Law* (New York, 1942); *La multiplicité des temps sociaux* (Paris, 1958); *Initiation à la sociologie de la connaissance* (Paris, 1948); monographs on the sociologies and philosophies of Marx, Saint-Simon, Proudhon, Comte, and Fichte; *Le concept de classe sociale, de Marx à nos jours* (Paris, 1954); and *Dialectique et Sociologie* (Paris, 1962). Most of these works have been translated into foreign languages. In addition to his numerous volumes, Gurvitch established and has been editing *Cahiers internationaux de sociologie* (one of the important journals of sociology).

[11] A comprehensive summary of its main points by Gurvitch himself takes more than a hundred pages.

or, in his terms, a "dialectization of dialectic" is necessary for an adequate grasp of the total social reality.

2. Of all sciences, "sociology needs most an application of dialectic method."

3. As a *method,* dialectic has the following characteristics:

A. The real task (and inspiration) of the dialectic method is the demolition of all acquired and crystallized concepts to prevent their "mummification" resulting from their incapacity to grasp the incessantly changing real totalities and to account simultaneously for the social ensembles (*Ganzheiten*) and their parts. For this reason to be fruitful the dialectic method must be *antidogmatic,* that is, free from any presumed philosophical or scientific position:

> The impenitent and intransigent dialectic, virulent and faithful to its vocation, cannot be either spiritualistic or materialistic or mystic. . . . As a method, dialectic is always a *negation,* not because it opposes the antinomic theses and antitheses— which opposition is only one of its operations of dialectization, namely, the procedure of polarization—but because dialectic *negates also the laws of formal logic* insofar as they are not included in a (social) ensemble which surpasses them because no element is ever identical with itself from the dialectic standpoint. . . . This does not mean that negation implied in dialectic method or, at least, in negation of negation, produces miracles, as Hegel thought. Dialectic negation is but a destruction of formal logic, of the general, of the abstract, of the discursive, in order to attain that what they screen. . . . According to Jean Wahl's happy formula, dialectic is . . . a way rather than a point of arrival. . . . It is a purificatory fire preparing the way for science and philosophy in opening the road to what is hidden.

According to F. Gonseth and M. Barzin, "dialectic démarche is purification of our knowledge under the pressure of experience with which it confronts itself. . . . It is the conception of science according to which every scientific proposition is in principle revisable."

B. Another characteristic of the dialectic method is that:

> Dialectic concerned with real movement as well as with the method deals simultaneously with ensembles and their con-

stituent elements, with totalities and their parts. It is concerned with the movements of the wholes and their parts, particularly with the movement between them. Any true dialectic refuses to annihilate unity in multiplicity or multiplicity in unity, because simultaneous movement of (social) ensembles and of their parts presupposes both these aspects.

C. "Dialectic taken in all its aspects is . . . a combat against artificial stability in the social reality as well as in knowledge. It is demolition of the obsolescent in the real world and of mummified concepts that hinder cognitive penetration into the real, particularly into the social reality. Dialectic combats simultaneously scepticism and dogmatism."

D. Dialectic is, on the one hand, manifestation; on the other, it is exposure of tensions, oppositions, conflicts, struggles, contraries, and contradictories (in the social realities and concepts). "It is manifestation and uncovering of the fact that the elements of the same ensemble mutually condition one another and that, with the exception of the genuine antinomies (like Being and Nothing, Absolute Necessity and Unlimited Creative Liberty), a majority of conflictual manifestations can also interpenetrate as well as combat one another. In brief, dialectic opens an infinity of intermediary degrees between the opposite terms which it endeavors to study in all their effective variety, like the intermediate degrees between the quantitative and the qualitative, liberty and determinism, the organized and the spontaneous, between the individual and collectivities, etc."

E. "As *a method,* dialectic is first of all a specific way of adequate cognition of the movements of the real social and historical totalities."

F. "As a *real movement,* dialectic is the way taken by the human-social and historical-totalities in the process of their making and remaking, in mutual engenderment of their ensembles and their parts, of their actions and their works, in the struggle of these totalities against the internal and external obstacles which they meet on their way."

G. "Finally, the third aspect of dialectic is *dialectic relationship* established between the object constructed by science, the method used and the respective reality." (Only dialectic is capable of fighting the various subjective evaluations infecting the individual and collective interpretations of the social realities and their change).[12]

On the multiplicity of dialectic operational procedures and their application in sociology, Gurvitch says that "One of the grave errors of all varieties of dialectic, elaborated up to the present, is a tendency to reduce all dialectic operational procedures to one, namely, *antinomy,* that is, to *polarization of the contradictories."* (Most dialecticians, including Damascius, Fichte, Proudhon, Kierkegaard, Plotinus, Leibniz, Hegel, Marx, and Sartre, have been guilty of an *"inflation and fetichism of antinomy";* the contemporary introduction of dialectic into the natural sciences has an inverse tendency, to reduce all dialectic methods to the operational procedure of *complementarity.*) Meanwhile there are, in the social sciences, at least, five different operational procedures of dialectic to be used in a study of the phenomena of the total social reality. These five procedures and movements are the dialectic of complementarity, the dialectic of mutual involvement, the dialectic of ambiguity and ambivalence, the dialectic of polarization, and the dialectic of reciprocity of perspectives.

The dialectic of complementarity discloses that two terms or elements that appear to be contrary or mutually exclusive are in fact twin brothers or doublets that include each other in the same conceptual or real ensemble. The front and the back view of the human head or two different sides of a mountain that appear to be quite different, even contrary, become complementary after we examine the head or reach the top of the mountain; these examples give a concrete image of the complementarity disclosed by this dialectic. The mutual complementarity of the ondulatory and corpuscular theories of light in modern physics, of comprehension and explication, of the immediate and the mediate, of the continuous and the discontinuous, of the absolute and the relative, of the abstract and concrete, of the superficial and profound, and of the positive and negative are other examples of dialectic complementarity. Each term (or

---

12 G. Gurvitch, *Dialectique et Sociologie,* pp. 5–28, 179–188.

real element) in each of these pairs cannot be adequately understood (or even exist in reality) without the other term or element. They dialectically complement each other.

The dialectic of mutual involvement consists of those terms or elements that at first glance appear to be opposite or heterogeneous but that in actuality overlap or partially interpenetrate or are immanent to each other. Without the dialectic of mutual implication we cannot adequately understand the relationship between body and mind or the total mental and the total social phenomena, because there is a mental element in the social phenomena and a social element in the mental.

The dialectic of ambiguity and ambivalence is applied to such contrasts as "friendly enemies" (friends who are at the same time enemies), as attractions which at the same time repulse, as comforts that simultaneously discomfort.

The dialectic of polarization is exemplified by the classic dialectic of thesis, antithesis, and synthesis, or by the dialectic of "identity of the opposites," or by *coincidentia oppositorum.* "In human social reality there are no contradictory or antinomic elements which remain such for ever, for all times, for all places, in all circumstances and changes." Tensions, conflicts, struggles, the contraries (conceptual and real) that cannot be understood by other dialectics may need to be clarified by the dialectic of polarization. (Hegelian dialectic is a classic example of this.)

The dialectic of reciprocity of perspectives endeavors to penetrate distinctions in elements or terms that do not lend themselves either to identification or separation but whose mutual immanence is so intense that it results in a parallelism or symmetry in their manifestations. The frequently observed reciprocity of perspectives between a collective opinion and the opinion of the individual—member of the same collectivity— can serve as an example of the reciprocity of perspective.

Such are the essential characteristics and operational forms of Gurvitch's dialectic. Despite the importance of dialectic, however, it does not explain social phenomena. "It leads us to the threshold of explanation in sociology but does not pass over this threshold. . . . The empirico-realist dialectic only sets forth the questions but does not furnish the answers to them. It only prepares the framework of explanation."[13]

Before our examination of how this dialectic (in cooperation with analytical, singularizing, and typological methods) is applied by Gurvitch to the study of social phenomena we need to know the conceptual framework of his system of general sociology. Its essential points are as follows.[14]

1. "The domain of sociology is the social reality—participation of the human in the human—irreducible to any other reality. Social reality affirms itself most of all in the 'total social phenomena' or in the dynamic, ever-changing, fluid (social) totalities [unified systems]."

2. "The total social phenomena are multidimensional and have different depth-levels. . . . [Despite their differentiation] these depth levels form an indissoluble ensemble in the total social phenomena without excluding however some discontinuity between different depth-levels or even a possibility of conflicts between them."

3. "Sociology is a qualitative and discontinuous typology, based upon the dialectic of nonstructurable, structurable, and structured total social phenomena studied in all their depth-levels, in all their sectors, in order to follow their movements of structuration, destructuration, restructuration, and bursting (*l'éclatement*). It finds their explanation in collaboration with history."

4. This sociology is divided into *microsociology* and *macrosociology. Microsociology* studies the simplest manifestation of social reality-sociability, that is, "the multifarious ways of being bound by a whole and in a whole [*par le tout and dans le tout*]." The two main forms of sociability are "we-ness" (*les nous*) and the "relationship to an *Alter*," We-ness entails the "we" of a family, of "we Americans," of "our labor union," of any group in which there has been a partial fusion of the

---

[13] *Ibid.*, pp. 189–200.

[14] Before formulating his conception of general sociology, Gurvitch outlines main preceding conceptions of this science. In this outline, some of the conceptions, including my own, are delineated inaccurately. For this reason, Gurvitch's criticisms of such conceptions represent a criticism of a "straw man" rather than that of the theories ascribed to the criticized sociologists. See G. Gurvitch, *Traité de Sociologie*, Vol. I, pp. 3–19, 28–64.

individual and the collective consciousnesses or intuition. The "relationship to an *Alter*" results from a partial opposition between "I", "Thou", "He", and "They" in interpersonal relationships. Neither form of sociability should be confused with social structures or groups. Sociability in both forms is the stuff of any social structure or group or collectivity, all varying in intensity and depth. There are $n+1$ forms of sociability. The main forms are *communion*—the most intense and most spontaneous form of "we-ness"; *community* (intermediary); and *mass*—the least intense and most constrained form of "we-ness."

5. *Macrosociology* deals with all the main depth-levels and sectors of the total social reality in its structurable and structured ensembles: groups, classes, and global societies. Stressing the pragmatic and modifiable character of his classification of these levels, Gurvitch distinguishes ten depth-levels of the total social reality, beginning with the most easily observable and ending with the most hidden. These are, *first,* the morphological or ecological surface level of social reality: geographical and technological environment, age-sex-race composition of population, birth-death-marriage rates, migrations, buildings, railways, and all varieties of cold "material culture." These phenomena are easily observable and often measurable. *Second,* the level of organized, centralized, and hierarchized patterns of collective conduct. This level externally constrains the conduct of individuals according to the pre-established rules. *Third,* the level of models, rules, signals, signs, and rules of conduct. These models, rules, and signs are guides and obligatory norms for individual and collective conduct. They are products as well as producers of culture. *Fourth,* the level of regular collective behavior external to the organized patterns of collective conduct. Ritual and procedural collective behavior is based upon rigorous regulations. Folkways, mores, customs, fashions, and fads are examples of this level of social reality. The web of social roles assumed, interpreted, and judged by collectivities and individuals constitutes the *fifth* level. Collective attitudes form the *sixth* level. Collective attitudes are imponderables in social reality and cannot be reduced to purely mental attitudes. They are dispositions that push individuals and groups

to react in a certain way, to behave in a certain fashion, to assume particular social roles, and to be guided by symbols.

Social symbols make up the *seventh* level. Social symbols serve as mediators between the content they symbolize and the collective and individual agents who create them and to whom they are addressed. Veiling what they reveal and revealing what they veil they now push individuals and collectivities to various actions, now inhibit their activities. In their totality they constitute an important layer of social reality.

The *eighth* level is made up of effervescent, innovating, and creative collective activities. By their unpredictability, nonconformity, novelty, creativity, and revolt against the crystallized, required, regular forms of collective conduct, these activities essentially differ from the regular and conformist collective attitudes and conduct. The innovating, revolutionary, and creative activities occupy a much larger place and play a more continuous role in social reality than is usually imagined. Collective ideas and values make up the *ninth* level. "Behind all the variety of collective activities and attitudes, all forms of social organization, all models, signs, roles and symbols, there is the world of collective ideas and values," objectified and externalized by all the preceding levels of social reality. This level of social reality is more hidden and less easily observable than all the preceding levels.

Tenth, is the level of collective mentalities and psychic acts. "Psychical life manifests itself on all levels of social reality and makes an integral part of it." In the total psychic phenomena we can distinguish the individual, the interpersonal, and the collective mentalities. All these in various degrees are permeated by social reality. This level of social reality is the most hidden and the most difficult for scientific study. Only through the empirico-realist dialectic can it be grasped and more or less adequately studied.

Each of these ten levels is connected with the total social reality and in various degrees interpenetrates the other levels.[15]

---

[15] For a thorough discussion of them, see Gurvitch, *Traité de Sociologie,* Vol. I, pp. 3–64, 135–185.

At the same time they are in perpetual conflict with one another.

- ## Macrosociology of Social Groupings, Structures, and Global Societies

Besides a study of depth-levels of social reality macrosociology investigates real social groupings, social classes, social structures, and global societies. A social group, according to Gurvitch, "is a real but partial collective unity directly observable and based upon continuous and active collective attitudes. It has a common task to accomplish, unity of attitudes, works and conduct which constitute a structurable social framework tending to a relative social cohesion of manifestations of sociability." Any real social group representing a cluster of microsocial forms of sociability and of depth-levels of social reality is a concrete real unity richer than $n+1$ forms of sociability, regulations, organization, and other depth-levels of social reality.

For classifying social groupings Gurvitch uses fifteen different criteria, such as *function* (unifunctional, multifunctional, and suprafunctional groupings); *size; duration; rhythm of change; degree of dispersion* (groupings at a distance, with artificial contacts, periodically meeting, etc.); *foundation of grouping's formation* (factual, voluntary, or imposed); *groupings open, closed, and conditionally accessible; unorganized and unstructured; organized and structured; central value* (parental, fraternal, local, economic, nonlucrative, mysticoecstatic); *degree of unity* (united, centralized, federalist, confederalist), and so on. Using these criteria a sociologist can give an exact characterization of each social grouping, particularly such "suprafunctional" complex social groups as social *class*. Gurvitch surveys various definitions of social class (including the Marxian) and finds that none of them, including Halbwachs' and Sorokin's (which he regards as the best ones), has fully succeeded in defining it. His own definition, formulated through a combination of eleven of his fifteen criteria, goes as follows:

Social class is a grouping: 1) suprafunctional; 2) vast in its membership; 3) permanent; 4) non-localized but dispersed; 5) factual (not voluntary or coercively imposed) in its emergence and existence; 6) open; 7) unorganized but structured; 8) combative in its orientation; 9) ordinarily resisting its penetration by the all-inclusive, global societies (except when a given social class is dominant in its power); 10) radically incompatible with other social classes; 11) exercising only conditional control and constraint over its members.[16]

Besides forms of sociability, depth-levels, and a multitude of social groupings—small and vast (like the social class)—the total social reality has an important category of phenomena that Gurvitch calls social structures. In sociology these play a role similar to that of the *Gestalt* in psychology. According to Gurvitch:

Each social structure is a precarious, incessantly re-made equilibrium between multiplicity of hierarchies in the macro-sociological total social phenomenon whose substitute social structure represents: equilibrium between specific hierarchies of depth-levels, manifestations of sociability, social regulations, social times . . . functional groupings, social classes and their organizations. This equilibrium of multiple hierarchies is armed and cemented by models, signs, symbols, social roles, values and ideas, in brief by culture proper to a given social structure. The structures of global societies are cemented by the total civilization which overflows them and in which the structures participate as its producers and beneficiaries.[17]

From this definition of social structures we gather that Gurvitch means by this term something very different from the current conceptions of social structures, which he finds faulty and inadequate.

Finally, Gurvitch's analysis of the total social reality in its sociability, depth-levels, groupings, social classes, and structures

---

[16] G. Gurvitch, *La Vocation actuelle de Sociologie*, p. 345; see, in this volume, a fuller development of his theory of groupings and the criteria of his classification of social groupings, pp. 268–348. An abridged version of this theory and classification and a slightly modified definition of social class is given in Gurvitch's *Traité de Sociologie*, Vol. I, pp. 184–204.

[17] *Traité de Sociologie*, Vol. I, pp. 216–235.

is terminated by that of the global societies—the vastest, most imposing, and richest-in-content total social phenomena or sociocultural supersystems. In their plenitude and authority they surpass all functional groupings, social classes, and structures. They are social "macrocosms of macrocosms." Each global society has juridical sovereignty over all social groupings (including the state) that are integrated in it. Each global society is structured, suprafunctional, and somewhat organized. The global societies participate in the creation of their civilizations, which are their cement. Civilizations, however, often overflow the boundaries of global societies and outlive them.

Gurvitch uses eight criteria to classify the global societies, of which he distinguishes fourteen types. Four of these are primitive or archaic in their structures: tribes organized into larger ensembles on the basis of either family bands or a chief with religious power or a military extended family or a monarchical clan of locality groupings.

Six types of historical global societies are: charismatic theocracies (like ancient Egypt); patriarchal societies (described in the Old Testament); feudal societies (like those existing in Europe from the tenth to the fourteenth centuries); city-states (like the Greek *polis* or the Roman *civitas* of 500 to 100 B.C.); societies of emerging capitalism; and societies with developed capitalism (like those in Europe in the nineteenth and at the beginning of the twentieth centuries).

The four contemporary types of global societies are: societies of developed capitalism (like the U.S. capitalist system); techno-bureaucratic fascist societies (Italy of 1922–1944, Germany of 1933–1945); state collectivism (U.S.S.R. and China since 1949); pluralistic collectivism (this type is not fully realized, as yet, but Yugoslavia and possibly the U.S.S.R. may be developing in this direction).[18]

Such is the conceptual framework of the total social reality as developed by Gurvitch. It gives us "histology" (in its microsociological analysis of sociability) and the gross (vertical and horizontal) anatomy and taxonomy of the total social

[18] *Ibid.*

reality, or, in other terms, a systematic theory of differentiation and stratification of this reality. Throughout his analysis Gurvitch continuously stresses the "fluid," ever-changing, precarious equilibria of each of his totalities and their incessant processes of structuration, destructuration, and restructuration. In this way his comprehensive theory contributes to the "physiology" of social systems.

● Gurvitch's Special Sociologies

Once grasped, the depicted framework of the total social reality easily explains the central features of Gurvitch's special sociologies, like his sociology of knowledge, sociology of moral life, sociology of law, and his theory of social times. The central problem of all these special sociologies is the functional correlation between the specific form of sociability or depth-level or groupings or social classes or social structures or global societies and the specific forms of knowledge, philosophy, ideology, moral phenomena, law, or time conception in each of these social ensembles.

Gurvitch's definition of the sociology of knowledge illustrates this point:

> Sociology of knowledge is a study of functional correlations that may be established between different genres and systems of knowledge, on the one hand, and [the] social framework, types of global societies, social classes, particular social groupings and diverse manifestations of sociability, on the other. Among the social totalities, partial and especially global social structures furnish the principal guiding mark for these studies.[19]

Gurvitch distinguishes two kinds of knowledge: on the one hand a perceptive knowledge of external worlds, of the Alter, of we-ness, of groups, of societies, common sense, and technical, political, scientific, and philosophical knowledge, and, on the other, a mystical and rational knowledge, empirical and conceptual, positive and speculative, intuitive and reflexive,

---

[19] *Ibid.*, Vol. II, pp. 120–121.

symbolic and adequate, collective and individual. He then formulates several functional correlations between his social ensembles and a specific variety of knowledge. For instance, he contends that in the hierarchy of various kinds of knowledge in the theocratic-charismatic global society, the first place is occupied by mythologico-philosophical knowledge, the second by technical and political, the third by knowledge of the external world, the fourth by common- and good-sense knowledge, the fifth by scientific, the sixth by the knowledge of an Alter, of "we," of social groupings and societies. In a patriarchal type of global society, the hierarchy of knowledges is quite different: here the first place is occupied by common sense, the second by that of an Alter, "we," and social groups, and the last, least important place by technical knowledge. Still more different are the hierarchies of knowledges in the feudal and the capitalist global societies. In the organized capitalist society, for example, the hierarchy of various knowledges is technical and political knowledge; scientific; knowledge of the external world; knowledge of an Alter, "we," and social groups; philosophical knowledge; and common-sense knowledge.[20]

Gurvitch's sociology of moral life, of law, and his theory of social times are developed along similar lines.[21]

In all of these special sociologies, Gurvitch's principles of the multidimensionality of social phenomena, their precarious equilibria, and their structuration, destructuration, and restructuration are systematically carried on, together with a logico-dialectical analysis of the phenomena studied.

GENERAL EVALUATION AND CRITICISM

Taken in its entirety Gurvitch's contribution to general and special sociologies is one of the most significant of our time. His system of general sociology is more systematic, original, and more completely developed than most of the contemporary theories of general sociology. His extraordinary erudition in philosophy, social sciences, and sociological theories, the com-

---

[20] *Ibid.*, pp. 120–135.
[21] *Ibid.*, pp. 137–206; *Sociology of Law*; and *The Spectrum of Social Time* (English ed., Dordrecht, Holland, 1964).

parative lucidity of his thoughts, reinforced by the exceptional diversity of his life experiences, make all his main works cognitively important, thought-provoking, and truly enlightening. By their verities as well as by their errors his theories notably enrich our knowledge of the total social reality. No historian of general and special sociologies in the mid-twentieth century can pass them by in silence. They already occupy one of the honored places in the sociology of that period.

My criticisms of his system of sociology should in no way detract from or cancel this general evaluation of Gurvitch's contributions. As any scientific, especially sociological theory, his theories have, side by side with their "virtues" and valid points, many flaws, shortcomings, and errors. Let us now examine these defects.

Despite his insightful analysis of the dialectics of Plato, Plotinus, Kant, Fichte, Proudhon, Marx, Sartre, and others, and notwithstanding his clarification of the essential characteristics and main operational forms of dialectic, Gurvitch's conception of dialectic has five serious defects: He ascribes to it several erroneous traits; he unnecessarily multiplies its "operational" forms; he is vague on several points; he overvalues its cognitive power and functions; he uses it only modestly himself in his analyses of social reality.

According to Gurvitch, dialectic method is, first of all, a "demolition of all acquired and crystallized concepts." It is always a negation, he says, including a "negation of the laws of formal logic." He depicts it as a sort of perennial revolutionary force incessantly overthrowing "mummified concepts," "laws of formal logic, the abstract, the discursive, the general in order to attain what they screen." This characterization of the dialectic method appears to be one-sided, nondialectic, and inaccurate. Dialectics of complementarity and polarity are not only demolitional but constructivist, not only negative but affirmative. Otherwise the terms "negation" and "demolition" become empty and meaningless.

Gurvitch's often-reiterated statement that the dialectic method "negates the laws of formal logic" (that is, the principles of identity, contradiction, and the excluded third) is very questionable. Dialectic in fact is not a negation of the laws of formal logic but is a special extension and modification of these laws. It only seems to negate these laws; in reality it affirms and uses them for its inferences. Hegel's classical identification of the category of Being with that of Nothing can serve as an example of this. If he had simply asserted that Being is identical with Nothing his statement would have certainly negated the logical law of contradiction. Instead, he assumed, first, that every concept contains in itself implicitly its opposite and as soon as it is defined or determined, this opposite becomes explicit; as a result, the two statements become contradictory and lead to the third, more adequate statement (thesis-antithesis-synthesis). Then, to obtain his concept of Pure Being, he abstracted from Being all differentia, all characteristics, and reduced Being to the "simple empty immediateness"—to qualityless, quantityless, propertyless, mere "is" or "is-ness," without any characteristics whatsoever, absolutely indeterminate, featureless, empty. This emptiness is not anything; it is mere absence of anything. Such an absence of everything is simple Nothing. Only after this—perfectly logical—operation does Hegel assert the identity of Pure Being with Nothing. In his initial assumption, as well as in all these dialectical operations, he did not violate any law of formal logic, including the law of contradiction.

The same can be said of Hegel's dialectic assertions that "all determination is negation" ("A is B" means A is not C, D, or N; "A is not B" contains negation explicitly). To define means to limit, to determine; this means to deny. Therefore, "affirmation in negation"; "to negate is to posit." All these statements, including Hegel's assertion of the "identity of opposites," were reached after logical operations similar to those with Being and Nothing. In all these operations none of the laws of formal logic was broken; on the contrary, they were skillfully used for arriving at these and many other conclusions.[22]

[22] See Hegel, *Science of Logic*, tr. by W. H. Johnston and L. G. Struthers (New York, 1929), Vol. I, Introduction and Book I.

The same can be stated of the dialectic logic of the Taoist and the Buddhist texts, of Plato and Plotinus, of Pseudo-Dionysius and J. S. Erigena, of Nicolas of Cusa, and of other eminent dialecticians.[23]

Another questionable characteristic ascribed to dialectic by Gurvitch is its freedom from any philosophical or scientific assumptions. It cannot, he says, be either spiritualistic or materialistic or mystic. If this statement means that the canon of dialectic logic per se is not tied up with this or that philosophy or dogmatic assumption, then the same can be said of the laws of formal or mathematical logic. This characteristic is not a *differentia specifica* of dialectic. It is the property of all forms of logic. If the statement means that the use of the dialectic method ensures against any and all philosophical or scientific assumptions, the statement is obviously untenable. First, his own analysis of the systems of great dialecticians from Plato to Sartre shows that all of them had many and different philosophical or scientific assumptions and that all of them committed a series of errors despite their use of the dialectic method. Second, to be free of all philosophy is also a "philosophy of having no philosophy." Such allegedly nonphilosophical or antidogmatic dialectic has been based upon idealistic, materialistic, mystic, critical (in the Hume-Kant sense), agnostic, sceptical, and all sorts of philosophies and dogmatic assumptions. There has not been any simple case of dialectic free from philosophical or other assumptions in the whole history of dialectic. Third, Gurvitch's own "empirico-realist dialectical sociology" has a long series of philosophical and dogmatic assumptions representing a combination of the philosophies and sociologies of Fichte, Marx, Scheler, Lask, Hartmann, Husserl, Bergson, Proudhon, Durkheim, Simmel, L. von Wiese, and others.

The second—less important—defect of Gurvitch's theory

[23] Niels Bohr, who introduced the principle of complementarity in modern physics, explicitly states that this principle and other principles of quantum mechanics do not eliminate or contradict the ordinary (formal) logic. See his "Quantum-Physics and Philosophy" ("Kvantovaya fisika i filosofia,") *Voprosy Filosofii*, No. 8 (1964), 54–55.

is the overclassification of the operational forms of dialectic. Here we meet one of the most conspicuous characteristics of his thought: his love for classifications. In a sense, various classifications make up the substance of Gurvitch's system of sociology. His five forms of dialectic—complementarity, mutual involvement, ambiguity-ambivalence, polarization, and reciprocity of perspectives—can easily be reduced to two or three forms—complementarity, polarity, and ambiguity—especially since his dialectics of mutual involvement, reciprocity of perspectives, and ambiguity are outlined vaguely. The logical analyses of these operational procedures can be handled well by deductive, inductive, and mathematical logics.

The next shortcoming of Gurvitch's dialectic is its vagueness on several points, specifically the "dialectic of real social movements" in the process of their making and remaking or change, and the "dialectic of dialectic relationships" between the objects constructed by science, dialectic method, and dialectic real movements.

Although I understand somewhat dialectic as a specified form of logic and method, I fail to grasp the meanings of these two forms of dialectic. If he means, by the dialectic of real movements, those changes in social or cultural or personality systems that immanently lead to consequences contrary to those that the system had at the preceding phase of its existence or that brought the system into conflict with other systems or that were unforeseen and unpredictable or that exhibit "three-phase rhythms" or that lead to the destruction of the system or that show an interdependence or dependence of the system from other systems and congeries, then let me point out that all these forms of the real movement of social totalities (systems) have been and can be described and studied without imputing to them a dialectic character.[24] An enormous variety of patterns,

[24] See, on all these and many other forms of change in sociocultural systems, my *SCP*, chs. 43–48; on the variety of sociocultural rhythms (so far little studied by sociology despite their cardinal importance), see the *Dynamics*, Vol. IV, chs. 8–14. Cf. also L. Schneider, "Toward Assessment of Sorokin's View of Change," and my "Reply," in G. K. Zollschan and W. Hirsch, *Exploration in Social Change* (Boston, 1964), pp. 371–432.

directions, and rhythms of these movements or processes cannot be reduced to Gurvitch's five operational forms of dialectic.[25]

It is unwarranted to impute the properties of dialectic logic or method to real social movements or processes, just as it is unwarranted to impute deductive or inductive logical rules or experimental or statistical procedures to real physico-chemical or biological or sociocultural processes. Deductive or inductive or dialectical properties are the properties of deductive or inductive or dialectical logic and method. They are not the properties of objective physico-chemical or sociocultural processes. To ascribe the characteristics of dialectic logic or

[25] Among sociocultural processes or "movements," there are rhythmical "movements" with the rhythms consisting of two-three-four-five and more phases or beats. Hegel, in accordance with his dialectic "triad" of thesis-antithesis-synthesis, viewed this three-phase logical law as applicable also to the real-social and historical-processes, as a universal formula according to which all processes pass through the sequence of the three phases of thesis-antithesis-synthesis. Through these phases passes the world history as the history of the *Geist* "in itself" (thesis), passing into the *Geist* in "its otherness," into objectified "nature" (antithesis) and, finally, into the stage of the *Geist* "in itself" and in its "otherness" (synthesis). Through three similar phases pass, according to Hegel, all the subprocesses of this all-embracing process of the world history: For instance, the subjective spirit (*Geist*) passes through the phases of anthropology—soul, phenomenology-consciousness, and psychology-mind. The objective spirit's triad of development is abstract right-morality-social ethics. The absolute spirit's subphases of self-realization are art-religion-philosophy. The main phases of art's development are symbolic-classic-romantic; of social ethics, the family-civil society-the State.

The first error of the Hegelian theory was the imputation of his dialectic triad to the real natural biological and sociohistorical processes. Its second error was the reduction of all rhythmical processes to one three-phase rhythm. As a result of these errors, most of the Hegelian three-phase triads of real social processes are quite artificial and do not fit his formula of thesis-antithesis-synthesis, like the triads of art-religion-philosophy, or the family-civil society-the State, or symbolic-classic-romantic art, or abstract right-morality-social ethics, and so on. The three phases of these triads do not represent really Hegelian "thesis-antithesis-synthesis." Furthermore, Hegel himself could not reduce all processes to this three-phase sequence or rhythm and had to admit processes with two-four-five-phase rhythms or sequences. His errors are somewhat similar to the defect of Gurvitch's dialectic. See Hegel's *Philosophy of History*, tr. by J. Sibree (New York, 1900), pp. 106 ff.

For a more detailed analysis of these problems, see the *Dynamics*, Vol. IV, pp. 408 ff., and ch. 5.

method to real movements is hardly possible; it is as meaningless as a qualification of the physical or biological or social processes as deductive or inductive or statistical.

If Gurvitch means, by the "dialectic of real social movements," the processes best described by the principles of complementarity or polarization, these principles should not be imputed to the respective real movements as their inherent property. Such an imputation would be but a modern variety of animism—that is, imputing to various phenomena the "spirit of complementarity or polarization." From the top of a mountain we see different, often contrasting, sides of it, but this contrasting many-sidedness of the mountain is not a reflection of the principle of complementarity. Under the impact of calamity or catastrophe, social groups uniformly undergo a process of religious and moral polarization: The majority of the group's members who in normal conditions are neither too saintly nor too sinful tend to polarize; some members become more criminal and less religious whereas other members become more religious and less criminal.[26] But this real process of religious and moral polarization is something quite different from the dialectic logic of polarization and can be and has been adequately studied without invoking this dialectic.

Some (decidedly not all) sociocultural systems in the process of changing become the opposite of their preceding form, but this sort of transformation is not identical with the dialectic canon of the polarization of thesis into antithesis.

To sum up, we cannot and should not impute the characteristics of dialectic to the real phenomena analyzed by dialectic, as it is done by Marx, Soviet dialecticians, and Gurvitch.

Still darker appears to me the meaning of Gurvitch's third form of dialectic—that of the dialectic relationship between the dialectic as method and the dialectic of real social movements (the "dialectization of dialectic").

In all frankness, I do not clearly understand what Gurvitch means by this operational form of dialectic. If he means by it

---

[26] See, on this polarization, my *Man and Society in Calamity* (New York, 1942), chs. 9, 10, 11, 12; and *The Basic Trends of Our Time* (New Haven, 1964), ch. 4.

a study of the relationship between the dialectic logic and all or some of the real social and cultural processes, or a study of the heuristic power of the dialectic method in understanding sociocultural processes, then let me point out that such studies have been done and can be done with or without involvement of dialectic method. In this kind of research, the dialectic method remains the same as in other applications of this method for a study of many other problems. There is no need to qualify this dialectic method as something basically different from Gurvitch's dialectic as method.

Throughout his *Traité de Sociologie, La Vocation actuelle de la Sociologie,* and *Dialectique et Sociologie,* Gurvitch repeatedly asserts the enormous heuristic power of the dialectic method. It is, he claims, capable of unraveling most of the "mysteries" of the total social reality and of its innumerable movements of structuration, destructuration, and restructuration of social totalities, ensembles, *cadres sociaux,* collectivities, depth-levels, groups, and global societies. Nobody can deny that the dialectic method and logic have rendered and can render valuable service in understanding many sociocultural systems and congeries and their dynamic processes. Granting this, Gurvitch's enthusiastic praise of this method appears to me notably exaggerated. I can simply point to three characteristics of Gurvitch's own theory that illustrate this exaggeration. The first of these is his own criticisms of the serious defects in the dialectic method of Plato, Plotinus, Damascius, Kant, Hegel, Fichte, Proudhon, Marx, Sartre, and others. If all the great dialecticians made many errors and constructed many an unscientific theory about social phenomena, this means that the dialectic method does not ensure any dialectician against blunders both gross and small. It means also that dialectic does not prevent any present or future dialectician from committing errors. This signifies the limited cognitive power of the dialectic method. The second corroboration of my statement is the fact that, despite his glorification of the dialectic method, Gurvitch praises three other (nondialectical) methods of studying social phenomena: systematic or analytic, individualizing or singularizing, and qualitatively and discontinuously typological (in part nondialectic). The third corroboration is that Gurvitch himself uses the dialectic method very sparingly, now and then fails to use it when it should be used, and here and there commits errors in using it.

These three evidences, furnished by Gurvitch himself, support my more conservative evaluation of the cognitive power of his dialectic method. More substantial corroboration of my evaluation is given by many eminent critics and denunciators of dialectics, such as the Taoist and Buddhist logicians and dialecticians, St. Thomas Aquinas and Duns Scotus, Kant, and all the thinkers who either denied the cognitive value of this method or decisively limited its heuristic capabilities. To this last group belong all those numerous thinkers who have contended that all sensory-perceptional and rational ways of cognition give to us only a superficial knowledge of the sensory-empirical surface of true reality and that true reality can be cognized only through the supersensory-superrational intuition of genius in all fields of creativity and cognition. This has been one of the most important and powerful currents in the history of human thought and many of its criticisms of all sensory-rational (including the dialectic) forms of cognition have never been satisfactorily answered.[27]

Several principles of Gurvitch's sociology are in agreement with those of my sociological system. Both of us consider sociocultural reality as a reality *sui generis* different from, and irreducible to physical and biological realities. Both of us view the total sociocultural reality and sociocultural phenomena as *multidimensional,* demanding for their adequate cognition a knowledge of all its main aspects as they are combined in the integrated systems (or structured totalities) and the unintegrated congeries (unstructurable and unstructured ensembles, in Gurvitch's terms). Both of us regard a real social group or cultural system as a real unity (system) irreducible to a mere nominalistic collection of its members in social groups or of its

---

[27] See a long list of its representatives in the *Dynamics*, Vol. II, pp. 639–642; and Vol. IV, ch. 16. See its characterization in *The Ways and Power of Love*, chs. 6, 19.

components in cultural systems. Any real social group or cultural system "is richer than $n+1$ combinations of its members or elements." Any unified system, social group, or cultural system has its own form of being, its own static and dynamic properties, its own logic, ways of change, and uniformities not found in a mere nominalistic combination of their elements and unaccountable from a nominalistic and singularistic standpoint.

Besides these real similarities there are many "ambivalent-ambiguous" similarities (in the terms of Gurvitch's dialectic) on a number of important points of both systems. For example, my conception of the "generic" model of sociocultural phenomena corresponds to Gurvitch's "microsociology of the manifestation of sociability" as the simplest social phenomenon. My classification of "open and closed," "unibonded, multibonded, and encyclopedic" groups is analogous to Gurvitch's "open and closed," "unifunctional, multifunctional, and suprafunctional" groups and ensembles. Our conception of social classes is fairly similar. My concepts of "organized," "as if organized," and "unorganized and disorganized" social groups are somewhat similar to Gurvitch's "structured," "structurable," and "unstructurable" social totalities. The pluralistic conceptions of social time-causality-space-determinism-liberty in both systems is mutually reconcilable. There is an essential similarity of the main methods of sociology (including dialectic) in both systems. We both stress an urgent need for the close cooperation of sociology and history. There are other real and "ambivalent" similarities.

There are differences also. For example, my conceptions, classifications, and theories are more empirical than Gurvitch's, which are more "formal" and less frequently subjected to empirical verification. My theoretical and empirical "constructs" and "models" are less cumbersome in their adequate simplicity than the corresponding needlessly complicated "constructs" of Gurvitch. In my sociology the theory of cultural systems is much more developed than in Gurvitch's sociology, which is mainly a theory of social systems. My system of sociology contains a much more systematic, developed, and empirically verified theory of sociocultural processes and change (including the systematic study of wars and internal disturbances as the sharpest forms of social conflicts) than Gurvitch's system. His theory of the structuration, destructuration, and restructuration of social totalities, of conflict, and of change is still in a somewhat fragmentary and rudimentary state. He has not developed it into a systematic and empirically verified theory of sociocultural dynamics.

These real and "ambivalent" similarities are briefly mentioned at this point in order to give the reader the correct perspective in regard to the criticisms that follow. The differences pointed out in the criticisms in no way preclude the many similarities on a number of important points in both systems of sociology.

Some of the weaknesses in Gurvitch's system of general and special sociologies are *general.* They mar his whole system of sociology. Others are *specific.* The most important of the general defects are his unwarranted stress on the empirical and realistic character of his system; the vagueness of many of his basic concepts and theories; his conspicuous proclivity to cumbersome classifications; the artificial or defective character of several classifications and of their classes or divisions; the dogmatic character of many of his propositions and correlations of an empirical nature.

1. Despite Gurvitch's claim that his system is an "empirico-realistic" one, there is very little real empirical research, data, or uniformities in practically any of his works. Some empirical material, like various types of concrete social groups or historical societies, is mentioned here and there, but mainly to illustrate his general and abstract propositions or divisions of his classifications. All in all his system of sociology is largely abstract, formal, and fairly remote from concrete empirical realities. The abstract character of a theory does not necessarily make it defective. In many cases such a character is a cognitive asset to a theory (as is the case with several of Gurvitch's abstract or formal theories). But a predominantly abstract theory like Gurvitch's can hardly claim to be particularly empirical. This does not mean that a theory cannot be simultaneously abstract and empirical. However, a happy synthesis of this sort is very difficult to achieve. Gurvitch, apparently, wanted to marry dialectic

to empiricism in order to avoid contradicting his own statements, first, that "dialectic . . . is but a destruction of formal logic, of the general, of the abstract, of the discursive," and, second, that sociology should have a close cooperation with history as the discipline dealing with concrete, empirical realities: concrete individuals, events, groups, and configurations. He wanted his theories to be simultaneously concretely empirical and abstractly dialectical, generalizing and singularizing. He wanted, in other words, to have his dialectic cake and at the same time to eat it empirically and realistically. Compelled to choose one of the horns of this dilemma, he made his choice in favor of the fairly abstract, formal, partly dialectic character of his sociological system at the cost of its truly empirical nature. Despite his claims he failed to synthesize dialectic with empirical-realism in his system.

2. Side by side with logically elegant and sufficiently clear propositions, Gurvitch's sociology contains a number of vaguely defined concepts and statements concerning the strategic points of his theory. He often uses the terms social totality, ensemble, group, organization, structure, structured, collectivity, cadre social, depth-level, and society interchangeably for denoting what is actually a social or cultural system. Despite the central importance of this concept in his system of sociology, he hardly ever gives us a careful analysis and definition of social and cultural *Ganzheiten* and frequently applies these terms to what I call congeries of nominal total social realities, ensembles, *cadres sociaux*, collectivities, societies, groupings, totalities, and depth-levels. In some places, he differentiates social systems (totalities, ensembles, *cadres sociaux*, collectivities) from civilizations or cultural systems; in other places he depicts civilization as the mere cement of social totalities, groups, and global societies.

3. Gurvitch's proclivity to construct cumbersome classifications has already been mentioned. His system of sociology consists largely of a multitude of various classifications. Some of these are logically elegant and heuristically fruitful; others are unduly complicated and cognitively fruitless. Taken together they compose the framework of his sociological system. For this reason, *classificatory system of sociology* is, perhaps, the most accurate name for Gurvitch's system.

Gurvitch classifies the total social reality into microsociological manifestations of sociability, subclassified into sociability by partial fusion and sociability by partial opposition. Each of these is in turn subdivided into active and passive, unifunctional, multifunctional, and suprafunctional. Various combinations of these forms of sociability are then classified according to the intensity and depth of the fusion of collective intuitions into three classes: Communion, Community, and Mass. Thus the merely microsociological social reality is cut into some twelve different slices or "manifestations."

Then come the much more complex and numerous, vertical and horizontal classifications of macrosociological divisions of the total social reality into ten depth-levels, each level again subdivided into two or more subclasses. Next comes the classification of the fifteen criteria for classifying social groupings, followed by classifications of these groupings, social classes, and social structures, each class of these subdivided in turn into several varieties. After these classifications comes the classification of eight criteria for classifying global societies and then the classification of these societies themselves. In brief, we have an extraordinary proliferation of vertical, horizontal, and crisscrossing classificatory plants in Gurvitch's sociological garden.

Some of these classificatory plants are beautiful cognitive flowers—logically impeccable and correctly differentiating diverse classes of empirical phenomena. Unfortunately, other plants in his garden are mere cognitive weeds, devoid of either logical or dialectical or empirical beauty. Examples of these weeds are given below. Here I am compelled to conclude that a multitude of classifications confuses rather than clarifies our knowledge of the total social reality.

4. Gurvitch's classification of the total social reality into ten depth-levels can serve as an example of his defective "weedy" classifications. The *fundamentum divisionis* of this classification in Gurvitch's sociology is the comparative ease with which each depth-level can be observed, beginning with the most easily visible and ending with the most hidden one. The most visible depth-level is the "morphological and ecological surface level" of social reality. Here is Gurvitch's description of this level or class of social phenomena:

By morphological and ecological surface is meant natural as well as technical milieux, objects, bodies and departments participating in social life and graspable by external perception. To this level belong also geographic and demographic basis of the total social phenomena: density of population, its distribution on the ground, its movements from villages to the cities and back, the attractions exerted upon it by different regions or urban centers; social seat or habitat of groups, territories of communities, parishes, counties, provinces, states, etc. Also monuments, buildings, churches, barracks, prisons, houses, factories, stores, studios; various means of communication; diverse vehicles, utensils, instruments, machines, industrial and agricultural produce, food, etc. All this material exteriorization of social reality is only social insofar as far as it is penetrated by collective human action.[28]

Gurvitch dumped into this level almost all the conditions of geographic and technological environments, demographic composition and vital processes of the population, social migrations and mobility, urban and rural centers, administrative divisions of the population's territories and almost all of what is usually called "material culture." The unscientific character of this division is obvious without any further comment. It is not a real class of social reality but a gigantic dump of congeries. Gurvitch's assumption that these are the conditions most easily observable by, and the least hidden from, external perception adds to its unscientific nature. As purely physical, material, phenomena, perhaps they are. But such physical phenomena as birth-death-marriage-morbidity rates, as migrations and mobility, as boundaries of counties-provinces-states, as means of communication and transportation, and as dispersion or concentration of population are hardly graspable by external perception: Long and industrious statistical research is necessary to obtain knowledge of these phenomena.

As social phenomena almost all of these are ungraspable, unobservable, and incomprehensible by and through external perception. A person who does not know the meaning of scientific laboratory, church, business office, apartment house, railroad station, store, factory, bank, symphony hall, prison,

[28] *Traité de Sociologie*, Vol. I, p. 158.

buildings of parliament, university, and theater, or the social meaning of any building, of any means of communication (radio, television, press), of county, municipality, and state, of marriage, divorce, crime, migration, and mobility cannot observe, properly understand, describe, and study the social phenomena in this depth-level. To properly understand the social nature of all these phenomena, an observer has to have an understanding of all the meanings-values-norms that these buildings, means of communications, gadgets, utensils, and other phenomena manifest, objectify, externalize, and materialize. Otherwise, the real social character of all the phenomena of this depth-level would be incomprehensible to the observer, because these meanings-values-norms can neither be easily observed nor grasped by external perception. Gurvitch himself confirms this by stating that "all the phenomena of this morphological-ecological level are material externalizations of social reality," and that "collective ideas and values . . . collective mental states are hidden behind all material externalizations or incarnations of this as well as of other depth-levels." The ninth depth-level, "collective ideas and values," is, he says, the most hidden from, and least accessible to, external observation.[29]

Practically none of the levels in Gurvitch's classifications are real classes or unities of social phenomena. They are, rather, veritable "congeries" or heaps of heterogeneous and poorly outlined psychosocial phenomena dumped into this or that depth-level. On the other hand, several more or less homogeneous social phenomena are divided and placed into two or more different depth-levels. For instance, regular collective conducts like ritual and procedural behavior, mores and folkways, based upon rigorous regulations, are separated from "organized collective behaviors," based upon "pre-established strict regulations" and placed in different depth-levels. The same is true of norms of conduct. "Signs and symbols" are separated into two different levels—"collective ideas and values," and "collective attitudes." Both are then separated from "collective mental states and psychic acts," thus forming a total of three different levels.

[29] *Ibid.*, pp. 158, 167.

Then among these levels suddenly pops up a "level of social roles" and "effervescent and innovating collective behaviors," each level outlined vaguely, without a clear indication as to whether it is a unified system or a pile of congeries.

With a slight variation these criticisms are applicable to Gurvitch's delineations and classifications of social groupings, especially of social structures, and global societies. As mentioned before, Gurvitch distinguishes social structure from social group, social organization, and institution, even from his concepts of unstructurable, structurable, and structured social ensembles and totalities. He does not give, however, a clear definition of his social structures and their specific characteristics.

Finally, despite his eight criteria for defining and classifying global societies, they remain poorly defined. The fourteen examples of historical global societies given by Gurvitch are not so much global societies as varieties of mainly politico-economic regimes of a few historical societies that do not meet even his own eight criteria and in no way are inclusive or global in Gurvitch's sense. His definition of global societies and his characterization of each of the fourteen global societies does not tell us anything about the kind of science, philosophy, religion, law, ethics, fine arts, social relationships, system of values, and way of life of any of these societies. Nor are Gurvitch's main *differentia* of the global societies—namely, that they are social totalities vastest and richest in content, surpassing in their plenitude and authority all functional groupings, social classes, and structures, and having juridical sovereignty over all social groupings, including the state—clear. A question arises as to what part or authority of the global society is the richest and most authoritative and has juridical sovereignty over all its groups, social classes, structures, and cultural systems. If we subtract from each of Gurvitch's global societies all the groups, classes, structures, and cultural systems that allegedly are controlled by it, what remains? Practically nothing. If his definition means that the politico-economic organization of the global societies has these characteristics and control, then this interpretation contradicts his own statement that the global society controls and has juridical sovereignty over even the state, the foremost political organization. Since, according to Gurvitch, global society surpasses the state in richness, plenitude, and sovereignty and controls it, he evidently means by global society a social ensemble different from the state. If his global society implies the supremacy of politico-economic factors and groups over all other factors and groups, then such an interpretation contradicts again Gurvitch's own rejection of all theories of "dominant, primary and most powerful factors and groups." If, finally, his definition means that in global societies all groupings, classes, structures, cultural systems are in harmonious relationship with one another and, in mutual cooperation, exert most powerful control and juridical sovereignty, then we must ask upon whom and what social groups and cultural systems does the global society exert this influence. If it exerts it on its own part, then the definition becomes platitudinous, because any whole is richer than its single part. Besides, such an interpretation decidedly contradicts one of the basic principles of Gurvitch: In any social totality there is always latent or actual conflict between its parts, and many conflicts are always present in intergroup relationships. We can conclude that his definition is largely indeterminate and meaningless. It does not indicate what remains of a global society if we exclude from it all its groups, classes, structures, and cultural systems; it does not state what part of it is richer and has juridical sovereignty over what other parts; and the meaning of his *differentia specifica* of the global societies is vague.

His fourteen global societies have hardly any *fundamentum divisionis* or hardly any important common characteristic to unify them into one real (not nominal) class or genus. There is hardly any basic similarity between the charismatic-theocratic global society of ancient Egypt, which lasted for a few millennia, and the fascist-technocratic societies of Italy and Germany, which lasted for a couple of decades. What are the similarities between the Greek and the Roman, the archaic, the patriarchal, the emerging and developed capitalist states, and the state collectivist societies? Some, like the state systems, have lived for centuries, whereas others expired after a few years or decades; some were powerful empires exerting their control over vast populations and territories, whereas others have been purely local and comparatively uninfluential organizations, like most of the feudal principalities, primitive groups, and patriarchal organizations. None has been truly universal and perennial. They have had quite different politico-economic organizations and still more different cultural, scientific, philosophical, religious, ethical, legal, and aesthetic systems and congeries. In brief, the fourteen global societies represent a somewhat incidental and nominal collection of heterogeneous historical (politico-economic) organizations arbitrarily unified by Gurvitch into one fictitious category. Taken as a whole, Gurvitch's "histology and anatomy" of the total social reality cannot be considered completely scientific; many of his divisions of this reality are quite incorrect and need to be redrawn along different and much simpler lines.

Similar defective definitions and classifications are scattered throughout his work. For instance, in his sociology of knowledge, he gives two different sixfold classifications of knowledge or mental acts. In both classifications, the six forms of knowledge are largely overlapping, knowledge of the same kind is divided and listed in two different classes, whereas two different forms of knowledge are put into the same class: Intuitive knowledge is separated from mystic; positive from empirical and adequate; rational from speculative; scientific from the perceptive knowledge of the external world and from the knowledge of groups and societies (as though all knowledge of the external world or of groups is unscientific); and knowledge of groups and societies from political knowledge.[30]

5. Finally, despite Gurvitch's claim that his dialectic and empirico-realist system of sociology is antidogmatic and free from philosophic and other speculative assumptions, in reality it is speculative, formal, and philosophical. Furthermore, it contains a number of dogmatic statements and conclusions. I have already pointed out that this philosophy of having no philosophy is a peculiar kind of philosophy of its own. By the same token, Gurvitch's contention to be free from any dogmatism still remains a dogmatism *sui generis*. In addition, I indicated that

[30] *Ibid.*, pp. 122–127.

Gurvitch's philosophy is a sophisticated combination of the philosophies of Fichte, Marx, Scheler, Lask, Hartmann, Husserl, and Bergson; in his system of sociology, a careful reader can easily discern dogmatic assumptions taken from Marx, Proudhon, Durkheim, Mauss, Scheler, Simmel, von Wiese, and other formal and philosophical sociologists. An abundance of dogmatic assumptions of an empirical character occur in the many functional correlations between his *cadres sociaux* on the one hand and one of his twelve forms of knowledge, fourteen types of the *genre de moralité*, systems of law, or varieties of social time on the other.[31] In his sociologies of knowledge, of moral life, of law, and of time conceptions, Gurvitch formulates a considerable number of generalized empirical uniformities between the types of *cadres sociaux* (or, in usual terms, social groups) and the types of knowledge, morality, law, and social time functionally connected with each of his social groups or totalities. However interesting and significant these uniformities and "functional correlations" are, all of them are set forth dogmatically, with no empirical evidence to corroborate their scientific validity.

Although some of these uniformities may be correct, others can be shown to be fallacious. Correct or fallacious, they remain purely speculative, dogmatic guesses until they are tested.

CONCLUSION

The above criticisms concisely outline the main shortcomings of Gurvitch's dialectic and system of general and special sociologies. These defects seriously mar his treatises about social time, determinism, and liberty. Nevertheless, his methodological, philosophical, and sociological contributions remain among the most significant of our time. Each of his main works notably increases our knowledge of social realities, opens new dimen-

---

[31] See these "functional correlations" in Gurvitch's *Traité de Sociologie*, Vol. II, chs. II, III, IV, and in his *The Spectrum of Social Time*, *passim*.

sions of the multidimensional sociocultural universe, and teaches us not only by its scientific verities but also by its errors.

SARTRE'S AND KÜHNE'S DIALECTIC SOCIOLOGIES AND PHILOSOPHIES

The resurgence today of dialectic philosophies and sociologies manifests itself in the rapidly increasing number of dialectic studies published and in the growing frequency of the use of the term dialectic in European and, in a lesser degree, American sociological publications. Indeed, the term has become fashionable.[32] Of recent dialectic sociologies and social philosophies besides the works of Gurvitch, J. P. Sartre's *Critique de la Raison dialectique*[33] and O. Kühne's *Allgemeine Soziologie*[34] deserve special mention.[35]

Sartre's treatise is primarily a philosophical work. It attempts to give a synthesis of dialectical philosophies, philoso-

---

[32] As random examples of this fashion the following works and articles can be mentioned here: Otto Kühne, *Allgemeine Soziologie* (Berlin, 1958); W. Heinrich, "Dualistishe Lehrgebäude in den Sozialwissenschaften"; H. Lefebvre, "Reflections sur le structuralism et l'histoire," *Cahiers internationaux de sociologie*, XXXV (1963), 3–24; F. Dumont, "Idéologie et savoire historique," *ibid.*, pp. 43–60; C. Lévy-Strauss, *Anthropologie structural* (Paris, 1958), *La pensée sauvage* (Paris, 1956), ch. X, and his "Introduction" to M. Mauss' *Sociologie et Anthropologie* (Paris, 1960); P. L. van den Berghe, "Dialectic and Functionalism," *ASR* 28(1963), 695–705; R. Dahrendorf, *Class and Class Conflict in Industrial Society* (Stanford, 1959); L. Schneider, "Toward Assessment of Sorokin's View of Change," and my "Reply" in Zollschan and Hirsch's *Explorations in Social Change*; L. Schneider, "The Role of the Category of Ignorance in Sociological Theory," *ASA*, 27(1962), 492–508; H. Znaniecki Lopata, "The Dysfunctional Effects of the Dissemination of Social Science Knowledge"; the works of the Soviet sociologists, of M. Merleau-Ponti, J. P. Sartre, and of A. Cuvillier, indicated before. Other works will be mentioned below.

[33] (Paris, 1960).

[34] (Berlin, 1958).

[35] The fairly vast dialectic literature published by the Soviet sociologists and philosophers represents, with a few exceptions, mainly an "orthodox" reiteration of the theories of Marx, Engels, and Lenin. For this reason, this vast literature can be passed by in this work without a special analysis and criticism.

phies of history, and the sociologies of Hegel, Marx and of Existentialism as it was developed in Sartre's earlier work, *L'Être et le Néant; Essai d'Ontologie phénoménologique* (Paris, 1950). It is out of place here to analyze Sartre's philosophical system and dialectic as developed in his *Critique de la Raison dialectique*. Let it suffice to say that Sartre's work has a number of fine analyses of some of the properties of dialectic thought, side by side with several doubtful ones. Sartre's dialectic differs from that of Gurvitch in several points: It is openly based on his postulated system of philosophy. On this point it contradicts Gurvitch's contention that dialectic is or should be free from any philosophical postulation or scientific assumption.[36] Sartre's dialectic in its interpretations of historical and social processes is more individualistic and less collectivistic than Gurvitch's. It is also more "methaphysical" or less "positivistic" than Gurvitch's dialectic (considered by Sartre to be a variety of positivism or empiricism remote from genuine dialectic). And Sartre's dialectic as method uses mainly the Hegelian dialectic of antinomies and syntheses and largely ignores what Gurvitch calls the dialectics of complementarity, mutual implication, and ambiguity and ambivalence.

In addition, Sartre ascribes to the dialectic's "creative and historical reasons" much greater power to comprehend historical and social phenomena and to determine objective historical and social processes than Gurvitch does. Sartre's dialectic evolves into a "sublime-philosophy of individual human existence which throughout all its alienations in the natural and social world, eventually returns to itself by recovering its liberty (from all its alienations)."[37] Gurvitch's dialectic is free from all ascendant or progressive, descendant or regressive philosophies of social and historical processes. In these points it is more scientific than Sartre's dialectic.

Sartre's dialectical sociology, sketched in his *Critique*, is a dialectical philosophy of history rather than of sociology. He only "hurriedly" outlines various ensembles, "serialities," col-

---

[36] Cf. Gurvitch, *Dialectique et Sociologie*, pp. 157–176.
[37] *Ibid.*, pp. 173–174.

lectives, and social classes as he develops the main conceptual framework of his philosophy of history. These sketches of various social totalities and their dialectic "totalizations" and "detotalizations" are too general to make a real contribution to the existing sociological knowledge of social, cultural, and personality systems (and congeries) or to add anything new to their anatomy and physiology.

Sartre's dialectical theory of the historical process, of daily human *praxis* and existence, depicts this process and *praxis* as a dialectical ongoing struggle of individuals and groups for their liberty and genuine human existence against incessant obstacles, "alienations," and "inertia" that inhibit the full realization of this "free," "nonalienated," truly human existence. These obstacles continuously endeavor to turn individuals and their *praxes* into a series of uncreative, alienated, or unfree forms of humanity performing antidialectic, "practico-inert" activities.

The perennial conflict of these two opposite forces of liberty and inertia, of unalienated creative existence and of an uncreative, "alienating inertia" in the lives of individuals and collectives, is the central theme of the historical process as well as of the daily existence of individuals and groups. At some periods, the forces of liberty prevail, at others the forces of inertia prevail. But all in all, throughout the whole process of human history, the forces of creative liberty are gaining. Eventually they will triumph, and will be free from all the forces of alienation and uncreative inertia.

The reasons for this optimistic variation on Hegelian philosophy are: "Individual dialectics (individual *praxis*, efforts, activities, production), which, after having created by the same stroke man's domination over nature (thesis) and the antihumanity of the domination of unorganized materiality over man (antithesis), create progressively by their unified efforts a truly human order (*le règne humain*)—that is, free relations among men (synthesis)." "The free actions of everyone, insofar as they are dialectic translucidities," are the first factor in this supreme historical trend.[38] The second and the third factors of this cen-

---

[38] J. P. Sartre, *Critique de la Raison dialectique* (Paris, 1960), Vol. I, pp. 377, 398.

tral trend are "universal reason" (*la raison universelle*) and "historical reason" (*la raison historique*), which Sartre regards as "immanent to individual *praxis* and to history." The force of these reasons is alienated in the "practico-inert" activities of individuals and ensembles, but they are recovered in different degrees in social classes and groups. In the long run, these rational, creative forces triumph over the force of inertia by producing through their dialectics less alienated or more free forms of social reality itself.[39]

Such is Sartre's philosophy of history in a nutshell. In Sartre's work, these ideas are greatly developed and presented, with all the finest reasoning of an eminent dialectician and social philosopher, along the lines of the logical, psychological, and sociological analyses in his *L'Être et le Néant*.

The central framework of Sartre's philosophy of history represents a variation on the Hegelian conception of history as a theodicy combined with Descartian rationalism, Hobbesian individualism, and the Marxian theory of alienation and *praxis*. It is too methaphysical, too abstract, and too distant from empirical psychosocial and cultural realities to be notably helpful in our cognition of *empirical* sociocultural phenomena. His philosophy of history hardly contributes much to sociology, but his numerous analyses of liberty and necessity, of the role of groups in history, of the perennial conflict of the creative and the "practico-inert," of the "liberating" and "alienating" forces in the *praxes* and the activities of individuals and groups, and of several other psychosocial and philosophical problems deserve to be studied by sociologists, anthropologists, and psychologists. These analyses open to us several hitherto little-known aspects of these phenomena and thereby enrich our knowledge of these problems. Sartre's attempt to unify into one sociophilosophical system the elements of Hegelian, Marxian, and Existentialist theories has also a considerable significance for social scientists and psychologists. In brief, some of Sartre's analyses that are sandwiched in between various parts of his metahistorical and metasociological philosophy of history represent a valuable contribution to the psychosocial sciences.

[39] *Ibid.*, pp. 159, 557, 755.

Otto Kühne's *Allgemeine Soziologie* represents a dialectic interpretation of social life—social systems (*Einheiten*), social processes, and social behavior of personality—in the terms of dualistic and dialectic polarities. Its starting assumption is that all of social life and all its systems (unities) and processes have a polar character and meaning.

Before developing and substantiating this assumption, Kühne sharply differentiates the "monistic" from the "dualistic" and/or "dialectical" unities or wholes (*Einheiten*). The monistic unities (*Einheiten*) represent just the opposite sides or parts of the same whole, like the right and the left halves of the same face of the same man or two sides of the same coin. The dualistic and dialectical unities represent two opposite phenomena fused together into a new unity. In such a unity the fused components do not lose their individuality; at the same time they mutually complement each other and by their fusion create a new unity or whole. Reciprocal relationships of husband and wife serve as an example of a dualistic-dialectical unity: In their new family unity each of them remains separate and retains his sameness; at the same time, however, both are united into a new family community (*Ehegemeinschaft*).

In the social-dialectical polar unities, the interaction of two fused elements (or forces) is not only causal but also meaningful (*sinnvolle*) and purposeful (*zweckbedingt*) or teleological. This "causal-meaningful-purposive" nature of Kühne's dialectic-dualistic social unities (or systems) is essentially similar to my "causal-meaningful" unity of all social and cultural systems.[40]

Kühne analyzes in great detail these dialectic-dualistic unities and makes quite clear how they differ from monistic unities and from what I call cultural congeries and unorganized social groups. He distinguishes also conceptual (contradictory and contrary) categories from the polar realities of social life itself: "Life itself knows generally no absolute and contradictory opposites (*Gegensätze*) like 'good' and 'not good.'" To the conceptually contradictory categories "good" and "not good"

---

[40] Otto Kühne, *Allgemeine Soziologie*, pp. 46 ff.

in real life correspond the polar "good" and "bad" of life itself. The contrary realities differ from each other not only quantitatively but also qualitatively:

> Such opposite realities are given in all spheres of human thought and action. In all such polarities one of its polar elements exists only through the other, and the whole polar unity exists only through, that is, simultaneously with, its parts. Yes, the polarity meets us everywhere in our daily life in multiform antithetic confrontations, like positive and negative, active and passive, inner and outer, [nature and *Geist*, form and content, means and end, high and low, I and thou].[41]

Having indicated the many polarities in human social life as a series of smaller fugues welding into larger fugues, Kühne builds a sort of a grand polar (or contrapuntal) fugue of the basic polarity of "I and the world around me" (*Ich und Umwelt*). His analysis of I and Thou (*Ich und Du*) leads him to a dialectic theory of personality, while his examination of the social world (*Umwelt*) results in his theory of the main forms of social *Ganzheiten*: communities, associations, organizations, and other social systems. Since each personality and social unity is made up of dialectically opposite elements and is inherently dynamic, his analysis of personality and of social *Ganzheiten* evolves into his theory of the main social processes. Just as all his narrower polarities in the sphere of personality-structure and behavior and in the sphere of the social world are dialectically derived from the basic polarity *Ich und Umwelt*, so also a multitude of polar social processes are inferred from two basic polar processes, social selection and adaptation (*Auslese und Anpassung*), immanently given and continuously working in social life.[42] These two processes are dialectically opposed to each other. They continuously inhibit each other and exert the opposite effects upon human personality, social *Ganzheiten*, and social life. The factor and process of social selection works in

---

[41] *Ibid.*, pp. 49–53.

[42] In *Allgemeine Soziologie*, see his classifications of "Gesellungs und Lebenssphäre in Gesellschaftsleben," pp. 89–95; of social processes, pp. 520–521; of the processes of "social selection," pp. 522–593; and of the processes of "adaptation," pp. 594–753.

favor of the individualization, inequalization, estrangement, and liberation of human beings from social bindings, from conformity, and from the limitations imposed upon them by various social groups and natural forces. If it is unchecked and given full freedom for its play the result is a triumph of crass egoism, excessive nonconformism, crazy individualism, disorganization of social bodies (community, association, society), and social chaos and anarchy with all their dire consequences. Fortunately, the free play of this factor is incessantly checked by the counteraction of the factor and process of social adaptation. This force works to limit the freedom and egoism of individuals and groups. Through various social bodies it builds in human beings the necessary minimum of conformity, social responsibility, sociality, legal and moral obligations, equality, and collective solidarity. If it were unchecked by the factor of social selection, it would produce an entirely standardized, conformist, equalitarian, collectivistic, and totalitarian society rigidly regimented in all important fields of social life and individual conduct.

In the life-history of many societies there are periods in which one of these polar factors-processes becomes dominant and produces respective transformations in the group and its members. Fortunately, however, these two basic factors-processes go on incessantly, continuously neutralize each other, and keep the social life more or less free from the disastrous results of being dominated by one or the other. If and when one of these factors-processes begins to become dominant, the dire consequences dialectically prepare the way for the increasing interference and influence of the opposite factor-process. Eventually, this factor checks the domination of the other and re-establishes the balanced unity.[43]

Such is the skeleton of Kühne's dialectic-dualistic system of general sociology. He thoughtfully analyzes such important problems of sociology as the methods of sociological investigation (which are fairly similar to my methods), social behavior, social types (which he calls polar mixed and contrary types, as opposed to M. Weber's ideal types, which Kühne finds fictitious,

---

[43] See Kühne's detailed analysis of the main forms of the processes of selection and adaptation in *Allgemeine Soziologie*, pp. 522–786.

artificial, and cognitively fruitless), and the dialectical synthesis of theoretical sociology with normative sociology.[44]

Taken as a whole, the *Allgemeine Soziologie* is a most significant dualistic system of general sociology built along the line of the dialectic of polarization.

Of its shortcomings, I shall mention only two at this point: first, like Sartre's and Gurvitch's sociologies, it is essentially formal and classificatory and fairly distant from empirical socio-cultural realities. These enter his system mainly to illustrate his concepts, definitions, and classifications. There is no systematic presentation of the causal or probabilistic or causal-meaningful uniformities and functional relationships of classes of empirical phenomena. Neither is there any original investigation of any important series or regions of empirical facts. After a careful study of Kühne's treatise, a sociologist hungry for empirical social realities remains unsatisfied. Like all the analytical and structural-functional theories such as Gurvitch's and Sartre's dialectical theories, Kühne's provides only a few empirical crumbs. Second, though Kühne's reasoning, concepts, definitions, and propositions are much clearer and more adequate from a logical and dialectical standpoint than those of the examined analytical and structural-functional theories, they are, nevertheless, vague on several points and questionable in their logical adequacy.

OTHER DUALISTIC AND TRIADIC SOCIOLOGIES

● Dualistic Types of Social Systems

Kühne's dualistic sociology is only one of many modern sociological models constructed by sociologists of the recent past and of the present:

[44] "The main task of sociology consists in elaboration and clarification of the bases and rules for humanly right (*ein menschen Gerechtes*) and humanly conscious (*Menschbewusstes*) thinking and acting in regard to the personal human world (*personlichen Mitwelt*) and the world of objective-phenomena around us (*sachlichen Umwelt*). . . . As sociologists we want to learn 'as human beings' life's right ways of (*Lebens-richtig*) thinking and acting in regard to the personal human world as well as the external world of phenomena. . . . Insofar sociology is a theory of an art of social living (*Soziale Lebenskunstlehre*)." *Allgemeine Soziologie*, p. 467.

One of the persistent aspects of sociological enterprise is the very old tradition of typing social entities antithetically. As Sorokin pointed out, the tradition may be traced back to the philosophical speculation of the Classical Greeks and to the epoch of Confucius.[45]

Despite the age of the tradition it still has a marked validity and appears to be one of the fundamental approaches to sociological phenomena. Such familiar conceptualizations as Maine's status society and contract society; Spencer's militant and industrial forms; Ratzenhofer's conquest state and culture state; Wundt's natural and cultural polarity; Tönnies' *Gemeinschaft* and *Gesellschaft* forms; Durkheim's mechanical and organic solidarity; Cooley's primary and secondary groups; MacIver's communal and associational relations; Zimmerman's localistic and cosmopolitan communities; Odum's folk-state pair; Redfield's folk-urban continuum; Sorokin's familistic vs. contractual relations; Becker's sacred and secular societies; as well as such non-personalized but common dichotomies as primitive-civilized; literate-nonliterate; and rural vs. urban are examples of this tradition. Obviously these varied polarizations are not interchangeable and do not abstract the "same thing" out of the social world, but they do have something in common. . . . They exemplify the view that it is necessary to distinguish fundamentally different types of social organization in order to establish a range within which transitional or intermediary forms can be comprehended.[46]

According to W. Heinrich, "Many systems of sociology and economics are marked by a strong dualism. It consists in that such theories view social or economic life as going on in two basic, polarly opposite spheres or forms of being."[47] For the

[45] See my Foreword to C. P. Loomis's English translation of F. Tönnies' *Gemeinschaft und Gesellschaft* published under the title *Fundamental Concepts of Sociology* (New York, 1940). In this Foreword, I briefly mention the dichotomic theories of Confucius, Plato, Aristotle, Cicero, St. Augustine, Joachim de Flore, Albertus Magnus, St. Thomas Aquinas, Nicolaus Cusanus, ibn-Khaldun, and, later on, the dualistic theories of the German historical school, Savigny, Puchta, and Hegel as predecessors of Tönnies' dualistic categories of *Gemeinschaft* and *Gesellschaft*.

[46] J. C. McKinney and C. P. Loomis, "The Typological Tradition," in J. S. Rouček, *Contemporary Sociology* (New York, 1958), pp. 557–558. See there an outline of each of these dichotomies and the authors' own dynamic variation of these, pp. 557–581.

[47] W. Heinrich, "Dualistische Lehrgebäude in den Sozialwissenschaften," p. 5.

cognition and clarification of social and economic phenomena, the dualistic theories construct a dualistic system of basic categories and use it for a study of society or economy.

To the above list of antithetic theories Heinrich and Cuvillier add a number of others, such as Ferguson's and Saint-Simon's militant and industrial types of society (later on developed by Spencer); Bachofen's *Mutterrecht* and *Vaterrecht* types of communities (which influenced Tönnies' theory of *Gemeinschaft* and *Gesellschaft*); Von Gierke's *Herrschaft* and *Genossenschaft;* Schurtz's *Geschlechtsverbände* and *Geselligkeitsverbände*; and several "polarity types" outlined by Fourrier, Owen, Proudhon, Kropotkin, and other socialist and anarchist ideologists.[48]

In more recent works, the construction of dualistic-polar models or types has been vigorously continued. It is exemplified by different variations on Tönnies's two types, by Freyer's *Standesgesellschaft* and *Klassengesellschaft*, Eucken's *Zentralverwaltungswirtschaft* and *Frein Verkehrswirtschaft*, Vierkandt's *Anerkennungsgemeinschaft* and *Machtgemeinschaft*, Geiger's *Verbanden* and *Gruppen*, Spengler's *Dasein* and *Wachsein* (with subdivision into polarities of woman-man, youth-old, country-city, culture-civilization, idea-power, *Volk-Masse, Mutterlichkeit-Geschlechtigkeit, Heimat-Vaterland*, etc.); by Rüstow's *Herrschaft und Freiheit*;[49] by Oppenheimer's polar categories of political means and economic means in economics; by Popper's open and closed societies; by Dahrendorf's binary class conflict of the ruling and the ruled strata in social groups;[50] and so on.

Most of these polarity-theories or polarity-metaphysics (as Heinrich calls some of them) contain also linear theories of historical trends leading in the course of time from the *Gemeinschaft* to the *Gesellschaft* type (Tönnies and others); from the *Herrschaft* to the *Genossenschaft*; from the *Herrschaft* to the

---

[48] See a concise characterization of these theories in W. Heinrich's "Dualistische Lehrgebäude," pp. 6–30; and A. Cuvillier, *Manuel de Sociologie*, Vol. I, ch. 4. On Fichte's, Proudhon's, and Marx's polarities, see Gurvitch, *Dialectique et Sociologie*, chs. 5, 7, 8.

[49] A. Rüstow, *Ortsbestimmung der Gegenwart* (3 vols.; Zurich, 1950–1957).

[50] K. R. Popper, *The Open Society and Its Enemies* (London, 1957). R. Dahrendorf, *Class and Class Conflict in Industrial Society* (Stanford, 1954).

Freiheit type (Rüstow and others); from high culture to civilization (Spengler and others); from the class society of the exploiters and the exploited to the classless "unalienated" communist or socialist society (Fourrier, Owen, Proudhon, Marx, and others), from the militant to the peaceful and harmonious social order; and from the autocratic to the democratic social systems.[51] In this respect almost all of these polarity philosophies of history belong to the "dominant stream of social thought of the eighteenth and the nineteenth centuries concentrated largely on a study of various linear trends and dynamic *laws of evolution and progress* allegedly governing the main course of human history. It paid little attention to the repeated sociocultural processes—those which are repeated either in social space (in various societies), or in time, or in both."[52]

● Triadic Models of Social Systems

Side by side with the surveyed dualistic models of social systems, a number of sociologists, social scientists, and philosophers of history of the recent past and of the present constructed a variety of the triadic—dialectical and nondialectical—types of social systems. Deliberately or not, they followed the classical example of Hegel's triadic dialectic of thesis, antithesis, synthesis and his triadic models of sociocultural systems. Applying this triadic dialectic in his analysis of historical and social realities, Hegel dissected these realities and their transformations into a series of triadic dynamic systems. During its historical

---

[51] See, on the linear trends and political ideologies of these dualistic theories, W. Heinrich's "Dualistische Lehrgebäude," *passim*.

[52] P. Sorokin, "Sociocultural Dynamics and Evolutionism," in G. Gurvitch and W. Moore, *Twentieth-Century Sociology* (New York, 1945), p. 97. See in this study a full survey and criticism of the main types of the linear trends of historical evolution and progress of mankind from the past and the present social orders to the future or the "eschatological terminal state" of mankind, pp. 96–120. At the present time, most of these linear theories of evolution and progress, including most of the linear trends surveyed here, are abandoned as scientifically untenable.

unfolding, each of these systems passes, according to Hegel, through the three dialectic phases and produces thereby three subtypes of sociocultural systems, like the triadic social systems of the family, the civil society, and the state (the Hegelian conception of these terms is different from their common meanings), the systems of art, religion, and philosophy, of the soul, consciousness, and mind, of abstract right, morality, and social ethics, and of symbolic, classic, and romantic art.

A number of recent and contemporary sociologists have followed the pre-Hegelian and Hegelian triadic tradition and formulated their own variations of the triadic models of sociocultural systems. Thus, in his later work, Tönnies introduces three triadic classifications: social entities (*soziale Wesenheiten*) classified into social relationships (*Verhältnisse*), collectives (*Samschaften*), and social organizations or corporations (*Korperschaften*); social norms into order, law, and morality; and social values into economic, political, and intellectual or spiritual values.[53]

Schmallenbach, modifying Tönnies' *Gemeinschaft* as predominantly traditional and his *Gesellschaft* as pre-eminently rational social systems, adds to them the *Bund* as a charismatic, partly instinctive and effective, and partly politically dominant social system that plays a particularly important role in popular social movements. With some modifications, Schmallenbach's triad of social systems has been reiterated by Brobeil, Monnerot, and by other social typologists.[54]

Further examples of triadic types of social bodies are Von Wiese's classification of social forms (*Gebilde*) into masses, groups, and abstract collectives (*abstrakte Kollektiva*); M. Weber's triadic types of political organizations based upon traditional, legitimate, and charismatic power (*Herrschaft*); Vierkandt's parental (*Sippe*), cultural (*Stamm*), and political

---

[53] F. Tönnies, *Einführung in die Soziologie* (Stuttgart, 1931), pp. 237–259, and *passim*.

[54] H. Schmallenbach, *Die soziologische Kategorie des Bundes* (Munich, 1922); W. Brobeil, *Die Kategorie des Bundes im System der Soziologie* (Frankfurt, 1936); J. Monnerot, *Les faits sociaux ne sont pas des choses* (Paris, 1946).

(*Staat*) social systems;[55] and my familistic, contractual, and coercive social relationships and systems and ideational, idealistic, and sensate cultural systems.

As mentioned, some of these triadic theories pretend to be derived dialectically; others do not.

Some of these models are viewed by their authors as "ideal types or constructs" (M. Weber and others); some are considered as the types of the real social or cultural systems given in the historical life of mankind (H. Freyer and others.) Some of them contain linear interpretations of the historical process; others have no systematic theory of historical trends or laws of evolution-progress.

Finally, like the dualistic polar theories, some of the triadic sociologies have been conceived by their authors or used by various social movements as foundations for political ideologies of neoliberalism, neoconservatism, socialism, communism, totalitarianism, federalism, anarchism, bureaucracy, and technocracy.

The preceding examination of Gurvitch's, Kühne's, and Sartre's dialectic sociologies and a concise survey of the main varieties of recent dialectical and nondialectical dualistic and triadic theories gives a fairly good idea of the dialectical current of sociological thought of our time. The criticisms of the sociologies of Gurvitch, Sartre, and Kühne can now be supplemented by a critical examination of the dualistic and the triadic conceptions and of the whole current of today's dialectical sociology.

CRITICISM

In the foregoing parts of this chapter, the widely different meanings given to the terms dialectic and dialectic logic and method have been mentioned. For this reason, those terms need a substantial clarification, for if they are used loosely they become indeterminate and largely meaningless. If they are specified, as is the case with Gurvitch's and Sartre's dialectics, they have been shown to be questionable in several points.

---

[55] See the outlines of these triadic theories in A. Cuvillier, *Manuel de Sociologie*, Vol. I, pp. 144–192. See there also the references to the works of these sociologists.

Even still more questionable are other recent interpretations of dialectic logic and method, like those of P. L. van den Berghe and Ralf Dahrendorf. Van den Berghe views the following elements as *differentia specifica* of the Hegelian-Marxian dialectic method:

> 1. Change is not only ubiquitus, but an important share of it is generated within the (social) system; i.e., the social structure must be looked at not only as the static framework, but also as the source of a crucial type of change; 2. change of intra-systemic or endogenous origin often arises from contradiction and conflict between two or more opposing factors. These "factors" can be values, ideologies, roles, institutions or groups. The minimum dialectic approach (if it can still be called that) seems applicable at three different levels of analysis: (a) the level of ideas and values corresponding to Hegel's use of dialectic; (b) the level of internal contradictions arising from institutional process of interaction; and (c) the level of group conflicts.[56]

Somewhat similar is Dahrendorf's concept of dialectic generally and of dialectic logic and method specifically: It also seems to view the *differentia* of immanent change and conflict as specific traits of dialectic theory.[57]

If we accept Van den Berghe's and Dahrendorf's definitions, then almost all theories of immanent ("endogenous")

---

[56] P. van den Berghe, "Dialectic and Functionalism," *ASR*, October, 1963, pp. 697–700.

[57] R. Dahrendorf, *Class and Class Conflict*. In passing, it can be noted that what Dahrendorf defines as social class is but a dichotomous social strata of the rulers and the ruled, a variation of the theories of Helvetius, R. Worms, Saint-Simon, F. Engels, L. Blanc, T. Veblen, J. Blondel, G. Mosca, and V. Pareto, who identified social class with the strata of the rulers and the ruled, of the exploiters and the exploited, of the privileged and the disfranchised, of the conquerors and the conquered, generally, with the relatively superior and inferior ranks of a social system. All such identifications of social class with these strata or with any of the unibonded (unidimensional) groups completely miss one of the most influential groups in modern industrial societies. The real social class is a vast group which "is 1, legally open, but actually semiclosed; 2, 'normal'; 3, solidary; 4, antagonistic to certain other social classes; 5, partly organized but mainly quasiorganized; 6, partly aware of its own unity and existence and partly not; 7, characteristic of the Western society of the eighteenth, nineteenth, and twentieth centuries; 8, a multibonded group bound together by two unibonded ties: occupational and economic similarity plus similarity of political status, different

change and of social conflict—that is, an overwhelming majority of sociological and historico-philosophical theories from Heraclitus to their own—become "dialectic," because almost all sociological and historico-philosophical theories deal with immanent ("endogenous") change and social conflict.[58] Both authors failed to indicate the specific characteristics of dialectic logic and theories.[59]

If the term dialectic is not limited to dialectic logic and method and is extended over, and applied to real social movements and group conflicts, as Van den Berghe does, then such an extension meets the same difficulties that have been pointed out in the criticism of Gurvitch's dialectics of social movements and the dialectic relationships between dialectic method and the dialectic of social movements. Just as we do not call deductive or inductive or mathematical sociocultural phenomena studied by these methods there is no reason to call dialectic social phenomena studied by the dialectic method or to call dialectic,

---

from that of other social classes." These similarities evolve the similarity of the style of living, of vital interests, and mentality of the members of the same social class. P. Sorokin, *SCP*, p. 271. See there a systematic survey and analysis of various theories of social classes and various forms of social stratification of which G. Mosca's-Dahrendorf's strata of the rulers and the ruled is only one of the forms. These two strata in no way can be considered as the real social classes defined above. *SCP*, pp. 261–275. Compare my definition of social classes with that of Gurvitch. See G. Mosca's *The Ruling Class* (New York, 1938). Mosca's ruling and ruled classes are fairly similar to Dahrendorf's "social classes."

[58] See a history of the immanent theories of social change in my *Dynamics*, Vol. IV, chs. 12, 13; the theories of social antagonisms and conflicts, *SCP*, chs. 5, 6, 7; *CST*, ch. 6; and L. A. Coser, *The Functions of Social Conflict* (New York, 1956).

[59] Van den Berghe failed also to define the specific characteristics of the "functional or structure-function" approach because his seven *differentia* of this approach (the holistic or systemic view of societies, multiple or reciprocal causation, imperfect equilibrium of social systems, always infected by various "dysfunctions," gradual change of the systems, generated by external, internal, innovating factors, and "value-consensus" as the main integrating factor) are the *differentia* common to practically all systemic sociological theories of the past as well as of the present. This fact additionally corroborates the conclusion given in the preceding chapters that recent "functional" sociologists have not presented any original system of sociology, but have only reiterated the systemic sociologies of the past and the present. See Van den Berghe's "Dialectic and Functionalism," p. 696.

deductive, or inductive every intragroup or intergroup conflict investigated by these methods. As a matter of fact most of the best studies of the main forms of social conflicts, beginning with the mildest ones like competition and ending with the sharpest ones like murder, revolution, and war, have been made without calling such studies dialectic. The same argument applies to the phenomena of alienation and estrangement, which are assumed to be dialectical by the Marxian and the non-Marxian writers. To sum up, Van den Berghe's and Dahrendorf's conceptions of dialectic method and dialectic social phenomena remain undefined and largely meaningless. The *differentia specifica* of their dialectic method and logic are common to deductive, inductive, mathematical, and to many empirical methods of studying sociocultural or psychological phenomena. Their application of the term dialectic to real social phenomena mixes the methods of study of such phenomena with their properties.

This conclusion is corroborated indirectly by the sharp denial of the very existence of a dialectic method and logic basically different from the laws of formal logic (deductive, inductive, and mathematical) by many past critics of dialectic, including St. Thomas Aquinas and Kant as well as a number of recent neo-Thomist, neo-positivist, and Cartesian logicians who, like R. Ruyer, call it the *"mythe de la raison dialectique.*[60] The eminent mathematician F. Gonseth sees dialectics as a mere "purification of knowledge under the pressure of experience with which it confronts itself,"[61] and the logician M. Barzin states that "what we call dialectic is a conception of science which, according to dialectic, is in principle subject to revision."[62] Are not these *differentia* equally applicable to any logical scientific method?

These discordant conceptions of the dialectic method and logic compel any investigator and user of this method to clarify his standpoint in this matter. My position can be summed up in the following statements:

1. Dialectic logic and method is a special modification of

---

[60] See his article in the *Revue de Métaphysique et la Morale,* Nos. 1–2 (1961), 1–34.
[61] *Dialectica,* June, 1948, p. 94.
[62] Quoted by Gurvitch in his *Dialectique et Sociologie,* p. 18.

the formal (deductive, mathematical, and inductive) logic and methods. The former in no way demolishes or cancels the latter logics and methods.

2. The relative specificity of dialectic logic and method consists in (a) making explicit the implicit tensions and multi-meaningfulness hidden in many concepts of class phenomena, especially of sociocultural class phenomena, and in (b) clarifying the correlations and mutual implications of the meanings of many concepts that otherwise, when taken alone, without reference to their correlative concepts, are meaningless, as the concept of the absolute is meaningless without its correlative concept of the relative, and as the concept of truth is meaningless without its correlative, error. Now for a few comments on these two *differentia* of dialectic logic and method:

a. Due mainly to the multidimensionality of sociocultural phenomena many concepts and definitions of various classes usually define only one or a few of their dimensions (statistical or ecological or sociogeographic or demographic or economic or political or artistic or religious or scientific) and leave undefined the other dimensions with which the defined dimension is logically or causally or causal-meaningfully connected. Because of this deficiency the unidimensional or duodimensional concepts and definitions of sociocultural or psychological class phenomena are inadequate, logically or empirically. This inadequacy manifests itself in the inner tensions and deficiencies of many of such class concepts.[63] Some of these tensions hide the dimensions contrary or even contradictory to the defined dimensions; most of the other tensions screen just different, contrasting, complementary (not contradictory) dimensions

---

[63] The classical example of this kind of deficiency is the Linnaean classification of plants on the basis of the number of stamens they have. Eventually, it was found to be inadequate and was replaced by a morphologico-genetic classification based upon more numerous, mutually complementary, characteristics of plants. "The aim of taxonomy is to produce a natural system of classification of organisms, i.e., a system that reflects the totality of similarities and differences, as well as the path of evolution." A. Cronquist, *Introductory Botany* (New York, 1961), p. 678; see there a history of taxonomic principles for classifying organisms into genera and species, ch. 33.

(logically and empirically) necessary for an adequate cognition of the defined class of phenomena.[64]

The kinds of theories that are marred by this deficiency are the extreme behavioristic or instinctivist or libidinal conceptions of human personality as well as the no less one-sided purely rationalist, idealistic, and spiritual conceptions of it. Most of the mechanistic or geographic or demographic or economic or technological interpretations of sociocultural realities and processes that try to reduce their multidimensionality and factors of their change to one dominant form or factor are also simplistic.[65]

Insofar as a logical or logico-empirical analysis helps to bring to light these hidden dimensions of reality and shows them to be causally or logically connected with dimensions defined in the concepts, it can be called *dialectic*—the dialectic of polarization when the hidden dimensions are contrary or contradictory to the defined ones, or the complementary dialectic when the hidden dimensions are just different from or contrasting to the defined ones. In both cases, these dialectic operations do not cancel the laws of formal logic, but simply represent a specific application of this logic for making the

[64] The discovery of these tensions in especially general concepts and categories (like Being and Nothing) was the starting point of the Hegelian dialectique of "thesis-antithesis-synthesis" in which Hegel extended these tensions to all class-concepts and turned the tensions into polar contraries and contradictories (antitheses). Both of these generalizations—the extension of the inner tensions to all concepts and the reduction of all tensions to antitheses—were overdrawn. Only a part of sociocultural class-concepts have the tensions and only a modest portion of these tensions are contrary or contradictory antitheses. A large part of the tensions "hide" different "complementary" dimensions overlooked by the unidimensional or duodimensional concepts and definitions. See E. Barthel, *Die Welt as Spannung und Rhythmus* (Leipzig, 1928). R. H. Williams' unpublished thesis "The Expression of Common Value Attitudes" (Harvard University, 1938), gives a survey of M. Weber's and Max Scheler's theories of conceptual and empirical tensions. See also the *Dynamics*, Vol. IV, pp. 66 ff., and chs. 12–16.

[65] In my *Contemporary Sociological Theories*, many simplistic theories are outlined and criticized. They are given in practically all the "schools of sociology" examined in that volume. Dahrendorf's concept of "social classes," mentioned before, suffers from the same defect: Instead of a many-dimensional social group (defined above), Dahren-

inadequate (unidimensional or duodimensional) concepts and theories more adequate (multidimensional).

b. The same can be said of the dialectic analysis of the correlationships and mutual complementation of many class concepts, especially of an antithetic kind, like absolute-relative, affirmative-negative, universal-singular, material-spiritual, eternal-temporal, realistic-nominalistic, rational-irrational, high-low, religious-atheistic, and so on. Each of these correlative concepts acquires a meaning only when its correlative, opposite, or contrasting meaning is given. Each of these concepts mutually defines the other. Many of the above-mentioned dualistic typologies of social entities are built according to this dialectic logic of correlation, polarities, or complementation. Those triadic typologies in which two types (the first and the second or the first and the third) are opposite (thesis and antithesis) or contrasting, the third type being either an important mixed form in the continuum between two opposite "poles" or an autonomous form different from both polar forms, are also constructed according to this logic.

Many class-concepts of a correlative, polar, and complementary kind are often constructed without involving the proper partner of such concepts or by relating such a concept to a wrong partner. The result is either a vagueness or an inadequacy of the definitions-concepts. In these conditions dialectic analysis can help in correcting such concepts by either supplementing them with their correlative partners or by indicating

---

dorf's definition indicates only one—and not the most important—characteristic of social class, namely, the contrasting distribution of political authority between the ruling and ruled strata of any social group, beginning with a small club or association and ending with vast national and international social groups. If we accept this unidimensional model of "social class," we have to conclude that the ruling tops (committees) of all social groups, beginning with small clubs and ending with empires, all belong to the same "ruling" social class, have the same vital interests, system of values, style of life, and solidarity of policies and activities. It is clear that both of Dahrendorf's "classes" are purely nominal collections of the most heterogeneous individuals with different—vital, mental, economic, occupational, political, cultural, and social characteristics, with different interests, systems of values, and ways of life. Such a collection is a mere nominal plurel and not a real social group or system. Still less is it a "social class."

the proper partner instead of the wrong one. In both cases a careful dialectic analysis can render a tangible service in comprehending complex sociocultural realities and processes.

3. In accordance with this specific character of the dialectics of complementation and polarization, it becomes comprehensible why, since ancient times, these two dialectical logics have been applied, first of all, to comprehend ultimate or total reality as the infinitely multidimensional and most general reality. All those great dialecticians from Lao-tse to Hegel who have dealt with the cognition of this reality have concluded that its nature forbids every formulation by concept or speech and that it is simply inexpressible, unutterable, indescribable, and indefinable in words, notions, or concepts. Many of these logicians called the true reality infinitude of infinitude, Tao, Nirvana, God, *coincidentia oppositorum,* divine nothing. As Nagarjuna summed up, "It escapes precision" (or definition). "Neither as Ens nor as a non-Ens can Nirvana be conceived." Whatever the specification or definition given to it, such a concept defines, at best, some of the ripples of the infinitely multidimensional ocean and cannot define the ocean itself in its quantitative and qualitative infinity. According to these dialecticians, all our concepts and categories, invented for the designation of finite realities, are inapplicable to this ultimate, total reality. J. S. Erigena put it beautifully: "God himself does not know *what* he is because God is not *what.*" Nor is the total ultimate reality either who, he, she, matter, or spirit, or any other finite Ens. Others, like St. Augustine and Nicolaus Cusanus, preferred simply to point out that the ultimate reality (God) is *coincidentia oppositorum,* which contains in itself all aspects, dimensions, or *differentia* and at the same time exceeds and transcends all of them.[66] It is above all definitions and all categories.[67]

---

[66] St. Augustine illustrates this by ascribing to God several antithetic characteristics, such as "Immutable, yet changing in all things; never new and never old, yet renewing all things. . . . Ever in action, and yet ever quiet." *Confessions,* tr. by T. Matthew (London, 1923), Bk. I, ch. IV, Bk. III, chs. VI, VII.

[67] See a fuller analysis of this problem in the *Dynamics,* Vol. IV, pp. 652 ff.; and in *The Ways and Power of Love,* pp. 363 ff.

Since the task of dialectic thinking is bringing into the open the hidden aspects and properties of multidimensional phenomena, the dialectics of polarization and complementation has naturally been applied to the infinitely multidimensional total-ultimate reality. In this application, dialectic discovered its own limitations and the impossibility of defining the infinite total reality by finite concepts, notions, and words. This has been one of the greatest discoveries of dialectic thought.

For the same reasons, dialectic logic has been fruitfully and most frequently applied to the analysis of general, multidimensional classes of sociocultural phenomena for the discovery of the hidden aspects of these phenomena missed in the inadequate concepts and theories that define only one or a few of the many aspects-dimensions-properties-factors-causal-meaningful relationships they actually have.

There is hardly a doubt that an artful use of the dialectic method will continue to be fruitfully applied in a study of particularly complex, multidimensional sociolcultural systems and processes. Its fruitfulness can be notably enhanced if and when it is used hand in hand with empirical methods of studying and testing the adequacy of the dialectic conclusions concerning the empirical aspects of the phenomena investigated. Although we should give dialectic methods of complementarity and polarization their due, we should not expect miracles from these methods. Their applicability and fruitfulness are limited as are those of other methods of cognition.

4. These conclusions are directly applicable to the dualistic polar and triadic dialectic theories discussed. So long as these theories bring to light the hidden complementarily or polarly contrasting types of sociocultural systems and their hidden aspects, processes, and relationships, they increase our knowledge of the sociocultural world and help us to orient ourselves in the bewildering jungles of the human universe. Some of the above binary and triadic theories meet this criterion fairly well; others meet it rather poorly. Which do which will be discussed in subsequent sections of this chapter.

As we have seen, Gurvitch, Sartre, Van den Berghe, and others apply the term dialectic to sociocultural realities and processes. Such an imputation of the characteristics of dialectic logic and method to the realities studied by this logic and method does not appear to be advisable on logical or empirical grounds. Just as we do not impute the properties of deductive or inductive or mathematical or experimental procedures to the phenomena studied by these methods, and just as we do not call the phenomena studied deductive or experimental or mathematical, we cannot impute the *differentia specifica* of dialectic logic and method to the phenomena analyzed by this method. Such an imputation is an erroneous identification of the methods of study with the phenomena studied by this method—i.e., an illogical identification of basically different things.

Empirically, such an identification leads only to confusion and hinders rather than helps the cognition of the sociocultural realities and processes. The mere addition of the term dialectic to various sociocultural systems and processes does not add anything to our knowledge of these systems and processes, especially when we consider the prevalent vagueness and different meanings attached to that term.

The main forms of cultural, social, and personality systems and processes far exceed in number and diversity the forms and processes called dialectic by the unduly enthusiastic partisans of this term. Their favorable examples of dialectic entities are the polarity opposite dualistic and triadic sociocultural entities (groups, systems, totalities, ensembles); their preeminently dialectic processes are the immanent processes of conflict, alienation, and those processes that develop according to the Hegelian schema of thesis-antithesis-synthesis or just thesis and antithesis—that is, the processes in which a given sociocultural entity changes during its existence into a form opposite to its initial form (without any subsequent synthesis).

An elementary knowledge of the main species of social, cultural, and personality systems undeniably shows that a large portion of these systems or entities are neither dualistic nor triadic in their structure and characteristics. Neither the family, nor occupational groups, nor religious groups, nor caste and social class, nor the state, nor most of the race-age-nationality-economic groups are either dualistic or triadic in their essential traits. Nor do most of the existing classifications of the main forms of each of these groups and social systems divide them into just two or three opposite or contrasting classes.[68] It is true that several social systems can be unified into two or three social supersystems, like *Gemeinschaft-Gesellschaft* or *Gemeinschaft-Gesellschaft-Bund*, but such supersystems are not given in all human populations; side by side with these supersystems in many populations there exist "multibonded" social supersystems made up of four, five, six or more different social groups or systems. Moreover, none of the concrete social groups loses its identity in the coalesced supersystem.

The same is true of cultural systems like science, philosophy, ethics, religion, law, and fine arts and subsystems of each of these cultural systems. They cannot be reduced to two or three systems because each of these cultural systems is different from the others. It is true that many of these systems in highly integrated cultures coalesce into two or three or more supersystems. But in this coalescence none of the systems loses its individuality, such dualistic or triadic supersystems occur only in a few high cultures. Side by side with these there may exist quadruple, quintuple, and even more complex cultural supersystems, or no supersystem at all (in the less integrated, eclectic cultures).

The correctness of these observations is well confirmed by the dialecticians themselves. Gurvitch and Sartre, for instance, in their micro- and macrosociologies, divide the total social reality not into two polar or three triadic totalities but into much more numerous classes: sociability, depth-levels, social classes, and global societies. Each of these is subdivided into several subclasses, like the fourteen types of global society of Gurvitch, or the ensembles, serialities, collectives, social classes, and groups of Sartre. Most of these unities are not depicted by Gurvitch and Sartre as being polarly dualistic or as conforming to the triadic formula of thesis-antithesis-synthesis.

---

[68] Most of the classifications of races, ethnic groups, political, economic, religious, philosophical, aesthetic, and other social and cultural systems classify these and other social and cultural systems into four, five, six, or more types or forms, each form subdivided into several subforms.

Even most of the surveyed dualistic and triadic typologies are not exactly contrary or contradictory to each other, nor do they conform to the Hegelian triad. *Gemeinschaft* is not an antithesis to *Gesellschaft* (or vice versa) nor is *Gemeinschaft* thesis, *Gesellschaft* antithesis, and *Bund* synthesis. They are, rather, types of social systems notably different from each other, as different as the Romanesque, Gothic, and Baroque styles in architecture, or the Classic and Romantic styles in literature, or the several genera and species of plants and animals. Tönnies modifies his seven essential *Gemeinschaft-Gesellschaft* types into different typologies, as do a number of other sociologists with their typologies.[69] A still more important fact, correctly pointed out by R. König and G. Wurzbacher,[70] is that there is no polar opposition between the *Gemeinschaft* and the *Gesellschaft,* that, factually, "no *Gemeinschaft* can exist without a *Gesellschaft,*" and that the essential elements of each type actually coexist and mutually complement each other in practically all historical societies and organized groups, with one of the types being predominant now and then. These considerations are applicable to practically all the surveyed binary and triadic typologies.[71]

These observations can be summed up as follows: An overwhelming majority of social groups, systems, and entities

---

[69] See, on these modifications, R. König's "Die Begriffe Gemeinschaft und Gesselschaft" in *Kölner Zeitschrift fur Soziologie und Sozial Psychologie*, Neue Folge, 7, Jg. (1955), 412.

[70] *Ibid.*, pp. 405, 412; G. Wurzbacher "Beobachtungen zum Anwendungsbereich der Tönniesschen Kategorien Gemeinschaft und Gesellschaft," *Kölner Zeitschrift*, Neue Folge 7, Jg. (1955), 453.

[71] This applies to Kühne's "polarities." So far as he distinguishes "conceptual polarities" from the relative contrasting and different entities of real social life his theory is somewhat free from the unwarranted imputation of the properties of dialectic method to the realities of social life itself. So far as he, inconsistently with this statement, makes here and there such an imputation, his "real-life polarities" are not contraries and contradictories, but, in most cases, are also different, sometimes contrasting, entities like "husband-wife" in the family, or even like his basic dualities of "I and the World around me," "I and Thou," and of "selection and adaptation." Each of the "poles" of these dualities is neither contradictory nor even contrary to the other. Their "fusion" into a new *Einheit* is similar to the fusion of H_2 and O into H_2O (water). Hydrogen and oxygen are neither contradictory nor contrary to each other.

are neither polar, nor triadic, neither contradictory nor contrary, and cannot be reduced to these allegedly dialectic types. Most of the existing classifications of these social bodies divide them into more than two or three forms, genera and species. Even the dialectic sociologists classify them into far more numerous classes. Almost all of the allegedly dialectic dualistic and triadic social entities are in fact not contradictory, contrary, and polar but represent merely different systems. And, finally, dialectic logic and method is something quite different from the social phenomena studied by this method, and there is no logical or empirical ground to impute the characteristics of this method to the sociocultural phenomena investigated by dialectic analysis.

With still greater reason these conclusions can be applied to the imputations and applications of the term dialectic to sociocultural processes and relationships, including those of conflict, of alienation, or of the immanent (endogenous) change of a sociocultural system into a form opposite (antithesis) to what it was in the first phase of its existence (thesis). Any of the basic sociocultural processes of how and why sociocultural systems originate or are conceived; how and why they become organized (or objectified or socialized); how and why they change and maintain their identity in their change; how and why they become stratified and differentiated; how they adapt themselves to crisis conditions and challenges; how and why the processes of social and cultural mobility or intra- and inter-group solidarities and antagonisms go on; how and why some sociocultural systems disintegrate and "die" and how some of them "resurrect"—these and practically all important processes have been and can be studied by various scientific methods, including the dialectic one, but none of them has the characteristics of these methods and none can be called "deductive," "inductive," "statistical," or "dialectic."[72]

Furthermore, only a part of these processes have two- and three-phase rhythms (allegedly conforming to the dialectic of thesis-antithesis or thesis-antithesis-synthesis). Besides two- and

[72] See an analysis and classification of the basic social and cultural processes in my *SCP*, chs. 21–48.

three-phase rhythmical processes there are many processes with four, five, six, and more numerous phases ("beats") in their rhythms.[73] Any attempt to reduce all sociocultural processes to the allegedly dialectic two- and three-phase rhythms, as some dialecticians attempt to do, has been, is, and will be doomed to failure because nobody can deny the existence of a multitude of multiphase rhythmical processes. Besides these there seem to exist also nonrhythmical processes. Obviously, to multiphase rhythmical and nonrhythmical processes no dialectic of thesis-antithesis or thesis-antithesis-synthesis is applicable and no grounds exist to call such processes dialectic.

Moreover, not even all the processes with double- and triple-phase rhythms are contradictory or contrary. The phases of such rhythms in many processes are merely different (but not contradictory), as are many rhythms in musical compositions. A few examples of double (not contradictory) rhythms are the daily and nightly activities of individuals and groups; the alternation of the left and right legs in walking; G. Tarde's repeated rhythm of the domination of custom and fashion in the cultural life of society; Saint-Simon's rhythm of the alternation of "the critical and the organic" periods; A. N. Whitehead's double rhythm of the alternation of intuitively creative and scholarly elaborative phases in the history of human thought; H. Spencer's, C. Bernard's, and G. Tarde's two-phase rhythm of the alternation of analytical (fact-finding) and synthesizing periods in the history of science and philosophical thought; and the Chinese double rhythm of Yin and Yang. The two phases of each rhythm are not contradictory thesis and antithesis but just essentially different phases of each of these rhythms. The same can be said of the ever-repeated alternation of the following styles in fine arts: Gothic and Greek, *Haptish* and *Optish* (A. Riggle), *Plastisch* and *Malerisch* (Schmarsow), *Fülle-Still* and *Form-Still* (Panofsky), and others.

Likewise, a multitude of three-phase rhythmic process

---

[73] See an analysis and examples of sociocultural rhythmic processes with double, triple, quadruple, and more complex rhythms in the *Dynamics*, Vol. IV, chs. 8, 9, 12, 13.

are neither contradictory nor contrary; for instance, G. Tarde's triple rhythm of invention, imitation, and opposition; R. Mayreder's ideological phase, organizational phase, and power phase in the life history of many social movements; my conception, objectification, and socialization in the emergence and growth of a great many cultural systems; P. Ligeti's architectural, plastic, and pictorial phases in the history of art and culture; C. Lalo's preclassical, classical, and postclassical phases through which music passes in various societies and in the same society in the course of time; Vico's ages of gods, of heroes, and of man through which fully developed societies pass and which recur in the same society.[74] Of course, there are also triple sociocultural rhythms in which two phases are contrary or contradictory and triple rhythms that conform to the Hegelian triad, but such triple rhythmical processes are only a small portion of the noncontradictory (just different) triple rhythmical processes.

What is said of the allegedly dialectic (contrary and contradictory) sociocultural processes can be said of the processes of alienation and conflict—the favorite "dialectic" processes of many dialecticians. Not every alienation is a repudiation of an existing value or person or situation or social order in favor of the opposite one. And not every alienation is factually followed by conditions contradictory to the preceding nonalienated state of the social, cultural, or personality system. Most individual, social, and cultural alienation processes represent a change in the given process or system or order or situation from the alienated to a *different* state of affairs. Only a small portion of these alienation phenomena pass into a state contrary to or contradictory to the alienated state. All the processes of alienation together make up only a small fraction of the total sociocultural processes.

The same can be said of the processes of social, cultural, and personal conflicts and antagonisms. No doubt these proc-

---

[74] See an analysis and examples of the contradictory and the noncontradictory triple rhythmical processes in the *Dynamics*, Vol. IV, pp. 408 ff.

esses and relationships (from mild competition and rivalry to murder and bloody wars) make up one of the basic, perennial, and universal forms of sociocultural processes and relationships. But it is only one of the three basic forms of these: no less basic, perennial, and universal are the processes and relationships of solidarity and neutrality.[75] Since by definition and by fact the solidary and neutral processes are neither contradictory nor made up of the opposite elements, this means that a larger portion of social processes and relationships is not dialectic.

Not even all the conflicting and antagonistic processes represent a conflict of values. As often as not, the parties in conflict fight for the same (scarce) value, for the same woman, say, or for a larger share of wealth or popularity or fame or power. Conflicts representing aspirations, conscious and subconscious wishes, and respective activities of individuals and groups are quite different from the logical thesis and antithesis of the dialectic method. This means that the properties of this method cannot be ascribed even to all conflicting or antagonistic processes of this type.

Finally, it is a curious and significant fact that practically none of the dialectical sociologists have seriously studied most of the basic sociocultural processes. Vague and general statements about totalizations and detotalizations, interpenetration (Gurvitch), routinization and deroutinization, inertia and creativity (Sartre), selection and adaptation (Kühne), and foggy references to undefined "equilibriums" of all sorts[76] take the place of substantial study of, for instance, the processes of how and why social or cultural systems originate, how and why they become organized, what the main forms are of their

---

[75] See an analysis and classification of the antagonistic, the solidary, and the neutral (mixed) sociocultural processes and relationships in my *SCP*, chs. 5, 6, 7, 17, 18, 19, 31, 32; and in L. A. Coser, *op. cit.*

[76] Once more I have to stress the use of the term "equilibrium" and its derivatives by the "structural-functional," "dialectic," and other sociologists. In almost all cases, its meaning remains undefined or represents a distorted meaning taken from the physical sciences. None of the five basic meanings of this term is applicable to sociocultural phenomena. See, on this, the *Dynamics*, Vol. IV, ch. 14.

adjustment to ever-changing internal and external conditions, what their mechanisms are for distributing their members among different strata of the system, what the forms and factors are of horizontal and vertical mobility, how the cultural systems are conceived, objectified, and socialized, how and why they change, what the ways and factors are of the growth or decline of social or cultural systems, how and why sociocultural antagonisms (rivalries, competitions, wars, revolutions, and crimes) arise and fluctuate, and what the life-spans are of various systems.

This is true even of the processes of conflict and alienation: The best existing studies of these processes and relationships are done not by structural-functional or dialectic sociologists but by scholars who hardly use these terms at all. One of the reasons for this is the logical and empirical impossibility of imputing the properties of either dialectic logic and method or of the "functional-structural" method to any sociocultural processes and realities.

CONCLUSIONS

The preceding critical examination of recent dialectic sociologies can be summed up as follows:

1. When the essential features of dialectic method and logic are more or less clearly defined, and when this method is artfully applied, it can fruitfully contribute, especially in cooperation with other logical and empirical methods, to an understanding of the multidimensional sociocultural phenomena, including the "nature" of human personality and of individual and collective human behavior and relationships.

2. This is well confirmed by the examined dialectic theories of Gurvitch, Sartre, Kühne, and by most of the surveyed dualistic and triadic theories. Despite my criticisms of their weak points, they have contributed to our knowledge of and orientation in the multidimensional, bewildering human universe about as much as have most of the empirical, analytic, func-

tional-structural, and historico-philosophical currents of contemporary sociological thought.

3. Although we must give the dialectic method its due, at the same time we must reject the imputation of the properties of this method to real sociocultural phenomena, and to social, cultural, and personality systems and processes. We also must avoid calling these realities dialectic. To study them by dialectic or deductive or inductive methods does not make them dialectic, deductive, or inductive.

4. The prevalent dialectical efforts to interpret sociocultural systems and processes in the terms of dualistic polarities or of the triadic thesis-antithesis-synthesis are applicable only to a small portion of these systems and processes, most of which are much more complex, multidimensional, and multirhythmic than the dualistic and triadic conceptions claim. A study of all the main sociocultural systems and of all the main varieties of repeated rhythms in the life-processes of these systems by a concerted attack by all methods of cognition, including the dialectic, promises a much greater cognitive harvest than the "mummified" interpretations of these phenomena in the terms of Hegelian-Marxian polarities, triads, and alienations.[77]

---

[77] A study of sociocultural rhythms, tempi, periodicities, and other basic characteristics of the processes in the life-history of main systems is still greatly neglected by sociologists. Meanwhile, even somewhat fragmentary studies of these phenomena by the past social thinkers delivered to us significant uniformities, important insights into, and knowledge of sociocultural phenomena. Still more significant have been the recent investigations in these fields. See the survey, analyses, and criticisms of the respective theories of sociocultural rhythms, periodicities, tempi, uniformities, and factors of change in sociocultural systems in the *Dynamics*, Vol. IV, chs. 7–16.

CHAPTER 15

Pseudo-Behavioral and Empirical

Sociologies

PSEUDO-BEHAVIORAL THEORIES OF SOCIAL SYSTEMS AND HUMAN BEHAVIOR

Despite the enormous vogue in the last few decades for all sorts of behavioristic interpretations of sociocultural phenomena and human behavior[1] and despite the publication of several behavioristic sociological studies, the general situation of the behavioristic sociological theories remains today essentially similar to what it was in the first quarter of this century.[2] Ivan Pavlov's classical studies of the objective behavior of animals and especially of their conditioned reflexes greatly stimulated

---

[1] This fad has gone so far in the United States that it has led to renaming the social and psychological sciences "behavioral sciences." It is hard to find either logical or empirical reasons for such a renaming, because, first, all sciences are "behavioral." (Chemistry studies the behavior of chemical elements and compounds; physics the behavior of the elementary particles, atoms, and material bodies; biology deals with the behavior of cells, organs, and organisms.) Second, it is difficult because the term "behavioral" fits much better the physical and the biological sciences than the psychological and social disciplines. The former study the behavior of physicochemical and biological phenomena as externally observable, transsubjective transpositions, motions, movements, and overt actions-reactions devoid of any inner, subjective experience, called consciousness, mind, ideas, sentiments, emotions, wills, memories, symbolic meanings, values, etc. The social and psychological disciplines cannot help but deal with these inner, immaterial, symbolic, and subjective experiences that do not lend themselves to direct external examination. Calling these psychosocial disciplines "behavioral sciences" signifies once more the irrational and nonlogical force of fashions and fads that penetrates even the sciences—the citadel of rational and logical thought.

[2] See my *Contemporary Sociological Theories* for an analysis and criticism of "behavioristic interpretations," pp. 617–635.

subsequent investigations of the behavior of rats, pigeons, dogs, monkeys, etc., by biologists and psychologists.[3] Some of these researchers, like Pavlov himself,[4] have been reluctant to extrapolate their conclusions beyond the limits supported by the results of their experimental and observational studies. They have been fairly conservative in applying their results to the behavior of human beings and to sociocultural phenomena. Others have been less cautious in this respect. They have increasingly proceeded to interpret human beings, their personality and their behavior, as well as many sociocultural phenomena, in terms of the conclusions derived from their studies of animal behavior.[5]

Following the lead of the liberal extrapolators of behavioral studies of animals, a number of sociologists who had hardly done any experimental or observational investigation of the conditioned reflexes or other forms of animal behavior, enthusiastically declared themselves "behaviorists" and, without any restraint or hesitation, began to interpret human behavior as well as almost all sociocultural phenomena "behavioristically."[6] In their behavioristic enthusiasms they began to interpret sociocultural phenomena, including sociocultural systems and processes, as merely the phenomena of human behavior—individual and social—and started to explain them largely in the terms of the behavior of the rats, dogs, pigeons, and monkeys studied by animal psychologists. Some of the behavioral sociologists

[3] See their names and bibliography in *CST*, pp. 617–635.

[4] In Pavlov's view, his studies of the conditioned reflexes belonged to the field of physiology rather than to that of psychology; he did not claim that the former can replace the latter or that the results of the investigations of the behavior of animals can be automatically transferred and applied directly to human beings or be the "key" to all the secrets of human personality and conduct.

[5] The investigators of animal behavior range all the way from the enthusiastic proponents, like John Watson, K. S. Lashley, W. S. Hunter, to the more moderate partisans of it, like G. Hall, B. F. Skinner, G. Mandler, W. Kessen, and E. Broadbent, to the conservative critics, like W. Kohler, K. Koffka, W. McDougall, M. Prince, R. Woodworth, and, more recently, C. Burt, B. B. Wolman, H. J. Eysenck, and many others. See the literature for the earlier period in *CST*; for the later period, see C. Hall, *A Behavior System* (New Haven, 1952); B. F. Skinner, *Verbal Behavior* (New York, 1957); G. Mandler and W. Kessen, *The Language*

have proceeded in this behavioristic dehumanization of man quite as naïvely as J. Watson did in psychology. Others have gone about it in a more sophisticated manner by dressing the operation in seemingly scientific apparel. Naïve or sophisticated, no behavioral sociologist has succeeded in delivering a genuinely behavioristic system of sociology. What they have delivered is a peculiar mixture of nonbehavioral—largely introspective and speculative—sociology served in behavioristic terminological trimmings. Despite their behavioristic contentions, all these theories largely deal with such nonbehavioristic phenomena and terms as consciousness, mind, ideas, sentiments, feelings, emotions, wills, duty, rights, memory, inventions, values, symbols, and other inner experiences of human beings, not to mention such phenomena as science, religion, ideology, law, ethics, authority, esteem, and so on—phenomena hardly found in the animal kingdom. Among the recent theories of this pseudobehavioristic kind, one of the best is George Homans' theories of social groups and of elementary forms of social behavior developed in his two books *The Human Group* (New York, 1950) and *Social Behavior: Its Elementary Forms* (New York, 1961).

GEORGE C. HOMANS: HUMAN GROUPS AND SOCIAL BEHAVIOR

The main scientific task of Homans' *The Human Group* is to study and formulate the interconnected uniformities in the behavior of human beings in small groups and in the properties and workings of human groups in general. The main scien-

---

of *Psychology* (New York, 1959); D. E. Broadbent, *Behaviorism* (London, 1961); Sir Cyril Burt, "The Concept of Consciousness," *British Journal of Psychology*, August, 1962; and P. H. Prabhu, "The State of Psychology as a Science Today," *Fiftieth Indian Science Congress* (Delhi, 1963).

[6] See on "fads" in modern sociology, my *Fads and Foibles in Modern Sociology*, ch. 3, and *passim*. See also G. Bergmann's "Sense and Nonsense in Operationism," in P. G. Frank (ed.), *The Validation of Scientific Theories* (Boston, 1961), pp. 52–54; and Sir Cyril Burt, *op. cit.*

tific objective of his *Social Behavior* is to explain the how's and why's of these "elementary forms of social behavior" in general and of the properties and behavior of human groups. In both works he deals with small groups:

> The difference between the two [works] that I want to underline goes deeper than the size of groups [which is somewhat smaller in *Social Behavior*]. It is a difference in intellectual aims: *The Human Group* did not try to explain much of anything, while *Social Behavior* will at least try to explain. . . . In [*The Human Group*] I tried to do two things. I chose from the literature five detailed field studies of human groups, ranging all the way from a group of industrial workers to an entire town. And of these studies I first asked what classes the observations made by the investigators might reasonably be divided into. . . . And I tried to show that the observations made by the different investigators might be divided into the same four classes: sentiments, activities, interactions, and norms. . . . The second question I asked of the five studies was what propositions about the relations between the four classes of variables the studies gave support to. . . . And I tried to show that several propositions did hold good in more than one of the studies. . . . This was as far, practically, as *The Human Group* went. The inevitable next step is to ask why the empirical propositions should take the form they do, and this to ask for explanations. [*Social Behavior* endeavors to give the explanations by deducing the found empirical uniformities and propositions from] a set of more general propositions, still of the same form as the empirical ones. . . . To deduce them successfully *is* to explain them.[7]

Homans says of *Social Behavior* that it "undertakes to explain elementary social behavior, and the explanation of a phenomenon is a process of showing that a proposition or propositions describing it may be deduced from a set of more general propositions under specified given conditions."[8] In con-

---

[7] G. C. Homans, *Social Behavior*, pp. 8–10. See, on the deductive method, H. L. Zetterberg, *On Theory and Verification in Sociology* (Totowa, N.J., 1965); H. L. Costner and R. K. Leik, "Deductions from Axiomatic Theory," *ASR*, December, 1964, pp. 819–836; D. C. Pelz and F. M. Andrews, "Detecting Causal Priorities," *ibid.*, pp. 836–848; and O. D. Duncan, "Axioms or Correlations," *ASR*, June, 1963. See also A. Perpina Rodriguez, *Métodos y Criterios de la Sociologia Contemporanea* (Madrid, 1958).

[8] *Social Behavior*, p. 205.

trast to this deductive method of explanation in *Social Behavior,* the "main method of exposition used [in *The Human Group*] is the case method."⁹ Such, in Homans' words, are the main tasks of these works and the methods used for their achievement.

Besides this difference in their methods, Homans' two studies have many other differences. In *The Human Group,* groups or social systems are treated mainly holistically: Group is regarded as a "unity" in which "the whole determines the parts [and] the parts determine the whole"; it is "an organized whole, or system"; sometimes he even calls it an "organism."¹⁰ In *Social Behavior,* this holistic approach is largely abandoned and replaced by a nominalistic-singularistic one: Two pigeons —"Person" and "Other"—are substituted for the group or social system:

> [Their] exchange where the activity of each reinforces (or punishes) the activity of the other, and where accordingly each influences the other [replaces the activities of a group as an organized whole]. . . . We need no new propositions to describe and explain the social. With social behavior nothing unique emerges to be analyzed only in its own terms. Rather, *from the laws of individual behavior follow the laws of social behavior* when the complications of mutual reinforcement are taken into account. Taking our departure, then, from what we know about animal behavior [B. F. Skinner's laboratory pigeons], we shall state a set of propositions that seem to us fundamental in describing and explaining human social behavior, or human exchange.¹¹

⁹ G. C. Homans, *The Human Group,* p. 18.

¹⁰ *Ibid.,* pp. 8, 9, and *passim.* His holistic conception of group is seemingly taken mainly from the works of M. P. Follet and A. N. Whitehead. We already know from Chapter 5 of this work that this holistic conception of social groups or systems was precisely formulated long ago by St. Thomas Aquinas and by other even earlier thinkers.

¹¹ *Social Behavior,* pp. 30–31. Both of these standpoints represent nothing new: They have been formulated many times in the history of sociology and psychology. The only new thing here is the fact that these opposite standpoints are proposed by the same scholar who seems to find them quite reconcilable. There is nothing new in calling the phenomenon of human interaction by the term "exchange." Economics, sociology, even philosophy, have used this term regularly for quite a long time. See J. Novicows "L'échange phénomène fondamental de l'associa-

The starting premises of Homans' two investigations also differ. In *The Human Group,* the basic assumption is that his task can be best accomplished by carefully analyzing the five field studies of different "small groups" done by five different anthropologists and sociologists. No animal behavior is involved. In *Social Behavior,* the starting assumption is that the pecking behavior of the pigeons (from the laboratory of B. F. Skinner) is a prototype of human behavior—of "Person and Other" "pecking" (remuneratively or punitively) at each other (in their interactional "exchange").[12] He directly applies the results of this experimental study to human beings. This model serves as the very basic principle of Homans' "deductive" explanation of the uniformities in human behavior that he finds in all five small groups and extrapolates over almost all the daily, ordinary (or "elementary" in his terms) behavior of human beings in general.

The essentials of the conceptual framework of *The Human Group* can be summed up as follows: The small human group is "the commonest of social units." Its general "elements" (which are at the same time "elements of behavior") consist of persons (at least two), their activities, their interaction, and their sentiments. Besides these four core elements, there are norms, evaluations, controls, symbolic meanings, emotions, interests, values, ideas, and associations. With the exception of norms, the others are mentioned incidentally and are studied little, if at all.[13] The study concentrates mainly on discovering and formulating the uniformities (or "mutual dependencies") in the relationships of these core elements, in the social behavior of interacting persons, and in the activities of a group as an organized whole. A greater part of the "analytical" theories of Homans consists in formulating the "mutual dependence of

---

tion humaine," in *Revue Internationale de Sociologie* (1911), No. 11. See also R. de la Grasserie, "De la Psycho-Sociologie," *Revue de Sociologie* (1912), Nos. 3 and 4; and M. Mauss, "Essai sur le don, form archaique de l'échange," reprinted in his *Sociologie et anthropologie* (Paris, 1950). See also P. M. Blau, *Exchange and Power in Social Life* (New York, 1964).

[12] *Social Behavior,* ch. 2.

[13] *The Human Group,* chs. 1, 2; compare pp. 8, 34–44, 121–130.

sentiment and activity," "of activity and interaction," of "interaction and sentiment," and of "sentiment and norms," and of
making several generalizations concerning the relationships of
the groups' members and their leaders. Cursory remarks are
made about social conflict, social order, social equilibrium,
democracy, and so on.

The main objectives and content of *Social Behavior* are
well outlined by Homans himself:

> In its method of exposition, this book will be much more
> nearly deductive [than *The Human Group*]. After a short
> chapter about the findings of behavioral psychology on the
> subject of animal behavior, I shall present in the two following
> chapters my set of general propositions. In the rest of the
> book I shall try to illustrate these propositions and show how
> they may be used to explain a number of familiar features of
> elementary social behavior—first those features that are least
> dependent on the presence of an organized group and last those
> that are most dependent. . . . Explanation [by deductive logic]
> is what I shall aim at. . . . I have come to believe that the
> empirical propositions [in *The Human Group*] may most
> easily be explained by two bodies of general propositions al-
> ready in existence: behavioral psychology and elementary
> economics. . . . In saying this I necessarily reject Durkheim's
> view that sociology is not a corollary of psychology.[14]

The bulk of the book is devoted to a formulation of a
series of deductive propositions (illustrated or corroborated by
the data of a few "experimental" studies of S. Schachter, N.
Ellertson, L. Festinger, and others that allegedly confirm the
deductive generalizations of Homans). The last part of the
volume deals quite cursorily with such problems as justice,
satisfaction, authority, equality, status-conformity-innovation,
institution, and other problems.

EVALUATION AND CRITICISM

Both volumes represent a well-written introduction to a
study of some of the utilitarian (or contractual) aspects of the
social behavior of economic man and of informal, small social

----

[14] *Social Behavior*, pp. 12–15.

groups. Here and there Homans' inquiries seriously touch a few important problems in these fields. But all in all his theories in his own opinion "owe much to elementary economics" and to a special brand of "behavioristic" psychology,[15] as well as to simplified utilitarian philosophy and ethics. As such, they hardly contribute a great deal to the existing knowledge of human personality, social behavior, and social systems.

The first defect of Homans' theories is the vagueness of many of his basic concepts. To begin with, his concept of small groups remains undefined. He includes in this class quite heterogeneous social groups radically different from one another in all their essential characteristics: in their complexity, unifying bonds and values, structure, culture, dynamic processes, behavior of their members, and even in their size (fluctuating in Homans' samples from a few individuals up to more than a thousand). Such a class (or genus) of social groups corresponds to a botanical genus of plants ranging from 5 to 55 inches in height or a genus of animal organisms weighing from 6 to 77 pounds. Not even in the pre-Linnaean classifications was such an illogical genus ever offered. Unfortunately, contrary to all logical and empirical canons of defining and classifying real classes (or genera and species), Homans and almost all the sociologists of "small groups" continue to unify very different human groups into one class (or genus) of "small groups."[16]

Another strategic concept in Homans' theories, the concept

---

[15] *Social Behavior*, pp. 12, 15, 68. Homans' own assessment of his works displays a peculiar ambivalence. On the one hand, he repeatedly contends in both books that his studies give a "new sociological synthesis," open a new field, a hitherto "neglected part of sociology," give an insight into "institutional growth," which "scholars seldom, it seems to me, examine in detail," and so on. On the other hand, he several times asserts that his theories are but modifications of those of elementary economics and behavioristic psychology, that "above all, we need humility," "that nothing we have said [in the book] can be taken to imply that this book tells the whole story about the group," that "*The Human Group* did not try to explain much of anything," and so on. *The Human Group*, pp. 1–7, 23, 442; *Social Behavior*, pp. 8, 388–389.

[16] See my criticisms of the concept of "small groups" in my *Fads and Foibles*, ch. 10, and above in Chapter 4. So far, none of these criticisms has been adequately answered by the investigators of the "small groups."

of "sentiments," is likewise defined poorly. It is used in the same vague sense in which it is used by Pareto, from whom Homans borrowed it. In some places Homans means by the term "drives, emotions, feelings, affective states, sentiments, attitudes," including even "hunger and thirst";[17] in other places, sentiments are used in a narrower sense than attitudes, drives, hunger, and thirst; in still other places they are identified with motives.[18]

In *The Human Group* they are defined as the "internal states of the human body" unobservable directly and different from overt "activity" (pp. 37 ff.); in *Social Behavior* we are told that "sentiments are not internal states of an individual." "They are not inferred from overt behavior: they are overt behavior and so are directly observable. They are, accordingly, activities" (pp. 34–36). Other meanings (like interests, values, etc.) are given to sentiments, but the above examples show that, as he himself correctly notes, he "lumped together under this word some psychological states [and psychological and overt actions] that psychologists would certainly keep separate" (*Human Group, p. 38*). The trouble with lumping together essentially different things is that propositions and functional correlations based on them are meaningless. If sentiments (A) are activities (A) then why try to establish a "mutual dependence" of sentiments and activities, as he tries to do in *The Human Group?* Does not the establishment of mutual dependence between these variables amount to a mere tautological identification of A with A? Further on we shall see indeed that most of his "mutual dependencies" and "deductive-inductive" propositions are tautological. If "sentiments" are overt behavior or actions then why, in Homans' classification of the core "elements" of human groups or of social behavior, are they defined as two elements different from each other?

A similar vagueness marks most of Homans' strategic concepts, like equilibrium, elementary behavior, unit-act, self-interest, punishment and reward, formal and informal, institu-

---

[17] *The Human Group*, pp. 37–38.
[18] *Social Behavior*, pp. 44–96.

tional and subinstitutional organizations, norms and expectations, and so on.[19] The inevitable consequence of this vagueness is, as we shall see, that it vitiates most of the propositions derived from manipulations of these defective concepts.

The second general defect of Homans' theories is his uncritical acceptance of the conceptions and propositions of his "favorite" authorities, B. F. Skinner, V. Pareto, L. Henderson, C. Barnard, F. J. Roethlisberger, E. Mayo, and all the authors whose field and experimental studies he uses for the inductive corroboration of his deductions and conclusions. Third, connected with this defect is Homans' limited knowledge of many basic works in the well-cultivated gardens of knowledge that he takes for wild jungles being penetrated by him and by a few other pioneers for the first time.

He unquestioningly accepts not only Skinner's interpretations of pigeons' behavior, but also Skinner's extrapolations of pigeons' behavior to human behavior. Homans seems to pay no attention to the extensive and serious criticisms of the experimental studies of animal behavior by other, more cautious, experimental researchers in this field, not to mention the criticisms by many psychologists and sociologists. B. B. Wolman correctly points out the "spectacular differences between Thorndike's and Guthrie's experiments" on the cats in the

---

[19] His operations with the term "equilibrium" are typical. He begins with LeChatelier's formula of equilibrium in physical chemistry, then replaces the essential concepts in the formula by his own, thus distorting LeChatelier's formula and making it largely meaningless; then he identifies "equilibrium" with "efficient control," and with a return of a disturbed social system to the *status quo*, which here and there acquires the meaning of an ideological approval of "social conservatism" and of "obedience to orders" of the superior authorities; finally, he ends with a "practical equilibrium" in the sense of "settled social relations" and with even an "unnatural equilibrium" in the sense of "a society of people apathetic, of institutions frozen in an unnatural equilibrium—unnatural in the sense that, out of the elements lying around here and there, something better might conceivably have been made." See *The Human Group*, pp. 301–308, 422; *Social Behavior*, pp. 84–85, 396–397. "Poor equilibrium!" is all one can say following these operations of Homans. O. Lange's *Catość i rozwój w świete cybernetyki* [*The Whole and Development in the Light of Cybernetics*] (Warsaw, 1962), can be recommended for all sociologists inclined to use the term "equilibrium" and

problem box: "It almost appears as if the two cats demonstrated behavior modes to suit the learning theories of their masters and to defeat all the opponent's learning theories. . . . One wonders how albino rats, pigeons, or cats would learn in situations which are different from puzzle box, maze or Skinner apparatus."[20] After a careful examination of the behavioristic theories of Watson, Hull, Skinner, Mandler-Kessen, and Broadbent, Sir Cyril Burt concludes that "as a basis for a general theory of human experience" behaviorism is "hopelessly inadequate" and that it is necessary to reinstate "consciousness as a useful and necessary concept, and to rehabilitate introspection as a valid scientific procedure."[21]

Some of the interpretations of human behavior in terms of behavior of rats, dogs, pigeons, and guinea pigs under artificial laboratory conditions are even more unpalatable. Homans should have explored these criticisms and the existing uncertainty in this field before accepting Skinner's questionable extrapolations. Instead, Homans unhesitatingly professes his beliefs in the infallibility of Skinner's *dicta* and accepts them as the major principles of his "deductive" explanations.

Similarly, he unquestioningly accepts the accuracy of the field studies of the Bank Wiring Observation Room, the Norton Street Gang, the Family in Tikopia, Hilltown, and the Electric Equipment Co., which he uses for constructing and corroborating his hypotheses. In using them, he makes two mutually contradictory statements: On the one hand he asserts that "our

---

related terms in their theories. See also *Studia Filozoficzne*, Nos. 3–4 (1963), where a discussion of these problems by a group of scholars and scientists is published. These works will show, among other things, that not all disturbed systems tend to return to their previous equilibrium, and that side by side with "homeostatic" systems—so frequently mentioned by Homans, Parsons, Merton, and other sociologists—many systems are "anti-homeostatic." See also A. Katchalsky, *Nonequilibrium Thermodynamics in Biophysics* (Harvard University Press, 1965), and articles of Kovalev, Petrov, Trincher in *Voprosy Filosofii*, 5(1964), 113–119, 3(1963), 6(1962).

[20] B. B. Wolman, *Contemporary Theories and Systems in Psychology* (New York, 1960), pp. 512–513; and P. H. Prabhu, *The State of Psychology*, p. 7. See other critical literature in *CST*, pp. 617–635.

[21] Sir Cyril Burt, "The Concept of Consciousness."

work presupposes the direct observation of human behavior," which assertion implies that his work is based on his own direct observation, and on the other hand he says that "our work relies on theirs"—that is, on the five field studies of these different investigators. Let us keep in mind that he has no means at his disposal to verify these studies; he simply accepts them as completely correct and true. He even assures us that anthropologists and sociologists who study either preliterate tribes or groups and communities in our society never make mistakes in their descriptions and interpretations of these respective groups.[22]

Anyone who knows anything about such anthropological and sociological investigations knows well that many of them are fantastic and incorrect and that only an insignificant portion of them are free from gross errors and misinterpretations. One can but envy Homans' trust in the infallibility of the five field studies on which his work relies. Since he neither made these field studies himself, nor verified their accuracy in any way, his claim that his theories are based upon the "direct observation of human behavior" is baseless. His theories are based upon hearsay stuff taken from other investigators.

The same trust is shown by him in several experimental researches that he uses in his *Social Behavior* to confirm his deductive propositions. As a matter of fact, all of these experimental studies are but pseudoexperimental: They do not meet either the very minimum conditions of a real experimental work or the basic canons of the inductive method. In none of them are all other conditions, except the experimented variable, kept constant; in none of them are these conditions controlled and accounted for by the experimenters. All of them have so many holes, doubtful machinations, and spurious assumptions that they hardly qualify even as good observational researches. (See, on the pseudoexperimental nature of these studies, *Fads and Foibles,* ch. 9. See also N. and A. Chapanis, "Cognitive Resonance," *Psychological Bulletin 1* (1964), 1–20; and S. E. Asch's review of L. Festinger's *A Theory of Cognitive Dis-*

---

[22] *The Human Group,* pp. 25, 19.

sonance, in *Contemporary Psychology* [1956], pp. 384–389.)

That Homans' knowledge of many of the fields he discusses so cavalierly is limited is evident in his reiterated claims to have discovered "small groups," "informal organizations," and new insights into the "institutional" and "subinstitutional" forms of behavior and norms, and to have achieved a "new synthesis" of sociological theory. It is also evident from the sources he refers to in his work. If he had known the classic and basic studies in the field, he would hardly have ventured to make these claims and would hardly have formulated several of his theories, which, as we shall see, were developed and formulated much more precisely and adequately by many a scholar hardly mentioned in his work.[23]

Fourth, these shortcomings are largely responsible for the deficiencies in Homans' main conceptions and theories. One of these defects is exemplified by his formula of the "elements" of human behavior and social groups. These elements consist of activity, interaction, and sentiment.[24] This classification is odd logically and empirically. Logically, interaction is but a *species* of action, and interactivity is but a species of activity. They are not two different genera; both belong to the same genus, activity. Insofar as Homans classifies interaction and activity as two different elements of human behavior, he presents as two different genera what is really a genus and one of its species. He makes a similar error in regard to the "elements" of sentiment and activity. In *Social Behavior,* sentiment is defined as, and identified with, activity. Thus we have the same element, activity, presented as two different elements, activity and sentiment.

Empirically, his classification is even more inadequate. It misses almost all the *differentia specifica* of human behavior and of social group. We must ask Homans: "Don't interacting human beings have, besides sentiments, also ideas, volitions, standards, values, norms—in brief, a rich series of inner experi-

---

[23] This sort of defect is fairly common among the works of many sociologists, psychologists, anthropologists, and social scientists. See *Fads and Foibles,* ch. 1.

[24] *The Human Group,* ch. 2, and *passim.*

ences or meanings quite different from sentiments? Since, of course, the answer is Yes, then we must ask him why he did not mention these uniquely human elements. The glaring empirical inadequacy of his conception of elements is so obvious that there is no need to criticize it further.[25] Let it suffice to say that if Homans had attempted to interpret human behavior and social groups in the terms of his elements, he would have missed almost all the specifically human characteristics of human social activities and of social and cultural systems. Fortunately, he did not. A few pages after presenting his formula of the elements, he introduces practically all the concepts of an introspective psychology and sociology (norms, values, ideas, justice, esteem, altruism, egoism, authority, interests, etc.) and forgets about his behavioristic concepts of human interactional behavior and of social systems. His "behavioristic" studies of the superorganic phenomena are all, in fact, pseudo-behavioristic.

"By their fruits ye shall know them." What sort of cognitive fruits have Homans' studies given to us? Most of his substantive propositions and generalizations can be classified into three defective classes: partially wrong and inadequate; platitudinous and tautological; indeterminate and vague.

One of the most important propositions of this class is the generalization that persons who interact frequently with one

[25] His classification of the "elements" fits animal behavior somewhat better. Most of the animal species—largely devoid of fully developed mental and creative experiences and guided in their activities mainly by reflexological-instinctive mechanisms—have, indeed, diverse "sentiments" in Homans' sense of this term. For this reason, "sentiment" can be specially mentioned as an "element" of animal behavior. A study of animal interactional behavior belongs to biology rather than to homosociology, and such a study has been made not by the homosociologists and the homopsychologists, but by biologists and animal sociologists and psychologists. If human behavior and the sociocultural-superorganic-human universe consisted only of Homans' "elements," there would be no need for homosociology. Animal behavior and reality could be much better investigated by biologists, animal sociologists, and physiologists than by homosociologists. W. M. Wheeler, an eminent biologist, organized, in cooperation with other biological investigators of animal behavior, a special course in Animal Sociology at Harvard. The course was excellent in its scientific richness and cognitive value.

another tend to like one another: "If the frequency of interaction between two or more persons increases, the degree of
their liking for one another will increase, and vice versa. . . ."[26]
"The more frequently men interact with one another, the more
nearly alike they become in the norms they hold, as they do in
their sentiments and activities."[27]

Only in two places does Homans qualify these generalizations with the following conditions: if the interacting persons
do not irritate each other; if one of the parties is not the boss
of the other; and if the group as a whole is maintaining itself
in its environment and is not breaking up.[28] Nowhere in his
works does he mention that this set of uniformities is but a
partial, very limited uniformity contrasted with two other—the
opposite and the neutral—sets of uniformities quite different
from his. The opposite set of the propositions says that "certain
kind of persons who interact frequently with one another fairly
often tend to dislike one another and, if the frequency of their
interaction increases, the degree of their disliking for one
another will increase, and vice versa." The neutral set of the
propositions says that "the relationships of persons who interact
frequently with one another fairly often remain unchanged or
neutral in their friendly or antagonistic character."

The opposite set of uniformities is illustrated and corroborated by such interactions as occur between enemy soldiers on
a battlefield, between jailer and jailed, rapist and raped, husband
and wife divorcing, and between those persons who develop
animosity to one another not at their first few interactions but
after many meetings.

The neutral set of uniformities quite frequently occurs in
big cities and anonymous aggregates of population. Many
people who live in a big apartment house may exchange "good
mornings" and nothing more with their next-door neighbors
for years and years at a time. We may buy our groceries in the
same supermarket for a decade without becoming friendly with

26 *The Human Group*, pp. 111–112, 113, 115, 116, and *passim*.
27 *Ibid.*, p. 126.
28 *Ibid.*, pp. 116–117. In most of his reiterations of these propositions, these qualifying conditions are not mentioned at all.

or hostile to the clerk. Similar "neutral" relationships are ordinarily maintained with a great many people, like plumbers, carpenters, garbage collectors, policemen, mailmen, and so on. Homans' uniformities are also contradicted by a certain familiar phenomenon: falling in love at first sight. This sentiment, as we all know, can change to indifference, enmity, and even hatred upon a longer acquaintance. Even in Homans' own case of the Bank Wiring Room, the increased interactions of the members of the team did not prevent a large number of antagonisms, centering around Maxmanian and Capek, from emerging.

Facts of this kind definitely contradict Homans' generalizations and quite clearly indicate two fallacies of his propositions: first, that he has extrapolated his uniformity far beyond its legitimate limits, completely overlooking its "opposite" and the "neutral" types; and, second, he has assumed the variable, frequency of interaction, to be the main factor in relationships between interacting parties (individuals and groups). This variable is neutral in this respect; the real factors in the establishment and maintenance of relationships are quite different. This is not the place to enter into an analysis of these factors. Instead, I must simply refer to the works of mine in which these problems are discussed in detail and in which my conclusions are corroborated by a vast body of relevant empirical evidence.[29]

Another of Homans' partially wrong and incorrect propositions is his generalization that "the higher the rank (or status) of a person within a group, the more nearly his activities conform to the norms of the group," and its corollary, "the more closely a man, in the activities he performs, realizes the norms of his group, the higher is his social rank in the group."[30] Undoubtedly these propositions are correct for some mainly preliterate and small informal groups whose members are fully

---

[29] See *SCP*, chs. 5, 6, 7; the *Dynamics*, Vol. III, chs. 9–14; *The Ways and Power of Love*, chs. 8–15, and *passim*; and my "Reply" in Allen, *P. A. Sorokin in Review*, pp. 454–469.

[30] *Social Behavior*, p. 9; *The Human Group*, p. 442. The proposition is reiterated many times in both books.

aware of the value of each other's activities, can freely select their leaders, and distribute their members among various ranks of the group. The propositions are quite inapplicable to almost all groups where the higher ranks are hereditary, where the boss(es) control the group coercively (as in many criminal gangs or dictatorial governments), where the "aristocracy" of the group decays, and where the higher ranks can be bought or obtained through monopolistic propaganda, dishonest machinations, and other conditions quite different from the real value of the activities rendered to the group by its different members.[31] If Homans' generalizations were taken at their enormously overextended face value, then there would not be any incapable, criminal, corrupt leaders and power elites in any human group. The fact is, however, that practically all scientific studies of various power elites, ruling classes, and leaders of big organizations show unquestionably that these upper ranks violate the norms of their groups more frequently and violently than the ruled populations. Thus, "when the morality and mentality of rulers and the ruled are measured by the same moral yardstick (and not by the double standard), then . . . the moral behavior of ruling groups tends to be much more criminal and sub-moral than that of the ruled strata of the same society. . . . The greater, more absolute, and coercive the power of rulers, political leaders, and big executives of business, labor, and other organizations, the more corrupt and criminal such ruling groups and executives tend to be."[32]

These conclusions are based on a systematic investigation of the criminality of 43 English monarchs and lord protectors, 34 Turkish sultans, all the kings of France, all the czars of Russia, 51 rulers of ancient Rome, 107 sovereigns of Byzantium, the khalifs of the Arabic dynasties, and the kings of Persia, Japan, and the Incas. We investigated, first, what percentage of these rulers committed the grave crime of murdering their father, mother, brother, sister, husband, wife, and other

---

[31] See some facts in my *Social Mobility*, pp. 305–316.

[32] P. Sorokin and W. Lunden, *Power and Morality* (Boston, 1959), pp. 36–37.

close relatives. We found that between 20 and 70 percent of these rulers were guilty of this crime; they violated the most sacred law norms of their respective societies 50 or 100 times more frequently than did their subjects. The same is true of other forms of murder and of less grave crimes against persons, property, mores, etc. Not so high but well above norm is the criminality of presidents of republics, high-ranking state officials, governors of states and provinces, mayors and top officials of big cities, captains of industry and finance, and the executives of big labor and other organizations.[33]

Beginning with Lao-tse, Confucius, Plato, Aristotle, Polybius, Kautilya, and Machiavelli and ending with modern investigators of the morality and criminality of the ruling groups, all have come to similar conclusions in regard to the "wrong" forms of government and leadership, which are more frequent than the "right" ones.[34]

In the light of these studies, Homans' uniformity is correct only in regard to a small portion of social groups and is grossly incorrect in regard to an overwhelming majority of large organized social systems.

Partially wrong also are such generalizations of Homans as: "Person while he is at the office values getting help more than he does struggling with his problems all by himself." (Two pages later on Homans himself mentions exceptions to this rule: "persons who are too proud to ask for help, who are aggressive, or self-reliant, etc." *Social Behavior,* pp. 43–46.) "No exchange continues unless both parties are making profit" (p. 61). (Yes, if we exclude the familistic, altruistic, coercive, and other relationships that in their totality are more numerous than Homans' "profitable" relationships.) "The more profitable to [two interacting persons] the average value of what each gives [to the other], the more time they will spend together in interaction" (p. 71). (Yes, if they have the time for that sort

---

[33] See the empirical and statistical evidence for these conclusions in *ibid.,* chs. 2, 3, 4.

[34] Cf. C. W. Mills, *The Power Elite* (New York, 1956); G. Mosca, *The Ruling Class* (New York, 1938); and R. Michels, *Les partis politiques* (Paris, 1911).

of interaction, which many persons don't. Actual studies of human behavior show that, out of every 24 hours, only a small fraction is spent in mutually profitable interaction; a greater portion is spent in activities that are neither "mutually profitable nor unprofitable"—activities performed under the pressure of circumstances and of other largely involuntary conditions and urgent needs.)[35]. Inaccurate also is Homans' statement that "aggressive behavior is simply released by a frustration or an attack" (*Social Behavior*, pp. 28–29). This "Freudian" axiom is incorrect in generalizing one of the many effects of frustration, attack, or calamity into an exclusive universal uniformity. As a matter of fact, frustration, attack, or calamity release quite different reactive activities in different persons and groups. They may engender altruistic, suicidal, apathetic, mentally disorganized, or desperately sensual activities. In a group that suffers a frustration of calamity, moral and religious polarization results: Some of the members become more criminal, cynical, irreligious, and atheistic, whereas others become more saintly, heroic, moral, and religious. This polarization is the *only* uniformity shown by practically all groups under conditions of frustration or calamity. Homans' rule, as well as the opposite generalization, that "by suffering we learn," are only partial uniformities.[36]

Homans' rules of theory-building, on pp. 16–17 of *The Human Group,* are platitudinous. Such statements as "We may speak of Person's activity as being valuable to him because it gets him a valuable reward, or of Other's activity as being valuable to Person because it rewards Person" (*Social Behavior,* p. 40), are tautological. So are the statements "Man will put more units of activity within given time to get a more valuable reward than he will to get a less valuable one" (p. 41), and "If in the past the occurrence of a particular stimulus-situation

---

[35] See P. Sorokin and C. Q. Berger, *Time-Budgets of Human Behavior* (Cambridge, Mass., 1939), chs. 8, 9, 10.

[36] See a vast body of empirical and historical evidence confirming this conclusion in my *Man and Society in Calamity* (New York, 1942), chs. 10–12; *Basic Trends of our Time* (New Haven, 1964), ch. 4; and *The Ways and Power of Love,* ch. 9, pp. 213–231.

has been the occasion on which a man's activity has been rewarded, then the more similar the present stimulus-situation is to the past one, the more likely he is to emit the activity, or some similar activity, now" (p. 53). (Certainly, if the Stimulus-Situation-Rewarded Activity, S-S-RA, recurs in the identical form or a form quite similar, then it is likely to be the same S-S-RA, or one quite similar. The rewarded activity is likely to be the same too, providing that the discharge of the first rewarded activity has not changed the man, as it usually does. Even a paramecium or an amoeba in the same constant environment reacts to the same stimulus-situation differently the second and third time, as the experimental studies of S. Metalnikov and other biologists show.)[37]

"Men express anger, when they do not get what their past history has taught them to expect. . . . The more to a man's disadvantage the rule of distributive justice fails of realization, the more likely he is to display the emotional behavior we call anger" (pp. 73–75). (Even this semitautological proposition is in no way a universal uniformity: As my preceding remarks on polarization and the multiform effects of frustration and calamity indicate, some persons and groups react to "distributive injustice" by displaying emotions different from anger and aggressiveness.) "The patterns of stimulus conditions that are capable of releasing emotional behavior in men are undoubtedly more complicated than those in pigeons" (p. 74). (Quite correct.) "The higher a man's esteem in a group, the higher his authority is apt to be. . . . A man who influences many others is also a man who influences them often and over a wide range of activities" (pp. 286–287). (Old logicians called this sort of definition *idem per idem*.)

These platitudinous and tautological propositions abound in the two books discussed.[38]

Practically all of Homans' propositions concerning value,

[37] See S. Metalnikov, *La lutte contre la mort* (Paris, 1937), p. 74 and chs. 1–7.

[38] Homans himself acknowledges the tautological character of some of his propositions. "It is our own choice which of our propositions we shall allow to become tautologies." *Social Behavior*, p. 41.

its unit and its measurements, are vague, because his concepts of value, unit, and measurement are not well defined: After a valiant attempt to define these, he admits that "Values like pride, altruism, aggression—values that are their own reward—are just the ones that give us most trouble in predicting and explaining the behavior of men." Finally, he concludes that a "man's past is where we must look for enlightenment; the past offers in principle the information we need to assess values independently of the amount of activity a man puts out to get these values at present" (pp. 40–45). This statement is fairly accurate, but it does not help at all to establish what value is for different people, or what its unit and measurement are.

The same can be said about most of Homans' propositions concerning norms, justice, authority, and satisfaction. His definition of norms does not specify that not all norms are regarded by us as obligatory and binding, but only those that are backed by "imperative-attributive" convictions. The violation of this type of norm is regarded by each of us as a crime or an injustice.[39] Because he does not differentiate these law-norms from many quite different other norms, most of Homans' propositions concerning norms, distributive justice, authority, formal-institutional and informal-subinstitutional behavior and organizations, conformity, expectations, and deviations are indeterminate and vague. This vagueness manifests itself in his second rule of justice: The value of what a member of a group receives from other members *should be* proportional to his investments" (p. 237). This leaves us wondering whether Homans is describing the uniformity as it really exists or as it *should* exist. This ambivalence is evident in many cases in which he considers what are or should be the characteristics of leaders, how frequently and urgently Person has to ask Other for help, how much help Other gives (or does not give) to

[39] See, on these norms, including the "official" and the "unofficial-intuitive" law-norms and convictions, my *SCP*, chs. 4, 31. If Homans had used respective theories of law-norms, he would have been able to give much more adequate formulation to many of his propositions and would not have been obliged to make his own formulations. This shortcoming is quite common among American sociologists; we met it before in examining the analytical, functional, and social-action theories.

Person, and under what conditions their "exchange" of help is most profitable (*Human Group,* ch. 16). One never knows whether Homans is describing these exchanges as they really happen or as they *should* happen. Even worse, in most of these discussions one does not find any deductive or inductive ground for Homans' conjectures of how Person and Other really behave in their exchange. Here is an example of such conjectures:

> How shall we measure this total profit? . . . Suppose both men are in the office for eight hours a day. If Other in fact gives Person two hours of help (thus giving up two hours he might otherwise have devoted to his own work) and gets two hours of approval for it, and gives the remaining six hours to doing his own work . . . we believe that he has achieved a greater total profit than he would have done if he reversed the distribution and gave six hours to Person and only two hours to his own work" (p. 71).

If we ask why it is more profitable for Other to give two hours of his time than six hours, we do not receive an answer based on empirical, deductive, or dialectic grounds. It is just a conjecture of Homans, as he himself acknowledges by saying that "we need not compare how he (Other) in fact distributed his activity with an unreal or ghost distribution, the whole point of which is that it never existed" (p. 71). Almost all Homans' propositions describing how Person and Other are exchanging their rewards and punishments are similar conjectures not corroborated by any empirical or genuine deductive evidence. A careful reader of Homans' book never knows whether he is reading propositions describing real uniformities as they occur in exchanges of rewards and punishments by individuals and groups or whether he is reading a Homans play, "Rewarding and Punishing Exchanges of Person and Other," as imagined by the author.

For a final example of the vagueness and sometimes even meaninglessness of Homans' propositions, let us look at his definition of profit and the new economic man:

> So long as men's values are altruistic, they can take a profit in altruism too. Some of the greatest profiteers we know are altruists. . . . The trouble with [the old economic man] was not that he was economic, that he used his resources to some

advantage, but that he was antisocial and materialistic. . . . What was wrong with him were his values: he was only allowed a limited range of values; but the new economic man is not so limited. He may have any values whatever, from altruism to hedonism (and even masochism) but so long as he does not utterly squander his resources in achieving these values, his behavior is still economic. Indeed if he has learned to find reward in *not* husbanding his resources, if he values *not* taking any thought for the morrow, and acts accordingly, his behavior is still economic. In fact, the new economic man is plain man (pp. 79–80).

Despite my liking for Homans' interpretation of profit and the new economic man, I find myself somewhat confused. If Homans' profit means an exchange in which Person obtains a maximum value from Other at no cost or at minimum cost to himself as well as an exchange in which Person gives to Other maximum value at no cost or at minimum cost to Other, if profit means ruining Other for Person's own benefit as well as sacrificing Person's fortune and life for the well-being of Other, if economic man is utterly egoistic as well as utterly altruistic, if he is perfectly normal as well as masochistic and sadistic, if economic activity signifies "husbanding" for the morrow as well as spending all resources for a given moment, then profit and economic man become a veritable *coincidentia oppositorum*, the incarnation of *A and non-A*. As applied to God, Tao, Nirvana, the Divine Nothing, or the total reality, negative definitions of this sort have been used and have a meaning and sense. But as applied to such finite and even prosaic phenomena as profit and economic man they are meaningless, for they imply that any exchange between Person and Other is profitable, that all the activities of Person and Other are "economic" activities, and that any kind of man is an economic man.

Sixth, let us finish the foregoing criticisms by a more general critical observation of *Social Behavior*.

1. Homans' two major premises are partly fallacious in the overgeneralized form in which he presents them. His first major premise is that human behavior is similar to that of the pigeons in Skinner's laboratory: "Taking our departure from what we know about animal behavior," he says "we shall state

a set of propositions that seem to us fundamental in describing and explaining human social behavior" (*Social Behavior*, p. 31).

His second major premise is that "*all* human behavior, no matter how subtle, is shaped by differential reinforcement of quite simple actions produced the first time as if by chance" (p. 19). Logically and empirically, an unrestricted identification of the behavior of animals with that of man is a gross error, for it ignores everything specifically human.

Homans' second premise is false because not all the behavior of pigeons is "shaped by differential reinforcements of quite simple actions"; and still less is *all* human behavior shaped by rewards and punishments. Only by completely disregarding the existing knowledge of how and by what factors the behavior of human beings is formed could Homan make such an assertion. In both cases, he generalized a partial similarity between human and animal organisms and behaviors into a total similarity. Homans' second premise is but a poorly formulated utilitarian-hedonistic doctrine long ago exposed as fallacious.[40]

The logical and empirical inadequacies of both of Homans' major premises are largely responsible for most of the mentioned shortcomings of his propositions. If the major or the minor

[40] Jeremy Bentham's formulation of this doctrine and his "moral arithmetic" for measuring the comparative value of different pains and pleasures, utilities and disutilities, is more precise than Homans' "rewards and punishments" and his measurements of their comparative value. According to Bentham's precept, that pleasure is greater which is (1) more intense, (2) more durable in time, (3) more certain, (4) more immediate and accessible, (5) more fruitful in pleasurable consequences, (6) more pure or free from painful consequences or elements, and (7) extended over a larger number of persons. These seven criteria are certainly more adequate than Homans' vague criteria for measuring the comparative value of punishments and rewards. See P. A. Pokrovsky, *Bentham i ego vremia* (*Bentham and His Time*) (Petrograd, 1916). For a criticism of Bentham's doctrine, see my paper "Novuy trud o Benthame" ("A New Work About Bentham"), in *Yuridichesky Vestnik* (1916). More sophisticated and penetrating is the analysis of the exchange of power and prestige in social life presented by Peter M. Blau in his book *Exchange and Power in Social Life* (New York, 1964). Most of Blau's conclusions are correct for a small fraction of interactions of individuals and groups. In their extrapolated form as presented by Blau, they become questionable and incorrect. In generalizing his conclusions beyond their legitimate limits, he commits the error of elevating a partial uniformity into a universal one.

premise of a syllogism is logically or empirically defective, defective also becomes the conclusion derived from these premises. Herein lies the main source of most of Homans' mistakes.

2. These premises, plus Homans' homemade modifications of economic man, economic value, marginal utility, cost, profit, and price, are largely responsible for the shortcomings of his theory of social behavior. His laborious translations of these economic theories into behavioral language makes one wonder why he did not use the respective theories themselves but offered us, instead, analogical variations on them. Homans' theorizings in this field are notably poorer—logically and empirically— than the classical theories of Smith, Rodbertus, Mill, Ricardo, Marx, Gossen, Menger, Walras, and Böhm-Bawerk, not to mention those of more recent economists. Regardless of whether one agrees or not with the deductive theories of the eminent economists, one cannot help being impressed with their logical and cogent explanation of certain important economic phenomena. The same cannot be said of Homans' theorizings in these fields.

3. If Homans had explicitly stated that his study deals only with one sector of social behavior and human groups, namely, with "exchange" relationships and with behavior shaped by rewards and punishments, if he had clearly indicated that his conclusions and propositions are applicable only to this sector and are inapplicable to familistic and coercive behavior, relationships, and groups, then several of his theories would have been free from the defects pointed out by the foregoing criticisms. Though his studies cover only contractual forms of behavior, relationships, and groups, he nevertheless contends several times that his propositions explain all human social behavior and all its elementary forms.

4. Homans' thesis that sociology is a part of psychology and that the real explanation of sociocultural phenomena has to be sought in animal and human psychology is one-sided and inadequate.[41] He gives no new logical or empirical evidence to corroborate this claim, which represents a mere reiteration of an

---

[41] This thesis is pointedly outlined in Homans' "Bringing Men Back In," *ASR*, December, 1964, pp. 809–818.

old controversy that by now is already dead and buried. (Its opposite thesis is that psychology is a part of sociology and that a scientific explanation of psychological phenomena should be sought in sociology.) Both disciplines have factually been and are separate and relatively independent from each other, but both need to cooperate, for their theories and explanations are often complementary. If Homans' thesis were to be systematically developed, it would evolve into a variety of the "instinctivist interpretations" of human and sociocultural phenomena—interpretations long in disrepute.[42]

5. Finally, Homans' theory of the human group or social system has two different conceptions: systemic (holistic) (in *The Social Group*), and singularistic-nominalistic (in *Social Behavior*). Taken together, both theories furnish only a somewhat fragmentary, largely conjectural, sketch of the anatomy and histology of social systems and hardly contribute anything systematic to their physiology and taxonomy.

Homans' studies have their own—and not insignificant—merits. First, his advocacy of the deductive method is a courageous and timely call to those American sociologists who mistakenly believe that only empirical, inductive, and "quantitative" methods are scientific, and who identify deductive or dialectic methods with speculative, philosophical, and unscientific procedures. Homans' endorsement of this method should remind these sociologists of the most important role that this method has played in the natural as well as in the psychosocial sciences, and in philosophy and the humanities.

Homans must also be commended for verifying his deductive propositions by relevant empirical facts. By verifying them, his whole method becomes "deductive-inductive"—that is, the proper method for investigating empirical phenomena. After the analytical, structural-functional, and dialectic theories discussed earlier, which are largely devoid of empirical realities, one turns to Homans' empirical and "experimental" studies with relish.

Paraphrasing Windelband's observation that "in the realm of philosophy it was not those who were right who contributed

---

[42] See a discussion of the "psychological school" and "instinctivist interpretations" in *CST*, ch. 11.

most, but those who had been wrong," I can say that we profit cognitively not only by Homans' correct conclusions but also by his errors, which vividly raise a number of important but neglected problems of sociology, make questionable some prevalent beliefs, and teach us to avoid Homans' own mistakes. Finally, his combined use of the data, theories, and methods of animal and human psychology, economics, and sociology for understanding important psychosocial realities deserves a warm commendation: It gives to all investigators of human behavior and social systems an example worthy of imitation.

PART FIVE

TAXONOMY AND CHANGE IN
SOCIOCULTURAL SYSTEMS

CHAPTER 16

Empirical Taxonomies of
Social Systems

TAXONOMY OF SOCIAL GROUPS

In the preceding chapters, it was noted several times that practically none of the examined theories of social systems offer any systematic taxonomy of empirical social systems. They give various typologies of social groups, and they suggest several formal characteristics of social groups, such as open and closed, small and large, primary and secondary, unifunctional and multifunctional, temporary and durable or permanent, localized and dispersed, formal and informal, organized and unorganized, solidary and antagonistic or neutral, and so on,[1] but none of them has developed an adequate taxonomy of empirical social groups or systems. Most of the recent theories mention, in passing, some of these, but they rarely give a systematic classification of even their most important genera and species. Except for several "evolutionary" pseudotaxonomies of the nineteenth and early twentieth centuries, the taxonomy of social groups continues to be one of the most neglected parts of general sociology.[2]

[1] The most detailed catalogue of such characteristics is given by Gurvitch, *Traité de Sociologie*, Vol. I, pp. 190 ff. See also my *SCP*, chs. 5, 8, 9.

[2] A general survey of the various classifications of social groups is given in my *SCP*, ch. 9. See also L. Wilson, "Sociography of Groups," in G. Gurvitch and W. E. Moore (eds.), *Twentieth-Century Sociology* (New York, 1945); R. Bierstedt, *The Social Order* (New York, 1963), chs. 10–17; L. Mendieta y Nuñez, *Théorie des Groupements Sociaux* (Paris, 1957), ch. 3, and *passim*. The lack of a systematic taxonomy of empirical social groups can be seen by perusing current sociological texts and the programs of the meetings of the American Sociological Association. Here are examples: In one text, only sex groups, the family,

Still more important is the fact that without a more or less adequate taxonomy of social systems, many important social groups, like social class, "community," and "society," cannot be adequately defined, nor can a correct theory of differentiation (and stratification) of mankind into concrete-empirical (not merely formal) groups be established, nor can a number of significant social processes be properly understood.

Fortunately, this general neglect has been somewhat remedied by a few recent works devoted to taxonomic classifications of empirical social groups. Through these it has been possible to study the main lines of social differentiation and stratification of mankind into real social systems that are "visible" and that by their activities and interactivities determine the basic processes of human social life. One of the best works of this sort is *Théorie des Groupements Sociaux* by Lucio Mendieta y Nuñez.

MENDIETA'S TAXONOMY OF EMPIRICAL GROUPS

Mendieta's monograph opens with the following statement:

> A study of social groupings is a fundamental problem of sociology because the social life appears to be shaped by these groupings much more than by singularistic individuals. Without denying the importance of interindividual relations the truth is that the most important changes in the history of humanity and the deepest transformations in societies are due to the actions of social aggregates called nations, states, classes,

---

city-country, caste and class, race and ethnic groups are specifically mentioned; in another, only the family-race-urban-rural-professional-economic-religious-criminal groups are described in separate chapters or sections; in the third text, only political-educational-religious-family-artistic-scientific groups and institutions are delineated in separate sections. The papers given at the annual meetings of the American Sociological Association cover only some social systems, like the family, race groups, political parties, or sometimes religious or military or professional or artistic groups. Rarely do they have any systematic taxonomy of groups or even any section devoted to this topic. This confusion is compounded by the interminable and largely fruitless "theorizing" on community, society, groups, and organizations. This confusion can easily be seen by reading such (otherwise good) works as M. R. Stein, *The Eclipse of*

crowds, commercial and industrial societies, scientific and cultural associations.[3]

According to Mendieta, his essay gravitates around the three essential concepts: society, social groupings, and social group: "*Society* is the whole humanity (or human race whose members live in continuous and multiple relations); it includes in itself different species of aggregates which we call *social groupings*, and, among these, we give the name of *social groups* to those groupings which possess an incontestable internal organization" (p. 30). He goes on to define a social grouping as:

> an ensemble of human individuals unified either by psychological bonds or by common material or spiritual interests, or by regulations of law, who maintain among themselves stable or temporary relations oriented in such a way that this ensemble forms a collective unity with the characteristics which distinguish it from its members individually considered. . . . It is a social formation endowed with its own life which however depends upon the presence of human beings who form it in pursuance of complexus of interactions established among them" (p. 58).

Mendieta then stresses the realistic character of his concepts of society, groupings, and groups in contrast to the abstract, unrealistic conceptions of Freyer, Geiger, Von Wiese, Ginsberg, and others, who reduce a society or group to a mere complex of social relations or psychic reality: "In our opinion," Mendieta says, "the tendency of modern sociologists to define society (or group) as an abstract ensemble of relationships contains in it a danger of its de-humanization. It appears to us as arbitrary as the statement that man is an ensemble of thoughts and actions, passing by in silence man's physical nature and organic conditions" (pp. 22–23).

After surveying various classifications of social groupings, the distinguished Mexican sociologist gives his own taxonomy of

---

Community (Princeton, N.J., 1960); D. Martindale, "Community Formation and Destruction," in G. K. Zollschan and W. Hirsch (eds.), *Explorations in Social Change* (Boston, 1964); and W. Heinrich, "Dualistische Lehrgebäude."

[3] L. Mendieta y Nuñez, *Théorie des Groupements Sociaux*, p. 13.

social groupings. First, he divides all social groupings into four main classes: the structural groups, the structural quasi-groups, the occasional or circumstantial pseudo-groups, and the artificial groups. The structural groups "compose the body social itself in which each of the groupings possesses an indubitable intrinsic organization in rapport with the whole society of which it is a part." The family, the tribe, and the state are examples of such groupings. They all are formed naturally, not artificially. The structural quasi-groups are devoid of internal organization but show a cohesion that allows them to detach themselves as ensembles from the rest of society. They are natural groupings by origin and growth. The occasional or circumstantial pseudo-groups are temporary and transitory groups that occasionally form and pass away. They are also natural in their formation. The artificial groups are formed artificially and are organized consciously or intentionally. Mendieta's classification of social groups is summed up in the following table:

Typological Classification of Social Groupings

Structural Groups of Society	Structural Quasi-Groups of Society	Occasional or Circumstantial Quasi-Groups	Artificial Groups
Horde	Community	Crowd	State groups
Family	Nation	Public	(army, bureaucracy, etc.)
Clan	Class		Religious
Tribe	Mass		Political
Confederation of tribes			Economic
Caste			Scientific
The state			Cultural
			Sportive
			Philanthropic
			Secret
			Pathological
			Mixed

In subsequent chapters, Mendieta gives a concise analysis of each of these groupings and of their reciprocal influence upon one another.

The last part of his study deals with "social mechanization,"

which he attributes to an increased differentiation and stratification of mankind into a multitude of the artificial groupings and
their social mechanisms:

> Our conception of social mechanism concerns all artificial
> groupings which . . . impose upon their members in an almost
> ineluctable manner and make them accomplish the prescribed
> actions under the pressure of the forces that control the
> groupings, even if these actions are contrary to the opinion,
> beliefs and individual interests of those who constitute the
> organization and independent from the qualities or defects of
> those who direct it.

In an artificial grouping the organization is so rigorous that
an order emanating from its chief puts automatically into motion
the whole hierarchy of those who form the organization and
make, as a rule, no effective opposition to the order possible:

> In such groupings the role performed by individuals is similar
> to that of a little part in a mechanical apparatus. An individual
> is but a mere cogwheel in the grouping of which he is a part.
> In other words, he loses his personality; his will is dominated
> by the superior orders and has to adapt itself exclusively to
> the movements or functions he is commanded to discharge
> (pp. 184–187).

The position of an individual in an army exemplifies his position in all rigorously organized artificial groups:

> In the past epochs, even the most powerful social mechanism,
> the State, had always before itself a grand mass of people who
> were free, in the sense of their being not attached to any social
> organization. An individual of such a society was something
> different from a mere cogwheel and, consequently, at a given
> moment, his independent conscience and his autonomous will
> could push him to unite in coalition with others in order to
> reduce to nothing the power of any artificial group of rigorous
> organization: the state, religious organization or political
> party, etc. Our epoch, on the contrary, is marked by growing
> social mechanization. The isolated individual does not count
> much any more or counts less and less each passing day. . . .
> He is compelled to become a member of some social organism
> to be able to defend his interests, sometime even his life. . . .
> The artificial groups which attract a great number of in-
> dividuals are all rigorously organized: army, bureaucracy,
> syndicates, political parties, religious associations, commercial

societies. . . . This tendency of social mechanization, that is, formation and growth of rigorously organized artificial groupings in our days does not obey the free will of persons; it obeys only the pressure of determined social factors and circumstances. In the civilized countries, each day the number of individuals who can stay outside of social mechanization decreases (pp. 188–189).

Once founded by free volitions, the artificial groups become increasingly organized, absorb an individual more and more, and impose themselves upon him and dominate him as superior beings. "The result is the individual's de-personalization, automatism, spiritual crisis and alteration of personality." For a society at large the effects of this social mechanization are, first, the intensification of social life and dynamism in all fields of human existence; second, the control and transformation of individuals according to the requirements of these artificial groups; third, the progressive undermining of the democratic spirit and individual liberty; fourth, the extraordinary increase of the power of the leaders who direct the rigorously organized artificial groups. Holding in their hands the steering wheel of social mechanism, they can move within fairly large margins the group's activities in the direction they find advisable to move. A sort of "Caesarism" (in Spengler's terms) emerges and grows in the populations differentiated and stratified into a multitude of such groups. Fifth, as a consequence of the preceding effects, such societies develop a standard, gregarious type of man obedient to the leaders of the artificial groups: "Democracy becomes increasingly supplanted by *leaderocracy* [and] an ever-increasing part of social life becomes determined not by the respective population but by a very limited number of individuals, sometime even by one leader, who impose their convictions, caprices, follies, sometime, but very rarely, grand ideas and noble sentiments upon them." Sixth, human history becomes increasingly determined by the activities of the few privileged leaders—not the heroes who by their great achievements and talents inspire the masses to follow them but the machinators-politicians who succeed in placing themselves at the head of the social mechanisms and holding them in their hands: "Great soldier, inventor, a genius are pushed to the back stage:

they are valued only insofar as they serve the leader." With very rare exceptions, most of today's leaders are mediocrities and "mystifiers" (*mystificateurs*) who pursue mainly their own interests screened by highfalutin ideologies they do not believe in but adroitly use for the beautification of their selfish and prosaic purposes (pp. 190–192).

As a result, Mendieta says, "modern social life develops in an atmosphere of lies, hypocrisy, cowardice, oppression, and lawlessness." The concentration of weapons in the hands of leaders of rigidly organized artificial groups makes it impossible for the oppressed individuals to resist successfully the pressures of the leaders or to overthrow them as they did in earlier periods.

On the other hand, the individuals and society at large exert a retroactive influence upon the artificial groups. Sooner or later in the process of their existence inner contradictions and conflicts with other groups arise. Reinforced by the extreme dissatisfaction of their members, they create crises that sometimes lead to the destruction of or to an essential correction of the "dysfunctional" results of the social mechanisms and their leaderocracy (ch. 17).

CRITICISM

As mentioned above, Mendieta's classification is one of the best in recent sociology. It has both sound and defective features. His conception of society, groupings, and groups is basically sound. Though less developed, it is somewhat similar to my conceptions of society, unorganized-semiorganized, organized, "as if organized," and disorganized social groups. If a sociologist uses the terms social group or groupings and distinguishes organized, as if organized, unorganized, and disorganized social groups, then the term society (at large) becomes identical with that of human population as an agglomeration of groups, whether the human population means a whole human race or a population of any territory differentiated into two or more groups.[4]

[4] See my conceptions of organized, unorganized, semiorganized, "as if organized," and disorganized groups and populations in *SCP*, chs. 4, 8, 16. This conception of society and community as an agglomeration of

Less satisfactory (logically and empirically) is Mendieta's classification of all groups into four classes. First, his division of groups into "natural" and "artificial" seems arbitrary and partly contrary to the facts. If by natural he means those groups which, "with an exception of the State, are formed without a previous agreement of their members" and by artificial those groups "intentionally organized," then to place the family, the confederation of tribes, the community, and the state into the natural structural class contradicts the fact that a multitude of families, several confederations of tribes, communities, and states have been organized intentionally by deliberate agreements and treaties according to the plans of the parties involved. On the other hand, some of the groups placed by Mendieta into the artificial class, like several religious, economic, cultural (e.g., language or ethnic groups), and pathologic (criminal and mentally and physically defective groups) have emerged fortuitously.

Besides their empirical inadequacy, the categories natural and artificial are somewhat vague and open to different interpretations. More precise and correct appears to be a theory of four ways in which human beings initiate their interactions and form organized groups. These four ways are "intentional or purposeful, sought by all interacting parties; intentional, sought by some of the parties and opposed or unsought by other parties; intentional or not, but opposed by all the parties directly involved (or coercively imposed by a third party); and unintentional or fortuitous on the part of all the parties concerned, whose interaction is started by various conditions—cosmic, biological, and sociocultural—and whose interactive relationship naturally crystallizes into organized forms—regardless of their purposes and aims."[5]

The second shortcoming of Mendieta's taxonomy is its incompleteness: Although it lists such comparatively unimportant groups as secret, philanthropic, pathological, and sportive, it does not mention at all racial, ethnic, occupational, and the sex

---

groups is quite different from the concept propounded by Parsons, Levy, Martindale, and others.

[5] *SCP*, pp. 369–372. See there a detailed and documented discussion of these four ways.

and age groups, which, in organized, semiorganized, and "as if organized" forms, occur in all populations. They are important, universal, and perennial lines of social differentiation and stratification, quite tangibly condition the behavior of millions of individuals, and notably determine the character of social processes and the course of human history.[6]

As a detail of this shortcoming, Mendieta's "cultural" groups represent largely a duplication of his specified artificial groups, whereas his "state-groups" mean really a few subgroups of the state like the army and the bureaucracy.

The third defect of Mendieta's classification is that it puts into the same class groups fundamentally different from one another. The state, caste, and the family are all called structured groups; community, nation, and mass are all called structured quasi-groups.

The fourth shortcoming is that his taxonomy tells very little about the componential structure of the groups or about their essential characteristics. It does not indicate which of the groups are unibonded and unifunctional and which are multibonded and multifunctional, which, in other words, are organized around one important value (economic or religious or artistic or occupational, or political) and respectively bind their members into unity by the bond of this value alone, and which are organized around two or more important values. The structural analysis of

---

[6] Perhaps this deficiency is due to a lack of definite criteria in selecting and enumerating the specified groups in Mendieta's classification and to an inadequacy in his formula of the comparative power and influence of social groups. He gives hardly any reasons for selecting the mentioned groups or for not mentioning a number of other groups. Only somewhat incidentally, on p. 182, he mentions that the power and influence of the artificial groups are determined by (a) a "degree or perfection of group's organization; (b) extension of the zone of its influence" (including the size of its membership); (c) the "attraction of the group's directive idea"; (d) the "effective character of the sanctions upon which is based the organization of the group." This formula of the power of a group appears to me less adequate than my own formula: "Five criteria give a rough, but fairly accurate, measuring stick of the comparative powerfulness of social groups. They are: (1) the size of the group membership, either of a single given group or of a formation of many similar interacting groups; (2) the totality of the meanings-values-norms at the disposal of the group (including the fund of scientific knowledge, tech-

groups by the kind and number of values around which they are
built (a sort of "sociological chemistry of groups," figuratively
speaking) is still largely neglected by sociologists. Without this
kind of analysis, however, no real understanding of either the
structure of groups, or of their stability, duration, or other important characteristics is possible. By having a "sociological
chemistry of groups," we would be able to give a fairly precise
formula of the structure and properties of every social group or
system; we would even be able to diagnose and prognosticate
their stability or instability. Such a structural analysis would
make also glaringly clear many blunders still prevailing in the
sociology of groups or social systems. For instance, most sociological theories of the family still regard it as one of the simplest
social groups; most of the recent theories of "small groups" still
contend that they are simple or "elementary" groups; and most
of the prevalent theories of social classes still identify them with
this or that *stratum* in the intragroup or intergroup social stratification. An elementary analysis of the structure of the family or
of many "small groups" or of social classes from the standpoint
of the values around which and for the realization of which they
exist and function shows at once that the family, despite its small
size, is one of the most complex, multibonded, and multifunctional groups in existence and that a social *class* is also a
multibonded and multifunctional group quite dissimilar from a
social *stratum,* with which it continues to be associated by to-

---

nological inventions, systems of philosophy and religion, laws and ethics,
rational economics and politics, fine arts, vitality and health, etc.); (3)
the totality of vehicles and instrumentalities possessed by the group for
influencing the individuals and groups (machines, tools, weapons, press,
telephone, radio, money, wealth, land, capital, books, libraries, orches-
tras, etc.); (4) the solidarity of the group; (5) the technical perfection
of its structural and functional organization." *SCP*, p. 169. From the
standpoint of the power of a group so measured, the influence and power
of the sex-age-race-ethnic-occupational groups has been and is incomparably greater on the behavior of individuals and groups, in shaping
their vital, mental, moral and social properties, and on their social
processes and the course of human history than those of the "secret-
philanthropic-pathological-sportive" groups in Mendieta's classification.
See an analysis and corroboration of these conclusions in *SCP*,
chs. 10, 11.

day's sociologists. The "sociological chemist" knows that the family is highly solidary, semiclosed, and multifunctional or multibonded, and that it represents a socially sanctioned union of husband and wife and parents and children bound together by, and functioning for the realization of, several important values, including the satisfaction of the husband's and wife's sexual needs, procreation, the procurement of means of subsistence for its members, the socialization and education of its younger generation, the protection of the lives, integrity, and values of its members from various inimical forces, the mitigation of their loneliness and psychosocial isolation, and the promotion of their happiness and self-realization. It is a multibonded and multifunctional group made up of heterogeneous and mutually supplementary values and bonds, including sex, age, race, and kinship bonds, and those values that are territorial, linguistic, religious, economic, occupational, educational, artistic, moral, and recreational. It is the only all-embracing community of bodies and souls, of minds, and activities. It is indeed, as the great Roman jurisconsult Modestinus called it, a *"consortium omnis vitae, divini et humani juris communicatio."*[7]

This abbreviated formula of the componential structure of the family clearly demonstrates that its structure is more complex than the structures of many vast economic, occupational, scientific, religious, or any other unibonded and unifunctional association. The values, norms, and functions of most unifunctional associations are compounded in the family. The family represents a most complex molecule or compound made up of the elements (values-bonds-functions) of several unifunctional or unibonded groups.[8]

This shortcoming of Mendieta's classification leads to a fifth questionable point, namely, the partial inadequacy of his concept of the social class. He rightly construes the social class as a

[7] *SCP*, p. 246. See there a more detailed analysis of the componential structure of the family, pp. 246–255.

[8] See a systematic theory of the unibonded (unifunctional) and multibonded (multifunctional) groups and an outline of sociological chemistry in my *SCP*, chs. 10–16. A knowledge of this theory is needed to fully comprehend these statements.

quasi-organized group whose members are united by the similarity of their economic and cultural values-bonds-functions (positions). As such, they have a similar economic standard and style of living, similar manners and mores, and similar mental outlook. In any society there are always three main classes, the upper, the middle, and the lower, together with interclass populations not consolidated into any social class. Following this schema, Mendieta describes the characteristics of each of the principal classes.[9]

The first part of this definition is correct insofar as it delineates social class as a multibonded-multifunctional, quasi-organized social group different from other unibonded and multibonded groups and their strata. In this respect his conception of social class is more sound than those that construe it as a nominal statistical plurel (exemplified by Warner-Lunt's six classes of "upper-upper, lower-upper, upper-middle, lower-middle, upper-lower, and lower-lower" in their studies of Yankee City) or that identify social classes with a stratified unibonded-unifunctional occupational or economic or political or educational group.[10] The errors of these theories consist in substituting a nominal (statistical) plurel for a real social group (system), identifying social class with one of the unibonded groups, and arbitrarily ranking all social classes in a unilinear hierarchy. These theories miss almost completely the idea of social class as a powerful, multibonded group *sui generis* that emerged in the West in the seventeenth century and subsequently has tangibly determined the behavior, mentality, and characteristics of millions of individuals, groups, social processes. In contrast to a caste or "social estate" system in a class society there is no unilinear, legally and socially sanctioned hierarchy of classes.[11] Legally and morally, the principle of the equality of all human beings before law, of "all men created equal," has prevented

[9] See L. Mendieta y Nuñez, *Théorie des Groupements Sociaux,* pp. 114–121.

[10] See a detailed survey and analysis of various theories of social class in my *SCP,* pp. 261–275; see there also the literature on this group.

[11] See an analysis of caste and "social estate" in my *SCP,* pp. 256–261.

and does prevent the establishment in a class society of a uni-linear, socially sanctioned hierarchy of classes. For instance, in class societies, there are no objective bases for deciding whether the peasant-farmer class or the class of industrial labor is su-perior, whether the class of industrial and financial capitalists or the class of the big landowners is superior. For these reasons, any ranking of social classes in a unilinear hierarchy is but an arbitrary opinion of the investigators or their informants.[12]

Fortunately, all three errors are increasingly being corrected by the scholars of social class. New conceptions increasingly approach the formula of social class exemplified by my own and Gurvitch's definition (see Chapter 14) of this group:

> Social class is: (1) legally open but actually semiclosed; (2) "normal"; (3) solidary; (4) antagonistic to certain other social classes; (5) partly organized but mainly quasi-organized; (6) partly aware of its own unity and existence and partly not; (7) characteristic of Western society of the eighteenth, nine-teenth, and twentieth centuries; (8) a multibonded group centered around and bound together by three unibonded values-ties" occupational, economic, and political—(by similarity of

[12] Many recent studies of social stratification and social classes in the United States have been contaminated by all three errors—i.e., they have identified social class with either a nominal-statistical plurel con-structed by the researcher, or with the unibonded (unifunctional) strati-fied group, or they have tried to rank social classes on a unilinear hier-archical ladder arbitrarily constructed by investigators or their informants. Fortunately, with the development of research on social classes, these errors have been increasingly avoided in favor of the more correct con-ceptions of social class as a multibonded group bound together by similarity of occupational, economic, political, and additional values. This trend has been exemplified by W. L. Warner and his associates in their later studies, where they introduce the criteria of occupation, source and amount of income, house type and dwelling area, plus the "social esteem" ratings of their informants. J. A. Kahl, J. A. Davis, P. Hatt, A. W. Kornhouser, A. Inkeles, P. Rossi, S. M. Lipset, P. Lazarsfeld, R. Centers, E. Monachesi, and others have found "a relatively high posi-tive correlation" between occupation, economic position, and political voting. Other studies of either purely occupational or economic or edu-cational or political or ethnic or racial stratifications in intra- and inter-unifunctional groups by G. S. Count, R. Dahrendorf, K. Svalastoga, M. Smith, W. A. Anderson, M. Deeg, D. Paterson, M. Welch, H. Him-melweit, A. Halsey, A. Oppenheim, the National Opinion Research Cen-ter's "Jobs and Occupations," the contributors to R. Bendix and S. M.

its members' occupational, plus economic, plus political positions). Through its legal openness and actual semiopenness the class differs from the closed caste as well as from the medieval orders or estates whose chronological successor it is. It differs also by the nature of its threefold compounded values-bonds from other multibonded groups, like the family, the tribe, the nation. . . . The coalescence of the three values-bonds of a class is "affined" or "normal": comparative poverty coalesces with manual (unskilled and semiskilled) occupations and with comparative disfranchisement (legal and actual) in respect to political rights and privileges; comparative wealth coalesces with more complex mental occupations and with privileged political status (legal and actual). To constitute a genuine social class a part of individuals similar in their occupation, economic, and political status must be tangibly organized and another part quasi-organized. When such an organization occurs, a class consciousness arises among the members of the social class.[13]

On the basis of the objective similarity of occupational, economic, and political positions of the members of the same class, they cannot help becoming similar, to a considerable extent, in their style of living, manners, and mores and in many of their physical, mental, moral, and behavioral characteristics.

In the light of these considerations, it is easy to see the shortcomings of Mendieta's concept of social class: the vagueness of the "cultural" values and bonds that coalesce individuals into a quasi-organized social class, the omission in his definition of the occupational similarity of the members of the same class, and the unnecessary reduction of all social classes to three unilinear hierarchical classes: high, middle, and low. We have already mentioned that almost all rankings of social classes on

---

Lipset's *Class, Status and Power,* T. H. Marshall, A. B. Hollingshead, C. Hunt, A. E. Edwards, the "Minnesota Occupational Scale," G. Lenski, R. W. Mack, C. Bird, J. L. Haer, N. Rogoff, H. Pfautz, O. D. Duncan, N. Gross, S. Sargent, T. E. Lasswell, C. A. Anderson, H. L. Zetterberg, and others have also produced significant knowledge of the intra- and intergroup stratifications in these unifunctional groups. See a good survey of most of the studies mentioned in this footnote in B. Barber, *Social Stratification* (New York, 1957); and H. M. Hodges, Jr., *Social Stratification* (Cambridge, Mass., 1964).

[13] *SCP,* pp. 271–272. See there a detailed discussion of this formula. See also the symposium "Les classes sociales dans le monde d'aujourd'hui" in *Cahiers internationaux de sociologie,* XXXVIII (1965).

a unilinear ladder are largely arbitrary. Social class can be defined without any hierarchical ranking whatsoever. In all other respects, however, Mendieta's conception of social class is essentially correct.

Mendieta's theory of social mechanization and its consequences for an individual and society at large seriously challenges the validity of the opposite theory, propounded by Durkheim, Tönnies, G. Richard, and others, that the division of social labor and the increasing differentiation of populations into diverse social groups increases the individuality, peculiarity, and relative freedom of individuals, replaces "mechanical" solidarity by "organic," favors the development of voluntary contractual relationships, decreases the autocracy and hereditary character of government, stimulates diversity and variety of different associations, and in brief, influences individuals and society at large in ways almost opposite to those outlined by Mendieta.[14]

Which of these theories is correct? Without entering into an analysis of this problem, let me just say here that *both theories are one-sided.* More correct is the proposition that both types of societies have their own forms of freedom and coercion, of inhibition and stimulation of creative potentials of their members, of "standardization" and diversification of their mentality and behavior; in brief, in both there is a "dialectical" coexistence of virtues and vices specific for the little differentiated and for the excessively differentiated societies at large. If in the *Gemeinschaft* type (or "mechanically" solidary type of social group) genuine "familistic" relationships prevail (as they sometimes do) then its members feel themselves free, mutually help one another, and regard their chiefs and leaders as *bonus pater familias.* If in this type of society, coercive and antagonistic relationships prevail (as in some such groups they do) then its members are oppressed, its government and leaders are despotic, and the group suffers from an abundance of inner antagonisms. If in the *Gesellschaft* (or "organically" solidary type of social group) genuine contractual relationships prevail, if respectively its members are free to join or not to join any of its associations, if its government is freely chosen and limited in its authority

[14] See a discussion of their theories in *CST*, pp. 467–495.

and power, if its written or factual constitution guarantees the "inalienable rights of man and citizen" for every member, then such a group and its members are largely free from the negative vices outlined by Mendieta. If, on the contrary, its contractual relationships degenerate into the pseudocontractual—that is, if they become largely coercive relationships as they have in Western societies in the twentieth century—then Mendieta's theory of "social mechanization" appears to be correct in its essential characteristics. We in the West live in an excessively differentiated world whose genuine contractual structure has now largely crumbled and has been increasingly replaced by a pseudocontractual structure of direct and indirect, mild and stern coercive relationships.[15] Most of Mendieta's negative descriptions of this world—similar to those of Spengler, Schubart, Berdyaev, and others—are roughly accurate.[16]

To sum up, though Mendieta's taxonomy of social groups appears to me less developed than my own,[17] his taxonomy and his theory of "social mechanization" both represent notable contributions to these fields of sociology.

R. BIERSTEDT'S CLASSIFICATION OF SOCIAL GROUPS

The essentials of Bierstedt's classification of groups can be summed up as follows: First, taking three properties of groups,

---

[15] Essentially correct also is Mendieta's portrait of contemporary "leaders," "leaderocracy," and "power elites." See a confirmation of his propositions in C. W. Mills, *The Power Elite* (New York, 1956); and Sorokin and Lunden, *Power and Morality*.

[16] These conclusions are based upon my analysis of the "familistic," "contractual," and "coercive" relationships, upon a systematic study of their proportions in the total network of social relationships in Western society from the eighth century to the present time, upon a detailed analysis of the decline of contractual relationships in the twentieth century and, finally, upon my criticism of Durkheim-Tönnies' typologies of the "mechanical" or *Gemeinschaft* and the "organic" or *Gesellschaft* forms of social system. See a detailed investigation of these problems in my *Dynamics*, Vol. III, chs. 1, 2, 3, 4, 7; *Crisis of Our Age*, ch. 5; *The Basic Trends of Our Time*, chs. 1, 3, 4; and *SCP*, chs. 29, 30, 31.

[17] See its abbreviated form at the end of Chapter 2 in this work and in its developed form in my *SCP*, ch. 9.

consciousness of kind, social interaction, and social organization, as his *fundamentum divisionis*, he divides all groups into four classes: statistical, which have none of these characteristics; societal, which have only "consciousness of kind," social, which have "consciousness of kind and interaction," and associational, which have all three characteristics.[18] We see at once that Bierstedt's "statistical" group is just a nominal plurel. His "societal" group is largely a fictitious plurel, because without direct or indirect interaction no real group is possible: Mere "consciousness of kind" is not enough to make a real group out of ten or tens of thousands of isolated individuals. His "social" group corresponds to what is usually called an unorganized group, and his "associational" group is an "organized" group. Since fictitious plurels are not real groups at all, we can leave Bierstedt's statistical and societal groups without any further analysis (as he himself largely does).

He correctly remarks that in their forms and contents social groups can be classified in many different ways. His own formal classification is fairly similar to mine and Gurvitch's. He distinguishes the following forms of groups: primary and secondary, in-groups and out-groups, large group and small groups, majority groups and minority groups, long-lived groups and short-lived groups, voluntary and involuntary, open and closed groups, horizontal and vertical, independent and dependent, unibonded and multibonded, organized and unorganized.

In his characterization of each of these group forms, Bierstedt deviates from current interpretations of these forms (for instance, in his interpretation of primary groups, he emphasizes, instead of the "face-to-face" characteristic, the "degree of intimacy, or social distance" as the most important *differentia* of primary social systems.)

Unfortunately, he hardly gives any systematic taxonomy of groups by their *content*. His most detailed enumeration of groups by their values, norms, and bonds is in *The Social Order* on p. 302, where, in passing, he mentions the following kinds of groups, "all of which have some importance in modern complex

[18] R. Bierstedt, *The Social Order* (New York, 1963), pp. 293–301.

societies: kin, family, ethnic, territorial, age, sex, political, governmental, language, religious, residential, class, occupational, recreational, propinquity, business, nationality, scientific, charity, insurance, educational, honorary, learned, and so on. The 'so on' is included because no list could ever be absolutely complete. Those mentioned, however, are major groups." Subsequently some of these groups are commented on in some detail, but most of them are not.

CRITICISM

The first doubtful point in his theory is his assumption (made in connection with his acceptance of F. Giddings' "consciousness of kind" as an important property of group) that "consciousness of kind [or of similarity] is a strong stimulus to social relations," whereas "consciousness of difference is frequently a barrier to social intercourse—excepting, of course, consciousness of difference in sex." Further on we are told that "those who recognize (important) similarities begin to gravitate together and to associate with one another" (pp. 295–296; see also pp. 467–469). Insofar as this proposition means that all important similarities of individuals and groups uniformly facilitate their solidarity, whereas all of their significant dissimilarities lead uniformly to prejudice, discrimination, and antagonism, it is incorrect. A careful study of this problem (including the existing statistical and experimental studies of the role of similarity and dissimilarity in interindividual and intergroup solidarities and antagonisms) shows that both of the opposite theories —the "attraction of like for like" and of "opposite poles attract" —are one-sided. Some important similarities, under certain specified conditions (when, for instance, respective values are scarce) generate antagonism (or indifferent, neutral relationships), whereas some complementary dissimilarities engender solidarity among the parties involved. In other cases, important similarities lead to friendly relationships, whereas important dissimilarities facilitate the development of inimical relationships. Which of a multitude of diverse similarities and dissimilarities of individuals or groups appear to be important to the parties involved and under which specified conditions they (or their combination) lead now to solidarity, now to antagonism is a problem somewhat better accounted for by a much more complex theory than either Empedocles' generalization that "like seek after like" or Heraclitus' opposite hypothesis that "the opposition unites." Contemporary reiterations of these ancient "opposite" theories by Durkheim, Tönnies, Bierstedt, and others can be dismissed as inadequate.[19]

The second doubtful point in Bierstedt's theory is his somewhat ambivalent attitude toward my theory of unibonded and multibonded groups and toward what I call the "sociological chemistry of groups." On the one hand, he accepts the theory, even the terms "unibonded" and "multibonded" groups. On the other hand, in his interpretation of these concepts he misconstrues them and then rejects the idea of a "sociological chemistry of groups."[20] He writes:

> Sorokin believes that on the basis of the distinction [between unibonded and multibonded groups] it might be possible to develop what he calls a "chemistry" of groups, in which some, the unibonded groups, would be elements and others, the multibonded groups, would be compounds. One might go on then to show that certain kinds of ties or bonds have an affinity with others, for example occupational and class ties—whereas others tend to repel each other and come together only rarely. An examination of this distinction, however, discloses that it probably does not add anything to what we have previously called the distinction between primary and secondary groups. Furthermore, the chemical analogy seems somewhat perverse, in that it is the primary group which is multibonded, the secondary group which is unibonded. It is the group with many bonds that is primary, primitive, and nuclear in the structure of society (p. 316).

In reply to this criticism, I have to note, first, that Bierstedt wrongly identifies my concept of unibonded and multibonded groups with MacIver's and Hiller's concept of "like and common

[19] See a detailed analysis of this problem and the relevant literature in *SCP*, ch. 7.

[20] For instance, in his interpretation, "kinship group" is multibonded; in mine, it is unibonded. See *SCP*, pp. 195–197, 251–253.

interests" and "distributive and corporate interests" and with "primary and secondary" groups.

The concepts of the unibonded and multibonded groups are quite different from MacIver-Hiller's categories and from the concepts of primary and secondary groups. These concepts were somewhat vague and self-contradictory even in Cooley's formulation and they remain vague in MacIver's, Page's, and Bierstedt's. If we view the "face-to-face" trait as the main characteristic of the primary group, then, as Bierstedt himself correctly remarks, *all* our "face-to-face" interactions, including those with plumber, postman, groceryman, and incidental acquaintances, become primary, and the concept becomes quite meaningless. If we dismiss the "face-to-face" trait as the main *differentia* of the primary groups (as Bierstedt largely does), then the concept of the primary group loses its most important characteristic and becomes an indeterminate group identified by Bierstedt now with the "intimate," now with the "family," now with the "primitive," now with the "personal," the "intrinsic," the "small group," even with the "social group" in Bierstedt's sense of this term (that is, with a largely nominal group having neither interaction nor organization). It also becomes identified with Durkheim's "mechanical solidarity," Tönnies' *Gemeinschaft*, and Sorokin's "familistic" groups. My concepts of the unibonded (unifunctional) and the multibonded (multifunctional) groups are certainly quite different from the vague concepts of primary and secondary groups.[21]

Neither can primary groups be identified with multibonded groups, nor secondary with unibonded groups, as Bierstedt claims. There are many multibonded groups, like nation,

---

[21] See their definitions and analysis in my *SCP*, pp. 170–178. H. Spencer's and E. Durkheim's morphological classifications of societies into "simple" (the "horde") and "doubly compound," "trebly compound," and so on are somewhat analogous to my unibonded and multibonded groups. They are, however, essentially different from mine. First, the Spencerian simple group and the Durkheimian horde (similar to Bierstedt's-MacIver-Page's "nuclear" primary group) is a fiction that never existed; and, second, Spencer's doubly and trebly compound societies and Durkheim's simple polysegmental and complex polysegmental become largely fictitious, based upon a trait of federations of unified

medieval order, and social class,[22] that are neither intimate nor face to face; nor do they have any other characteristics of primary groups. Moreover, there are many multibonded groups compounded of two or more mutually antagonistic unibonded-group values. In such multibonded groups, the mutually antagonistic compounded values incite their members to mutually contradictory actions, ideas, and impulses, and make such a multibonded group a house divided against itself, unstable and easily disintegrated. Such, for instance, was the two-bonded population of Europe in the eleventh century, whose members were simultaneously subjects of King Henry IV and members of the Catholic Church. During the feud between Henry IV and Pope Gregory VII, this two-bonded population, as Catholics, had to follow the injunction of the Pope and to oppose the king's; as the king's subjects, however, they had to obey the orders of the state and to denounce the Pope. The mutually antagonistic values of the state and the Church forced each member of this population in opposite directions and split the multibonded group into three different factions: those in whom loyalty to the Pope prevailed, those in whom loyalty to the king was stronger, and those who remained neutral. Another example of an innerly antagonistic two-bonded group is the conscientious objectors or pacifists. When they are drafted into the armed forces, they are expected to participate wholeheartedly in war and to defeat the enemy, although their moral convictions make such a task abhorrent. All such innerly antagonistic multibonded groups are quite different from primary groups in any sense of that term.

---

societies. The Spencerian classification puts into one class such groups as ancient Mexico, the Assyrian Empire, the Egyptian Empire, Great Britain, France, Germany, and Russia. The absurdity of this speaks for itself. See *SCP*, p. 164. See H. Spencer, *Principles of Sociology* (London, 1885), Vol. I, pp. 540 ff.; and E. Durkheim, *The Rules of Sociological Method* (Chicago, 1938), ch. 4. The error of these classifications is that they classify multibonded (compounded) groups or populations representing agglomerations of several unibonded and multibonded groups, instead of unibonded (elementary) and multibonded (compounded) groups in my sense.

[22] See their structural formulas and analysis in *SCP*, pp. 242–246, 251–255.

On the other hand, there are several unibonded groups—fanatical religious sects, revolutionary political parties, and certain kinship groups—whose members are so completely dedicated to the realization of the one main value of the group that they are bound into an intimate, personal, intrinsic, and solidary group that is as closely integrated as any multibonded group, including the family. In short, each pair of categories, unibonded-multibonded and primary-secondary, embraces many different aspects or forms of groups, just as the categories voluntary-involuntary and long-lived and short-lived embrace quite dissimilar aspects or forms of social systems.

For this reason, Bierstedt's assertion that the classification of groups into unibonded-multibonded "probably does not add anything to the distinction between primary and secondary groups" is quite incorrect. The distinction between the unibonded (unifunctional) and multibonded (multifunctional) groups certainly adds a great deal to the classification of groups by their form as well as by their content. First, it points out a very important aspect or form of groups largely neglected by formal anatomists and taxonomists of groups. Second, it defines precisely the content or sociocultural portrait of each social group by pointing out the value(s) for realization of which the group is organized as being value(s) of sex, age, race, occupation, politics, or religion. It also indicates whether they are two-bonded (religious plus political, sexual plus occupational); "three-bonded" (religious plus occupational plus ethnic, economic plus occupational plus political); or four-bonded, five-bonded, and so on. Third, the categories unibonded-multibonded allow the sociocultural structure of any real group to be expressed in a fairly precise formula. The definitions of the family and social class given above are examples of such formulas. These formulas precisely define around what sort of value(s) a given group is established, what behavioral and social functions it performs for the realization of these values, what kind of rights, duties, ideologies, and forms of behavior it imposes upon its members, whether it is innerly antagonistic or solidary or neutral, and so on. Fourth, if fully developed, the concept of unibonded-multibonded groups can serve as the best basis for a systematic taxonomy of social groups. This taxonomy would consist of a detailed classification, first, of all important unibonded (unifunctional) groups with subdivisions of each group into its species; second, of a detailed enumeration of all important two-bonded (two-functional) groups with their species; third, a detailed classification of all important three-bonded, four-bonded, and still more complex multibonded groups. Combined with other formal characteristics of each group, such a fully developed classification would give to us, for the first time, a truly systematic and scientifically adequate taxonomy of social groups or systems on a par with botanical or zoological taxonomies of living forms, with the classification of elements and compounds in chemistry, and with the classification of elementary particles and atoms in physics.

Fifth, when the multibonded groups are studied and classified as to which of them are "innerly solidary" (that is, built around two or more mutually complementary values), "innerly antagonistic" (built around two or more antagonistic values), or "innerly neutral" (built for the realization of two or more mutually indifferent values), we will have a much greater understanding of a large part of the mentality and behavior of human individuals and of many basic sociocultural processes. Whether a person is a member of an innerly solidary or innerly antagonistic multibonded group makes a great difference in his mentality and behavior. If one belongs only to an innerly solidary group, one's personality tends to be well integrated and one's behavior tends to be consistent and resolute, for it is forced in one direction by all mutually complementary compounded values of the respective multibonded group. If one belongs to an innerly antagonistic multibonded group, one's personality is bound to be fragmented and one's behavior either inconsistent or irresolute, for it is forced in opposite directions by mutually opposite compounded values. In brief, without a knowledge of the kind of multibonded groups to which an individual belongs (voluntarily or not), no psychologist or psychiatrist or sociologist can explain all the mental and moral characteristics and behavior of the individual.

A knowledge of multibonded groups greatly helps also in

understanding the comparative stability, life-span, and other *differentia* of various groups and in understanding the what's, how's, and why's of many social processes: As a rule, other conditions being equal, the innerly solidary multibonded group tends to be more stable and longer lived than the innerly antagonistic multibonded group. If an innerly antagonistic ("abnormal") multibonded group emerges in any society, one can predict its pending disintegration and its replacement by a corresponding "normal" (innerly solidary) multibonded group, either in an orderly or, more often than not, in a violent, revolutionary way. The values of wealth and political privilege seem to combine easily, and quite frequently produce "normal," two-bonded economically rich and politically privileged groups. However, there occasionally appear two "abnormal," two-bonded groups: one politically more privileged but economically poorer, and one economically richer but politically less privileged. The French nobility and the French bourgeoisie on the eve of the French Revolution in 1789 and the Russian nobility and the Russian bourgeoisie on the eve of the Russian Revolution in 1917 illustrate this point: In both countries, the bourgeoisie was economically richer but politically disfranchised, and the nobility was economically poorer but politically more privileged. Both "abnormal" groups in both countries were short-lived and were replaced, in a violent way, by "normal" (innerly solidary) groups—a politically privileged and economically rich bourgeoisie in France and the new Soviet Communist ruling class in Russia. Prosaically viewed, the main process of both revolutions consisted in the disintegration of these two abnormal (two-bonded) groups and their replacement by groups with a "normal" combination of wealth and political privilege and comparative poverty and political disfranchisement. Abbé Sieyès summed up this aspect of the French Revolution well by saying that before the Revolution the bourgeoisie was nothing and after the Revolution it became everything.

In some cases, wealth obtains political privileges; in other cases, the politically privileged take wealth by violence from the conquered wealthy group. The result in both cases is a replacement of innerly antagonistic, abnormal group(s) by the innerly solidary, normal ones. On a large and small scale, similar processes go on all the time, now in a gradual and orderly, now in a violent and disorderly way. The civil-rights movement in the United States today, the conflict between the former colonial powers and the subjugated colonial populations, the civil wars going on in many countries all over the world are basically processes in which abnormal multibonded groups are being replaced by normal, innerly solidary, multibonded groups.

These examples illustrate the cognitive services of the discussed classification of groups into multibonded-unibonded for a better knowledge of many social processes.

Finally, such a classification would permit an elaboration of an adequate system of "affinities" of unibonded group values to one another. Such a system of affinities can tell us which unibonded group value easily combines with which other group value, how frequently such "affine" compounds take place, how frequently such "affine" multibonded groups are observed in various populations, and how stable and long- or short-lived such multibonded groups are. It can also tell us with which of the group values a given group value does not combine at all or combines rarely and with difficulty, how stable and durable such "abnormal" multibonded groups are, and under what conditions they appear and disintegrate. Even a rough theory of group affinities of this sort can give us a much greater knowledge of the properties of various groups, especially of multibonded groups, than the vague generalities supplied by today's theories of groups and by such incidental classifications of groups as we have.

The heuristic importance of classifying groups into unibonded and multibonded groups is equal, at least, to that of any of the prevalent classifications.[23] I have called the theory of multibonded-unibonded groups the "sociological chemistry of groups." If Bierstedt or anyone else does not like this expression, it can easily be dropped without involving any change in the

[23] For a greater development of the theory of multibonded and unibonded groups and of the basic problems involved in it, see my *SCP*, chs. 13, 14.

exposition of my theory. The only role this figurative expression plays is to facilitate the reader's grasp of the essential properties of multibonded-unibonded groups and their classification.

Because Bierstedt so hastily dismissed the scientific importance of this theory, he made a series of mistakes in his analysis of social stratification, social classes, castes, and other multibonded groups. First, he had to identify social class with a higher or lower stratum either in a unibonded or in a multibonded group. It was shown above that such an identification is a gross error, for it misses the point that a social class is a powerful, specific, multibonded group *sui generis* that emerged in Western society in the seventeenth century and since has played a most important role in the West and to some extent in the East.[24] Because he started by wrongly identifying social class with *stratum*, Bierstedt could not avoid making many errors in developing his theory of stratification and his concepts of social class, caste, medieval estates, and other multibonded groups. Here is a brief enumeration of some of these mistakes:

1. "Class is almost, but not quite a universal phenomenon in human society. It is a phenomenon that is absent only in the smallest, the simplest, and the most primitive societies."[25]

Here social class is identified with a stratum in general without any specification of the kind of stratification and group in which the stratum is a social class. This is a very vague definition of social class as well as of stratum. If the term social class is taken in this general sense, then Bierstedt's statement that "it is absent only in the smallest, the simplest, and the most primitive of societies" is incorrect: Even in the most primitive known groups members are stratified by age, sex, and by personal rank. Even the family, especially the patriarchal family, is juridically and factually stratified. The *pater familias* has the right of life and death (*jus vitae ac necis*) over the children, and the husband has a complete authority over his wife (*manus mariti*) in

---

[24] Besides the literature on this given in *SCP*, see S. Mallet, *La nouvelle classe ouvrière* (Paris, 1963); and M. Bouvier-Ajam and G. Mury, *Les classes sociales en France* (2 vols.; Paris, 1963). See also J. S. Mathur, *Indian Working-Class Movement* (Allahabad, 1964).

[25] R. Bierstedt, *The Social Order*, p. 436.

many patriarchal societies. In a milder form, stratification exists also in "modern" families.[26] If by social class is meant the specific multibonded group that appeared only in the seventeenth century in the West, then this group is in no way universal or perennially present in almost all human societies, as Bierstedt states.

2. On pages 454 ff. of his work, we read: "Among various criteria that appear to be related to class status in our own complex society we may briefly discuss the following: 1) wealth, property or income; 2) family or kinship; 3) location of residence; 4) duration of residence; 5) occupation; 6) education; and 7) religion. We should like to emphasize that no single criterion, taken by itself, embraces the whole of the phenomenon of class."

Here, in contrast to the previous definition, social class is defined as a complex multibonded group whose members are unified by *seven* value-bonds, including such detailed bonds as location and duration of residence, religion, and education. There is no doubt that in some American cities, there are small septibonded groups. However, any *local* multibonded group is a small group; it plays hardly any tangible role in determining the mental, moral, and social characteristics of millions of individuals and groups in the course of human history. Such local groups have little similarity to such social classes as the peasant or farmer class, the proletariat, the capitalist class, or the class of big landowners, or even with such influential "interclass" groups as the intelligentsia. Moreover, most of Bierstedt's "septibonded" groups are nominal statistical groups arbitrarily constructed and ranked by social stratifiers in various communities like Yankee City, Plainville, and so on.[27] Such local and mainly nominal plurels are in no way identical with the vast

---

[26] See *SCP*, pp. 240 ff. See also C. C. Zimmerman, *Family and Society* (New York, 1935).

[27] See particularly H. W. Pfautz and O. D. Duncan, "A Critical Evaluation of Warner's Work in Community Stratification," *ASR*, Vol. 15 (1950), 483–498; and P. K. Hatt, "Stratification in the Mass Society," *ASR*, Vol. 15 (1950), 216–222. See also Bierstedt, *The Social Order*, pp. 460 ff.

social classes as they have functioned during the eighteenth, nineteenth, and twentieth centuries. In addition, Bierstedt's septi-bonded class is radically different from his previous (quoted) definition of class in terms of an unspecified stratum generally.

An additional small mistake in his conception of the septi-bonded class is his statement that "class status in general is a family rather than an individual phenomenon. It also comes to be a hereditary one; that is, class status, once attained tends to endure through several generations" (pp. 456, 436–440). This statement is true only for caste, medieval estate, and agricul-tural, patriarchal, and closed societies with a weak mobility; it is largely incorrect in regard to many modern, "open," industrial-ized, and, particularly, revolutionary societies. In such societies, with their strong social mobility, the members of a great many families are dispersed among different strata and classes and the intergenerational status of families changes rapidly and contrast-ingly, as Bierstedt himself notes on pages 441 ff. of his work.[28]

Not quite correct either is his identification of a caste system with a closed-class system: "We regard a closed class system and a caste system as synonymous" (p. 441). A social class (as defined before) differs from a caste or a medieval estate or other closed, unibonded and multibonded group not only in its semi-openness but also in the bonds that bind its members together. The Hindu caste "is a closed, solidary, organized, or quasi-organized multibonded group made up of racial, kinship, occupational, economic, territorial, religious, and language bonds, the state bond playing an insignificant role."[29] The mem-bers of a social class, on the other hand, are bound together mainly by similar occupational, economic, and political ties; religious, racial, kinship, territorial, and language bonds play no important role. Different also are the bonds making up the

[28] See on this O. D. Duncan and R. W. Hodge, "Education and Occupational Mobility," *AJS*, Vol. 28 (1963), 629–644; K. Svalastoga, *Prestige, Class and Mobility* (Copenhagen, 1959); P. Sorokin, *Social and Cultural Mobility* (Glencoe, Ill., 1959), chs. 17–20; B. Barber, *Social Stratification*, chs. 13–16; and H. M. Hodges, *Social Stratification*, chs. 12–13. See the data and literature in these works.

[29] *SCP*, pp. 256 ff.

medieval estate, tribe, clan, family, community, nation, and other multibonded groups.[30] Here again, Bierstedt's disregard of the theory of multibonded and unibonded groups is responsible for his inadequate conception of the differences between caste, social class, and other groups discussed in his book.

Bierstedt's theory of the factors and forms of social stratification is also inadequate; it does not spell out any specific factor of why stratification appears in any organized group, why it assumes a specific form in a given group, why it eventually changes in its profile and height, or why it allows for mobility. All we learn about these problems in Bierstedt's work is that "people do different things . . . and pursue different vocations. These different occupational statuses then come to be ranked with respect to one another in terms of the contributions the individuals who occupy them make to the welfare of the tribe or the community. . . . K. Davis suggests that stratification results when some activities are judged to be of more service to a society than are others" (pp. 437–438).

This whole theory is even more artificial and inadequate than the Hobbesian contract theory of how and why the institution of government, in the form of absolute monarchy, was established. The Bierstedt-Davis theory does not answer any of the basic questions involved: Why do different individuals in preliterate tribes or in today's complex societies engage in different activities? Why do only a few of these different activities acquire "functional importance," whereas other activities that are just as necessary for the group's well-being do not? Who and on what basis is doing the "ranking" of the group's members and distributing them among its various strata? What is the mechanism of such a selection and distribution? What are the intragroup, intergroup, and external (cosmic and biological) factors of all these processes? Why do the profile, height, and population of the hierarchical strata of the group change in the course of time? And, finally, does the group's mechanism of

[30] See the formulas of the compounded bonds of the medieval estate, tribe, clan, nation, and other multibonded groups in *SCP*, pp. 242–261.

social selection and distribution of various members among different strata always work "functionally" or does it sometimes select and distribute members quite "disfunctionally," that is, does it place in the upper strata members who, according to their merits, should be placed in the lower strata, and vice versa? None of these questions is really answered by the Bierstedt-Davis theory. If anything, their theory seems to assume that all groups distribute their members among their hierarchical strata according to their merits and the functional importance of their activities for the welfare of the group. According to this theory, Socrates, Christ, and al-Hallaj were "justly" condemned to death for their "disfunctional" activities, and mad and wily politicians and mass murderers were "justly" placed at the top of their stratified hierarchy for their "functional" activities.[31] For their "useless" achievements many a great genius, like Mozart and Schubert, was "justly" condemned to the stratum of the poor, whereas many a voiceless crooner has been made a rich and glamorous popular idol. According to this theory, it was quite right that some of sociology's greatest builders, like Bruno, Vico, Comte, and Marx, were either executed or condemned to poverty. We know well that this sort of extremely "disfunctional" distribution of individuals among wrong strata has been and is going on continuously in many groups. We know also that when the harmful results of such a "disfunctional" selection and distribution accumulate and become disastrous for a respective group, the malfunctioning mechanism and its stratified hierarchy are often overthrown by a violent revolution. The very fact of revolutions is convincing evidence that such a malfunctioning selection and distribution of individuals among the group's various strata is not a rare phenomenon: One of the perennial factors of all great revolutions is exactly this disfunctional selection and distribution.

It is regretful that Bierstedt and other investigators of social stratification have not used the considerable fund of

---

[31] The criminality of monarchs, presidents, and power-elites is many times greater than that of the ruled. See Sorokin and Lunden, *Power and Morality*, chs. 2, 3, 4.

knowledge available for a study of the real problems of social stratification.[32] If they had, they would not have introduced theories of stratification based on the "functional importance" of the activities of the inhabitants of various strata for the well-being of their societies. All the power elites in today's societies, all the top politicians, multimillionaires, big executives, marshals, generals, admirals, crooners, band leaders, bosses of criminal corporations, submediocre but "successful" artists, writers, and journalists, and all the other uncreative "celebrities" of our time should be grateful to these sociologists for glorifying their activities.

I cannot help feeling that these theories are as idolatrous and unscientific as many a Communist ideology similarly glorifying the Communist leaders as the benefactors of the human race. As a conservative Christian anarchist, I find both ideologies scientifically fallacious, morally objectionable, and aesthetically distasteful.

Let me repeat that, despite all the criticisms, Bierstedt's work is one of the most excellently written and clearly formulated texts in general sociology. Several of the theories accepted by him are sound and correct; others are doubtful and defective. But even these are valuable in that they stimulate a further study of their doubtful points.

GENERAL CONCLUSIONS

The preceding survey of recent taxonomic theories indicates that this division of general sociology has been largely neglected. Most of the surveyed currents of sociological thought hardly touch it at all; although others, like the dialectic sociology of Gurvitch and Sartre, or the sociologies of Mendieta and Bierstedt, do treat it, even these theories fail to deliver a truly systematic and scientifically adequate classification of social groups by their "content." To develop a truly scientific taxonomy remains the task of future sociologists.

[32] See an analysis of these problems in my *Social and Cultural Mobility*, chs. 14–19; and in *SCP*, chs. 23–26.

CHAPTER 17

Recent Studies of Social Change

THE CONTINUED NEGLECT OF THE "PHYSIOLOGY" OF SOCIAL SYSTEMS

Despite a considerable study of various aspects of social change, despite an analysis and formal classification of social processes,[1] one field of social dynamics has been largely neglected by sociologists. This field roughly corresponds to that of physiology in the biological sciences. In figurative terms it can be called the "physiology of social systems." It investigates the totality of the repeated basic processes taking place in the life-course of organized groups, beginning with their birth (or establishment) and ending with their death (or disappearance).

Like the taxonomy of social systems, the "physiology" of social systems has been investigated even less by today's sociologists than by those of the second half of the nineteenth and of the early twentieth centuries.[2]

The midcentury sociologists have preferred to concentrate

---

[1] Here are a few formal classifications of sociocultural processes by various sociologists of the first quarter of the twentieth century: invention, imitation, opposition (G. Tarde); organization, disorganization, ascendancy, domination, leadership, formalization, individualization, socialization, conflict, hostility, suggestion (C. H. Cooley). See the still more detailed enumeration of various sociocultural processes by C. A. Ellwood, E. Bogardus, E. A. Ross, L. von Wiese, G. Duprat, and others in my *SCP*, p. 368; and in *CST*, ch. 9. See also A. Cuvillier, *Manuel de Sociologie*, Vol. I, pp. 219–225.

[2] The leaders of the organismic and organic school, like H. Spencer, P. Lilienfeld, and others, paid considerable attention to the physiological processes of social groups. Spencer fairly carefully analyzed and classified the processes of growth, differentiation, and integration of social systems, and the "sustaining, distributing and regulating" functions and mechanisms necessary for their survival and the maintenance of their identity. Their theories preconceived and formulated practically all the

on structural-functional theories of how social systems maintain or lose their "equilibriums" and undefined "boundaries";[3] on nomenclatures of psychological processes like "cognitive-mapping," "tension-management," and "goal-attaining" (Loomis); on dialectic processes of "structuration, destructuration, and restructuration" (Gurvitch); on outlines of various "formal" processes (Tarde, Cooley, Ellwood, Ross, Von Wiese); or on the "manner in which social and cultural forms arise and are destroyed" (Martindale).[4]

None of these theories gives us even a roughly adequate knowledge of the physiology of social systems. None of them answers comprehensively such questions as: How do social groups live? Which differentiated processes does their life-process consist of?[5] What are the mechanisms regulating and controlling these processes? How do these heterogeneous processes succeed in harmoniously cooperating with one another in maintaining the life-process of the whole social system? And how and why do they sooner or later fail in this task and disintegrate? More specifically, these theories provide neither a systematic theory

---

sound propositions of the "structural-functional" schemes concerning the requirements that any social system must meet for its survival. In contrast to the structural-functional "ghost models of social systems"— hardly related at all to concrete sociocultural and historical realities— the organicists not only developed a general theory of the basic physiological processes of groups, but documented it by concrete historical and anthropological examples. See H. Spencer, *Principles of Sociology* (London, 1885), Vol. 1, pp. 435–591. The term "social physiology" was used by Buchez and also by Comte. See F. Isambert, "Physiologie Social chez Buchez," *Cahiers internationaux de sociologie*, XXXVI (1964), 101–116.

[3] Parsons' latest definition of "equilibrium" reduces it to "the maintenance of the identity and continuity of social systems" and of their "normative patterns." This definition does not add anything to the concept of "the maintenance of the identity and continuity of social systems"; it is parasitical and void of cognitive value. See Parsons' definition of equilibrium in his "An Outline of the Social System," in Parsons-Shils-Naegele-Pitts' *Theories of Society*, Vol. I, p. 37.

[4] D. Martindale, *Social Life and Cultural Change* (Princeton, N.J., 1962), p. viii, and *passim*.

[5] The physiology of the human organism answers these questions by differentiating its life-process into the specialized physiologies of the organism's main systems: cardiovascular, respiratory, reproductive, excretory, neurophysiology, physiologies of blood, muscle, digestive system, endocrinology, etc.

of the total life-process of a social group nor a classification of the special processes of which this total life-process is made up. The following questions remain unanswered:

1. How and why do social groups originate? How and why do their member: pass from a state of isolation to that of meaningful interaction and contact?

2. How and why do they organize? How and why do official law-norms emerge? How and why do recommended, required, and prohibited relationships arise? How and why does intragroup and intergroup differentiation and stratification appear, with a government and hierarchy of respective ranks and authorities?

3. How do social groups maintain their integrity, identity, and continuity? In accordance with the componential structure of the groups, an adequate answer to this question requires a knowledge of three subprocesses: How do the groups maintain the identity of their component of meanings-values-norms because of which and for the realization of which the groups are organized and function? How do they acquire, exchange, maintain, and lose their means of subsistence and their biophysical media (vehicles) that objectify and materialize their values-meanings-norms? How do they maintain their membership? How do they supply, produce, recruit, exchange, and lose their members?

4. How and why do groups exchange, test, select, and distribute their members among their strata and positions?

5. How and why do they maintain, in critical conditions, now the method of self-adjustment (each individual "tightening his belt"), now the method of group-adjustment (suiting the groups' environment to meet its needs)? How and why do these methods fluctuate in time and social space?

6. How and why does the groups' creativity fluctuate in time and space?

7. How and why do the groups change in size, in stratified profile, and in the proportion of the familistic, contractual, and compulsory relationships in the total network of social relationships?

8. How and why do some social relationships migrate from one kind of group into a different kind—for instance, from the

network of relationships of religious bodies into that of the states, or vice versa?

9. How and why do the unibonded groups, values, and bonds compound into different multibonded groups, values, and bonds? How and why do various multibonded values-bonds-groups dissociate into diverse sets of unibonded values-bonds-groups?

10. How and why do the forms of groups' government change? How and why does the amount and severity of government regimentation and the kind and extent of freedom of groups and of their members fluctuate in time and in social space?

11. How and why do groups change now in orderly and now in violent revolutionary manner?

12. How and why do war and peace, solidarity and conflict, fluctuate in intergroup relationships?

13. How and why do the groups disintegrate and "die"?

14. How and why do some of the groups revive?[6]

These questions do not cover all the "physiological" processes of social systems. They give, however, a sufficiently clear idea of their scope.

Some of these processes—like social mobility, social differentiation and stratification, social conflicts and solidarities, growth and decline of social systems—have, of course, been substantially investigated by midcentury sociologists and psychosocial scholars. But the investigated processes cover only a small portion of the important "physiologies" of social groups. Out of context, these studies often fail to grasp important forms of these processes, to uncover some of the hidden functions they play in the life-process of the whole system, and to give an adequate explanation of many what's, how's, and why's concerning these processes, their *differentia specifica*, their interrelationships with one another, their rhythms, functions, causes, and consequences, and the mechanisms that control the operations of each and of the whole ensemble of these processes in maintaining, conditioning, and making up the total life-course

---

[6] *SCP*, pp. 367–368; an analysis of the how and why of each of these processes is given in chs. 21–34.

of the whole social system. A rough outline of these processes is given in my *Society, Culture and Personality* (chs. 21–34), but a full development remains the task of the coming generations of sociologists.

GENERAL CHARACTERISTICS OF RECENT STUDIES OF SOCIAL CHANGE

The midcentury sociologists have intensely investigated various problems of social change, especially in the fields of special sociologies. The range of the problems of social change studied is so wide and so diverse that in a single chapter there is no possibility either to survey briefly the kinds of problems investigated, to outline the theories, conclusions, and uniformities arrived at, or to list the vast literature produced by the investigators of these problems. Instead of a minute examination of these studies, this chapter merely sums up some of their high points and general characteristics.

The first general characteristic of the recent studies of social change is their concentration on discovering constant and repeated sociocultural processes, repeated either in social space (in various groups) or in time or in both. Eighteenth- and nineteenth-century studies of social change, on the other hand, concentrated on discovering the laws of evolution and progress governing the main course of human history:

> The dominant stream of social thought of the preceding two centuries concentrated largely on a study of various *linear trends* believed to be unfolding in the course of time [in the evolution of inorganic, organic, and sociocultural worlds]. The main ambition and central preoccupation of scientific, philosophical, social and humanistic thinkers in these centuries consisted in the discovery of the eternal laws of progress and evolution and in an elaboration of the main stages or phases through which the trend passes as it comes to fuller realization in the course of time. Discovery and formulation of such trends was the focal point of biology, sociology, philosophy of history and of other social and humanistic sciences.[7]

[7] P. Sorokin, "Sociocultural Dynamics and Evolutionism," in G. Gurvitch and W. E. Moore, *Twentieth-Century Sociology* (New York, 1945), pp. 97–98. See also C. C. Zimmerman, *Patterns of Social Change*

It was a focal point of the philosophies of history of Herder, Fichte, Kant, Hegel. The discovery and formulation of the laws of evolution and progress or of irreversible historical trends was a central theme of the sociologies of Turgot, Condorcet, Saint-Simon, Comte, Spencer, Buckle, Bachofen, Lubbock, Morgan, Letourneau, Ratzenhofer, Tönnies, Durkheim, Ward, Novicow, De Roberty, Marx, Engels, Gobineau, Cost, Lilienfeld, and others. In a much more weakened form, this preoccupation with the evolutionary laws and historical stages of development lingered on into the first quarter of the twentieth century and found its expression in several historical trends formulated by Hobhouse, Giddings, Small, Sumner, Ogburn, Hart, Keller, and other sociologists, anthropologists, historians, psychologists, and philosophers.[8] In later decades of the twentieth century this preoccupation became dormant and continues to be such up to the present time. (Recent attempts to revive it by White, Parsons, and a few others have been so far unsuccessful.)[9]

> In contrast to this dominant interest of the preceding period, the main interest of the philosophic, social, and humanistic disciplines of the recent period has been increasingly concentrated on a study of sociocultural processes and dynamic relationships which are either *constant*, appearing whenever and wherever a certain class of sociocultural phenomena are given, or *are repeated* in space, time, or both, in the form of more or less uniform rhythms, fluctuations, oscillations, "cycles" and their periodicities.[10]

This concentration on the *constant relationships* and *repeated processes* has manifested itself in several forms. First, in

---

(Washington, D. C., 1956); M. C. Elmer, *Contemporary Social Thought* (Pittsburgh, 1956); A. W. Gouldner, "Some Observations on Systematic Theory," in H. Zetterberg's *Sociology in the U.S.A.* (Paris, 1956); and C. S. Mihanovich, *Social Theorists* (Milwaukee, 1953).

[8] See a more detailed outline of their historical trends in Sorokin, *ibid.*, pp. 96–119.

[9] See L. White, *The Science of Culture* (New York, 1949); "Energy and Evolution," *American Anthropologist* (1943), 335–356; "Lewis Henry Morgan," in H. E. Barnes, *An Introduction to the History of Sociology* (Chicago, 1948); and T. Parsons, "Evolutionary Universals in Society," R. N. Bellah, "Religious Evolution," and S. N. Eisenstadt, "Social Change, Differentiation and Evolution," *ASR*, June, 1964.

[10] Sorokin, "Sociocultural Dynamics and Evolutionism," p. 97.

the valid logical, empirical, and historical criticisms of the assumptions, propositions, and trends of the theories of evolution and progress.[11] On logical, historical, and empirical grounds, no eternal linear trends in their unilinear, oscillatingly linear, branchingly linear, and spirally linear forms have actually been proved by the partisans of evolutionary-progressive theories. Eternal trends have been replaced by the principle of limit, according to which all sociocultural trends are temporary and are given only in some of the sociocultural processes. Eventually such trends are broken and replaced by "turns" and "basic deviations" and different temporary trends. Typical in this respect are the trends studied by the President's Research Committee on Social Trends,[12] or the important trends of our time outlined in my little volume,[13] or the trend toward the "homogenization" of society in the United States, well demonstrated by T. Lynn Smith. All the trends investigated in these works as well as many other trends studied recently are regarded as temporary and not eternal. Most of the sociocultural processes have been found to be multiform and multidirectional; in some links they are temporarily linear, in some others rhythmical or cyclical, in still others curvilinear, and now and then fanciful and unpredictable.

The second manifestation of the recent studies of social change is their emphasis on the constant or uniform relationships between specified cosmic or geographic or biological or psychological factors and specified sociocultural processes[14] and

[11] See the development of these criticisms in *ibid.*, pp. 104–106; in the *Dynamics*, Vol. I, ch. 4, Vol. IV, chs. 12–16, and *passim* throughout all four volumes.

[12] See the Committee's *Recent Social Trends in the United States* (2 vols.; New York, 1933), and a series of monographs published by the Committee.

[13] See P. Sorokin, *The Basic Trends of Our Time* (New Haven, 1964). See also T. Lynn Smith, "The Homogenization of Society in the United States," in *Memoire de XIXe Congrès International de Sociologie* (Mexico City, 1960), Vol. II, pp. 245–275.

[14] See a critical analysis of the main theories of constant (uniform) relationships between specified cosmic, geographic, biological, and psychological factors and specified sociocultural phenomena and processes in my *CST*, chs. I–VII, IX.

between two or more sociocultural variables like economics and religion, anomie and suicide, science and law, poverty and crime, technology and fine arts, and so on.[15]

Third, this concentration on constant and repeated features of sociocultural change has manifested itself also in intensive study of such constant and repeated processes in the sociocultural universe as isolation, interaction, amalgamation, acculturation, invention, imitation, adaptation, conflict, estrangement, differentiation, stratification, organization, disorganization, integration, disintegration, diffusion, convergence, and several "physiological" processes going on in social and cultural systems.

The fourth manifestation of this concentration has been a progressively increasing research in repeated sociocultural rhythms, oscillations, fluctuations, cycles, and periodicities in the flow of sociocultural processes.[16]

Contemporary sociology concentrates on the constant and repeated uniformities and relationships in social change; it differs in this respect from the sociology of the eighteenth, nineteenth, and early twentieth centuries, which concentrated on evolutionary theories of social change.

The second important feature of the recent theories of social change has been their increasing awareness of the essential dissimilarity between changes in social systems (organized groups) and changes in social congeries (unorganized and disorganized groups); and, in accordance with this dissimilarity, their increasing use of different methods and different explanatory hypotheses in their studies of these types of change.

In the foregoing chapters, the profound differences between a unified system (of atoms or cells or interacting individuals or cultural or social phenomena) and its ununified congeries or plurels was comprehensively discussed. It was shown that, at the present time, this profound difference is clearly recognized by the physical, the biological, the psychological, and the social

[15] See a critical analysis of these theories in *ibid.*, chs. VIII, IX, X, XII, XIII. See also "Sociocultural Dynamics and Evolutionism," pp. 107–119; and the *Dynamics*, all four volumes.

[16] See the theories of social rhythms and cycles in the *Dynamics*, Vol. IV, chs. 6–11, and *passim*.

sciences. It was mentioned, too, that all these disciplines increasingly use different methods, techniques, and explanatory principles in studying changes in physical, biological, psychological, social, and cultural systems and congeries.

This is not the place to discuss comprehensively the intricate problems of why the methods of study and the explanatory theories of change in social systems and congeries have to be and are essentially different. The matter was discussed in Chapter 5 and in subsequent chapters of this work. A more systematic analysis is given elsewhere in my works and also in the works of other competent investigators of these problems.[17] Some of these problems will be touched on in subsequent examinations of some of the recent theories of social change.[18]

The third characteristic of the recent theories of social change is a lack of what may be called truly grand theories. Despite an enormous amount of research in this field, hardly any original theory has emerged, hardly any new general principles of change have been formulated, and hardly any new uniformity has been discovered that is as comprehensive and impressive as

---

[17] See my *SCP*, chs. 43–47; *Fads and Foibles*, pp. 150–173; and the *Dynamics*, Vol. IV, chs. 4, 5, 6, 12, and *passim*. See also G. Gurvitch, *La vocation actuelle de la sociologie* (Paris, 1963), pp. 54 ff.; G. Granai, "Le problème du changement social et la théorie sociologique," *Cahiers internationaux de sociologie*, XXXVI (1936), 33–46; and G. Gurvitch, "Objet et méthode de la sociologie," and "Les règles de l'explication en Sociologie," in his *Traité de Sociologie*, Vol. I, pp. 1–27, 236–254. See also J. Lhome, "Sociologie des systèmes, régimes et structures économiques," *ibid.*, pp. 383–419; A. Marshall, "Sociologie des fluctuations économiques," *ibid.*, pp. 419–439; R. Bastide, "Sociologie et psychologie," *ibid.*, pp. 65–82; F. Braudel, "Histoire et sociologie," *ibid.*, pp. 83–99; G. Th. Gilbaud, "Sociologie et statistique," *ibid.*, pp. 114–134; V. Kelle and M. Kovalson, "O klassifikatzii obschestvennykh nauk," in *Voprosy Filosofii*, No. 11, 1964; O. F. Anderle (ed.), *The Problems of Civilizations* (The Hague, 1964), *passim*; T. F. O'Dea, "Sociological Dilemmas," in E. A. Tiryakian (ed.), *Sociological Theory, Values, and Sociocultural Change: Essays in Honor of P. A. Sorokin* (New York, 1963), pp. 71–89; and S. N. Eisenstadt, "Institutionalization and Change," *ASR* (1964), 235–247.

[18] Unfortunately, these "substantive" or, in E. Tiryakian's term, "methodological" problems have been studied much less in recent years than the purely technical or formal research methods. While the latter have been developed to a degree of "methodolatry" (S. S. Stevens' expression), the substantive methodological problems (involving their logi-

the theories and laws of evolution and progress of the preceding periods. Even more, in the field of social change there has hardly appeared a work comparable to the examined works of Spengler, Toynbee, Kroeber, and Northrop in the field of culturology and cultural change. Despite their shortcomings, the scope, breadth, depth, insight, and all-around comprehensiveness and generality of the latter theories have hardly been rivaled by any of the recent theories, most of which have been either fragmentary, or abstract and speculative, or purely descriptive, or pedestrian.

This pedestrian character of the recent theories of social change has, however, been brightened in at least one important spot, namely, in their particularly intense and fruitful study of the fundamental conceptions of sociocultural time, sociocultural space, sociocultural causality, sociocultural tempi, periodicities, rhythms, and the sociocultural categories of cognition that underlie any significant theory of social change and serve as the unavoidable foundation for any model or conceptual framework of social becoming and transformation. In this field of the basic categories of social cognition generally, and of social and cultural change specifically, the achievements of the recent *Wissensoziologie* and sociocultural dynamics have been unique and truly revolutionary. They have already notably changed the naïve and unreflective use of these categories in the preceding theories of sociocultural change and are likely to call forth a

---

cal, philosophical, epistemological implications) have been cultivated much less and are still largely passed by in silence by most of the studies on sociological research techniques and formal methods. Cf. E. A. Tiryakian, "Methodology and Research," in J. S. Rouček, *Contemporary Sociology*, pp. 151–166; S. S. Stevens, "Problems and Methods of Psychophysics," in *Psychological Bulletin*, July, 1958, pp. 177–196; J. C. Taylor, "Experimental Design: A Cloak for Intellectual Sterility," *British Journal of Psychology*, May, 1958, pp. 106–116; P. H. Prabhu, "The State of Psychology as a Science Today," *Fiftieth Indian Science Congress* (Delhi, 1963), pp. 8 ff. See also C. C. Zimmerman, "Contemporary Trends in Sociology; A. H. Hobbs, *The Claims of Sociology* (Harrisburg, 1951); N. Robbio, *Philosophy of Decadentism* (Oxford, 1948); and P. H. Furfey, *The Scope and Method of Sociology* (New York, 1953). See the literature on technical research procedures and formal methodology represented by the works of F. L. Ackoff, S. Stouffer, J. T. Doby, P. Lazarsfeld, M. W. Riley, Morris Rosenberg, F. Kaufman, S. Chapin, H. Zetterberg, and others in their works.

radical revision of many basic sociological theories in the future. Whereas the sociologists and social thinkers of the preceding periods thought of time, space, and causality as being quite simple, clear, uniform, and comprehensible—as innate forms of our mind—the recent studies have shown that there are many different social times, different social spaces, different causalities, even quite different forms and criteria of truth and of the methods of cognition of, especially, sociocultural realities. Side by side with the Aristotelian or Kantian interpretation of the basic categories of cognition as the forms of our mind, the recent studies have shown that they are not only the formal categories of our mind, they are also sociocultural categories largely shaped and determined in their meanings and concrete content by the social and cultural conditions of the collective life of human beings. With a change in these conditions, their meanings, comprehension, and criteria also tend to change. This intensive and revolutionary investigation of the basic categories of the cognition of sociocultural realities is the fourth characteristic of the recent *Wissensoziologie* and theories of sociocultural change. These theories largely redeem the noted inadequacies and shortcomings of the bulk of the recent theories of social change. Some of them are: G. Gurvitch, *The Spectrum of Social Time* (Paris, 1958); *Déterminismes sociaux et liberté humaine* (Dodrecht, 1964); "Les variations des perceptions collectives des étendues," *Cahiers internationaux de sociologie*, XXXVII (1964), 79–106; respective chapters in his *Traité de Sociologie*; and *La vocation actuelle de la Sociologie* (Paris, 1950). P. Sorokin, *Sociocultural Causality, Space, Time* (Durham, N.C., 1943; New York, 1964); *The Dynamics*, all volumes, but particularly Vol. II, chs. 1–12, and Vol. IV, chs. 6–11, 16; P. Sorokin and C. Q. Berger, *Time-Budgets of Human Behavior* (Cambridge, Mass., 1939); P. Sorokin "Theses on the Role of Historical Method in the Social Sciences," *Transactions of the Fifth World Congress of Sociology*, Vol. I, pp. 235–254. R. M. MacIver, *Social Causation* (Boston, 1942); *The Challenge of the Passing Years* (New York, 1962). W. E. Moore, *Man, Time and Society* (New York, 1963); *Social Change* (New York, 1963). M. Heirich, "The Use of Time in the Study of Social Change," *ASR*, June, 1964, pp. 386–397. G. K. Zollschan and W. Hirsch, *Explorations in Social Change* (Boston, 1964).

See also (besides the works of E. Durkheim, M. Scheler, M. Weber, and K. Mannheim), W. Stark, *The Sociology of Knowledge* (Glencoe, Ill., 1958). F. Adler, "Stark's Sociology of Knowledge," *Kyklos* (1959), pp. 216–226, 500–509. J. J. Maquet, *The Sociology of Knowledge* (Boston, 1951). R. Merton, *Social Theory and Social Structure* (rev. ed.; Glencoe, Ill., 1957), chs. 12–19. B. Barber, *Science and the Social Order* (New York, 1962). The articles of J. B. Ford, R. Merton, B. Barber, M. Riley, and W. E. Moore, and my "Reply to My Critics," and "Sociology of My Mental Life," in P. J. Allen, *Pitirim A. Sorokin in Review* (Durham, N.C., 1963). W. Hirsch, "Knowledge, Power, and Social Change," in Zollschan-Hirsch's *Explorations in Social Change*, pp. 798–816. B. Barber and W. Hirsch (eds.), *The Sociology of Science* (New York, 1962).

Such are some of the conspicuous midcentury theories of social change. With the exception of the one noted "bright spot," the bulk of the studies can be classified into three categories: abstract, speculative essays on social change generally; studies that try to map hurriedly the main problems of social change and, now and then, to suggest some of the answers or scientific solutions to these problems; and investigations that concentrate on a substantial study of one or a few important problems of social change crowned by formulating an important uniformity in the area investigated. Let us examine more closely each of these kinds of theories.

ABSTRACT, ANALYTICAL, AND FUNCTIONAL SPECULATIONS ON SOCIAL CHANGE

The theorists of social change usually pretentiously define and prescribe what sorts of categories, analytical schemes, models, principles, and universals have to be used in a scientific study of social change, even though they may never have undertaken such a study themselves. They play the part of scientific legislators who, through either charismatic inspiration or their analytical, psychoanalytical, normative, phenomenological, existential, or functional speculation, believe they have discovered the true methods to scientific study of social change. They rarely, if ever, take upon themselves the task of finding out whether their speculative schemas, models, and categories are applicable to a study of the empirical forms of social change, much less the task of testing their "revelations" by the relevant empirical evidence. They leave these prosaic tasks to other empirical researchers of social change.

When carefully examined, most of these "analytical speculations" turn out to be either platitudes dressed up in ponderous pseudoscientific verbiage or a series of empirically inadequate or inapplicable propositions contributing little, if anything, to our understanding of empirical social change. There has been in recent decades a proliferation of speculative theories of social change. This "analytical theorizing" represents a modern form of medieval scholasticism at its decadent phase.[19] The best examples of this kind of theorizing are the essays of G. K. Zollschan and his collaborators, the studies of A. Boskoff, D. Lockwood, and J. M. Beshers on social-system models of change and by the sketch of I. Sosensky, "The Problem of Quality in Relation to . . . Social Change," in G. K. Zollschan and W. Hirsch (eds.), *Explorations in Social Change*. Other good examples are T. Parsons' paper, "Evolutionary Universals in Society," R. N. Bellah's "Religious Evolution," both in *ASR*, June, 1964, and P. A. Slater's "On Social Regression," *ASR*, June, 1963.

There is nothing particularly new in Zollschan's theory of institutionalization, according to which "changes in action . . . may be conceptualized as responses to exigencies"—that is, to

---

[19] This similarity is well outlined by Zollschan and Hirsch in their statement that "all this is rather reminiscent of the Angelology of Duns Scotus, in which the weighty questions posed in the *Liber Sententiarum* of Petrus Lombardus concerning the number of angels who could dance on the head of a pin was tempered by considerations of whether angels might interpenetrate." Zollschan and Hirsch, *Explorations in Social Change*, p. 293.

a "discrepancy between . . . a desired or expected state of affairs and an actual situation. . . . To eventuate in social-system changes exigencies must trigger a series of phase processes, namely articulation (of the need)-action-institutionalization" (*Explorations*, p. 89). This formula is a verbal variation of an old notion that some of our actions are triggered by an unsatisfied need which we try to remedy by this or that (right or wrong) action. The whole sequence is but a variation on the general formula of "stimulus-response" or of Toynbee's "challenge and response" or of the "purposeful (goal-attaining) action." Each of these forms of actions has been investigated and analyzed in such great detail that any further analytical, functional, or dialectic speculation can hardly give us any essentially new knowledge, despite the fancy terminology ("affective-cathectic," "evaluative," and "cognitive discrepancies"), the complex tables, and the paradigms of the "phases of articulation-activation-institutionalization and their coordinates," the "deprivation equilibrium," the "valence-cognitive-normative dissonances," the "salience-specification-justification requisites of articulation," and so on. This sort of verbiage only confuses the reader without enlightening him either about the source, the mechanism, or the nature of the action.

Zollschan-Petrucci's theory is further vitiated by several incorrect propositions: First, it implies and asserts that their formula of the "exigency-articulation-action-institutionalization" is applicable to all meaningful actions, but it mistakenly takes a specific form of meaningful actions for a general type of all meaningful actions, which are quite different in their motivation, sequence of phases, and nature from the exigency-triggered species of action. Several species of meaningful actions are not triggered by any exigency, but are generated either by a free creative *élan* or by "normative" or "fundamental" motivation, which is quite different from an "exigency" motivation (unless we extend the meaning of exigency to all sorts of actions, in which case the term exigency becomes meaningless).

A further shortcoming of the formula of "action-institutionalization" is its failure to explain why some of the exigency-triggered actions become "institutionalized," whereas many others never reach this stage; like ripples on the surface of a pond, they either disappear from the social world after their performance by a few individuals or remain noninstitutionalized, purely individual actions, or sometimes even criminal actions. They often undergo quite different, frequently opposite kinds of institutionalization: Some of them assume the positive, more creative, more religious, more moral forms of institutionalization, whereas others assume its negative, less creative, more irreligious, more cynical and criminal forms.[20]

Zollschan's essay does not indicate what kinds of changes the exigency-triggered actions generate in political, economic, scientific, artistic, legal, and other fields of social life (as I have done in my works and as other scholars have done). In all these respects, the old formulas and theories of Spencer, Savigny-Puchta, Kovalevsky, Waxweiler, Ross, Westermarck, and Sumner give a much more adequate explanation of this problem. The gist of their theories is well formulated by Waxweiler:

> In a group of interacting individuals many actions are performed; the best ways of acting are repeated; repeated actions become customs; when customs become conscious they turn into a juridical rule; a totality of such rules pertaining to one field of activity composes a social institution; and a totality of such institutions composes the social organization of the group. In a shortened way the scheme is expressed in the formula: action-repetition-habit-custom-rule-institution-organization.[21]

The Zollschan-Petrucci theory, while contributing something to the psychology of exigency-triggered actions, hardly contributes much to our knowledge of institutionalization, social stability, and social change.

The same can be said of D. Willer and G. K. Zollschan's "Prolegomenon to a Theory of Revolution" (*Explorations*,

---

[20] See my *Man and Society in Calamity*, chs. 9–15; *The Ways and Power of Love*, pp. 213, 223, 226 ff.; and *The Basic Trends of Our Time*, ch. 4.

[21] E. Waxweiler, "Avant-propos," in *Bulletin Mensuel* of the Solvay Institute of Sociology, No. 1 (1910). See, for a discussion of other theories of the institutionalization of certain forms of interactive activities, my *CST*, pp. 697 ff.

pp. 125–151), R. Dahrendorf's "Ueber Einige Probleme der Soziologischen Theorie der Revolution," in *Archives Européenes de Sociologie*, II, No. 1 (1961), and—to a lesser degree—of J. C. Davies, "Toward a Theory of Revolution," *ASR*, February, 1962, pp. 5–19.[22]

The first two of these studies are almost entirely speculative. Neither is based upon any systematic investigation of any sample of historical revolutions nor does either try to test its propositions by an adequate body of relevant empirical facts. Neither refers much to the important historical, sociological, and psychosocial classical treatises on revolutions. By neglecting the empirical realities of revolutions and the vast and quite significant literature in the field, these and other speculative studies do not add much to our knowledge of revolutions. Here and there they lightly touch upon an interesting problem and now and then formulate a few hypotheses worthy of a systematic development and empirical verification but, unfortunately, these occasions are rare. They seem more preoccupied with verbally polishing their analytical schemes. A careful study of, say, Taine's *The Origins of Contemporary France* (New York, 1876–1894) gives an incomparably better knowledge and deeper comprehension of the psychology and sociology of revolutions, of their causes and consequences, than all the "analytical" studies taken together. Even such a special, historico-sociological analysis of a counterrevolution as C. Tilly's *The Vendée* (Cambridge, Mass., 1964) contributes much more to a comprehension of the violent forms of counterrevolution than, for instance, the dry, speculative discussion of the "Conditions for the Outbreak or Prevention of Revolutions" in Willer-Zollschan's "Prolegomenon."

More factual and less speculative is J. Davies' essay "Toward a Theory of Revolution." Its main thesis combines the theories of De Tocqueville and Marx:

> Revolutions are most likely to occur when a prolonged period of objective economic and social development is followed by

---

[22] See other theories of this "abstract-speculative-analytical" kind in my *SCP*, chs. 31, 32, 33. See there a more substantial criticism of this sort of speculative theorizing on revolutions.

a short period of sharp reversal. The all-important effect on the minds of people in a particular society is to produce, during the former period, an expectation of continued ability to satisfy needs—which continue to rise—and, during the latter, a mental state of anxiety and frustration when manifest reality breaks away from anticipated reality.

Political stability and instability are ultimately dependent on a state of mind, a mood, in a society. . . . It is the dissatisfied state of mind rather than the tangible provision of "adequate" or "inadequate" supplies of food, equality, or liberty which produces the revolution.[23]

To corroborate this theory Davies analyzes three historical rebellions: Dorr's Rebellion of 1842, the Russian Revolution of 1917, and the Egyptian Revolution of 1952. The theory remains, nevertheless, an unproved speculation, for it is based upon an unverifiable and hardly measurable factor, "the dissatisfied state of mind." In his three examples, Davies does not attempt to measure this state of mind before or at the time of the explosion of these rebellions; his diagrams and curves of the "expected need satisfaction" and "intolerable and tolerable gaps between what people want and what they get" are purely arbitrary. They are not based upon any actual data; they merely illustrate graphically but do not prove his theory. He deals only with three historical rebellions out of 1,622 major internal disturbances that occurred in the history of Greece, Rome, Byzantium, Italy, Spain, France, Russia, Poland, Lithuania, and the Netherlands in the period from the sixth century B.C. up to A.D. 1925. (These are all systematically investigated and roughly measured in my *Dynamics*, Vol. III, chs. 12, 13, 14, and concisely summed up in my *SCP*, chs. 31, 32, 33.) If his three examples clearly confirmed his hypothesis, this sample would still be too small to be representative of all 1,622 revolutions and rebellions. Davies himself even indicates "one negative case of a rebellion that did not occur—[whereas, according to his hypothesis, it should have exploded]—the depression of the 1930's in the United States" (Davies, pp. 16–17).

---

[23] *ASR*, February, 1962, pp. 6 ff. Davies' thesis is in agreement with Zollschan's more general formula of the exigency-triggered theory of revolution.

Furthermore, his data are too fragmentary to give sufficient factual support to his theory. For instance, his data about the rebellions in Russia, especially from 1861 to 1917, mention only a small fraction of the total rebellions that occurred during this period. If he had consulted my much more complete and systematic study of *all* the important internal disturbances that occurred in Russia from 926 to 1925, he would have seen the inadequacies of his data.[24]

If not even his selected three cases clearly confirm his hypothesis, still less can they account for the 1,622 revolts studied —statistically and systematically—in my *Dynamics*.[25] Davies' hypothesis does not explain at all most of these 1,622 revolutionary explosions, a large portion of which took place under conditions contrary to his hypothesis, whereas a considerable number that should have occurred, according to his hypothesis, did not occur at all. To sum up, his hypothesis is inadequate.

Among several attempts to formulate a more adequate theory of revolutions and wars, my own theory can be mentioned here. It is based on a critical examination of all the main theories

---

[24] For instance, he states that after the abolition of serfdom and the Great Reforms of 1861, "instead of declining, rural violence increased." According to my much more complete data, during the quarter 1826–1850 there occurred seven important internal disturbances. The total index of their magnitude was 76.15. In the quarter 1851–1875 there were only three rebellions with a total magnitude of 39.80. In the quarter 1876–1900 there were only four "disturbances" with a total magnitude of 34.77. See Davies' paper, *ibid.*, p. 16, and my *Dynamics*, Vol. III, pp. 460–464.

[25] Despite its many shortcomings, my study of the frequency, magnitude, fluctuation, causes, and consequences of *all* the important internal disturbances recorded in the annals of history of Greece, Rome, and eight main European countries from 600 B.C. to A.D. 1925, still remains the most complete and most systematic investigation of its kind. As such, it should be consulted by any competent investigator of revolutions, regardless of whether he accepts or rejects my conclusions; otherwise, he runs a risk of using a few fragmentary data for the more complete and systematic ones given in my study. Unfortunately, neither Zollschan, nor Davies, nor several other essayists on revolution seem to have consulted it; as a result, they built their theories of revolution upon a few arbitrarily selected cases, which by no stretch of the imagination can be considered adequate sample representatives of all or even of most of the revolutions studied.

of revolutions and on the completest series of revolutions studied (some 1,622 cases). My logically developed propositions are tested by this vast body of empirical evidence. If my theory does not account for all the phenomena of revolutionary change, it does so more adequately and for a much larger portion of revolutions (their main forms, their frequencies and magnitudes, their movements in the course of many centuries in each country studied, their main cause and supplementary factors, and their consequences in the sociocultural life of respective populations) than Davies', Dahrendorf's, Zollschan's, and practically all the recent "analytical," "functional," and other largely speculative studies of revolutions.[26] So far, the central propositions of my theory of revolutions (and of wars) have withstood all criticism. If my historico-statistical and empirical series are ever repeated, I am reasonably certain that my main statistical tables and curves, and also my main conclusions, will be confirmed in their essentials, as was a study which I made of all the wars in the history of Greece, Rome, and the main European countries from 600 B.C. to A.D. 1925 by the studies of Q. Wright and B. Urlanis.[27] Despite my respect for a logical and phenomenological analysis of the phenomena studied, a mere weaving of analytical-speculative yarns about revolutions or of any other form of social change cannot and does not add much to our knowledge of empirical social change.

Similar criticisms can be applied to the studies of A. Boskoff and D. Lockwood on social system models of change.[28] Instead of making a logical and empirical investigation of change in an important social system or of a vast class of social phe-

---

[26] See my study of revolutions in the *Dynamics*, Vol. III, chs. 12, 13, 14; and in my *SCP*, chs. 31, 32, 33. See also N. Timasheff's criticisms of my theory and my "Reply" to it in P. Allen's *P. A. Sorokin in Review*, pp. 247–275, and 454–461, and Timasheff's *War and Revolution* (New York, 1965). By its logico-empirical study of wars and revolutions, this work favorably contrasts with the criticized abstract theories.

[27] See my study of wars in the *Dynamics*, Vol. III, chs. 9, 10, 11; and in *SCP*, chs. 31, 32, 33. See also Q. Wright, *A Study of War* (2 vols.; Chicago, 1942); and B. Urlanis, *Voiny i narodonaseleniye Evropy* (*Wars and the Population of Europe*) (Moscow, 1960).

[28] Published in Zollschan-Hirsch's *Explorations in Social Change*, pp. 213–257.

nomena, they are preoccupied with various scholastic interpretations of structural-functional theories. They study which of these interpretations is correct, what the relationship is of structural-functional speculations to the dialectic materialism, what categories, concepts, and analytical schemas are to be used in investigation of social change, and so on. It is highly doubtful that this sort of analytical and functional "angelology" contributes much to our knowledge of the empirical realities of social change.

Other examples of speculative theories of social change are supplied by T. Parsons' recent essay, "Evolutionary Universals in Society," and R. N. Bellah's paper, "Religious Evolution."[29] In his earlier works, particularly in *The Social System*, Parsons repeatedly contended that "we simply are not in a position to 'catch' the uniformities of dynamic processes in the social system except here and there." We are not in a position, he goes on, "to develop a complete dynamic theory in the action field and . . . therefore, the systematization of theory in the present state of knowledge must be in 'structural-functional' terms."[30] Nevertheless, Parsons means his theory to be a "contribution to the revival and extension of evolutionary thinking in sociology" (p. 359). As such, it seems to mark an abrupt change in his position in regard to the possibility of scientifically studying the dynamic aspects of sociocultural processes.

However, a closer study of the essay shows that it is not really a "contribution to the revival and extension of evolutionary thinking in sociology," but a mere reiteration, in different terms, of his old speculative theory of the requirements that a social system must meet to keep its equilibrium, to survive, and to continue its existence. In the present essay, he speculates about which "new developments" a social system must have in order to increase its "adaptive capacity," to pass "from the primitive social conditions to those of the 'archaic' civilizations," and to move forward on the all-too-familiar way of a progressive evolution. Such "new developments" or prerequisites are called

[29] Both are published in *ASR*, June, 1964, pp. 339–374.
[30] T. Parsons, *The Social System*, pp. 19–21.

by him "universals." They are the "innovations endowing their possessors (respective societies) with a very substantial increase in generalized adaptive capacity, so substantial that species (societies) lacking them are relatively disadvantaged in the major areas in which natural selection operates, not so much for survival as for the opportunity to initiate further major developments" (pp. 339, 356).

He indicates four required "universals" necessary for a progressive transition from an animal to a truly human society: religion, communication with language, kinship organization based on incest taboo, and technology. In order for a society to pass from primitive conditions to the level of the "archaic" civilizations, he adds two other prerequisites: the development of social stratification and of "patterns of cultural legitimation." To pass from the archaic stage to the modern, a society must have "bureaucratic organization of collective goal-attainment, money-and-market systems, a generalized universalistic legal system, and a democratic association with elective leadership and mediated membership support for policy orientation" (pp. 342–357).

No lengthy criticism is needed in order to see that Parsons' essay represents a peculiar mixture of elementary trivialities with defective speculations concerning the "universals" or prerequisites for human sociocultural progress. His four universals (religion, language, technology, and kinship organization) differentiating *homo sapiens* and human societies from animals and animal societies can be found in any elementary textbook in anthropology, ethnology, sociology, archeology, and human prehistory. His six prerequisites for the progressive evolution of societies from the primitive to the modern and the future supermodern sociocultural orders are inadequate, vague, and arbitrary. Among his prerequisites he does not mention, for instance, such "universals" as science, philosophy, ethical and law norms, aesthetics and fine arts, or even the familistic and wise "autocracies" that have been and are at least as important as many "dysfunctional" forms of bureaucracy, stratification, legitimation, money-and-market economies, and corrupt democracies. Also, he does not specify the good and the bad forms of each of his "universals" (as was wisely done by such eminent social thinkers as Confucius, Lao-tse, Plato, Polybius, Aristotle, Hobbes, Grotius, Locke, Rousseau, De Maistre, Saint-Simon, Comte, Jefferson, Marx, and Lenin). He seems to assume that *all* bureaucracies, *all* stratifications, *all* legitimate governments, *all* money economies, and *all* forms of his other prerequisites have been functional, useful, creatively stimulating, and perfectly adaptive for *all* societies in which they existed. Besides this utterly untenable assumption, his theory implies two still more fallacious dogmas: first, that all his prerequisites are perfectly fit for *all* the contrastingly different societies, and, second, that through mere speculation he can prescribe the perfect evolutionary pair of shoes to fit perfectly *all* human beings. The logical and factual absurdity of these assumptions is so obvious that no further comment is necessary.

Similar criticisms are applicable also to R. N. Bellah's essay, "Religious Evolution" (*ASR*, June, 1964, pp. 358–374), which does not enrich our knowledge of the empirical history of religions or contribute anything significant to either the psychology or the sociology of religion. Bellah's definition of religion differs slightly from several other definitions, including my own.[31] His first, most central point on the evolution of religions is that religious symbols and religious collectivities move from compact or less differentiated to more differentiated forms. The assertion is a less exactly formulated reiteration of Spencer's general formula of evolution-progress and of Spencer's much more detailed factual analysis of religious evolution according to this formula.[32] Likewise, Bellah's theory of the five stages of religious evolution

[31] Compare Bellah's definition on p. 359 with the definition on pp. 225 ff. of my *SCP*. Bellah's and Parsons' essays completely ignore the significant literature and research produced in recent years in the history and sociology of religion. It is astounding that both scholars offered their home-made trivialities and antiquated speculations without consulting this literature and research. See a bibliography of these in my "Western Religion and Morality of Today." See also L. Schneider (ed.), *Religion, Culture, and Society*; P. H. Benson, *Religion in Contemporary Culture* (New York, 1960); and W. H. Clark, *The Psychology of Religion* (New York, 1957).

[32] See Spencer's formula of evolution-progress in his *First Principles* (New York, 1895), p. 396. His detailed factual theory of religious evolution is given in his *Principles of Sociology* (London, 1885), Vol. I, Part 1, and in Vol. III, Part 6, chs. 1–16.

("primitive, archaic, historic, early modern and modern") is a homemade, largely speculative, arbitrary, and historically incorrect theory of the *diverse* evolutionary stages undergone by various religions during their historical existence. He makes several factual errors, including a statement about the "nonrejection of the world" by primitive and modern religions and the "rejection of the world" by all religions that emerged in the first millenium B.C. and during the subsequent 2,000 years. If he had checked his hypothesis against the relevant data about the fluctuation of the ideational, idealistic, and sensate systems of truth, reality, and value (in which the ideational religions and philosophies roughly correspond to his religions that "reject" the empirical world, the idealistic religions and philosophies correspond to the religions that accept the supersensory, rational, and noble sensory realities and values of the world, and the sensate religions and philosophies correspond to the religions that accept the empirical world), Bellah would have realized the incorrectness of his generalizations in regard to the Greco-Roman and Western worlds as well as to the Chinese, Hindu, and Egyptian, religions.[33] As a matter of fact, some "primitive" religions, like the Zuni and the Hopi, "reject" the world, whereas Confucianism and the materialistic and "Epicurean" philosophies-religions of India, China, and ancient Egypt "accept" it and its values as the only real ones.

As C. C. Zimmerman has said of these structural sociologies, they "are primarily classificatory, and describe relative static conditions. . . . [They] have abandoned the major study of social change [and of living realities]. They have done so by making 'structure,' not the time-course of society, the major problem of sociology. According to their postulates, change is only a minor sociological pre-occupation."[34] No wonder, there-

---

[33] See the statistical and empirical evidence for my theory of the fluctuation of the ideational, idealistic, and sensate systems of truth and cultural supersystems in my *Dynamics*, Vol. II, chs. 1–12, and *passim* throughout all four volumes.

[34] C. C. Zimmerman, "Contemporary Trends in Sociology," pp. 8–9. See also A. W. Gouldner's, "Some Observations on Systematic Theory," and Zetterberg's article in H. L. Zetterberg, *Sociology in the U.S.A.* (Paris, 1956), pp. 34–42.

fore, that their efforts to "revive and extend the evolutionary thinking in sociology" have remained, so far, cognitively fruitless.

More fruitful cognitively have been the recent surveys of the basic problems of social change supplemented by suggestions of cognitive solutions of some of these problems. One of the better studies of this kind is W. E. Moore's *Social Change*.[35] In Moore's own words, "the intent of this book is to underscore the normality of change as well as its special contemporary characteristics and magnitudes, to explore causes and directions, and to establish such a measure of understandable order as our present knowledge and thinking permit" (p. 5). Moore then outlines the main problems of social change: the normality and qualities of change, small-scale and revolutionary changes, the dynamics of modern, industrial societies, and, finally, the problems of social evolution. In each of these broad divisions, he briefly sketches, analyzes, and criticizes some of the existing theories and sets forth several of his generalized propositions. Within some 120 pages, he succeeds in inspecting and appraising quite a large number of important problems of social dynamics.

The main virtues of his work are, first, a skillful and concentrated packing into a little volume of a far greater assortment of theories and considerations concerning the phenomena of social change than is usually done within similar space by other investigators of these phenomena; second, his essentially sound criticism of the deficiencies of the "equilibrium," the "functional," and the "evolutionary" concepts of social systems and change, including a criticism of the naïve forms of the theories of diffusion, acculturation, and technological and economic determinism; and, third, the plausibility, of some of his numerous hypotheses.

---

[35] Englewood Cliffs, N.J., 1963; see also his "Predicting Discontinuities in Social Change," *ASR*, June, 1964, pp. 331–338.

The main drawbacks are, first, a too cursory treatment of the problems inspected in his book and articles. His touch-and-go discussion of many complex problems does not allow him (or anybody else following this path) to analyze these problems thoroughly, or to furnish the minimum of logical and empirical evidence for corroborating his criticisms and conclusions, or to examine all the important theories and studies in the field. His work represents a thoughtful and well-planned *program* for studying the main aspects of social change rather than such a study itself. I hope eventually he will produce a significant monographic study of, at least, some of the problems outlined in the book. The second drawback is his uncritical acceptance of some of the questionable dogmas of the current "structural-functional" speculative sociologies. The third is a number of somewhat vague and questionable statements. For instance, he states that "many features of social life persist from day to day and from year to year. In terms of these persistent patterns of action, tomorrow will be about the same as today and yesterday, and next year will be about the same as this year and last" (*Social Change*, p. 3). The statement is roughly correct, but it does not tell us to what extent, in what fields of social life, and for how long a time such persistent patterns continue. If he had used the existing studies of the time-budgets of human behavior, he could have formulated his propositions in a more precise, quantitative form.[36]

Another of his questionable generalizations is his statement that there is much greater autonomy of change in aesthetic and religious systems compared with other cultural and social systems in the same culture. My detailed, systematic, even quantitative study of the fluctuations of the style and content of fine

[36] See an excellent survey of time-budget studies in A. Szalai, *Comparative Time-Budget Research* (Budapest, 1964). See also P. A. Sorokin and C. Q. Berger, *Time-Budgets of Human Behavior* (Cambridge, Mass., 1939), chs. 13 and 14, where the problem of the "extent to which an individual can predict his own activities a day, two days, a week, and a month in advance" is experimentally studied, as are the problems of the extent to which these activities persist and change from day to day. At the present time, a vast literature in this field exists and gives a possibility of formulating fairly precise, quantitatively measured, and empirically confirmed propositions concerning the persistency, change, and predictability of human behavior and social processes.

arts and religious beliefs in the Greco-Roman and Western cultures for the period from the ninth century B.C. to A.D. 1925 shows that in their forms and contents the aesthetic and religious systems have been changing in close connection with, and in the same ideational or idealistic or sensate directions as, the scientific, philosophical, ethical, legal, and even political systems of these total cultures. All these cultural systems have been changing together, interdependently. The economic, familistic, contractual, and coercive systems in these cultures, however, have followed a more autonomous path.[37] Since Moore gives practically no empirical evidence to confirm his propositions and since the total body of evidence corroborating my conclusions is systematic, vast, and substantial, my conclusions will stand until Moore or some other scholar either supplies adequate proofs in favor of Moore's propositions or demonstrates the inadequacy of my proofs.

Despite these defects, Moore's study is a notable contribution to our knowledge of a multitude of complex problems of social change.[38]

Another slender volume touching upon several problems of sociocultural change, sharply criticizing many assumptions of the natural-science sociologists, and radically challenging the predictive capacity of the historical and social sciences is Karl R. Popper's *The Poverty of Historicism* (Boston, 1957). Popper's central thesis is that "it is impossible for us to predict the future course of history." His reasons are as follows:

1. The course of human history is strongly influenced by the growth of human knowledge.
2. We cannot predict, by rational or scientific methods, the future growth of our scientific knowledge.
3. We cannot, therefore, predict the future course of human history.

[37] See the statistical and empirical evidence confirming these conclusions in the *Dynamics*, Vol. II, pp. 628–632; Vol. III, chs. 4, 8; and *passim* in all four volumes.

[38] With necessary modifications, similar criticisms and assessments apply to S. N. Eisenstadt's *The Political Systems of Empires* (New York, 1963), and to his "Social Change, Differentiation, and Evolution," *ASR*, June, 1964. (See the criticism of the former in the *British Journal of Sociology*, December, 1964, pp. 357–359.

4. This means that we must reject the possibility of a theoretical history; that is to say, of a historical social science that would correspond to theoretical physics. There can be no scientific theory of historical development serving as a basis for historical prediction. . . . The argument does not, of course, refute the possibility of every kind of prediction. It only refutes the possibility of predicting historical developments to the extent to which they may be influenced by the growth of our knowledge. If there is such a thing as growing human knowledge, then we cannot anticipate today what we shall know only tomorrow. My proof consists in showing that no scientific predictor can possibly predict, by scientific methods, its own future results. . . . This means that no society can predict, scientifically, its own future states of knowledge (*Poverty*, pp. ix–xi).

I prefer to replace Popper's "scientific knowledge" by a broader concept, "human creativity," because, as I have stated several times,[39] all forms of human creativity (artistic, religious, philosophical, technological, ethical, political, and economic) are essentially unpredictable, and all discoveries, inventions, and new creations, especially great ones, tangibly influence the course of human history and notably change the ways of life of individuals and social groups.[40] This rewording makes Popper's thesis in essential agreement with my own conclusions, with two reservations: (1) Because human creativity is largely unpredictable, we cannot conclude that scientific or other creativity can never a curately foresee and predict its own future creativity or future changes in various fields of social and cultural phenomena. And (2), as I pointed out in *Fads and Foibles* (p. 276), "Correct predictability is neither a necessary nor a sufficient criterion of the scientific nature of a theory. A vast number of scientific propositions are not predictive. Many correct predictions are made on the basis of a nonscientific theory; a number of wrong predictions are made on the basis of scientific assumptions." As

[39] See my "The Factor of Creativity in Human History," *Main Currents in Modern Thought*, May-June, 1962, pp. 99–104; and in *Fads and Foibles*, ch. 11.

[40] See an example of the tangible influence of several ideologies among various sociological theories in my "Practical Influence of 'Impractical' Generalizing Sociological Theories," in *Sociology and Social Research*, October, 1962, and T. Abel's "Comments" on it, *ibid.*, January, 1963.

a matter of fact, it is exactly through scientific and other creativities that we can make roughly accurate short-time and middle-range predictions in several fields of mass phenomena that are frequently repeated in time and space and in the future phases of the immanent development of several social and cultural systems and forms of human behavior. However, a far larger portion of sociocultural changes, especially of unique and unrepeated phenomena, remain unpredictable and are likely to remain so for as long as factors of human creativity and unique configurations of unrepeated phenomena continue to function.[41]

Popper's volume contains several other important ideas. It can be profitably read by the natural-science sociologists who often do not see the perfectly dogmatic character of many of their assumptions and the doubtful nature of many of their methods and theories. Popper's book exposes these.

His book also has serious shortcomings. There are, for instance, many ambiguities and inconsistencies scattered throughout, beginning with his concept of "historicism" and ending with his insufficient knowledge of today's sociology. However, these shortcomings can be passed by without any discussion. Popper's theses on predictability and his views concerning several problems of social and historical change are the main points of interest.

MONOGRAPHIC STUDIES OF A BASIC PROBLEM AND UNIFORMITY OF SOCIAL AND CULTURAL CHANGE

D. Martindale's *Social Life and Cultural Change*[42] represents one of the best studies of this kind in recent sociological literature.

Before examining the central problem of Martindale's work, we have to briefly inspect his general theory of social and cul-

---

[41] See on this *Fads and Foibles*, ch. 11; and Popper, *The Poverty of Historicism, passim*.

[42] (Princeton, N.J., 1962); see also his "The Formation and Destruction of Communities" and "The Roles of Humanism and Scientism in the Evolution of Sociology," in Zollschan-Hirsch's *Explorations in Social Change*, pp. 61–87, 452–490.

tural change—or "the formation of communities [that is, self-sufficient societies] and the kind of social thought which arises in connection with communities"—or, more exactly, the kind of social conditions and societies that stimulate an explosion of creativity in their intellectuals and that favor the routinization and decline of the intellectuals' creativity and, through that, the explosion or decline of the creativity of the respective self-sufficient communities.

Martindale's treatise opens with a brief sketch of three recent theories of social and cultural change: the culture-lag theory represented by W. Ogburn's theory; the cyclical theories exemplified by Sorokin's, Toynbee's, and Spengler's conceptions; and the "functional theories," which "have treated social and cultural change as of little general significance." He finds all three theories deficient and offers, instead, his version of a theory of social behaviorism that "seems to hold the greatest promise for an adequate theory of social and cultural change" (*Social Life*, pp. 2, 3).

In regard to these points of Martindale's theory, I have to make two observations: First, his characterization of myself as a "positivistic organicist" and of my theory of social and cultural change as "cyclical" is grossly incorrect; and, second, his "social behavioristic" theory of sociocultural change is, in most of its essential points, a reiteration of my theory.

In my *Contemporary Sociological Theories*, I sharply criticized the organismic analogies of the bioorganismic school (ch. 4, pp. 194–218). I repeated this criticism in my later works. For this reason, I cannot be called a positivistic *organicist*.[43] Similarly, I have never joined the positivistic denomination in sociology and in my works have been critical of many essential theses of positivistic philosophy, sociology, ethics, and other

---

[43] My criticism of the organismic analogies of H. Spencer, P. Lilienfeld, A. Schäffle, and other leaders of the bioorganismic school does not hinder my high estimation of the important scientific contributions of this school to sociology and related sciences. These contributions have nothing to do with the organismic analogies that were considered by Spencer himself as a "mere scaffolding" for building his theories and were dropped by him (and by other organicists) after their theories were built. In this totality, the substantial contributions of the organicists were

psychosocial disciplines (although I accept some of the points stressed by Comte and other leaders of "positivism"). For this reason also, I cannot be classified as a positivistic organicist. The term integral is the term that I selected and used for many years to characterize my brand of philosophy, sociology, psychology, ethics—my whole *Weltanschauung*. This term means something quite different from "positivistic organicism," with which Martindale repeatedly tries to identify me. I did not and do not belong to this denomination. So much for this *pro domo sua* point.

Similarly, my theory of sociocultural change cannot be called cyclical. As a matter of fact, several essential *differentia* of my theory are identical with the characteristics that he ascribes to his social behavioristic theory of sociocultural change:

> While the social behavioristic theory of social and cultural change accepts some changes as *semilinear*, some as *random* and *accidental*, it places particular importance on those social and cultural changes which are *semicyclical* in nature. The formation and destruction of communities and civilizations [and of many other social groups and of a multitude of social processes—P.S.] are semicyclical in nature. . . . The study of these [semicyclical or rhythmical] types of changes holds out the special value of supplying a recurrent subject matter for the discovery of the laws, if any, of social and cultural change (*Social Life*, pp. 2, 22, 31, 32, 66, 495 ff., 501 ff.).

Such is Martindale's formula for "social behavioristic" theory of change. The formula for my allegedly "cyclical" conception of change follows:

> Any sociocultural phenomenon changes from something to something. This "from-to," from a state A to a state B, is the direction of the change. . . . There are three main patterns of direction: linear, cyclical, and variably recurrent. . . . This

---

notably greater and more scientific than, for instance, those of the recent "structural-functional" theorists: These, in their sound parts, are but a pale reiteration of the essential theses of the organic school; in their questionable parts, they are infected by most of the analogical diseases of the bioorganismic school and by the still more questionable mechanistic analogies regularly used by the structural functionalists or functional structuralists of today.

variably or creatively recurrent pattern comprises in itself a *combination of linear* and *relatively cyclical* directions. In part it may have a linear link, but its direction is changed in the next link; it contains in itself a *rhythmic repetition* of some relative cycles, but these cycles are never identical, nor do they return back to their previous position; each cycle is an ever-new variation of the preceding cycle, or, more exactly, rhythm or oscillation.[44]

In the *Dynamics*, I say that:

The most general pattern of the sociocultural change is that of incessantly varying recurrent processes. . . . This means:
    1. Identically recurrent sociocultural processes are impossible.
    2. Eternally linear sociocultural processes are also impossible.
    3. But a linear trend (of various durations) limited in time is to be expected and is factually found in almost all sociocultural processes. . . .
    8. Thus history ever repeats itself and never repeats itself; both seemingly contradictory statements are true and are not contradictory at all, when properly (dialectically) understood.
    9. This means that the strictly cyclical (identically recurrent) conception of sociocultural processes; the unlimitedly linear; the unicist, in the sense of the nonexistence of any recurrent rhythms in the processes totally "brand-new" at any moment; the static conception that there is no change—all these conceptions of sociocultural change are fallacious. The valid conception is that of an "incessant variation of the main recurrent themes which contains in itself, as a part, all these conceptions, and as such is richer than any of them."[45]

This summary of my detailed analysis of the patterns of sociocultural change shows, first, that Martindale made a gross error in calling my theory "cyclical," and, second, the essential similarity between Martindale's theory and mine. Both theories are also similar in their treatment of "meaningful social interaction as the primary social reality," in that both say that most sociocultural changes are accomplished through individuals,

---

[44] *SCP*, pp. 675–676 and ch. 45.
[45] The *Dynamics*, Vol. IV, pp. 731–732; see a most detailed analysis of these problems, *ibid.*, Vol. I, chs. 4, 5; Vol. II, chs. 4, 5, 10; and Vol. IV, chs. 12–15.

particularly through "a special stratum of individuals—the innovators or conservers of their time" (*Social Life*, pp. 2–3).

Our theories also differ in several points: Despite some inconsistencies, his theory remains essentially "nominalistic," "atomistic," and "singularistic," whereas mine covers changes in sociocultural systems as well as in singularistic congeries. His theory concentrates on explaining "how social and cultural forms are established and formed into (self-sufficient) communities and civilizations, and how these societies and civilizations may decay or be destroyed" (*Social Life*, pp. 2, 31 ff.), whereas mine covers all the main sociocultural processes in all the important micro- and macrosociological cultural systems and social groups. His definition of "community" as a "set or system sufficient to solve all the basic problems of ordinary ways of life . . . through all the routine problems of an ordinary year and through the cycle of an ordinary life from birth to death" is essentially similar to Parsons-Levy's self-sufficient "society." It also has all the shortcomings of the latter. If "tribal communities of hunters-gatherers-fishers" and Aristotle's city-states were largely self-sufficient, much less self-sufficient were the first cities of the early empires, the feudal communities of China, Japan, Europe, and of the Moslem world, and especially the modern nation-states, indicated by Martindale as historical examples of his self-sufficient communities ("The Formation and Destruction of Communities," pp. 69–78). In our time, when the whole human world has become "interdependent," none of today's "nation-states" is really "autarkical," including the largest of them: the United States, Russia, and China. All of them are compelled to be in trade-economic-political-military-scientific-cultural interactions with one another. All the recent attempts to establish a self-sufficient Fortress America or other autarkical nation-states have failed dismally. Among the existing nation-states there are hardly any that are really self-sufficient. If Martindale would stress that most of the nation-states can survive and can solve, in one way or another (even if it means increasing the mortality rate and lowering the standard of living), "the routine problems of an ordinary year" so also can most of the families, villages, towns, cities, and most of the unibonded and multibonded groups, for their life-spans are much longer than the life-span of a generation ("from birth to death").[46] On the basis of this criterion of survival, all these unibonded and multibonded groups have to be called "self-sufficient communities"; thus the concept of Martindale's "community" and of its boundaries becomes quite indeterminate and void.

If we accept Martindale's thesis that the main task of sociology is to study the "formation and destruction of communities," the field of sociology is radically narrowed to just two processes among many. Even these two processes can hardly be studied, because Martindale's "self-sufficient communities" have largely vanished from today's world. The field of study, then, dwindles to a few self-sufficient, primitive, preliterate tribes, if such still exist.

If we accept Martindale's *differentia* of "survival for a year or for a generation" as a criterion of community, then most of the unibonded and multibonded groups become communities, Martindale's differentiation of community from all the other social groups becomes fictitious, and his concept of community becomes void and meaningless. These reasons explain why Martindale's community and Parsons-Levy's society are largely fictitious models, little applicable to today's world of groups and cultural systems, and useless in a study of the structural and dynamic properties of this superorganic universe. Faulty also, in my opinion, is Martindale's treatment of culture (and cultural systems and congeries) as a mere "form of interaction." I am quite certain that such a conception of culture cannot account at all for all the essential features of systems of science, philosophy, religion, fine arts, ethics, law, economics, and politics in their purely meaningful and materialized forms. Unacceptable also is Martindale's thesis that "potential human genius is constant" in all social groups at all periods of human history. This thesis is clearly contradicted by a vast body of biological, psy-

---

[46] See, on the actual life-spans of economic and cultural organizations, families and universities, cities and states, and religious and multibonded groups, *SCP*, chs. 34 and 47. If anything, the typical life-span of Martindale's "nation-states" is shorter than that of many unibonded and multibonded groups.

chological, sociological, and historical evidence and by the daily experience of almost all observers of human nature and creativity. On his part, Martindale finds my theory of "integral truth" as being "not only outside of the circle of positivism but outside of science as well" and my theory of ideational, idealistic (integral), and sensate supersystems and their fluctuations "evaluative" rather than explanatory and scientific: "In Sorokin's constructions historical phenomena are not being studied to understand them, but to evaluate them," he says. ("Formation and Destruction," pp. 16–19).[47]

Such are some of the main similarities and dissimilarities between Martindale's and my theories of sociocultural change.

Having cleared up these preliminary issues we can now turn to an examination of the central problem of his study: What kind of social conditions and societies generate an explosion

[47] At this point, my reply to these criticisms can be limited by the following observations: First, D. Martindale's and H. Spier's criticisms of my integral system of truth and cultural supersystems is stated quite dogmatically, without any logical or empirical proofs supporting their statements. Second, both of them seem to profess the naïve and obsolescent version of an empirical (sensate) theory of truth largely abandoned by modern science and by the dominant currents of modern philosophy, like phenomenologism, existentialism, intuitivism, neo-Thomism, and even logical positivism, dialectical materialism, and so on. Both of them seem to be unaware of the fact that what I call the integral system of truth has been increasingly recognized and is already a dominant system of truth in today's science and philosophy as well as in the psychosocial disciplines. Third, my theory of ideational, idealistic (integral), and sensate cultural supersystems and of their fluctuations represents not an "evaluation," but a systematic investigation of cultural and social realities based upon quantitative and qualitative historical data whose adequacy and accuracy, so far, have not been shown to be spurious by any critics, including Martindale and Spier. No one has even attempted to show any serious errors in my numerous statistical tables and in my other empirical proofs or conclusions given in the *Dynamics* to corroborate my theory of these supersystems and their fluctuations during some twenty-six centuries of Greco-Roman and Western sociocultural history. It is not my theory, and its logical and empirical corroborations, but, rather, the purely dogmatic assertions of some of my critics that have been "evaluative" and "devoid of understanding of historical phenomena." See a development of these observations in my "Reply to the Critics" in P. Allen's volume, *P. A. Sorokin in Review*, pp. 380–408; and in my "Comments on Schneider's Observations and Criticisms," in Zollschan-Hirsch's *Explorations in Social Change*, pp. 401–431.

of creativity of their intellectuals and—through them—of their respective communities. And what kind of social conditions favor the routinization and decline of creativity of the self-sufficient communities?[48]

1. The creative epochs of humankind are the periods of the formation of new (self-sufficient) communities. At such times the sphere permitted for individuality of the intellectuals tends to be widened, and its products tend to be rewarded.

2. The quality and quantity of creativity are related to the type of community in which they occur. In general, the brilliant creative periods have coincided with the creation of the more complex human communities.

3. During the periods of the maturity of a community and the completion of its cultural synthesis, the encouragement of free creativity tends to come to an end. The sphere of social life left open for the free construction of individuals is narrowed, and a restricted array of intellectual forms tends to be fixed.

4. The standards of the acceptability of thought, or truth in this restrictive sense, tend to vary as between the creative and conformist epochs of human civilization; (a) during creative epochs there is a strong tendency to determine truth in terms of standards and criteria established in the proper conduct of the thought process, and (b) during conformist epochs of human civilization there is a tendency to establish socially acceptable truth by institutional procedures (*Social Life*, p. 91).

The main corroborations of these conclusions consist in Martindale's analysis of the four "great creative periods in human culture." Each of these periods coincided with that of a great transition from the preceding basic type of (self-sufficient) community to its subsequent type.

The first of these creative periods happened sometime between 14,000 and 8000 B.C., when "humankind moved out of

---

[48] Though Martindale repeatedly stresses that "the major events in human history consist of the formation and destruction of (self-sufficient) societies and civilizations," factually these "events" are studied only insofar as they are connected with the explosion and decline of creativity in the areas of "socialization, the mastery of nature, and social control." His study is a "sociology of creativity," rather than a sociology of the formation and decay of self-sufficient "communities."

a world of tribal communities of hunters and gatherers into a world of peasant villages within which active food production was carried on." This period is marked by the domestication of plants and animals, by pottery making, expansion of the size of communities, new social differentiation, and by other important inventions and creations.

The second great creative period occurred between 5000 and 3500 B.C., when the first cities were built and the first civilizations, with their differentiation of social classes and their new forms of religions, political institutions, and governments, emerged.

The third great explosicn of creativity took place in the Axial Period, sometime between 900 and 200 B.C., when Confucius, Lao-tse, Zarathustra, Buddha, the Hebrew prophets, and the great Greek and Hindu philosophers developed great world religions and philosophical systems, when important scientific discoveries and inventions were made, and when a number of new social institutions were introduced.

The fourth period of great creativity happened in modern times in the West, especially after the fifteenth century A.D. It continues up to the present time. "We are still midway in the course of our own destiny. . . . The eventual forms into which our civilization will finally crystallize are not yet fully known." This last creative period saw the great transition from feudal communities and institutions to nation-states, Western megalopolitan cities, and to new social, political, and economic organizations. "It is already clear that there are numerous points in which our own development recapitulates features of the Axial Period. . . . All of the Axial civilizations had their origins in barbaric, semifeudal periods. So did our own. The great creative period in ancient civilizations lay in a time of community destruction and the formation of new communities. This process is paralleled and, in fact, is still under way in our own time." (*Ibid.*, pp. 89–91, 397 ff., 421 ff.; "The Formation and Destruction of Communities," pp. 76–87).

In the process of its establishment, a new form of community passes through phases of "stabilization, consistency and closure." When it is firmly established, it tends to limit the creative freedom of its intellectuals, to suspect them, and "to exercise a greater control over their thoughts." As a result, the creative *élan* of such societies weakens and routinized conformist standards increasingly replace it. (See "Formation and Destruction," pp. 71–87; *Social Life*, chs. 3, 19.)

Much of Martindale's book is devoted to corroborating these theses by a fairly detailed survey of the positions of intellectual and religious, philosophical and social thought of the Axial Period in China, India, Israel, ancient Greece and Rome, and the modern period in the West. Such are the essential points of his sociology of creativity and its interrelations with the processes of formation and destruction of the basic forms of (self-sufficient) communities.

CRITICISMS

Though Martindale's sociology of creativity contains some truth, he does not produce enough empirico-historical evidence to support it.

1. For his first and his second great creative periods, he gives practically no real evidence to indicate that these periods were indeed greatly creative or that their creativity was due to the destruction of the community of hunters and gatherers and the formation of a new peasant-village community, or, for the second period, to the replacement of the peasant-village community by that of the city-community. Nor does he give much information as to where in the population such replacements of these communities took place or where, exactly, they were followed by great explosions of creativity. Even the time periods given by him (between 14,000 and 8000 B.C. for the first transition-explosion of creativity and between 5000 and 3500 B.C. for the second) are too long to serve as evidence confirming his conclusions. In brief, we discount these two periods entirely as corroborations of his theses. For his Axial and Western periods he gives a considerable body of proofs. But even this is far from sufficient to prove adequately his generalizations. Here again the time period (from 900 to 200 B.C.) of the Axial explosion and the transition from the city-community through the ancient empires to the feudal communities is too extended to

warrant the connection between creativity and change of forms of community. The same is true of Western creativity. In this period, almost all the medieval centuries are indefinitely outlined as either "preparatory" for the explosion of the Western creativity after the fifteenth century or somehow "lost" as little creative. If we include the medieval period in the creative period of Western culture, its total length extends again over some 1,200 years—too long a period to serve as an inductive proof for Martindale's propositions. If we exclude the medieval period, such an exclusion becomes quite arbitrary and makes it quite hard to explain how, from what sources, and why the Western creative period (from 1600 on to the present time) arose.

2. For the second and the Axial periods of creativity Martindale deals only with the Chinese, the Indian, the Hebrew, and the Greco-Roman civilizations and "communities" and hardly mentions such "full-blown civilizations of the first generation" (in Toynbee's terms) as the Egyptiac, Andean, Sumeric, Minoan, Mayan, Babylonic, Hittite, Syriac, and others.[49] Some of these "full-blown" civilizations, like the Egyptiac, were highly creative in some periods of their history. As such, Martindale should have examined them.

3. A more important shortcoming of Martindale's theory is that his main evidence for even the Axial and the Western periods of creativity is limited to a survey of the religious and philosophical creativities of these periods. He passes by, without substantial examination, the scientific, technological, ethical, legal, aesthetic, political, economic, and other creativities. This omission seriously vitiates the validity of his conclusions. Actually, different societies, even the same society at different periods of its history, are creative only in one or a few fields of creativity and uncreative in other fields. For instance, the Western medieval "community" was highly creative in religious, philosophical, and ethical fields and in that of ideational fine arts; it was much less creative in science, technology, eco-

[49] See A. Toynbee's "resurvey" of civilizations in his *Reconsiderations*, pp. 540–561, and R. Coulborn, "Toynbee's *Reconsiderations*: A Commentary," *Journal of World History*, VIII (1964), 15–53.

nomics, and sensate fine arts. In contrast, Western society in its modern sensate period has been comparatively uncreative in religious and ideational fine arts, ethics, and philosophy and highly creative in science, technology, economics, politics, and sensate philosophy and arts. Greece was, in the period from the sixth to the third century B.C., highly creative in philosophy, fine arts, and science and much less creative in military arts, politics, economics, and law. Ancient Rome, in contrast, was highly creative in military arts, law, and government, and much less creative in religion, philosophy, and fine arts. Likewise, long-existing civilizations and "communities," like the Egyptiac, the Indian, and the Chinese, have been creative in different fields at different periods. The same can be said of all creative societies and civilizations.

Furthermore, great civilizations have had not one but several creative periods in the same field of creativity. For instance, ancient Egypt had creative explosions in religion in the periods *c.* 3500–3000 B.C., 2500–2300 B.C., 1580–1400 B.C., 1370–1352 B.C.; in politics and economics *c.* 2895–2540 B.C., 2000–1785 B.C., 1580–1200 B.C., 663–525 B.C.; in science *c.* 4241 B.C., 1900–1500 B.C., and so on in practically all fields of creativity. India, China, Japan, Greece, Rome, the Arabic-Islamic world, France, Germany, Great Britain, Italy, Russia, and all great creative societies whose creativity history is more or less known have had similar recurrent creative renaissances in the same field of creativity.[50]

On the other hand, none of these creative societies has been creative in all fields of creativity at the same period.

The actual fluctuations of creativity—its declines and growths—have been much more complex, more numerous, and considerably different from the greatly simplified picture presented by Martindale. It is hardly possible to select one "community-civilization" that in one period of its existence has been greatly creative in all fields. If one is selected, without specifying the fields of creativity in which it has been particularly

[50] See systematic statistical and historical evidence for these statements in the *Dynamics,* all four volumes; *SCP,* pp. 548–551; A. Kroeber, *Configurations of Culture Growth* (Berkeley and Los Angeles, 1944); and Chs. 8–11 of the present work.

creative (as Martindale does), the selection is arbitrary, indeterminate, and questionable. If the creativity of a certain period in the life-course of a community-civilization is corroborated only by a high creativity in one or a few fields, this does not mean that the society or period has been creative in *all* forms of creativity. And, vice versa, if a given community-civilization or period is found to be uncreative in one or a few fields of creativity, this does not mean that such a society or period has been uncreative in other fields of creativity. An investigation must be made of all forms of its creativity in order that its encyclopedic creative sterility can be established. Since Martindale did not make an encyclopedic study of all forms of creativity in the community-civilizations that existed in the long periods in between his four great periods of creativity (from 8000 to 5000 B.C., from 3500 to 900 B.C., and from 200 B.C. to 1600 A.D.), much less in his exceedingly long periods of creativity (from 14,000 to 8000 B.C., from 5000 to 3500 B.C., from 900 to 200 B.C., and, finally, from 1600 up to the present), his conclusion that there were only four great periods of creativity in the long period from 14,000 B.C. to the present becomes highly questionable. Still more questionable becomes the scientific correctness of practically all the theses derived from such a one-sided examination.

Martindale seems to be even more parsimonious than Toynbee in regard to the creative periods and communities in human history. He is also as pessimistic as Toynbee in viewing enormous stretches of the history of many societies as creative deserts. Toynbee, at least, finds more than twenty great civilizations with their creative periods; Martindale finds only four great periods of creativity. Toynbee contends that the Chinese, Egyptian, Hellenic, and some other civilizations have been "petrified" and uncreative for centuries, and that almost all of his civilizations, with the exception of the Western, have died or are in a state of agony. Martindale finds only four great creative periods in the whole of human history. Many centuries, even millennia, of this history he finds creatively sterile. The actual situation has fortunately been more cheerful and more creative than is pictured by either Toynbee or Martindale.

4. The central point of Martindale's theory is the causal

relationship between the destruction of the old and the formation of the new community on the one hand, and the explosion
of creativity, triggered by this factor, on the other. How valid is
this point?

At the beginning of my examination of Martindale's theory,
I stated that it contains some truth, but truth that has to be
considerably changed and reinterpreted. If his thesis is correct,
then we should expect, first, an explosion of creativity in any
society undergoing a great revolution because any great revolution consists in the destruction of many cultural systems, social
groups, institutions, and ways of life and their replacement by
new cultural systems, social groups, institutions, and ways of
life—in brief, any great revolution means a destruction of the
old and the formation of a new "community."

Second, if Martindale's hypothesis is correct, then we should
expect a low creativity in all societies and periods free from
radical and violent transformations in their social and cultural
forms.

Are these expectations, following from Martindale's thesis,
supported by the effects of the great revolutions and by the
comparatively orderly and slow-changing periods in the life-
course of various societies? The answer is that they are only
partially confirmed by the relevant facts and even these confirming facts need to be formulated and interpreted in forms
essentially different from Martindale's. On the basis of our study
of some 1,622 revolutions and important internal disturbances
in the history of Greece, Rome and eight European countries
from 600 B.C. to A.D. 1925, we found that:

1. All great revolutions produce destructive as well as constructive (creative) effects in practically every aspect of the
cultural and social life of the revolutionary society. These
changes are common to all fully developed revolutions. This
dialectically opposite two-sided uniformity can be called the
"Law of Polarization."

2. The frequency of revolutions tends to be comparatively
high in two periods of a given society—in the period of cultural
and social growth and in that of decay. The creative effects of
revolutions in the period of growth (compared by Marx to the

birth throes of a new creative order) tend to be dominant over its destructive effects, whereas in revolutions in the period of decay (compared with the agony of death) the destructive (uncreative) effects tend to be dominant over the creative changes.

3. Similar "polarized" changes are caused not only by the factor of revolution (or of the destruction of the old and the formation of a new "community"), but also by great calamities, catastrophies, or frustrations. Great personal calamities and misfortunes reinforce the creativity of some individuals and depress or destroy the creativity of many others. Beethoven's great personal calamity, deafness, did not suppress but invigorated his creativity. His greatest masterpieces were created in the postcalamity period of his life. On the other hand, great personal catastrophies harmfully effect many ordinary persons, engendering mental disorders, submissiveness, apathy, passivity, cynical sensualism, criminality, suicide, and generally inhibiting their creativity. Likewise, in some societies great calamities generate predominantly constructive-creative changes, whereas in others they have mainly uncreative-destructive consequences.

4. While some of the orderly and slowly changing periods of the historical life of some societies are marked by low creativity, some other such periods are free from radical reconstructions and display a high creativity in various fields of sociocultural life.[51]

These greatly simplified formulas show to what extent Martindale's thesis is correct and to what extent it is fallacious. It is correct insofar as it contends that *some* of the periods of the basic reconstruction of societies or "communities" release their creative potentials and are marked by explosions of creativity. It is incorrect insofar as it ascribes this release of creative forces to *all* processes of the destruction of the old and the formation of the new "communities" (or to *all* great revolutions), includ-

---

[51] See the analysis, development, and systematic corroboration of these propositions in the *Dynamics*, Vol. III, chs. 9–14; in *SCP*, chs. 31–33; in *Man and Society in Calamity*, chs. 1–15; in *The Ways and Power of Love*, pp. 217–223, 226 ff.; in *The Sociology of Revolution* (Philadelphia, 1925); and in Kroeber, *The Configurations of Culture Growth*, *passim*.

ing those that represent the agony of respective "communities." It is incorrect insofar as it views *all* periods of history free from basic reconstructions as comparatively uncreative: Factually, only a portion of such periods are marked by low creativity; another portion displays a high creativity. It is incorrect insofar as it overlooks the dialectic uniformity of the scientific, religious, moral, artistic, and—generally—creative polarization taking place in practically all basic reconstructions of societies, in all revolutionary and calamitous periods in the lives of individuals and social groups. Instead of this polarization or release of constructive and destructive, creative and uncreative forces in such periods, he seems to adhere to the theory that all great destructions and formations of societies release only creative forces and uniformly cause the explosion of creativity in such periods. As mentioned before, such a theory is untenable logically and is contradicted empirically by a vast body of relevant facts. His theory is inadequate also insofar as it states that the "creative potential [of individuals and groups] is constant" and insofar as it tries to explain the explosion of creativity by the greater freedom "permitted the intellectuals" and the decline of creativity by the limitations of the intellectuals' freedom. His thesis of the "constancy of the creative potential" of individuals and groups runs contrary to what we know of heredity.[52] Although the factor of heredity cannot be discounted completely in determining the anatomical, physiological, mental, and behavioral characteristics of individuals and collectivities, Martindale's thesis seems to run contrary to the facts as generally accepted by biologists, psychologists, and sociologists. It is highly improbable that Martindale (who gives practically no proof of his thesis) can supply a convincing evidence for the scientific validity of his thesis.

Hardly more valid is his idea that explosions and declines of creativity can be explained by the comparative freedom of the intellectuals. A minimum of cultural freedom is certainly needed for the release of creative potential (though there are cases of persons of genius who realized their creative potential

[52] See on this problem my *CST*, chs. V, VI.

under extremely unfavorable conditions). A very great, even unlimited freedom, is not enough to produce creators like Moses, Buddha, Confucius, Lao-tse, and Jesus, Homer, Shakespeare, and Dante, Plato, Aristotle, St. Thomas Aquinas, and Kant, Phidias and Michelangelo, Bach, Mozart, Beethoven, Galileo and Newton, and so on. If Martindale's thesis were sound, we should have at the present time a galaxy of persons of genius in almost all fields of social and cultural creativity, because in "free" countries nobody limits the creative achievements of anyone in almost any field of constructive creativity. And yet, with the exception of the fields of science and technology, we have an abundance of mediocre creators and a superabundance of pseudo-creators and a great scarcity of men and women of genius. In contrast, in ancient Egypt and in several autocratic societies, there existed hardly any political freedom or any tangible cultural freedom; yet, despite this, these "unfree" societies have produced geniuses in many fields. More generally, if we take a statistical series of the movement of scientific discoveries and inventions, of the periods of eminent creativity in religion, philosophy, fine arts, ethics, laws, statesmanship, economics, and the practical arts in Egypt, Babylonia, Iran, India, Greece, Rome, China, the Arabic world, and in the main Western countries, and if, in each country, we compare the creative and uncreative periods with the political and social freedom during these periods, we will see that *the curves of creative periods and of the periods of freedom do not parallel each other but develop fairly independently of each other*: Periods of creativity occur in periods of unfreedom or very limited freedom as well as in periods of greater freedom, and some of the periods of freedom are creative whereas others are marked by low creativity.[53] If the freedom factor is the decisive factor in creativity, we could "hatch" an enormous number of great creators by giving them freedom. As a matter of fact, such freedom already exists in many countries in many fields of creative activity. Unfortunately, we can hardly expect that even governmental or

---

[53] The data for such comparison are given in my *Dynamics*, in *SCP*, and in Kroeber's *Configurations of Culture Growth*.

congressional enactment and enforcement of such freedom would produce geniuses.

In short, the Martindale theory of the factors of creativity is quite inadequate. Though we still know very little about the great mystery of creativity, we know enough to assert firmly that Martindale's and Danilevsky's factor of freedom is only one of several causative factors. Creativity, that most marvelous, most mysterious, and most important miracle, distinguishes the human race from all other species. It is the highest and sublimest form of energy known to us in the whole universe. In man's endowment with this energy lies the answer to the ancient question, "What is man that Thou art mindful of him?" Let us not fool ourselves with the idea that we have deciphered its mysteries.

Finally, Martindale's theory of creativity and cognition is defective in its concept of creative and cognitive mental processes as consisting only of sensory perception and of rational (logico-mathematical) thought. He flatly denies the third mental process, "intuitional enlightenment," whose "flash," "genius," or "operation" is necessary for especially great discoveries and creative achievements.

Among other things this process makes visible and open the most hidden aspects, forms, characteristics, and uniformities of physical, biological, and psychosocial realities otherwise inaccessible to sensory observation and rational thought. Martindale seems to flatly deny the reality and supreme functions of this 'intuitional" process; by denying it, he also rejects my integral theory of cognition and creativity.

In several of my studies, I stressed the fact that mediocre discoveries and midgety creations have been made and can be made through a careful use of sensory observations and rational, logical, deductive-inductive, dialectic, and mathematical reasoning. But, according to my theory, truly great discoveries and creative achievements have not been made and cannot be made without the flash of genius or the grace of intuitional enlightenment. My integral theory contends, first, that each of these three "channels" of cognition and creativity is unreliable and insufficient to deliver to us an adequate knowledge of important problems or to fully equip and empower potential creators to realize their potential, because the history of scientific discoveries and creative achievements is full of wrong sensory perceptions and observations, of illogical reasonings and nonrational inferences, and of spurious intuitions, revelations, and enlightenments. Second, it contends that a skillful combined use of all three channels delivers to us more reliable and richer results than those obtained through only one of them. Third, it contends that all great discoveries, inventions, or creative masterpieces have been accomplished by the cooperation of all three channels. The initial idea usually has been given by a flash of intuition; this idea has then been tested, developed, and completed by a skillful use of sensory observation in all its forms—clinical, statistical, experimental—and by logicomathematical verification, analysis, and development. Actually, the whole mental process of discovery or creation is an exceedingly complex process in which the intuitional, the sensory, and the rational operations are interwoven. The actual mental process of discovery or creation is an intricate maze of operations of all three processes. This maze is incomparably more complex than the current simple schema of the methods of scientific research that allegedly start with "fact-finding observations" of the phenomena studied and then analyze the accumulated empirical data by applying the canons of "deductive-inductive" logic and "seductive" mathematical inference. I seriously doubt that a strict adherence to this simplistic schema of research has ever discovered an important truth or created even a third-class masterpiece.

Martindale's denial of the "intuitional" source of cognition and creativity is seemingly based upon his insufficient knowledge of the past history and present state of this problem. This is not the place to give either this history, or a detailed account of the present recognition of this way of cognition and creativity in today's science, or to furnish a vast logical and empirical body of evidence fully corroborating its reality and its "strategic operations" in important scientific discoveries and inventions, in creations of great religions, philosophical, ethical and legal systems, in masterpieces of the fine arts, even of masterful social, political, and economic organizations and reconstructions.

Instead, I can only summarize the basic points of the

problem and refer to a few works in which an adequate analysis and information and evidence supporting my statements can be found:

1. Under different names and characterizations what is here called "intuition" was discovered long ago, at least in the eighth century B.C. in India, China, Greece, and other ancient civilizations. Since that time it has been acknowledged by many great philosophers, scientists, religious creators, great artists, and other eminent thinkers and creators in practically all civilized countries. Among the religious creators who viewed it as the highest cognitive and creative grace are practically all the founders and creators of almost all the world's religions, like Lao-tse, the authors of the Upanishads and the Bhagavad-Gita, Buddha, Mahavira, Moses, Jesus, St. Paul, St. Augustine, Mohammed, al-Ghazali, and al-Hallaj, to mention but a few.

Among the great philosophers Plato, Aristotle, Plotinus, Erigena, Albertus Magnus, St. Thomas Aquinas, Eckhart, Descartes, Bruno, Spinoza, Kant, Fichte, Hegel, Schopenhauer, Mill, Von Hartmann, Nietzsche, Emerson, Bradley, Croce, Bergson, Royce, Unamuno, Jung, Lossky, Whitehead, Husserl, Scheler, and all the Existentialist, neo-Thomist, and Phenomenologist philosophers can be mentioned.

Among eminent scientists Galileo, Kepler, Newton, Leibnitz, Ampère, Gauss, Liebig, Faraday, Planck, Hadamard, Poincaré, Kroenecker, Gonseth, Eddington, Langmuire, Weil, Bohr, Birkhoff, De Broglie, Bernard, Berthelot, Dirac, the whole "intuitional" school in mathematics, and many others recognized "intuition as the foundation for the rational superstructure erected by means of deductive and inductive reasoning. . . . [It is] heuristically valuable . . . of supreme importance . . . and beyond reason."[54]

Recent investigations of how eminent living mathematicians, inventors, physicists, chemists, and biologists made their discoveries disclosed the fact that almost all questioned scientists and inventors acknowledged that the first start to their discov-

---

[54] G. Birkhoff, "Intuition, Faith, and Reason in Science," *Science*, December 30, 1938, p. 603.

eries and inventions was given by an intuitional "flash" in an un-expected situation and moment.[55]

Likewise, many eminent painters, sculptors, musicians, and writers regarded intuitional inspiration as the main factor of their creativity.

Among eminent social thinkers the importance of intuitional cognition has been stressed by the Taoist, the Confucianist, the Indian, the Buddhist, the Zen, and the Arabic thinkers, by the Platonist and neo-Platonist Greek and Roman social philosophers, by most of the Church Fathers, by almost all great medieval Scholastics, by G. Vico, and so on up to Spengler, Toynbee, Northrop.[56]

The total body of the extant mathematical, logical, and empirical evidence supporting the role of intuition in scientific discoveries, inventions, and creative achievements is already so great as to leave no firm ground for either a dogmatic denial of its reality or for viewing it as something "supernatural and mystical" or as a speculation "outside of science," as Martin-dale asserts. For the same reasons neither my nor many other versions of the integral theory of cognition and creativity can be dogmatically "outlawed" as unscientific. As a matter of fact,

[55] See J. Hadamard, *The Psychology of Invention in the Mathematical Field* (Princeton, N.J., 1945); H. Poincaré, *Inventions Mathématiques* (Paris, 1908); J. Rossman, *Psychology of Inventors* (Washington, 1931).

[56] See a history of the various conceptions, sponsorship, and analysis of intuition in K. W. Wild, *Intuition* (Cambridge, 1938); N. Lossky, *Sensory, Intellectual and Mystical Intuition* (Paris, 1918); E. Meyerson, *Du Chéminement de la Pensée* (3 vols.; Paris, 1931); F. Gonseth, *Fondements de Mathématiques* (Paris, 1926); M. Bunge, *Intuition and Science* (Englewood Cliffs, N.J., 1962); P. Sorokin, *The Ways and Power of Love*, chs. 6, 19; the *Dynamics*, Vol. IV, ch. 16; P. Allen, *P. A. Sorokin in Review*, pp. 380–400; M. Polanyi, *Personal Knowledge*; K. Motwani, "Study of Sociology in India," *Indian Journal of Social Research*, December, 1964; E. W. Sinnott, *Two Roads to Truth* (New York, 1953); F. S. C. Northrop, *The Meeting of East and West* (New York, 1946); H. Margenau, *Open Vistas* (New Haven, 1961); R. G. H. Siu, *The Tao of the Sciences* (New York, 1957); B. Sjövall, *Höjdpsykologi* (Stockholm, 1959); R. G. Johnson, *Watcher on the Hill* (London, 1959); A. Koestler, *The Act of Creation* (New York, 1964); and V. A. Asmus, *The Problem of Intuition in Mathematics and Philosophy* (in Russian; Moscow, 1963). See in these works a vast literature on the problem of intuition.

in its several variations the integral theory has already become if not *the* dominant, then at least as important and as generally accepted as any other theory of cognition and creativity, and certainly more accepted by the physical, biological, and psychosocial sciences than Martindale's obsolescent version of John Locke's sensory theory of cognition and creativity.

GENERAL CONCLUSIONS

Each of the theories examined makes a small contribution to our knowledge of social change; hardly any of them *greatly* enriches our understanding of the most essential aspects, forms, principles, relationships, uniformities, causes, and consequences of social changes of the past as well as of the present. They are all either too abstract or too fragmentary. All are pedestrian, and Alexandrian rather than classical, enlightening, and imaginative. Hardly any of them compares favorably with the recent theories of cultural change of Spengler, Toynbee, Kroeber, and others. Let us hope that the material which the recent theories of social change furnish, and the questions they raise, will notably help in the discovery and formulation of truly grand theories of social change in the future.

CHAPTER **18**

The Shape of Sociology to Come

This examination of the main currents of sociological thought has emphasized mainly the shortcomings and differences of the various theories, to the neglect of their virtues and similarities. If the examination ended at this point, it would support the widely diffused opinion that sociology consists of a multitude of mutually discordant views with very few, if any, theories accepted by all or most sociological denominations.

This opinion is contradicted, however, by a considerable agreement of diverse sociological theories in the past and by a growing concordance of these theories at the present. Most of these theories are beginning to converge toward a set of principles and propositions acceptable to all. Let us examine this convergence by comparing the basic theories of integral sociology with the corresponding views of other currents of recent sociological thought. In this comparison, integral sociology is used as a whetstone to make the similarities or dissimilarities of the other sociologies sharper and to permit us to outline their concordance or discordance in a concise and concrete form.

1. Explicitly or implicity, all currents of sociological thought now accept the meaningful, normative, value-laden, superorganic character of sociocultural phenomena as a realm of reality different from inorganic and organic realities. They also agree that so far this meaningful form of reality is found in its fully developed form only in the world of "mindfully" (symbolically) interacting human beings. A few extremely mechanistic or biological theories that try to reduce sociocultural reality to inorganic or organic realities either completely miss it in their verbal reductionism or acknowledge the specific character of this reality as a *sui generis* combination of biophysical realities different from all the other physical and biological phenomena.

2. Whether or not the recent currents of sociology spell out

clearly the componential structure of sociocultural phenomena, they all admit (directly or circuitously) three distinct components of these phenomena: the meaningfully interacting human individuals that create, realize, and exchange in their meaningful actions-reactions (interactions) meanings-values-norms; the meanings-values-norms (often called symbols or images) that are superimposed upon the inorganic and the organic phenomena and by that transform them into a superorganic reality; and the biophysical media in which and through which the interacting individuals objectify, materialize, and exchange their immaterial (symbolic) meanings-values-norms. These biophysical media serve as vehicles of meaningful interactions and as solidified conserves of the meanings-values-norms accumulated in the countless meaningful interactions during the historical existence of the human race. This component of the vehicles and the materialized conserves is often called the material culture or material substratum of society. Though some sociological theories mention only either the meaningfully interacting individuals, with their behavior or roles, or only the material substratum of sociocultural phenomena as their component or unit, they all bootleg the other two components into their theories as necessary elements of all superorganic or sociocultural phenomena. By its theory of the three-componential structure of sociocultural phenomena, the integral theory spells out clearly what other theories state indistinctly and incidentally.

3. From this three-componential theory follows the thesis that sociocultural phenomena have three different levels of realization: a purely meaningful-ideological level, existing in the mind; a behavioral level, realized in the overt meaningful actions-reactions of interacting individuals; and a material level, objectified by and solidified into biophysical media of vehicles and conserves. These three levels are recognized, again under different terms (material culture, material basis of society, ideologies, ideological superstructure, social behavior, social roles), by practically all the sociological theories of our time.

4. From the same three-componential theory follows the thesis that, viewed from a different standpoint, all sociocultural phenomena have cultural, social, and personal aspects. Though

in their empirical forms these aspects are distinctly different from one another, nevertheless, like the Christian Trinity of God the Father, God the Son, and God the Holy Ghost, they all represent three main concrete forms of being of multidimensional superorganic phenomena. For this reason, the empirical forms of cultural, social, and personal aspects of sociocultural realities are closely interdependent. None of these forms can be adequately understood without understanding the other two. This theory of integral sociology is, again in diverse formulations, professed by many recent sociologists, psychologists, and psychiatrists, or indistinctly "mumbled" by other sociological and psychological theories.

5. The same can be said of integral sociology's clearly defined and empirically demonstrated theory of cultural systems (with their subsystems and supersystem) and congeries, of social systems (organized groups) and social congeries (unorganized and disorganized plurels of individuals), and of integrated personality systems and unintegrated and disintegrated personality types. Chapter 5 of this work outlined the recent upsurge of systemic theories in all sciences, and other chapters described the growth of systemic theories in recent sociology. In their own variations, all the systemic theories of today's sociology support the integral theory of social-cultural-personal systems. On the other hand, integral sociology's theory of atomistic-singularistic congeries is supported by all the recent singularistic-atomistic theories surveyed in the preceding chapters of this work. The objective ground for the systemic as well as for the singularistic theories is the undeniable fact of the existence in the total sociocultural universe of causal or meaningful or meaningful-causal unities (systems) as well as of singularistic congeries, whose parts are united only by spatial and/or time adjacency devoid of any causal or causal-meaningful relationships. Insofar as some sociocultural realities exist in the form of the singularistic-atomistic congeries, the singularistic-atomistic approaches to the study of these congeries are fully justified scientifically and notably contribute to our knowledge of this kind of sociocultural reality. The confused and incorrect theories result not from applying singularistic-atomistic methods and principles to the study of

congeries but from failing to distinguish between congeries and systems. This failure often leads to a misapplication of the methods proper for a study of congeries to that of systems and the methods proper for an investigation of systems to that of congeries. (See on this Chapter 4 and point 8 below.) Such a misapplication inevitably results in the kinds of mistakes pointed out in my criticism of the singularistic-atomistic theories in Chapters 3 and 4 of this work. A clear distinction between socio-cultural systems and congeries prevents this sort of error and thereby reinforces the validity of these theories. As mentioned, this distinction is now accepted by most of the recent sociologies.

6. From the acceptance of this distinction three other principles that are also increasingly recognized by most of today's sociologists follow. The first of these principles consists in distinguishing cultural systems and congeries from social systems and congeries. Cultural and social systems with their congeries are separate dimensions of the total superorganic reality and must be studied separately. That they are being studied separately is evident in the establishment of the theories of culturology as contrasted with those of sociology; in the macro- and microsociological theories of cultural systems (civilizations, *Hochkulturen*, and supersystems) as differentiated from those of social systems; in two kinds of *Wissensoziologie*—one taking for its independent variable the category of social groups (to explain cultural systems and congeries), the other taking for its independent variable the category of cultural systems (to explain social groups and phenomena as dependent ones). Integral sociology has systematically carried on separate studies of both kinds of systems and then unified the results in a higher synthesis, thereby clarifying the relationships of cultural and social systems to each other and restoring their interdependence in the same total superorganic reality.[1]

The increasing acceptance of this distinction and synthesis implies the decreasing acceptability of the theories that make one of these dimensions a mere feature of the other, thereby

---

[1] This is shown clearly in my *SCP*, where the social, the cultural, and the personality systems are analyzed separately, with a continuous stress on their interdependence as the different dimensions of the total many-dimensional superorganic reality.

denying their profound differences and independence. This error is still committed by some of the singularistic and behavioristic and even by some of the systemic theories that otherwise acknowledge the essential difference between, and irreducibility of, the cultural, social, and personal dimensions.

7. The second principle following from the distinction of systems and congeries is the growing efforts to classify the cultural as well as the social systems in a logical order, beginning with the smallest units and sub-sub-sub . . . systems, continuing with the larger systems, and ending with the vastest cultural and social supersystems. In the field of cultural systems, this trend is exemplified by Danilevsky's, Spengler's, Toynbee's, Northrop's, and Sorokin's theories of "civilizations" and cultural supersystems.

In the field of social systems, it is manifested in attempts to grade social systems, beginning with the smallest social units and ending with the largest of social supersystems, like Parsons' and Levy's self-sufficient society, Martindale's self-sufficient community and nation-state, and Gurvitch's global society.

Despite the fragmentary and incidental character of practically all of these classifications, the desire to find the logical hierarchy in their systems is common to almost all of today's sociologists.

I am no exception. My classification and taxonomy of cultural systems are crowned by the vast ideational, idealistic (integral), and sensate cultural supersystems and by my taxonomy of social groups, beginning with the smallest dyadic groups and ending with vast and powerful—unibonded and multibonded—groups. A knowledge of these systems and supersystems is necessary for an understanding of the structural and dynamic aspects of the sociocultural universe and of the great role they have played in determining the mentality and behavior of millions of individuals, the character of social processes, and the historical destiny of humankind. This reason explains also the more systematic, less fragmentary, and possibly more adequate character of integral sociology's classifications of cultural as well as social systems than those of other systems of sociology.

8. The third principle resulting from the distinction be-

tween systems and congeries concerns the proper methods of studying them. Since a congeries is made up of either one unique singularistic-atomistic phenomenon or a mass of such phenomena, the problem of the proper methods of study (and also of the kinds of cognitive results expected from each method) can be summed up by indicating the proper method for, and the kind of cognitive results expected from, a study of (a) unique and unrepeated sociocultural phenomena, (b) a singularistic-atomistic mass of phenomena repeated in time and/or space; and (c) social and cultural systems.

Unique (unrepeated) sociocultural phenomena can only be described and understood by empathy and inner experience, for they are not amenable to generalized conclusions or to the formulation of uniformities. "Singularistic causalities," as some call them, are unique in that they are incapable of being extended to other phenomena. Unique sociocultural realities correspond to the single atom or particle in the microphysical world. The physicists call this world the "microcosm of lawlessness," and the "realm of discontinuity and uncertainty." "No theory has yet been proposed to render vagaries [of single atoms or particles] understandable in detail, none is able to predict them. . . . Indeed Heisenberg's principle says precisely that such predictions are impossible. . . . Discontinuity and ambiguity mark the microscopic subatomic world." This describes well unique sociocultural phenomena. They are a poor hunting ground for uniformities, generalized propositions, or scientific predictions.

Mass singularistic psychosocial phenomena, frequently repeated in time and space (like births, deaths, marriages, divorces, fluctuations of prices, etc.), lend themselves to statistical mass observation and once in a while to inductive or experimental tests. They correspond to ever-repeated macrophysical phenomena, like large aggregates of atoms, that are susceptible to mass observation by statistical and inductive methods. In the physical as well as in the psychosocial sciences, these methods often discover chance uniformities in the relationships of such phenomena. On the basis of the discovered uniformities, their future states can often be predicted with varying degrees of accuracy within specified conditions and time-space limits. These mass phenomena represent a good ground for factorial analysis, diverse probabilistic correlations, covariations, and even for causal-functional uniformities. In this field, an investigator can theoretically take for his independent and dependent variables any singularistic phenomena he finds promising and can try to discover and measure the degree of probablistic relationship between his variables, which may range all the way from zero to a tangible positive or negative correlation or uniformity.

As was shown in Chapters 4 and 5, the modern biophysical sciences sharply separate the class of biological and psychosocial systems from the "lawless physical microcosm" of single atoms or particles and from the large aggregations of atoms or particles of macrophysics with their probabilistic relationships and uniformities. Subatomic phenomena display discontinuities, irregularities, and uncertainties, and the large macrophysical aggregates manifest statistical chance uniformities, but biological and sociocultural systems, no matter how small an aggregation of atoms they represent, display orderly relationships and, now and then, uniformities quite different from the other two classes. Physicists call this order by different names. A. Eddington calls it the "inner law of direction." M. Planck calls it an order determined by a "free will." E. Schrödinger calls it "conscious mind," or Athman, and H. Margenau calls it "conscious, voluntaristic decision." Schrödinger's analysis of genes and biological organisms well demonstrates this difference between a biological system and microphysical and macrophysical phenomena. Genes, he says, represent a small aggregation of atoms, and belong to the microphysical world; as such, they should display the discontinuity, uncertainty, unpredictability, and "lawlessness" of microphysical phenomena. Instead, genes appear to be highly integrated systems. They contain in themselves a "plentitude pattern" or the "plenotype" of the respective organism—the totality of its hereditary characteristics. Even more, genes preserve their specific individuality unimpaired from generation to generation. Amidst ever-changing environmental conditions they carry on their integrity and plenotype, and, through it, predetermine the essential characteristics of an organism and the stages of its life-course. Thus, "incredibly small groups of atoms, too small to display exact statistical laws, do play a domineering role in the very orderly and lawful events within a living organism."

These properties of an organism as a system that bears in itself its individuality and perpetuation, the ability to direct its change and passage through immanently predetermined phases in its life-career, are applicable, with slight variation, to all sociocultural systems. From the moment of their emergence, they also bear in themselves the main phases of their life-career, and this life-career consists largely of an unfolding or realization of their potentialities. Like genes and organisms, they have a tangible margin of autonomy from external forces. The external forces can hinder or facilitate the full realization of their potentialities (their inherent "plenotype"), and now and then they can even destroy a system, but they cannot radically change their inherent properties or the succession of states or phases in their history, if such a succession is an inherent part of their life-career. In Spengler's terms, "they have destiny as an organic necessity of potentiality passing into actuality . . . in the time process, flowing from the past through the present to the future." The forms of change of a family are different from those of a political party or a business corporation. The forms of change of a "univariant" sociocultural system are different from those of "bivariant" or "multivariant" systems. The forms, phases, rhythms, periodicities, and directions of their quantitative and qualitative changes differ in each system according to its nature. In this sense any personal or sociocultural system largely molds its own destiny.

These properties of systems require several modifications in the methods used to study them:

a. A system has to be studied as a unified, meaningful-causal whole with triple interdependence.

b. The study has to proceed not only from parts to the whole and from each part to the other parts but still more so from the whole to the parts (along the lines of the triple interdependence).

c. An explanation of the important structural properties of the whole system as well as those of its essential parts, and an explanation of its "physiological" (repeated) processes as well as of the phases through which the system passes in its life-course—its rhythms, periodicities, and other changes—has to be sought, first of all, in the system itself, in its "immanent" potentialities and the self-direction of its life-functions, in the nature of its components of meanings-values-norms, in its "vehicles and material conserves," and in its human members and their relationships to one another; second, in the relation-ships of the system to other systems of which it is a subsystem or a larger system; and third, in the total sociocultural environ-ment of the system. Residual problems may be "explained" now and then by the biophysical milieu of the system and by the interference of some extraordinary—unforeseen and unpre-dictable—factors, forces, and events of the sociocultural and biophysical universes.

d. This means that the system's structural dynamic proper-ties or its life-course cannot be "explained" by merely environ-mental factors, or by taking the system's part as the "factor" of the whole system (e.g., its "economic" or "ideological" or "technological" part). Nor can it be explained by the formulas of "stimulus-response," "challenge-reaction," or by other pro-cedures that largely neglect the system as a unified whole.

e. This means that a statistician who has almost unlimited liberty in choosing his independent and dependent variables in a study of congeries is greatly limited in an investigation of sociocultural systems. He cannot take for his variables a part of one system (for instance, the Newtonian law of graviation in a system of physical science) and correlate it with a part of a different system (for instance, the financial fund of a business corporation). Nor can he take as his variable any part of any system isolated from its system. This sort of operation is as unscientific as the operations of a biologist who tries to study and correlate the swimming behavior of a fish with the buzzing of bumblebee or the heartbeats of a human with the flying behavior of a bird or to explain the anatomical, physiological, and psychological changes of a human organism when it passes from the state of childhood to that of maturity by one of these changes, like the increase in the organism's height or the appearance of his mustache.

This should give an idea of how the principles and methods

of studying systems differ from those of studying congeries. Though all the main methods of scientific cognition can be used in a study of systems, these methods and principles must undergo considerable modifications.[2] The methods of studying sociocultural congeries and systems outlined above are in an essential agreement with the corresponding conclusions of the biophysical sciences. In today's sociology, these conclusions, with some variations, are also supported by most sociologists competent in the problems of epistemology, methodology, and logic.

9. The "intuitional" method has also been widely accepted as one of the channels of the integral theory of cognition and creativity. Among the recent currents of sociology, it is explicitly recognized, with variations, by the dialectic and macrosociological theories of culture, and by some of the singularistic and systemic sociologies. Many of the "positivistic-behavioristic" sociologists who emphatically reject it factually do accept it to some extent, calling it intuition, imagination, insight, inspiration, luck, inductive leap, horse sense, sudden enlightenment, and so on. Still more significant is the fact that many of the opponents of "intuition" now and then use this term in their writings, although most of them prefer substitutes like imagination, insight, and other names that imply some sort of cognition different from sensory perception-observation and logico-mathematical reasoning. The main difference between the partisans and detractors of intuition and the integral method of cognition is that the latter bootleg it into their theories without spelling out the essential features of their substitutes for "intuition." Convincing evidence of the intuitional way of cognition and creativity is responsible for the dwindling numbers of those who in the past have rejected it. In diverse variations, the integral theory of cognition and creativity is becoming increasingly accepted by sociologists in the West and particularly in the East.[3]

---

[2] See a more detailed analysis of these problems in my *Fads and Foibles*, pp. 150–172. See there also the literature on these problems.

[3] For the Eastern sociologies, see K. Motwani, "Study of Sociology in India," *Indian Journal of Social Research*, December, 1964, pp. 225–

10. An essential agreement also exists concerning the abstract-empirical character of important "substantive" sociological theories. No significant theory *can be purely abstract and devoid of relevant empirical content, nor can it consist of a mere collection of empirical facts devoid of an adequate explanatory theory.* The recent "fact-finding" research in sociology has been enormous and has accumulated a mountain of empirical data; but only a modest part of this research has resulted in significant conclusions or has discovered uniformities of a "middle-range" generality. The bulk of this research has produced purely local, temporary, "informational" material devoid of general cognitive value. The main reason for these meager results has been a lack of an adequate theory in this kind of empirical research.

Many recent abstract theories suffer from an ascetic detachment from empirical sociocultural realities. These abstract schemes represent a peculiar mixture of those "ghostly" models of social systems that are devoid of empirical content and frequently peppered with mechanistic analogies of equilibrium, inertia, thermodynamic laws, and speculative prerequisites of systems' self-preservation.[4] The meshes of the abstract nets are so large that practically all the empirical fish slip through, leaving nothing in the hands of the fisherman-researcher.

In their preoccupation with verbal equilibriums, inertias, and abstract prerequisites for the continuity of systems, these speculative schemas are constructed in such a static way that they can hardly register most of the changes in the fished sociocultural waters. As a result of their ascetic detachment from the empirical sociocultural facts they are not helpful in the cognition of empirical realities.

The deficiencies of the empirical and abstract theories

235; see also his *Manu Dharma Shastra* (Madras, 1958). See the editorials by Raj Pal Mohan in *Indian Sociological Bulletin* (1964); by G. C. Hallen in *Indian Journal of Social Research* (1964); and the works of R. Mukerjee, S. Radhakrishnan, and P. H. Prabhu, "The State of Psychology as a Science Today." For China, see R. G. H. Siu, *The Tao of Science* (Massachusetts Institute of Technology, 1957).

[4] These mechanistic analogies are cognitively much more misleading than the organismic analogies of the preceding period.

are both due to the use of exclusively empirical channels of cognition by the "theory-less" empirical researchers and to their neglect of the other two channels of cognition, the logico-mathematical and the intuitional, as well as to the neglect of the sensory-observational and intuitional ways of cognition by the abstract theories.

At the present time, the inadequacy of both of these one-sided theories is generally acknowledged and sociologists of all denominations try to avoid it.

11. Despite the considerable variety in the surveyed socio-logical theories, they are mutually exclusive or contradictory only on some of their wrong points; on a number of their points they are mutually complementary rather than exclusive. The preceding critical examination of these theories has shown that each of them has, side by side with its defective and question-able points, a body of correct propositions that are quite recon-cilable with and complementary to the valid propositions of other theories. Considering the multidimensionality of the total sociocultural reality, it is but natural that each of the currents of sociological thought should stress different aspects of it. Insofar as these aspects are real and are accurately depicted by different theories, each theory is sound and reconcilable with the sound parts of other theories. Even more, these sound parts can be unified and incorporated into a more "multidimensional" and more adequate integral theory that gives a fuller and more accurate knowledge of the superorganic universe than each of the existing theories. Some imperfect attempts to build such integral theories are already being made. My own integral system of sociology is one of these imperfect endeavors. There is hardly any doubt that much better, finer, and more adequate integral systems of sociology will be built in the future.

In their sound parts, the singularistic-atomistic theories of social, cultural, and personal congeries are reconcilable and complement the sound body of systemic theories: Each class of these theories gives a real knowledge of the singularistic and systemic forms of the total superorganic reality. The sound part of macrosociological theories of vast sociocultural systems and supersystems complements the microsociological studies of small groups and small cultural unities. Sociologies of cultural systems and congeries complement sociologies of social systems and congeries. Valid contributions of the analytical, structural-functional, dialectic, empirical, integral, and other currents of sociological thought are quite reconcilable with one another. The same can be said of dualistic, triadic, and other typologies: Each of these "opens" a particular dimension of sociocultural reality and thereby enriches our knowledge of it. Each of them is like the different kaleidoscopic forms of the same bits of colored glass changing with each turn of the optical tube. The dimensions of the *Gemeinschaft-Gesellschaft,* the militant-industrial, the sacred-secular, the familistic-contractual-compulsory, the primary-secondary, and other dyadic and triadic typologies of sociocultural realities do not contradict but complement one another. In their totality they deliver to us a fuller knowledge of more dimensions of the human universe than each of these typologies alone. If all these typologies are logically and empirically integrated into a vast unified system, our knowledge of the total superorganic reality will become richer and more adequate.

This applies to almost all other differences in the seemingly discordant sociological theories of social change, in the taxonomic classifications of social groups and cultural systems, in the repeated physiological processes in the systems, in their evolutionary trends, and in practically all other surveyed theories. Almost all of them contain a part of the truth—some larger, some smaller—and these sound parts can, are, and will be increasingly integrated into the more scientifically adequate integral theories of the future sociology.

In some divisions of sociology, the existing, partially true theories are already sufficiently numerous and correct as to permit their tentative synthesis into a multidimensional integral theory. In other divisions of sociology, particularly in its taxonomy of social and cultural systems and in its physiology of the repeated processes—their natures, rhythms, tempi, periodicities, reasons, functions, and interrelationships—the existing, partially true theories are still too few and too uncertain for such an integral synthesis at the present time. A great deal of research in these fields has to be done before such a synthesis becomes possible. The preceding survey shows that even in these less-developed fields of sociology an intensified study of their basic problems is proceeding crescendo and that several significant theories with their relevant empirical evidence have already been formulated. Several others are in a *statu nascendi.*

To sum up, the growing agreement of different currents of sociological thought is likely to continue in the future.

12. This hypothesis raises the question of the shape of sociology to come, of the predominant character of the next phase of general sociology. Any prognosis of the future course of science or of any creative activity can be but conjectural. My guess is that the next period of general sociology is likely to be the period of great sociological syntheses, of grand integral systems of sociology. In this sense, the next period will markedly differ from the period from 1925 to 1965. In the terms of H. Spencer's, Claude Bernard's, G. Tarde's, and A. N. Whitehead's theory of alternating analytical (fact-finding) and synthesizing periods repeating themselves in science and philosophy, the examined period has been preparatory, analytical, and fact-finding rather than synthesizing. The main achievements of the recent period consist largely in excavating and analyzing an enormous mass of relevant and irrelevant empirical facts, in testing and correcting preceding sociological theories, in elaborating various techniques of sociological research, and in formulating a few "middle-range" generalizations and significant sociological and historico-philosophical theories, like the macrosociological theories of vast cultural systems or civilizations and the dialectic and the integral systems of sociology.

In creating vast sociological syntheses and grand systems of sociology, the examined period has been notably poorer than that of the second half of the nineteenth and the early twentieth centuries. The theories of Comte, Spencer, Marx, Durkheim, Weber, Simmel, Dilthey, Scheler, von Wiese, W. I. Thomas, Ward, Sumner, Tarde, Tönnies, Pareto, and other leaders of sociology of this period not only established sociology as a science, but still serve as the basic frameworks and referential systems for today's general sociology. In their totality, these systems make the preceding period much more synthesizing than the recent period examined. The "preparatory" character of today's sociology accounts for its concentration on technique ways, for its preoccupation with fact-finding labor, and for the comparative dearth of significant syntheses and grand systems of sociology. Today's sociology has excavated so many facts that it often does not know what to do with them. Likewise, in its analysis of various—important and unimportant—techniques of research, it has become as finicky as the angelology of the medieval Scholastics. In its revolt against the "grand systems of sociology," it has increasingly neglected a study of the fundamental problems of sociology and has progressively wasted its creative energy in research on comparatively trivial, cognitively unimportant problems.

Further research along these lines will yield not bigger and better scientific harvests but progressively diminishing returns, not new breakthroughs but an increasing stagnation and routinization of sociology.

Whether we like it or not, today sociology's has come to a crossroad: One road leads it to the new peak of great syntheses and more adequate systems of sociology, the other leads it to a hackneyed, rubber-stamped, greatly mechanized set of dogmas devoid of creative *élan* and cognitive growth.

My guess is that, of the two roads, sociology will choose the road of creative growth and will eventually enter a new period of great syntheses. I hope that this prognosis may be as lucky as my previous prognostications of the changes in the sociocultural life of mankind that I made at the end of the 1920's.[5] With this hope, I say finis to this critical examination of the main currents of recent sociological thought.

[5] See these prognostications in the *Dynamics,* Vol. III, ch. 16, Vol. IV, ch. 17, and *The Crisis of Our Age.*

INDEXES

Date Due